D0976198

Guide to
SOUTHERN TREES

BY

ELLWOOD S. HARRAR, Ph.D., Sc.D.
Dean, School of Forestry, Duke University

AND

J. GEORGE HARRAR, Ph.D.
President, The Rockefeller Foundation

SECOND EDITION

DOVER PUBLICATIONS, INC.
New York

Published in Canada by General Publishing Company, Ltd., 30 Lesmill Road, Don Mills, Toronto, Ontario.

Published in the United Kingdom by Constable and Company, Ltd., 10 Orange Street, London WC 2.

This Dover edition, first published in 1962, in an unabridged republication of the work originally published by the McGraw-Hill Book Company, Inc., in 1946. In this Dover edition the nomenclature has been revised to conform to current practice.

International Standard Book Number: 0-486-20945-8

Library of Congress Catalog Card Number: 62-52799

Manufactured in the United States of America
Dover Publications, Inc.
180 Varick Street
New York, N. Y. 10014

To

MOTHER AND DAD

PREFACE

Dixie—steeped in tradition, acclaimed in song, reverenced in verse—is a land of trees. Once the center of the nation's lumber industry, it is now a leader in conservation and modern practices in forestry.

During the past decade the creation in the southern states of national, state, and community forests, national and state parks, wilderness areas, and game refuges and bird sanctuaries; the organization of forestry agencies both public and private; and the activity of conservation societies have done much to stimulate the layman's interest in trees. There exists today a real appreciation of the biological and recreational value of forests in terms of bountiful game, good fishing, and other out-of-door pursuits, not the least of which is a knowledge of the trees themselves. Thus the authors, believing that there is a need for a nontechnical book covering the trees of the greater South, undertook the preparation of this little volume.

Guide to Southern Trees describes the more than 350 arborescent species indigenous to that great region in the United States lying south of the Mason and Dixon's line, the Ohio River, and the extension of the Missouri-Arkansas boundary to the western limits of southern forests. Minimum use is made of technical terminology. Included are notes of unusual interest and historical significance pertaining to many of the trees described, together with pertinent information on the usage of valuable products other than lumber derived from the leaves, flowers, fruit, wood, or bark of many of them. It is hoped that teachers of biology or natural science, nature leaders, and amateur naturalists will find this book especially useful in the examination and identification of southern trees.

The authors are grateful for the friendly interest shown and timely suggestions offered by their colleagues during the preparation of the manuscript. We are particularly indebted to Dr. H. J. Oosting for free access to the Duke University Herbarium; Dr. J. H. Buell, Appalachian Forest Experiment Station, Dr. Wilbur Duncan, University of Georgia, Dr. Erdman West, Florida Experiment Station, Dr. C. A. Brown, University of Louisiana, and F. J. LeClair, nurseryman, Soil Conservation Service, Chapel Hill, N.C., for supplying botanical materials from their respective regions; W. M. Buswell, curator, for use of the University of Miami Herbarium; and W. A. Dayton, U.S. Forest Service, for taxonomic information pertaining to certain of the generic groups included here.

The illustrations were prepared by Mrs. Helene S. Millar from living materials and authentic herbarium sheets. We wish also to acknowledge the assistance of Mrs. Marion Harrar in reading proof and for the preparation of the Index and of Miss Margaret Trapnell, Key West, Fla., for typing a large portion of the manuscript. Figures 1 through 8 are adapted from *Textbook of Dendrology* by W. M. Harlow and E. S. Harrar.

E. S. HARRAR,
J. G. HARRAR.

CONTENTS

	PAGE
PREFACE	vii
INTRODUCTION	1
KEYS TO THE GENERIC GROUPS	26
THE CONIFERS	45
THE BROADLEAVED TREES	101
GLOSSARY	677
SELECTED REFERENCES	684
INDEX	689

GUIDE TO SOUTHERN TREES

INTRODUCTION

Southern forests are both temperate and tropical. From the mangrove swamps of the Florida Keys to the alpine forests of the Appalachian highlands there is to be found a greater diversity of trees than in any other North American area of comparable magnitude. Many roads, trails, and waterways permit of easy access to nearly every section of the South. Anyone possessing an interest in trees will find southern woodlands fascinating areas in which to explore and study.

Here are vast forests of the renowned southern yellow pines, around which has centered an enormous lumber industry. These pines also supply tremendous quantities of wood for local pulp and paper mills and two of them, slash and longleaf, have been the world's principal source of naval stores since early colonial times. Notable too, are extensive stands of baldcypress, Atlantic whitecedar, red spruce, and white pine.

Magnificent mixed hardwood forests characterize many sections. These include, among others, such valuable trees as black walnut, yellowpoplar, sweetgum, birches, West Indian mahogany, numerous red and white oaks, and several hickories and provide many of the raw materials used by manufacturers of flooring, cooperage, veneer, plywood, excelsior, and many other wooden commodities. The large southern furniture industry likewise looks to these forests for

1

the bulk of its timber supply. Many of our nation's crack trains run on rails spiked to ties hewn from southern trees. The countless thousands of poles and crossarms that carry the maze of communication and transmission networks across the United States, piling, posts, and mine timbers are but a few of the other products derived from these versatile and seemingly inexhaustible southern timberlands.

Kinds of Trees

Three distinct kinds of trees are found in the South. Those with needlelike or scalelike foliage and conelike fruits,[1] such as are developed by the pines, hemlocks, cedars, and cypresses, belong to that important group of plants known as the *conifers*. The great majority of these retain their foliage for 2 years or more and hence have become generally known to many as the *evergreens*. Lumbermen, in an effort to distinguish the conifers from other tree types, have long since designated them the *softwoods*.

The broadleaved trees, that is, the maples, oaks, elms, and similar forms, comprise the largest group of southern trees and include a number of interesting and important forms. In temperate regions most of the trees in this category lose their foliage each fall and develop a new canopy with the advent of another growing season. Those trees exhibiting this behavior are usually described as *deciduous*. There are a few southern trees, however, such as magnolia, laurelcherry, and rhododendron, that feature persistent foliage. These are described as *broadleaved evergreens* and in tropical forests occur in great profusion. To lumbermen the broadleaved species are the *hardwoods*.

The palms and yuccas constitute the third group.

[1] See also the yews and torreyas.

There are about a dozen arborescent forms of this class indigenous to the South, but they are of comparatively little value as a group. The majority are restricted to the coastal plains and are particularly characteristic of the flora of lower peninsular Florida and the Florida Keys. Space does not permit of their inclusion here, but the reader who has a special interest in them is referred to the various manuals and guides[1] included in the Selected References (page 684).

Classification of Trees

Ever since man first began to take an interest in his surroundings, he has endeavored to arrange and classify, in a more or less systematic order, the objects of his interest. In fact, much of the pioneer work in the natural and physical sciences was devoted to assembling and classifying vast numbers of related materials and objects such as plants, animals, rocks, minerals, chemical elements and compounds, and a host of other things.

Considerable space could be devoted here to a discussion of plant systematics, the concepts which have prevailed in the past and those on which our modern classifications are based. It is not necessary, however, to fortify oneself with much information of this sort before beginning the study of trees, although one wishing a philosophical background will find the historical literature in this field both interesting and stimulating reading. It is sufficient to state here that contemporary plant arrangements are founded on apparent genealogical relationships as evidenced by reproductive processes and the structure of the reproductive organs, which in the seed plants are, of course, the flowers.

[1] For an excellent account of the southern palms and yuccas, see C. S. Sargent, Manual of the Trees of North America, pp. 96 - 118. Dover Publications, Inc.

The unit in plant classification is the *species*. A species may be defined as a collection of individuals so nearly resembling one another that they suggest common parentage. Upon walking along a forest trail one might observe the repeated occurrence of a certain kind of tree, which suggests that all such trees might be the offspring of some venerable forest giant. Collectively, all trees of this form, regardless of their generation, constitute the species. Individuals within the species that exhibit prominent, yet minor variations from the apparent normal, for example, a weeping or columnar habit or variations in the color of leaves or flowers or length and shape of the fruits, are regarded as *varieties* of the species.

A collection of related species, the oaks for example, constitute a *genus*. Similarly a number of related genera comprise a *family*. Related families make up an *order*, and in a like manner orders are grouped into *subdivisions*, subdivisions into *divisions*, and divisions, of which there are four, constitute the *plant kingdom*. A typical classification, using the shipmast locust, which is a variety of black locust, as an example, is given below:

```
Kingdom................Plant
  Division..................Spermatophyta
    Subdivision..............Angiospermae
      Order....................Rosales
        Family...................Leguminosae
          Genus....................Robinia
            Species...................Robinia pseudoacacia L.
              Variety..................R.  pseudoacacia  var.
                                        rectissima Raber
```

Tree Names

Every southern tree has one or more names by which it is known in various parts of its range and a technical or scientific designation by which it is known universally.

Common names usually suffice when used within rather restricted areas, but considerable confusion often arises when they are applied to a species of wide distribution. For example, *loblolly pine* is known in various parts of its range by no less than 25 other names, several of which are also applicable to species with which it is commonly associated. Thus, in certain sections, this tree is called *longleaf, slash, shortleaf, Virginia,* and *spruce pine,* actually the preferred common names of several other well-known southern trees. The confusion increases when we find that a number of other names are also applied to these trees and that many of those are used to designate still other species.

Again, common names have their shortcomings because of their general application to unrelated groups of trees. The real pines, as we know, are a group of conifers with fascicled needles belonging to the genus *Pinus.* Yet several unrelated genera of the Southern Hemisphere, notably *Araucaria* and *Podocarpus,* include a number of "pines," and the Australian casuarinas or beefwoods, which actually belong to the broadleaved group, are called "Australian-pines" merely because their foliage is more or less scalelike.

The use of common names is also restricted to people of one language; thus in Germany pine is *Kiefer,* in France *pin,* and in Italy *pino.*

In order to overcome or lessen the confusion resulting from restricted use or loose application of common names, a universal binomial system of plant nomenclature has been devised. This system involves the use of Latin names and is ideal for this purpose since Latin is a dead language and the laws governing its syntax will remain unchanged with the passing of time.

The scientific or technical name of a plant consists of two parts, namely, a generic name and a specific name. These are usually followed by the full or abbreviated name of the person or persons responsible for the original published description of the plant. Thus the technical designation for loblolly pine is *Pinus taeda* L., *Pinus* being the generic name, *taeda* the specific name, and L. the initial for Linnaeus, a great Swedish botanist of the eighteenth century and the person who originally described this species. All other pines are likewise members of the genus *Pinus*, but no other may have the same specific designation, that is, *taeda*. Thus longleaf pine is *P. palustris* Mill., slash pine *P. caribaea* More., and shortleaf pine *P. echinata* Mill.

While it is desirable for one working with trees to know them by their scientific names, it is by no means an essential requirement of tree identification. They are included in this book, however, for technical accuracy and for those readers who desire to know trees by their botanical designations.

How to Study Trees

The study of trees can be made a fascinating and instructive avocation. It is not necessary to be a technically trained botanist to appreciate fully tree characteristics; anyone possessing an interest and the ability to note small but significant details can soon learn to recognize and identify plants as readily as any professionally trained observer. It is well for the beginner, however, to familiarize himself first with the trees about his home or in his neighborhood and to be able to identify them at any season of the year. Once the pertinent summer and winter characteristics of a small group of this sort are mastered, the ability to recognize and identify large numbers becomes merely a matter of additional time and study in woodlands farther afield.

The principal features of trees used in the determination of a species are habit, leaves, flowers, fruits, twigs, and bark. In many instances a single character may suffice for accurate identification of a specimen, but in other cases several features may be necessary to attain the same end. Tree habitats, too, are often helpful. After doing a certain amount of field work one soon appreciates the fact that there are definite plant associations or societies and that the composition of these varies with locality. Thus one notes that certain forms are typically swamp species; others may be found only on sandy soils, on western slopes, in brackish waters, or on soils of limestone origin. In the course of time an alert observer will make his own correlations of this sort. He will know that it is futile, for example, to look for swamp chestnut oak along the summit of a hill, and he will never expect to find red spruce or cucumbertree in swales of the coastal plains.

Habit

The habit of a tree, that is, its general appearance, is often a useful feature leading to specific identification. In open situations the crowns of trees are usually well developed and assume shapes that are diagnostic. Most of us can recognize an American elm at a considerable distance because of its graceful, vase or fanlike crown. Isolated hickories develop long, narrow, oblong crowns; those of oaks are usually globular; egg-shaped crowns prevail in maples; and conical heads are a feature of the alders.

Trees growing in the forest, on the other hand, are competing for space in the forest canopy so that their crowns are much smaller and often without special character. In such instances, features of the bole may become manifestly more significant. For example, the butts of many trees growing in swamps or on land subject to periodic inundation are commonly swollen or churn-shaped. The bole above the butt may be fluted, excessively tapered, or clothed for the greater part of its length below the living canopy in snags and dead branches. Unusual roots, such as the knees developed on baldcypress or the aerial systems produced by the figs, are also pertinent.

Leaves

These essential organs are chiefly concerned with several vital processes in the metabolism of a plant; but since they occur in many different shapes and forms, they are also extremely useful in determining the identity of trees. Upon examination it will be observed that a leaf consists of an expanded portion, commonly termed a *blade,* and its supporting stalk, the *petiole.* Leaves having a single blade are said to be *simple;* if the petiole is lacking and the blade is attached at its base directly to the twig, the leaf is *sessile.* Leaves with two or more blades are designated as *compound.* In such cases the blades are known as *leaflets* and the stalk to which they are attached is called a *rachis.* When the leaflets are disposed laterally along a rachis, the leaf is *pinnately* compound. If the leaflets themselves are compounded, the blades are described as *pinnules* and a *bipinnate* leaf results. A division of the pinnules gives rise to a *tripinnately* compound leaf. *Odd* or *even* pinnate leaves are those having an odd or even number of leaflets, respectively. *Palmately* compound leaves are characterized by several leaflets radiating from a common point of attachment at the end of a rachis. Compound leaves with only three leaflets are described as *trifoliate.*

The leaves of many trees are attended by a pair of

small scalelike or leafy structures known as *stipules*. These are attached to the twig at either side of a petiole or rachis, but they are normally present for such a short time that they are of little diagnostic value. Trees featuring stipules are *stipulate;* those without them, *exstipulate*.

Leaves are inserted on twigs in one of three ways, and their arrangement for any given species is usually constant. The point of leaf attachment on the twig is designated as a *node*. When only a single leaf occurs at such points, the leaves are said to be *alternate*. Upon closer scrutiny, however, it may be seen that they are actually arranged in a spiral about the twig. When a pair of leaves occur at a node, one on either side of the twig, they are *opposite*. A *whorled* condition results when three or more leaves appear at a common node. Occasionally trees may be encountered in which the leaves are nearly but not quite opposite. This disposition is described as *subopposite*.

Leaf Shapes.—The shape of a leaf blade or a leaflet is ordinarily characteristic for a species and hence is of tremendous value in the identification of a tree. Compound leaves, particularly those of the pinnate type, frequently develop terminal leaflets that are manifestly different from their associated laterals. In cases of this sort it is often necessary to describe both types. The common shapes of leaves or leaflets of southern trees are illustrated in Fig. 1. The first three of these are characteristic of the cone-bearing trees, whereas all of them are to be found among the broadleaved forms.

Leaf Apices and Bases.—The tip of a blade, that is, that portion farthest removed from the petiole, is termed the *apex*, while that part of the blade nearest to the petiole is known as the *base*. The common apices and bases that are features of leaves of southern trees are illustrated in Fig. 2.

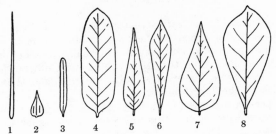

1. Needlelike. 2. Scalelike. 3. Linear. 4. Oblong. 5. Lance-shaped. 6. Inverted lance-shaped (Oblanceolate). 7. Ovate. 8. Obovate.

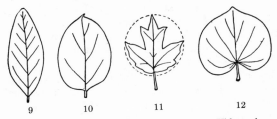

9. Elliptical. 10. Oval. 11. Circular. 12. Kidney-shaped

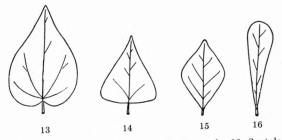

13. Heart-shaped. 14. Triangular. 15. Diamond-shaped. 16. Spatula-shaped.

Fig. 1.—Leaf shapes. (*Drawn by L. E. Partelow.*)

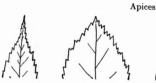

1. Acuminate.   2. Acute.   3. Bristle-tipped.   4. Spine-tipped.
                                     (Mucronate)   (Cuspidate)

5. Obtuse.   6. Rounded.   7. Flattened.   8. Notched.
                                  (Truncate)   (Emarginate)

Bases

9. Wedge-shaped.   10. Acute.   11. Heart-shaped.   12. Inequi-
    (Cuneate)   (Cordate)   lateral.

13. Obtuse.   14. Rounded.   15. Flattened.   16. Earlike.
                                                  (Auriculate)

Fig. 2.—Leaf apices and bases.

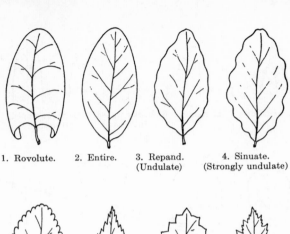

1. Rovolute.   2. Entire.   3. Repand.   4. Sinuate.
                              (Undulate)   (Strongly undulate)

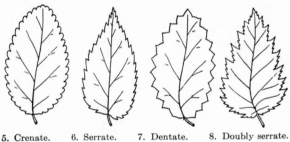

5. Crenate.   6. Serrate.   7. Dentate.   8. Doubly serrate.

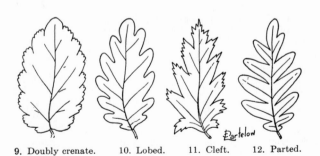

9. Doubly crenate.   10. Lobed.   11. Cleft.   12. Parted.

Fig. 3.—Leaf margins.

Leaf Margins.—The edge of a leaf blade is known as the *margin*. The margin is commonly a distinctive feature of a leaf and in many instances may serve as the basis for separation of closely related forms. A number of characteristic margins are illustrated in Fig. 3.

Leaf Venation.—Three types of venation characterize the leaves of the hardwoods discussed in this book. These are illustrated in Fig. 4. When three

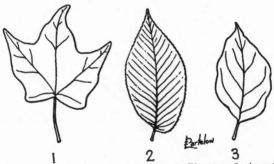

FIG. 4.—Leaf venation. 1. Palmate. 2. Pinnate. 3. Arcuate.

or more secondary veins branch from the base of a leaf, the leaf is described as *palmately* veined (Fig. 4, 1). A *pinnately* veined leaf (Fig. 4, 2) features a herringbone pattern in which the numerous secondary veins, on either side of the midrib, are parallel and extend to the margin or nearly so. An *arcuate* venation (Fig. 4, 3) is one in which the secondary veins curve near their point of departure from the midrib and parallel the leaf margin for some distance.

Leaf Surfaces.—Hairs, of whatever color and form, resin cysts or glands, waxes, blooms, or minute scales often encountered on leaf surfaces are very useful features and often of positive diagnostic value. It is also well to note the texture of leaves since some possess a distinctly leathery character while others are papery in nature.

Flowers

All trees, except for a short time in their youthful development, bear flowers at one time or another during the year. In a few species, such as the lob-

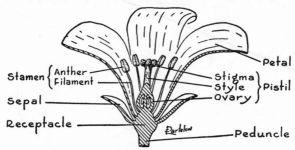

FIG. 5.—Flower structure.

lollybay, magnolias, yellowpoplar, and stewartias, they are large and showy and a conspicuous part of the tree while in bloom. Ordinarily, however, tree flowers are comparatively inconspicuous and often go unnoticed by the casual observer. Yet a knowledge of the features and peculiarities of tree flowers is essential as all natural classifications of woody, seed-bearing plants are based on their structure.

Figure 5 illustrates the organization of a *complete* flower, that is, one with *sepals*, *petals*, *stamens*, and a *pistil*. The omission of any one of these whorls results in an *incomplete* flower. A complete flower, or a flower in which the sepals and/or the petals are wanting, is known as a *perfect* flower. The term "perfect" as used here refers to the presence of both sex organs and presupposes that both types are capable of normal activity. If either of the sex organs is abortive or wanting, the flower is *imperfect* or *unisexual*. Unisexual flowers having stamens are termed *staminate*, while those bearing one or more active pistils are said to be *pistillate*. If a flower consists merely of reproductive organs, it is said to be *naked*.

The nature of flowers and the manner in which they appear on a tree are important. In trees like oaks, hickories, and birches, the flowers are unisexual, but both types occur on the same individual, usually on separate branches. This condition is described as *monoecious*. When unisexual flowers occur on separate individuals, that is, the male on one tree, the female on another, the species is said to be *dioecious*. This arrangement is a feature of the hollies, willows, and some of the ashes. Where both perfect and unisexual flowers occur on the same individual, a *polygamous* condition results.

Finally, flowers of whatever form may also be classed as *regular* or *irregular*. Regular flowers are those which have their parts so arranged that any number of planes passed through their central axis invariably results in two symmetrical halves, one the mirror image of the other. When flowers can be divided into two symmetrical halves by only one properly orientated plane, they are irregular. The flower of the black locust is an excellent example of an irregular condition (see page 372).

Flower Arrangement.—Flowers may appear singly or in a characteristic cluster known as an *inflorescence*. When an inflorescence terminates a shoot, it is said to be *terminal;* when it appears in a leaf axil, it is described as *axillary*. Inflorescences may also appear from separate flower buds, which are usually crowded toward the tips of twigs.

When the rachis of an inflorescence terminates in a blossom that opens slightly in advance of its nearest associates, the inflorescence is described as *determinate*. However, when the blossoms open along the rachis progressively from base to apex or from the outside toward the center in flat-topped clusters, the inflorescence is *indeterminate*.

Figure 6 depicts a number of the common types of inflorescences that are featured by many southern trees.

Fruit

A fruit, in the botanical sense, is the seed-bearing organ of a plant. Because of differences in size, shape, structure, and color, fruits often serve as one of the best and most reliable means of distinguishing among closely related forms. Unfortunately, however, the application of fruit characteristics in tree identification is limited. Because they never bear fruits, staminate trees of dioecious species must always be distinguished by other features. Many fruits are perishable and can be found only during a short time after ripening. Finally, several species require more than a single season in which to mature the fruits, and others produce them only at irregular intervals of 2 to 5 years or more. Thus, often many months may elapse before one has an opportunity to observe the fruits of certain trees.

The fruits of coniferous trees are very different in form and structure from those of the hardwood groups. It is therefore best to consider those of each class separately.

Fruits of Coniferous Trees.—The fruits of cone-bearing trees are basically different from those of the hardwood species in that the seeds are not produced within an ovary. Those of the southern conifers fall readily into one of two types, namely, (1) those which

1a. Cylindrical
cyme.

1b. Flat-topped
cyme.

2. Spike.

3. Catkin or
ament.

4. Raceme.

5. Panicle.

8a. Globose head.

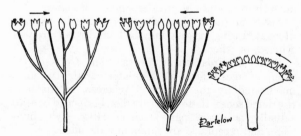

6. Corymb.

7. Umbel.

8b. Flat-topped head.

FIG. 6.—Flower arrangement (arrows show direction of flowering).

17

consist merely of a single seed, partly or wholly surrounded by a thin or very succulent, fleshy layer, an *aril;* and (2) those which are composed of two to many woody, leathery, papery, or fleshy seed-bearing scales characteristically inserted on a central stalk to form a *cone.*

Cone scales may be thick or thin; rigid or flexible; boat-shaped, club-shaped, or thin and flattened. The exposed portion of any scale of a closed cone is known as the *apophysis.* This may be ridged, grooved, channeled, or depressed or may have a small boss or other protuberance such as a prickle, spine, claw, or scar. Notable, too, is its margin, which may be smooth or toothed, reflexed or revolute.

Pine cones ripen during their second or rarely their third season, and the apophyses reveal this fact in a most interesting manner. A small scarlike structure, the *umbo,* found on the apophyses of all pine cones, of whatever origin, is in reality that part of the scale formed during the first season subsequent to pollination. When the umbo terminates a scale, it is described as *terminal;* when it occurs on the back of the apophysis, it is said to be *dorsal.* Umbos frequently terminate in prickles, spines, or claws.

Seeds of the conifers may terminate in a single, elongated wing, or they may be laterally 2- (rarely 3-) winged, or wingless.

Fruits of Broadleaved Trees.—The fruits of this group of trees exhibit much greater variability than is manifested by the conifers. Whereas, in the most restricted sense, these fruits are merely ripened ovaries, actually, accessory parts such as calyx, style, involucre, and receptacle are commonly included.

The fruits of southern trees exhibit a wide range of structural characteristics, which, for convenience, may be classified in the following manner:

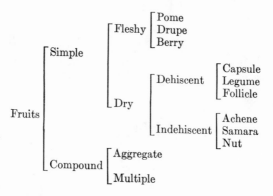

A *simple* fruit is the product of a single pistil. When more than one pistil is involved, the fruit is said to be *compound*. If the pistils of a compound fruit are traceable to the same flower, an *aggregate* results; but when the pistils of two or more separate flowers unite, the fruit is described as a *multiple*. The fruits of yellowpoplar and magnolia are excellent examples of aggregates, while those of mulberry, sweetgum, and sycamore illustrate the multiple.

The common types of fruits produced by southern broadleaved trees are described briefly below:

1. Pome—a fleshy, succulent fruit, the product of a compound pistil; the outer wall fleshy, the inner wall papery or cartilaginous and encasing numerous seeds.

2. Drupe—a fleshy, usually 1-seeded fruit, the product of a simple pistil; the outer wall fleshy, often succulent, the inner wall bony.

3. Berry—a fleshy, several-seeded fruit, the product of a compound pistil; both inner and outer walls fleshy with the seeds embedded in the pulpy mass.

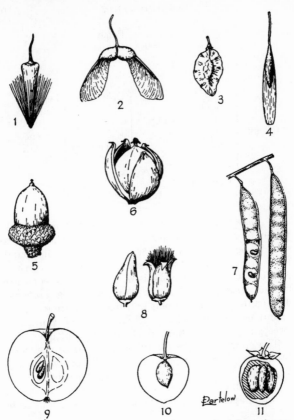

Fig. 7.—Fruits of some broadleaved trees. 1. *Achene* of sycamore. 2. *Double samara* of maple. 3. *Single samara* of elm.
4. *Single samara* of ash. 5. *Acorn* (*nut*) of oak. 6. *Nut* of hickory.
7. *Legume* of black locust. 8. *Capsule* of willow. 9. *Pome* of
apple. 10. *Drupe* of cherry. 11. *Berry* of persimmon.

4. Capsule—a dry, dehiscent fruit, the product of a compound pistil, at maturity splitting along two or more lines of suture.
5. Legume—a dry, dehiscent fruit, the product of a simple pistil, at maturity splitting along two lines of suture.
6. Follicle—a dry, dehiscent fruit, the product of a simple pistil, at maturity splitting along a single line of suture (see magnolias, pages 276–288).
7. Achene—a dry, indehiscent, 1-celled, 1-seeded fruit, the product of a simple pistil.
8. Samara—a winged achene.
9. Nut—a dry, indehiscent fruit, commonly the product of a compound pistil, but usually 1-seeded and 1-celled; with a bony, woody, leathery, or papery wall, often partly or wholly surrounded by an involucre.

Twigs

Twig characters are exceedingly useful in the identification of trees except for a short time each spring when the buds are bursting and their structural identity is being obliterated. Diagnostic features of twigs include the size and nature of buds, leaf scars, stipule scars, and lenticels; character of pith, color, odor, and taste are also helpful features. Spurs, spines, thorns, corky wings, ridges or excrescences, hair or waxy blooms when present are likewise pertinent.

Buds.—Buds contain the growing points of stems, that is, the embryonic axes. Those which develop only leaves are known as *leaf* or *branch* buds. In many species, notably elms and soft maples, the flowers appear from separate structures called *flower* buds. When both leaves and flowers appear from the same axis, the buds are *mixed*. A bud that appears at the apex of a twig is described as *terminal*, while those occurring at the nodes are called *lateral* buds.

The twigs of many species, however, continue to grow until checked by external conditions. In such cases the growing tip usually dies and sloughs off back to the last fully developed lateral bud. This lateral bud then takes the place of a terminal bud and is described as a *pseudoterminal* bud. Pseudoterminal buds, unlike most true terminals, are no larger than their lateral associates. Their identity can be readily established by noting the *twig scar*, which usually appears on the side of the twig opposite the leaf scar.

The presence of more than one bud at a node is not uncommon. When this condition exists, the bud directly above the leaf scar is considered to be the true lateral bud and the others are designated as *accessory* buds. Accessory buds that appear on either side of the lateral bud are said to be *collateral;* when they appear over the real lateral bud, they are described as *superposed.*

Buds may be either *scaly* or *naked.* Naked buds are those which have no special covering. These are common to trees growing in tropical regions but of only sporadic occurrence elsewhere. The buds of several species are covered with a single caplike scale. Others feature two, or sometimes three, outer scales that meet at their edges without overlapping. Scales of this sort are described as *valvate.* Most common, however, is the *imbricate* arrangement, in which numerous scales overlap one another in a shinglelike fashion. In a few species, for example, black locust, the buds are embedded in the callous layers of leaf scars; buds so disposed are said to be *submerged.*

Leaf Scars.—When a leaf drops off, there remains at the original point of attachment a characteristic pattern termed a *leaf scar.* Within the leaf scar are one or more minute scars that are actually the ruptured strands of conductive tissue that passed from the twig into the leaf. These scars are known as *bundle scars.*

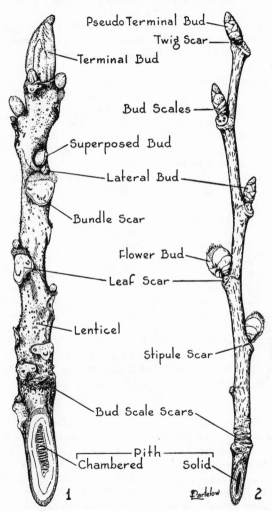

Pseudo Terminal Bud

Twig Scar

Terminal Bud

Bud Scales

Superposed Bud

Lateral Bud

Bundle Scar

Flower Bud

Leaf Scar

Lenticel

Stipule Scar

Bud Scale Scars

Pith
Chambered   Solid

1   2

Parlelow

FIG. 8.—Twig Features. Butternut (left); slippery elm (right).

23

Leaf scars exhibit a wide range of sizes, shapes, and bundle-scar patterns and hence are useful features for tree identification, particularly during the winter season.

Stipule Scars.—Stipule scars are minute, often slit-like scars that, when present, appear in pairs at either side of a twig at the top of a leaf scar. In a few species, such as sycamore and yellow-poplar, they completely encircle the twig. Stipule scars are not a universal feature of twigs, since, as has been previously indicated, many trees are exstipulate.

Lenticels.—Lenticels are minute to comparatively large dots, slits, or diamondlike or wartlike patches of loosely organized tissue concerned with aeration. When of unusual form or color they have some diagnostic value, but in most instances they are of little use for purposes of identification.

Pith.—In the medial or central portion of a twig is a mass of soft tissue known as *pith*. Pith may be of a lighter or darker hue than the layer of wood surrounding it and is often tinted with light shades of pink, yellow, green, or brown. Upon careful examination of transverse sections of twigs it will be seen that the pith conforms to one of a number of characteristic patterns; these are usually constant for a given species. Star-shaped pith is a feature of oaks, hickories, cottonwoods, and many other groups; oval, circular (terete), triangular, or irregular outlines also are of frequent occurrence.

The composition of pith is sometimes a useful feature; it may be determined by examining longitudinal sections of twigs cut through this tissue. Pith of uniform texture is called *continuous* or *homogeneous*. When denser, disclike thickenings bridge an otherwise continuous pith at frequent and regular intervals, it is described as *diaphragmed*. *Chambered* pith is a feature of a few trees and consists of empty chambers separated by thin or thick, transverse partitions. When the pith is loosely packed or exceedingly porous, a *spongy* condition results. Hollow twigs in which the pith has disappeared, as a result of enzymatic action, are said to be *excavated*.

Spurs.—Spurs are merely twigs in which there has been little or no internodal development. Because of this the leaves, which may be opposite or alternate, appear to be in whorls at the ends of such structures. Spurs frequently grow for years and bear a new complement of foliage or flowers each season. These structures are characteristic of many of the common fruit trees, birches, and hollies.

Spines and Thorns.—Structures of this sort are common to many trees, and their origin, position, and form are often diagnostic. *Stipular* spines, that is, modified stipules, are common to several plant families. Spines arising from the cortex of twigs (cortical) are a feature of a few species. Thorns are actually another form of twig modification and are frequently furnished with minute buds and leaf scars.

Bark

The bark of a tree is usually distinctive, but it is exceedingly difficult to describe its appearance in any but the most general terms. Persons earning their livelihood in the forest soon learn to recognize most trees solely by the appearance of the bole. Anyone interested in the study of trees should likewise endeavor to become familiar with bark characteristics since they are very useful at any time of the year and serve as still another check on the identification of a given specimen. On the other hand, it is well to remember that the appearance of the bark on young trees and on mature trunks of the same species may be quite different and that variations in environment may be reflected in the character of the bark of trees growing on different sites or in widely separated areas.

KEYS TO THE GENERIC GROUPS

I. THE CONIFERS

1. Fruit, a woody, papery, or fleshy cone, composed of a few to many seed-bearing scales, characteristically inserted on a central stalk........................ 2
1. Fruit, a single seed, partly or wholly surrounded by a fleshy, often succulent aril........................ 9

    2. Foliage, needlelike or linear, spirally disposed along the twig................................ 3
    2. Foliage, scalelike, occasionally awl-shaped; scale-like leaves, opposite in pairs, the awl-shaped opposite or in whorls of 3......................... 7

3. Leaves, needlelike, borne in fascicles of 2 to 5; cones, maturing at the end of 2 seasons......**Pines** (p. 46)
3. Leaves, linear, solitary; cones, maturing at the end of a single season.................................. 4

    4. Leaves, deciduous; cones, globular, their scales club-shaped; seeds, laterally 3-winged...........
                                Baldcypresses (p. 82)
    4. Leaves, persistent; cones, egg-shaped or cylindrical, their scales thin and more or less flattened; seeds, with a single terminal wing.............. 5

5. Leaves, 4-angled in transverse section, upon falling leaving basal, peglike projections (sterigmata) attached to the twigs..............**Spruces** (p. 71)
5. Leaves, flattened, upon falling not leaving basal, peglike projections attached to the twig............... 6

    6. Leaves, sessile; leaf scars, prominent, circular; cones, erect, their scales and bracts deciduous from the central stalk at maturity.............
                               Balsam firs (p. 78)

6. Leaves, stalked; leaf scars, inconspicuous, not circular; cones, pendent, remaining intact at maturity...................**Hemlocks** (p. 75)

7. Cones, berrylike; seeds, wingless; twigs, 4-angled; leaves, both scalelike and awl-shaped usually present
Redcedars (p. 92)
7. Cones, woody or leathery; seeds, laterally 2-winged; twigs, flattened; leaves, scalelike only.............. 8

8. Foliage, coarse, yellow-green; cones, egg-shaped; cone scales, thin, flattened, woody.............
Northern white-cedar (p. 87)
8. Foliage, fine, blue-green; cones, globular; cone scales, club-shaped, leathery..................
Atlantic white-cedar (p. 90)

9. Leaves, pale yellow below; fruit, a seed partially surrounded by a scarlet, cuplike aril, maturing at the end of 1 season....................**Florida yew** (p. 99)
9. Leaves, silvery white below; fruit, a seed wholly incased in a thin, purple, fleshy covering, maturing at the end of 2 seasons..........**Florida torreya** (p. 97)

II. TREES WITH OPPOSITE, SIMPLE, DECIDUOUS, LEAVES

1. Leaves, palmately lobed............**Maples** (p. 462)
1. Leaves, unlobed................................. 2

2. Leaves, heart-shaped..........**Catalpas** (p. 654)
2. Leaves, ovate, elliptical, lance-shaped, or oval... 3

3. Stipules or their scars, present..................... 4
3. Stipules or their scars, wanting................... 5

4. Terminal buds, present, ½″ long, resinous; leaf scars, circular to heart-shaped.................
Pinckneya (p. 660)
4. Terminal buds, wanting, the laterals minute, dry; leaf scars, semicircular........................
Common buttonbush (p. 662)

5. Leaves, entire.................................... 6
5. Leaves, toothed................................. 7

    6. Leaf venation, arcuate; leaf scars, V-shaped, with 3 equidistant bundle scars....................
                    Flowering dogwood (p. 565)
    6. Leaf venation, pinnate; leaf scars, circular, raised, with a single bundle scar...............
                    Fringetree (p. 635)

7. Bud scales, valvate; petioles, grooved..............
                    Viburnums (p. 670)
7. Bud scales, imbricate; petioles, terete.............. 8

    8. Leaves, serrate above the middle; lateral buds, superposed..............**Swamp-privet** (p. 633)
    8. Leaves, serrate from base to apex; lateral buds, solitary................**Eastern wahoo** (p. 452)

III. TREES WITH PERSISTENT, OPPOSITE, SIMPLE LEAVES

1. Leaves, glandular-dotted below, aromatic when bruised... 2
1. Leaves, neither glandular below nor aromatic....... 4

    2. Flowers, without petals......**Lidflowers** (p. 547)
    2. Flowers, with petals.......................... 3

3. Flowers, borne in axillary fascicles or racemes; fruit, with a minute crown..........**Nakedwoods** (p. 545)
3. Flowers, borne in cymes; fruit, with a large, conspicuous crown.....................**Eugenias** (p. 541)

    4. Trees, furnished with aerial roots..............
                    Mangrove (p. 530)
    4. Trees, without aerial roots.................... 5

5. Leaf margins, toothed, at least above the middle.... 6
5. Leaf margins, entire............................. 7

6. Leaves, oval to elliptical; bark smooth..........
Florida crossopetalum (p. 458)
6. Leaves, obovate; bark, broken into shreddy scales
West Indies falsebox (p. 460)

7. Stipules or their scars, present................... 8
7. Stipules or their scars, absent....................11

8. Leaves, rounded at apex, usually notched....... 9
8. Leaves, obtuse to acuminate at apex, usually ending in a short, pointed tip....................10

9. Twigs, clothed in dense, velvety pubescence; leaf margins, wavy..................**Leadwood** (p. 495)
9. Twigs, obscurely hairy; leaf margins, thickened.....
Darling-plum (p. 498)

10. Leaves, ovate-lanceolate, smooth above and below
Caribbean princewood (p. 665)
10. Leaves, oval to ovate or elliptical, pubescent at least on lower surfaces......**Velvetseeds** (p. 667)

11. Petioles, furnished with a pair of apical glands.......
White-mangrove (p. 538)
11. Petioles, without glands..........................12

12. Leaves, covered below in minute, branlike scales.
Florida tetrazygia (p. 550)
12. Leaves, smooth, hairy, or woolly below.........13

13. Leaves, woolly-pubescent below..................
Black-mangrove (p. 646)
13. Leaves, smooth below..........................14

14. Leaves, 1″ to 2″ long....**Longleaf blolly** (p. 273)
14. Leaves, 3″ to 5″ long..........................15

15. Twigs, light yellow, many-angled; leaves, obscurely veined......................**Devilwood** (p. 637)
15. Twigs, reddish brown, terete or slightly 4-angled; leaves, conspicuously veined....................
Fiddlewood (p. 648)

IV. TREES WITH OPPOSITE, COMPOUND LEAVES

1. Leaves, palmately compound......**Buckeyes** (p. 478)
1. Leaves, pinnately compound, occasionally trifoliate. 2

    2. Leaves, deciduous............................ 3
    2. Leaves, persistent............................ 4

3. Leaves, entire or finely toothed; leaf scars, shield-shaped, with many bundle scars.......**Ashes** (p. 621)
3. Leaves, coarsely toothed; leaf scars, V-shaped, with 3 to 7 bundle scars..............**Boxelder** (p. 464)

    4. Leaves, even-pinnate, with 2 to 4 pairs of leaflets
          Holywood lignumvitae (p. 387)
    4. Leaves, trifoliate...........**Sea amyris** (p. 399)

V. TREES WITH ALTERNATE, SIMPLE DECIDUOUS, LEAVES[1]

1. Leaves, lobed................................... 2
1. Leaves, unlobed.................................10

    2. Leaves, mitten-shaped, 3-lobed, and unlobed, all 3 forms usually occurring on the same tree........ 3
    2. Leaves, of uniform appearance, or nearly so..... 4

3. Sap, watery; leaves, exhaling an aromatic odor when crushed, their margins entire......**Sassafras** (p. 306)
3. Sap, milky; leaves, not aromatic, their margins conspicuously toothed............**Mulberries** (p. 254)

    4. Leaves, palmately lobed..................... 5
    4. Leaves, pinnately lobed..................... 6

5. Twigs, furnished with corky wings; stipule scars, minute, slitlike.................**Sweetgum** (p. 315)

[1] To avoid confusion, trees with tardily deciduous leaves have been included in this key and in the key for persistent, alternate, simple leaves.

5. Twigs, free of corky wings; stipule scars, encircling the zigzag twigs.................**Sycamore** (p. 321)

6. Twigs, furnished with stout, sharp-pointed thorns
Hawthorns (p. 336)
6. Twigs, unarmed (except in a few of the apples)... 7

7. Stipule scars, encircling the twig................... 8
7. Stipule scars, if present, minute, not encircling the twig.. 9

8. Leaves, 4-lobed, broadly truncate at the base; bud scales, valvate.......**Yellow-poplar** (p. 289)
8. Leaves, furnished at the base with a pair of ear-like lobes; bud scales, imbricate...............
Magnolias, in part (p. 276)

9. Leaf scars, with many scattered bundle scars........
Oaks, in part (p. 173)
9. Leaf scars, with 3 bundle scars....................
Apples, in part (p. 325)

10. Leaf margins, entire..........................11
10. Leaf margins, variously toothed...............31

11. Twigs, armed with stout thorns..................12
11. Twigs, unarmed...............................13

12. Leaves, broadly oval to lance-shaped; inner bark, bright orange...........**Osage-orange** (p. 257)
12. Leaves, oblong or elliptical; inner bark, red-brown
Buckthorn bumelia (p. 601)

13. Leaves, kidney-shaped; fruit, a legume............
Eastern redbud (p. 374)
13. Leaves, usually longer than broad; fruit, not a legume 14

14. Sap, milky...............**Manchineel** (p. 418)
14. Sap, watery..................................15

15. Winter buds, naked...............................16
15. Winter buds, scaly...............................18

16. Leaves, 10″ to 12″ long, obovate to lance-shaped
     Pawpaw (p. 292)
16. Leaves, 3″ to 5″ long, elliptical, oval, or oblong..17

17. Leaves, thick, leathery, glabrous; winter buds, soli-
     tary at each node..............**Pond-apple** (p. 295)
17. Leaves, thin, papery, very hairy below; winter buds,
     commonly superposed at each node................
     Snowbells (p. 611)

18. Stipules or their scars, present.................19
18. Stipules or their scars, absent..................21

19. Stipule scars, encircling the twig.................
     Magnolias, in part (p. 276)
19. Stipule scars, inconspicuous, not encircling the twig.20

20. Pith, homogeneous; fruit, an acorn............
     Oaks, in part (p. 173)
20. Pith, chambered at the nodes; fruit, a small, thin-
     skinned drupe............**Hackberries** (p. 248)

21. Terminal bud, present...........................22
21. Terminal bud, absent............................28

22. Twigs, green, aromatic; leaves, unlobed, mitten-
     shaped, and 3-lobed, all appearing on the same
     tree......................**Sassafras** (p. 306)
22. Twigs, variously colored; if green, not aromatic;
     mitten-shaped and 3-lobed leaves, wanting......23

23. Leaves, dotted on lower surface with numerous
     resinous glands.................**Marlberry** (p. 587)
23. Leaves, nonresinous below........................24

24. Pith, diaphragmed............**Tupelos** (p. 555)
24. Pith, homogeneous...........................25

25. Leaves, with arcuate venation.....................
     Alternate-leaf dogwood (p. 563)
25. Leaves, with pinnate venation.....................26

26. Leaves, pubescent above and below, lance-shaped;
     twigs, clothed in dense, velvety pubescence when
     young.....................**Corkwood** (p. 115)
26. Leaves, smooth above, occasionally slightly hairy
     below, oblong to ovate or obovate; twigs, smooth,
     or with sparse, fine hairs.....................27

27. Leaves, tardily deciduous; twigs, lenticellate........
     Swamp cyrilla (p. 438)
27. Leaves, early deciduous; twigs, without lenticels.....
     Elliottia (p. 569)

28. Leaf apices, acute to acuminate.................29
28. Leaf apices, obtuse or rounded.................30

29. Buds, minute, with 2 or 3 outer scales; twigs, grayish
     Gulf graytwig (p. 266)
29. Buds, large, with several outer scales; twigs, brown..
     Persimmons (p. 607)

30. Leaves, 4″ to 6″ long, obovate to nearly circular,
     their petioles ¾″ to 1″ long **Smoketree** (p. 424)
30. Leaves, ½″ to 2″ long, oblong-oval, nearly
     sessile..............**Tree sparkleberry** (p. 582)

31. Winter buds, naked.............................32
31. Winter buds, scaly.............................35

32. Leaves, inequilateral at the base, their margins
     coarsely toothed...........**Witchhazels** (p. 317)
32. Leaves, equilateral at the base, their margins
     finely toothed.............................33

33. Leaves, elliptical to oblanceolate; buds, solitary.....34
33. Leaves, oval to obovate; buds, superposed..........
     Snowbells (p. 611)

34. Stipules or their scars, wanting...............
                    Franklinia (p. 521)

34. Stipules or their scars, present................
                    Carolina buckthorn (p. 500)

35. Terminal buds, present.........................36

35. Terminal buds, wanting.........................45

36. Primary veins, extending from midrib to leaf
    margin....................................37

36. Primary veins, uniting within the blade.........43

37. Twigs, armed..................................38

37. Twigs, unarmed................................40

38. Fruit, a 1-seeded drupe...Plums, in part (p. 339)

38. Fruit, a pose................................39

39. Seeds, enclosed in a papery structure **Apples** (p. 325)

39. Seeds, enclosed in a bony structure...............
                    Hawthorns, in part (p. 336)

40. Leaves, triangular; buds, resinous..............
                    Aspens and Poplars (p. 106)

40. Leaves, not triangular; buds nonresinous........41

41. Buds, ovoid to nearly globular; leaf scars, with a
    single bundle scar..........**Hollies,** in part (p. 442)

41. Buds, elongated; leaf scars, with 3 bundle scars.....42

42. Buds, lustrous, chestnut-brown; leaves coarsely
    dentate...............**American Beech** (p. 164)

42. Buds, dull, greenish red or purplish red; leaves,
    finely toothed..........**Serviceberries** (p. 333)

43. Fruit, a drupe; twigs, emitting an aromatic or fetid
    odor when bruised................................
                    Cherries and Plums, in part (p. 339)

43. Fruit, a nut; twigs comomnly astringent............44

44. Fruit, an acorn..........**Oaks,** in part (p. 173)

44. Fruit, a nut, several often enclosed in the same
    spiny bur.....**Chestnut and Chinkapins** (p. 166)

45. Stipules or their scars, present...................46

45. Stipules or their scars, absent...................54

46. Winter buds, covered by a single caplike scale...
                    Willows (p. 101)

46. Winter buds, covered by 2 or more scales.......47

47. Sap, milky...................**Mulberries** (p. 254)
47. Sap, watery.......................................48

    48. Bark, peeling horizontally into thin, papery sheets......................**Birches** (p. 149)
    48. Bark, smooth, blocky, furrowed, or longitudinally scaly.......................................49

49. Winter buds, mucilaginous......**Basswoods** (p. 507)
49. Winter buds, nonmucilaginous...................50

    50. Leaves, with pronounced, inequilateral bases....51
    50. Leaves, rounded at the base or nearly so........53

51. Leaf margins, doubly serrate..........**Elms** (p. 230)
51. Leaf margins, singly serrate.....................52

    52. Leaves, with 3 or 4 prominent veins extending from the base, their margins glandular........
          Hackberries, in part (p. 248)
    52. Leaves, with several pairs of lateral veins extending from the midrib, their margins glandular....
          Planertree (p. 244)

53. Bark, gray-blue, smooth, fluted...................
          American hornbeam (p. 158)
53. Bark, brown to black, scaly ....
          Eastern hophornbeam (p. 160)

    54. Leaves, leathery.....**Common sweetleaf** (p. 618)
    54. Leaves, thin and papery.....................55

55. Leaves, acidulous to the taste; twigs, greenish red, commonly zigzag...............**Sourwood** (p. 577)
55. Leaves, not acidulous to the taste; twigs, brown or dark gray, not contorted......................56

    56. Fruit, a woody, ovoid, hairy capsule............
          Stewartias (p. 522)
    56. Fruit, a dry, 2- to 4-winged drupe..............
          Silverbells (p. 613)

VI. TREES WITH ALTERNATE, PERSISTENT SIMPLE, LEAVES

1. Leaves, lobed...................................2
1. Leaves, unlobed.................................3

2. Leaves, palmately lobed, 1' to 2' in diameter....
   Papaya (p. 527)
2. Leaves, pinnately lobed, 1'' to 5'' in length......
   Oaks, in part (p. 173)

3. Leaf margins, entire (occasionally toothed on vigorous
   shoots)... 4
3. Leaf margins, variously toothed...................43

4. Leaves, exhaling an aromatic aroma when
   bruised...................................... 5
4. Leaves, not aromatic......................... 9

5. Leaves, rounded, obtuse, or emarginate at apex.....
   Canella (p. 525)
5. Leaves, acute to acuminate at apex............... 6

6. Twigs, furnished with small, wartlike excrescences; leaf scars, U-shaped, with 5 to 7 bundle
   scars.....................**Pond-apple** (p. 295)
6. Twigs, smooth or hairy; leaf scars, usually semicircular, with a single bundle scar.............. 7

7. Leaves, abruptly long-tapered at apex; margins, thin,
   wavy........................**Gulf licaria** (p. 309)
7. Leaves, acute to gradually long-tapered at apex;
   margins, thick, slightly curled.................... 8

8. Twigs, somewhat 3-angled in transverse section..
   Perseas (p. 300)
8. Twigs, terete........**Jamaica nectandra** (p. 303)

9. Stipules, persistent, insheathing the twig above the
   node........................**Seagrapes** (p. 268)
9. Stipules, deciduous or wanting....................10

10. Stipules or their scars, present.................11
10. Stipules or their scars, absent..................20

11. Stipule scars, encircling the twig....................12
11. Stipule scars, not encircling the twig...............13

12. Leaves, clothed below in orange-red, woolly pubescence; sap, watery...................... **Southern magnolia** (p. 277)
12. Leaves, smooth below; sap, milky...**Figs** (p. 259)

13. Twigs, angular in transverse section..............14
13. Twigs, terete...................................16

14. Leaves, rounded or emarginate at apex, furnished below with above and yellow, pubescence....... **Cuba colubrina** (p. 506)
14. Leaves, acute at apex.........................15

15. Petioles, biglandular; twigs, remotely winged........ **Button-mangrove** (p. 536)
15. Petioles, eglandular; twigs, unwinged............. **Jamaica caper** (p. 313)

16. Sap, milky...................**Drypetes** (p. 416)
16. Sap, watery................................17

17. Leaves, rounded or emarginate at apex............. **Icaco coco-plum** (p. 356)
17. Leaves, acute at apex..........................18

18. Leaves, glandular below...................... **Bahama colubrina** (p. 503)
18. Leaves, without glands.......................19

19. Leaf scars, with 3 bundle scars; twigs and leaves, exhaling an almondlike odor when bruised.......... **Laurelcherries** (p. 353)
19. Leaf scars, with a single bundle scar; twigs and leaves, without characteristic odor.**Hollies,** in part (p. 442)

20. Twigs, armed................................21
20. Twigs, unarmed.............................23

21. Sap, milky.................**Saffron-plum** (p. 601)
21. Sap, watery...................................22

22. Leaves, obovate, bluish green, in clusters near the tips of twigs............**Oxhorn bucida** (p. 534)
22. Leaves, oblong to elliptical, lustrous, dark green, scattered along the twigs...**Tallowwood** (p. 263)

23. Sap, milky......................................24
23. Sap, watery.....................................27

24. Leaves, rounded or emarginate at apex.........
    Wild-dilly (p. 602)
24. Leaves, acute at apex........................25

25. Leaves, clothed below with copper-red pubescence...
    Satinleaf (p. 604)
25. Leaves, glabrous below or nearly so................26

26. Leaves, oval to oblong, mostly rounded at the base
    False-mastic (p. 594)
26. Leaves, mostly oblanceolate, wedge-shaped at the base....................**Willow bustic** (p. 596)

27. Leaves, glandular-dotted below....................28
27. Leaves, without glandular dots below..............29

28. Leaves, 3″ to 6″ long; twigs, terete............
    Marlberry (p. 587)
28. Leaves, 1½″ to 3″ long; twigs, many-angled....
    Joewood (p. 584)

29. Leaves, clothed above and below with woolly or bristlelike pubescence............................30
29. Leaves, glabrous above, hairy or scaly below........31

30. Leaves and twigs, woolly-pubescent............
    Mullein nightshade (p. 651)
30. Leaves and twigs, furnished with short, stiff, raised hairs..............**Geiger-tree** (p. 640)

31. Twigs, angular................................32
31. Twigs, terete.................................34

32. Twigs, stout; leaves, 6″ to 8″ long............
　　　　　　　　　　Black-calabash (p. 657)
32. Twigs, slender; leaves, 1½″ to 2½″ long........33

33. Twigs, 4-angled......**West Indies falsebox** (p. 460)
33. Twigs, many-angled......**Florida-boxwood** (p. 456)

34. Leaves, acute to acuminate at apex............35
34. Leaves, obtuse, often emarginate at apex.......39

35. Leaves, with minute, pale- to rusty-red scales below..36
35. Leaves, smooth or hairy below...................37

36. Winter buds, scaly..........**Tree lyonia** (p. 579)
36. Winter buds, naked.....**Guiana rapanea** (p. 590)

37. Twigs, stout; leaves, 4″ to 12″ long..............
　　　　　　　　　　Rosebay rhododendron (p. 572)
37. Twigs, slender; leaves, 1½″ to 4″ long............38

38. Leaves, elliptical, often falcate................
　　　　　　　　　　Gulf graytwig (p. 266)
38. Leaves, oblong-ovate, not falcate..............
　　　　　　　　　　Mountain-laurel (p. 574)

39. Leaves, usually less than 2″ in length..............40
39. Leaves, usually 2½″ to 3½″ in length............42

40. Petioles, channeled......**Longleaf blolly** (p. 273)
40. Petioles, terete............................41

41. Leaves, subsessile, with emarginate apices..........
　　　　　　　　　　Buckwheat-tree (p. 440)
41. Leaves, petiolate, with rounded apices............
　　　　　　　　　　Guttapercha mayten (p. 454)

42. Leaves, oblong to elliptical, ¼″ to 1″ wide......
　　　　　　　　　　Swamp cyrilla (p. 438)
42. Leaves, oval to obovate, 1¼″ to 2″ wide........
　　　　　　　　　　Bahama strongbark (p. 642)

43. Twigs, armed..................................**44**
43. Twigs, unarmed..............................**46**

    44. Sap, milky..........**Bumelias,** in part (p. 598)
    44. Sap, watery..............................**45**

45. Leaves, clustered near the tips of twigs............
               Oxhorn bucida (p. 534)
45. Leaves, normally disposed along the twigs..........
               Tallowwood (p. 263)

    46. Sap, milky..................................**47**
    46. Sap, watery................................**48**

47. Leaves, mostly heart-shaped, with petioles 2″ to 4″
    long........................**Manchineel** (p. 418)
47. Leaves, mostly elliptical, with petioles ¼″ to ½″ long
               Oysterwood (p. 421)

    48. Leaves, dotted above and below with minute
    glands, exhaling an aromatic aroma when bruised
               Southern bayberry (p. 113)
    48. Leaves, without surface glands, occasionally
    exhaling a strong but not aromatic odor when
    bruised....................................**49**

49. Stipules or their scars, wanting...................**50**
49. Stipules or their scars, present...................**51**

    50. Twigs, with chambered pith...................
               Common sweetleaf (p. 618)
    50. Twigs, with continuous pith...................
               Loblolly-bay (p. 519)

51. Leaf scars, with a single bundle scar..............
               Hollies, in part (p. 442)
51. Leaf scars, with 3 or more bundle scars............**52**

    52. Leaves, glabrous, exhaling almondlike odor when
    crushed...............**Laurelcherries** (p. 353)

52. Leaves, bristly-pubescent above, woolly below, without characteristic odor when bruised........
Florida trema (p. 246)

VII. TREES WITH ALTERNATE, TRIFOLIATE LEAVES

1. Leaves, deciduous........**Common hoptree** (p. 396)
1. Leaves, persistent.............................. 2

2. Leaflets, sessile..............**Inkwood** (p. 490)
2. Leaflets, petiolate............................ 3

3. Twigs, armed; sap, watery; leaflets, deltoid.........
Eastern coralbean (p. 379)
3. Twigs, unarmed; sap, milky; leaflets, ovate.........
Florida poisontree (p. 435)

VIII. TREES WITH ALTERNATE, PINNATELY COMPOUND LEAVES

1. Leaves, deciduous.............................. 2
1. Leaves, persistent.............................13

2. Twigs, armed........................... 3
2. Twigs, unarmed.......................... 4

3. Leaf rachises, spiny; leaflets, ovate-lanceolate, their margins toothed.............**Hercules-club** (p. 393)
3. Leaf rachises, smooth or furnished with glandular hairs, leaflets, mostly oval, their margins entire....
Locusts (p. 370)

4. Leaflets, alternate or nearly so.................
Yellowwood (p. 377)
4. Leaflets, opposite........................... 5

5. Pith, chambered................**Walnuts** (p. 118)
5. Pith, homogeneous............................ 6

6. Stipules or their scars, present................ 7
6. Stipules or their scars, wanting................ 9

7. Leaflet margins, sharply serrate; buds, resinous......
$$\text{American mountain-ash (p. 331)}$$
7. Leaflet margins, entire; buds, nonresinous.......... 8

    8. Leaves, 5- to 11-foliate; leaflets, oval, pubescent along the midrib below......................
$$\text{Florida fishpoison-tree (p. 381)}$$
    8. Leaves, 13- to 19-foliate; leaflets, elliptical, with scattered hairs below, or smooth..............
$$\text{Texas sophora (p. 384)}$$

9. Leaflets, long-stalked.........**Gumbo-limbo** (p. 409)
9. Leaflets, sessile, or nearly so......................10

    10. Leaflets, toothed.............................11
    10. Leaflets, entire...............................12

11. Bud scales, valvate; buds, in part superposed.......
$$\text{Pecans (p. 123)}$$
11. Bud scales, imbricate; buds, nearly encircled by the leaf scar.................**Sumacs,** in part (p. 427)

    12. Leaflets, bright, waxy green, not fragrant (poisonous to touch); bud scales, purplish.............
$$\text{Poison sumac (p. 428)}$$
    12. Leaflets, dull to lustrous, fragrant; bud scales, brown to black..............**Hickories** (p. 123)

13. Leaves, even-pinnate............................14
13. Leaves, odd-pinnate............................17

    14. Leaves, with 2 to 4 leaflets **Butterbough** (p. 488)
    14. Leaves, with 6 to 12 leaflets...................15

15. Leaflets, ovate to lanceolate, acuminate at apex.....
$$\text{West Indies mahogany (p. 412)}$$
15. Leaflets, oblong to obovate, obtuse at apex.........16

    16. Leaves, 6″ to 10″ long; leaflets, rounded or mucronate at apex........**Paradise-tree** (p. 406)

16. Leaves, 2″ to 3″ long; leaflets, rounded or emarginate at apex........**Biscayne prickly-ash** (p. 396)

17. Stipules, present.............**Mescal-bean** (p. 386)
17. Stipules, wanting...............................18

18. Leaflet margins, toothed.....................19
18. Leaflet margins, entire.......................20

19. Twigs, armed with short spines...................
Lime prickly-ash (p. 391)
19. Twigs, unarmed..........**Florida cupania** (p. 492)

20. Leaves, with 21 to 41 leaflets.................
Mexican alvaradoa (p. 402)
20. Leaves, with 5 to 19 leaflets..................21

21. Sap, milky.............**Florida poisontree** (p. 435)
21. Sap, watery...................................22

22. Leaflets, sessile or nearly so..**Soapberries** (p. 484)
22. Leaflets, petiolate..........................23

23. Leaf rachises, hairy, glandular; leaflets, often falcate, obtuse at apex...............**Yellowheart** (p. 394)
23. Leaf rachises, smooth, not glandular; leaflets, oblong-oval, acuminate at apex........**Bitterbush** (p. 404)

IX. TREES WITH ALTERNATE, TWICE PINNATELY COMPOUND LEAVES

1. Leaves, persistent.......**Bahama lysiloma** (p. 361)
1. Leaves, deciduous............................ 2

2. Leaves, 1- and 2-pinnately compound on same plant; twigs, branches, and trunk, armed with 3-branched, occasionally simple, vascular thorns, 1″ to 5″ long............**Honeylocusts** (p. 366)
2. Leaves, wholly 2-pinnate; twigs, unarmed or, if armed, the spines simple, usually less than ½″ long.. 3

3. Rachises and twigs, armed with simple spines; leaflets, toothed...............**Devils-walkingstick** (p. 553)
3. Rachises and twigs, unarmed; leaflets, entire........
Kentucky coffeetree (p. 363)

X. TREES WITH WHORLED LEAVES

1. Leaves, deciduous............................... 2
1. Leaves, persistent............................... 3

2. Leaves, broadly heart-shaped, 5″ to 12″ long; twigs, stout.................**Catalpas** (p. 654)
2. Leaves, lance-shaped to elliptical, 2″ to 6″ long; twigs, slender....**Common buttonbush** (p. 662)

3. Twigs, many-angled............**Joewood** (p. 584)
3. Twigs, terete.........**Florida crossopetalum** (p. 458)

THE CONIFERS

THE PINE FAMILY

Pinaceae

The Pine Family is the largest and most important of the coniferous groups. It includes nine genera and about 200 species, many of them large and valuable trees, widely scattered in the Northern Hemisphere from the almost inaccessible montane forests of the tropics, to those beyond the Arctic Circle. A few forms are also found south of the equator.

Many of the products of the Pinaceae are intimately associated with our daily lives and activities. Most of the many fine structural timbers with which we build our homes are traceable to this family. It produces the bulk of the pulpwood used in the manufacture of our newspapers and favorite magazines; its chemical derivatives such as rayon, cellophane, turpentine, and plastics are legion. In times of illness our physician may prescribe certain pharmaceutical preparations that are obtainable only from members of this group of plants.

Because of their grace and pleasing form, trees of several genera are highly prized as ornamentals. Our parks, our streets, and our homes have been given added charm and beauty where members of this group have been used in landscaping.

Four genera and 16 species are included in the flora of the South. Several of them are very important species and have played a notable role in the economic development of the region.

Synopsis of Southern Genera

Genus	Leaves	Cones
Pinus	needlelike, in fascicles of 2 to 5	pendent; bracts, shorter than the seed scales; maturing in 2 seasons
Picea	linear, 4-sided or more or less flattened, sessile, leaving peglike projections on the twig upon falling	pendent; bracts, shorter than the seed scales; maturing in 1 season
Tsuga	linear, flattened, petioled, more or less 2-ranked	similar to *Picea*, but smaller
Abies	linear, flattened, sessile, sometimes 2-ranked	upright; scales and bracts, deciduous from the cone axis at maturity; bracts, longer or shorter than the seed scales; maturing in 1 season

THE PINES

Pinus L.

The pines, numbering about 90 species, comprise one of the largest and most important genera of coniferous plants. They are widely scattered through the forests of the Northern Hemisphere from the Arctic region in North America and Europe, to subtropical Asia, northern Africa, the West Indies, British Honduras, and the Philippine Islands. They attain their best development in western North America where sugar pine, ponderosa pine, and western white pine reach gigantic proportions. Several of the smaller western species are found at high altitudes, at or near the timber line, where they play a stellar role in the protection of valuable watersheds against excessive runoff and erosion. The nut or piñon pines, a small group of southwestern trees, produce large, sweetish seeds, which are collected and placed on the market as "pine nuts." The American naval-stores industry centers around the slash and longleaf pines of the southeastern United States.

Scotch pine (*P. sylvestris* L.), a native of Europe, has been planted extensively in the Northeast in areas where the blister rust has been a serious menace to the continued development of the white pine. Austrian pine (*P. nigra* Arnold), Japanese black pine (*P. thunbergii* Parl.), and the maritime pine (*P. pinaster* Ait.) are among the more common exotics used in ornamental planting in the Southeast.

Eleven species, including the eastern white pine, are included in the flora of southern forests.

KEY TO THE SOUTHERN PINES

1. Leaves, in clusters of 5, with a deciduous basal sheath; cone scales, unarmed, furnished with a terminal scar.................**Eastern white pine** (p. 49)
1. Leaves, in clusters of 2 or 3 (rarely, in part, 4 or 5), with a persistent basal sheath; cone scales, usually smooth at the apex, but armed on the back with a spine, prickle, or claw............................ 2

   2. Leaves, in clusters of 2....................... 3
   2. Leaves, in clusters of 3, or of 2 and 3 on the same tree... 6

3. Cone scales, knoblike near the apex, armed on the back with a stout hook or claw; leaves, blue-green..
                    Table-mountain pine (p. 63)
3. Cone scales, thin at the apex or only slightly thickened, armed on the back with a small pine or prickle; leaves, dark green or yellow-green................. 4

4. Cones, about 2″ long, armed with weak, often deciduous prickles..........**Spruce pine** (p. 70)
4. Cones, about 3″ long, with slender, mostly persistent prickles.............................. 5

5. Cones, opening at maturity; cone scales, with a terminal, purple stripe on the inner lip; leaves, yellow-green, twisted.................**Virginia pine** (p. 65)
5. Cones, remaining closed at maturity, persistent on the branches for many years; leaves, dark green, not twisted........................**Sand pine** (p. 70)

6. Leaves, in clusters of 3........................ 7
6. Leaves, in clusters of 2 and 3..................10

7. Leaves, mostly 12″ or more in length, borne on stout branchlets; buds, white; cones, about 9″ long, sessile, usually leaving the basal portions on the branches when falling away.............**Longleaf pine** (p. 51)
7. Leaves, usually less than 9″ in length, borne on slender branchlets; buds, brown to reddish brown; cones, less than 6″ long, if sessile not leaving basal portion on the branches when falling away....................... 8

8. Cones, narrowly conical....**Loblolly pine** (p. 55)
8. Cones, ovoid to nearly globular................ 9

9. Leaves, 3″ to 5″ long; cones, ovoid, the scales armed with stout, sharp prickles.........**Pitch pine** (p. 60)
9. Leaves, 6″ to 8″ long; cones, broadly ovoid to nearly globular, the scales armed with weak, deciduous prickles........................**Pond pine** (p. 62)

10. Cones, stalked, about 5″ in length; leaves, 8″ to 12″ in length................**Slash pine** (p. 58)
10. Cones, sessile, about 2″ to 6″ in length; leaves, 3″ to 9″ in length............................11

11. Cones, about 2″ in length; leaves, 3″ to 5″ in length; bark, with resin pockets.......**Shortleaf pine** (p. 67)
11. Cones, about 5″ in length; leaves, 6″ to 9″ in length; bark, without resin pockets.....**Loblolly pine** (p. 55)

Eastern White Pine

Pinus strobus L.

Habit.—A large tree, commonly 100' or more in height and 2' to 4' in diameter; in open situations, usually developing a rapidly tapering bole clothed in a broad, conical crown of living branches that extends almost to the ground; in the forest, producing a tall, cylindrical shaft that is commonly clear for two-thirds or more of its length and then supports a short, usually irregular crown composed of numerous horizontally spreading or ascending, plumelike branches; root system, moderately deep and wide-spreading; taproot, usually wanting except in youth.

Leaves.—Needlelike, 3" to 5" long, in clusters of 5, the basal sheath early deciduous, dark bluish green, slender, flexible, triangular in cross section, marked by 3 to 5 whitish, longitudinal lines along the ventral surfaces, beginning to drop off at the end of the 2d season.

Flowers.—The male, yellow; the female, pink, their scales, tinged with purple along the margin.

Cones.—4" to 8" long, narrowly oblong, often somewhat curved, stalked; scales, thin, their exposed portions (closed cone) smooth or with several parallel ridges, unarmed, but with a terminal scar (umbo); seeds, about $\frac{1}{4}$" long, reddish or grayish brown, usually mottled, the wing about $\frac{3}{4}$" long, straw-colored, streaked with brown.

Twigs.—Orange-brown, smooth or sparsely hairy; buds, covered with several thin, reddish- or orange-brown scales.

Bark.—Dark green and smooth on young stems, at length becoming 1" to 2" thick, then divided into narrow, roughly rectangular blocks by deep, narrow fissures.

Habitat.—Most abundant and reaching best development on moist, sandy loams or loamy clays, but

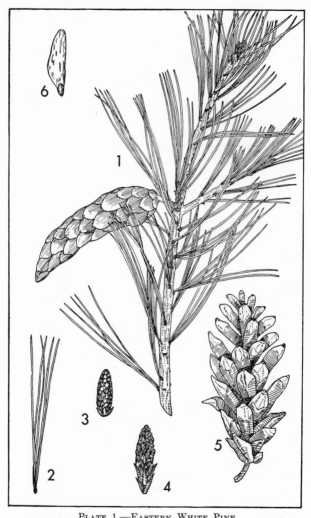

PLATE 1.—EASTERN WHITE PINE
1. Foliage and closed cone ×½. 2. Fascicle of needles ×½.
3. Cluster of male flowers ×½. 4. Cluster of female flowers ×1.
5. Open cone ×1. 6. Seed ×1.

able to become established on dry, rocky ridges and even in wet sphagnum bogs. Found in pure stands or in a mixture with many other species; in the South occurring along the slopes of the Appalachians and in widely scattered areas in the Piedmont, commonly in association with eastern hemlock and a variety of broadleaved species.

Distribution.—Southern Canada, the Lake states, the Northeast, and the Appalachian Mountains to northern Georgia.

Importance.—Eastern white pine was the principal source of American softwood timber from the time when the first New England colonies were established until the turn of the present century. While vast quantities of this valuable species have long since been logged, burned, or otherwise destroyed, it is still among the leaders in the production of saw timber. The wood of old-growth white pine is of excellent quality and is suitable for many purposes, particularly planing-mill products such as fancy moldings, sashes, doors, and interior trim. Boxboards, matches, and pattern stock consume large quantities of this wood.

Because of the demand and ever-ready market for white pine timber, the tree has been established in countless plantations, not only in the northeastern United States, but in England and Germany as well.

White pine is not suitable for street or roadside planting although it makes an excellent ornamental for parks and lawns. It is occasionally used in this manner in the South, particularly along the Piedmont plateau and in the Sand Hills towns of North Carolina.

Longleaf Pine

Pinus palustris Mill.

Habit.—A tree, 80′ to 100′ in height and 2½′ in diameter; characterized by a long, clear, symmetrical

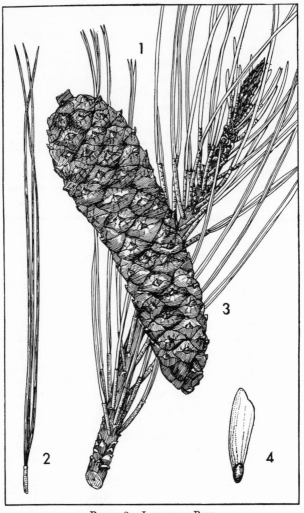

PLATE 2.—LONGLEAF PINE
1. Foliage $\times\frac{1}{2}$. 2. Fascicle of needles $\times\frac{1}{2}$. 3. Closed cone $\times\frac{1}{2}$. 4. Seed $\times\frac{1}{2}$.

bole, a small, open crown with long, bright-green tufts of needles at the tips of stout branchlets, and a deep taproot supported by numerous wide-spreading lateral roots.

Seedling trees differ from those of associated conifers in that little or no stem elongation occurs during the first 3 to 7 or more years of their development. During this interval the aerial portion of the stem consists merely of a dense cluster of needles, in general appearance not unlike a large tuft of grass. It is not strange, therefore, that this phase of the tree's development is known as the *grass stage*. Through this period of apparent inactivity above ground, a prodigious root system is being developed below; once this has become thoroughly established, normal stem elongation begins.

Leaves.—Needlelike, 8″ to 18″ long, in clusters of 3,* with a persistent basal sheath, in dense tufts at the ends of the stout branchlets, bright green, slender, pendulous, flexible, 3-sided, beginning to fall off in the 2d season.

Flowers.—Male, dark rose-purple, many-clustered; female, dark purple, in pairs or clusters of 3 or 4.

Cones.—6″ to 10″ long, narrowly ovoid or cylindrical, sessile, when falling leaving a few basal scales attached to the branchlets; the scales, thin, flat, rounded at the apex, the exposed portions (closed cone) reddish brown, often wrinkled, armed on the back with a small, reflexed prickle, which curves toward the base of the scale; seeds, about ½″ long, mottled, the wing, about 1½″ long, striped, oblique at the ends.

Twigs.—Orange-brown, stout; buds, stout, large, and conspicuous, covered by many silvery-white, fringed, long-spreading scales.

---

* Trees with 5 needles in a fascicle have been observed in the Gulf states.

Bark.—Orange-brown, coarsely scaly, the scales thin and papery; plated on the largest trees.

Habitat.—Flat, sandy, and gravelly soils of the coastal plains; often on thin soils underlaid with hard-pan; toward the southern parts of its range, ascending low knolls and ridges.

Distribution.—South Atlantic and Gulf coastal plains from southeastern Virginia to eastern Texas. Not found in the Mississippi River Valley; sea level to 1,900' in northern Alabama.

Importance.—This is the largest and most impor-tant of the southern yellow pines. It was well known in early colonial times, although it was not so exten-sively used during that era as the northern white pine. History records that some of the choicest stands of longleaf pine were set aside by the English Crown for the exclusive use of the British Navy. These trees were ideal for masts and spars for the sailing ships that carried England's trade to the seven seas. Here was also a tree that supplied quantities of resinous materials admirably suited for calking the planking of hulls and decks.

When the supply of high-grade white pine began to dwindle, lumbermen turned their attention to the southern pinelands, and by 1909 the South was the principal lumbering center of the nation. It supplied about half the total annual cut, much of which was longleaf pine.

The naval-stores industry, which had its beginning as noted above, has been greatly expanded and today is one of our greatest forest industries. The resinous exudations of both longleaf and slash pines are now fractionally distilled and the resulting products find numerous and diversified uses. They are employed in the manufacture of paints, varnishes, furniture and shoe polishes, japans, soaps, cloth-printing inks, pharmaceutical preparations, greases, specialty lubricants, linoleums, sealing wax, roofing materials, brewer's pitch, and sweeping compounds. The rosin, so essential to the papermaker, is another major product of the industry, and some of the heavy oils used in the flotation of the precious-metal ores are other products. A considerable portion of the annual cut is also consumed in the production of kraft paper and paperboards.

Remarks.—An interesting hybrid between longleaf and loblolly pines, the Sonderegger pine (*P. palustris* × *P. taeda*), is known to occur in North Carolina, Louisiana, Texas, and possibly elsewhere. Seedling trees of this form are not infrequently found in seed beds of longleaf pine. Here they are easily distinguished since, unlike the longleaf pine, they produce vigorous, lengthy aerial shoots during their initial season of growth.

Several years ago a plantation of Sonderegger pine was established on the Duke Forest, Durham, North Carolina, where careful recordings are being maintained on the growth and development of this form.

Loblolly Pine

Pinus taeda L.

Habit.—A tree not uncommonly 90′ to 110′ in height and 2′ to 4′ in diameter; characterized by a long, clear, cylindrical, and occasionally buttressed bole, a well-developed lateral root system, and a large, open crown of spreading and ascending limbs.

Leaves.—Needlelike, 6″ to 9″ long, in clusters of 3 (occasionally 2), with a persistent basal sheath, yellow-green to gray-green, slender but rather stiff, occasionally twisted, beginning to drop off at the end of the 2d season.

Flowers.—The male, in large clusters, yellow; the female, in clusters of 2 or 3 or solitary, yellow.

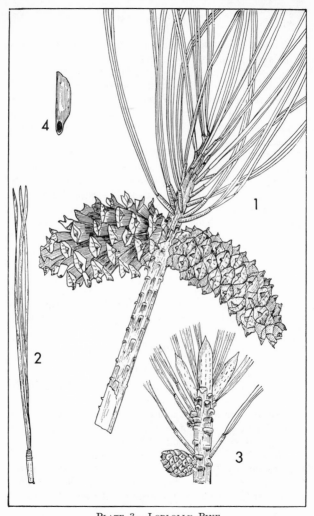

PLATE 3.—LOBLOLLY PINE

1. Foliage and cones $\times \frac{1}{2}$. 2. Fascicle of needles $\times \frac{1}{2}$. 3. Buds and one-year-old cone $\times 1$. 4. Seed $\times \frac{1}{2}$.

Cones.—3″ to 6″ long, narrowly conical to ovoid-cylindric, sessile; the scales, thin, their exposed portions (closed cone) tawny, flattened, wrinkled, armed on the back with a short, stout, sharp spine; seeds, about ¼″ long, rough or pebbly to the touch, dark brown, mottled with black, the wings about ¾″ long, broadest above the middle, lustrous, light, yellowish brown to nearly gray-black.

Twigs.—Reddish brown to dark yellow-brown; buds, covered by numerous narrow, wedge-shaped, reddish-brown scales, free and commonly reflexed at the tips.

Bark.—Nearly black and scaly on very young stems; on older trees, 1″ to 2″ thick and divided into irregular dark-brown, scaly blocks; on the very largest trees, similar to that of shortleaf pine trees of comparable size, but without the resin pockets so characteristic of that species.

Habitat.—Widely scattered on a variety of sites through the forests of the coastal plains and lower Piedmont plateau, in either pure or mixed stands; very aggressive on fallow fields and cutover lands, and often fully restocking such areas in a remarkably short time; occurring as an occasional tree in virgin forests in moist situations and along streams, in association with hardwoods; west of the Mississippi Valley forming extensive pure stands on gently rolling uplands.

Distribution.—The coastal plains and lower Piedmont plateau from southern New Jersey to central peninsular Florida, southern Oklahoma, and southeastern Texas; not found in the lower Mississippi Valley.

Importance.—Loblolly pine grows more rapidly over long periods of time than does any other of the southern yellow pines. The wood, however, is inferior in quality to that produced by either longleaf or shortleaf pines, but ordinarily it is used for the same purposes.

Recently it has been found to be suitable for the production of bond and similar papers and now is an important raw material for the newly developed southern sulphite pulp and paper industry.

Slash Pine

Pinus caribaea Morelet

Habit.—A rapidly growing tree, often 80′ to 100′ in height and 18″ to 30″ in diameter, with a clear, symmetrical bole, very deep root system, and dense, round-topped crown of horizontal and ascending branches.

Leaves.—Needlelike, 8″ to 12″ long, in clusters of 2 and 3 on the same tree and commonly on the same branch, with a persistent basal sheath, dark, glossy green, tufted at the ends of the branches, stout, rather stiff, dropping off in their 2d season.

Flowers.—The male, in many-flowered clusters, dark purple; the female, commonly solitary, on long stalks, pinkish.

Cones.—2″ to 6″ long, ovoid-conic, stalked; the scales, thin, their exposed portions (closed cone) lustrous brown, armed on the back with a small, sharp, commonly curved prickle; seeds, about $\frac{1}{4}$″ long, more or less triangular, black, ridged; the wings, about 1″ long, encircling the seed, thin, and translucent.

Twigs.—Orange-brown, stout; buds, covered with several silvery-brown scales, free at the tips.

Bark.—Deeply furrowed on young stems, ultimately becoming 1″ to 2″ thick on older trees, then broken into large, flat plates covered with large, thin, papery, silvery-orange scales.

Habitat.—Low ground, hammocks, swamps, and along streams; very aggressive and commonly usurping cutover lands formerly occupied by other species.

Distribution.—Gulf states southward through sev-

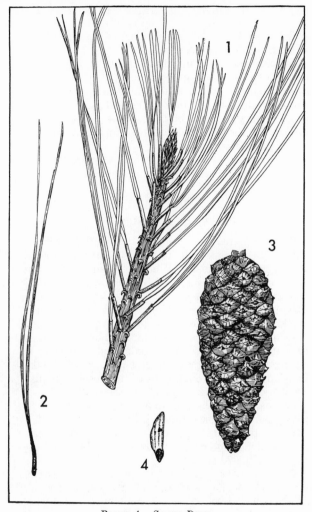

PLATE 4.—SLASH PINE
1. Foliage ×½. 2. Fascicle of needles ×½. 3. Closed cone
×½. 4. Seed ×½.

eral of the West Indian islands to Guatemala and
Honduras in Central America.

Importance.—Probably best known to those associated with the naval-stores industry. It is said that
slash pine actually excels longleaf pine in the production of crude resin and that the refined products are of
equal quality to those of that species. The wood is
principally used for railroad ties, fuel, general construction, and pulp.

The tree is occasionally used as a roadside ornamental in several sections of the Deep South.

Pitch Pine

Pinus rigida Mill.

Habit.—A tree of widespread distribution, exhibiting notable variation in form and stature; on good
sites, commonly 60′ to 70′ in height and 1′ to 2′ in
diameter, then characterized by a clear, symmetrical
bole and small, open crown; on exposed, dry, rocky
sites, usually producing a short, stocky bole, which is
quickly lost in a large, grotesque crown of contorted
branches. Saplings possess a taproot, but this ceases
to function as the trees grow older and ultimately is
replaced by a widespread lateral root system. Like
the shortleaf pine, young trees of this species are also
capable of producing sprouts from the root collar.

Leaves.—Needlelike, 3″ to 5″ long, in clusters of 3,
with a persistent basal sheath, yellow-green, stiff, often
twisted, supported at right angles to the twig, commonly
in tufts along the bole from adventitious buds, falling
off during the 2d season.

Flowers.—The male, in many-flowered clusters,
yellow, occasionally with a purplish tinge; the female,
short-stalked, greenish yellow, sometimes tinged with
pink.

Cones.—2″ to 3½″ long, ovoid, sessile or nearly so;

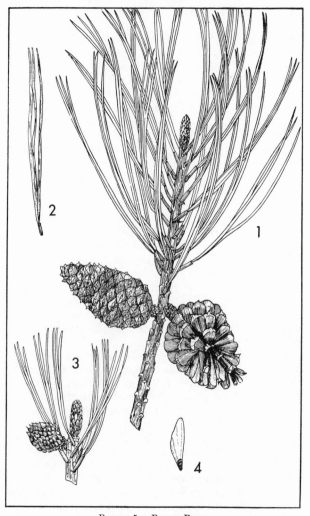

PLATE 5.—PITCH PINE

1. Foliage and cones ×½. 2. Fascicle of needles ×½.
3. One-year-old cone ×½. 4. Seed ×⅔.

the scales, thin, their exposed portions (closed cone) light brown, smooth, armed on the back with a stout, rigid prickle; seeds, about ¼" long, oval to somewhat 3-angled, dull black or mottled with gray, rough or pebbly to the touch, the wings, about ¾" long, light brown commonly with darker, longitudinal streaks.

Twigs.—Stout, ridged, at first bright green but becoming orange-brown during the 1st winter; buds, conical, about ¾" long, covered by several reddish-brown scales, occasionally free at the tips, resinous.

Bark.—Very dark, scaly on young stems; on the largest trees 1" to 2" thick, yellowish brown, and separated into large, irregular, flat plates by narrow seams and fissures.

Habitat.—Variable; in the North on the poorest of sterile, sandy soils or occasionally on the margins of cold swamps; in the South on moist, sandy loams of mountain slopes, commonly forming pure stands but reaching its best development with mixed hardwoods.

Distribution.—The Northeast and the Appalachian Mountains to northern Georgia; at or near sea level in the North, often above 3,000' of elevation toward its southern limits.

Importance.—Pitch pine at one time was a source of naval stores; hence the name. It has not been exploited in this manner, however, for many years. The wood is commonly used for charcoal, fuel, pulp, crossties, and mine props but is seldom cut into lumber.

Remarks.—Pond pine (*P. rigida* var. *serotina* Loud.) is a natural variety of the pitch pine and occurs along the coastal plain in swamps and low wet flats, known locally as "pocosins," from southern New Jersey to northern Florida and central Alabama. The needles are longer than those of pitch pine (6" to 8"), and the cones nearly globular. Some authorities see fit to give this form specific rank with the designation of *P. serotina* Michx. It is becoming an important pulpwood species; the larger trees, when encountered during logging, are taken along with the more desirable species and indiscriminately mixed with them.

Table-Mountain Pine

Pinus pungens Lamb.

Habit.—A tree, in dense stands 50′ to 60′ in height and 2′ to 3′ in diameter, with a long, clear bole, crowned at the summit with several short branches forming a narrow, rounded head; in open situations, seldom more than 20′ to 30′ in height with correspondingly smaller diameters, then characterized by a short bole almost hidden by a crown of horizontal or pendulous, cone-laden branches that extend nearly to the ground.

Leaves.—Needlelike, 1½″ to 2½″ long, in clusters of 2, with a persistent basal sheath, dark blue-green, rigid, generally twisted, falling off during the 2d or 3d years.

Flowers.—The male, clustered, yellow; the female, yellow, clustered, long-stalked.

Cones.—2″ to 3½″ long, ovoid-conic, commonly asymmetrical at the base, borne in clusters of 3 to 8, gradually opening and shedding their seeds over a period of 1 to 3 years, but commonly remaining on the branches for 15 to 20 more; the exposed portions of the scale (closed cone), light brown, lustrous, commonly knoblike, armed with a stout hook or claw, the inner lip of each scale with a broad, mahogany-red band; seeds, about ¼″ long, 3-angled, light brown, pebbly to the touch, the wings, about 1″ long, brown.

Twigs.—Stout, at first light orange, eventually dull, dark brown; buds, about ½″ long, cylindrical, resinous, covered with several brown, closely appressed scales.

Bark.—Dark brown tinged with red, that on the lower portions of the trunk plated and superficially

PLATE 6.—TABLE-MOUNTAIN PINE.
1. Foliage and cones ×⅔.   2. Seed ×1.

scaly, the upper trunk and larger limbs with thin, loosely appressed scales.

Habitat.—Dry, gravelly or rocky mountain slopes and tablelands; toward the southern limits of its range, forming extensive pure stands.

Distribution.—The Appalachian region from south-central Pennsylvania to northern Georgia and eastern Tennessee; not infrequently found above 4,000' in elevation.

Importance.—The wood of this species is used for fuel and occasionally in the manufacture of charcoal. In certain sections the trees play an important role in the protection of valuable watersheds.

Virginia Pine

Pinus virginiana Mill.

Habit.—A tree of modest proportions, seldom more than 40' to 60' in height and 12" to 20" in diameter. Even in dense stands the boles do not prune readily and are usually characterized by numerous, persistent snags and dead branches for a considerable length below the living crown. Open-grown trees usually have open, flat-topped or pyramidal crowns; the root system is characteristically wide-spreading.

Leaves.—Needlelike, 1½" to 3" long, in clusters of 2, with a persistent basal sheath, yellow-green, stout, twisted, falling off at irregular intervals during the 3d and 4th seasons.

Flowers.—The male, in many-flowered clusters, golden brown to orange-brown; the female, usually in 2's on opposite sides of the twig, stalked, pale green or tinged with pink.

Cones.—1½" to 2½" long, ovoid-conic; the scales, thin, their exposed portions (closed cone) reddish brown, armed on the back with a persistent, slender prickle, the inner lip furnished with a broad, purplish

PLATE 7.—VIRGINIA PINE
1. Foliage and cones ×½. 2. Seed ×1.

stripe; seeds, about $\frac{1}{4}''$ long, oval, light brown, pebbly to the touch, wings, about $\frac{1}{2}''$ long, brown, usually broadest near the middle.

Twigs.—Those of the 1st season, green, commonly covered with a purplish, waxy bloom, at length gray-brown; buds, ovoid, sharp-pointed, resinous.

Bark.—Thin and smooth on young stems, eventually about $\frac{1}{2}''$ thick, then broken into dark-brown, flat, platelike scales separated by shallow fissures; upper trunk and larger limbs, clothed with orange-brown, papery scales.

Habitat.—Heavy clays, sandy and impoverished soils of slopes and flats; commonly preempting fallow fields and forming pure stands; also occurring as an occasional tree in mixed hardwoods and with shortleaf and loblolly pines.

Distribution.—Southern New York, west through central Pennsylvania to southern Ohio and Indiana, thence south to Georgia and South Carolina; rare in the southern Atlantic coastal plain.

Importance.—This species is rapidly becoming an important source of pulpwood. In the past it has been used for crossties, boxboards, charcoal manufacture, and fencing.

Shortleaf Pine

Pinus echinata Mill.

Habit.—A tree, 80' to 100' in height and 2' to 3' in diameter, characterized by a long, clear, symmetrical, unbuttressed bole, small, narrow, pyramidal crown, and a huge taproot. This pine, unlike most other conifers, possesses unusual regenerative powers during its early juvenile development. When the original stem of a seedling or sapling has been destroyed, sprouts arise from the root collar and are capable of ultimately attaining commercial proportions.

PLATE 8.—SHORTLEAF PINE

1. Foliage and closed cone ×⅔. 2. Cluster of female flowers
×1. 3. Cluster of male flowers ×½. 4. Open cone ×⅔.
5. Seed ×1.

Leaves.—Needlelike, 3″ to 5″ long, in clusters of 2 and 3 on the same branch, the basal sheath persistent, dark yellow-green, slender, flexible, often persistent through the 4th season, occasionally in tufts along the bole from adventitious buds.

Flowers.—The male, in large clusters, yellowish brown to pale pink; the female, in small clusters of 2 or 3 or solitary, light pink.

Cones.—1½″ to 2½″ long, conical or ovoid, nearly sessile, releasing their seeds at maturity, but persisting on the branches for many years, the scales thin, rounded at the apex, the exposed portions (closed cone) reddish brown, armed on the back with a small, sharp, straight or curved, occasionally deciduous prickle; seeds, about ¼″ long, brown, commonly mottled with black, the wings ½″ long, broadest near the middle, straw-colored, occasionally with yellow-brown streaks.

Twigs.—Those of the 1st season, pale green, usually covered with a purplish bloom, at length smooth and reddish brown; buds, covered with several slender, red-brown scales.

Bark.—Nearly black and roughened on young stems, that of older trees reddish brown and separated into irregular, flat, scaly plates, with many small resin pockets scattered through the corky layers.

Habitat.—Most common in pure or mixed stands on dry upland soils although occurring on many different sites and on a variety of soils.

Distribution.—Eastern United States from central New Jersey south and west to northern Florida, southern Missouri, eastern Oklahoma, and southeastern Texas; found neither on the upper slopes of the Appalachian Mountains nor in the Mississippi Valley.

Importance.—This is another of the four important southern yellow pines. The wood is firm and moderately heavy and well suited for many uses, notably structural timbers, planing-mill products, excelsior, cooperage, and pulp.

The tree is occasionally used as an ornamental, but its use for decorative purposes should be discouraged, especially in lawns, because of the unsightly litter of dry needles, old cones, and dead branches, which drop off almost constantly.

Sand Pine

Pinus clausa Vasey.

Sand pine, so called because of its occurrence on the sandy coastal soils in Florida and Alabama, is a small tree seldom ever more than 25' high or 12'' in diameter. The trees often occur in limited pure stands where their long, fibrous roots greatly retard the migration of shifting sands. Sand pine may be identified by its dark green flexible needles, 2'' to 3½'' long, borne in fascicles of 2; its 2'' to 3½'' long, ovoid-conic cones which remain closed and persistent on the branches for many years; and its reddish-brown scaly bark.

Spruce Pine

Pinus glabra Walt.

The spruce pine is a tree of modest proportions (80' to 90' high and 1½' to 2½' in diameter) found on moist, sandy loam soils along the southern coastal plains from the Santee River valley in South Carolina to north-central Florida, thence west to southeastern Louisiana. It occurs as an occasional tree or in small groves in association with sweetgum, beech, several hickories, and shortleaf and loblolly pines. The wood is occasionally used for pulp, for fuel and for saw timber. Spruce pine is easily distinguished by its slender, dark-green, twisted needles, 1½'' to 3'' long which are borne in fascicles of 2; its 1'' to 2'' long, oblong-ovoid to nearly globular cones, armed with minute, deciduous prickles; and its silvery-gray, deeply furrowed bark.

THE SPRUCES

Picea Diet.

The spruces comprise a group of about 40 species of trees, the majority restricted to cooler regions of the Northern Hemisphere. Their principal center of distribution appears to be in China, where there are no less than 18 species. The loftiest trees, however, are found near the tidewater along the Pacific rim of western North America. Here the Sitka spruce [*P. sitchensis* (Bong.) Carr.] not infrequently attains heights in excess of 200′ with diameters of 3′ to 4′ or more.

Many of the spruces because of their pleasing symmetry, lustrous and colorful foliage, and pendulous branchlets are highly desirable for ornamental planting. In the South, the Colorado blue spruce (*P. pungens* Engelm.) and several of its varieties, and the oriental spruce (*P. orientalis* Link.) are the two most commonly used for decorative purposes.

Norway spruce [*P. abies* (L.) Karst.] has been used extensively in plantations throughout the Northeast. The resinous bark exudations of this species furnish the Burgundy pitch of commerce, the basic substance for numerous varnishes and medicinal compounds.

KEY TO THE SOUTHERN SPRUCES

1. Leaves, dark yellow-green; cones, about 1¾″ long, ovoid-oblong, usually falling off after the 1st season..
   Red spruce (p. 72)
1. Leaves, blue-green, often covered with a waxy bloom, fetid; cones, about 1″ long, ovoid, persistent for many years after releasing their seed...**Black spruce** (p. 74)

Red Spruce

Picea rubens Sarg.

Habit.—A tree, often 70′ to 100′ in height and 1′ to 2′ in diameter; in the open, developing a broad, conical crown, which extends nearly to the ground; in the forest, producing a long, cylindrical shaft, which rises above a shallow, wide-spreading root system and passes through a short, conical crown.

Leaves.—Linear, $\frac{1}{2}$″ to $\frac{5}{8}$″ long, dark yellow-green, blunt or acute at the apex, 4-sided, persisting for 5 or 6 years.

Flowers.—Those of both sexes, either terminal or subterminal; the male, ovoid, sessile or nearly so, scarlet; the female, cylindric, green or tinged with red.

Cones.—$1\frac{1}{4}$″ to 2″ long, ovoid-oblong, chestnut-brown; scales, rigid, rounded, entire or slightly eroded along the margin; seeds, about $\frac{1}{8}$″ long, dark brown, with broadly oval, straw-colored terminal wings.

Twigs.—Orange-brown, more or less pubescent, furnished with numerous peglike projections (sterigmata); buds, ovoid, pointed, with reddish-brown scales.

Bark.—Seldom over $\frac{1}{2}$″ in thickness, gray to reddish brown, separating at the surface into more or less appressed, scaly plates.

Habitat.—Occasionally encountered in peat bogs and swamps with red maple, tamarack, black spruce, and balsam fir; more abundant and attaining larger proportions, however, on moist but well-drained flats and slopes, where it occurs either in pure stands or as a component of mixed coniferous and hardwood forests, then with beech, yellow birch, sugar maple, white pine, eastern hemlock, and balsam fir as its

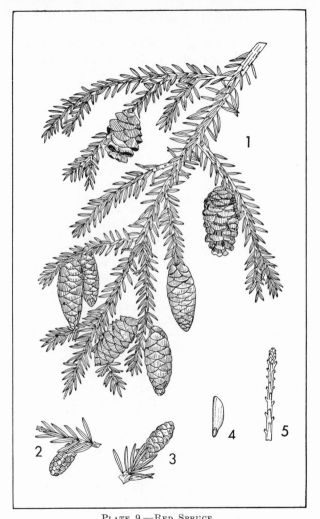

PLATE 9.—RED SPRUCE

1. Foliage and cones ×½. 2. Male flower ×1. 3. Female flower ×1. 4. Seed ×1. 5. Portion of naked twig showing sterigma ×1.

principal associates; in the South restricted to high
mountain slopes and ridges of the Appalachian region.

Distribution.—The Northeast, and the Appalachian
Mountains to northern Georgia; occasionally on bluffs
overlooking the ocean in the North, to 6,000′ of elevation in the South.

Importance.—Red spruce is one of the most important of eastern conifers. Vast quantities of the
wood are consumed annually in the production of
both mechanical and chemical pulps. During the
First World War the wood was found to be suitable
for aircraft construction, although the Sitka spruce
of the Pacific Northwest eventually replaced it.
Much of the annual cut is manufactured into planing-
mill products, boxcar siding, floors and roofing,
lard and butter tubs, pails, and construction lumber.
Because of its strength and lightness, it is suitable for
ladder stock, canoe ribbing, paddles, and small boats.
The highly resonant quality of the wood is responsible
for its wide use as sounding boards in pianos and in
other stringed instruments.

Spruce beer was brewed from the tips of leafy
shoots during the colonial period, and great claims
were made for its beneficial effects. The resinous
exudation of the bark has been collected and sold to
tourist trade as "spruce gum." The seeds form a
considerable portion of the diet of red squirrels and
chipmunks.

Black Spruce

Picea mariana (Mill.) B.S.P.

Black spruce is a small tree of widespread transcontinental distribution through Canada. Its presence in the mountains of Virginia has been established
beyond all doubt, but reports of its occurrence in the
North Carolina highlands have never been sub-
stantiated. This species differs from the red spruce

in several respects. Its leaves are shorter, blue-green, and commonly covered with a waxy bloom; the cones are only about 1″ in length, egg-shaped, and, after the seeds have been released, often persistent on the branches for 20 to 30 years.

THE HEMLOCKS

Tsuga Carr.

The hemlocks constitute a group of about 13 species of graceful, pyramidal-shaped trees confined to the forests of North America and Asia. Most of them are used ornamentally throughout the cooler regions of the Northern Hemisphere. An astringent derived from the bark of several species is suitable for tanning leather and at one time was the principal source of commercial tannin extract. The wood is used for general construction and pulp.

Four hemlocks are indigenous to the United States, and 2 are native to the southeastern United States.

KEY TO THE SOUTHERN HEMLOCKS

1. Leaves, 2-ranked; cones, about ½″ long; terminal leader, usually drooping.....**Eastern hemlock** (p. 75)
1. Leaves, spreading from the twig in all directions; cones, about 1¼″ long; terminal leader, usually erect......
   Carolina hemlock (p. 78)

Eastern Hemlock

Tsuga canadensis (L.) Carr.

Habit.—A tree, 60′ to 80′ in height and 2′ to 3′ in diameter; in the open, producing a handsome, broadly conical crown, which nearly obscures a rapidly tapering bole; in the forest, developing a large, irregular crown with massive branches. This tree does not prune itself readily; the bole under the living crown is usually characterized by numerous dead snags and

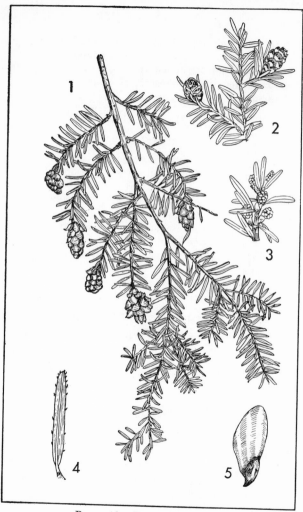

PLATE 10.—EASTERN HEMLOCK

1. Foliage and cones ×½. 2. Female flowers ×1. 3. Male flowers ×1. 4. Leaf ×2. 5. Seed ×4.

limbs. Of particular note is the terminal shoot, which assumes a gracefully weeping habit.

Leaves.—Linear, ⅓″ to ⅔″ long, 2-ranked, yellow-green above, with 2 silvery-white bands below, rounded or slightly notched at the apex, dropping off in their 3d season.

Flowers.—The male, stalked, borne in the leaf axils of year-old foliage, light yellow; the female, solitary, terminating the growth of the season, light green.

Cones.—½″ to ¾″ long, oblong-ovoid, light brown, dull; scales, nearly circular, smooth along their margins; seeds, 1/16″ long, with 2 or 3 resin cysts, their wings, terminal, broad, pale brown.

Twigs.—Those of the current season, slender, yellowish brown, pubescent; at length, reddish brown to purplish and smooth; buds, ovoid, minute, covered with several hairy scales.

Bark.—Scaly or flaky on young stems; on old trees, deeply furrowed and when blazed exhibiting alternating layers of purplish and reddish-brown tissues.

Habitat.—To be encountered on a variety of soil types, but attaining its best development in cool moist situations; in the South, most abundant along mountain slopes and streams, sometimes in limited pure stands, but more commonly with hickories, yellow-poplar, basswoods, and numerous oaks.

Distribution.—Southern Canada, the Northeast, the Lake states, and the Appalachian region to northern Georgia; seldom below 800′ of elevation in the South.

Importance.—Eastern hemlock bark for many years was the principal source of tannin extract. In the early days it was common practice to strip the standing tree of its bark, but no attempt was made to harvest the timber. As a result of this wasteful procedure, vast "silver forests" composed of dead, naked, weatherworn hemlocks could be seen in many sections of the East. The wood of eastern hemlock is perishable, brash, and of inferior quality generally but is used for pulp, boxboards, crating, and construction. There are no less than 15 horticultural varieties of this species, among them dwarfed and prostrate forms. In some localities the hemlock is used as a hedge because it reacts well to shearing.

Carolina Hemlock

Tsuga caroliniana Engelm.

The Carolina hemlock is a beautiful tree of the Appalachian Mountains, where it may be observed on cliffs, rocky slopes, and ridges, usually above 3,000' in elevation. It occurs sporadically from southwestern Virginia to northern Georgia and may be distinguished from the eastern hemlock, with which it is often associated, by its linear, lustrous, green needles, which extend from all sides of the twigs, and its light-brown, oblong cones, often 1″ to 1½″ in length. This tree contributes little or nothing to the nation's timber supply, but its pyramidal crown of spreading or pendulous branches is a prized ornamental plant in many localities far removed from its natural range. It propagates readily and is hardy at least as far north as central New York.

THE BALSAM FIRS

Abies L.

The balsam firs comprise a group of about 40 species, all trees, widely scattered through the forests of North and Central America, Africa, Europe, and Asia. Included in the genus are several important timber and pulpwood species, although none of them produces wood comparable in quality with that of the spruces. Canada balsam, an oleoresin derived from the pitch blisters on the bark of certain species, is used as a cementing matrix for lenses of microscopes and other optical apparatus.

When grown in the open, many of the firs develop dense, broad, conical crowns that extend to the ground. The pleasing symmetry of such trees, together with their silvery-blue or green foliage and their ease of propagation, is largely responsible for their widespread use as ornamentals.

Ten balsam firs are included in the coniferous flora of the United States, and two of them are natives of the southern Appalachian region. These are readily distinguishable from other conifers of the South on two counts. First, the leaves are sessile and upon falling leave circular scars on the twigs. Second, the cones, which are borne in an erect position, disintegrate at maturity and leave their naked, central, spikelike axes attached to the branchlets.

KEY TO THE SOUTHERN BALSAM FIRS

1. Cones, about 2½″ long; the bracts, extending beyond the margin of the seed scales, reflexed...............
   Fraser fir (p. 79)
1. Cones, about 3½″ long; the bracts, much shorter than the seed scales....................**Balsam fir** (p. 81)

Fraser Fir

Abies fraseri Poir.

Habit.—A small, handsome tree, 30′ to 40′ in height and 12″ to 20″ in diameter; in the forest, producing a symmetrical but noticeably tapered bole, narrow, pyramidal crown of horizontally disposed branches, and a shallow, spreading root system.

Leaves.—Linear, ½″ to 1″ long, flat, dark green, lustrous, grooved above, silvery white below, blunt or slightly notched at the apex, sessile and twisted at the base; those on sterile branchlets, mostly 2-ranked;

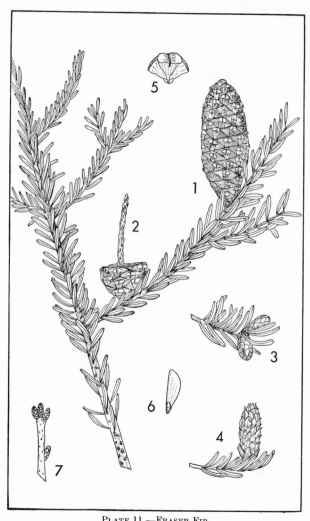

PLATE 11.—FRASER FIR.

1. Foliage and cone ×½. 2. Partially disintegrated cone ×½.
3. Male flowers ×1. 4. Female flower ×1. 5. Cone scale and
bract ×1. 6. Seed ×1. 7. Buds ×1

crowded toward the upper side on cone-bearing branchlets.

Flowers.—The male, pendent, yellow or yellowish red; the female, erect, with elongated, yellow-green bracts terminating in a long, slender tip.

Cones.—2″ to 2½″ long, erect, oblong-ovoid, dark purple; the scales, much wider than long, partly covered by their exserted, reflexed bracts; seeds, about ⅛″ long, with broad, terminal, purplish wings.

Twigs.—Stout, hairy for 2 or 3 seasons, at first yellow-brown but darkening with age; buds, blunt, resinous, covered with several orange-brown, overlapping scales.

Bark.—Thin, smooth, gray, and with numerous resin blisters on young stems; on the largest trees, divided into gray-brown, scaly plates.

Habitat.—Moist, cool mountain slopes between elevations of 4,000′ and 6,700′. Commonly in association with red spruce, yellow birch, and sugar maple.

Distribution.—The mountainous regions of southern Virginia, North Carolina, and Tennessee.

Importance.—Fraser fir plays an important part in the protection of high southern watersheds. Attempts to use the tree as an ornamental at low elevations have not been successful. The wood is used locally for construction and for pulp.

Balsam Fir

Abies balsamea (L.) Mill.

Balsam fir, an important tree of widespread distribution through Canada and the northeastern United States, is of rare occurrence in the South, being found only on the highest mountains of Virginia and West Virginia. Balsam fir is readily separated from Fraser fir on the basis of cone characteristics previously indicated (see key, page 79).

THE BALDCYPRESS FAMILY

Taxodiaceae

Students of fossil plants assert that at one time the Baldcypress Family was very abundant and formed vast forests throughout the world, particularly in the Northern Hemisphere. The modern family, however, numbers but 14 species included in 8 genera. These are found distributed in the timbered regions of Tasmania, Formosa, Japan, China, and North America. Two genera, each with two species, are included in the arborescent flora of the United States. One of these, *Sequoia*, embraces the world-famous redwoods and big trees of California. The other, *Taxodium*, includes the equally famous "trees with knees," the baldcypresses of southern river bottoms and coastal swamps.

THE BALDCYPRESSES

Taxodium Rich.

The baldcypresses were once widely distributed through the prehistoric forests of North America and Europe, but most of them have long since become extinct. The modern genus includes but three species. One of them (*T. mucronatum* Ten.) is a native of Mexico, while the two remaining forms are found along the Atlantic and Gulf coastal plains of the southeastern United States. This genus, unlike other coniferous groups of the South, is characterized by deciduous foliage.

KEY TO THE SOUTHERN BALDCYPRESSES

1. Leaves, linear, spreading, 2-ranked.................
   Baldcypress (p. 83)
1. Leaves, nearly scalelike, appressed against the twig, in several ranks...................**Pondcypress** (p. 85)

Baldcypress

Taxodium distichum (L.) Rich.

Habit.—An unusually interesting tree, 100′ to 150′ in height and 3′ to 6′ or more in diameter; in youth, developing a heavily buttressed, excessively tapered, and commonly fluted bole and an open, narrowly pyramidal crown; old trees are characterized by a more nearly cylindrical bole and irregular, often ragged, flat-topped crown, which is often festooned with Spanish moss. Of particular note is the distinctive and unique root system. This consists of numerous "sinkers," which afford good anchorage, but which are supported by a wide-spreading, lateral system of shallow roots. From these there arise the peculiar conelike structures known as *knees*.

Leaves.—Deciduous, with their supporting twigs (a feature rare among conifers) linear, ½″ to ¾″ long, 2-ranked, yellow-green.

Flowers.—The male, in long, pendulous clusters, purplish brown, each with 6 to 8 stamens; the female, solitary or in clusters of 2 or 3 near the ends of the branchlets of the previous season, consisting of several overlapping bracts, each fused at the base with a fleshy scale bearing 2 ovules.

Cones.—¾″ to 1″ in diameter, nearly globular, usually disintegrating at maturity; the scales, club-shaped, leathery, yellowish brown; seeds, irregularly 3-angled, 3-winged.

Twigs.—Terminal twigs, persistent, light green through the growing season but becoming reddish brown during the winter; lateral twigs, usually deciduous with the foliage at the end of the 1st season; buds, nearly globular, covered with several overlapping, pointed scales.

Bark.—Fibrous, scaly, or commonly peeling off in

PLATE 12.—BALDCYPRESS

1. Foliage $\times\frac{1}{2}$. 2. Cluster of male flowers $\times\frac{1}{2}$. 3. Male flowers $\times 2$. 4. Female flower $\times 1$. 5. Cluster of cones $\times\frac{1}{2}$. 6. Seed $\times\frac{3}{4}$.

long, thin, narrow strips, reddish brown, but often weathering to an ashy gray.

Habitat.—Typically, a tree of permanent swamps, where it occurs in extensive pure stands or occasionally with water tupelo. On somewhat higher ground it mingles with bottom-land hardwoods such as American elm, red maple, green ash, sweetgum, and certain of the oaks. Best growth is made on deep, moist, sandy loams, but it is rarely found on such sites because of its inability to compete with the hardwoods.

Distribution.—Atlantic and Gulf coastal plains, lower Mississippi River Valley and bottom lands of adjacent drainage areas.

Importance.—The wood of baldcypress is very durable and is employed principally for construction of docks, bridges, silos, tanks, caskets, and general millwork. It is commonly used in greenhouse construction and for seed flats. Small amounts are also consumed in the manufacture of shingles, cooperage, poles, piling, and crossties. A resin obtained from the cones is used locally as an analgesic for lesions of the skin. The knees are occasionally fashioned into wooden novelties and offered to the tourist trade. This tree also enjoys a limited ornamental use.

Pondcypress

Taxodium distichum var. *nutans* (Ait.) Sweet

By some authorities, pondcypress is considered to be only a variety of the baldcypress. It attains neither the grandeur nor the widespread occurrence of baldcypress. It is readily distinguished by its nearly scalelike leaves, which are appressed along the twig in several ranks. Pondcypress, as its name suggests, is found commonly in shallow ponds, chiefly in the pine barrens, from the Dismal Swamp of Virginia, to Florida and Alabama.

THE CEDAR FAMILY

Cupressaceae

The Cedar Family comprises a group of 15 genera and about 130 species of trees and shrubs widely distributed both north and south of the equator. It includes several important timber trees and many forms of particular interest to horticulturalists. The North American flora (exclusive of Mexico) includes 5 genera and 26 species. Five species, distributed among 3 genera, are components of southern woodlands.

Synopsis of Southern Genera

Genus	Leaves	Cones	Branchlets
Thuja	scalelike, opposite in pairs, lateral pairs keeled, facial pairs flattened, glandular on the back	ovoid-oblong, with 8 to 10 thin, leathery scales; seeds, winged	flattened
Chamaecyparis	similar to the above but smaller	globular, with 4 to 8 leathery to semifleshy scales; seeds, winged	flattened
Juniperus	of 2 sorts, the scalelike opposite in pairs, the awl-shaped in whorls of 3 or opposite	globular, berrylike, with 3 to 8 fleshy scales; seeds, wingless	4-angled

THE THUJAS

Thuja L.

These are a small genus embracing five species of trees and shrubs, each with many horticultural varieties. Two species are indigenous to the United States. Western redcedar (*T. plicata* D. Don), a forest giant of the Pacific Northwest and northern Rocky Mountain region, is the principal timber tree used in shingle manufacture, both in the United States and in Canada. The remaining species, the northern white-cedar, has its southern limit in the Appalachian region of North Carolina and Tennessee.

Northern White-Cedar

Thuja occidentalis L.

Habit.—A tree, seldom more than 40′ to 50′ in height or 2′ to 3′ in diameter; in youth, developing a long, narrow, pyramidal crown, which becomes irregularly oblong with age. The branches, unlike those of most evergreens, often simulate a shepherd's crook and curve gracefully upward at their tips. The bole is usually buttressed at the base, noticeably tapered, and commonly fluted. Anchorage is afforded by a shallow, wide-spreading system of fibrous roots.

Leaves.—Scalelike, opposite in pairs, ⅛″ to ¼″ long, dull green, glandular on the back; the foliage sprays, flattened, often fanlike.

Flowers.—Monoecious, minute, terminal, solitary; the male, with 4 to 6 yellowish-pink stamens; the female, pink, with 4 fertile scales, each bearing 2 ovules.

Cones.—⅓″ to ½″ long, oblong, erect, light brown, dull, composed of 8 to 12 scales, 4 of which are fertile; scales, oval to broadly elliptical, the apex rounded or

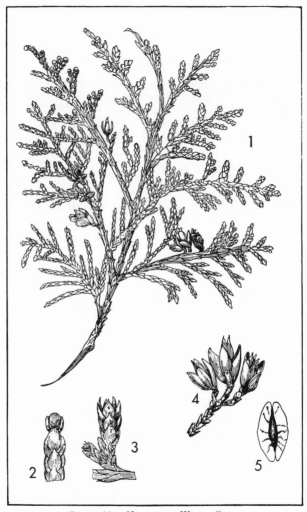

PLATE 13.—Northern White-Cedar
1. Foliage and Cones ×½. 2. Male flower ×4. 3. Female
flower ×4. 4. Cones ×1. 5. Seed ×4.

tipped with a small spine; seeds, about ⅛″ long, with a pair of lateral, straw-colored wings, which are about as wide as the seed.

Twigs.—At first yellowish green and flattened, with age becoming reddish brown and terete; buds, minute, hidden by the leaves.

Bark.—Thin, fibrous, often peeling off in long, narrow strips, reddish to grayish brown, on the larger trees forming a network of anastomosing ridges separated by shallow fissures.

Habitat.—Most abundant and reaching maximum size on limestone soils, ridges, and outcrops; found in either pure or mixed stands, in the second instance with yellow birch, black ash, white pine, hemlock, and sugar maple; in the North, also inhabiting swamps and even sphagnum bogs.

Distribution.—Southern Canada, Lake states, the Northeast, and the Appalachian Mountains of North Carolina and Tennessee; disjuncts from the main range, in Ohio and southeastern Missouri.

Importance.—This is a comparatively rare tree in southern forests. Michaux (51) recorded in his North American Silva that the crushed foliage blended with hog lard was used as a salve for easing the pains of rheumatism. A decoction also prepared from the leaves was thought to be useful in the treatment of scurvy; in appreciation of its remarkable restorative powers, members of the Jacques Cartier Canadian expedition carried it back to France. In this manner eastern arborvitae was the first American tree to be introduced into Europe and even today is an important ornamental of that continent.

The wood of this cedar is soft, very durable, and aromatic. At present it is used largely for poles, posts and piling, woodenware, small-boat construction, and cooperage. No less than 50 horticultural varieties are now in general use for decorative purposes.

THE WHITE-CEDARS

Chamaecyparis Spach.

The white-cedars comprise a group of six species, three of which are indigenous to North American forests. The Atlantic white-cedar, however, is the only southern representative of the group.

Atlantic White-Cedar

Chamaecyparis thyoides (L.) B.S.P.

Habit.—A tree, seldom over 60′ to 80′ in height and 10″ to 15″ in diameter; featured by a cylindrical bole, which, in dense stands, is often clear of branches for three-fourths its length. The crown is usually small and narrowly conical with slender limbs and graceful, pendulous branchlets; the root system is shallow and spreading.

Leaves.—Scalelike, $\frac{1}{16}''$ to $\frac{1}{8}''$ long, blue-green, glandular on the back, turning brown in their 2d year but persisting for many seasons; the foliage sprays, flattened and fanlike.

Flowers.—Monoecious, minute, terminal, solitary; the male, with 10 to 12 dark-brown or nearly black stamens; the female, pink, globular, with 6 thickened, fleshy scales, each bearing 2 to 4 ovules.

Cones.—About $\frac{1}{4}''$ in diameter, globular, rather fleshy, bluish or purplish at maturity, covered with a waxy bloom; the scales, thickened, each terminating in a reflexed boss or stubby protuberance; seeds, usually only 1 or 2 on each scale, about $\frac{1}{8}''$ long, laterally winged.

Twigs.—At first light green tinged with red, ultimately becoming reddish brown to dark brown and terete; buds, minute, hidden by the leaves.

Bark.—Thin, ashy gray to reddish brown, divided by narrow fissures into flat, anastomosing ridges.

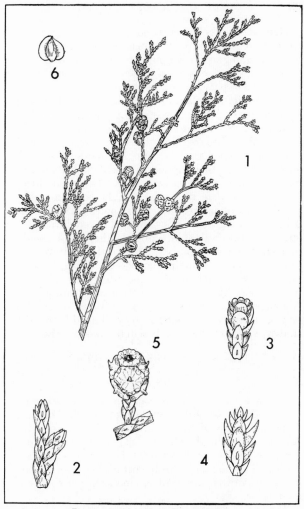

PLATE 14.—ATLANTIC WHITE-CEDAR
1. Foliage and cones ×½. 2. Foliage detail ×2. 3. Male
flower ×3. 4. Female flower ×3. 5. Cone ×2. 6. Seed ×2.

Habitat.—Largely restricted to wet sites such as fresh-water swamps, bogs, stream banks, and bottom lands; forming extensive pure stands or in admixture with baldcypress, sweet bay, slash pine, spruce pine, black tupelo, perseas, and red maple.

Distribution.—Atlantic and Gulf coastal plains from southern Maine to eastern Louisiana.

Importance.—Atlantic white-cedar has been an important timber tree since the early development of our cities along the Atlantic seaboard. "Juniper shingles" were to be found in the Philadelphia and Baltimore markets as early as 1800. Large quantities of the wood were also used for charcoal and gunpowder manufacture. Michaux notes (1819) that persons owning tracts of swampland covered with this species possess valuable timber holdings and should manage them judiciously. The wood is suitable for many purposes including cooperage, piling, marine and boat construction, shingles, crossties, poles, and posts. Large trees that have been wind-thrown and subsequently immersed for many years in swamp or bog waters are not infrequently "mined," and the timber, which is still perfectly sound, sawed into boards.

THE REDCEDARS or JUNIPERS

Juniperus L.

The redcedars comprise a group of about 50 small trees and shrubs scattered through North America, Asia and many of its neighboring islands, northern Africa, Abyssinia, the Canary Islands, the Azores, and the West Indies. *J. communis* L., the pasture juniper, is a small circumpolar shrub with many varieties, one of which (var. *montana* Ait.) is found in our southern mountains.

The leaf and wood oils of this group are of considerable economic importance and are employed in the manufacture of scented soaps, perfumes, sweeping compounds, and a variety of medicinal preparations. The frankincense of Biblical times was obtained from *J. phoenica* L. Some of the heaviest of the wood oils have been used in refining the ores of precious metals.

The redcedars are also an important horticultural group and include a number of beautiful ornamental plants, several with variegated foliage. Of the 13 junipers native to the United States, 2 attain tree size in southern forests.

KEY TO THE SOUTHERN REDCEDARS

1. Cones, about ⅓″ in diameter, with 1 to 4 seeds; branches, horizontal or ascending.....................
   Eastern redcedar (p. 93)
1. Cones, about ⅛″ in diameter, with 1 to 2 seeds; branches, pendulous.......**Southern redcedar** (p. 95)

Eastern Redcedar

Juniperus virginiana L.

Habit.—A small tree, 40′ to 50′ in height and 1′ to 2′ in diameter. The crown is dense and narrowly pyramidal or in some forms columnar and in the open extends nearly to the ground. The bole is noticeably tapered, often deeply fluted at the base, and terminates below in a deep root system.

Leaves.—Of two sorts: (1) on old trees, scalelike, about $\frac{1}{16}$″ long, dark green, in 4 ranks, usually appressed, (2) on young stems or vigorous shoots, often awl-shaped, opposite in pairs or ternate, light green, sharp-pointed, the upper surface commonly silvery white, both types usually turning brown in their 2d winter but persistent for several years.

Flowers.—With a single sex on each tree (dioecious); the male, with 10 or 12 golden-brown stamens; the female, globular, composed of several fleshy, purplish scales, each bearing 1 or 2 basal ovules.

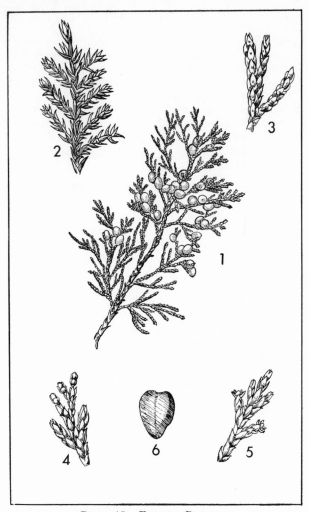

PLATE 15.—EASTERN REDCEDAR

1. Foliage and cones ×½. 2. Awl-shaped foliage ×1. 3. Scalelike foliage ×1. 4. Male flowers ×1. 5. Female flowers ×1. 6. Seed ×5.

Cones.—¼″ to ⅓″ in diameter, globular, berry-like, dark blue at maturity, but commonly covered by a light-bluish-gray, waxy bloom; the scales, with a sweetish, resinous flesh; seeds, about ⅙″ long, ovoid, sharp-pointed, wingless.

Twigs.—Terete or angled, reddish brown once the persistent dead foliage has fallen away; buds, minute, hidden by the leaves.

Bark.—Thin, fibrous, light reddish brown, separating into long, narrow, fringed scales or strips.

Habitat.—Found on a variety of soils but making its best growth on light loams of limestone origin; occurring more abundantly, however, on dry, shallow, rocky soils; forming nearly pure, open, parklike stands or in admixture with hardwoods.

Distribution.—Eastern United States and southern Ontario.

Importance.—This is an important tree in spite of its small stature and knotty timber. The heartwood, because of the moth-repellent properties of certain infiltrated oils, is used for closet linings, wardrobes, and chests. Planing-mill shavings find a ready market for kennel bedding, and even the sawdust is processed to remove the oils, which have a number of industrial and pharmaceutical uses. At one time this species was the principal pencil wood; hence the name *pencil cedar*, which still persists in some localities. Today, however, less than 10 per cent of the total output is utilized in this manner. Quantities of the wood are also consumed in paneling, millwork, woodenware, poles, posts, and novelties. Many varieties of eastern redcedar are employed in landscaping.

Southern Redcedar

Juniperus silicicola (Small) Bailey

This form is very similar to eastern redcedar but is characterized by somewhat more slender, pendulous branches and smaller cones. Unlike the eastern redcedar, which is usually found on dry soils, this species normally occurs in swamps or on moist sites. It is restricted to the coastal-plain region of southern Georgia and Florida, and reappears in eastern Texas.

THE YEW FAMILY

Taxaceae

This is a small family and includes but 3 genera (1 a monotype) and 11 species. Two genera, each with a single species, are found in the South.

Synopsis of Southern Genera

Genus	*Leaves*	*Flowers*	*Fruit*
Torreya	linear, with 2 silvery-white bands below	male flowers, solitary	a single seed with a fleshy seed coat; maturing in 2 seasons
Taxus	linear, pale yellow-green below	male flowers, in globular, headlike clusters	a single seed partly enveloped in a fleshy, scarlet cup; maturing in 1 season

THE TORREYAS

Torreya Arn.

This small genus includes five trees and shrubs of sporadic occurrence in North America, China, and Japan. Two species are found in the United States, one (*T. californica* Torr.) on the western slopes of the Sierra Nevada, the other in southwestern Georgia and western Florida.

Florida Torreya   Stinkingcedar

Torreya taxifolia Arn.

Habit.—A small tree, sometimes 30′ to 40′ in height and 1′ to 2′ in diameter; characterized by a short bole and an open, pyramidal crown composed of whorls of spreading branches, slightly pendulous at their tips.

Leaves.—Linear, about 1½″ long, rounded on the back, 2-ranked, sometimes remotely falcate, fetid, dark green, lustrous above, silvery white below, with a stout, sharp point at the apex, short-stalked at the base, persisting for several years.

Flowers.—With a single sex on each tree (dioecious); the male, solitary, globular, with 16 to 20 yellow stamens; the female, solitary, consisting of a single, purple ovule, subtended by several pointed scales.

Fruit.—1″ to 1¼″ long, ovoid, consisting of a single, reddish-brown seed covered by a layer of thin, leathery, purplish flesh; ripening at the end of 2 seasons.

Twigs.—Bright green or yellow-green, hairy, becoming reddish brown and smooth with age; buds, brown, angular, about ¼″ long, with several overlapping scales.

Bark.—Irregularly fissured and scaly, dark brown, often tinged with orange.

Habitat.—A rare tree of local occurrence; found on bluffs and slopes covered by rich, moist soils of limestone origin; usually occurring as an occasional tree in association with Florida yew and many hardwoods, including swamp white oak, southern magnolia, holly, buckeyes, palmetto, beech, yellow-poplar, and redgum.

Distribution.—Largely restricted to the banks of the Apalachicola River and its tributaries in western Florida; also reported from Decatur County in southwestern Georgia.

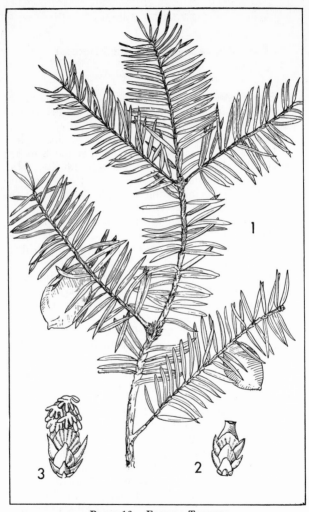

PLATE 16.—FLORIDA TORREYA
1. Foliage and fruit $\times\frac{1}{3}$. 2. Female flower $\times 4$. 3. Male flower $\times 4$.

Importance.—Of no commercial value; occasionally used as an ornamental, particularly in Tallahassee, Fla., and the vicinity; used locally for fence posts owing to the durable nature of the wood when in contact with soil.

Florida Yew

Taxus floridana Nutt.

Habit.—A small, bushy tree or a large shrub, rarely more than 20′ to 25′ in height or 8″ to 12″ in diameter, with a short bole that soon becomes lost in a crown of spreading branches. The root system is moderately deep and widespread.

Leaves.—Linear, about ¾″ long, flat, 2-ranked, scythe-shaped, dark green above, pale yellow-green below, pointed at the apex, persistent for several years.

Flowers.—With a single sex on each tree; the male, in globose, headlike clusters, each with 4 to 8 yellow stamens subtended by several ovate scales; the female, solitary, composed of a single yellow ovule, subtended by several bracts.

Fruit.—About ½″ long, ovoid, consisting of a single tawny or yellowish-brown, wrinkled seed, partly enclosed in a sweet, fleshy, scarlet cup; ripening at the end of 1 season.

Twigs.—Light green to brownish green, turning reddish brown in their 2d season; buds, with numerous loosely overlapping scales.

Bark.—Smooth on young stems, on older trees separated into thin, flat, irregularly shaped, purplish-brown scales.

Habitat.—Bluffs, coves, and ravines along water-courses.

Distribution.—Western Florida along the Apalachicola River from Bristol to Aspalaga.

Importance.—Of no commercial or medicinal value.

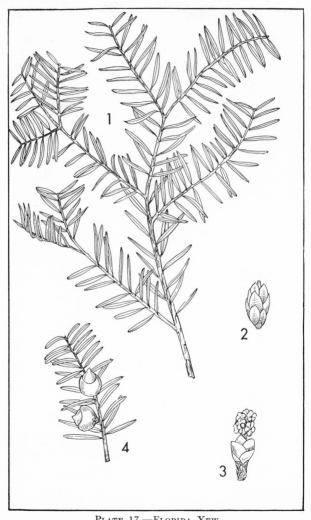

PLATE 17.—FLORIDA YEW

1. Foliage $\times \frac{1}{2}$.   2. Female flower $\times 4$.   3. Male flower $\times 4$.
4. Fruit $\times \frac{1}{2}$.

THE BROADLEAVED TREES

THE WILLOW FAMILY

Salicaceae

The Willow Family consists of 4 genera and about 200 species of trees and shrubs, the majority scattered through the cooler regions of the Northern Hemisphere. Included in the family are the willows, cottonwoods or poplars, and aspens. Those attaining the stature of trees produce timber of secondary importance, while others, either because of the weeping or columnar habit or because of their handsome foliage, are extensively employed for ornamental purposes.

Synopsis of Southern Genera

Genus	Leaves	Flowers	Buds
Salix	usually many times longer than broad	nectareous	covered by a single caplike scale
Populus	about as broad as long	not nectareous	covered by several overlapping scales

THE WILLOWS

Salix L.

The willows comprise a group of about 170 species of trees and shrubs, largely restricted to the North Temperate Hemisphere. A few forms, however, may be found in the tropics, while others occur at the northern limits of tree growth. As a group the willows require relatively large amounts of water and thus are commonly found along banks of streams and in swamps. Their matted roots form a natural barrier to erosion, and the ease with which many willows may be propagated from cuttings further adds to their value in flood control and revetment work.

Willow baseball bats were once very popular. The branches from several species are used in basketry, and the bark is a source of tannic acid and salicin. Weeping varieties are commonly planted as ornamentals, and certain shrubby forms serve as a source of food for both cattle and large game animals when a more suitable browse is not available.

There are more than 65 species of willow native to North America, one-third of which are arborescent. Four willows attain tree size in the South, but only the black willow reaches commercial proportions and abundance. Several others, exotics originally used for ornamental purposes, have long since escaped cultivation. Among these mention should be made of the graceful weeping willow (*S. babylonica* L.), the white willow (*S. a ba* L.), and the golden willow [*S. alba* var. *vitellina* (L.) K. Koch.].

KEY TO THE SOUTHERN ARBORESCENT WILLOWS

1. Twigs of the current season, readily separated from the parent branch (brittle-jointed).................... 2
1. Twigs of the current season, not easily separated from the parent branch (not brittle-jointed).............. 3

    2. Leaves, lanceolate, green above and below; stamens, 3 to 5; capsule, about ⅛″ long..................
                               Black willow (p. 103)
    2. Leaves, linear-lanceolate, pale whitish below; stamens, 3 to 9 (mostly 5 to 7); capsule, about ¼″ long....................**Harbison willow** (p. 105)

3. Leaves, narrow, more than 4 times longer than broad, with long-tapered apices and pale lower surfaces; stamens, 3 to 7 (mostly 5 or 6); capsule, about ¼″ long....................**Coastalplain willow** (p. 106)

3. Leaves, broad, less than 4 times longer than broad, with short, acute apices and silvery-white lower surfaces; stamens, 2; capsule, about ½″ long.................

Pussy willow (p. 106)

Black Willow

Salix nigra Marsh.

Habit.—A small tree, 30′ to 40′ in height and 12″ to 14″ in diameter, with stout, clustered stems forming a broad, irregular, open crown; the root system, shallow and spreading.

Leaves.—Alternate, simple, deciduous, 3″ to 6″ long, ¼″ to ¾″ wide, lanceolate, often scythe-shaped; apex, long-tapered; base, rounded; margin, finely glandular-serrate; glabrous above and below; petiole, short; stipules, foliaceous.

Flowers.—Dioecious, each sex borne in terminal catkins on leafy, pubescent branches; staminate flowers, with 3 to 5 stamens, their filaments hairy; pistillate flowers, with an ovoid ovary, short style, and 2 stigmas.

Fruit.—A conic, glabrous, reddish-brown, 2-valved capsule, about ¼″ long.

Twigs.—Reddish brown, at first pubescent, but soon becoming glabrous, brittle at the joints; terminal buds, absent; lateral buds, appressed, ⅛″ long, covered by a single, caplike scale; leaf scars, V-shaped, with 3 bundle scars; stipule scars, slitlike, inconspicuous; pith, homogeneous.

Bark.—Dark brown to black, deeply divided; forming shaggy scales on old trunks.

Habitat.—Moist, alluvial banks of streams and lakes; also in wet bottoms and permanent swamps.

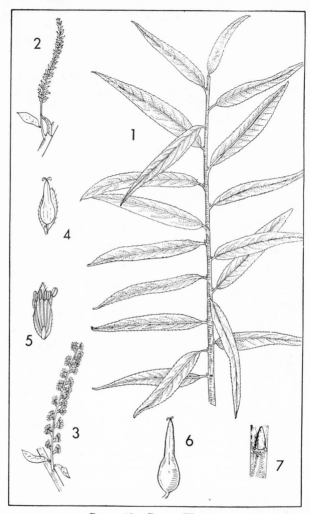

PLATE 18.—BLACK WILLOW

1. Foliage ×⅓. 2. Female catkin ×½. 3. Male catkin ×½.
4. Female flower ×4. 5. Male flower ×4. 6. Fruit ×4. 7. Leaf
scar ×1½.

Distribution.—Southern New Brunswick west to Lake Superior and northern Minnesota; southward along the coast to South Carolina and Georgia in the East, and through Arkansas and Louisiana to eastern Texas in the West.

Importance.—This is the most important American willow. Its wood, while not strong or even durable, is suitable for many purposes as it is subject to little or no twisting and checking while drying. Among the more common uses, mention should be made of toys, artificial limbs, charcoal, cheap furniture, crating boards, and excelsior.

Remarks.—In the Deep South, particularly in Louisiana, Arkansas, and eastern Texas, the species is largely replaced in the forest by its variety *S. nigra* var. *altissima* Sarg., a much larger tree, sometimes 100′ to 120′ tall. The variety is readily distinguished by its hairy twigs and hairy leaves with longer petioles and more acutely wedge-shaped bases.

Harbison Willow

Salix harbisonii Schneid.

The Harbison willow is a shrub or small tree, sometimes 30′ tall, with lance-shaped, finely glandular-toothed leaves, 2″ to 5″ in length. It occurs along stream banks and in moist situations on the Atlantic coastal plain from the Dismal Swamp in southeastern Virginia to northern Florida. It also extends west through Florida to the Apalachicola River Valley. While some authorities regard this form as merely a hybrid between the black and coastalplain willows, most southern taxonomists agree that it is worthy of a species designation. It differs principally from black willow in that its leaves are pale white below and from the coastalplain willow by its smooth, brittle-jointed twigs. This willow is of little or no commercial value.

Coastalplain Willow

Salix longipes Shuttl.

This is also a shrub or small tree of the Atlantic coastal plain but occurs over a much wider area than the Harbison Willow. Its lanceolate, often scythe-shaped leaves, with finely glandular-toothed margins, often exceed 5″ in length, while its twigs are usually hairy but not brittle at the joints. It is found from along the North Carolina coast to the lower Florida peninsula and reappears in Cuba.

A well-known variety, Ward willow (var. *wardii* Schneid.), with large, obtuse stipules, smooth twigs, and leaves with acute apices, extends westward from the banks of the Potomac River to the west-central states.

Pussy Willow

Salix discolor Muhl.

The pussy willow is exceedingly rare in the South and occurs only as a shrub, although it attains tree size farther to the north. It has been found along streams in the mountains of Virginia and North Carolina and may be distinguished by its more or less oblong leaves, 1½″ to 4″ long, with a bluish-silvery-white bloom on the lower surface. The so-called "pussy willow" that is frequently encountered in the spring at low elevations is the prairie willow (*S. humilis* Marsh.), a small shrub of both dry and moist situations occurring from Virginia to Florida.

THE ASPENS AND POPLARS

Populus L.

This group comprises about 35 species of which 15 are natives of North America. Several forms, including the Chinese poplar and the European silver and

Lombardy poplars, are widely used ornamentals for both city planting and along open highways. The wood of several species is suitable for pulp and other products such as excelsior, musical instruments, plywood, cooperage, and crating.

The genus is represented in the South by two poplars and a single aspen. While both of these groups include closely related species and are placed by botanists in the same genus, poplars may be distinguished from aspens by their highly resinous, aromatic winter buds and staminate flowers with 12 to 60 stamens. In contrast, the winter buds of the aspens are only slightly resinous, and the staminate flowers exhibit only 6 to 12 stamens.

KEY TO THE SOUTHERN POPLARS AND ASPENS

1. Leaves, essentially circular in outline; buds, only slightly resinous, dull, gray, hairy, particularly on the margin of the scales; male flowers, with 6 to 12 stamens
   Bigtooth aspen (p. 112)
1. Leaves, ovate to triangular in outline; buds, resinous, aromatic, lustrous, reddish brown; male flowers, with 12 to 60 stamens................................. 2

   2. Leaves, 3″ to 5″ long, triangular; petioles, flattened.
   Eastern poplar (p. 107)
   2. Leaves, 4″ to 7″ long, oval; petioles, rounded in cross section................**Swamp poplar** (p. 110)

Eastern Poplar   Eastern Cottonwood

Populus deltoides Marsh.

Habit.—A medium-sized to large tree, 50′ to 100′ in height and 3′ to 4′ in diameter, with an irregular, open, spreading crown; in open situations, the trunk usually divides near the ground into several massive limbs to form a broad, rounded head, 80′ to 100′ in diameter.

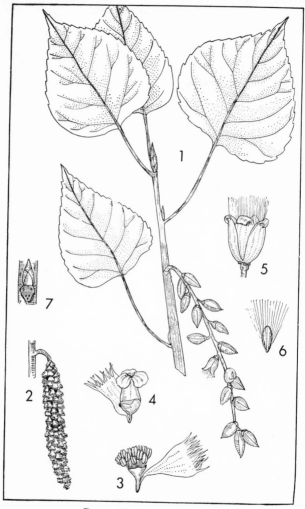

PLATE 19.—EASTERN POPLAR

1. Foliage and fruit ×½. 2. Male catkin ×½. 3. Male
flower ×5. 4. Female flower ×5. 5. Open capsule ×1½.
6. Seed ×1½. 7. Leaf scar ×1.

Leaves.—Alternate, simple, deciduous, triangular, 3″ to 5″ long, 3″ to 5″ broad; apex, acute; base, heart-shaped; margin, coarsely crenate-serrate; light green above, paler and glabrous below; petioles, smooth, flattened, glandular; stipules, linear, 1″ long.

Flowers.—Unisexual, each sex borne on separate trees, appearing before the leaves in 3″ to 5″ catkins; staminate flowers, with 40 to 60 stamens; anthers, red; pistillate flowers, with a subglobose ovary bearing 3 or 4 sessile, divergent, greatly enlarged stigmas.

Fruit.—A green, conical capsule, about ¼″ in length; borne on few-fruited, pendent stalks, 8″ to 12″ in length.

Twigs.—Yellowish brown, stout, with prominent lenticels; terminal buds, ovoid, acute, brown, resinous, about ¾″ long, with 6 or 7 scales; lateral buds, smaller, more or less divergent; leaf scars, lunate to triangular, with 3 bundle scars; pith, homogeneous, star-shaped in cross section.

Bark.—At first yellowish green, smooth, and thin, becoming thick, gray, and deeply furrowed between broad, flattened ridges on the largest trunks.

Habitat.—On moist alluvial soils along streams, near lakes, and on rich, moist bottom lands.

Distribution.—From southern Quebec and Ontario, west to Montana; south to Texas in the West; in the East, through western Massachusetts, south to Florida.

Importance.—The rootwood was once employed by Indians for making fire by friction, and the logs were used by early settlers for building stockades. Throughout the plains states the tree has been found to make a suitable windbreak, in spite of the rather brittle nature of its branches. For many years this species was a favored street and shade tree, but the rapidity with which its roots entered and clogged storm and even sanitary sewers ultimately resulted in legislation against its use in many localities.

Swamp Poplar Black Cottonwood

Populus heterophylla L.

Habit.—A moderately large tree, often 70′ to 90′ in height and 2′ to 3′ in diameter, its branches forming a narrow, open, round-topped, or irregular crown.

Leaves.—Alternate, simple, deciduous, ovate, 4″ to 8″ long, 3″ to 5″ wide; apex, gradually narrowed, pointed, or rounded; base, rounded, or heart-shaped; margin, irregularly serrate, the teeth glandular; dark green above, pale and smooth below; midrib, yellow; petiole, oval to circular in cross section, about 3″ long; stipules, 1″ long, lanceolate.

Flowers.—Unisexual, borne on separate trees, appearing before the leaves in 1″ to 3″ catkins; staminate flowers, with 12 to 20 stamens; anthers, large, dark red; pistillate flowers, consisting of an ovoid ovary and short style with 2 or 3 divergent, greatly enlarged stigmas.

Fruit.—An ovoid, acute, brown, 2- or 3-valved capsule, borne on an elongated pedicel, about ½″ long; seeds, minute, obovoid, dark red or brown, bearing tufts of white hairs.

Twigs.—Slender or stout, brownish gray, with prominent lenticels; terminal buds, broadly ovoid, bright reddish brown, slightly resinous, about ⅝″ long; lateral buds, smaller; the flower buds plump and blunt; leaf scars, broadly triangular, with 3 bundle scars; pith, orange, star-shaped in cross section, homogeneous.

Bark.—Reddish brown, divided by deep fissures into narrow, flattened, superficially scaly ridges.

Habitat.—Lowland forests of the southern coastal plains, a common constituent of swamps; usually mixed with other species.

Distribution.—From southern Connecticut to northern Florida and through the Gulf states to western

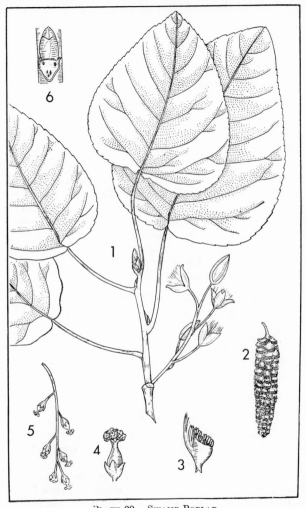

PLATE 20.—SWAMP POPLAR

1. Foliage and fruit ×½. 2. Male catkin ×⅔. 3. Male
flower ×2. 4. Female flower ×2. 5. Female catkin ×½.
6. Leaf scar ×1.

Louisiana, north in the Mississippi drainage basin to southern Illinois, Indiana, and Ohio.

Importance.—Occasionally used for cheap lumber.

Bigtooth Aspen

Populus grandidentata Michx.

This is a small northern tree of rare occurrence south of the North Carolina–Virginia border. It may be distinguished by its circular, coarsely and irregularly toothed leaves with flattened petioles, essentially nonresinous buds, and smooth, thin, olive-green to gray-green bark. This tree is commonly found on burned-over areas and on dry, sandy or stony sites. Its inner bark is a source of food for both beaver and snowshoe rabbit, and the foliage is browsed upon by deer and other similar large game animals. The early American pioneer found that decoctions made from the inner bark could be used as a substitute for quinine.

THE SWEETGALE FAMILY

Myricaceae

The Sweetgale Family includes 2 genera, 1 a monotype, and about 40 species of deciduous and evergreen shrubs and small trees with aromatic foliage and wax-coated fruits.

THE BAYBERRIES

Myrica L.

This group of plants is widely scattered over the temperate regions of the world. Bayberry (*M. carolinensis* Mill.) is a small evergreen shrub of wide distribution through the eastern and southern states. The waxy coating of its fruits is refined and used for making candles and scented soaps. The southern bayberry is the only American species of the genus attaining tree size.

Southern Bayberry

Myrica cerifera L.

Habit.—A shrub, or in some localities a tree, 20' to 40' in height, with a trunk 8" to 10" in diameter, the slender, divergent branches forming a narrow, round-topped head.

Leaves.—Alternate, simple, persistent, aromatic when bruised or crushed, oblanceolate, 2" to 4" long, ½" wide; apex, acute or rarely rounded; base, wedge-shaped; margin, coarsely serrate-toothed; yellow-green, covered with minute, dark glands above, with bright-orange glands below; petioles, short, stout.

Flowers.—Unisexual, each sex borne on separate plants in axillary, oblong catkins with acute scales, ¼" to ¾" long; stamens, few, yellow; ovary, tapered, surmounted by 2 slender, divergent stigmas.

Fruit.—A globose drupe, ⅛" in diameter; covered with a bluish wax; borne in short spikes that are often persistent until spring; seeds, small, pale.

Twigs.—Slender, with small, pale lenticels; at first tomentose and glandular, becoming dark brown and glabrous during their 2d season; terminal buds, wanting; lateral buds, oblong and acute, ⅛" long, with several overlapping scales; leaf scars, more or less 3-angled, with 3 bundle scars; pith, continuous.

Bark.—Thin, smooth, and gray-green with gray patches.

Habitat.—In sandy soils near the seacoast.

Distribution.—From New Jersey south along the coast into southern Florida, and through the Gulf states to Texas.

Importance.—The waxy coating of the fruits of this species is occasionally used in making candles. These burn with a bluish flame and when extinguished leave a lasting, fragrant aroma.

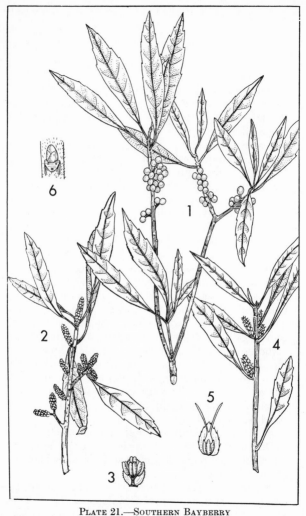

PLATE 21.—SOUTHERN BAYBERRY

1. Foliage and fruit ×⅓. 2. Male catkins ×⅓. 3. Male
flower ×3. 4. Female catkins ×⅓. 5. Female flower ×3.
6. Leaf scar ×1½.

THE CORKWOOD FAMILY

Leitneriaceae

This family embraces but a single species, the Florida corkwood, a tree of the Deep South. The tree produces a wood of extremely low density but, because of its limited distribution, has little or no industrial use.

Florida Corkwood

Leitneria floridana Chapm.

A Monotype

Habit.—Shrubby or treelike, occasionally becoming 18′ to 20′ in height and 4″ to 5″ in diameter above a swollen base; the bole tapers rapidly and soon becomes lost in an open, spreading crown.

Leaves.—Alternate, simple, deciduous, lanceolate, 4″ to 6″ long, 1½″ to 3″ wide; apex, acute; base, wedge-shaped; margin, entire and undulate; bright green and glabrous above, pale and pubescent below; petioles, 1″ to 2″ long.

Flowers.—Unisexual, each sex borne on separate trees in short, stubby catkins; staminate catkins, about 1″ long, terminally clustered, the flowers with 3 to 12 stamens, each with yellow, 2-celled anthers; pistillate catkins, about ½″ long, scattered, the flowers with rudimentary sepals surrounding a short-stalked pistil with a pubescent, 1-celled ovary and flattened style.

Fruit.—An oblong, compressed, rugose, chestnut-brown, dry drupe, about ¾″ long and ¼″ broad; seed, flattened, with rounded ends, lighter colored than the fruit husk.

Twigs.—Light reddish brown to purplish, hairy, ultimately becoming darker and glabrous; terminal buds, conic, ⅛″ long, with triangular, imbricate,

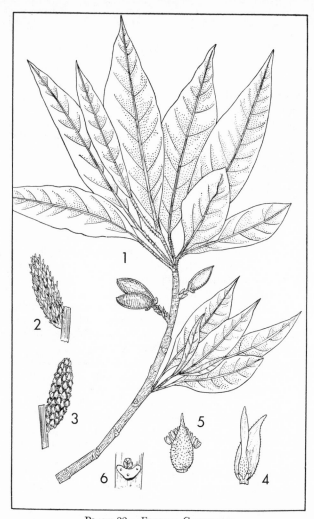

PLATE 22.—FLORIDA CORKWOOD

1. Foliage and fruit ×½. 2. Female catkins ×1. 3. Male
catkins ×1. 4. Female flower ×5. 5. Male flower ×5. 6. Leaf
scar ×1½.

tomentose scales; lateral buds, of two sorts: (1) flower buds, clustered near the ends of twigs, cylindrical, about ½″ long, covered by several large, overlapping scales; (2) leaf buds, ovoid, with 3 exposed scales, about twice as broad as high; leaf scars, half elliptical, with 3 bundle scars; pith, white, continuous.

Bark.—Thin, brownish gray, forming narrow, rounded ridges separated by shallow fissures.

Habitat.—In swamps, on swamp borders, and on muddy, saline shores.

Distribution.—In Georgia, western Florida, Texas, Arkansas, and Missouri.

Importance.—The wood is of no commercial importance, but has sometimes been used locally as a cork substitute, particularly in the construction of floats for fishing nets.

THE WALNUT FAMILY

Juglandaceae

This group, which includes about 40 species of trees widely scattered through the forests of the Northern Hemisphere, is well represented in the southern forests by the walnuts, hickories, and pecans.

Synopsis of Southern Genera

Genus	*Flowers*	*Fruit*	*Pith*
Juglans	staminate catkins, unbranched	a corrugated nut, enclosed in a thick, indehiscent husk	chambered
Carya	staminate catkins, 3-branched	a smooth or few-ribbed nut, enclosed in a dehiscent husk	homogeneous

THE WALNUTS

Juglans L.

Of the 15 known species of walnut, 5 are indigenous to the United States, and 2 of these flourish in the South. Not only is the group productive of many fine cabinet timbers, but the nut meats of several species are very toothsome and used extensively in candies, pastries, and ice cream.

KEY TO THE SOUTHERN WALNUTS

1. Leaflets, broadest at the base; fruit, spherical, solitary or paired; pith, yellowish gray or cream-colored. . . .
   Black walnut (p. 118)
1. Leaflets, mostly broadest near the middle; fruit, oblong, in clusters; pith, dark brown to deep purplish brown.
   Butternut (p. 121)

Black Walnut

Juglans nigra L.

Habit.—A large tree, 70′ to 100′ in height, with a trunk 2′ to 4′ in diameter; in dense stands, commonly producing a long, clear bole that supports a small, narrow, open crown; in the open, developing a short trunk and massive, spreading crown; root system, deep and widespread.

Leaves.—Alternate, deciduous, odd–pinnately compound, 1′ to 2′ long, with 15 to 23 nearly sessile leaflets; leaflets, ovate-lanceolate, 3″ to 4″ long, about 1″ wide; with acute apices, unequally rounded bases, and finely toothed margins; glabrous above, pubescent below; rachis, hairy.

Flowers.—Unisexual, appearing with the leaves in separate inflorescences on the same tree; the male, in stout catkins 3″ to 5″ long, each flower with a 6-lobed calyx and 20 to 30 nearly sessile stamens protected by a rusty-brown bract; the female, in 2- to 5-flowered

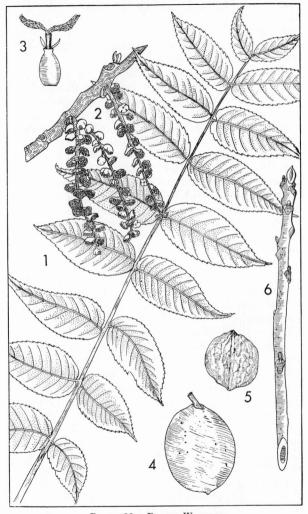

PLATE 23.—BLACK WALNUT

1. Leaf ×⅓.   2. Male catkins ×⅓.   3. Female flower ×3.
4. Fruit ×⅓.   5. Nut with husk removed ×⅓.   6. Twig ×½.

spikes, each flower about ¼" long, with 2 yellow-green, divergent, feathery stigmas and a short style surmounting a subglobular ovary.

Fruit.—An ovoid to nearly globular, corrugated nut, 1½" to 2¼" in diameter; enclosed in a thick, succulent, yellowish-green husk; seed, oily, sweet, and edible.

Twigs.—Stout, brown to orange-brown, with many raised, orange lenticels; terminal buds, ovoid, with few pubescent scales; lateral buds, smaller, woolly, gray; leaf scars, large, shield-shaped, with 3 U-shaped bundle scars; pith, yellowish gray, chambered.

Bark.—Gray-brown to nearly black, sometimes with a purplish or reddish-brown tinge, soon becoming fissured; on the largest trees, deeply furrowed between sharp or broadly rounded ridges; considerable variation exists between trees of the North and those of the South.

Habitat.—On deep, moist, fertile soils of bottom lands and gentle slopes, where it occurs as an occasional tree in association with other hardwoods.

Distribution.—From Massachusetts through southern Ontario, to central Nebraska; thence south to Texas in the West and Georgia in the East.

Importance.—Black walnut has long been recognized as one of the most valuable of North American trees, and it is indeed unfortunate that ruthless cutting has caused its almost complete extinction in certain localities. American colonists used the wood for fence rails and fuel, and its early recognition as a cabinet wood of the first order is attested to by the beautiful creations of the master craftsmen of the Queen Anne, William and Mary, and Colonial periods. During the Civil War the wood was employed in the manufacture of gunstocks and later in the First and Second World Wars for both gunstocks and airplane propellers. Even in these modern times black walnut is the most popular wood for fabrication of solid and veneered furniture.

Butternut   White Walnut

Juglans cinerea L.

Habit.—A tree, 40′ to 60′ in height and 1′ to 2′ in diameter (occasionally larger); the bole usually divides 20′ to 30′ above the ground into several stout, ascending limbs, which further divide into secondary branches forming a broad, nearly symmetrical, round-topped crown.

Leaves.—Alternate, deciduous, odd–pinnately compound, 15″ to 30″ long, with 11 to 17 nearly sessile leaflets; leaflets, oblong-lanceolate, 3″ to 4″ long, 1″ to 2″ wide, tapering at the apex, more or less unequally rounded at the base, toothed along the margin; wrinkled above, pale, hairy below; rachis, covered with sticky, glandular hairs.

Flowers.—Unisexual, both sexes borne in separate clusters on the same tree, appearing with the leaves; staminate flowers, in 3″ to 5″ catkins, each with a 6-lobed calyx, a rusty-brown bract, and 8 to 12 nearly sessile, brownish stamens; pistillate flowers, in 6- to 8-flowered spikes, bright red, ½″ long, with bright-red, plumose stigmas.

Fruit.—An ovoid-oblong, corrugated, 4-ribbed nut, 1½″ to 2½″ long, enclosed in a thin, leathery, indehiscent husk with 2 to 4 obscure ridges and covered with a coat of sticky, matted hairs; seed, irregularly shaped, sweet, oily, edible.

Twigs.—Stout, at first pubescent, green, ultimately reddish brown and covered with light-yellow lenticels, terminal buds, ¾″ long, blunt, hairy; lateral buds, about ⅛″ long, ovoid, hairy; leaf scars, raised, 3-lobed, with a woolly cushion or ridge on the upper margin; bundle scars, large, black, arranged in 3 U-shaped clusters; pith, chambered, brownish black to deep purplish brown.

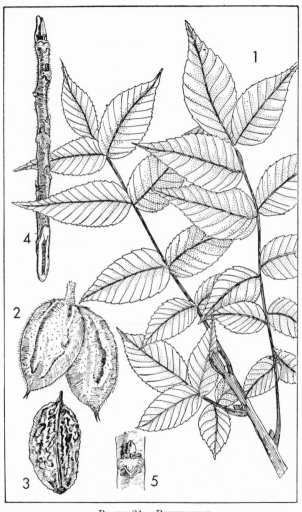

PLATE 24.—BUTTERNUT

1. Foliage ×⅓. 2. Fruit ×½. 3. Nut with husk removed ×½. 4. Twig ×½. 5. Leaf scar ×1.

Bark.—At first smooth and light gray, finally gray-brown and broken into broad, flat ridges by deep furrows.

Habitat.—Fertile soil near water or in areas with abundant rainfall, often found along roads and streams and in fields adjacent to woodlands.

Distribution.—New Brunswick through southern Quebec and Ontario, to eastern South Dakota; south to eastern Arkansas in the West and to northern Georgia in the East; not on the Atlantic coastal plain south of Delaware.

Importance.—Commonly used for interior trim and furniture. Butternut dye is made from the fruit husks, sugar may be obtained from the sap, and medicinal compounds have been extracted from the inner bark of the roots.

THE HICKORIES AND PECANS

Carya Nutt.

This is truly an American group of trees, only 3 of the 23 known species occurring outside the United States. Of these, 1 is a tree of Mexico; the other 2 are natives of the Orient. While the pecan hickories and true hickories are incorporated into one botanical group, they exhibit certain specific differences that serve readily to distinguish between them; these are indicated below.

	True Hickories	*Pecan Hickories*
Leaves	mostly with 5 to 7 leaflets	mostly with 7 to 17 leaflets
Fruit husks	unwinged, creased or ribbed at the sutures	broadly winged at the sutures, at least above the middle
Winter buds	with 6 or more overlapping scales	with 4-to 6-valvate scales

Hickory wood is strong and tough and is used for tool handles, agricultural implements, ski, and wagon-wheel spokes, hubs, and rims. Prior to the substitution of steel, it was also employed in the manufacture of automobile-wheel spokes and golf-club shafts. Throughout the South, hickory is the favorite wood in the smokehouse; it is claimed by many that meat cured with hickory-wood smoke possesses a superior flavor and is of better fuality than that similarly processed with other fuels.

Pecan timber in contrast is softer and more highly figured and is used for flooring and furniture.

KEY TO THE SOUTHERN HICKORIES AND PECANS

1. Bud scales, overlapping; fruit husks, depressed, smooth, or ridged along the sutures................ 2
1. Bud scales, valvate; fruit husks, broadly winged along the sutures, at least above the middle.............13

    2. Fruit husks, commonly ½″ to 1″ in thickness; bark, separating into long, shaggy plates, free at the ends.. 3
    2. Fruit husks, ¼″ or less in thickness; bark, smooth or variously furrowed and ridged, occasionally scaly at the surface but not broken into long, shaggy plates................................ 5

3. Leaves, mostly 7- to 9-foliate; twigs, tinged with orange; shell of nut, very thick....................
                               Shellbark hickory (p. 126)
3. Leaves, 5- to 7-foliate; twigs, reddish brown; shell of nut, thin.. 4

    4. Leaves, 8″ to 14″ long; fruit, 1½″ to 2½″ long; husk, about ½″ thick; nut, oblong to obovoid; buds, ovoid..........**Shagbark hickory** (p. 128)
    4. Leaves, 4″ to 8″ long; fruit, ¾″ to 1½″ long; husk, about ⅜″ thick; nut, ovoid; buds, cylindrical.......**Southern shagbark hickory** (p. 131)

5. Twigs, stout; leaves, with a strong, spicy odor, woolly below; rachis, woolly......................
Mockernut hickory (p. 131)
5. Twigs, slender; leaves, fragrant or odorless, smooth, somewhat hairy, or dotted with minute scales below; rachis, smooth or hairy............................ 6

6. Leaves, 7- to 9-foliate........................ 7
6. Leaves, 5- to 7-foliate........................ 8

7. Leaflets, with minute, silvery-white scales below; nut, compressed.............**Sand hickory** (p. 133)
7. Leaflets, smooth or sparsely hairy below; nut, full round.....................**Ashe hickory** (p. 134)

8. Fruit, 1¼″ to 1⅜″ in diameter............... 9
8. Fruit, about ¾″ in diameter.................10

9. Twigs, smooth; fruit husks, about ¼″ thick; leaves, mostly 7-foliate............**Swamp hickory** (p. 134)
9. Twigs, hairy; fruit husks, about ⅟₁₀″ thick; leaves, 5- and 7-foliate..............**Black hickory** (p. 135)

10. Fruit, pear-shaped; the husk, indehiscent or splitting tardily to about the middle............
Pignut hickory (p. 135)
10. Fruit, obovoid to elliptical; the husk, splitting freely to the base or tardily dehiscent..........11

11. Rachis and lower leaflet surfaces, hairy; fruit husk, tardily dehiscent............**Valley hickory** (p. 138)
11. Rachis and lower leaflet surfaces, smooth or nearly so; fruit husk, splitting freely at maturity.............12

12. Leaflet margins, finely, often obscurely toothed; fruit, ellipsoidal...........**Red hickory** (p. 138)
12. Leaflet margins, coarsely toothed; fruit, obovoid.
Scrub hickory (p. 141)

13. Leaves, with 7 to 9 leaflets........................14
13. Leaves, with 7 to 17 leaflets........................15

14. Fruit husks, 4-winged above the middle; nut, thin-
shelled, brittle........**Bitternut hickory** (p. 141)
14. Fruit husks, 4-winged from base to apex; nut,
thick-walled, bony......**Nutmeg hickory** (p. 144)

15. Leaves, 7- to 17-foliate; nut, full round; seeds, sweet..
Pecan (p. 144)
15. Leaves, 7- to 13-foliate; nut, compressed; seeds,
bitter..16

16. Leaflets, glandular above, woolly below.........
Bitter pecan (p. 147)
16. Leaflets, smooth above, hairy below..........
Water hickory (p. 147)

Shellbark Hickory   Bigleaf Shagbark Hickory

Carya laciniosa Schneid.

Habit.—A large tree, 90′ to 120′ tall, with a trunk 2′ to 3′ thick; the crown, composed of short, stout limbs of nearly equal length, forming a characteristic oblong head.

Leaves.—Alternate, deciduous, pinnately compound, 12″ to 24″ long, with 7 or rarely 5 to 9 obovate, sessile leaflets; leaflets, 5″ to 9″ long, 3″ to 5″ wide, the terminal usually the widest; with acute to long-tapered tips, wedge-shaped or unequally rounded bases, and finely serrate margins; dark green and lustrous above, pale yellow-green and covered with velvetlike hairs below; rachis, stout, grooved, hairy or smooth.

Flowers.—Unisexual, both sexes borne in separate clusters on the same tree; the staminate, in 3-branched catkins, 5″ to 8″ long, each flower with hairy, yellow stamens; the pistillate, in 2- to 5-flowered spikes.

Fruit.—A large, 4- to 6-ribbed, light-reddish- or yellowish-brown, globular to ellipsoidal nut, 1″ to 2″ in length; incased in a chestnut-brown to orange-brown, unwinged, dehiscent husk, ¼″ to ½″ in thickness; seed, sweet.

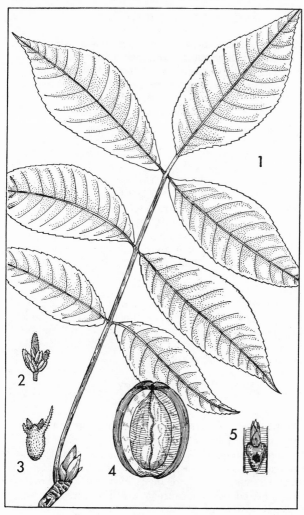

PLATE 25.—SHELLBARK HICKORY
1. Leaf ×⅓. 2. Male flower ×2. 3. Female flower ×3.
4. Fruit with part of husk removed ×½. 5. Leaf scar ×1.

Twigs.—Stout, dark brown, hairy, marked with pale, elongated lenticels; terminal buds, about ¾″ long, egg-shaped, blunt, with 3 or 4 dark-brown, loosely fitting, overlapping, hairy scales; lateral buds, smaller, leaning away from the twig; leaf scars, triangular to half-round, with many scattered bundle scars; pith, homogeneous.

Bark.—Smooth on young stems; blue-gray to slate-gray, dividing into long, firm, thin, curved plates, which give the bole a shaggy aspect.

Habitat.—Most abundant throughout the southern area on deep, rich, moist, alluvial soils in association with other bottom-land hardwoods; toward the northern limit of its range, a tree of upland slopes and flats.

Distribution.—Southern Maine west to southeastern Minnesota and eastern Nebraska; south to Delaware, thence south over the Piedmont plateau to northwestern Florida; in the West, south to northeastern Texas and northern Louisiana.

Importance.—One of the more important species of hickory and used for handle stock, basketry, and agricultural implements of all sorts. The wood makes an excellent fuel, and the nuts are edible and occasionally found in markets locally.

Shagbark Hickory

Carya ovata K. Koch.

Habit.—A moderately large tree, 60′ to 80′ in height and 1′ to 2′ in diameter (max. 120′ by 4′); in the forest, developing a long, clear bole with a small, open crown; in open situations, distinguished by the long, oblong crown so characteristic of many hickories. The root system includes a long taproot, which renders the tree unusually windfirm.

Leaves.—Alternate, deciduous, pinnately compound, 8″ to 14″ long, with 5 (rarely 7) obovate, sessile or

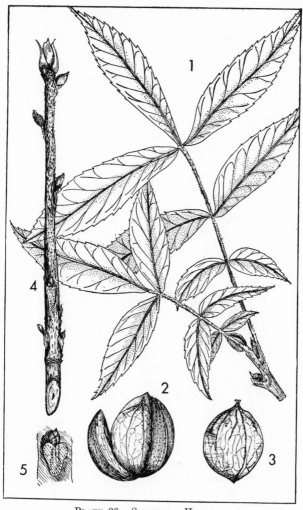

PLATE 26.—SHAGBARK HICKORY
1. Foliage ×½.   2. Fruit ×1.   3. Nut with husk removed ×1.
4. Twig ×⅔.   5. Leaf scar ×1½.

nearly sessile leaflets; leaflets, 5″ to 7″ long, 2″ to 3″ wide, the terminal slightly larger than the laterals; with long-tapered apices, wedge-shaped bases, and finely serrate margins; dark yellow-green and smooth above, lighter and hairy below; rachis stout, grooved, smooth or hairy.

Flowers.—Unisexual, both sexes borne in separate clusters on the same tree; the staminate, borne in hairy catkins of 4″ to 5″ in length; individual flowers, with 4 hairy stamens; pistillate flowers, in 2- to 5-flowered, rusty-red, woolly spikes.

Fruit.—A 4-ribbed, thin-shelled, oblong, light-brownish-white nut, about 1″ long; incased in a nearly black, dehiscent husk, about ½″ thick, depressed at the apex and depressed or rounded at the base; seed, sweet, light brown.

Twigs.—Stout, orange-brown, with large, orange lenticels; terminal buds, about 1″ long, egg-shaped, blunt, clothed with 6 to 8 dark-brown, loosely appressed, overlapping scales; lateral buds, similar but smaller, usually leaning away from the twigs; leaf scars, heart-shaped, with many scattered bundle scars; pith, homogeneous.

Bark.—Bluish gray to slate-gray in color, smooth on young stems, but on larger trunks separating into long, flattened, shaggy plates.

Habitat.—Best development of this tree occurs on moist, alluvial, river-valley soils. It is not restricted to such sites, however, and may be found on neighboring slopes and ridges. In bottom lands, it often forms nearly pure, open, parklike groves; in mixed stands, its common associates are pin, swamp white, and overcup oaks, red and silver maples, and American elm.

Distribution.—Central New York through southern Michigan to southern Nebraska; south to northern Alabama, northern Louisiana, and eastern Oklahoma.

Importance.—The wood is used for the same purposes as that of other hickories. The nuts have a
limited commercial value.

Southern Shagbark Hickory

Carya carolinae-septentrionalis Engelm. & Graebn.

This is a large tree of limited distribution occurring
sparsely through northeastern Mississippi, eastern
Tennessee, and the Piedmont plateau and neighboring
foothills of the Appalachian highlands from North
Carolina to Georgia. The tree resembles the better
known shagbark hickory with which it is occasionally
associated on moist sites. The southern shagbark
hickory, however, is characterized by smaller, less
hairy leaves; smaller fruits with thinner husks and less
pronounced longitudinal ridges along the nuts; and
slender twigs with cylindrical buds clothed in a number
of shiny-black scales, a feature of real diagnostic value.
When cut, the logs are mixed with those of other
hickories and thus lose their identity in the trade.

Mockernut Hickory

Carya tomentosa Nutt.

Habit.—A moderately large tree, 50′ to 70′ in height
and 1′ to 2′ in diameter; unlike most other hickories,
with a broad, rounded crown.

Leaves.—Alternate, deciduous, pinnately compound,
with 7 to 9 sessile or nearly sessile, glandular-resinous, fragrant leaflets, 8″ to 12″ long; leaflets, 5″ to 8″
long, 3″ to 5″ wide, the terminal and upper pair the
largest; with acute to long-tapered apices, unequally
rounded or broadly wedge-shaped bases, and finely to
coarsely serrate margins; dark yellow-green above,
covered with pale-yellow-green to orange-brown hairs
below; rachis stout, grooved, covered with glandular
hairs, fragrant when bruised.

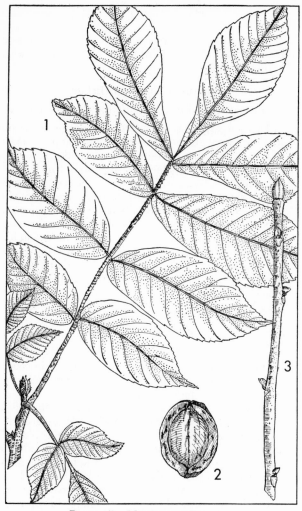

PLATE 27.—MOCKERNUT HICKORY.
1. Leaf ×½. 2. Fruit ×⅔. 3. Twig ×⅔.

Flowers.—Unisexual, both sexes borne in separate clusters on the same tree; the staminate, borne in 3-branched aments, 4″ to 5″ long; each flower, with 4 bright-red, hairy stamens; the pistillate, borne in 2- to 5-flowered spikes; each flower, with dark-red stigmas.

Fruit.—A 4-ribbed, thick-walled, obovoid to ellipsoidal nut, 1″ to 1½″ long; enclosed in a deeply 4-channeled, reddish-brown husk, ⅛″ to ¼″ thick; seed, sweet.

Twigs.—Stout, reddish brown to grayish brown, those of the current season hairy, dotted with pale, slitlike lenticels; terminal buds, about ½″ to ¾″ long, nearly globular, the outer scales soon dropping off and exposing the silky, buff-colored scales below; lateral buds, similar but smaller, commonly divergent, often superposed; leaf scars, 3-lobed to heart-shaped, with many bundle scars arranged in 3 groups or scattered; pith, homogeneous.

Bark.—Firm, sometimes almost horny, with blue-gray, rounded, interlacing ridges separated by shallow furrows.

Habitat.—Abundant in mixed hardwood forests on dry upland slopes; found in association with other hickories, many oaks, sweetgum, yellowpoplar, and black locust.

Distribution.—Eastern United States from southern Maine west through southern Michigan and northern Illinois to eastern Nebraska; south to northern Florida in the East and to eastern Texas in the West.

Importance.—Similar to that of shagbark hickory.

Sand Hickory

Carya pallida Engelm. & Graebn.

Sand hickory, characteristically a tree of dry, sandy soils, extends southward from Cape May, N.J., over the upper coastal plain and Piedmont plateau to Florida, thence west through the Gulf states. It has been reported also from Tennessee. The leaves are usually 7- (rarely 9-) foliate; the leaflets, supported on a hairy rachis, are resinous, fragrant, long-tapered, and furnished below with a myriad of minute, silvery scales. The fruit, $\frac{1}{2}''$ to $1\frac{1}{2}''$ long, is obovoid to nearly globular and often depressed at the summit; its husk is both hairy and profusely dotted with minute, yellow scales, and at maturity it opens tardily from the apex base to release the angular, laterally compressed, thin-shelled nut.

Ashe Hickory

Carya ashei Sudw.

Ashe hickory was first recognized as a distinct species by the late W. W. Ashe, who discovered it in Walton, Santa Rosa, and Escambia Counties of western Florida about a decade ago. The tree closely resembles red hickory and is often mistaken for that species. It may be distinguished by its 7- to 9-foliate leaves, deeply divided, horn-shaped stigmas, and small fruit, circular in cross section. The wood is used locally for fuel but is otherwise of little or no commercial value.

Swamp Hickory

Carya leiodermis Sarg.

Swamp hickory, a tree of the lower Mississippi basin and adjoining river valleys in Louisiana, Arkansas, and Mississippi, occurs on low, wet sites with other bottom-land hardwoods. This hickory is characterized by 7- (rarely 5-) foliate leaves. The leaflets, usually hairy below, are borne on slender, hairy rachises. The nearly globular to obovoid fruits, $1\frac{1}{2}''$ to $1\frac{3}{4}''$

long, are occasionally depressed at the apex and consist of a thin-shelled, slightly compressed nut, incased in a relatively thick (¼″) husk, which, at maturity, splits along 4 lines of suture from base to apex. Unlike most other hickories, the bark of this tree is relatively smooth except on the very largest trees.

Black Hickory

Carya texana Buckl.

Black hickory is a small, unimportant tree of the dry, sandy, sterile soils of central Oklahoma and northern and eastern Texas, where it is encountered as an occasional tree in association with other hardwoods. Pertinent botanical features are: (1) leaves, 5- to 7- (mostly 7-) foliate, 8″ to 12″ long; leaflets, with axillary pubescence below; (2) fruits, globose, 1¼″ to 1¾″ in diameter; husk, thin, hairy, at maturity splitting freely from apex to base to release a slightly compressed nut, 4-angled above the middle; (3) buds, hairy, dotted with minute, chafflike, silvery scales; (4) deeply furrowed, black bark.

A variety, Arkansas black hickory (var. *arkansana* Sarg.), with obovoid to pear-shaped fruit, is widespread on dry, sandy soils, rocky ridges, and heavy clays from southwestern Indiana to eastern Oklahoma and south through western Louisiana and eastern Texas.

Pignut Hickory

Carya glabra Sweet

Habit.—A tree of modest proportions, seldom more than 60′ to 80′ in height or 1′ to 2′ in diameter; like most other hickories, featuring a long, clear, symmetrical bole, which rises from a deep anchorage and passes through a narrow, oblong crown.

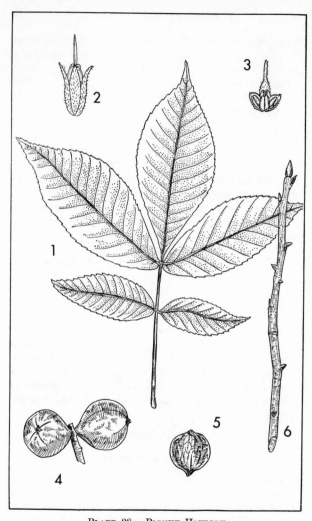

PLATE 28.—PIGNUT HICKORY
1. Leaf ×½. 2. Female flower ×4. 3. Male flower ×4.
4. Fruit ×½. 5. Nut with husk removed ×½. 6. Twig ×½.

Leaves.—Alternate, deciduous, pinnately compound, 8″ to 12″ long with 5 (rarely 7) sessile, lance-shaped leaflets; leaflets, 4″ to 6″ long, 2″ to 3″ broad, the terminal leaflet the largest, usually ovate, stalked, and about as broad as long; with acute to long-tapered apices, rounded bases, and finely serrate margins; yellow-green and smooth above, paler and smooth below or occasionally hairy along the midrib; rachis, slender, smooth, and free of hair.

Flowers.—Unisexual, both sexes borne in separate clusters on the same tree; the staminate, in 3-branched catkins of 2″ to 2½″ in length, the individual flowers with 4 yellow stamens; the pistillate, in few-flowered, woolly spikes.

Fruit.—Pear-shaped, about 1¼″ long; nut, thick-walled, unridged, compressed, incased in a thin husk, which even at maturity is incompletely dehiscent along 2 to 4 lines of suture; seed, small, usually sweet.

Twigs.—Stout, reddish brown, smooth, dotted with pale lenticels; terminal buds, broadly ovoid to nearly globular, almost ½″ long, covered by a few loosely fitting, reddish-brown scales, which usually slough off during the winter months, exposing the tawny inner scales; lateral buds, smaller, at nearly right angles to the twig; leaf scars, heart-shaped to nearly triangular, with many bundle scars clustered into 3 nearly equidistant groups; pith, homogeneous.

Bark.—Deeply furrowed between narrow, interlacing ridges, which are often scaly at the surface.

Habitat.—Most abundant on upland slopes and ridges in association with oaks and other hickories; in the South, occasionally on low ground with other bottom-land hardwoods.

Distribution.—Southwestern Vermont west through New York to southern Michigan; south through central Illinois to Louisiana; in the East, south along the coast to Virginia, thence along the Piedmont plateau and mountains to Georgia, Alabama, and Mississippi.

Importance.—Similar to that of other hickories.

Remarks.—Several distinct varieties of this species are recognized. A form (var. *megacarpa* Sarg.) with large fruits, 1″ to 2″ in length, and larger leaflets with resinous scales occurs widespread through the coastal plains and the Ohio and Mississippi valleys. A form with flattened fruits (var. *reniformis* Ashe), occurs through the central Piedmont plateau. A third with sharply angled fruits (var. *angulata* Sarg.) has also been described.

Valley Hickory

Carya villosa Ashe

Valley hickory, a small tree of the lower Mississippi Valley and adjacent areas, is considered by several authorities to be only a variety of the black hickory, which it superficially resembles. This tree, however, is readily separated from the black hickory by its hairy leaf rachises and small fruits with more or less indehiscent husks.

Red Hickory

Carya ovalis Sarg.

Habit.—A large tree, sometimes 80′ to 100′ in height, and 2′ to 3′ in diameter; the crown, cylindrical to pyramidal.

Leaves.—Alternate, deciduous, pinnately compound, 6″ to 10″ long, with 7 (often 5) sessile, lance-shaped leaflets; leaflets, 6″ to 7″ long, 1″ to 2″ wide, the upper 5 of nearly equal length; with acuminate or rarely blunt-rounded apices, unequally rounded bases, and finely or obscurely toothed margins; dark yellow-green above, paler and with tufts of axillary hairs below; rachis, slender, smooth or nearly so.

Flowers.—Unisexual, both sexes borne in separate

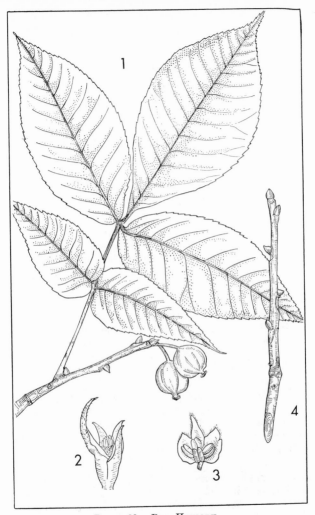

PLATE 29.—RED HICKORY

1. Foliage and fruit ×½. 2. Female flower ×5. 3. Male
flower ×5. 4. Twig ×½.

clusters on the same tree; the staminate, borne in 3-branched, hairy catkins, 6″ to 7″ long; each flower, with 4 yellow, hairy stamens; the pistillate, borne in 1- or 2-flowered spikes; each flower, with yellowish, hairy stigmas.

Fruit.—A slightly compressed, thin-walled, oblong nut, about 1″ long, 4-angled above the middle; enclosed in an ellipsoidal husk, which at maturity splits into 4 thin valves, slightly raised at the lines of suture; seed, sweet.

Twigs.—Slender, reddish brown, slightly hairy or smooth, dotted with pale, slitlike lenticels; terminal buds, about ½″ long, ovoid, blunt, or sharp-pointed, the outer, lustrous, reddish-brown scales soon dropping off and exposing the pale, woolly scales below; lateral buds, similar to the terminal but smaller; leaf scars, heart-shaped to remotely 3-lobed, with several bundle scars arranged in 3 groups or scattered; pith, homogeneous, star-shaped in cross section.

Bark.—Intermediate in character between that of shagbark and pignut hickories.

Habitat.—In mixed hardwood forests in association with other upland hickories, numerous oaks, and occasionally yellowpoplar; occurring on a variety of soils and sites but attaining maximum development on cool, moist slopes.

Distribution.—Central New York west to central Iowa, south to northeastern Arkansas and northern Mississippi, in the East, south to northern Alabama and Georgia; not on the coastal plain.

Importance.—Similar to that of other commercial hickories.

Remarks.—The red hickory has numerous varieties several of which occur in the South. Pearnut red hickory (*C. ovalis* var. *obovalis* Sarg.) may be distinguished by its pear-shaped fruits 1″ in length. This form is widely distributed through the Deep

South. Carolina red hickory (*C. ovalis* var. *hirsuta* Sarg.) is characterized by short-stalked pear-shaped fruits and pubescent leaflets, leaf rachises, and winter buds. This form is restricted to the mountains of North Carolina. Northern red hickory (*C. ovalis* var. *obcordata* Sarg.) is characterized by nearly globular fruits, the husks of which are obscurely winged along the sutures. This form also occurs widely through the South from North Carolina south through the Gulf states.

Scrub Hickory

Carya floridana Sarg.

This tree frequents the dry, sandy hills and ridges of peninsular Florida. On the best sites the tree attains a height of 50′ to 70′, but on dry, sterile soils it acquires a shrubby habit. Scrub hickory is characterized by 5- (rarely 7-) foliate leaves; the leaflets are sessile and coarsely toothed along the margin. The fruits exhibit considerable variation in size and shape, ranging from ¾″ to 1¾″ in length and from nearly globular to pear-shaped. The fruit husks are very thin, tardily and irregularly dehiscent, and profusely dotted with minute, golden scales.

Bitternut Hickory

Carya cordiformis K. Koch.

Habit.—A medium-sized, rapidly growing tree, 50′ to 60′ in height and 2′ to 3′ in diameter (max. 100′ by 4′), with stout, spreading limbs forming a gracefully full-rounded crown; bole, often buttressed at the base; root system, deep and widespread.

Leaves.—Alternate, deciduous, pinnately compound, 6″ to 10″ long; with 7 to 11 sessile to nearly sessile, lance-shaped leaflets; leaflets, 3″ to 6″ long, about 1″ wide, with long-tapered tips, rounded or wedge-shaped

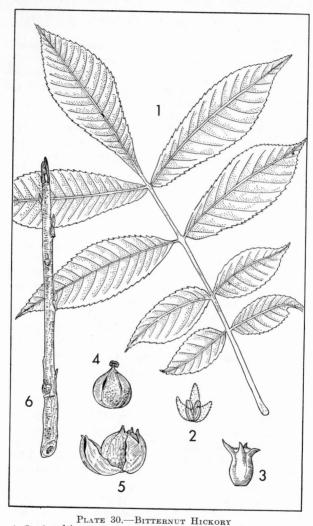

PLATE 30.—BITTERNUT HICKORY

1. Leaf ×½. 2. Male flower ×4. 3. Female flower ×4.
4. Fruit ×½. 5. Nut with husk partially dehiscent ×½.
6. Twig ×⅔.

bases, and finely to coarsely serrate margins; lustrous, bright green, and smooth above, pale green and either smooth or hairy below; rachis, slender, slightly grooved above, hairy.

Flowers.—Unisexual, both sexes borne in separate clusters on the same tree; the staminate, in 3-branched, 3″ to 4″ catkins, each with 4 yellow stamens sub-tended by a 2- or 3-lobed calyx; the pistillate, mostly solitary or paired, sessile, yellowish, woolly.

Fruit.—A nearly globelike nut, enclosed in a yellowish, thin-skinned husk, 4-ribbed above the middle, solitary or paired, thin-shelled, about 1″ in length; seed, bitter, deeply grooved.

Twigs.—Moderately stout, gray-brown to greenish brown, hairy through the early summer, dotted with numerous pale, oblong lenticels; terminal buds, present, about ½″ long, 4-angled, the sulphur-yellow scales valvate and covered with minute, chafflike scales; lateral buds, smaller, short-stalked, often leaning away from the twig; leaf scars, 3-lobed to heart-shaped, with numerous bundle scars scattered or arranged in 3 groups; pith, brownish white, homogeneous.

Bark.—Light brown to slate-gray, smooth for many years even on moderately large trunks; on the largest boles, with shallow furrows between flattened, interlacing ridges; occasionally scaly at the surface.

Habitat.—Most frequently encountered along streams and in wet bottom lands, where it occurs in small numbers in association with other moisture-loving broadleaved trees; occasionally found on slopes remote from streams but usually of small stature on such sites.

Distribution.—A tree of widespread occurrence ranging from southeastern Maine to central Minnesota, south to Florida in the East and through Kansas and Nebraska to eastern Texas in the West.

Importance.—The wood is inferior to that of many of the hickories but is frequently used for the same purposes; it is a good fuel wood.

Nutmeg Hickory

Carya myristicaeformis Nutt.

Nutmeg hickory, so-called because of the resemblance of its small, bony, thick-walled nut to that of the real nutmeg, is a large tree of sporadic occurrence and distribution. Only in Dallas County, Alabama, and in southern Arkansas does it occur commonly in the forest. Elsewhere, it is usually encountered as an occasional tree along streams, in swamps, or in river bottoms. This species has been reported from eastern South Carolina, central Alabama, northern Mississippi, central Arkansas, western Louisiana, southeastern Oklahoma, and eastern Texas. It has also been recorded from the mountains of northeastern Mexico. Nutmeg hickory is characterized by 7- to 9-foliate leaves, usually silky white below; ellipsoidal fruits about 1″ in length, distinguished by very thin husks (⅓₂″), which at maturity split nearly to the base to release the small, bony nuts; and twigs covered with minute, golden-brown scales.

Pecan

Carya illinoensis (*Wangenh.*) K. Koch

Habit.—A large tree, often 100′ to 140′ in height and 3′ to 4′ in diameter (rarely 180′ by 6′); the long, clear bole of the forest tree rises above a buttressed base and passes through a narrow, inverted, pyramidal crown; in the open the crown is broad, more or less rounded, and often covers the greater part of the trunk.

Leaves.—Alternate, deciduous, pinnately compound, 10″ to 20″ long, with 9 to 17 sessile or nearly sessile,

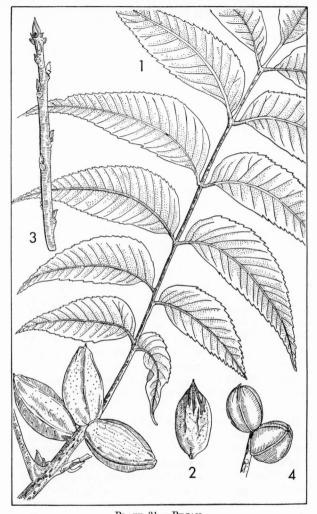

PLATE 31.—PECAN
1. Leaf and fruits ×½. 2. Nut with husk removed ×½.
3. Twig. ×⅔. 4. Fruit of the Nutmeg Hickory ×½.

lance-shaped, scythelike leaflets; leaflets, 4″ to 8″ long, 1″ to 2″ wide, with sharp, pointed tips, unequally rounded or wedge-shaped bases, and serrate or doubly serrate margins; dark yellowish green and smooth above, paler and at first hairy below; rachis, slender, smooth or at times hairy.

Flowers.—Unisexual, both sexes borne in separate clusters on the same tree; staminate flowers, in 3-branched, 3″ to 5″ aments, each with 5 or 6 yellow stamens subtended by a 2- or 3-lobed calyx; pistillate flowers, borne in few- to several-flowered spikes, yellow, hairy, and slightly 4-angled.

Fruit.—An ellipsoidal nut, enclosed in a thin-skinned husk, 4-winged from base to apex, borne in clusters of 3 to 12; nut, reddish brown, thin-shelled, 1½″ to 2½″ long, smooth or slightly 4-ridged; seed, sweet, deeply 2-grooved.

Twigs.—Moderately stout, reddish brown, more or less hairy, with conspicuous, orange-brown lenticels; terminal buds, present, about ½″ long, acute, yellowish brown, the scales valvate; lateral buds, similar but smaller, often more or less stalked, usually leaning away from the twig; leaf scars, obovate, the many bundle scars scattered or arranged in various clusters or patterns; pith, homogeneous.

Bark.—Moderately thick, light brown or grayish brown, divided by narrow fissures into flattened, scaly, interlacing ridges.

Habitat.—Rich, moist soils of well-drained river bottoms; usually occurring as an occasional tree with sweetgum, American elm, persimmon, honeylocust, hackberry, poplars and water oak.

Distribution.—Southwestern Indiana to southeastern Iowa, thence south through western Tennessee, to central Alabama, and south and west through southeastern Kansas to east and central Texas; reappearing in the mountains of Mexico.

Importance.—Widely planted throughout the South both as an ornamental and for its fruit. Several "papershell" varieties of superior flavor are now widely cultivated in our southern states, some of which are hardy as far north as Virginia. The wood is used for flooring, furniture, and fuel.

Bitter Pecan

Carya × lecontei Little

This is a large, symmetrical tree occasionally attaining a height of 80′ to 100′ and a diameter of 20″ to 30″. It frequents the wet, low grounds and river swamps of the Gulf coastal plain from Mississippi to eastern Texas and the river valleys of Louisiana and eastern Arkansas. The tree closely resembles the pecan but may be distinguished from that species by its much smaller leaves (10″ to 12″ long), compressed nuts with bitter seeds and smaller, compressed winter buds. This tree is now regarded as a hybrid between *C. illinoensis* and *C. aquatica.*

Water Hickory

Carya aquatica (Michx. f.) Britton

Water hickory is a large tree found in deep swamps of the southern coastal plains from southeastern Virginia to Florida, thence west through the Gulf states to eastern Texas. It also extends inland along the Mississippi River northward to Missouri and Illinois. This tree, which is occasionally 100′ in height and 24″ in diameter, may be distinguished by its 9″ to 15″ leaves with 7 to 13 scythelike leaflets, glandular on the upper surface; conspicuously flattened fruits, the husks of which are longitudinally 4-winged from base to apex and covered with bright-yellow scales; and slender twigs with small, yellowish buds. The wood is of an inferior quality to that of other pecan hickories; it is difficult to work, often brash, and dimensionally unstable. It is occasionally used locally for fuel, posts, and props.

THE BIRCH FAMILY

Betulaceae

The Birch Family comprises a group of 6 genera and nearly 100 species of deciduous trees and shrubs that, except for a few alders in Mexico, Central America, and the Peruvian Andes Mountains, are restricted to the cooler regions of the Northern Hemisphere. The genus *Corylus* L. produces the hazelnuts and filberts of commerce, and on the west coast *Alnus rubra* Bong. is an important timber tree.

Three genera, *Betula*, *Carpinus*, and *Ostrya*, are represented in southern forests by one or more arborescent forms.

Synopsis of Southern Arborescent Genera

Genus	Flowers	Fruit
Betula	staminate catkins, pre-formed; scales of pistillate catkins, persistent	small, laterally winged nutlets, borne in a conelike structure whose scales (bracts) are deciduous at maturity
Carpinus	staminate catkins, appearing in the early spring from specialized flower buds; scales of pistillate catkins, deciduous	small, unwinged nuts, each subtended by a characteristic 3-lobed bract, borne in leafy, spikelike clusters
Ostrya	staminate catkins, preformed; scales of pistillate catkins, deciduous	small, unwinged nuts, each enclosed in a papery, bladderlike sac, borne in conelike clusters

THE BIRCHES

Betula L.

This is a group of about 40 species of deciduous trees and shrubs restricted to the Northern Hemisphere from the Arctic Circle to The Himalayas in the Old World and in North America from the arctic regions to the southern United States. Many of them, because of their habit, handsome foliage, or showy and distinctive bark, are used ornamentally.

Fifteen birches are included in the North American flora, and four of the arborescent forms are found in southern forests.

KEY TO THE SOUTHERN BIRCHES

1. Fruit clusters, pendent; bark, chalky white..........
    Mountain paper birch (p. 157)
1. Fruit clusters, erect............................... 2

2. Twigs, aromatic; fruit clusters, nearly sessile...... 3
2. Twig, not aromatic; fruit clusters, borne on long, slender stems; bark, divided into loose, papery scales, tinged with pink........**River birch** (p. 149)

3. Leaves, heart-shaped at the base; fruit clusters, oblong; bark, on young stems black, not separating into thin layers........................**Black birch** (p. 152)
3. Leaves, mostly rounded or inequilateral at the base; fruit clusters, ovoid; bark, on young stems bronze, separating into thin layers.......**Yellow birch** (p. 154)

River Birch

Betula nigra L.

Habit.—A medium-sized tree, 70′ to 80′ in height and 15″ to 30″ in diameter. The trunk, even in the forest, usually divides 15′ to 20′ from the ground into

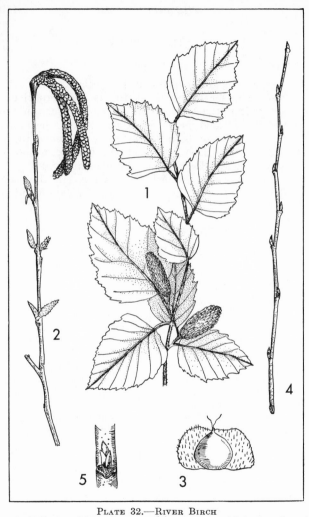

PLATE 32.—RIVER BIRCH

1. Foliage and fruit clusters ×½.   2. Twig with both male and female catkins   ×1.   3. Nutlet   ×6.   4. Twig   ×1.   5. Leaf scar ×1½.

several large, arching branches to form an irregularly spreading crown. The roots are shallow and wide-spread.

Leaves.—Alternate, simple, deciduous, 1½″ to 3″ long, 1″ to 2″ wide, rhombic-ovate; apex, acute; base, wedge-shaped; margin, deeply doubly serrate; bright green above, pale and hairy below; petioles, slender, somewhat flattened, hairy, about ½″ long.

Flowers.—Unisexual, both forms on the same tree but in separate catkins; staminate catkins, about 1″ long, reddish brown; pistillate catkins, about ⅓″ long, green, hairy.

Fruit.—A cylindrical, erect, stalked strobile incasing many small, winged nutlets, 1″ to 1½″ long; strobile scales, longer than broad, hairy on the back, par-ticularly toward the apex, deciduous from the central axis at maturity; nutlets, pubescent at the apex, broader than their lateral wings.

Twigs.—Slender, zigzag, orange-brown or reddish brown, commonly with short, stiff, reddish-brown hairs, without either aromatic odor or taste; terminal bud, lacking; lateral buds, ovoid, sharp-pointed, covered by several lustrous, chestnut-brown, over-lapping scales; leaf scars, nearly oval, with 3 bundle scars; stipule scars, minute, slitlike; pith, homogeneous.

Bark.—Reddish brown on very young stems, soon becoming white or salmon-pink and papery; ulti-mately, gray to gray-brown and coarsely scaly.

Habitat.—The only birch in the South to be found at low altitudes; most common along streams and in wet bottoms in association with American elm, syca-more, red and silver maples, hackberry, boxelder, willows, poplars, and yellow-poplar.

Distribution.—Southern New England west through Pennsylvania, and southern Wisconsin to south-eastern Minnesota; south to northern Florida in the East and eastern Texas in the West.

Importance.—A tree of secondary importance. The wood is used locally for fuel and occasionally for woodenware and turnery. The tree has a limited ornamental use.

Black Birch

Betula lenta L.

Habit.—A tree of modest proportions, commonly 50′ to 70′ in height and 15″ to 30″ in diameter; in the forest, producing a graceful, spherical crown and long, clear, columnar bole, which rises from a deep, spreading root system.

Leaves.—Alternate, simple, deciduous, 2½″ to 5″ long, 1½″ to 2″ broad, ovate to oblong-ovate; apex, acute; base, heart-shaped; margin, sharply singly or remotely doubly serrate; dull, dark green above, paler and with tufts of hair in the axils of the principal veins below; petioles, stout, hairy, ½″ to ¾″ long.

Flowers.—Unisexual, both forms on the same tree, but in separate catkins; staminate catkins, ¾″ to 1″ long, reddish brown; pistillate catkins, ½″ to 1″ long, light green, tinged with pink.

Fruit.—An oblong or oblong-ovoid, sessile or short-stalked, erect strobile, incasing many small, winged nutlets, 1″ to 1½″ long; strobile scales, either hairy at their base or along their upper margin or entirely devoid of hair, tardily deciduous from the central axis at maturity; nutlets, smooth, obovoid, slightly wider than their lateral wings.

Twigs.—Slender, zigzag, light reddish brown, with an aromatic odor and taste similar to wintergreen; terminal bud, absent; lateral buds, sharp-pointed, divergent, covered by several lustrous, chestnut-brown, overlapping scales; spurs, numerous on old growth; leaf scars, semiovate or crescent-shaped, with 3 nearly equidistant bundle scars; stipule scars, minute, slitlike; pith, homogeneous.

PLATE 33.—BLACK BIRCH

1. Foliage and fruit clusters $\times\frac{1}{3}$.   2. Male catkin $\times1\frac{1}{2}$.
3. Female flower $\times3$.   4. Male flower $\times3$.   5. Leaf scar $\times1\frac{1}{2}$.
6. Nutlet $\times4$.

Bark.—Smooth, reddish brown to nearly black, with prominent, horizontal lenticels on young stems; breaking up into large, thin, irregularly scaly plates on old trunks.

Habitat.—Most abundant on deep, rich, moist but well-drained soils; also occurring on rocky ledges and dry, rocky soils; always encountered as an occasional tree in association with other hardwoods, notably maples, yellow-poplar, beech, basswood, and numerous oaks. This species reaches its best development in Kentucky and Tennessee.

Distribution.—Appalachian Mountains and adjacent regions, southern Michigan, and New England.

Importance.—The wood of black birch is similar to that of yellow birch and is used for the same purposes. The twigs are a source of birch oil.

Yellow Birch

Betula alleghaniensis Britton

Habit.—The largest and most important of the American birches; a tree, 60′ to 90′ in height and 20″ to 40″ in diameter; under forest conditions, producing a long, clear, cylindrical bole, small, irregularly rounded crown, and shallow, wide-spreading root system.

Leaves.—Alternate, simple, deciduous, 3″ to 4½″ long, 1½″ to 2″ wide, ovate to ovate-oblong; apex, acute or long-tapered; base, rounded or inequilateral; margin, sharply doubly serrate; dull, dark green and smooth above, pale yellow-green below, with tufts of hair in the axils of the principal veins; petioles, slender, pubescent, about ½″ to ¾″ long.

Flowers.—Unisexual, both forms on the same tree in separate catkins; staminate catkins, ¾″ to 1″ long, light golden brown; pistillate catkins, ½″ to ⅔″ long, green, tinged with red.

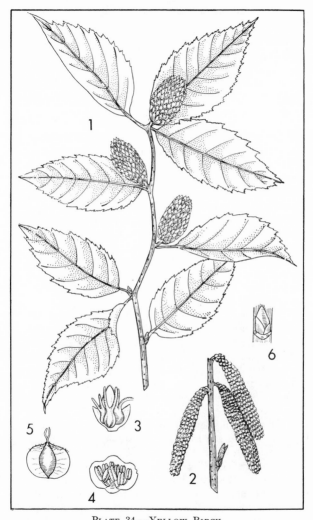

PLATE 34.—YELLOW BIRCH

1. Foliage and fruit clusters ×½. 2. Male catkins ×½.
3. Female flower ×4. 4. Male flower ×4. 5. Nutlet ×4.
6. Leaf scar ×1½.

Fruit.—An ovoid, sessile or short-stalked, erect strobile, incasing many small, winged nutlets, 1″ to 1½″ long; scales, pubescent on the back, tardily deciduous from the central axis at maturity; nutlets, oval to ovate, about as wide as their lateral wings, pubescent at and near the apex.

Twigs.—Slender, zigzag, yellow-green to dark brown, with an aromatic odor and taste not unlike wintergreen; terminal bud, absent; lateral buds, ovoid, acute, covered with several overlapping, chestnut-brown scales which are hairy along the margin; spurs, numerous on old growth; leaf scars, crescent-shaped, with 3 nearly equidistant bundle scars; pith, homogeneous; stipule scars, slitlike.

Bark.—Smooth, golden gray to bronze; characterized by long, horizontal lenticels on young stems, eventually separating at the surface and peeling horizontally into thin, curly, papery sheets; on the largest trees, divided into irregularly shaped, reddish-brown plates.

Habitat.—Of widespread occurrence in northeastern forests, where it usually appears on sandy loams in association with sugar maple, beech, white pine, red spruce, and hemlock; occasionally forming dense thickets on burned-over land; in the South, largely restricted to moist, cool, northerly mountain slopes between 3,000′ and 5,000′ in elevation.

Distribution.—Southeastern Canada, the Lake states, New England and Appalachian Mountains to northern Georgia. Near sea level in the North, to over 5,000′ in elevation in the South.

Importance.—Yellow birch produces a fine, moderately heavy wood suitable for many purposes. With beech and sugar maple it is used in the hardwood distillation industry, which now centers in the Lake states region. It is one of the principal furniture woods of the United States and may be stained and finished to simulate either black walnut or mahogany. Some of the largest and finest logs are cut into veneers of both cabinet and commercial rank. In the latter instance they are manufactured into aircraft veneers, baskets, crates, picnic dishes, and lard, butter, and meat containers. The twigs contain an essential oil, not unlike wintergreen, that is obtained in commercial quantities by steam distillation. Michaux records (1819) that wood sent to Ireland and Scotland in the form of planks was highly esteemed for joinery and that in Maine and Nova Scotia it was used for the underwater planking of ships. He also observed that the bark was used in tanning hides but that only a fair leather resulted.

Mountain Paper Birch

Betula papyrifera var. *cordifolia* Fern.

This is a variety of the transcontinental paper birch of the North. It is a rare form in southern forests and occurs only at high elevations in the mountains of North Carolina, usually above 5,000'. It is readily identified by its heart-shaped leaves, pendulous fruit clusters, and chalky-white bark, marked by prominent, horizontally linear lenticels.

THE HORNBEAMS

Carpinus L.

This group includes about 25 species of deciduous trees and shrubs. Unlike other genera of the birch family, the hornbeams do not develop preformed staminate catkins, the inflorescences appearing in the spring from specialized flower buds. A single species (*C. caroliniana* Walt.), found in eastern and southern forests, is the only American representative of this group.

American Hornbeam   Bluebeech

Carpinus caroliniana Walt.

Habit.—A large shrub or small, bushy tree that under optimum growing conditions seldom attains a height of more than 25′ to 35′ or a diameter of more than 15″ to 20″. The short, fluted, and commonly twisted trunk rises from a shallow, spreading anchorage of lateral roots and is soon lost in a number of spreading branches, which are pendulous at the tips.

Leaves.—Alternate, simple, deciduous, 2″ to 4″ long, 1″ to 2″ wide, ovate; apex, long-tapered; base, rounded, heart-shaped, or wedge-shaped; margin, sharply doubly serrate, the teeth glandular except at the base; dull blue-green and smooth above, pale yellow-green and with tufts of white hair in the axils of principal veins below; petioles, slender, hairy, about ⅓″ long.

Flowers.—Unisexual, each sex borne on the same tree but in separate catkins; staminate catkins, about 1″ long, the scales red above the middle, green below; pistillate catkins, about ½″ long, the scales green and hairy.

Fruit.—A small, ovoid, wingless nut, subtended by a 3-lobed, leafy bract; borne in spikelike clusters 3″ to 6″ in length.

Twigs.—Slender, zigzag, deep red to reddish purple; terminal buds, absent; lateral buds, ovoid, sharp-pointed, about ⅛″ long, the scales overlapping, chestnut brown, commonly greenish toward the base; leaf scars, small, crescent-shaped, with 3 bundle scars; stipule scars, small, crescent-shaped or lens-shaped; pith, homogeneous.

Bark.—Tight, thin, smooth, blue-gray, fluted or occasionally with small knoblike excrescences.

Habitat.—An understory tree found on deep, rich,

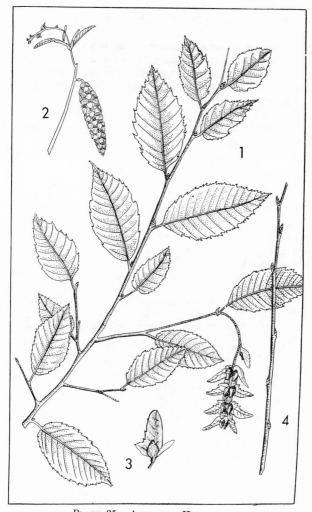

PLATE 35.—AMERICAN HORNBEAM

1. Foliage and fruit cluster ×⅓. 2. Male and female flower clusters ×1. 3. Single fruit ×1. 4. Twig ×½.

moist loams, along streams, in swamps and wet bottoms in association with many hardwoods.

Distribution.—Widespread through southeastern Canada and the eastern and southern United States.

Importance.—This species is generally considered to be a weed tree throughout its range. The wood is hard, tough, heavy, and difficult to dry but is used in limited quantities for tool handles.

THE HOPHORNBEAMS

Ostrya Scop.

Of the seven known hophornbeams two are North American species. One (*O. knowltonii* Cov.) is restricted to small, isolated areas in Utah and Arizonia. The other (*O. virginiana* K. Koch.) is a widespread eastern and southern species. This group is so named because of its hoplike fruit.

Eastern Hophornbeam

Ostrya virginiana K. Koch.

Habit.—Ordinarily, a small tree, seldom more than 20′ to 30′ in height and 15″ to 20″ in diameter, with a small, columnar bole, round-topped or vaselike, open crown, and moderately deep root system.

Leaves.—Alternate, simple, deciduous, 3″ to 5″ long, 1½″ to 2½″ wide, oblong-lanceolate; apex, acute to long-tapered; base, rounded, heart-shaped inequilateral or sometimes even wedge-shaped; margin, sharply serrate; dull yellow-green above, paler and with axillary, hairy tufts below; petioles, hairy, about ¼″ long; stipules, on vigorous growth, often persistent through the growing season and well into the winter.

Flowers.—Unisexual, both forms on the same tree but in separate catkins; staminate catkins, about ½″

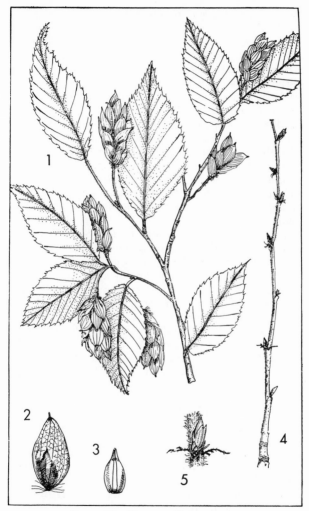

PLATE 36.—EASTERN HOPHORNBEAM
1. Foliage and fruit clusters ×½. 2. Single fruit ×1. 3. Nutlet ×1½. 4. Twig ×¾. 5. Leaf scar ×1½.

long, reddish brown; pistillate catkins, about ¼″ long, borne on hairy stalks, the scales light green, tinged with red above the middle.

Fruit.—A small, brown nut, about ¼″ long, completely enclosed in a papery sac; in conelike clusters 1½″ to 2″ in length.

Twigs.—Slender, zigzag, yellowish brown to orange-brown, commonly more or less hairy through their 1st winter; terminal buds, absent; lateral buds, ovoid, oblique, covered by several overlapping, often striate, chestnut-brown scales; leaf scars, crescent-shaped to semielliptical, with 3 bundle scars; stipule scars, slitlike, the pairs usually of unequal length; pith, homogeneous.

Bark.—Reddish brown and cherrylike on young stems; on old trunks, gray to brown, broken into narrow, oblong, platelike scales, which are free at the ends, thus giving the bole a shreddy appearance.

Habitat.—On slopes and ridges and occasionally in bottoms; usually an understory species in association with many hardwoods.

Distribution.—Southeastern Canada, the eastern and southern United States.

Importance.—Like the American hornbeam, another weed tree; the wood is used locally for posts, tool handles, and mallets.

THE BEECH FAMILY

Fagaceae

The Beech Family embraces 9 genera and about 600 species of trees and shrubs, many of them evergreen. These are scattered throughout the forests of the world but occur in much greater numbers in the Northern Hemisphere.

Of the 5 genera indigenous to North America, 3 are represented by 1 or more species in the forests of the South. The genus *Quercus*, which includes the oaks, is probably the most important hardwood group within our region. In fact, some authorities look upon all our southern hardwood forests as oak forests in admixture with other species.

Synopsis of Southern Genera

Genera	Leaves	Flowers	Fruit
Fagus	deciduous	staminate, in heads; pistillate, in 2- to 4-flowered spikes	triangular nuts, in pairs within a spiny bur; matures in 1 season
Castanea	deciduous	in erect aments or bisexual spikes	flattened, conical nuts, in 2's or 3's, within a thick bur covered with rigid, compound spines; matures in 1 season
Quercus	persistent or deciduous	staminate, in aments; pistillate, solitary or in few-flowered spikes	acorns; matures in 1 or 2 seasons

THE BEECHES

Fagus L.

The beeches are restricted to forests of the Northern Hemisphere. Of the 10 known species, only 1 (*F. grandifolia* Ehrh.) is native to North America. The European beech and several of its varieties are widely planted ornamentals. Included in this group is the bronze beech (*F. sylvatica* var. *atropunicea* West) with its beautiful bronze-purple foliage. There are also weeping, and cut-leaved forms. The fruit, known as *mast* or *beech mast*, is fed to swine and is a source of vegetable oil.

American Beech

Fagus grandifolia Ehrh.

Habit.—A medium-sized tree, 60′ to 80′ in height and 2′ to 3′ in diameter (rarely 120′ by 4′); in the open, branching fairly close to the ground and forming a large, open, spreading crown; by contrast, the bole of the forest tree is clear and straight and supports a small, narrow crown; the root system is very shallow, and numerous root suckers arising under the canopy of the parent tree are characteristic of old growth.

Leaves.—Alternate, simple, deciduous, often clustered at the ends of branchlets, 2½″ to 5″ long, 1″ to 2½″ wide, oblong-ovate; apex, gradually tapering to a point; base, wedge-shaped; margin, serrate; dark green above, yellow-green below, lustrous and glabrous; secondary veins, oblique and parallel; petioles, ¼″ to ½″ long; stipules, 1″ to 1½″ in length.

Flowers.—Monoecious, appearing with the leaves; staminate, in rounded heads, about 1″ in diameter, supported on slender, hairy stalks, 1″ to 2″ long; calyx, bell-shaped, hairy, 4- to 8-lobed; stamens, 8 to 10, with green anthers; pistillate, in 2- or 4-flowered spikes borne on stalks ½″ to 1″ long; calyx, hairy, with 4 or 5 lobes; pistil, composed of a 3-celled ovary and 3 divergent, stigmatic styles.

Fruit.—A 3-angled nut, borne in 2's or sometimes in 3's; enclosed within a bur covered with soft, simple (unbranched) spines.

Twigs.—Slender, at first pale green and downy, but at maturity yellowish brown and smooth; usually zigzag; terminal buds, sharp-pointed, spindle-shaped, lustrous brown, about 1″ long; lateral buds, similar;

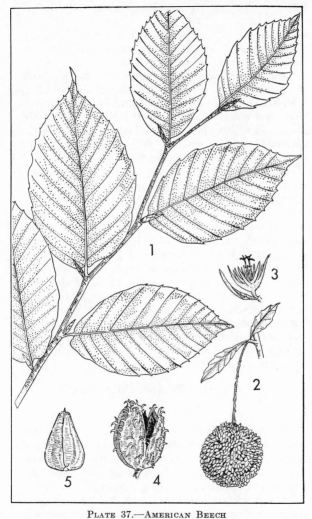

PLATE 37.—AMERICAN BEECH
1. Foliage ×½. 2. Head of male flowers ×1. 3. Female
flowers ×1. 4. Fruiting bur ×1. 5. Fruit ×1.

leaf scars, half-round, with 3 bundle scars, the lower often redivided; stipule scars, minute, nearly surrounding the twig; pith, continuous.

Bark.—Thin, smooth, steel-gray, and showing little or no change with increased diameter of the bole.

Habitat.—Rich soil on mountain slopes, bottom lands and swamp margins; in the North, commonly associated with yellow birch and maple; in the South, associated with sweetgum, yellow-poplar, numerous bottom-land oaks, and sycamore.

Distribution.—Southeastern Canada to Wisconsin, south to northern Florida and eastern Texas.

Importance.—The beech produces a wood of many uses. With birch and maple it is used in the hardwood distillation industry to obtain charcoal, wood alcohol, and acetate of lime. Limited quantities are also employed in the soda process of pulp manufacture. Veneers, flooring, furniture, brush backs, clothespins, spools, toys, cooperage, crates, turned articles, and laundry appliances are only a few of the many products manufactured of this wood. As a fuel wood it has few superiors, and when thoroughly dry it makes an excellent cooking fire. The nuts contain a high percentage of oil and are consumed in vast quantities by small game animals and birds.

THE CHESTNUTS AND CHINKAPINS

Castanea Mill.

The chestnuts comprise a group of 11 species distributed through northern Africa, Asia, Europe, and North America. Several are a source of valuable timber, tannin extract, and edible nuts, and others are prized ornamental trees of long standing.

The American chestnut has been one of the finest of American trees. Unfortunately, however, a parasite, introduced into the United States in 1904, has since destroyed the bulk of our chestnut forests as no practical control measures have ever been devised to prevent its spread. Grafts consisting of oriental scions on American rootstock have been used for planting, but it is not expected that this method of regeneration will ever replace the vast stands of chestnut which once occurred in the East and South.

At least 7 chestnuts and chinkapins occur in the South, 6 of which are arborescent.

KEY TO THE SOUTHERN ARBORESCENT CHESTNUTS AND CHINKAPINS

1. Burs, with 2 or 3 (sometimes 4) nuts; nuts, usually flattened on 1 side; leaves, smooth above and below..
American chestnut (p. 168)
1. Burs, with a single rounded nut; leaves, usually woolly or hairy below.................................... 2

2. Leaves, woolly below.......................... 3
2. Leaves, silky below, those in the lower crown sometimes nearly glabrous at maturity................ 5

3. Leaves, 4″ to 7″ long, with small, sharp, marginal teeth.................................... 4
3. Leaves, 6″ to 10″ long, with bristle-tipped, marginal teeth.....................**Ozark chinkapin** (p. 173)

4. Burs, densely covered with clustered spines; leaves, velvety pubescent below.........................
Allegheny chinkapin (p. 170)
4. Burs, sparingly clothed with clustered spines; leaves, feltlike below......**Ashe chinkapin** (p. 172)

5. Leaves, 4″ to 9″ long, glaucous below...............
Alabama chinkapin (p. 173)
5. Leaves, 2½″ to 6″ long, lustrous below............ .
Florida chinkapin (p. 172)

American Chestnut

Castanea dentata (Marsh.) Borkh.

Habit.—Ordinarily, a large tree, 60' to 80' in height, with a straight trunk 3' to 4' in diameter (max. 120' by 10'); in the open, developing a short, massive trunk with a large, majestic crown of spreading branches; in the forest, producing a long, clear, slightly tapered bole and short, narrow crown; the root system often characterized by a taproot; when felled, producing numerous sprouts about the root collar of the stump.

Leaves.—Alternate, simple, deciduous, oblong-lanceolate, 7" to 8" long, 2" wide; apex, long-tapered; base, wedge-shaped; margin, coarsely serrate; yellow-green, glabrous above, paler below; petioles, short, stout, ½" long.

Flowers.—Unisexual, appearing after the leaves; male catkins, erect, 6" to 8" long, the stalk supporting many sessile flowers; calyx, bell-shaped, brown, remotely pubescent, 6-lobed; stamens, 10 to 20, with long, white filaments and yellow anthers; pistillate flowers, situated at the base of bisexual catkins, in clusters of 3 to 5, enclosed in an involucre of green, hairy scales; calyx, hairy; ovary, 6-celled; styles, 6, divergent, stigmatic.

Fruit.—A smooth, light-brown, edible nut, about 1" long, slightly compressed on one side, and pubescent near the apex; borne in clusters of 2 or 3 and incased in a 2- to 4-valved, leathery involucre covered with stiff, needle-sharp, branched spines; seed, sweet.

Twigs.—Moderately stout, chestnut-brown, somewhat angled, glabrous, with white lenticels; terminal buds, present or absent; lateral buds, ovoid, obliquely sessile, with 2 or 3 visible, overlapping, dark-brown scales; leaf scars, half-round, with 3 bundle scars which are frequently broken into many smaller ones;

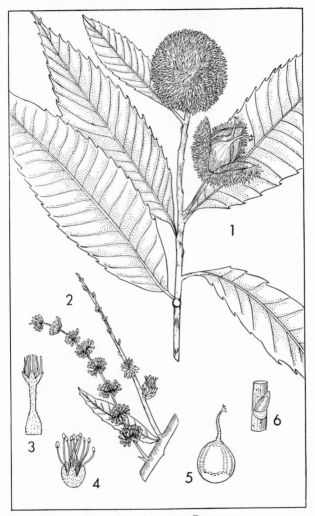

PLATE 38.—AMERICAN CHESTNUT

1. Foliage and fruit ×½. 2. Catkins ×½. 3. Female flower
×3. 4. Male flower ×4. 5. Nut ×¾. 6. Leaf scar ×1.

stipule scars, elongated; pith, continuous, star-shaped in cross section.

Bark.—1″ to 2″ thick, dark brown, fissured, forming broad, flat ridges, which often separate into small scales.

Habitat.—On rich, well-drained soil from lowlands to elevations of over 4,000′; usually occurring in association with other hardwoods.

Distribution.—Southern Maine, west to eastern Michigan; south along the coast to central Virginia, thence inland along the upper Piedmont plateau to southern Alabama; in the West, south through Ohio, southern Indiana, and Illinois to east-central Arkansas.

Importance.—Prior to decimation by the chestnut blight, this species was of immense importance to the lumber industry and was used in the manufacture of furniture, musical instruments, caskets, boxes, and core stock for veneers; it was also an important source of tannin, and the nuts were used widely as food by both man and beast.

Allegheny Chinkapin

Castanea pumila (L.) Mill.

Habit.—A shrub or small tree, 10′ to 30′ in height and 6″ to 18″ in diameter (rarely up to 50′ by 3′); in the Southeast, often shrubby and forming thickets through the development of innumerable stolons.

Leaves.—Alternate, simple, deciduous, 3″ to 5″ long, 1½″ to 2″ wide, oblong to elliptical; apex, acute; base, unequal; margin, coarsely serrate, with rigid teeth; at first, tomentose above and below, later yellow-green above, pubescent below; yellow in the fall; petioles, short, stout, flattened.

Flowers.—Unisexual, staminate aments with stout stems, 4″ to 6″ long, flower clusters crowded or scattered; bisexual aments, silvery, tomentose, 3″ to 4″ long, the pistillate flowers basal.

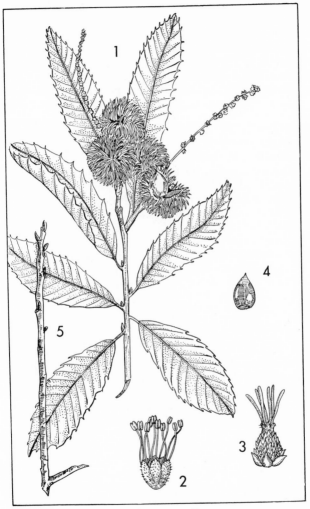

PLATE 39.—ALLEGHENY CHINKAPIN
1. Foliage and fruit ×½. 2. Male flower ×5. 3. Female
flower ×5. 4. Nut ×½. 5. Twig ×½.

Fruit.—A smooth, brown, edible nut, about ¾″ long, pubescent near the apex, usually borne singly and incased in a 2- or 3-valved involucre covered with stiff, needle-sharp, branched spines; seed, sweet.

Twigs.—Slender, at first pubescent, becoming orange-brown and glabrous during the 1st winter; buds, ⅛″ long, becoming red, pubescent; other features similar to those of the preceding species.

Bark.—Up to 1″ thick, reddish brown, broken into loose, platelike scales.

Habitat.—In sandy or rich soil on hillsides and swamp borders.

Distribution.—From southern Pennsylvania east to New Jersey and south to western Florida; in the Gulf states, and through Arkansas to Oklahoma and Missouri.

Importance.—Chinkapin nuts are a source of food for many small game animals. The wood is very durable in contact with the soil and is used locally for poles, posts, and crossties.

Ashe Chinkapin

Castanea pumila var. *ashei* Sudw.

This is a small tree of the coastal plains that frequents hammocks and dry, sandy soils from Virginia south to Florida and eastern Texas. It is characterized by small, oval to elliptical leaves, small, 1-fruited burs with short, stubby spines, and smooth bark.

Florida Chinkapin

Castanea floridana (Sarg.) Ashe

This chinkapin is widespread along the coastal plains and lower Piedmont plateau from Virginia to Florida and eastern Texas. Some authorities consider it to be merely an arborescent variety of the shrubby *C. alnifolia* Nutt. and as such give it the designation of *C. alnifolia* var. *floridana* Sarg. The burs are even less spiny than those of the Ashe chinkapin, and it may be further distinguished from that tree by its thinner, lustrous leaves.

Alabama Chinkapin

Castanea alabamensis Ashe

A small tree, reported only from Alabama, where it may be encountered at low elevations along creeks and on wooded slopes. The coarsely dentate, bristle-tipped leaves with glaucous lower surfaces readily serve to distinguish this form.

Ozark Chinkapin

Castanea ozarkensis Ashe

This small tree is found on the Ozark-Ouachita plateau, in southern Missouri, Oklahoma, Louisiana, and Mississippi, and on the adjacent coastal plain. It is readily identified by its large, bristle-tipped leaves, with brown or tawny, pubescent lower surfaces, and spiny burs, which are about 1" in diameter.

THE OAKS

Quercus L.

The oaks comprise a genus of nearly 300 species of deciduous and evergreen trees and shrubs. Our southern forests, except for the subtropics, abound with members of this group, and there is hardly a section in which several of them may not be found.

Economically, the oaks are of major importance. In the United States they furnish more timber than any other related group of broadleaved trees. The barks of 2 Mediterranean species supply the cork of commerce; several others are a source of tannin extract and yellow dye pigments. The acorns of many species are edible and are consumed in great quantities by squirrels, pheasants, wild turkeys, grouse, and domestic hogs.

Oaks have played an important role in both ancient and modern history. Many have been the center of much religious activity. As the host of the mistletoe, it held an important place in Druid rites. More recently, oaks have served as witnesses of the progress in our own nation, and specific trees connected with historical events are legion.

At least 35 species reach arborescent stature in the South.

KEY TO THE SOUTHERN OAKS

1. Leaf apices and lobes, usually rounded; if pointed, not bristle-tipped; acorns, maturing in a single season; inner shell of nut, glabrous; seeds, usually germinating in the fall, often sweetish............
   The white oaks 2
1. Leaf apices and lobes, usually bristle-tipped; acorns, maturing at the end of 2 seasons; inner shell of nut, usually woolly or silky; seeds, usually germinating in the spring, normally bitter to the taste.............
   The red oaks 15

2. Leaves, evergreen............**Live oak** (p. 179)
2. Leaves, deciduous............................ 3

3. Leaves, shallowly to deeply pinnately lobed or with coarsely toothed or scalloped margins............... 4
3. Leaves, entire or occasionally in part 3-lobed at or near the apex....................................13

4. Leaves, lobed................................. 5
4. Leaves, toothed or scalloped along the margin...10

5. Leaves, having the appearance of a cross........... 6

5. Leaves, oval, oblong, elliptical, or obovate, but never crosslike.. 7

    6. Leaves, mostly 4″ to 6″ long; twigs of the current season, reddish brown, glabrous...............
                                    Post oak (p. 181)
    6. Leaves, mostly 2″ to 4″ long; twigs of the current season, brownish gray, woolly.................
                               Sand post oak (p. 183)

7. Leaves, with only the central or lower pairs of sinuses extending nearly to the midrib.................... 8
7. Leaves, with all sinuses of nearly equal depth....... 9

    8. Nut, almost wholly enclosed in a cup composed of thin, reddish-brown, wedgelike scales; twigs, without corky ridges; complementary leaf lobes, usually oblique............**Overcup oak** (p. 183)
    8. Nut, about half enclosed in a deep cup with a marginal fringe of elongated, matted scales; twigs, commonly ridged with cork; complementary leaf lobes, usually opposite.........**Bur oak** (p. 185)

9. Leaves, usually 7- to 9-lobed, the sinuses extending nearly to the midrib; acorn cup, rather shallow, composed of numerous thickened, warty scales..........
                                White oak (p. 187)
9. Leaves, mostly 5-lobed, the sinuses very shallow; acorn cup, moderately deep, composed of numerous thin, loosely appressed, hairy scales...............
                                Bluff oak (p. 190)

    10. Acorns, borne on long, slender stalks that are often twice as long as the leaf petioles..........
                          Swamp white oak (p. 190)
    10. Acorns, sessile or borne on short stalks that are never longer than the leaf petioles..............11

11. Leaf margins, serrate, the teeth incurved and glandular; acorns, sessile or nearly so, about ¾″ long, nut about half incased in the cup..**Chinkapin oak** (p. 192)
11. Leaf margins, scalloped, occasionally glandular.....12

12. Leaves, coated with silvery-white and yellowish, woolly hairs on the lower surfaces; bark, thin, scaly.............**Swamp chestnut oak** (p. 194)

12. Leaves, green below, sometimes coated with thin. silky hairs; bark, thick, deeply furrowed between thick, flattened ridges.....**Chestnut oak** (p. 196)

13. Acorn cup, shallow, saucerlike; leaves, 5″ to 7″ long
Durand oak (p. 199)

13. Acorn cup, moderately deep, bowl-shaped or top-shaped; leaves, 2″ to 5″ long......................14

14. Leaves, yellowish pubescent below.............
Oglethorpe oak (p. 199)

14. Leaves, light green or silvery white below.......
Chapman oak (p. 199)

15. Leaves, evergreen................................16
15. Leaves, deciduous...............................17

16. Leaves, elliptical, 3″ to 4″ long, falling off irregularly during the spring prior to emergence of new leaves.................**Laurel oak** (p. 200)

16. Leaves, oblong to obovate, 1″ to 2″ long; falling away during their 2d year...**Myrtle oak** (p. 202)

17. Leaves, pinnately 3- to 11-lobed...................18
17. Leaves, entire or more or less 3-lobed at the apex....29

18. Leaves, green above, silvery white or rusty red below...19

18. Leaves, green above and below, commonly with tufts of hair in the axils of the principal veins below.......................................21

19. Leaves, 2″ to 5″ long, mostly 5-lobed, the lobes acute; silvery white below..............**Bear oak** (p. 203)

19. Leaves, 5″ to 12″ long, variable, 3- to 11-lobed, the lobes acute or obtuse, grayish white to rusty red below..20

20. Leaves, dimorphic, those in the lower crown mostly 3-lobed, with a long, scythelike, central lobe, those in the upper crown 5- (occasionally 7-) lobed................**Southern red oak** (p. 203)

20. Leaves, of more uniform appearance, mostly 7- to 11- lobed, the lobes at nearly right angles to the midrib................**Swamp red oak** (p. 205)

21. Leaves, dull green, thin and papery, 7- to 11-lobed; acorn cup, saucerlike, the scales thin and fused......
Northern red oak (p. 206)

21. Leaves, lustrous, firm, 3- to 9-lobed; cup and cup scales, variable...................................22

22. Cup scales, free at the margins to form a fringe..23

22. Cup scales, closely appressed; in some species, having the appearance of being fused..........24

23. Leaves, mostly 7-lobed; acorns, coated with soft, rusty-brown hairs; buds, strongly angular, coated with gray, woolly hair...........**Black oak** (p. 208)

23. Leaves, mostly 3- to 5-lobed, often falcate; acorns, coated with chalky-white hair toward their summit; buds, coated with rusty-red hairs.............
Turkey oak (p. 211)

24. Leaves, 3- to 5-lobed, 2″ to 4″ in length.........25

24. Leaves, 5- to 9-lobed, mostly 5″ to 9″ in length..26

25. Leaves, 5-lobed; acorns, about ¾″ long; the cup, deep, toplike or bowl-shaped...........**Texas oak** (p. 213)

25. Leaves, 3- to 5-lobed; acorns, about ½″ long; the cup, shallow, saucerlike.............**Georgia oak** (p. 213)

26. Acorn cup, saucerlike.........................27

26. Acorn cup, bowl-shaped......................28

27. Nut, about 1¼″ long, oblong-ovoid................
Shumard oak (p. 213)

27. Nut, about ½″ long, nearly hemispherical..........
Pin oak (p. 214)

28. Nut, characterized by several concentric rings about the apex, about as long as broad.........
Scarlet oak (p. 216)
28. Nut, not featured by concentric apical rings, noticeably longer than broad **Nuttall oak** (p. 219)

29. Leaves, mostly lanceolate to oblong-elliptical........30
29. Leaves, usually broadest at the apex or diamond-shaped, sometimes more or less indistinctly 3-lobed...33

30. Leaves, hairy or woolly on the lower surface....31
30. Leaves, smooth on the lower surface............32

31. Leaves, pale blue-green, 2″ to 5″ long, woolly below..
Bluejack oak (p. 219)
31. Leaves, dark green, 4″ to 6″ long, sometimes covered with brown, silky hairs on the lower surface........
Shingle oak (p. 220)

32. Leaves, more or less lanceolate, 2″ to 5″ long, deciduous in the fall........**Willow oak** (p. 222)
32. Leaves, mostly elliptical or rarely 3-lobed at the apex, 3″ to 4″ long, falling away during the last of the winter and in the spring prior to leaf emergence.................**Laurel oak** (p. 200)

33. Leaves, diamond-shaped...**Diamondleaf oak** (p. 224)
33. Leaves, more or less spatulalike or kite-shaped, commonly more or less 3-lobed at the apex.............34

34. Acorn cup, bowl-shaped; leaves, 6″ to 8″ long, tawny on the lower surface...................
Blackjack oak (p. 224)
34. Acorn cup, saucerlike; leaves, mostly 2″ to 5″ long, pale green below........................35

35. Leaf bases, rounded..........**Arkansas oak** (p. 226)
35. Leaf bases, wedge-shaped........**Water oak** (p. 227)

Live Oak

Quercus virginiana Mill.

Habit.—A tree, 40′ to 50′ in height with a trunk 3′ to 4′ in diameter above a buttressed base; branching close to the ground into a few massive, wide-spreading limbs, forming a broad, low, dense, round-topped crown (sometimes shrublike).

Leaves.—Alternate, simple, evergreen, falling during the spring after the new foliage has appeared, 2″ to 5″ long, ½″ to 2½″ wide; oblong-obovate or elliptical; apex, obtuse; base, acutely wedge-shaped; margin, entire or rarely toothed; dark, lustrous green above, usually pale-pubescent below; petiole, stout, ¼″ long.

Flowers.—Unisexual; staminate flowers, in hairy, 3″ catkins; pistillate flowers, in few-flowered, 1″ to 3″ spikes.

Fruit.—An acorn, usually borne on long-stalked clusters of 3 to 5; nut, maturing in 1 season, ellipsoid or obovoid, brownish black, 1″ long; cup, top-shaped, enclosing one-third of the nut.

Twigs.—Slender, rigid, becoming gray-brown and glabrous; terminal buds, present, about ⅛″ long, nearly globular, covered with several light-brown scales with pale margins; lateral buds, similar but smaller; leaf scars, half-round, with scattered bundle scars; pith, homogeneous.

Bark.—Dark red-brown, up to 1″ thick, somewhat furrowed, and separating into small, appressed scales.

Habitat.—On sandy soils along the Atlantic and Gulf coastal plains.

Distribution.—From coastal Virginia south through Florida; west along the Gulf through southern Mississippi and Louisiana, to west-central Texas; found also in Mexico and Cuba.

PLATE 40.—LIVE OAK
1. Foliage and fruit $\times \frac{1}{2}$. 2. Nut with cup removed $\times \frac{1}{2}$.

Importance.—In the days of sailing ships the United States Navy procured large holdings of live oak forests for the exclusive use of the government's ship-yards. The large, massive, and arching limbs were highly sought after for ship ribs and knees. The wood was also used in the manufacture of hubs and wooden cogs. Small amounts of bark have been used in the tannin industry, and oil expressed from the acorns has been used in cooking.

Post Oak

Quercus stellata Wang.

Habit.—A small or medium-sized tree, usually about 50' tall with a trunk 18" to 22" in diameter (occasionally nearly 100' by 3'); more rarely a short, scrubby tree or shrub; branches, stout and twisted, forming a spreading, irregular head.

Leaves.—Alternate, deciduous, leathery, oblong-obovate, often having the appearance of a cross, 3" to 4" broad; apex, rounded; base, wedge-shaped; margin, variable, usually unequally 5-lobed, the 2 large, central lobes usually squarish to give the leaf a crosslike appearance; dark green and pubescent above, woolly below; petioles, very short.

Flowers.—Unisexual, appearing with the leaves; the staminate, in pendent spikes 2" to 4" long, each with 4 to 6 stamens; pistillate flowers, sessile or short-stalked.

Fruit.—Sessile or short-stalked acorns, occasionally borne in pairs; ovoid, ¾" long, striate, more or less pubescent at the apex; cup, bowl-shaped, enclosing one-third of the nut.

Twigs.—Stout, brown, somewhat tomentose; terminal buds, small, subglobose, brown, ⅛" long; lateral buds, smaller; leaf scars and pith, similar to those of other white oaks.

PLATE 41.—POST OAK
1. Foliage and fruit $\times \frac{1}{2}$. 2. Nut with cup removed $\times \frac{1}{2}$.

Bark.—Thick, gray, at first blocky or scaly, later deeply irregularly fissured with platelike scales.

Habitat.—On dry, sandy soil or rocky slopes and ridges, less commonly in rich bottom lands.

Distribution.—From Massachusetts to Iowa and south to Texas; in the East, south to Florida.

Importance.—A timber species. The wood is similar to that of *Q. alba* and is used for the same purposes.

Sand Post Oak

Quercus stellata var. *margaretta* Sarg.

The sand post oak is a small, scrubby tree characteristic of sandy slopes and ridges and pine barrens from coastal Virginia to Florida and west to southern Arkansas. The tree may be distinguished from the post oak by its smaller leaves and woolly twigs. It is of no commercial value but is often used locally for fuel.

Overcup Oak

Quercus lyrata Walt.

Habit.—Usually a small, irregular tree with crooked or twisted branches; occasionally reaching 100′ in height and 2′ to 3′ in diameter above a buttressed base, but usually much smaller; the crown is characteristically irregular and open, the root system shallow and widespread.

Leaves.—Alternate, simple, deciduous, oblong-ovate, 6″ to 10″ long, 1″ to 4″ wide; apex, variable, acute, round, or acuminate; base, wedge-shaped; margin, 5- to 9-lobed, extremely variable; the sinuses, irregular in width and depth; dark green, glabrous above, pale-pubescent or nearly glabrous below; petiole, slender, about 1″ long.

Flowers.—Unisexual, the staminate in slender,

PLATE 42.—OVERCUP OAK
1. Foliage and fruit ×½. 2. Nut with cup removed ×½.
3. Twig ×¾.

hairy catkins, 4″ to 6″ long; the pistillate mostly solitary, sessile, woolly.

Fruit.—An acorn, in pairs or solitary, nearly sessile; the nut, ovoid or subglobose, brown, up to 1″ long; almost entirely enclosed in a nearly spherical, scaly, unfringed cup.

Twigs.—Slender, gray-brown, glabrous; terminal buds, ovoid, chestnut-brown, woolly, about ⅛″ long; lateral buds, similar but smaller, persistent stipules often present near the tips of twigs; leaf scars and pith, similar to those of other white oaks.

Bark.—Up to 1″ thick, gray-brown, rough, irregularly ridged or flattened, often appearing spirally distorted.

Habitat.—A bottom-land species commonly occurring on poorly drained, clay soils subject to prolonged inundation; most generally associated with willow, water and swamp chestnut oaks, persimmon, elms, green ash, and waterlocust.

Distribution.—The Atlantic and Gulf coastal plain from southern New Jersey to northern Florida and west to Texas; through the Mississippi drainage basin to Missouri, Illinois, and Indiana.

Importance.—Of limited value for rough lumber.

Bur Oak   Mossycup Oak

Quercus macrocarpa Michx.

Habit.—A large tree, mostly 70′ to 80′ in height and 2′ to 3′ in diameter, sometimes becoming 170′ by 7′; trunk, straight, clean; crown, large, spreading, forming a broad, symmetrical head; shrubby at the northern and western limits of its range.

Leaves.—Alternate, deciduous, simple, oblong-obovate, 6″ to 12″ long, 3″ to 6″ wide, 5- to 9-lobed, with a large, somewhat triangular or obovate, coarsely toothed terminal lobe; lower lobes, separated from

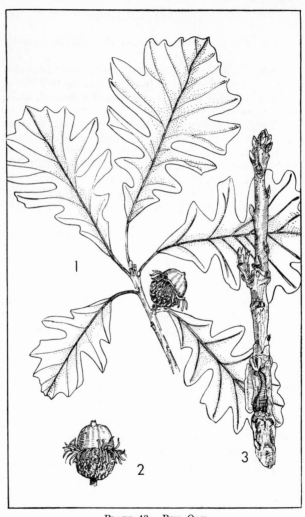

PLATE 43.—BUR OAK
1. Foliage ×⅓. 2. Acorn ×⅓. 3. Twig ×1.

terminal lobe by deep sinuses; apex, rounded; base, wedge-shaped; dark lustrous green above, pale-pubescent below; petioles, about 1″ long, stout.

Flowers.—Unisexual, appearing with the leaves; the staminate, in slender, 4″ to 6″, hairy, stalked catkins; the pistillate, sessile or subsessile, solitary or in several-flowered spikes.

Fruit.—An acorn, usually solitary, stalked; nut, varying in size from ¾″ to 2″ in length, ovoid, with pubescent apex; cup, deep, bowl-shaped, with a conspicuous fringe, enclosing up to three-fourths of the nut.

Twigs.—Stout, light brown, pubescent, later becoming dark brown and developing corky ridges up to 1″ in width; terminal buds, ovoid, obtuse up to ¼″ long, reddish-brown-pubescent; lateral buds, similar but small; leaf scars and pith, similar to those of other white oaks.

Bark.—Up to 2″ thick, deeply fissured and broken into irregular, thick, brown scales.

Habitat.—Low, rich, moist soils on bottom lands; on dry, rocky elevations in the foothills of the Rocky Mountains.

Distribution.—Southern Canada and the eastern United States except for the Atlantic and Gulf coastal plains.

Importance.—The wood of bur oak is similar to that of other white oaks and is used for the same purposes. In some localities this species is used ornamentally in both parks and dooryards.

White Oak

Quercus alba L.

Habit.—A large tree, 80′ to 150′ in height with a trunk 3′ to 5′ in diameter; in the forest, developing a

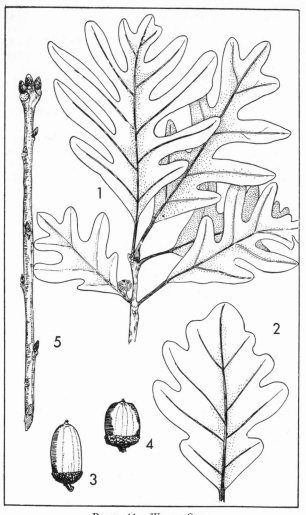

PLATE 44.—WHITE OAK

1. Foliage ×½. 2. Leaf of variety *latiloba* ×½. 3 and 4.
Typical variations in shape of nut ×¾. 5. Twig ×¾.

tall, clean, straight trunk with a small crown; in the open, usually with a shorter bole and a broad, rugged, spreading head.

Leaves.—Alternate, simple, deciduous, oblong-obovate, 5″ to 9″ long, 2″ to 4″ wide, mostly deeply 7- to 9-lobed, with oblique, rounded sinuses reaching nearly to the midrib; apex, usually 3-lobed; base, wedgeshaped; glabrous, bright green above, paler below; midrib, yellow; petioles, stout, up to 1″ long.

Flowers.—Unisexual, appearing with the leaves; the staminate, in 3″, loose, pendulous catkins; pistillate flowers, solitary, short-stalked, bright red.

Fruit.—An acorn, solitary or in pairs, either sessile or short-stalked; nut, about ¾″ long, oblong-ovoid, light brown; cup, bowl-shaped, enclosing up to one-fourth of ut; cup scales, thickened, warty, more or less fused.

Twigs.—Slender to moderately stout, with pale lenticels, at first pale, ultimately gray; terminal buds, short, about 3⁄16″ long, globular, glabrous, reddish brown; lateral buds, similar but small, often clustered near the tips of twigs; leaf scars, half-round, with several scattered bundle scars; pith, continuous, star-shaped in transverse section.

Bark.—Light gray, variable, at first broken into scaly rectangles, later becoming thicker and divided into ridges separated by shallow fissures.

Habitat.—Variable, but attaining largest size on moist, rich soil usually in admixture with other species; also found in commercial size and abundance on sandy soils and stony ridges.

Distribution.—Southeastern Canada and the eastern United States except for lower peninsular Florida, and northwestern Minnesota.

Importance.—The most important timber species among the white oaks. Widely used for ship-building and general construction work and in the manufacture of furniture, agricultural implements, tools, barrels, baskets, and ties; also used for fuel.

The acorns are a substantial part of the squirrel's diet, and it is recorded that Indians found them palatable after prolonged boiling.

Bluff Oak

Quercus austrina Small

The bluff oak is a relatively unimportant southern species belonging to the white oak group. In general, it resembles *Q. alba* but is usually smaller. It is separated from allied species on the basis of leaf and fruit characters. The leaves are 3″ to 8″ long and 2″ to 4″ broad, usually with 5 compressed, rounded lobes. The ovoid acorns are solitary or borne in pairs and are usually pubescent at the apex. The cup is bowl-shaped, enclosing one-third to one-half of the nut.

Bluff oak is found only in the Deep South through South Carolina, Alabama, Georgia, Florida, and Mississippi, where it grows in rich, moist soil on bluffs near streams.

Swamp White Oak

Quercus bicolor Willd.

Habit.—A medium-sized tree, 60′ to 70′ in height and 2′ to 3′ in diameter (rarely 100′ by 7′); crown, narrow, open, round-topped or irregular; in the open, somewhat drooping.

Leaves.—Alternate, simple, deciduous, obovate, 5″ to 6″ long, 2″ to 4″ wide; apex, rounded; base, wedge-shaped; margins, irregularly shallowly lobed and somewhat wavy-toothed; dark lustrous green above, pale-pubescent below; petioles, stout, about ½″ long.

Flowers.—Unisexual, appearing with the leaves; the staminate, in hairy catkins, 3″ to 4″ in length; the

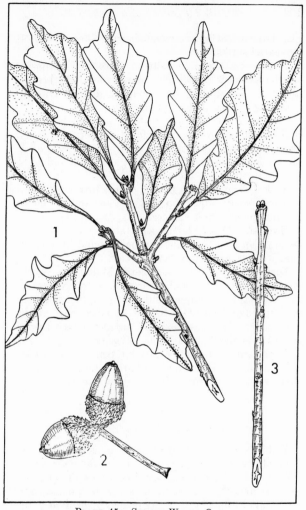

PLATE 45.—SWAMP WHITE OAK
1. Foliage ×⅓.   2. Acorns ×¾.   3. Twig ×¾.

pistillate, in several-flowered, hairy spikes, borne on elongated stalks.

Fruit.—An acorn, usually in pairs and borne on slender stalks 2″ to 4″ long; nut, ovoid, light brown, about 1″ long; cup, bowl-shaped, slightly fringed, enclosing the basal third of the nut.

Twigs.—Stout, at first reddish orange, becoming dull purple or brown and exfoliating; terminal buds, short, globose, brown, glabrous, about ⅛″ long; lateral buds, similar but smaller; leaf scars and pith, similar to those of other white oaks.

Bark.—Gray to dark brown, deeply furrowed, forming long, scaly ridges (on young stems and branches, forming papery, reflexed scales).

Habitat.—Moist, fertile soils along streams or in swamps and bottom lands, usually found in association with other bottom-land species.

Distribution.—From southern Maine to southeastern Minnesota, south through Iowa, Nebraska, and Kansas to Oklahoma and Arkansas; thence northeast through Kentucky to the Appalachians; in the East, south along the coast to Chesapeake Bay, thence inland over the Appalachians to Georgia.

Importance.—Used for interior trim, as a cabinet wood and boat timber and for barrels, ties, and fences. Somewhat similar in quality to the white oak.

Chinkapin Oak   Yellow Oak

Quercus muehlenbergii Englem.

Habit.—A tree of modest proportions, seldom more than 60′ to 80′ in height or 2′ to 3′ in diameter (max. 160′ by 4′); a buttressed base rises from a shallow root system, and the tapering bole supports a dense, narrow, round-topped crown; frequently a shrub near the northern limits of its range.

Leaves.—Alternate, simple, deciduous, 4″ to 7″

PLATE 46.—Chinkapin Oak
1. Foliage ×⅓. 2. Acorns ×¾.

long, 1″ to 4″ wide; oblong-lanceolate; apex, acute; base, wedge-shaped; margin, coarsely serrate; glabrous, yellow-green above, silvery-pubescent below; midrib, stout, yellow; petioles, slender, about 1¼″ long.

Flowers.—Unisexual; the staminate, in 3″ to 4″ hairy aments; the pistillate, in short, white, woolly spikes.

Fruit.—An acorn, mostly solitary, occasionally in pairs, nearly sessile; nut, ovoid, dark brown to black, ¾″ long; cup, bowl-shaped; enclosing up to one-half of the nut; the scales, brown, more or less fused, woolly.

Twigs.—Slender, lenticellate, at first reddish or purple, becoming gray or gray-brown; terminal buds, orange-brown, acute; lateral buds, similar but smaller; leaf scars and pith, similar to those of other white oaks.

Habitat.—On dry, rocky soil, and limestone ridges toward the northern limits of its range; farther south, on deep, rich valley soils in association with other hardwoods.

Distribution.—The eastern United States except for Atlantic and Gulf coastal plains.

Importance.—Limited commercial value.

Swamp Chestnut Oak   Basket Oak   Cow Oak

Quercus prinus L.

Habit.—A tree, usually 60′ to 80′ in height, with a trunk 2′ to 3′ in diameter (rarely 120′ by 7′); in the forest, with a short, compact, round-topped head; in the open, branching 15′ to 30′ above the ground to form a low, spreading, open crown.

Leaves.—Alternate, simple, deciduous, 5″ to 8″ long, 3″ to 4″ wide; apex, acute to rounded; base, wedge-shaped; obovate to oblong; margin, coarsely wavy-toothed, the teeth often glandular-tipped; dark

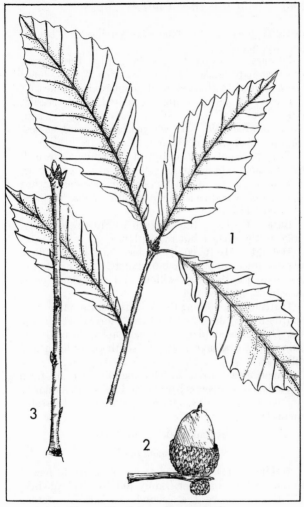

PLATE 47.—SWAMP CHESTNUT OAK
1. Foliage ×½. 2. Acorn ×1. 3. Twig ×1.

lustrous green above, pale silvery-pubescent below; petioles, about ¾″ long.

Flowers.—Unisexual, appearing with the leaves; the staminate, in slender, hairy catkins 2″ to 3″ long; the pistillate, in short-stalked, few-flowered spikes.

Fruit.—An acorn, solitary or paired, nearly sessile; nut, 1″ to 1½″ long, oblong, lustrous brown; cup, thick, bowl-shaped, with wedge-shaped scales, enclosing up to one-third of the nut.

Twigs.—Stout, red or brown, becoming brownish gray; terminal buds, about ¼″ long, oval, acute, dark red; lateral buds, similar but smaller, crowded toward the tips of twigs; leaf scars and pith, similar to those of other white oaks.

Bark.—Up to 1″ thick, irregularly furrowed, scaly, gray on the surface but red within.

Habitat.—Moist, poorly drained bottoms and flood plains subject to periodic inundation; usually found in association with water, willow, and cherrybark oaks, sweetgum, and red ash.

Distribution.—Along the Atlantic coastal plain from southern New Jersey to northern Florida, west along the Gulf coastal plain to Texas; north through the Mississippi drainage basin, to southern Indiana and Illinois.

Importance.—Used in the manufacture of farm implements, cooperage, posts, and baskets; similar in quality to white oak, but not produced in the same quantity.

Chestnut Oak   Rock Oak

Quercus montana L.

Habit.—A medium-sized tree, 60′ to 70′ in height and 3′ to 4′ in diameter (rarely 100′ by 6′); branching 15′ to 30′ above the ground into heavy, arching limbs, forming a broad, open, irregular, spreading crown.

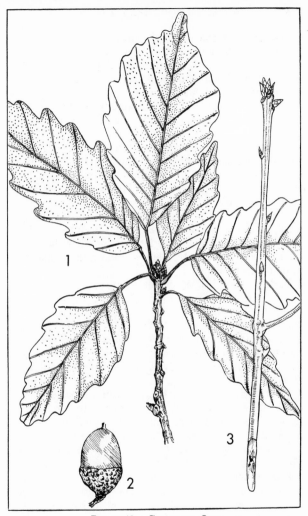

PLATE 48.—CHESTNUT OAK

1. Foliage $\times\frac{1}{3}$.   2. Acorn $\times\frac{3}{4}$.   3. Twig $\times 1$.

Leaves.—Alternate, simple, deciduous, obovate or oblong; 5″ to 9″ long, 2″ to 3″ wide; apex, acuminate; base, wedge-shaped; margin, scalloped; yellowish green above, pale-pubescent below; midrib, stout, yellow; petioles, about 1″ long.

Flowers.—Unisexual; the staminate, in hairy catkins, 3″ to 4″ long; the pistillate, in 2- or 3-flowered, short, stout stalks.

Fruit.—An acorn, solitary or less frequently in 2's and 3's, short-stalked; nut, ovoid, about 1″ long, bright, lustrous brown; cup, bowl-shaped or toplike, usually enclosing one-third of the nut; the scales, close and more or less fused.

Twigs.—Stout, at first purplish brown, becoming reddish brown; terminal buds, narrowly ovoid, acute, ½″ long, chestnut-brown; lateral buds, similar but smaller, often divergent; leaf scars and pith, similar to those of white oak.

Bark.—Dark brown or black, up to 1½″ thick; deeply and coarsely furrowed, forming broad ridges covered with small scales.

Habitat.—A tree of hillsides and mountain slopes. On poor, dry, thin, rocky soils, forming pure open stands; on better sites, usually occurring in admixture with other species, notably pitch pine, numerous oaks, chestnuts, and hickories.

Distribution.—From southern Maine through Vermont, New York, west to southern Indiana and Illinois, south to Georgia and Alabama; on the coastal plain to the District of Columbia, thence inland and south to Georgia; most abundant in the Appalachian Mountains and the Ohio Valley.

Importance.—Used for fence posts, ties, and fuel; a source of tannin extract. The interlacing roots serve to retard the forces of erosion, particularly on thin soils where other vegetation is comparatively scarce.

Durand Oak

Quercus durandii Buckl.

This is a white oak that superficially resembles certain of the water oaks. The trees, which are often 60' to 90' in height and 2' to 3' in diameter, are nowhere abundant and hence contribute little to the supply of white oak lumber. Durand oak may be distinguished by its yellow-green, obovate to oblong-elliptical, 5" to 7" long leaves with entire or apically 3-lobed margins and white, hairy or woolly lower surfaces. The acorns mature in a single season and consist of an ovoid, lustrous-brown nut, about ½" long, incased only at the base in a shallow, saucerlike cup with appressed scales that are slightly thickened on the back.

This species is restricted to the Deep South and is found from Richmond County, Georgia, westward to southern Arkansas and eastern Texas.

Oglethorpe Oak

Quercus oglethorpensis Duncan

This oak has only recently been discovered and to date has been reported only from Elbert, Oglethorpe, and Wilkes Counties, Georgia. Belonging to the white oak group, it may be distinguished from related forms by its (1) elliptical leaves, 2" to 5" long, with yellowish, hairy lower surfaces; (2) hairy, purplish-brown twigs; and (3) ovoid acorns, ½" in length, which are about one-third enclosed in a toplike cup with appressed scales.

Chapman Oak

Quercus chapmanii Sarg.

This oak is usually encountered as a large, bushy shrub, but under ideal conditions for growth it attains a height of 35' to 50' and a diameter of 10" to 12". It is nowhere abundant and occurs most frequently on dry, sandy barrens near salt water, both on the mainland and adjacent islands from Beaufort County, South Carolina, to central and western Florida.

Chapman oak resembles, superficially at least, certain of the willow oaks, but its fruit, unlike that of the latter group, matures in a single season. Its leaves, which are about 3½" long, are mostly obovate to oblong with entire margins, silvery green to silvery white below, and furnished with short, hairy petioles. The sessile acorns are either paired or solitary, with an ovoid nut, ¾" long, half enclosed in a hairy, bowl-shaped cup with knobby or warty scales. The tree is of no commercial value.

Laurel Oak

Quercus laurifolia Michx.

Habit.—Usually a medium-sized tree, 50' to 60' tall, but occasionally reaching 100' in height, with a trunk 3' to 4' in diameter, its slender branches forming a broad, round-topped, dense crown of pleasing symmetry.

Leaves.—Alternate, simple, persistent until early spring; elliptical or rarely oblong-obovate, 2" to 4" long, ½" to 1" broad; apex, acute; base, wedge-shaped; margin, entire or rarely irregularly lobed; lustrous green above, pale below; midrib, yellow; petioles, stout, yellow, ¼" long [occasionally, forms with three-lobed apices (var. *tridentata* Sarg.) are to be observed].

Flowers.—Unisexual; the staminate, in hairy, red-stemmed catkins 2" to 3" long; the pistillate, usually solitary, on short, stout, glabrous stalks.

Fruit.—An acorn, mostly solitary, commonly sub-sessile; nut, ovoid or hemispherical, brownish black,

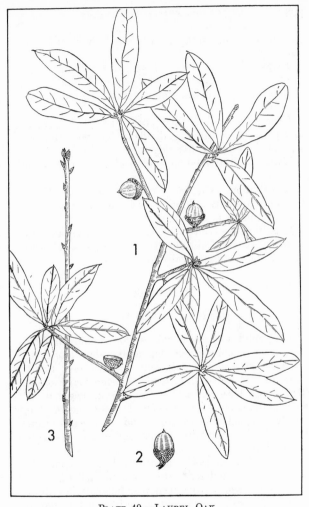

PLATE 49.—LAUREL OAK
1. Foliage and fruit ×½. 2. Elongated variety of nut ×¾.
3. Twig ×¾.

½″ long; cup, thin, saucer-shaped, with reddish, pubescent scales.

Twigs.—Slender, deep red, glabrous; terminal buds, small, ovoid, acute, reddish brown; lateral buds, similar but smaller; leaf scars and pith, similar to those of other red oaks.

Bark.—Up to ½″ thick, dark reddish brown; at first smooth, becoming divided into deep fissures separated by broad, flat ridges.

Habitat.—Scattered on sandy soil near streams and swamps.

Distribution.—On the coastal plain from North Carolina to central Florida and west to Louisiana; most abundant in Florida.

Importance.—Laurel oak is a common ornamental in many parts of the South. The wood is of little value although used locally for fuel.

Myrtle Oak

Quercus myrtifolia Willd.

This small, evergreen oak, seldom found far from salt water, usually occurs on sandy ridges along our southern shores and adjacent islands from South Carolina to Mississippi inclusive of peninsular Florida. The largest trees are seldom over 35′ in height or 4″ to 8″ in diameter. This species often forms extensive, nearly impenetrable thickets, and in exposed situations its grotesque wind forms lend added charm to the seascape.

Myrtle oak is easily identified by its small, 1″ to 2″, oval to oblong-ovate, evergreen leaves, hairy twigs, small acorns with nearly globular, striate nuts, about ½″ in diameter, and saucerlike to top-shaped cups, which incase about one-half of the nut.

The trees are of no commercial value.

Bear Oak   Scrub Oak

Quercus ilicifolia Wang.

Bear oak is a small, scrubby, poorly formed tree 15′ to 20′ in height and 5″ to 7″ in diameter. The bole is contorted and often divided near the ground into several lesser stems with short, tough, twisted, interwoven branches. The tree is usually encountered on barren, sandy soils, rocky slopes, plateaus, and mountaintops, where it commonly forms extensive thickets, thus affording excellent cover for small game birds and animals. Bear oak is common to the New England and Middle Atlantic states and extends into the South along the eastern slopes of the Appalachians to southwestern Virginia; it reappears on King and Crowder Mountains near Gastonia, N.C.

This species may be identified by its shallowly 3- to 7-lobed (mostly 5-lobed) leaves, silvery white below, and small, sessile or stalked acorns, which are borne in great profusion along the twigs. The finely striate, ovoid nut, about ½″ long, is one-half embedded in a bowl-shaped cup, whose scales are free at the tips and form a fringe along the margin.

The small size and poor form of bear oak preclude its becoming a source of commercial timber.

Southern Red Oak

Quercus falcata Michx.

Habit.—A tree, 70′ to 80′ in height with a trunk 2′ to 3′ in diameter; branches, spreading, forming a broad, open, round-topped head.

Leaves.—Alternate, simple, often tardily deciduous, 5″ to 9″ long, 4″ to 5″ wide; extremely variable, with 2 basic types: (1) obovate, with 3 bristle-tipped apical

PLATE 50.—SOUTHERN RED OAK
1. Foliage and fruit $\times\frac{1}{2}$.   2. Twig $\times\frac{1}{2}$.

lobes, or (2) deeply 5- to 7-lobed, with a divided terminal lobe (on same or different trees); lustrous dark
green above, rusty-pubescent below; petioles, flattened,
slender, 1″ to 2″ long.

Flowers.—Unisexual; the staminate, in 3″ to 5″,
hairy catkins; the pistillate, solitary or in few-flowered
spikes, borne on short, stout, hairy stalks.

Fruit.—An acorn, solitary or in pairs; nut, hemispherical or nearly globular, ½″ long, often striate,
orange-brown; cup, thin, saucer-shaped or sometimes
toplike, and enclosing one-third of the nut; cup scales,
pale-pubescent except on the margins.

Twigs.—Stout, at first orange-pubescent, becoming
glabrous and dark red in their 2d season; terminal
buds, ¼″ to ⅛″ long, reddish brown, stout, ovoid,
acute; lateral buds, only slightly smaller, divergent;
leaf scars and pith, similar to those of other red oaks.

Bark.—Up to 1″ thick, dark brown or black, the
rough, scaly ridges separated by deep fissures.

Habitat.—Characteristically an upland species and
an inhabitant of dry, infertile soils; occurring as an
occasional tree or in small groves in admixture with
other hardwoods and occasionally pine.

Distribution.—On the coastal plain and the Piedmont region from New Jersey to Alabama, north to
southern Illinois and Indiana, south through Missouri,
Arkansas, and Texas, also in southern Ohio and central
Florida.

Importance.—Similar to that of other commercially
important red oaks.

Swamp Red Oak

Quercus falcata var. *pagodaefolia* Ell.

Swamp red oak is a common bottom-land species of
the southern coastal plains and Mississippi Valley
region, although it is by no means restricted to such

sites.   In fact, the largest trees are encountered most frequently on moist, loamy ridges, old fields, and flats. The trees often attain heights and diameters of 100′ to 130′ and 3′ to 5′, respectively, which thus classes them with the largest of the southern red oaks.

This form is readily distinguishable from the southern red oak by its more nearly uniform, 5- to 11-lobed leaves and its gray-black, flaky or scaly bark, which superficially resembles that of large, black cherry trunks.   Because of this resemblance the tree is also known as *cherrybark oak* in some localities, although this name is usually reserved for another variety, *Q. rubra* var. *leucophylla* Ashe, a form exhibiting considerable leaf variation.

Both swamp red oak and cherrybark oak reach their best development in the lower Mississippi Valley, where they produce long, clear boles of excellent red oak timber in a comparatively short time.

Northern Red Oak

Quercus rubra L.

Habit.—A medium-sized tree, 60′ to 80′ in height, with a trunk 2′ to 3½′ in diameter (rarely 150′ by 5′); in the open, producing a short, stout trunk and massive crown; in the forest, developing a tall, clear bole with a small, round, compact head.

Leaves.—Alternate, simple, deciduous, oblong, 5″ to 9″ long, 4″ to 5″ wide; apex, acute; base, wedge-shaped; margin, with 7 to 11 bristle-tipped lobes between deep, oblique sinuses; dark green, glabrous above, paler below; petioles, stout, reddish, about 1½″ long.

Flowers.—Unisexual; the staminate, in pubescent, 4″ to 5″ catkins; the pistillate, solitary or paired, on short stalks.

Fruit.—An acorn, solitary or in pairs; the nut, pale

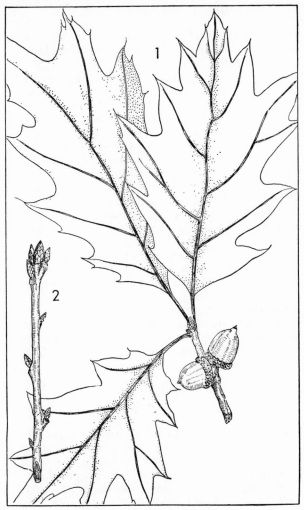

PLATE 51.—NORTHERN RED OAK
1. Foliage and fruit ×½.   2. Twig ×1.

brown, ovoid, about 1″ in length, ¾″ in diameter; cup thick, shallow, saucer-shaped, with red-brown pubescent scales.

Twigs.—Stout, glabrous, dark brown; terminal buds, ovoid, ¼″ long, acute, with dark-reddish-brown, hairy scales; lateral buds, similar but smaller; leaf scars, half-round with several scattered bundle scars; pith, continuous, star-shaped in transverse section.

Bark.—At first smooth and greenish, at length becoming gray-brown or black, and broken into flat-topped ridges separated by shallow furrows.

Habitat.—A component of many mixed hardwood forests; in the South, usually found on rich, moist, but well-drained loams in association with other upland oaks, ashes, numerous hickories, and black cherry.

Distribution.—Nova Scotia west to eastern Minnesota; south to Georgia in the East and to Arkansas in the West; absent in the coastal plain below the Chesapeake Bay region.

Importance.—In point of timber production this is the most important of the red oaks. The trees develop rapidly in youth and, because of the deep, rich-red color of their autumnal foliage, in many localities are commonly used as ornamentals.

Black Oak

Quercus velutina Lamarck

Habit.—A tree, 70′ to 85′ in height (rarely 150′), with a trunk 3′ to 4′ in diameter; in the open, developing a low, wide-spreading crown; in the forest, forming a narrow, oblong, sometimes irregular head.

Leaves.—Alternate, simple, deciduous, 5″ to 7″ long, 3″ to 5″ broad; ovate or obovate; apex, long-tapered or acute; base, flat or wedge-shaped; margin, variable, with 5 to 7 broad or narrow, toothed, bristle-

PLATE 52.—BLACK OAK

1. Foliage ×½. 2. Leaf from lower crown ×¼. 3. Acorn
×1. 4. Twig ×1.

tipped lobes; sinuses, variable in depth; dark lustrous green above, copper-green below, with prominent axillary tufts of hairs; petioles, stout, about 3″ to 5″ long.

Flowers.—Unisexual, appearing with the leaves; the staminate, in interrupted, 4″ to 6″ hairy catkins; the pistillate, in 2's or 3's on short, hairy stalks.

Fruit.—An acorn, solitary or in pairs; nut, variable, oval, obovoid, or hemispherical, ½″ to ¾″ long, light brown, striate, ripening the 2d season; cup, bowl-shaped or toplike, with chestnut-brown scales loosely imbricated above and free at their tips to form a fringe around the cup margin, incasing about one-half of the nut.

Twigs.—Stout, glabrous, reddish brown, becoming dark brown with pale lenticels; terminal buds, ovoid, up to ½″ long, acute, angular, and gray-tomentose; lateral buds, similar but smaller; leaf scars and pith, similar to those of other red and black oaks.

Bark.—At first smooth, dark brown, with orange-yellow inner bark; becoming 1″ to 1½″ thick, almost black, and dividing into broad, scaly ridges separated by deep, vertical furrows.

Habitat.—An upland tree on dry slopes and ridges or on moist, rich soil in mixed stands, rarely on rich bottom lands.

Distribution.—From southern Maine through southern Ontario and into Michigan, Wisconsin, and Iowa; south to Florida and west to Texas.

Importance.—The bark of black oak is an important source of tannic acid and a yellow dye known as *quercitron.* Its wood is suitable for the same purposes as that of other red and black oaks. Black oak is seldom used as an ornamental since the leaves never develop the vivid fall colorations so characteristic of scarlet, eastern red, and white oaks and several other species of the group.

Turkey Oak

Quercus laevis Walt.

Habit.—A small tree, 20′ to 30′ (rarely 50′ to 60′) in height, with a trunk up to 2′ in diameter, but usually smaller; crown, rather broad, open, irregular, or round-topped (often shrubby on the poorest sites).

Leaves.—Alternate, simple, deciduous, 3″ to 12″ long, 1″ to 8″ wide, oblong or obovate, occasionally triangular, mostly 5- but sometimes 3- to 7-lobed; lateral lobes, somewhat scythe-shaped and spreading, occasionally with dentate tips; terminal lobes, irregular; apex, 3-toothed; base, wedge-shaped; lustrous yellow-green above, paler below, glabrous, or with tufts of rusty-red axillary hairs; petioles, short, stout, and grooved, about ½″ to 1″ long.

Flowers.—Unisexual, appearing with the leaves; the staminate, in slender, 4″ to 5″, hairy catkins; the pistillate, on short, stout, hairy stalks.

Fruit.—An acorn, usually solitary, stalked; nut, ovoid, up to 1″ long, brown, woolly at apex; cup, top-shaped, somewhat pubescent, enclosing one-third of the nut.

Twigs.—Stout, red, becoming dark brown and glabrous; terminal buds, slender, conical, acuminate, ½″ long, rusty-pubescent; lateral buds, divergent, smaller, but otherwise similar; leaf scars and pith, similar to those of other red oaks.

Bark.—Dark gray, becoming nearly black, red within, irregularly fissured and scaly.

Habitat.—An upland tree found on dry, sandy, sterile soils. Commonly associated with longleaf pine and bluejack and dwarf post oaks.

Distribution.—From southeastern Virginia to central Florida, thence west to Louisiana.

Importance.—Usually considered a weed tree; used locally for fuel and in construction about farms.

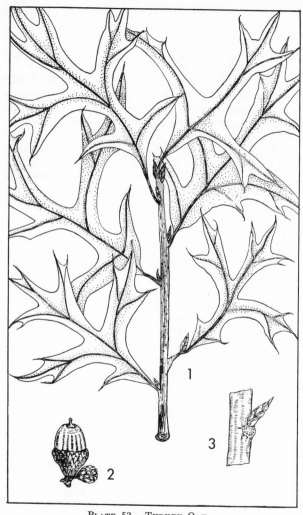

PLATE 53.—TURKEY OAK
1. Foliage ✕⅓.   2. Acorn ✕¾.   3. Leaf scar ✕1.

Texas Oak

Quercus texana Buckl.

This small tree, restricted to central and western Texas, seldom attains a height of more than 35′ and in some localities is actually never more than a large shrub. Its botanical features are similar to those of the Shumard oak, but it may be distinguished by its smaller, 5-lobed leaves, pubescent, staminate catkins, and acorns with deep, toplike cups and ovoid, striate nuts.

Georgia Oak

Quercus georgiana M. A. Curt.

The Georgia oak is so similar to pin oak that the two are easily confused in the field. However, the leaves of *Q. georgiana* are smaller and mostly 3- to 5-lobed, and the acorns are nearly one-half enclosed by the thick, light-reddish-brown cup. It is found only on sandy or stony mountain slopes in Georgia.

Shumard Red Oak

Quercus shumardii Buckl.

Habit.—Usually a large tree, 90′ to 125′ in height, with a slightly buttressed trunk 4′ to 5′ in diameter; the bole is symmetrical and commonly clear for the greater part of its length and supports a rather broad, open crown; the root system is extensive and moderately shallow.

Leaves.—Alternate, simple, deciduous, obovate, 6″ to 8″ long, 4″ to 5″ broad; apex, acuminate; base, wedge-shaped or flattened; margin, with 7 to 9 bristle-tipped lobes, often subdivided into secondary lobes by rounded sinuses; dark green and glabrous above, paler below and with tufts of axillary hairs; petioles, slender, glabrous, 2″ long.

Flowers.—Unisexual; the staminate, in glabrous, 6″ to 7″ aments; the pistillate, solitary or paired, borne on pubescent stalks.

Fruit.—An acorn, solitary or in pairs; the nut, oblong-ovoid, up to 1¼″ in length and 1″ in diameter; cup, saucer-shaped, with somewhat pubescent scales.

Twigs.—Moderately stout; glabrous, gray-brown; terminal buds, ¼″ long, ovoid, acute, gray-brown, usually angled; lateral buds, similar but shorter; leaf scars and pith, similar to those of eastern red oak.

Bark.—Thick, with whitish, scaly ridges separated by deep, darker colored fissures.

Habitat.—Most abundant on deep, rich, bottom-land soils and along stream and swamp borders; usually occurring as an occasional tree in mixed hardwood forests.

Distribution.—From eastern Pennsylvania near the Maryland line, south through Virginia and North and South Carolina to Georgia and Florida; also in Ohio, Indiana, Iowa, and Texas.

Importance.—A very important timber species used for flooring, furniture, interior trim, and cabinetry. The lumber of this species is mixed indiscriminately with boards of other red oaks and hence soon loses its identity in the trades.

Pin Oak

Quercus palustris Muench.

Habit.—A tree, usually 70′ to 80′ in height and 2′ to 3′ in diameter (rarely 120′ by 5′); in the open, the trunk is usually more or less disfigured by small, slender, tough branches, and even in the forest the bole is apt to bear numerous dead branches below the broad, pyramidal, profusely branched crown.

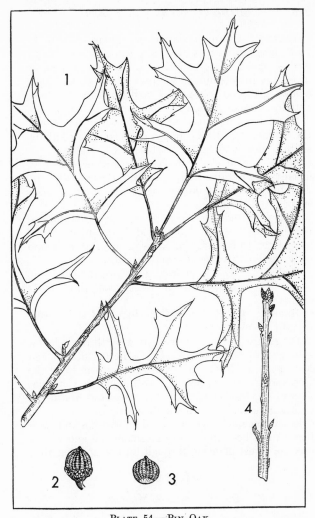

PLATE 54.—PIN OAK
1. Foliage $\times\frac{1}{2}$. 2. Acorn $\times\frac{1}{2}$. 3. Nut without cup $\times\frac{1}{2}$.
4. Twig $\times1$.

Leaves.—Alternate, simple, deciduous, obovate, 3″ to 7″ long, 2″ to 5″ wide; apex, acute; base, broadly wedge-shaped; margin, with 5 to 7 lobes separated by deep, irregular sinuses; lustrous green above, paler below, glabrous except for axillary tufts of hair; petioles, slender, yellow, 1″ long.

Flowers.—Unisexual, appearing with the leaves; the staminate, in 3″ hairy catkins; the pistillate, solitary and in 2's or 3's on short, hairy stalks.

Fruit.—An acorn, solitary, in pairs, or clustered, usually short-stalked; nut, hemispherical, $\frac{1}{2}$″ long, dark brown, with mahogany-red streaks; cup, saucer-shaped, red-brown.

Twigs.—Slender, lenticellate; gray or reddish brown; terminal buds, short, ovoid, reddish brown, about $\frac{1}{8}$″ long; lateral buds, similar but smaller; leaf scars and pith, similar to those of other red oaks.

Bark.—At first smooth, gray-brown, becoming somewhat shallowly fissured between thin, scaly ridges.

Habitat.—On rich, moist, bottom-land soils; occasionally on moist uplands.

Distribution.—In Connecticut west through Pennsylvania, western New York, southern Ontario, and Michigan, to Iowa and Nebraska; south from the Chesapeake Bay region to central North Carolina; west of the Appalachians in Tennessee and Kentucky, to Arkansas and eastern Oklahoma.

Importance.—In the past used for shingles and clapboards, but best known as an ornamental and widely used for street planting through Europe and America.

Scarlet Oak

Quercus coccinea Muench.

Habit.—A tree, 70′ to 80′ in height, and 2′ to 3′ in diameter (rarely 100′ by 4′); in the forest, developing

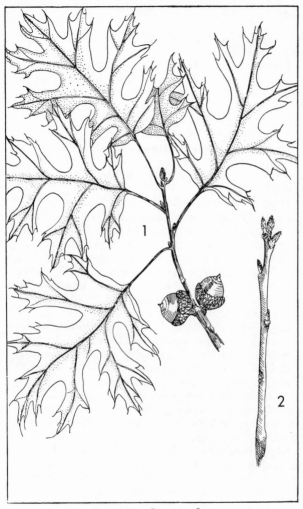

PLATE 55.—SCARLET OAK
1. Foliage and fruit ×⅓.   2. Twig ×1.

an irregular, narrow crown, but very wide-spreading in open situations.

Leaves.—Alternate, simple, deciduous, ovate or oblong-ovate, 3″ to 7″ long, 2″ to 5″ wide; apex, acute; base, flattened; deeply 7- (rarely 9-) lobed; lobes, irregularly dentate and bristle-tipped; lustrous bright green above, paler below, with axillary tufts of hairs; petioles, slender, 1″ to 2½″ long.

Flowers.—Unisexual, appearing with the leaves; the staminate, in 3″ to 4″, slender, glabrous aments, at first bright red; the pistillate, in few-flowered, short-stalked spikes.

Fruit.—An acorn, solitary or paired, sessile or short-stalked; nut, oval, often with concentric rings about the apex; up to one-half enclosed in the deep, reddish-brown, bowl-shaped cup, 1″ to 1¼″ in diameter.

Twigs.—Slender, at first light-colored, becoming dark brown, glabrous; terminal buds, ¼″ long, ovoid, dark brown, with pubescent scales; lateral buds, similar but smaller; leaf scars and pith, similar to those of other red oaks.

Bark.—Almost black, broken by shallow fissures into irregular ridges, sometimes becoming scaly.

Habitat.—On dry, light, sandy soils in association with upland oaks and hickories.

Distribution.—Southern Maine westward to Minnesota, south along the coast to the Chesapeake Bay, and thence inland along the Piedmont plateau to Alabama; in the West, south through eastern Nebraska to eastern Oklahoma.

Importance.—An ornamental of recognized merit, particularly because of its brilliant, scarlet fall coloration. The wood is cut and mixed indiscriminately with other red oak timbers, although actually somewhat inferior to that of several related species.

Nuttall Oak

Quercus nuttallii Palmer

The Nuttall oak is usually a medium-sized tree about 70' in height with a trunk 2' in diameter. Occasionally, however, specimens 120' by 4½' may be found. In most respects this species is similar to the scarlet oak although the bark is much more similar to that of the pin oak. In the absence of fruit, however, Nuttall oak is usually mistaken for scarlet oak. The leaves are dull green, and the fruit, which is solitary or clustered and oblong-ovoid, is about 1" long. The toplike or bowl-shaped acorn cup encloses nearly one half of the nut.

The Nuttall oak is a bottom-land species, usually growing on poorly drained clay soils along with gum, elms, ashes, maples, and water oaks. This species has been found only in Mississippi, Arkansas, and Alabama, and its range is still imperfectly known at the present time.

Bluejack Oak

Quercus cinerea Michx.

Bluejack oak, which is never more than a large shrub in many localities, seldom exceeds a height of 30' to 35' or a diameter of 5" to 10". It may be distinguished from other willow oaks by its 3"- to 5"-long, oblong-oblanceolate, blue-green leaves with woolly lower surfaces, its small, nearly globular acorns with apical hairs and longitudinal striations, and its slender twigs with prominent ovoid buds, ¼" or more in length.

This tree is most frequently encountered on dry, sterile, sandy soils and ranges along the coastal plains from Cape Henry, Virginia, to eastern Texas. It is also widespread through the sand hills of the Carolinas and of lower peninsular Florida and extends inland through eastern Texas to southeastern Oklahoma. Turkey oak, dwarf post oak, and longleaf pine are its most constant associates. Poor bole form and small size preclude this species from commercial exploitation other than as a source of a hardwood fuel.

Shingle Oak

Quercus imbricaria Michx.

Habit.—A medium-sized tree, usually 50′ to 60′ in height (rarely 100′), with a trunk 3′ to 4′ in diameter, bearing a short, narrow, round-topped crown.

Leaves.—Alternate, simple, deciduous, oblong-lanceolate or oblong-obovate; 4″ to 6″ long, 1″ to 2″ wide; apex, acute or rounded; base, wedge-shaped or rounded; margin, entire, sometimes wavy; dark lustrous green above, brown-pubescent below; petioles, short and pubescent.

Flowers.—Unisexual; the staminate, in 2″ to 3″, woolly catkins; the pistillate, mostly solitary, on short, slender, hairy stalks.

Fruit.—An acorn, solitary or in pairs, borne on stout stalks; nut, up to ¾″ long, subglobose, dark brown; cup, bowl-shaped or toplike, enclosing up to one-half of the nut; cup scales, pubescent.

Twigs.—Slender, at first reddish green, becoming dark brown and glabrous; terminal buds, small, ovoid, acute, remotely angled, light brown; lateral buds, similar but smaller; leaf scars and pith, similar to those of others in the red oak group.

Bark.—Thin, brown, smooth, becoming up to 1½″ thick, and broken into broad, flattened ridges separated by shallow fissures.

Habitat.—On fertile soil of moist hillsides and

PLATE 56.—SHINGLE OAK
1. Foliage $\times\frac{1}{3}$. 2. Acorns $\times\frac{2}{3}$.

bottom lands in association with numerous other oaks, hickories, and elms.

Distribution.—The Appalachian, Ohio River, and central Mississippi River Valley regions.

Importance.—Once an important source of hand-split shingles and clapboards; contributing little to the present-day supply of red oak timber; because of its dense, lustrous, dark-green foliage, commonly used as an ornamental.

Willow Oak

Quercus phellos L.

Habit.—A medium to large-sized tree, 80′ to 130′ high, with a 3′ to 6′ trunk; in the forest, with a long, clear, symmetrical bole and spherical crown; in open situations, developing a short trunk and a dense, broad, oblong or oval head.

Leaves.—Alternate, simple, deciduous, 2″ to 5″ long by ½″ to 1″ wide, linear-lanceolate to ovate-lanceolate; apex, acute; base, acute; margins, entire, sometimes wavy, on young, vigorous growth sharply and irregularly lobed; light green, glabrous above, paler below; petioles, slender, ¼″ long.

Flowers.—Unisexual, appearing with the leaves; the staminate, in 2″ to 3″, hairy catkins, borne on slender stalks; the pistillate flowers, solitary or in pairs, short-stalked.

Fruit.—An acorn, solitary or in pairs, usually short-stalked; nut, hemispherical, ½″ long, somewhat stellate-pubescent, bluntly pointed at the apex, yellowish brown; cup, greenish brown, thin, saucer-shaped.

Twigs.—Slender, red-brown, glabrous, with dark lenticels (sometimes spurlike), becoming deep brown; terminal buds, about ⅛″ long, acute, ovoid, brown; lateral buds, similar but smaller; leaf scars and pith, similar to those of other red oaks.

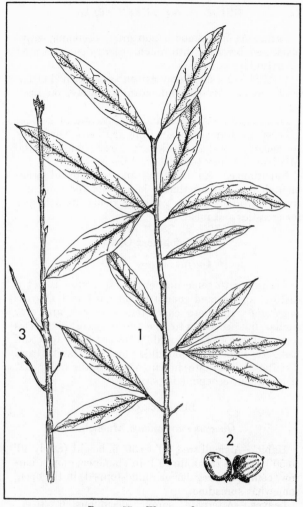

PLATE 57.—WILLOW OAK
1. Foliage ×½.   2. Acorns ×⅔.   3. Twig ×½.

Bark.—At first smooth and gray, becoming gray-black and breaking into rough, scaly ridges separated by irregular fissures.

Habitat.—Most abundant on wet, rich bottom lands, along streams and swamps; rarely, on drier sites.

Distribution.—Atlantic and Gulf coastal plains and Mississippi drainage basin from southern New York to central Florida and eastern Texas; north in the Mississippi Valley to southern Illinois.

Importance.—An excellent and widespread ornamental; also cut for timber in spite of the comparatively low-grade product that it yields; used locally for crossties and fuel.

Diamondleaf Oak

Quercus obtusa Ashe

According to some authorities, *Q. obtusa* is not a distinct species and should be included with *Quercus laurifolia*. In most characters the two are very similar, but according to Ashe the leaves of this species tend to taper from the middle toward both apex and base, to form a diamondlike figure. Habitat and distribution are quite similar to those of the water oak. It is without economic importance.

Blackjack Oak

Quercus marilandica Muench.

Habit.—A small tree, 20' to 30' in height (rarely 40' to 50'), with a trunk up to 1' in diameter; crown, narrow, compact, irregular or round-topped; in the open, somewhat spreading.

Leaves.—Alternate, simple, deciduous, 6" to 7" long, 2" to 3" broad; mostly obovate or triangular; apex, 3-lobed, entire or dentate, bristle-tipped; base,

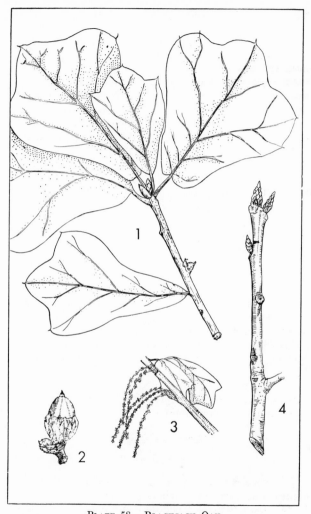

PLATE 58.—BLACKJACK OAK

1. Foliage ×⅓.   2. Acorn ×⅔.   3. Male catkins ×½.   4.
Twig ×1.

tapering; margin, entire; dark yellow-green above, orange-pubescent below; midrib, thick, orange; petiole, stout, ½″ long.

Flowers.—Unisexual, appearing with the leaves; the staminate, in 2″ to 4″, interrupted, hairy catkins; the pistillate, solitary or in pairs, short-stalked.

Fruit.—An acorn, solitary or in pairs, usually stalked; nut, oblong or ovoid, about ¾″ long, light brown, striate; cup, top-shaped, light brown, covered with loose, rusty-red scales, enclosing one half of the nut.

Twigs.—Stout, pubescent, becoming glabrous and gray-brown, with pale lenticels; terminal buds, narrowly conical, ½″ long, sometimes prominently angled, rusty-brown; lateral buds, similar but smaller; leaf scars and pith, similar to those of other red oaks.

Bark.—Dark brown or nearly black, rough, about 1″ thick, broken into squarrose, scaly plates.

Habitat.—Usually on dry, sandy, sterile soils, where it forms nearly pure, parklike groves, or in association with other species, notably eastern redcedar and black, southern red, and post oaks.

Distribution.—From southern New York and New Jersey through Pennsylvania, Ohio, Michigan, and Illinois to Iowa; south through Oklahoma to Texas in the West; south to Florida in the East.

Importance.—Occasionally used for ties, posts, and fuel; rarely, for rough lumber.

Arkansas Oak

Quercus arkansana Sarg.

This species is similar in most respects to *Q. marilandica* but becomes much larger (up to 70′ by 2′). It is found only in the woods and on the hills of Hempstead County, Arkansas. The leaves are remotely 3-lobed and usually bear a distinct bristle at the rounded apex of each lobe. This species is of little or no economic value at present.

Water Oak

Quercus nigra L.

Habit.—A tall, slender tree, 50′ to 80′ in height, with a trunk 2′ to 3½′ in diameter and a round-topped, symmetrical crown of ascending branches.

Leaves.—Alternate, simple, deciduous, sometimes not falling until late winter, variable in shape but mostly spatulalike, oblong-obovate, or oblong-lanceolate, 2″ to 4″ long, 1″ to 2″ wide (occasionally 6″ long); apex, acute to broadly obtuse; base, usually wedge-shaped; margin, variable, (1) entire, (2) 3-lobed at the apex, or (3) variously lobed, the latter form being largely restricted to vigorous sprouts and juvenile plants; dull bluish green above, paler below, often with rusty axillary tufts; petioles, short, stout, flattened.

Flowers.—Unisexual; the staminate, in 2″ to 3″, hairy, stalked catkins; the pistillate, mostly solitary, also on short, hairy stalks.

Fruit.—An acorn, solitary or occasionally in pairs, often short-stalked; nut, ovoid to hemispherical, light brown to nearly jet-black, with a pubescent apex; about ½″ long; cup, thin, saucer-shaped, reddish brown, pubescent.

Twigs.—Slender, glabrous, at first dull red, becoming brown; terminal buds, ¼″ long, ovoid, acute, reddish brown, prominently angled; lateral buds, similar but smaller; leaf scars and pith, as for other red oaks.

Bark.—At first smooth and brown, becoming gray-black with rough, scaly ridges.

Habitat.—Typically a bottom-land species, but seldom occurring in permanent swamps; usually

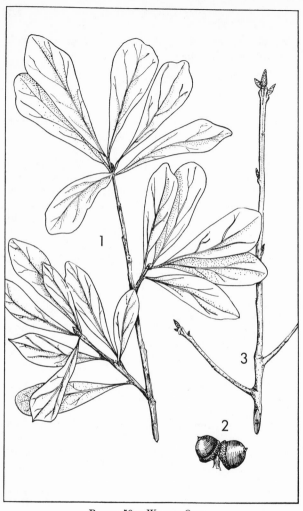

PLATE 59.—WATER OAK
1. Foliage ×½.　2. Acorns ×½.　3. Twig ×1.

associated with other hardwoods and under favorable conditions often the most abundant species in the stand.

Distribution.—Atlantic and Gulf coastal plains from Virginia to central Florida and west to eastern Texas; also in the Mississippi drainage basin as far north as southern Illinois and western Kentucky.

Importance.—Used to some extent as fuel and, in the absence of better species, as a source of timber. Water oak, because of its rapidity of growth during the first few years of its development, ease of propagation, and pleasing form, is a favorite street and lawn tree in many southern cities.

THE ELM FAMILY

Ulmaceae

The Elm Family is widely distributed through temperate and tropical forests of both hemispheres but is not represented in the timbered areas of sub-arctic regions. The 150 or more species of trees, shrubs, and herbs are grouped into 14 or 15 genera, 4 of which have 1 or more representatives in southern woodlands.

Synopsis of Southern Genera

Genus	Leaves	Flowers	Fruit
Ulmus	deciduous, doubly serrate	perfect	samara
Planera	deciduous, singly serrate-crenate, the teeth glandular	polygamo-monoecious	nutlike
Trema	persistent, singly serrate	monoecious, dioecious, or rarely perfect	drupe
Celtis	deciduous, entire or singly serrate	polygamo-monoecious	drupe

THE ELMS

Ulmus L.

The elms comprise a group of 18 to 20 species widely distributed through the forests of North America, Europe, and Asia. Many of them, because of their graceful form, pleasing symmetry, ease of propagation, and rapidity of growth, are used extensively as ornamentals. The wood of most species is tough and strong and has many diverse uses. Crude cloth and rope were fabricated from the inner bark fibers by primitive peoples, and certain compounds having definite pharmaceutical properties have been derived from the bark of other species.

The elms have enjoyed a prominent place in American history, and several nationally known trees that were silent witnesses to memorable events in the development of our country are still standing. Notable among these is the now famous Great Elm (*U. americana*) at Palmer, Mass. Here, General Washington, standing in the shade of this venerable giant, addressed his troops just 3 days before he took command of the Continental Army. On the Capitol grounds are several elms well known to Washington visitors. These include the John Quincy Adams Elm, planted there during his administration, and the Washington Elm, a native tree that witnessed the erection of the Capitol. Other well-known elms include the Penn Treaty Elm, blown down in 1810, the Washington Elm (now dead) at Cambridge, Mass., and the Friendship Elm, planted in 1860 in Central Park in New York, N.Y., by King Edward VII, then Prince of Wales.

Six elms are indigenous to North America, and five of them form a part of the broadleaved forests of the South.

KEY TO THE SOUTHERN ELMS

1. Twigs, with 2 or 3 corky ridges or wings, more or less continuous except at the nodes...................... 2
1. Twigs, without corky emergences................... 4

    2. Flowers, appearing in the spring from separate buds in advance of the leaves......**Winged elm** (p. 239)
    2. Flowers, emerging from leaf axils during late summer or early fall............................ 3

3. Leaves, elliptical to ovate, rounded at the apex, scabrous on the upper surface; flowers, in fascicles of 3 to 5..........................**Cedar elm** (p. 242)
3. Leaves, oblong-obovate, acuminate at the apex, essentially glabrous on the upper surface; flowers, in many-colored racemes..............**September elm** (p. 234)

    4. Leaves, scabrous on the upper surface; samara, rounded, depressed, or slightly notched at the apex, pubescent only on the seed cavity; twigs, stout, scurfy, gray; the buds, brown, often tinged with purple, coated with rusty-brown hairs........
              Slippery elm (p. 237)
    4. Leaves, essentially glabrous on the upper surface; samara, deeply notched, ciliate on the margin; twigs, slender; the buds, brown, glabrous or nearly so.... 5

5. Leaves, oblong-ovate, 4″ to 6″ long, with pronounced unequal bases; samara, glabrous except for a ciliate margin.....................**American elm** (p. 231)
5. Leaves, oblong-lanceolate, 1½″ to 2½″ long, with unequally rounded or heart-shaped bases; samara, hairy on wings, seed cavity, and margin.............
              Winged elm (p. 239)

American Elm

Ulmus americana L.

Habit.—A tree, 80′ to 120′ in height and 2′ to 5′ in diameter. The bole, which is often heavily buttressed

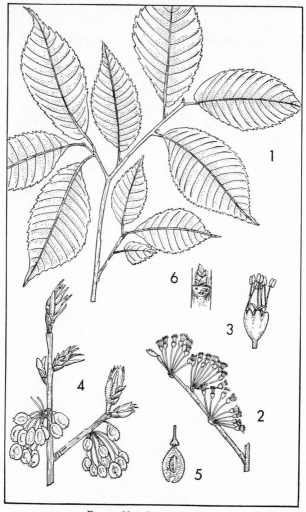

PLATE 60.—AMERICAN ELM

1. Foliage $\times\frac{1}{3}$. 2. Flower clusters $\times\frac{2}{3}$. 3. Flower $\times 5$.
4. Fruit clusters $\times\frac{1}{2}$. 5. Fruit $\times 1$. 6. Leaf scar $\times 1\frac{1}{2}$.

at the base, usually divides several feet above the ground into a number of gracefully arching limbs with more or less pendulous branchlets to form an attractive, vaselike or spreading crown of rare beauty and unusual symmetry.

Leaves.—Alternate, simple, 4″ to 6″ long, 2″ to 3″ wide, oblong-ovate to elliptical; apex, acute to acuminate; base, rounded-inequilateral; margin, coarsely doubly serrate; dark green and essentially smooth on the upper surface (occasionally scabrous on vigorous shoots), pubescent or rarely glabrous below; petioles, short, stout, about ¼″ in length.

Flowers.—Perfect, without petals, long-stalked, borne in clusters of 3 or 4 from separate buds before leaf emergence, each flower bud producing 5 to 8 such clusters; calyx, bell-shaped, reddish green, with 7 to 9 lobes; stamens, 5 or 6, with long, slender filaments and bright-red anthers; pistil, pale green, compressed; the 2-celled ovary, surmounted by 2 divergent styles.

Fruit.—A green, less commonly orange-red samara, consisting of a flattened seed surrounded by a wing, oval to obovate, about ½″ long, with a deep, terminal notch, hairy only along the margin of the wing, maturing with the bursting of the leaf buds.

Twigs.—Slender, those of the current season reddish brown to dark brown, smooth or sparsely pubescent, marked by pale, inconspicuous lenticels; terminal buds, absent; lateral buds, ovoid, covered by several chestnut-brown, overlapping scales, about ⅛″ long, those at the upper nodes usually leaf buds, those at the lower nodes flower buds; leaf scars, elevated, semicircular, with 3 nearly equidistant bundle scars; stipule scars, inconspicuous.

Bark.—Ashy gray, divided into broad, flat-topped ridges, separated by deep, elliptical to diamond-shaped fissures; when blazed, exhibiting alternating layers of buff-colored and reddish-brown tissue.

Habitat.—On bottom lands, alluvial flats, margins of streams, ponds, and lakes and on moist fertile slopes and uplands in association with other broadleaved species.

Distribution.—Newfoundland west through southern Canada to Saskatchewan and the Rocky Mountains, south to central Florida and eastern Texas.

Importance.—American elm is a valuable tree from the standpoint of both lumber production and ornamental use. It is a favorite and highly prized street and shade tree in many cities of the United States. It grows rapidly in youth and commonly attains an age of 150 to 175 years. The wood is tough, splits with difficulty, and is admirably suited for the manufacture of cooperage, kitchenette furniture, flooring, baskets, vehicle parts, and woodenware. The extinction of this species is threatened by the Dutch elm disease.

September Elm

Ulmus serotina Sarg.

Habit.—A tree, 40′ to 60′ in height and 2′ to 3′ in diameter, resembling American elm in its general form, although it never attains the grandeur and stately proportions of that species. Where the two occur as forest associates, red elm may be readily distinguished by its corky-winged twigs and branchlets.

Leaves.—Alternate, simple, 3″ to 4″ long, 1″ to 2″ wide, obovate-oblong or oblong; apex, acute to acuminate; base, extremely unequal; margin, doubly serrate-crenate; lustrous yellow-green and glabrous on the upper surface, pale-pubescent on the principal veins and midrib below; petioles, short, stout, about ¼″ long.

Flowers.—Perfect, without petals, on short, jointed stalks, borne in the leaf axils during the late summer and early fall in few- to many-flowered racemes; calyx,

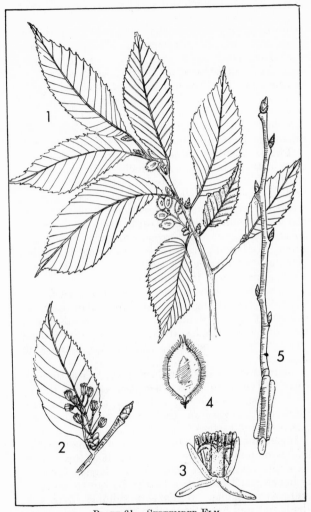

PLATE 61.—SEPTEMBER ELM

1. Foliage and fruit ×⅓. 2. Flower cluster ×⅓. 3. Flower
×5. 4. Fruit ×1⅓. 5. Twig ×1.

reddish brown, 6-lobed, the lobes extending to the base; stamens, 6, with long, slender filaments and reddish-purple to orange-red anthers; pistil, greenish, pubescent, surmounted by 2 divergent styles.

Fruit.—A light-greenish samara, consisting of a flattened seed surrounded by a narrow wing, elliptical to oblong, about ½″ long, with a deep terminal notch; seed hull and wings, covered with silvery-white hairs, ciliate on the margin, maturing in early November.

Twigs.—Slender, those of the current season usually lustrous brown, occasionally somewhat hairy, marked by elongated, white lenticels; those of the 2d and 3d seasons characterized by 2 to 3 corky ridges or wings, which are more or less continuous except at the nodes; terminal buds, absent; lateral buds, ovoid, sharp-pointed, covered by several dark-brown, glabrous, overlapping scales, about ¼″ long; leaf scars, elevated, semicircular or nearly so, with 3 bundle scars; stipule scars, inconspicuous.

Bark.—Light grayish brown or reddish brown, with scaly, flat-tipped ridges separated by shallow fissures.

Habitat.—Most abundant on dry, rocky soils underlaid with limestone; less frequently encountered along streams, in rich bottoms, and on the margins of swamps.

Distribution.—Southern Kentucky, south through eastern Tennessee to northeastern Georgia; thence west through southern Illinois in the North and northern Alabama in the South to northeastern Arkansas and eastern Oklahoma.

Importance.—September elm occurs sporadically and is of minor commercial availability throughout its entire range. The wood is used largely for fuel, although small quantities find their way to sawmills and veneer plants. It makes a suitable street and shade tree and has been used in these ways in several cities of Alabama and Georgia.

Slippery Elm

Ulmus rubra Muhl.

Habit.—A tree, seldom more than 50′ to 70′ in height or 12″ to 30″ in diameter. Its general form is not wholly unlike that of the American elm although this tree never develops the graceful character and stateliness of that species. The limbs and branchlets of slippery elm are ascending, and at maturity the crown is usually spreading and flat-topped.

Leaves.—Alternate, simple, 5″ to 7″ long, 2″ to 3″ wide; obovate, ovate, or broadly elliptical; apex, acuminate; base, broadly rounded-inequilateral; margin, coarsely doubly serrate; dark green and noticeably roughened (scabrous) on the upper surface, pubescent below; petioles, stout, short, about ⅓″ in length.

Flowers.—Perfect, without petals, short-stalked, often nearly sessile, borne in 3-flowered clusters before leaf emergence, from separate buds, each flower bud producing several such clusters; calyx, bell-shaped, green, pubescent, with 5 to 6 lobes; stamens, 5 or 6, with long, slender, yellow filaments and reddish-purple anthers; pistil, reddish, compressed; the 2-celled ovary, surmounted by 2 exserted, divergent styles.

Fruit.—A green, short-stalked samara, consisting of a flattened seed surrounded by a broad, netted-veined wing, oval to orbicular, about ¾″ long, with a rounded, slightly notched, or merely depressed apex; the wing margin, naked; faces of the seed cavity, rusty-woolly; matures when the leaves are about half developed.

Twigs.—Moderately stout, those of the current season ashy gray, scabrous and further roughened by raised lenticels; exceedingly difficult to break because of the plastic nature of the bark; terminal bud, absent; lateral buds, ovoid (leaf buds) to subglobose (flower

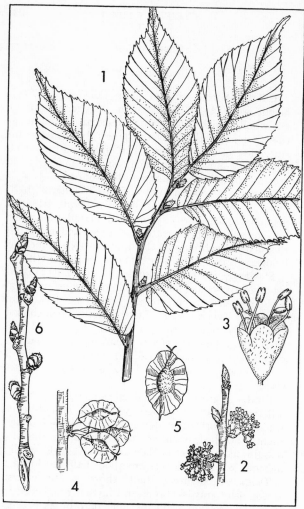

PLATE 62.—SLIPPERY ELM

1. Foliage ×⅓. 2. Flower clusters ×½. 3. Flower ×5.
4. Fruit cluster ×⅔. 5. Fruit ×1. 6. Twig ×1.

buds), blunt, covered by 10 to 12 chestnut-brown to purplish, overlapping scales with rusty-red, woolly hairs; about $\frac{1}{4}''$ long, those at the upper nodes leaf buds, those at the lower nodes flower buds; leaf scars, elevated, oval to semicircular, with 3 bundle scars; stipule scars, inconspicuous.

Bark.—Dark reddish brown to ashy gray, divided into flat, nearly parallel or anastomosing (often superficially scaly) ridges by shallow fissures; when blazed, uniformly reddish brown; inner bark, fragrant and mucilaginous when first exposed.

Habitat.—Most abundant on deep, rich soils of slopes and flats; also found in commercial size and abundance on limestone outcrops.

Distribution.—Southern Quebec, west through Ontario to southeastern North Dakota; south to western Florida and eastern Texas; not on the Atlantic coastal plain below Virginia.

Importance.—The timber of slippery elm exhibits many of the properties of American elm and is generally used for the same purposes. The mucilaginous inner bark was famous in pioneer days as a thirst quencher and appeaser of appetites. It was also used in powdered form as a poultice. Its water extractives contain certain pharmaceutical compounds suitable for the treatment of throat ailments, inflammation, and fever. Moose are known to browse on the young twigs and foliage of this species, and in certain sections of Canada the tree is called the *moose elm*.

Winged Elm

Ulmus alata Michx.

Habit.—A tree, 40′ to 50′ in height and 12″ to 30″ in diameter; the short bole, usually terminated by several ascending limbs with laterally spreading branchlets, resulting in an oblong, nearly spherical

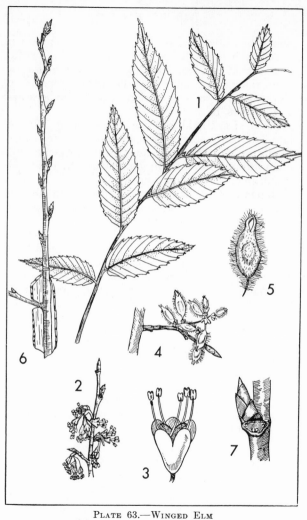

PLATE 63.—WINGED ELM

1. Foliage ×½. 2. Flower clusters ×½. 3. Flower ×5.
4. Fruit cluster ×1. 5. Fruit ×3. 6. Twig ×1. 7. Leaf scar ×2.

or less frequently a pyramidal crown of pleasing proportions.

Leaves.—Alternate, simple, deciduous $1\frac{1}{2}''$ to $3\frac{1}{2}''$ long, $1''$ to $1\frac{1}{2}''$ wide; oblong-lanceolate to oblong-ovate or elliptical, often falcate; apex, acute to acuminate; base, unequally rounded or cordate; margin, coarsely doubly serrate, dark green and smooth on the upper surface, pale-pubescent below; petioles, short, stout, about $\frac{1}{3}''$ long.

Flowers.—Perfect, without petals, long-stalked, borne in clusters of 3 to 5, appearing from separate buds before leaf emergence; calyx, bell-shaped, yellowish red, 5-lobed; stamens, 5, with long, slender filaments and orange-red anthers; pistil, pale green, woolly, compressed; the 2-celled ovary, surmounted by 2 divergent styles that extend just above the corolla lobes.

Fruit.—An orange-red samara, consisting of a single, flattened seed surrounded by a narrow wing, oval to oblong, about $\frac{1}{3}''$ long; notched at the apex, hairy on the seed cavity, wing, and margin.

Twigs.—Slender, those of the current season grayish brown to reddish brown, glabrous, or more or less pubescent on vigorous growth, with minute, orange-red lenticels; commonly furnished with 2 corky wings or ridges, which appear during either the 1st or the 2d year; terminal buds, absent; lateral buds, ovoid, acute, covered by several dark-brown, smooth or remotely pubescent, overlapping scales about $\frac{1}{8}''$ long; the flower buds, usually restricted to the lower nodes; leaf scars, elevated, semicircular, with 3 bundle scars; stipule scars, inconspicuous.

Bark.—Light brownish gray, divided into flat, often superficially scaly ridges by narrow, shallow fissures; when blazed, exhibiting alternating patches of brown and buff-colored tissues.

Habitat.—Common throughout much of the South; usually found on dry, gravelly soils at low elevations; less frequently, near streams and on alluvial flats or even in swamps.

Distribution.—Southeastern Virginia west through the lower Ohio River Valley and southern Missouri in north-central Oklahoma; south to central Florida and eastern Texas.

Importance.—This is not a timber tree of primary importance. When milled, the boards are mixed with those of other elms and thus lose their identity in the trade. Because of its rapid growth, pleasing habit, and relative freedom from serious diseases or insect pests, it is a favorite ornamental and street tree in many southern communities. The inner bark is fibrous and in the past has been used locally for baling twine.

Cedar Elm

Ulmus crassifolia Nutt.

Habit.—A medium-sized tree, 80′ to 100′ in height and 2′ to 3′ in diameter; characterized by a heavily buttressed base, an angular or strongly fluted bole, and a dense, long, narrow, rounded crown of crooked limbs and interlacing branchlets. The limbs in basal portions of the crown are either pendulous or nearly horizontal while those above are sharply ascending.

Leaves.—Alternate, simple, 1″ to 2″ long, ½″ to 1″ wide, narrowly ovate to elliptical; apex, rounded or acute; base, unequally cuneate, oblique, or less frequently rounded; margin, coarsely, often unequally, doubly serrate; lustrous dark green and with minute excrescences on the upper surface, with silky hairs below; petioles, short, stout, woolly, about ⅓″ in length.

Flowers.—Perfect, without petals, short-stalked,

borne in clusters of 3 to 5 in the leaf axils late in the summer or early fall; calyx, bell-shaped, hairy, greenish to reddish green, with 6 to 9 deep lobes; stamens, 5 or 6, with long, slender filaments and red to purplish-red anthers; pistil, greenish, pubescent, compressed; the 2-celled, pubescent ovary, surmounted by 2 exserted, divergent styles.

Fruit.—A green samara, consisting of a flattened seed surrounded by a broad wing, oblong or nearly so, about ½″ long, with a deep terminal notch, hairy on wing, seed-cavity cover, and the margin; maturing from early September to early November.

Twigs.—Slender, those of the current season light reddish brown and commonly somewhat pubescent, marked by minute lenticels, featured by a pair of lustrous-brown, corky wings, which are continuous except at the nodes (or in some instances with only sporadic cork formation); terminal bud, absent; lateral buds, broadly ovoid, sharp-pointed, covered by several overlapping, chestnut-brown scales, which are slightly hairy on their back, about ⅛″ long; leaf scars, elevated, semicircular or nearly so, with 3 bundle scars; stipule scars, inconspicuous; pith, homogeneous.

Bark.—Silvery gray to brownish gray, often tinged with purple; broken into thin, flat, brittle scales, which are loose at their edges; differing from that of other southern elms in not being fissured and hence a primary diagnostic feature.

Habitat.—Widely distributed on flood plains, alluvial flats, dry clay ridges and hummocks, and along streams in association with other hardwoods, notably willow, swamp chestnut, overcup, swamp red, and Nuttall oaks, hackberry, persimmon, water hickory, and sweetgum.

Distribution.—Northwestern Mississippi, through southern Arkansas and western Louisiana to western Texas.

Importance.—This is the common elm of Texas, where it is used as a street and shade tree. The wood is frequently too knotty or gnarled to be worked. Small quantities, however, are sawed into lumber, which is used chiefly in the fabrication of vehicle stock.

Planertree   Waterelm

Planera aquatica Gmel.

A Monotype

Habit.—A large shrub or small tree, rarely more than 30′ to 40′ in height or 14″ to 20″ in diameter; in form quite similar to American elm with its graceful, vaselike crown.

Leaves.—Alternate, simple, deciduous, 2″ to 2½″ long, ½″ to 1″ wide, oblong-ovate; apex, acute; base, unequally wedge-shaped; margin, crenate-serrate, with glandular teeth; dull, dark green above, paler below; petioles, stout, short, about ¼″ long.

Flowers.—Perfect and imperfect, appearing with the leaves in 2 to 5 axillary clusters; calyx, bell-shaped, greenish yellow sometimes tinged with red, with 4 to 5 lobes; petals, wanting; stamens, several or none, when present, exserted; pistil, with an ovoid ovary, short style, and 2 elongated, greatly reflexed stigmas.

Fruit.—Nutlike, oblong-ovoid, covered with many soft knoblike processes, which grow out of tubercles on the ovary wall, about ½″ long.

Twigs.—Slender, slightly zigzag, those of the current season light reddish brown and hairy, dotted with minute, whitish lenticels, at length silvery gray and smooth; terminal buds, absent; lateral buds, ovoid, minute, covered by several tiny, chestnut-brown, hairy, overlapping scales; leaf scars, broadly oval to triangular, with 3 bundle scars; stipule scars, minute; pith, homogeneous.

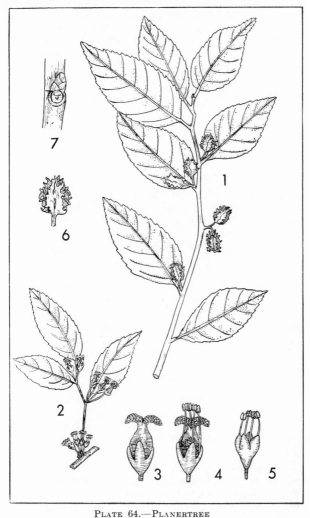

PLATE 64.—PLANERTREE

1. Foliage and fruit ×½.   2. Flower clusters ×½.   3. Female
flower ×5.   4. Perfect flower ×5.   5. Male flower ×5.   6. Fruit
×1.   7. Leaf scar ×2.

Bark.—Light gray-brown, dividing into large, shreddy scales, which drop off to expose the reddish-brown inner bark.

Habitat.—A swamp tree, not infrequently occurring along stream banks or on lands subjected to periodic inundation.

Distribution.—South Atlantic and Gulf coastal plains, from southeastern North Carolina to eastern Texas; occurring sporadically through the Mississippi River drainage system to northern Kentucky and the lower Wabash River Valley in Illinois.

Importance.—This tree is of little or no commercial value. The wood, because of its low density, is occasionally used for floats by local fishermen.

THE TREMAS

Trema Lour.

The tremas comprise a group of about 20 species of subtropical and tropical trees and shrubs with evergreen foliage. Two species, one a small tree, are indigenous to the lower Florida peninsula and neighboring Keys

Florida Trema

Trema micrantha (L.) Blume

Habit.—Ordinarily a shrub, but occasionally becoming arborescent, with a single, erect stem supporting a small, ovoid crown of ascending branches; at best rarely over 25' to 30' in height or 12" to 24" in diameter.

Leaves.—Alternate, simple, persistent, 3" to 4" long, 1" to 2½" broad, ovate; apex, abruptly long-tapered; base, rounded, heart-shaped, or oblique; margin, finely serrate; dark green and with short, bristly hairs above, covered with woolly hair below; petioles, stout, woolly, about ⅓" long.

PLATE 65.—FLORIDA TREMA

1. Foliage ×½. 2. Flower ×3. 3. Fruit ×3. 4. Leaf scar ×1½.

Flowers.—Unisexual, apetalous, both sexes borne in mixed, axillary, many-flowered clusters; calyx, composed of 5 oblong sepals; petals, wanting; stamens, 5; pistil, with a sessile, 1-celled ovary and elongated, completely divided style with linear, fleshy stigmas.

Fruit.—A small, orange or yellow, nearly spherical drupe, containing a solitary, bony nutlet, about ⅛″ in diameter.

Twigs.—Stout, somewhat zigzag, those of the current season red-brown and clothed with dense, woolly hair, later becoming smooth and dotted with small, yellowish-white lenticels; terminal buds, wanting; lateral buds, ovoid, woolly, the flower-buds superposed; leaf scars, triangular, with 3 bundle scars; pith, continuous, white.

Bark.—Dark brown, thin, featured by numerous wartlike excrescences and breaking up into small, appressed, paperlike scales.

Habitat.—Rich hammocks near tidewater; commonly usurping burns formerly occupied by other species.

Distribution.—Lower peninsula of Florida and neighboring Keys, the West Indies, and Mexico.

Importance.—The wood is of no commercial value, but the fleshy fruits are a source of food for the many small birds of the region.

THE HACKBERRIES

Celtis L.

The hackberries comprise a group of about 70 species of trees and shrubs widely distributed through the tropics and north temperate regions of the world. At the present time there appears to be considerable disagreement among systematic botanists as to the limits of certain forms, specific identification being, in some instances, extremely difficult. Sudworth (73) lists 6 aborescent species for the United States, 3 of which occur in the South.

KEY TO THE SOUTHERN HACKBERRIES

1. Fruit, dark purple, the stalks much longer than the leaf petioles....................**Hackberry** (p. 249)
1. Fruit, yellow or orange-red, the stalks shorter or only slightly longer than the leaf petioles................ 2

    2. Leaves, oblong-lanceolate, 2½″ to 5″ long, mostly entire along the margin; fruit, yellow or orange, the stalks shorter or only slightly longer than the petioles.....................**Sugarberry** (p. 252)
    2. Leaves, ovate, 1½″ to 2½″ long, entire or sharply serrate; fruit, dark orange-red (rarely purplish), the stalks shorter than the petioles...............
                Georgia hackberry (p. 253)

Hackberry

Celtis occidentalis L.

Habit.—Sometimes attaining gigantic proportions, but ordinarily a tree, 40′ to 60′ in height and 12″ to 20″ in diameter; in the open, developing a short bole and large, spherical crown; forest trees, in contrast, producing a long, columnar, occasionally buttressed bole and a narrow, round-topped crown; root system, superficial or moderately deep and widespread.

Leaves.—Alternate, simple, deciduous, 2½″ to 4″ long, 1½″ to 2″ broad, ovate to ovate-lanceolate; apex, long-tapered; base, commonly asymmetrically heart-shaped; margin, sharply serrate, sometimes only above the middle; light green, smooth or with short, bristly hairs above, pale green and hairy along the principal veins below; petioles, smooth, about ½″ long.

Flowers.—Perfect and imperfect, without petals, long-stalked, appearing with leaf emergence; the

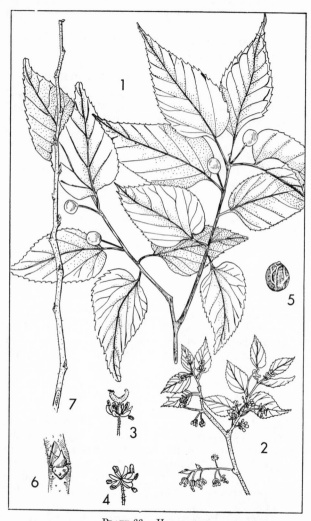

PLATE 66.—HACKBERRY

1. Foliage and fruit $\times\frac{1}{2}$. 2. Flower clusters $\times\frac{1}{2}$. 3. Female flower $\times 2$. 4. Male flower $\times 2$. 5. Pit $\times 1\frac{1}{2}$. 6. Leaf scar $\times 2$. 7. Twig. $\times 1$.

staminate, in few-flowered clusters in the axils of the lower leaves; the perfect and pistillate flowers, mostly solitary, in the axils of leaves near the tips of twigs; calyx, 4- or 5-lobed; stamens, 4 to 6 (mostly 5); pistil, with an ovoid, sessile ovary surmounted by a short style and 2 elongated, hairy, reflexed stigmas.

Fruit.—A globular, purple drupe, about $\frac{1}{3}''$ in diameter, with a large, reticulate, bony pit, thick skin, and thin layer of sweetish flesh; borne on stalks, $\frac{1}{2}''$ to $1''$ in length.

Twigs.—Slender, zigzag, those of the current season greenish brown to light reddish brown, smooth, marked by numerous pale lenticels; terminal buds, absent; lateral buds, about $\frac{1}{4}''$ long, ovoid, sharp-pointed, appressed, covered by a few overlapping, chestnut-brown scales; leaf scars, oval to crescent-shaped, with 3 bundle scars; stipule scars, minute; pith, commonly chambered at the nodes, homogeneous between them.

Bark.—Gray-brown to silvery gray, featured by many corky warts and ridges, particularly on the lower portions of the bole; scaly on old trees.

Habitat.—In the North most commonly encountered on dry ridges and limestone outcrops; to the south, frequenting rich, moist, alluvial soils in association with other hardwoods of the region.

Distribution.—Eastern and southern United States.

Importance.—Hackberry is a common tree of secondary importance to the American lumber industry. Recently, selected material cut into rotary veneer stock has been offered to the trade under the name of *beaverwood*. The wood is also used in the manufacture of furniture, and the tree is occasionally planted for decorative purposes in both the United States and Europe. The fruit is a source of food for many game birds particularly quail, turkey, pheasant, and grouse.

Sugarberry

Celtis laevigata Willd.

Habit.—A medium-sized tree, 60′ to 80′ in height and 2′ to 3′ in diameter, with a straight but short bole, broad, open crown of slender, spreading branches, pendulous at their tips, and a moderately deep, spreading root system.

Leaves.—Alternate, simple, deciduous, $2\frac{1}{2}''$ to 5″ long, 1″ to $2\frac{1}{2}''$ wide, oblong-lanceolate; apex, gradually tapering to a long, narrow point; base, obliquely wedge-shaped or asymmetrically rounded; margin, entire (or with a few serrate teeth near the apex, a feature of vigorous growth); light green, smooth or occasionally roughened above, somewhat paler and smooth below; petioles, slender, smooth, about $\frac{1}{3}''$ long.

Flowers.—Similar to those of common hackberry.

Fruit.—An orange or yellowish drupe; about $\frac{1}{4}''$ long, nearly spherical, with a wrinkled, bony pit, thick skin, and thin layer of flesh; borne on short stalks, about $\frac{1}{4}''$ to $\frac{1}{2}''$ in length.

Twigs.—Similar to those of common hackberry, except for the buds, which are only $\frac{1}{16}''$ to $\frac{1}{8}''$ long.

Bark.—Similar to that of common hackberry.

Habitat.—Stream banks, river bottoms, and moist alluvial flats of clay and silt loam; usually occurring as an occasional tree in association with many species, but most commonly with sweetgum, pecan, green ash, American and cedar elms, overcup, Nuttall and water oaks, and honeylocust.

Distribution.—Southeastern United States from coastal Virginia to eastern Texas including Florida and the keys.

Importance.—The wood is used for slack cooperage, furniture and crating.

Georgia Hackberry

Celtis tenuifolia Nutt.

This is a large shrub or small tree occurring on dry, rocky soils of the Piedmont plateau and lower mountain slopes of North Carolina, South Carolina, and Georgia. It also has been reported from southern Illinois, southern Missouri, western Florida, and coastal New Jersey. The small, ovate, roughened leaves, seldom more then 2″ in length, and dark, orange-red fruits serve to distinguish this tree from other hackberries of the region.

THE MULBERRY FAMILY

Moraceae

The Mulberry Family is a large group of tropical and subtropical plants embracing 55 genera and about 1,000 species of herbs, shrubs, and trees. A few forms extend into the milder parts of the Temperate Zones. Several species are productive of important fruits, fibers, and rubber; notable are the breadfruits, figs, mulberries, hops, and hemp.

Four arborescent species included in 3 genera are natives of the South. The paper mulberry [*Broussonetia papyrifera* (L.) Vent.], a native of eastern Asia, but commonly used as an ornamental throughout much of the South, has escaped cultivation and is becoming rapidly naturalized in many localities.

Synopsis of Southern Arborescent Genera

Genus	*Leaves*	*Flowers*	*Fruit*	*Buds*
Morus	deciduous, toothed and lobed	dioecious	succulent	scaly

Genus	Leaves	Flowers	Fruit	Buds
Maclura	deciduous, entire	dioecious	firm, with a milky sap	scaly
Ficus	persistent, entire	monoecious	succulent	naked

THE MULBERRIES

Morus L.

This group comprises 12 to 15 species of trees and shrubs widely distributed through the Northern Hemisphere. The white mulberry (*M. alba* L.), a native of Asia, was introduced along the Atlantic seaboard during colonial times when an attempt was made to establish the silkworm industry in this country.

Two mulberries are indigenous to the United States, and one of them occurs widespread through many sections of the South.

Red Mulberry

Morus rubra L.

Habit.—Ordinarily a small tree, but occasionally attaining a height of 60' to 70' and a trunk of 12" to 18" in diameter; the branches are stout and spreading and form a dense, broad, round-topped crown.

Leaves.—Alternate, simple, deciduous, of 3 general types, (1) unlobed, (2) mitten-shaped, (3) 3-(rarely 5-) lobed, all of which commonly appear on the same tree; mostly circular in shape or nearly so, 3" to 6" in diameter; apex, acute to abruptly short-tapered; base, flattened or heart-shaped; margin, coarsely serrate; dark bluish green and smooth above, paler and hairy below; petiole, short, about 1" long.

Flowers.—Unisexual, appearing with the leaves, each sex borne on separate trees in lax, green, hairy

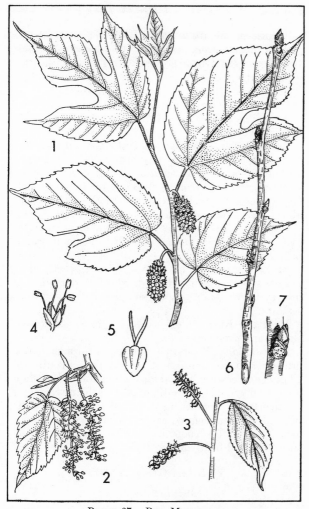

PLATE 67.—RED MULBERRY

1. Foliage and fruit ×⅓.   2. Clusters of male flowers ×½.
3. Clusters of female flowers ×½.   4. Male flower ×4.
5. Female flower ×4.   6. Twig ×⅔.   7. Leaf scar ×1½.

spikes, the staminate, 2″ to 3″ long, the pistillate, about 1″ long; male flowers, with a deeply 4-lobed calyx and 4 green stamens; female flowers, with 4 sepals insheathing a flat, sessile ovary; male flowers sometimes appearing with the female on the same spike.

Fruit.—A cluster (multiple) of dark-red to purplish, sweet, edible drupelets, 1″ to 1¼″ long; seeds, minute, light brown, ovoid.

Twigs.—Slender, zigzag, at first hairy but smooth through their 1st winter, gray-brown, with scattered, gray lenticels, on vigorous growth with papery scales or shreds resulting from the peeling of the epidermal layers; terminal buds, absent; lateral buds, ovoid, about ¼″ long, covered with several overlapping, shining olive-brown scales; leaf scars, half-round to oval, concave, with numerous scattered bundle scars; pith, homogeneous.

Bark.—Smooth, light gray on young stems, ultimately about ¾″ thick, then divided into dark-brown or gray-brown, thin, narrow, longitudinally elongated scales.

Habitat.—Rich, moist soils on flats, protected slopes, and even ridges.

Distribution.—Western New England through southern Ontario to southern South Dakota, south to Florida and eastern Texas; most abundant in the Ohio River Valley and the southern Appalachian region.

Importance.—Sometimes planted for its fruit but of limited ornamental value. The wood is occasionally used for cooperage, fence posts, crossties, furniture, and boat construction.

THE OSAGE-ORANGE

Maclura Nutt.

The osage-orange of the Southwest is the only member of this genus. Originally restricted to portions of

Texas, Arkansas, and Oklahoma, it is now used extensively throughout the East and has become naturalized in many localities.

Osage-Orange

Maclura pomifera (Raf.) Schneid.

A Monotype

Habit.—A large shrub, or occasionally a tree, sometimes reaching 50′ in height and 2′ to 3′ in diameter; the bole is usually short, often malformed, and supports a number of stout, ascending, often contorted branches, which collectively form an open, nearly spherical head.

Leaves.—Alternate, simple, deciduous, mostly ovate, 3″ to 6″ long, about 3″ wide; apex, long-tapering; base, rounded, flattened, or, more generally, broadly obtuse; margin, entire; lustrous dark green above, paler below; petioles, 1″ to 2″ long.

Flowers.—Unisexual, appearing after the leaves, each sex borne on separate trees, the male in long-stalked, axillary racemes, 1″ to 1½″ long, the female in short-stalked heads, about 1″ in diameter; male flowers, with a 4-lobed calyx and 4 stamens; the female, with a 4-lobed calyx, a nearly globular, sessile ovary, and greatly elongated, hairy, filamentous styles.

Fruit.—About 3″ to 5″ in diameter, having the appearance of a green orange, actually a compact cluster (multiple) of green, oblong, firm drupelets; when bruised, exuding a milky sap.

Twigs.—Slender to moderately stout, green to orange-brown and smooth, armed with short, stout axillary thorns or, in one variety, thornless; terminal buds, lacking; lateral buds, small, inconspicuous, often somewhat sunken, with 4 or 5 overlapping, light-brown scales; leaf scars, triangular to kidney-shaped,

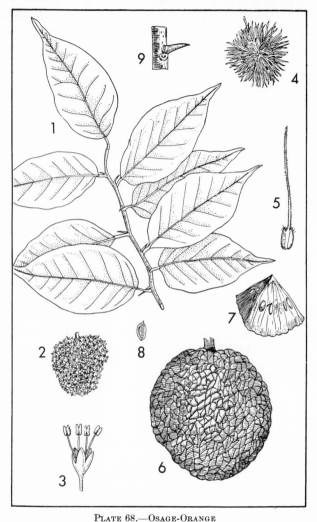

PLATE 68.—OSAGE-ORANGE

1. Foliage ×⅓.   2. Cluster of male flowers ×¾.   3. Male flower ×3.   4. Cluster of female flowers ×¾.   5. Female flower ×3.   6. Fruit ×⅓.   7. Section of fruit ×⅓.   8. Seed ×½. 9. Leaf scar ×1½.

with 3 to 5 bundle scars; stipule scars, very small, triangular; pith, homogeneous.

Bark.—Orange-brown, about 1″ thick, deeply furrowed between the broad, interlacing, rounded, fibrous ridges.

Habitat.—Within its natural range largely restricted to bottom lands of high moisture retention, but encountered on a variety of sites in its extended naturalized range.

Distribution.—Northeastern Texas, southern Arkansas, and southern Oklahoma; naturalized in many sections of the South and East.

Importance.—Because of the thorny nature of its branches the osage-orange has been used for hedges, and many of the old southern plantation boundaries were delineated by rows of this tree. While it responds readily to pruning and trimming it does not enjoy the same popularity as a decorative tree that it did years ago.

Osage-orange wood, one of the heavier and tougher of American timbers, is admirably suited for bow-staves. While originally used in this manner by the American Indians, it is also a favorite bow wood of many amateurs of archery. The bright-yellow wood contains a dye principle that has been commercially exploited in the past.

THE FIGS

Ficus L.

The figs comprise a large group of about 800 species of trees, shrubs, and vines, the majority indigenous to the South Pacific islands. The figs of commerce are traceable to *F. carica* L., originally a native of the Mediterranean basin but now widely cultivated in California and several sections of the southeastern United States. The common rubber plant of our

botanical conservatories as well as the banyan tree
are both members of this genus.

The fruit of the fig is an interesting structure.
Unlike other native plants of the mulberry family,
the flowers of the fig are borne on the *inside* of a closed
receptacle. After fertilization the small female flowers
and their stems become fleshy and embedded in the
then hollow and greatly enlarged fleshy receptacle.

Two species, both restricted to subtropical Florida,
are the only figs found in the United States.

KEY TO THE SOUTHERN FIGS

1. Leaves, elliptical, pointed at both ends; fruit, stalkless
   or nearly so............**Florida strangler fig** (p. 260)
1. Leaves, ovate, heart-shaped at the base; fruit, long-
   stalked....................**Shortleaf fig** (p. 262)

Florida Strangler Fig

Ficus aurea Nutt.

Habit.—A tree, 50′ to 60′ in height and 2′ to 4′ in
diameter. Beginning its life as a parasite, the seed
lodges in cracks and crevices along the bark of other
trees and germinates. Aerial roots subsequently put
out, ultimately reach the ground, and develop an inde-
pendent, subterranean system. When many such
roots are developed, they cover the supporting tree
to form a trunk and eventually strangle the host.
Branches touching the ground also take root and
produce new shoots; thus, over a long period of time
a compound structure covering a considerable area of
land surface may eventually result.

Leaves.—Alternate, simple, evergreen, thick and
leathery, falling off during the 2d season, oblong to
elliptical, 2″ to 5″ long, 1″ to 3″ wide; apex, acute;
base, wedge-shaped; margin, entire; yellow-green,
lustrous above, paler below; petioles, short, stout,

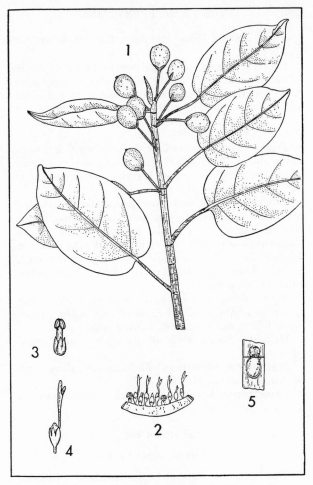

PLATE 69.—FLORIDA STRANGLER FIG
1. Foliage and fruit ×⅓. 2. Flowers on portion of receptacle ×2.
3. Male flower ×5. 4. Female flower ×5. 5. Leaf scar ×1.

grooved, about 1″ long; stipules, foliaceous, encircling the twig.

Flowers.—Unisexual, both types borne on the inside of the same axillary, nearly sessile, closed receptacle; male flowers, with a single stamen and a 2- or 3-lobed calyx; female flowers, with a 4- or 5-lobed calyx and an ovoid ovary; both types of flowers, separated by 5 reddish-purple, chafflike scales.

Fruit.—A paired or solitary cluster of small drupelets embedded in the enlarged, fleshy receptacle and forming a bright-red or yellow, berrylike structure, about ⅝″ in diameter; seed, ovoid, minute.

Twigs.—Stout, greenish orange to yellowish, dotted with pale lenticels; buds, naked; the terminal, about ¾″ in length; the laterals, globular, about ⅛″ in diameter; leaf scars, oval, with a nearly continuous or broken ring of bundle scars; pith, large, continuous; stipule scars, surrounding the twig; fruit scars, circular, often paired.

Bark.—Smooth, ashy gray, on the larger trunks separating into small, thin, appressed scales, which upon falling expose the black inner bark.

Habitat.—Sandy soils of hammocks and ocean shores.

Distribution.—Southern Florida, the Keys, and Bahama Islands.

Importance.—Occasionally used ornamentally in some of the Florida cities.

Shortleaf Fig

Ficus laevigata Vahl

This is another fig that begins its life as a parasite on other trees. It is found along the coral reefs and Keys of Florida and in the Bahamas and Cuba. Shortleaf fig may be distinguished from the strangler fig by its broader leaves with heart-shaped bases, long-stalked, floral receptacles, and larger fruits, often 1″ or more in diameter. The tree is of no value.

THE TALLOWWOOD FAMILY
Olacaceae

The Tallowwood Family numbers about 27 genera and nearly 150 species of trees, shrubs, and lianas scattered throughout the tropical forests of the world. The trees of this group are small of stature and of little or no economic importance, except locally. Two genera, each with a single species, are to be found in the lower Florida peninsula, the Keys, and certain of the neighboring West Indian islands.

Synopsis of the Southern Genera

Genus	Leaves	Flowers	Fruit	Twigs
Ximenia	notched or spine-tipped at the apex	stalked, white or yellowish white	a naked, yellow or yellowish-red drupe	armed with stout thorns
Schoepfia	long-tapered at the apex	sessile, pink or red	a scarlet drupe, nearly wholly enclosed in the enlarged disc	unarmed

THE TALLOWWOODS
Ximenia L.

These are a small genus comprising five species of widely distributed tropical trees and shrubs. One of them, *X. americana* L., extends northward into southern Florida.

Tallowwood   Hog-plum
Ximenia americana L.

Habit.—A large shrub, with long, thorny, vinelike branches, or occasionally arborescent and then devel-

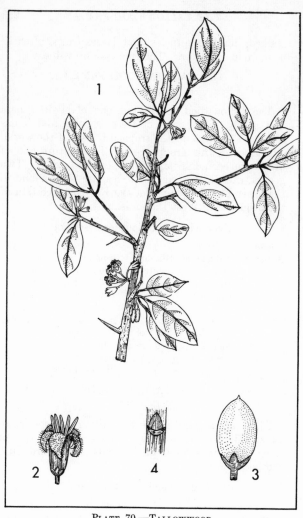

PLATE 70.—TALLOWWOOD
1. Foliage and flowers ×½. 2. Flower ×2. 3. Fruit ×⅔.
4. Leaf scar ×1½.

oping a single bole 25' to 35' in height and 2' to 3' in diameter.

Leaves.—Alternate, simple, persistent, leathery, without stipules, 1" to 2½" long, ½" to 1" wide, oblong to elliptical; apex, notched or spine-tipped; base, long-tapering; margins, slightly thickened and somewhat curled under; lustrous above, pale and dull below; petioles, short and slender, winged at the apex, about ⅓" long.

Flowers.—Perfect, regular, bell-shaped, fragrant, borne in 2- to 4-flowered, axillary, stalked clusters; calyx, with 4 or 5 sharp-pointed, triangular lobes; petals, 4, yellowish white, densely hairy, particularly on their inner surfaces, curled back at their tips; stamens, 8, shorter than the petals; pistil, with a nearly spherical, 4-grooved, glandular ovary, united styles, and globular stigmas.

Fruit.—An ovoid, yellow or yellowish-red drupe, about 1¼" long; with a thin, astringent pulp and a profusely pitted, reddish stone; seeds, yellow.

Twigs.—Slender, armed with straight, stout spines, light reddish brown, angular or terete; buds, small and rather inconspicuous, covered by several overlapping, reddish-brown scales; leaf scars, lunate to triangular, with 3 bundle scars; stipule scars, wanting; pith, homogeneous.

Bark.—Smooth and close, dark reddish brown, very astringent.

Habitat.—Sandy, gravelly, and coral-rock soils bordering fresh-water lakes and tidewaters; hammocks, sand dunes, and pinelands.

Distribution.—A cosmopolitan, circumtropical species; in the Western Hemisphere occurring in the lower Florida peninsula and neighboring Keys, thence south through the West Indies to Brazil.

Importance.—The wood of this species is pleasantly scented and in India has been used as a substitute for sandlewood.   Locally it has been used for fuel and in the manufacture of charcoal.   The bark contains appreciable quantities of a water-soluble astringent suitable for tanning leather, and the fruits are a source of hydrocyanic acid.   The fleshy pulp of the plumlike fruits is edible and is a source of food for many small indigenous and migratory birds.

THE GRAYTWIGS

Schoepfia Schreb.

This is a group of about 15 species of shrubs and small trees found in China, Japan, the East Indies, Peru, Brazil, Mexico, the West Indies, and the United States.   A single species, the gulf graytwig, occurs in southern Florida.

Gulf Graytwig   Whitewood

Schoepfia chrysophylloides Planch.

Habit.—A large shrub or small bushy tree with ascending, thornless branches; seldom more than 30' in height and 12" to 18" in diameter.

Leaves.—Alternate, simple, persistent or tardily deciduous, leathery, without stipules, 1½" to 2½" long, ½" to 1¼" wide, ovate-elliptical, occasionally scythe-shaped; apex, tapering to a sharp point; base, asymmetrically tapered; margin, entire; light green and shiny above, paler and dull below; petiole, stout, short, winged at the apex, about ⅓" long.

Flowers.—Perfect, regular, borne in axillary, sessile clusters of 2 or 3 (mostly 2), or solitary; calyx, cuplike, almost completely filled with an enlarged, fleshy disc; petals, 4, united, the free tips reflexed; stamens, 4, their anthers sessile; pistil, 1, the ovary almost completely embedded in the disc, the style extremely short, the stigma 3-lobed.

PLATE 71.—GULF GRAYTWIG

1. Foliage and fruit $\times\frac{1}{2}$.   2. Cluster of flowers $\times\frac{1}{2}$.   3. Flower $\times 4$.   4. Fruit $\times 4$.   5. Leaf scar $\times 2$.

Fruit.—An ovoid, scarlet drupe, almost wholly incased in the much enlarged, floral disc, about ½″ long, with a thin, fleshy pulp and a hard, but brittle stone; seeds, reddish brown.

Twigs.—Slender, zigzag, unarmed, rather brittle, at first smooth and green, ultimately becoming grayish yellow or ashy gray and scurfy; buds, minute, with 2 or 3 tiny, visible scales; leaf scars, small and very inconspicuous, more or less triangular, with 1 to 3 bundle scars; lenticels, rather prominent after the 1st season; stipule scars, wanting.

Bark.—Thin, grayish brown, and smooth on young stems; divided by narrow, longitudinal, and irregularly transverse ridges into small patches or blocks on the larger stems.

Habitat.—Sandy, gravelly, or coral-rock soils near tidewater and hammocks.

Distribution.—The lower peninsula of Florida, the Keys, Cuba, Jamaica, the Bahamas, and Guatamala.

Importance.—Of no commercial value.

THE KNOTWEED FAMILY

Polygonaceae

This family, which includes the buckwheats, rhubarb, docks, and waterpeppers, consists of about 40 genera and nearly 1,000 species. Those of the Temperate Zone are mostly herbaceous, while a few trees, shrubs, and woody climbers occur in the tropics. The Polygonaceae are represented in our southern forests by two species from the genus *Coccolobis*.

THE SEAGRAPES

Coccolobis P.Br.

The seagrapes comprise a group of over 150 species of evergreen trees and shrubs scattered through the tropical forests of the Americas and the West Indies. Two species, both arborescent, are included in the flora of southern Florida and the Keys.

KEY TO THE SOUTHERN SEAGRAPES

1. Leaves, nearly circular in outline, broader than long, heart-shaped at the base; fruit, in dense, pendulous clusters; pith, excavated . . . . **Seagrape** (p. 269)
1. Leaves, oblong to obovate, longer than broad, rounded or wedge-shaped at the base; fruit, in erect, open clusters; pith, continuous. . . . . **Doveplum** (p. 271)

Seagrape

Coccoloba uvifera (L.) L.

Habit.—A large shrub, or occasionally a small tree, seldom more than 15′ to 25′ in height or 12″ to 20″ in diameter, with a massive, spherical crown and short, often contorted trunk; in exposed situations, branching at or near the ground and assuming a bushy habit.

Leaves.—Alternate, simple, persistent, leathery, 4″ to 5″ long, 5″ to 6″ broad, nearly circular; apex, rounded, notched, or occasionally sharp-pointed; base, deeply heart-shaped; margin, without teeth or lobes, but wavy; lustrous dark green and smooth above, somewhat lighter below and with pale hairs along the stout, reddish midrib and principal veins; petioles, stout, flattened, enlarged at the base, about ½″ long; stipules insheathing the twig above the node.

Flowers.—Perfect, appearing intermittently throughout the year, solitary or in 2- to 6-flowered fascicles, borne in stout, terminal or axillary racemes, 5″ to 15″ long; calyx, white, bell-shaped, 5-lobed, the lobes pubescent on their inner surfaces, longer than the stamens; petals, absent; stamens, 8, red, attached at their bases to the calyx; pistil, with a 3-angled ovary, short style, and 3 short, stigmatic lobes.

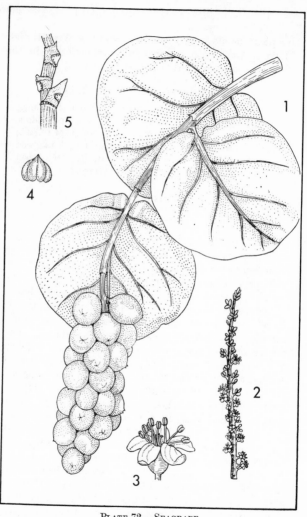

PLATE 72.—SEAGRAPE
1. Foliage and fruit ×⅓. 2. Flower cluster ×¼. 3. Flower
×5. 4. Seed ×1. 5. Leaf scars and stipular sheath ×1.

Fruit.—A thin-walled, red nutlet enclosed in an enlarged, purplish or greenish-white calyx tube with a fleshy, astringent pulp; borne in long, dense, pendulous, grapelike clusters; seed, 3- to 6-lobed, red-brown.

Twigs.—Stout, yellowish green to light orange, hairy, furnished with elongated, pale lenticles; buds, sessile, naked, conical, concealed by the leaf base; leaf scars, nearly circular, with 3 to 5 bundle scars, not on the stem (Plate 72) but borne on a persistent basal sheath, the ocrea, that encircles the stem at the node; the ocrea, upon falling, leaving an annular, encircling stipular scar; pith, large, whitish, excavated at the nodes.

Bark.—Very thin, smooth, light brown, mottled with lighter colored patches of irregular contour.

Habitat.—Typically a tidewater tree or shrub of sandy shores and beaches.

Distribution.—Southern peninsular Florida, the Florida Keys, Bermuda, the Bahamas, the West Indies, and in South America from Colombia to Brazil.

Importance.—The bark of the common seagrape yields a dark-red, astringent juice known as *kino*, at one time used in quantity in the preparation of medicinal compounds and dyes. The wood is used locally for fuel and occasionally in cabinetry. Common seagrape, because of its large leaves, abundance of fruit, and dense, shrubby habit on dry, sandy soils, is used extensively throughout its range for decorative purposes.

Doveplum   Pigeon Seagrape

Coccoloba laurifolia Jacq.

Habit.—A medium-sized tree, 60′ to 80′ in height and 12″ to 24″ in diameter; characterized by a long, clear bole and short, dense, round-topped crown of spreading branches.

Leaves.—Alternate, simple, persistent, leathery, 3″ to 4″ long, 1½″ to 2½″ broad, mostly ovate to ovate-lanceolate; apex, acute or rounded; base, rounded or wedge-shaped; margin, slightly wavy, rolled under; bright green above, pale green below; petioles, stout, flattened, enlarged at the base, about ½″ long, falling away during their 2d or 3d season.

Flowers.—Perfect, appearing in the early spring, solitary or in few-flowered fascicles, borne along a slender, erect, terminal or axillary stalk forming a raceme, 2″ to 3″ in length; calyx, white, cup-shaped, 5-lobed, shorter than the stamens; petals, absent; stamens, orange to orange-yellow, their bases much enlarged and attached to the calyx; pistil, with a 3-angled, oblong ovary, short style, and 3 elongated, stigmatic lobes.

Fruit.—A thin-walled, light-brown nutlet, incased in a dark-red calyx tube with a thin, fleshy, astringent pulp; borne in short, open, erect, racemose clusters; seed, 3- to 6-lobed, red-brown.

Twigs.—Slender, zigzag, often contorted, yellowish orange, smooth, furnished with small, elongated lenticels; buds, sessile, naked, conical, concealed by the leaf base; leaf scars, nearly circular, with 3 to 5 bundle scars, not on the stem but borne on a persistent basal sheath, the ocrea, that encircles the stem at the node; the ocrea, upon falling, leaves an annular, encircling, stipular scar; pith large, whitish, continuous.

Bark.—Thin, smooth, dark reddish brown; scaly on the largest trees.

Habitat.—Hammocks and sandy soils near tide-water.

Distribution.—Southern Florida, West Indies, the Bahamas, and Venezuela.

Importance.—The fruit of this species is much sought after by doves of the region; hence the name *doveplum*. The heavy, dark-reddish-brown wood has a limited use in furniture manufacture, and the tree is used as an ornamental throughout its range.

THE FOUR-O'CLOCK FAMILY

Nyctaginaceae

The Four-o'clock Family embraces about 20 genera and over 250 species, the majority herbaceous. A few shrubs, lianas, and trees occur in the tropics. The beautiful and highly colored Bougainvilleas of South America are used extensively for decorative purposes in the warmer regions of the United States. This family does not include any commercially important timber trees.

THE BLOLLIES

Torrubia Vell.

This genus numbers about 15 tropical species of trees and shrubs. Four extend into southern Florida, one of which becomes arborescent.

Longleaf Blolly

Torrubia longifolia (Heimerl) Britton

Habit.—A large shrub, or occasionally a small tree, 30′ to 40′ in height and 12″ to 20″ in diameter; in dense forests, developing a short, compact, round-topped crown; in open situations, producing a spreading crown of irregular contour supported by 2 or more, often greatly contorted stems.

Leaves.—Opposite or alternate, simple, persistent, 1″ to 2″ long, ½″ to 1″ wide, oblong-obovate; apex, rounded or notched; base, wedge-shaped; margin,

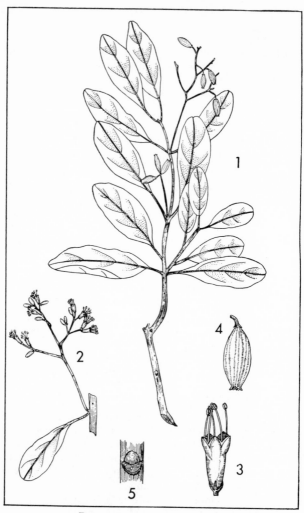

PLATE 73.—LONGLEAF BLOLLY

1. Foliage and fruit ×½.   2. Cluster of flowers ×½.   3. Flower
×3.   4. Fruit ×2.   5. Leaf scar ×2.

thickened, wavy; light green, smooth above, paler, glabrous below; petioles, stout, grooved, about ½″ long.

Flowers.—Perfect or unisexual, appearing in the fall in few-flowered, terminal or axillary clusters; calyx, funnel-shaped, 5-lobed, greenish yellow; petals, none; stamens, 5 to 8; pistil, with an ovoid ovary and long, narrow style crowned with 5 to 8 short, triangular, stigmatic lobes.

Fruit.—A light-brown, cylindrical nutlet enclosed in an enlarged, red, fleshy calyx tube with 10 longitudinal, rounded ribs, about ½″ long.

Twigs.—Slender, orange-yellow, smooth; buds, ovoid to hemispherical, rusty-red and woolly; leaf scars, raised, lunate to semicircular, with 3 to 5 bundle scars; stipule scars, absent; pith, homogeneous.

Bark.—Thin, even on the largest trunks, reddish brown, superficially scaly.

Habitat.—Near tidewater and in hammocks somewhat removed from the seacoast.

Distribution.—Southern peninsular Florida and neighboring Keys, Cuba, and the Bahamas.

Importance.—Of no commercial or medicinal value.

Remarks.—This species is easily confused with a Bahamian form, *T. obtusata* Britt., which has larger, thicker leaves.

THE MAGNOLIA FAMILY

Magnoliaceae

The Magnolia Family comprises 10 genera and approximately 80 species ranging from small shrubs to magnificent trees widely distributed in temperate and subtropical areas of both North America and Asia. Representatives of 4 genera are to be found in the United States, and 2 of these include arborescent forms, all of which occur in our southern forests.

Because of their handsome foilage and large, showy flowers, many are suitable for ornamental planting.

Synopsis of Southern Arborescent Genera

Genus	Leaves	Flowers	Fruit
Magnolia	unlobed	stamens, opening on side toward center of flower	a conelike cluster of follicles
Liriodendron	4-lobed	stamens, opening on side toward the petals	a conelike cluster of terminally winged samaras

THE MAGNOLIAS

Magnolia L.

There are about 35 species of *Magnolia*, 9 of which are natives of the United States. All are found in the southern states, and most of them, because of their beautiful, tropiclike foilage and large, showy flowers and fruits, are widely planted as ornamentals. A few are hardy as far north as Massachusetts, but they flourish best in the South and are particularly well known in the Carolinas and Virginia. Only 2 species are valued as timber trees; the dried flower buds of others have had a limited medicinal use.

KEY TO THE SOUTHERN MAGNOLIAS

1. Leaves, evergreen...................................... 2
1. Leaves, deciduous.................................... 3

    2. Leaves, 6″ to 10″ long, with rusty-red, woolly hairs on the lower surface; fruit, orange-red, woolly.....
                    Southern magnolia (p. 277)
    2. Leaves, 4″ to 6″ long, with a whitish bloom on the lower surface, aromatic when crushed; fruit, dark red, smooth...................**Sweetbay** (p. 280)

3. Leaves, more or less wedged-shaped at the base...... 4
3. Leaves, with earlike appendages at the base.......... 7

    4. Petals, greenish yellow to canary-yellow.......... 5
    4. Petals, chalky white............................ 6

5. Leaves, 6″ to 12″ long; petals, greenish yellow; twigs, smooth.....................**Cucumber-tree** (p. 282)
5. Leaves, 3″ to 6″ long; petals, canary-yellow; twigs, hairy.................**Yellow cucumber-tree** (p. 284)

    6. Leaves, 10″ to 20″ long, clustered near the tips of twigs, smooth and green below, falling in the early autumn; buds, smooth, purplish.................
            Umbrella magnolia (p. 285)
    6. Leaves, 4″ to 6″ long, evenly disposed along the twig, with a whitish bloom on the lower surface, tardily deciduous through the winter and early spring; buds, silky..............**Sweetbay** (p. 280)

7. Winter buds, smooth; leaves, mostly less than 12″ long; flowers, pale yellow or cream-colored................ 8
7. Winter buds, silky or woolly; leaves, mostly more than 15″ long; flowers, chalky white.................... 9

    8. Leaves, 10″ to 12″ long, spatula-shaped; petals, pale yellow, 5″ to 6″ long.....**Fraser magnolia** (p. 285)
    8. Leaves, 5″ to 9″ long, kite-shaped or like that of an inverted spearhead; petals, cream-colored, about 3″ long...............**Pyramid magnolia** (p. 287)

9. Leaves, 20″ to 30″ or more in length; fruit, nearly spherical..................**Bigleaf magnolia** (p. 288)
9. Leaves, 15″ to 20″ or more in length; fruit, nearly cylindrical..................**Ashe magnolia** (p. 288)

Southern Magnolia   Evergreen Magnolia
Magnolia grandiflora L.

Habit.—A moderately large tree, 60′ to 90′ in height with a trunk 2′ to 3′ in diameter (rarely 130′ by 4½′); bole, straight and clear for a considerable por-

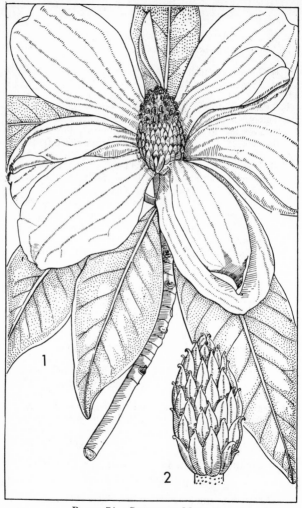

PLATE 74.—SOUTHERN MAGNOLIA
1. Foliage and flower $\times\frac{1}{2}$.   2. Fruit $\times\frac{1}{2}$.

tion of its length and passing through a narrow, pyramidal crown; open-grown trees, developing a rapidly tapering bole, which is completely clothed in a broad, evergreen, conical crown of pleasing symmetry.

Leaves.—Alternate, simple, persistent, leathery, oval, ovate, or oblong, 5″ to 8″ long, 2″ to 3″ wide; apex, bluntly pointed or, rarely, tapered to a sharp point; base, wedge-shaped; margin, entire; bright lustrous green above, clothed with rusty-red, woolly hairs on the lower surface; petiole, short, stout, covered with matted, rusty-red hairs; stipules, leafy, encircling the twig.

Flowers.—Complete, large and showy, 6″ to 8″ broad, appearing after the leaves; sepals, 3; petals, white, 6, 9, or 12, 3″ to 4″ long; stamens, many; pistils, many, spirally inserted on a spikelike receptacle.

Fruit.—An ovoid to nearly cylindrical aggregate of hairy, orange-red follicles, 3″ to 4″ in length, 1½″ to 2″ in diameter; seeds, red, about ½″ long, slightly flattened, suspended from the open pods by slender, elastic threads.

Twigs.—Moderately stout, often clothed with rusty-red, woolly hairs; terminal buds, woolly, 1″ to 1½″ long; lateral buds, similar but smaller; leaf scars, more or less shield-shaped, with a marginal row of bundle scars; stipule scars, prominent, encircling the twig above the leaf scar; pith, often indistinctly diaphragmed.

Bark.—Light brown to gray-brown and irregularly scaly.

Habitat.—On rich bottom lands or on gentle, protected slopes in admixture with other hardwood species.

Distribution.—Coastal plain from North Carolina to Florida, west through Louisiana and Arkansas to eastern Texas.

Importance.—One of the South's finest evergreens; used ornamentally throughout the region; cut in limited quantity for lumber.

Sweetbay

Magnolia virginiana L.

Habit.—A small tree, 20′ to 30′ in height with a trunk 1′ to 1½′ in diameter, supporting a head of nearly erect or spreading branches; in many localities, merely a shrub.

Leaves.—Alternate, simple, in the North falling in November, persistent until spring in the Deep South, where they remain green until dropped; oblong to elliptical, 4″ to 6″ long, 1″ to 3″ wide; apex, bluntly pointed or rounded; base, wedge-shaped; margin, entire or somewhat wavy; bright lustrous green above, with a whitish bloom below; petioles, short; stipules, leafy.

Flowers.—Complete, white, fragrant, 2″ to 3″ broad, borne on short, slender, smooth stalks and appearing after the leaves; sepals, 3; petals, 9 or 12, obovate; stamens, many; pistils, many, spirally inserted on a spikelike receptacle.

Fruit.—An ovoid to ellipsoidal aggregate of smooth, dark-red follicles, about 2″ in length and 1″ in diameter; seeds, oval, flattened, red, about ¼″ long, suspended from the open pod by slender, filamentous, elastic threads.

Twigs.—Slender, bright green, hairy, becoming reddish brown and smooth after the 1st winter; terminal buds, ovoid, clothed with white, silky hairs, about ¾″ long; lateral buds, similar but smaller; leaf scars, half-round to crescent-shaped, with numerous bundle scars arranged in a marginal band; stipule scars, encircling the twig; pith, diaphragmed.

Bark.—Gray-brown, superficially scaly on the largest trunks.

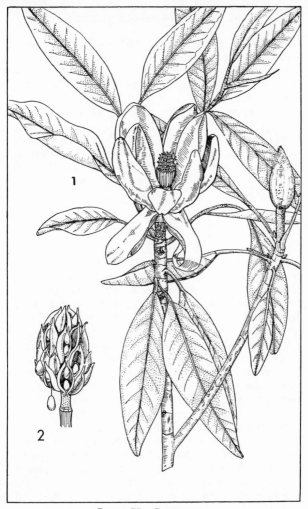

PLATE 75.—SWEETBAY
1. Foliage and flower ✕½.   2. Fruit ✕½.

Habitat.—Swamps, swales, and moist, low ground, occasionally in thickets.

Distribution.—Atlantic coastal plain from Massachusetts to Georgia; west to Franklin County, in Pennsylvania.

Importance.—Generally regarded as a weed tree; used sparingly as an ornamental.

Remarks.—A form with narrow leaves and woolly twigs and fruit stalks has been observed in Florida. This is often a tree 75′ to 90′ in height and up to 3′ in diameter and is designated as *M. virginiana* var. *australis* Sarg.

Cucumber-Tree

Magnolia acuminata L.

Habit.—A tree, 70′ to 80′ in height and 3′ to 4′ in diameter above a slightly buttressed base; the bole of the forest tree is symmetrical and usually clear for a considerable portion of its length, the crown short, dense, and pyramidal, the root system shallow and spreading.

Leaves.—Alternate, simple, deciduous, mostly elliptical to oval or ovate, 6″ to 12″ long, 3″ to 6″ wide; apex, acute; base, wedge-shaped or rounded; margin, entire, often somewhat wavy; smooth, yellow-green above, somewhat hairy below; petioles, slender, about 1″ long; stipules, leafy, encircling the twig.

Flowers.—Complete, bell-shaped, 2″ to 3″ broad, borne on stout stalks ½″ to 1″ long, appearing after the leaves; sepals, 3; petals, 6, greenish yellow, tongue-shaped; stamens, many; pistils, many, spirally arranged upon a spikelike receptacle.

Fruit.—A nearly cylindrical aggregate of dark-red follicles, 2″ to 3″ in length; seeds, red, about ½″ long; at maturity, suspended from the ovary wall by a slender, gummy filament.

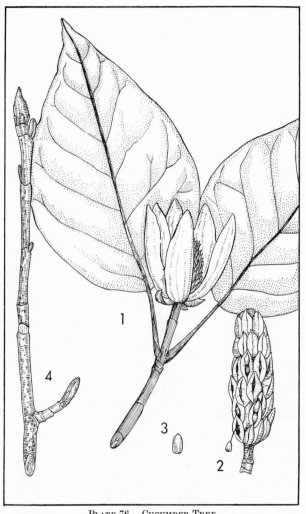

PLATE 76.—CUCUMBER-TREE
1. Foliage and flower ×⅓. 2. Fruit ×½. 3. Seed ×½.
4. Twig ×⅔.

Twigs.—Moderately stout, reddish brown, with many small lenticels; terminal buds, present, about ¾″ long, densely clothed with silky, silvery-white hairs; lateral buds, similar but smaller; leaf scars, horseshoe-shaped, with 5 to 9 bundle scars; stipule scars, encircling the twig; pith, homogeneous.

Bark.—Dark brown, broken into longitudinal, scaly ridges separated by narrow fissures.

Distribution.—Central New York, west through the Ohio River Valley to eastern Oklahoma; south to northern Georgia, south-central Alabama, central Mississippi, and Arkansas.

Habitat.—Moist, deep, fertile, loose-textured soils on low, gentle slopes and on stream banks in association with a diversity of broadleaved species.

Importance.—A tree of limited ornamental use. The wood is similar to that of yellow-poplar and is used for the same purposes.

Yellow Cucumber-Tree

Magnolia acuminata var. *cordata* (Michx.) Sarg.

This is a small and exceedingly rare tree, of natural occurrence but commonly cultivated as an ornamental in many localities because of its canary-yellow or orange-colored flowers. Michaux first described this tree about 125 years ago, but it was not until 1913 that it was rediscovered growing naturally out of cultivation. It is now known to exist in several localities in the following Georgia counties, namely, Oconee, Oglethorpe, Richmond, Clarke, and Hancock. Ashe (2) has reported its occurrence in Moore County, North Carolina.

Yellow cucumber-tree is readily identified by its deciduous, 4″ to 6″, oblong-obovate leaves, small, canary-yellow or rarely orange-colored blossoms, and small, oblong, smooth, dark-red fruits, 1″ to 1½″ in length.

Umbrella Magnolia

Magnolia tripetala L.

The umbrella magnolia derives its name from the characteristic manner in which its enormous leaves are usually disposed. Instead of being normally spaced along a branchlet, they occur in crowded, spirally arranged clusters near the tips of the twigs and simulate an open umbrella.

This is a large shrub or small tree seldom over 35′ tall and is usually found near streams or in moist bottom lands along the coastal plain and Piedmont plateau from Virginia to Georgia. It has also been observed infrequently in the mountains to the west.

Umbrella magnolia is characterized by large, broadly elliptical leaves, 10″ to 20″ long; large, ill-scented, cream-colored flowers, 10″ to 12″ wide, with 3 sepals and 6 or 9 petals; rose-red fruits, 2″ to 4″ long; and large, smooth, purple terminal buds. Its bark is light gray and smooth. This tree enjoys a limited ornamental use locally and abroad.

Fraser Magnolia   Mountain Magnolia

Magnolia fraseri Walt.

Habit.—A small mountain tree, 30′ to 40′ in height with a trunk 1′ to 1½′ in diameter; sometimes branching at or near the ground into a number of stout stems to form a large, dense clump or producing a single stem, which supports a short, spreading head.

Leaves.—Alternate, simple, deciduous, obovate or in the form of a spatula, 10″ to 12″ long, 6″ to 7″ wide (sometimes much larger); apex, usually blunt-pointed; base, with a pair of earlike appendages; margin, entire or wavy; lustrous bright green above, paler and smooth below; petioles, 2″ to 4″ long; stipules, foliaceous, surrounding the twig.

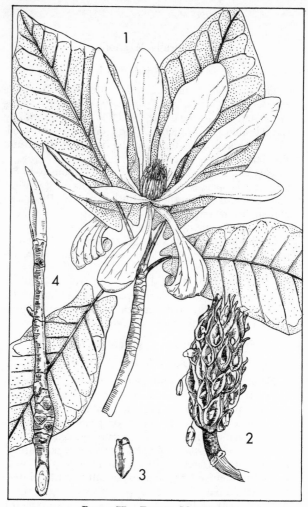

PLATE 77.—FRASER MAGNOLIA
1. Foliage and flower ×⅓. 2. Fruit ×⅓. 3. Seed ×½.
4. Twig ×½.

Flowers.—Complete; borne on stout stalks about 1″ long, pale yellow, aromatic, 8″ to 10″ in diameter; sepals, 3, 4″ to 5″ long, early deciduous; petals, 6 or 9, pale yellow; stamens, many; pistils, many, spirally arranged upon a spikelike receptacle.

Fruit.—An oblong, bright-red, smooth aggregate of follicles, 4″ to 5″ long; seeds, obovoid, flattened, red, about ¾″ long.

Twigs.—Stout, brittle, swollen near the tip, reddish brown, marked with prominent lenticels; terminal buds, 1″ to 2″ long, smooth, purple; lateral buds, similar but very much smaller; leaf scars, large, broadly U-shaped to shield-shaped, with numerous scattered bundle scars; stipule scars, encircling the twig; pith, homogeneous.

Bark.—Thin, smooth, dark brown, becoming somewhat scaly on the largest trees.

Habitat.—On cool soils on sheltered mountain slopes and in coves, and in protected valleys along watercourses.

Distribution.—Virginia and Kentucky south along the Appalachians to Georgia and west to Alabama.

Importance.—Cultivated to some extent as an ornamental in the southeastern United States and warmer portions of Europe.

Pyramid Magnolia

Magnolia pyramidata Pursh.

The pyramid magnolia is a small tree of local and rare occurrence found only in low, moist situations from southern Georgia west through northwestern Florida to Louisiana. This tree closely resembles the Fraser magnolia but may be distinguished from that species by its smaller (5″ to 9″ long, 3″ to 4″ wide), kite-shaped leaves, small, cream-colored flowers, and rose-tinted, oblong fruits, which are seldom more than

$2\frac{1}{2}''$ long.   This magnolia has been used sparingly as an ornamental in warmer localities of Europe.

Bigleaf Magnolia

Magnolia macrophylla Michx.

This is another of our southern magnolias of rare and local occurrence.   It occurs sparsely, usually as an occasional tree or in small clumps, along the western edge of the Piedmont plateau from North Carolina to Florida, thence westward to Kentucky and Louisiana. Individual trees $50'$ in height and up to $12''$ in diameter have been observed.   The tree is readily identified by its enormous leaves ($20''$ to $30''$ long, $9''$ to $12''$ wide), large, chalky-white flowers ($10''$ to $18''$ wide), and nearly globular, rose-red, hairy fruits.   Like other magnolias this species is also cultivated as an ornamental.

Ashe Magnolia

Magnolia ashei Weatherby

This shrub or small tree occurs only in Okaloosa, Santa Rosa, and Walton Counties, Florida, where it is usually found bordering the watercourses of that area.   It is similar in appearance to the bigleaf magnolia but can be distinguished by its somewhat shorter and slightly wider leaves, smaller flowers, and oblong to cylindrical fruit clusters up to $5''$ in length.

THE YELLOW-POPLARS

Liriodendron L.

This is a small genus of trees comprising but two species.   One, the Chinese tuliptree, is a native of central Asia; the other, yellowpoplar, is a large tree of widespread distribution through eastern North America.

Yellow-Poplar   Tuliptree

Liriodendron tulipifera L.

Habit.—One of the largest of eastern forest trees, often 100′ to 200′ in height and 4′ to 6′ (rarely up to 12′) in diameter; in the forest, developing a long, clear shaft surmounted by a broad, spreading, often oblong crown; in open situations, developing a long, narrow, pyramidal crown of pleasing symmetry; root system, deep and widespread.

Leaves.—Alternate, simple, deciduous, tuliplike, 4″ to 6″ long and broad, usually 4-lobed with the 2 lower lobes the broadest; apex, flattened or notched; base, flattened or somewhat rounded; margin of the lobes, entire; dark lustrous green and smooth above, paler below; petioles, slender, 4″ to 6″ long; stipules, foliaceous, persistent through the growing season on vigorous shoots.

Flowers.—Complete, appearing after the leaves, cup-shaped, 1½″ to 2″ wide; sepals, 3, greenish white; petals 6, in 2 rows of 3, light green, with brilliant orange, rounded bases; stamens, many; pistils, many, spirally inserted on a spikelike receptacle.

Fruit.—A conelike aggregate of terminally winged samaras; each samara, about 1½″ long.

Twigs.—Slender to moderately stout, reddish brown, sometimes with a purplish bloom, with many small lenticels; terminal buds, about ½″ long, flattened, the two outer valvate scales giving it the appearance of a duck's bill, green, purplish, or brownish red; lateral buds, similar but smaller; leaf scars, nearly circular, with many scattered bundle scars; stipule scars, encircling the twig, giving the whole a jointed appearance; pith, diaphragmed.

Bark.—On young stems, dark green, becoming gray with small, white patches, later streaked with narrow,

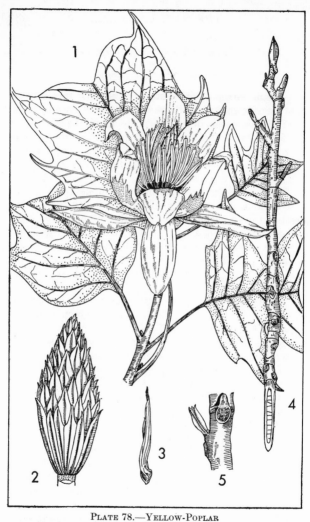

PLATE 78.—YELLOW-POPLAR

1. Foliage and flower ×½. 2. Aggregate of samaras ×⅔.
3. Single samara ×⅔. 4. Twig ×1. 5. Leaf scar ×1⅓.

irregular lines, finally deeply furrowed between ashy-gray, interlacing, rounded ridges; inner bark, with a spicy aroma but bitter to the taste.

Habitat.—Most abundant on moist but well-drained, loose-textured soils of flats and slopes. Often forming small, nearly pure thickets during juvenile development, but occurring only as an occasional tree in old stands. Its most common associates are sweet-gum, cucumbertree, basswood, numerous oaks and hickories, black cherry, black walnut, and white pine.

Distribution.—Southern New England (Rhode Island) west to Michigan, south to Florida and Louisiana.

Importance.—This is one of the most important of southern hardwoods. The wood is comparatively soft, easily worked, and suitable for a variety of products. Because of its porosity, lightness, strength, and ability to take glue, it is commonly used for cores and crossbands in the fabrication of built-up furniture. Compressed yellow-poplar wood has the ability to return to its normal shape when pressure is removed, and because of this property it is an ideal material for barrel bungs. Yellow-poplar is also used for interior trim, aircraft construction, paneling, wooden novelties, and many other purposes. The tree makes a desirable ornamental. The Indians of Pennsylvania and Virginia used the long, clean boles in making dugout canoes.

THE CUSTARD-APPLE FAMILY

Annonaceae

This family comprises a group of over 70 genera and 600 species of evergreen and deciduous trees and shrubs, the majority tropical and most abundant in the forests of the Old World. Various parts of these plants, that is, leaves, flowers, fruits, roots, and barks, contain aromatic substances that are extensively used in the tropics as spices and in the preparation of medicinal extracts and perfumes. Many species produce large, palatable fruits, and others are used in decorative plantings because of their showy flowers and handsome foliage.

Two genera, each with a single arborescent species, represent this family in our southern forests.

Synopsis of Southern Genera

Genus	Leaves	Flowers	Fruit
Asimina	deciduous	with purple or white petals, imbricate in the bud	simple, developed from a single pistil with many ovules
Annona	persistent or tardily deciduous	with yellow or white petals, valvate in the bud	compound, developed from several pistils, each with a single ovule

THE PAWPAWS

Asimina Adans.

These are a North American genus with eight species, one of which becomes arborescent. The seven remaining species are small shrubs scattered along the south Atlantic and Gulf coastal regions of the southeastern United States.

Pawpaw

Asimina triloba (L.) Dunal

Habit.—A large shrub, or sometimes a small tree, 25′ to 35′ in height and 10″ to 15″ in diameter. The bole is usually slender and passes through a short, dense, round-topped head. In open situations, the

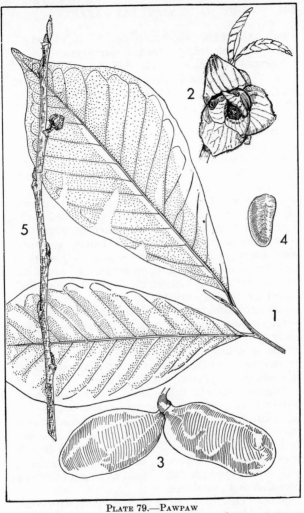

PLATE 79.—PAWPAW
1. Foliage ×⅓. 2. Flower ×2. 3. Fruit ×½. 4. Seed ×1.
5. Twig ×¾.

crown assumes a graceful, pyramidal habit, which makes this tree desirable for ornamental use.

Leaves.—Alternate, simple, deciduous, 10″ to 12″ long, 4″ to 6″ broad, obovate-oblong; apex, acute; base, wedged-shaped; margins, entire; light green above, paler below; with short, stout petioles, about 1″ long.

Flowers.—Appearing before or with the leaves from separate buds above the leaf scars on twigs of the previous season; perfect, solitary, about 2″ in diameter when fully developed; calyx, composed of 3 light-green, ovate, hairy, early-deciduous sepals; petals, 6, in 2 series of 3, longer than the sepals, purple, deeply veined, the outer 3 ovate, rounded, or pointed at the strongly reflexed apex, the inner 3 pointed, glandular, erect; stamens, many, inserted on a globular receptacle with short filaments and separated anther sacs; pistils, 3 to 15, crowning the receptacle and extending beyond the stamen masses, the ovary, 1-celled, with numerous ovules, surmounted by an oblong style, which terminates in a slightly curved, stigmatic apex.

Fruit.—An oblong to nearly cylindrical, yellow berry with white or yellowish flesh, rounded or pointed at the extremities, 3″ to 5″ long, 1″ to 1½″ thick, containing several shiny, dark-brown, flattened seeds; the pulp (when yellow), sweet and edible.

Twigs.—Slender, light brown, rusty-pubescent; terminal buds, naked, rusty-pubescent, about ½″ long; lateral buds, about ⅛″ long, superposed; flower buds, globose; leaf buds, oblong; leaf scars, crescent-to horseshoe-shaped, with 5 or 7 (mostly 5) bundle scars; stipule scars, absent; pith, white, continuous, with firmer, greenish diaphragms, at length becoming brownish and chambered.

Bark.—Thin, dark brown to silvery gray, with large, grayish blotches, marked by numerous wartlike excrescences or smooth.

Habitat.—Deep, rich, moist soil along streams and in bottoms; usually an understory species in association with other hardwoods; in some localities, particularly the lower Mississippi River Valley, forming vast, dense thickets on moist bottom lands.

Distribution.—New Jersey west to southern Michigan, thence south to northern Florida and eastern Texas.

Importance.—Pawpaw is of no importance in the production of timber. The fruits, however, are occasionally offered for sale locally; but, because of their perishable nature, they are never on the market for any length of time. Moreover, there appear to be two types of fruit, one with a yellow flesh, the other with a white pulp. The latter is rather tasteless and the less desirable of the two. Susceptible persons may develop a dermatitis from handling either of them. Michaux (51) reports, "At Pittsburgh some persons have succeeded in making from it a spirituous liquor; but, notwithstanding this experiment, very feeble hopes can be entertained of cultivating the tree with profit for this purpose." Sargent (65) asserts that the fibrous inner bark makes an excellent fish stringer.

THE POND-APPLES
Annona L.

The pond-apples comprise a group of about 50 trees and shrubs, mostly aromatic evergreens, widely distributed through the warmer and tropical regions of both hemispheres. A single arborescent form is found in peninsular Florida and adjacent Keys.

Pond-Apple
Annona glabra L.

Habit.—A small to medium-sized tree, 40′ to 50′ in height and 12″ to 20″ in diameter above the large,

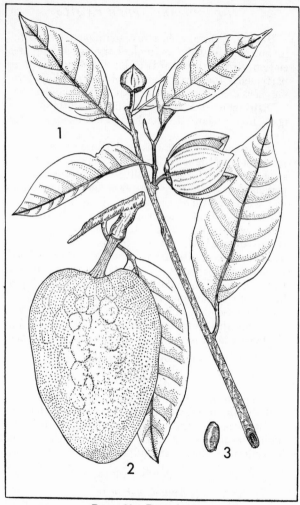

PLATE 80.—POND-APPLE
1. Foliage and flowers ×½. 2. Fruit ×½. 3. Seed ×½.

swollen, buttressed base. The bole tapers rapidly and is ultimately lost in a spreading crown of contorted branches.

Leaves.—Alternate, simple, tardily deciduous, leathery, 3″ to 5″ long, 1½″ to 2″ broad, oblong to elliptical; apex, acute; base, rounded or wedge-shaped; margin, entire; bright green above, pale below; with short, stout petioles, about ½″ long.

Flowers.—Appearing with or after the leaves from separate flower buds; about 1″ in diameter when fully developed; perfect, solitary, drooping; calyx, composed of 3 green sepals, loosely united at the base, deciduous; petals, 6, in 2 series of 3, longer than the sepals, yellow to dirty white, the outer 3 the larger and with a bright-red spot near their base on the inner surface, ovate, thick and fleshy, 3-angled at the apex; stamens, many, clustered on the receptacle, with short filaments; pistils, many, separate or united, inserted at the apex of the receptacle, the ovary 1-celled, surmounted by a slender style with an apical, oblong stigma.

Fruit.—Compound, an aggregate of berries, 3″ to 5″ long, 2″ to 3½″ wide, ovoid, yellow, aromatic; the numerous seeds, obovoid, winged along the margin, about ½″ long.

Twigs.—Slender, yellowish brown, commonly angular, with small wartlike excrescences; terminal buds, naked, rusty-pubescent, about ¼″ long; lateral buds, minute, hairy; leaf scars, raised, U-shaped to horseshoe-shaped, with 5 to 7 slitlike, sunken bundle scars; stipule scars, absent; pith, brownish, continuous.

Bark.—Thin, dark reddish brown, on the largest trunks divided by broad, shallow fissures into flat, superficially scaly ridges.

Habitat.—Along streams and in swamps and shallow ponds, ordinarily as an understory tree; occasionally forming extensive pure stands.

Distribution.—Southern peninsular Florida, the Keys, the Bahamas, and the West Indies.

Importance.—This tree is of no commercial importance. The fruit while palatable is almost tasteless and is seldom eaten.

THE LAUREL FAMILY

Lauraceae

The Laurel Family includes about 45 genera and approximately 1,000 species of trees and shrubs, the majority evergreen. While most of the Lauraceae are tropical, a few extend into the Temperate Zones.

Many aromatic substances present in the leaves, stems, roots, and fruits have been commercially exploited. From Bois de Rose (*Aniba panurensis* Mey.) is obtained linaloa oil, a compound used in the manufacture of expensive perfumes. To *Cinnamomum camphora* Nees. is traceable the true camphor of commerce, and cinnamon and cassia barks are products of two other Asiatic members of this genus, namely, *C. zeylanicum* Breyn. and *C. cassia* Bl., respectively. A number of commercial oils and drugs, notably oil of anise and oil of sassafras, are also produced by members of this family. The avocado or alligator pear, now so widely cultivated throughout the tropics, is the fruit of *Persea gratissima* Gaet., a small tree originally native to the American tropics but now rapidly becoming naturalized in many other tropical countries.

A few commercial timbers of the Lauraceae find their way into the lumber markets of the world, but most of them are used only locally. *Endiandra palmerstoni* White, the walnut bean or Oriental walnut of eastern Australia, resembles American walnut (*Juglans nigra* L.) sufficiently closely (superficially at least) to permit of its substitution for this species. *Ocotea rodioei* (Schomb., Mez.), the British Guiana Demerara greenheart, long since has proved its worth in marine construction; this is exported in quantity, particularly to European ports, and small amounts are utilized along the American seacoasts; the gates of the Panama Canal locks were originally fabricated of this wood. The South African stinkwood (*O. bullata* Mey.) because of its strength, durability, color, and pleasing figure is also a cabinet wood and building timber of recognized merit.

Six genera, 4 with arborescent forms, have representatives in our southern forests.

Synopsis of Southern Arborescent Genera

Genus	*Leaves*	*Flowers*	*Fruit*
Persea	persistent, entire	perfect; stamens, 12; calyx, yellow to creamy white	blue-black; the persistent, lobed calyx, green
Ocotea	persistent, entire	perfect; stamens, 12; calyx, creamy white	blue-black, borne on a persistent, red calyx base
Sassafras	deciduous, lobed	imperfect, mostly dioecious; stamens, 9; calyx, yellowish green	blue; the persistent, lobed calyx, scarlet
Misanteca	persistent, entire	perfect; stamens, 9; calyx, purplish	dark blue, ⅓ enclosed in a red, woody, capsular calyx tube

THE PERSEAS

Persea Mill.

The perseas form a natural group of about 50 tropical and subtropical evergreen trees with naked buds and entire, aromatic leaves. Except for a single species that occurs in the Canary Islands, the group is restricted to the New World. Two species, both trees of secondary importance, are included in the woody flora of the South.

KEY TO THE SOUTHERN PERSEAS

1. Stalks supporting flower clusters, about 1″ long; leaves, mostly oblong, with a waxy bloom on the lower surface; twigs, only slightly hairy. . **Red bay persea** (p. 300)
1. Stalks supporting flower clusters, about 2½″ long; leaves, mostly elliptical, with rusty-red hairs on the midrib and principal veins below; twigs in their 1st season, clothed with a thick coat of rusty-red, woolly hairs . . . . **Swamp bay persea** (p. 303)

Red Bay Persea

Persea borbonia Spreng.

Habit.—A beautiful evergreen tree, sometimes 60′ to 70′ in height and 2′ to 3′ in diameter; in the forest, developing a clear, cylindrical bole and dense, pyramidal crown with ascending branches. The fleshy, yellowish roots are moderately deep and widespread.

Leaves.—Alternate, simple, persistent, aromatic, 3″ to 4″ long, 1″ to 1½″ wide, oblong-lanceolate to oblong; apex, pointed or rounded; base, rounded or broadly wedge-shaped; margin, entire, thickened, and curling under; bright green and lustrous above, paler and furnished with a waxy bloom on the lower surface; petioles, stout, rigid, grooved above, red-brown, about ½″ long.

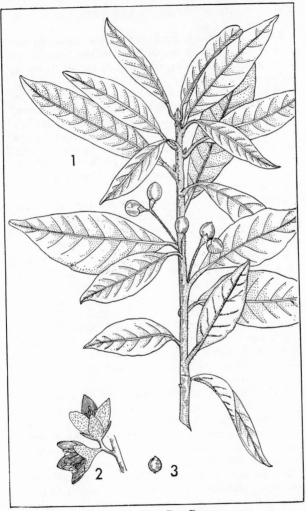

PLATE 81.—RED BAY PERSEA
1. Foliage and fruit ×½. 2. Flowers ×1. 3. Pit ×½.

Flowers.—Perfect, appearing in the spring in the axils of the new foliage, in few-flowered panicles on short, supporting stalks; occasionally terminal; calyx, bell-shaped, yellow or creamy white, 6-lobed, the lobes in 2 series, hairy on the back and on the margins, those of the inner series the longer; corolla, none; stamens, 12, divided into 3 series of 4, the inner row usually sterile, poorly developed, glandular at the base; filaments, flattened; anthers, 4-celled; pistil, with a nearly globular, sessile, 1-celled ovary surmounted by a slender style that terminates in a disclike stigma.

Fruit.—A small, bright-blue or shining-blue-black, obovoid drupe, seated on the persistent calyx base, with a large ovoid pit surrounded by a thin layer of rather dry flesh.

Twigs.—Slender, those of the current season somewhat 3-angled and minutely fluted, light brown, smooth except for a coating of pale or rusty-red hair when they first appear, at length becoming terete; terminal buds, naked, elongated, with 3 or 4 visible, scalelike leaves; lateral buds, smaller, about ¼″ long, ovoid, sessile, solitary or superposed; leaf scars, linear to elliptical, with a single occasionally decompounded, linear bundle scar; stipule scars, absent; pith, rounded, whitish, homogeneous.

Bark.—Reddish brown, divided by deep, irregular fissures into broad, flat, superficially scaly ridges.

Habitat.—On rich, moist soils along streams and borders of swamps in association with both conifers and broadleaved species; occasionally appearing on dry, sandy soils in association with longleaf pine.

Distribution.—Atlantic and Gulf coastal plains from southern Delaware to eastern Texas; north through Louisiana to southern Arkansas; also in southern peninsular Florida.

Importance.—This tree is probably known to many because of its aromatic leaves, which are the "bay leaves" used in spiced food products of all kinds and in soups. The wood is used sparingly in cabinetry and in interior finishing; at one time employed in boat construction.

Swamp Bay Persea

Persea palustris Sarg.

Swamp bay persea is a small tree, 30′ to 40′ in height and 10″ to 15″ in diameter, that frequents pine-barren swamps and river bottoms along the Atlantic and Gulf coastal plains from southern Virginia to southeastern Louisiana. It may be distinguished from the red bay persea by the rusty-red hairs on lower leaf surfaces, its densely hairy twigs, and flower or fruit clusters borne on long, supporting stalks.

THE NECTANDRAS

Nectandra Roland

These are a group of about 200 species of trees and shrubs largely confined to tropical forests of the New World extending from southern peninsular Florida to Brazil and Peru, but with a few species indigenous to South Africa and the Canary Islands. Several are important timber trees, and their woods are suitable for many purposes. A single species, the gulf ocotea, occurs in southern Florida.

Jamaica Nectandra

Nectandra coriacea (Sw.) Griseb.

Habit.—A large shrub, or sometimes a small tree, 20′ to 30′ in height and 12″ to 18″ in diameter; characterized by a small, symmetrical bole and narrow, rounded crown with short, spreading branches.

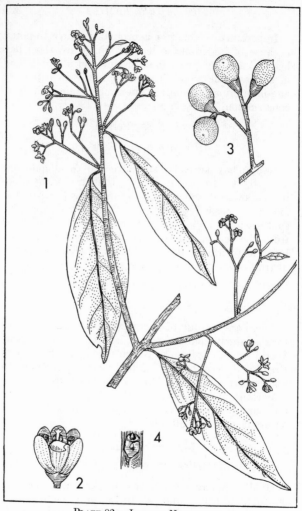

PLATE 82.—JAMAICA NECTANDRA
1. Foliage and flowers ×½.   2. Flower ×3.   3. Fruit cluster
×⅔.   4. Leaf scar ×1½.

Leaves.—Alternate, simple, persistent, leathery, 3″ to 6″ long, 1″ to 2″ broad, oblong to lance-shaped; apex, long-pointed; base, rounded or broadly wedge-shaped; margin, thickened, entire, and slightly rolled under; lustrous dark green above, the lower surface light green, often with a reddish tinge and commonly with pale hairs on the principal veins; petioles, flattened, about ½″ long.

Flowers.—Perfect, appearing in the early spring in the axils of the new leaves or occasionally from those of the previous season, borne in long panicles supported on slender, red stalks, 2″ to 4″ long; calyx, deciduous, bell-shaped, creamy white, 6-lobed, the lobes with dense, woolly inner surfaces, hairy along their margins and on their backs; corolla, none; stamens, 12, about one-half as long as the calyx lobes, in 3 series of 4, the inner series with abortive anthers and glandular; pistil, with an ovoid ovary, short, stout, erect style, and flattened, remotely lobed stigma.

Fruit.—A nearly spherical, lustrous, dark-blue or blue-black drupe, seated on the base of the red calyx tube; often tipped with the persistent base of the style; with a thin-shelled, reddish-brown pit surrounded by a layer of thin, dry flesh.

Twigs.—Slender, terete, reddish brown, smooth; buds, minute, frequently superposed; leaf scars, small, semicircular, with a single transverse or circular bundle scar; stipule scars, absent; pith, homogeneous, whitish, terete.

Bark.—Thin, dark reddish brown, and smooth except for numerous small irregular excrescences.

Habitat.—Seashores and hammocks in admixture with other species.

Distribution.—Southern tip of the Florida peninsula, and adjacent Keys; also in the Bahamas.

Importance.—Of no commercial or industrial value.

THE SASSAFRAS

Sassafras Nees.

This is a small genus including only three species of deciduous trees, one in China, another in Formosa, and the third a native of the eastern and southern United States.

Sassafras

Sassafras albidum (Nutt.)Nees.

Habit.—A medium-sized tree, occasionally 60′ to 80′ in height and 2′ to 3′ in diameter. A cylindrical bole rises above a moderately deep and spreading root system and often becomes lost in an ovoid to columnar crown with short, stout, contorted branches. In many localities scarcely ever more than a large shrub.

Leaves.—Alternate, simple, deciduous, aromatic, 4″ to 6″ long, 2″ to 4″ broad; of three sorts, all of which may be found on the same tree, namely, (1) entire and elliptical, (2) mitten-shaped (either right- or left-handed), and (3) 3-lobed; all are usually acute at the apex, wedge-shaped at the base, yellow-green above, pale green and commonly hairy along the veins below; petioles, stout, about 1″ long.

Flowers.—Unisexual, each sex borne on separate trees, usually appearing in racemes from terminal buds with the unfolding of the leaves; calyx, yellowish green, 6-lobed; corolla, none; stamens, 9, divided into 3 series of 3, the inner series sterile and glandular; pistil, with an ovoid ovary surmounted by an elongated style, which is crowned by a disclike, remotely lobed stigma.

Fruit.—A small, blue, ovoid drupe seated upon the thickened, scarlet calyx lobes and supported on scarlet stalks 1″ to 2″ long; the flesh, thin; pit, light brown.

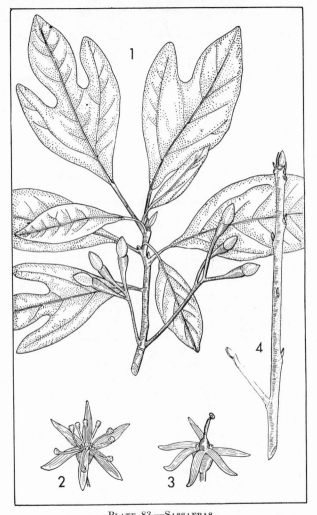

PLATE 83.—SASSAFRAS

1. Foliage and fruit $\times\frac{1}{2}$. 2. Male flower $\times 3$. 3. Female flower $\times 3$. 4. Twig $\times 1$.

Twigs.—Slender, those of the current season yellowish green, often clothed with appressed, velvety hair, at length reddish brown and smooth except for lenticels and roughened, corky patches; with an aromatic odor and spicy taste; terminal buds, globular, about ¼″ in diameter, with 3 or 4 visible scales, each with a single, central rib along its back; lateral buds, much smaller; leaf scars, half-round to crescent-shaped, raised, with a transverse bundle scar, which is often divided into 3 parts; stipule scars, lacking; pith, white, mucilaginous, remotely 5-angled in transverse section, continuous.

Bark.—Often 1″ or more in thickness, dark red-brown to cinnamon-red, divided by deep, irregular fissures into broad, flat ridges with heavy, thick, appressed scales; the inner bark, aromatic.

Habitat.—On dry, sandy soils, usually in association with other species; commonly found along fence rows and in abandoned fields; in the South, becoming a part of the montane flora and in the southern Appalachians ascending mountain slopes up to 4,000′.

Distribution.—Widely distributed throughout the eastern and southern United States from Maine to Iowa, south to Florida and Texas.

Importance.—Oil of sassafras, distilled from the bark, roots, and twigs, is used in the manufacture of flavoring extracts, scented soaps, and perfumes and in the preparation of certain pharmaceutical compounds. Michaux (51) reports at length upon the medicinal virtues of the sassafras and indicates that because of them the tree was among the first American plants to be introduced into Europe. During early colonial times a "spring tonic" was brewed from the roots and twigs, which sold on the market for 7 or 8 cents a pint under the name of *sassafras tea.*

Throughout the South during this same period, the countrypeople made a beer by boiling the twigs in water. To this infusion molasses was added and the whole allowed to ferment. In Louisiana the crushed dry leaves were used to thicken pottage.

Sassafras wood is extremely durable and is used for poles, posts, and crossties. Small quantities are also used for cooperage and cabinetry.

THE LICARIAS

Licaria Aubl.

These are a small genus of tropical evergreen trees consisting of only three species. Two are indigenous to Mexico, and the third extends northward from the West Indies to southern Florida.

Gulf Licaria

Licaria triandra (Sw.) Kosterm.

Habit.—A small tree, sometimes 35′ to 45′ in height and 12″ to 18″ in diameter; characterized by a broad crown with spreading and pendulous branches.

Leaves.—Alternate, simple, persistent, leathery, 3″ to 4″ long, 1″ to 2″ broad, broadly elliptical, oval, or ovate-lanceolate; apex, long-tapered and pointed; base, wedge-shaped; margin, entire, often wavy; lustrous dark green above, pale below; petioles, stout, about ½″ long, occasionally with minute wings near their apex.

Flowers.—Perfect, appearing in the spring in the axils of the new leaves in few-flowered clusters supported on short stalks; calyx, funnel-shaped, purplish, with 6 triangular, fleshy lobes; corolla, none; stamens, 9, in 3 series of 3, the inner rank sterile; pistil, with a smooth ovary, short, thick style, and headlike stigma.

Fruit.—An olive-shaped, dark-blue drupe, about 1″ long, one-third embedded in a thickened, light-red, cuplike calyx tube; with a thin, dry, flesh and a large, brittle pit.

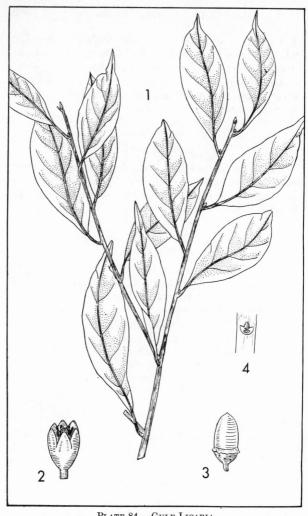

PLATE 84.—GULF LICARIA

1. Foliage ×½. 2. Flower ×3. 3. Fruit ×⅔. 4. Leaf scar ×2.

Twigs.—Slender, reddish brown, smooth at maturity, at first somewhat 3-angled but becoming terete in their 2d season, and with prominent, wartlike lenticels; buds, small, globular, with 2 or 3 overlapping scales; leaf scars, half-round to somewhat oblong, with a single, transverse, vascular bundle scar; stipule scars, absent; pith, continuous, whitish.

Bark.—Thin, reddish brown to gray-brown, superficially flaky.

Habitat.—Hammocks and occasionally near tidewater.

Distribution.—Dade County (Florida), Jamaica, and Cuba.

Importance.—Of no commercial or industrial importance.

THE CAPER FAMILY

Capparidaceae

The Caper Family comprises a group of about 35 genera and nearly 500 species of trees, shrubs, and herbs widely scattered through the warmer regions of the world. As a group, the family is of little economic importance. A few species are cultivated for decorative purposes, others produce timber that is used locally, and still others contain compounds suitable for pharmaceutical preparations.

Seven genera are represented by one or more species in our southern flora, but only one of them (*Capparis* L.) includes arborescent forms.

THE CAPERS

Capparis L.

These are a tropical genus of trees and shrubs, numbering more than 100 species and most abundant in South and Central America. Commercial capers,

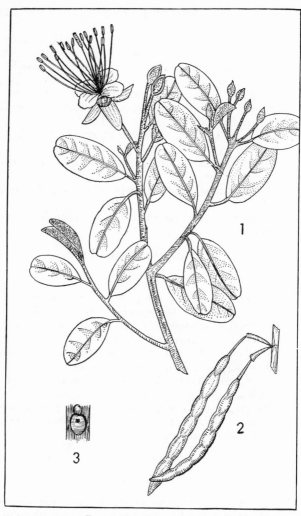

PLATE 85.—JAMAICA CAPER
1. Foliage and flowers ×½. 2. Fruit ×⅕. 3. Leaf scar ×2.

a widely used condiment, are the pickled flower buds of *C. spinosa* L., a shrub of the Mediterranean basin. Two West Indian species, one the shrubby dog caper (*C. flexulosa* (L.) L.), the other a small tree, range northward into southern Florida.

Jamaica Caper

Capparis cynophyllophora L.

Habit.—A small tree, commonly shrubby, scarcely ever more than 15' to 20' in height or 5" to 8" in diameter. The bole is commonly clothed for the greater part of its length in an evergreen, rounded crown.

Leaves.—Alternate, simple, persistent, somewhat leathery, 2" to 3" long, 1" to 1½" broad, oblong to broadly oval; apex, rounded or notched; base, rounded, occasionally flattened or remotely cordate; margins, entire, with a tendency to curl; yellow-green and smooth above, with minute, yellowish-brown scales on the lower surface; petioles, stout, about ½" long, covered with minute, yellowish-brown scales.

Flowers.—Perfect, regular, appearing in the early spring in terminal cymes; calyx, with 4 ovate, acute sepals, scaly on the back, glandular on the inner face; petals, 4, alternating with the sepals, white; stamens, 20 to 30, with deep-purple filaments and yellowish anthers, commonly 1" to 2" in length; pistil, with a long-stalked, 2-celled ovary and a circular disclike, sessile stigma.

Fruit.—A long-stalked, elongated, fleshy, podlike structure constricted at regular intervals throughout its length in such a way as to simulate a string of sausages, 9" to 12" long; the light-brown seeds, about 1" in length.

Twigs.—Slender, angular, yellowish gray, covered with minute, yellowish-brown scales; buds, naked; leaf scars, triangular to nearly oval, with a single crescent-shaped or linear bundle scar; stipule scars, absent; pith, white, continuous.

Bark.—Thin, red-brown, shallowly fissured and irregularly plated at the surface.

Habitat.—Sandy and gravelly soils near tidewater.

Distribution.—Southern Florida and many of the Keys, Jamaica, the Bahamas, and other West Indian islands.

Importance.—Of no commercial or industrial value.

THE WITCHHAZEL FAMILY
Hamamelidaceae

This family of trees and shrubs consists of 20 genera and about 50 species widely scattered through forests of North America, Africa, Asia, Madagascar, and the Malayan Archipelago. Two of the three North American genera have arborescent representatives in southern forests.

Storax, used in the preparation of soaps, is obtained from certain members of this family. Perfumes, incense, and various medicinal compounds are other commercial derivatives, and at least 3 genera include notable timber-producing species.

Synopsis of Southern Genera

Genus	Leaves	Flowers	Fruit	Buds
Liquidambar	lobed	unisexual, apetalous	borne in heads; seed, winged	scaly
Hamamelis	unlobed	bisexual, with a corolla	solitary; seed, unwinged	naked

THE SWEETGUMS
Liquidambar L.

The sweetgums comprise a group of four species, all large trees. Two of these are natives of Asia, a third is indigenous to South America, and the fourth occurs widespread through the eastern and southern United States.

Sweetgum Redgum

Liquidambar styraciflua L.

Habit.—A large tree, becoming 80′ to 150′ in height and 3′ to 5′ in diameter, with a buttressed base, long, clear, cylindrical bole, and pyramidal or oblong crown.

Leaves.—Alternate, simple, deciduous, 6″ to 7″ in diameter, more or less star-shaped, with 5 to 7 deeply palmate lobes; aromatic when bruised or crushed; apex, long-tapered; base, flattened or slightly heart-shaped; margin, finely serrate; glabrous, lustrous green above, paler below, with axillary tufts of hair; petioles, slender, often 4″ or more in length; stipules, about ½″ long.

Flowers.—Monoecious, in headlike clusters; the staminate clusters, borne in terminal, hairy racemes, 2″ to 3″ long; pistillate heads, globose, solitary, axillary, borne on long, slender stalks; staminate flowers, naked, with many stamens; pistillate flowers, composed of a minute calyx, 4 sterile stamens, and a 2-celled ovary.

Fruit.—A persistent, woody head of many 2-celled capsules, 1″ to 1½″ in diameter, each capsule usually containing 2 seeds; seeds, black, terminally winged, about ¼″ long.

Twigs.—Slender to moderately stout, yellowish to reddish brown, with a few scattered lenticels, aromatic, frequently more or less covered with corky outgrowths, which may become large and winglike after a season or two; terminal buds, acute, up to 1″ long, with several overlapping, orange-brown scales; lateral buds, similar but smaller; leaf scars, half-round, with 3 circular bundle scars; pith, homogeneous, star-shaped

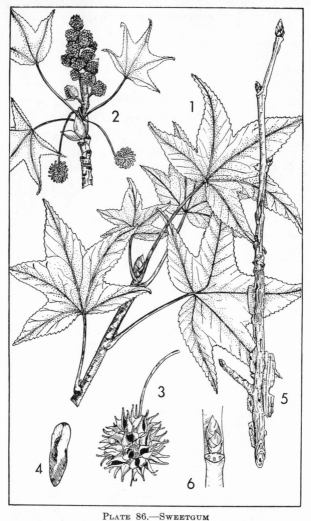

PLATE 86.—SWEETGUM

1. Foliage ✕⅓. 2. Heads of male (erect) and female (drooping) flower clusters ✕½. 3. Fruit ✕¾. 4. Seed ✕4. 5. Twig ✕¾. 6. Leaf scar ✕1.

in cross section; stipule scars, slitlike, comparatively inconspicuous.

Bark.—Gray to gray-brown, with deep furrows separating narrow, rounded, scaly ridges.

Habitat.—Typically a southern bottom-land tree that occurs most abundantly on moist, rich, alluvial soils in association with many other species; also common on abandoned fields, where it not infrequently forms dense, even-aged thickets; rarely found in abundance where soil drainage is poor.

Distribution.—Connecticut west through southeastern New York, southern Ohio, southern Missouri to eastern Oklahoma; south to central Florida in the East and eastern coastal Texas in the west.

Importance.—A valuable commercial hardwood used for many purposes, notably veneer, furniture, interior trim, and woodenware. The wood is often distributed and sold under the trade name of *satinwalnut*. Widely planted as an ornamental because of its brilliant autumn colors.

THE WITCHHAZELS

Hamamelis L.

This genus of shrubs and trees includes six species. These are equally divided between eastern Asia and eastern North America. Two witchhazels, both large shrubs or small trees, are natives of the South.

KEY TO SOUTHERN WITCHHAZELS

1. Leaves, smooth; winter buds, hairy, yellowish brown. .
    Common witchhazel (p. 318)
1. Leaves, warty; winter buds, woolly, reddish brown. . .
    Southern witchhazel (p. 320)

Common Witchhazel

Hamamelis virginiana L.

Habit.—A large shrub with several divergent stems, or less frequently a small tree, up to 30′ in height, with a single erect bole sometimes 1′ in diameter. The crown is usually spreading, of rather irregular contour, and often clothes the greater portion of the trunk.

Leaves.—Alternate, simple, deciduous, obovate, 4″ to 6″ long, 2″ to 3″ wide; apex, acuminate; base, unequal; margin, often coarsely shallowly lobed above the middle; dark green and glabrous above, paler below with hair on the midrib and principal veins; petiole, short and slender; stipules, lanceolate.

Flowers.—Perfect, opening from September to December, usually in 3-flowered terminal clusters, each flower with 2 or 3 bracts, a 4-parted calyx, and 4 long, straplike petals; stamens, 8, in 2 rows, the outer whorl usually sterile; pistil, with a 2-celled ovary surmounted by 2 spreading, tubular styles, each with a small, terminal stigma.

Fruit.—A 2-beaked, woody capsule, furnished at the base with a persistent calyx, about ½″ long; at maturity, splitting open along 2 lines of suture and forcibly ejecting the lustrous-black, oblong, unwinged seeds.

Twigs.—Slender, more or less zigzag, at first quite scurfy, later becoming glabrous, orange-brown to reddish brown or tawny, usually with numerous pale, inconspicuous lenticels; terminal buds, stalked, naked, hairy, tawny, about ½′ long; lateral buds, similar but smaller; leaf scars, half-round to 3-lobed, each with 3 bundle scars; stipule scars, inconspicuous, slit-like; pith, continuous.

Bark.—Thin, light brown, relatively smooth or scaly, the inner bark purplish.

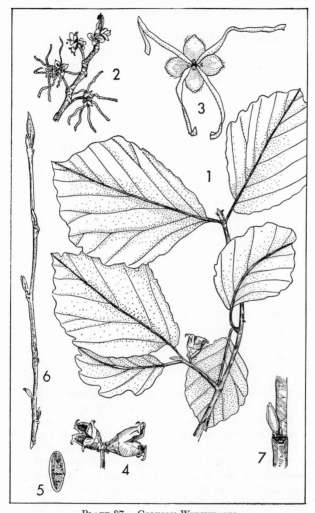

PLATE 87.—COMMON WITCHHAZEL

1. Foliage and fruit $\times\frac{1}{2}$. 2. Cluster of flowers $\times 1$. 3. Single
flower $\times 3$. 4. Fruit $\times 1$. 5. Seed $\times 2$. 6. Twig $\times\frac{3}{4}$. 7. Leaf
scar $\times 1\frac{1}{2}$.

Habitat.—On the banks of streams and margins of lakes, ponds, and swamps, and on moist, upland, forest soils, where it occurs as an understory species in mixed hardwood stands.

Distribution.—New Brunswick, Canada, west through southern Ontario to Minnesota and northeastern Iowa; south to Georgia in the East and Arkansas in the West.

Importance.—Common witchhazel is of no value as a timber tree, and its use as an ornamental is very limited; nevertheless, this species is one of the most widely known southern trees because of its purported supernatural powers when in the hands of "water diviners." Not only is it claimed that the witchhazel fork has the ability to indicate the presence of water when in the hands of such fakers, but in the past it has also been used by the unscrupulous in attempts to locate buried treasure and precious metals and ores.

The analgesic principle of witchhazel lotions and Hamamelis salves, used in treating minor skin irritations, is derived from the inner bark of this species.

Southern Witchhazel

Hamamelis macrophylla Pursh.

This small tree of the Deep South occurs along stream banks and borders of woodlands through southern Georgia, central and western Florida, central and southern Alabama and Mississippi, Louisiana, and eastern Texas. It attains greater stature than the preceding species and is easily identified by its somewhat smaller leaves with noticeably roughened lower surfaces, woolly, rusty-reddish-brown winter buds, and yellow flowers, which appear through the winter months. The twigs of this species are also used in the manufacture of salves and lotions.

THE SYCAMORE FAMILY

Platanaceae

The Sycamore Family, with only one genus, *Platanus,* comprises six or seven species of trees. Three of them are found in the United States, and one is widespread through our southern forests. The others, *P. wrightii* S. Wats. and *P. racemosa* Nutt., are natives of the Southwest and California, respectively. The London plane, so commonly used for street planting in this country, is probably a hybrid between our native sycamore and the oriental plane.

Sycamore   Buttonwood   Planetree

Platanus occidentalis L.

Habit.—A large tree, 100′ to 170′ in height, with a straight or leaning trunk, 3′ to 14′ in diameter; usually branching about 20′ to 80′ above the ground into a massive, spreading, open, somewhat irregular, pendulous head.

Leaves.—Alternate, simple, deciduous, broadly ovate, 4″ to 7″ (rarely up to 14″) in diameter, palmately 3- to 5-lobed, with broad, shallow sinuses; apex, long-tapered; base, flat or heart-shaped; margin, wavy, with short or long, tapering teeth; light green, glabrous above, with pubescence along the veins below; petioles, stout, 3″ to 5″ long, enclosing the lateral buds in their swollen bases; stipules, leafy, surrounding the twig, often persisting through the season.

Flowers.—Minute, appearing with the leaves in dense, stalked, unisexual heads; staminate heads, dark red, axillary, each flower with 3 to 6 minute sepals and 3 to 6 long-pointed petals; stamens, with short filaments and 2-celled anthers; pistillate, green or reddish green, on long, terminal stalks, each flower with 3 to

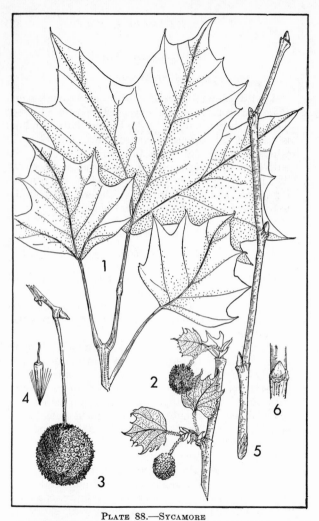

PLATE 88.—SYCAMORE

1. Foliage ×½. 2. Heads of male and female flowers ×½.
3. Head of fruit ×¾. 4. Single achene ×1. 5. Twig ×¾.
6. Leaf scar ×1.

6 small sepals and 3 to 6 large petals; sterile stamens, present; ovaries, narrowed into bright-red styles.

Fruit.—A persistent multiple of achenes, forming a head, 1″ in diameter, borne on slender stalks, 3″ to 6″ long; achenes, elongated, obovoid, with a blunt apex and persistent style; seed, oval, yellow-brown.

Twigs.—Slender, zigzag, orange-brown, becoming gray; terminal buds, wanting; lateral buds, conic or slightly curved, divergent, with a single, brown, resinous scale; leaf scars, horseshoe-shaped, surrounding the bud; bundle scars, 5 to 9, large, distinct; stipule scars, encircling the twig; pith, homogeneous.

Bark.—Thin, at first creamy white, becoming brown, and later mottled by the formation of large, deciduous, platelike scales; inner bark, whitish or greenish; bark near the base of old trunks, becoming brown, furrowed, and scaly.

Habitat.—Moist, rich soil on margins of streams and lakes or on rich bottoms.

Distribution.—From southern Maine through New York to Ontario, Michigan, central Iowa, and eastern Nebraska; south to Texas and thence east to northern Florida.

Importance.—Occasionally planted as an ornamental but of greater value as a source of wood for boxes, crates, baskets, yokes, furniture, butcher's blocks, automobile parts, cooperage, and woodenware; also suitable for planting along watercourses, where its interlacing roots serve to retard erosion of stream banks and levees.

THE ROSE FAMILY

Rosaceae

The Rose Family includes many valuable economic plants in the more than 100 genera and 2,000 species of herbs, shrubs, and trees that it embraces. From the standpoint of timber production it is relatively unimportant; but to the horticulturist and floriculturist the Rosaceae are of foremost interest, and innumerable varieties of plants with showy flowers have been developed for decorative purposes. Included in this group are such well-known ornamentals as the laurelcherries, mountainashes, hawthorns, flowering crabs, spireas, ninebarks, roses, cotoneasters, firethorns, flowering quince, and pearlbushes. To this family are traceable also the valuable pome and stone fruits such as apple, pear, quince, cherry, plum, peach, and raspberry. Notable among the perennial herbaceous forms are the strawberries. The black cherry is the only arborescent tree in the South productive of timber of cabinet rank.

Seven genera of the family are represented in the South by one or more arborescent species.

Synopsis of Southern Arborescent Genera

Genus	Leaves	Flowers	Fruit
Malus	simple, deciduous	on spurs in few-flowered terminal racemes	a pome with papery carpels
Sorbus	pinnate, deciduous	in large, terminal, compound cymes	a pome with papery carpels
Amelanchier	simple, deciduous	in terminal racemes	a pome with papery carpels
Crataegus	simple, deciduous	in terminal, cymose corymbs	a pome with bony carpels

Genus	Leaves	Flowers	Fruit
Prunus	simple, deciduous	in fascicled axillary umbels or corymbs, or in terminal racemes	a 1-seeded drupe with globular or flattened stone
Laurocerasus	simple, persistent	in axillary racemes	a 1-seeded drupe with a globular stone
Chrysobalanus	simple, persistent	in terminal or axillary, cylindrical cymes	a 1-seeded drupe with an angular stone

THE CRABS AND APPLES

Malus Mill.

This is a group of approximately 25 trees and shrubs widely distributed through the forests of the Northern Hemisphere. The common apple (*M. pumila* Mill.) was originally introduced from Europe during early colonial times and has long since escaped cultivation over much of the eastern United States. Pomologists have developed over 3,000 varieties of this species, many of which may be found in the nation's orchards. Measured in terms of culture and production, the apple is by far the most important fruit of temperate climates. The small-fruited apples used in jelly making are popularly known as the *crabs* or *crabapples*. The horticulturist has also exhibited a keen interest in this group and has developed numerous varieties with showy flowers and fruits.

Nine crabs attain tree size in the southern states.

KEY TO THE SOUTHERN CRABS

1. Lower surfaces of leaves, hairy at maturity.......... 2
1. Lower surfaces of leaves, free from hair at maturity 4

2. Flower stalks and sepals, free of hair..............
$$\text{Buncombe crab (p. 328)}$$
2. Flower stalks and sepals, hairy or woolly.......... 3

3. Leaves, oblong to lance-shaped, sharply serrate.......
$$\text{Missouri crab (p. 329)}$$
3. Leaves, elliptical, ovate, or oblong-ovate, nearly entire
or often finely toothed........Louisiana crab (p. 329)

4. Leaves, usually rounded or bluntly pointed at the
apex....................Southern crab (p. 326)
4. Leaves, usually acute or long-tapered at the apex.. 5

5. Leaves, triangular-ovate, broadest at the base........ 6
5. Leaves, oval, elliptical, lance-shaped, or ovate, broadest
near the middle.................................. 7

6. Leaves, heart-shaped at the base, pale green below.
$$\text{Biltmore crab (p. 329)}$$
6. Leaves, rounded at the base, with a pale, waxy
bloom below................Dunbar crab (p. 329)

7. Leaves of flower-bearing branches, oval or ovate, with
incisely serrate margins....Wild sweet crab (p. 330)
7. Leaves of flower-bearing branches, mostly lance-shaped
to elliptical, with finely singly or doubly serrate margins... 8

8. Fruit, 2″ to 2½″ in diameter; leaves, mostly elliptical......................Bigfruit crab (p. 330)
8. Fruit, 1″ to 1¼″ in diameter; leaves, mostly lance-
shaped....................Lanceleaf crab (p. 330)

Southern Crab

Malus angustifolia Michx.

Habit.—A shrub or small tree, 20′ to 30′ in height,
with a short trunk 8″ to 10″ in diameter; with rigid,
spreading branches forming a broad, rounded crown.

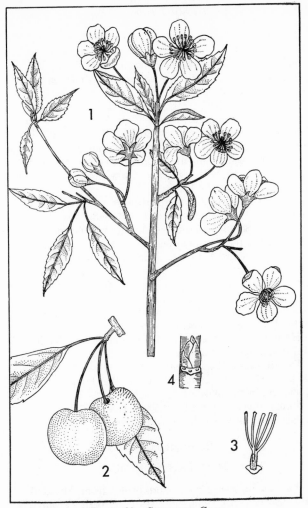

PLATE 89.—SOUTHERN CRAB

1. Foliage and flowers ×½. 2. Fruit ×¾. 3. Detail of pistil ×1½. 4. Leaf scar ×1½.

Leaves.—Alternate, simple, deciduous, ovate to elliptical, 1″ to 3″ long, ½″ to 2″ wide; apex, blunt or acute; base, wedge-shaped; margin, coarsely serrate; dull green above, lighter below; petioles, short, rather stout, occasionally twisted.

Flowers.—Perfect, fragrant, about 1″ in width, borne on slender stalks about 1″ in length, in 3- to 5-flowered clusters; calyx, tubular, 5-lobed at the summit; petals, 5, pinkish, obovate, narrowed to a claw at the base; stamens, 20, in 3 series, shorter than the petals; pistil, with a 5-celled ovary surmounted by 5 styles united at the base.

Fruit.—A nearly globular, green or yellowish-green pome, about 1″ in diameter, usually broader than long.

Twigs.—Slender to stout, reddish brown and smooth, dotted with pale, orange lenticels; buds, small, dark brown, obtuse, with 4 outer, hairy, overlapping scales; leaf scars, linear, with 3 bundle scars; pith, homogeneous, obscurely angled in transverse sections; stipule scars, minute, slitlike.

Bark.—Thin, red-brown, divided by deep, longitudinal fissures into flat, scaly ridges.

Habitat.—Thickets, moist depressions, stream banks, and margins of woodlands.

Distribution.—Southeastern Virginia west to Illinois, south to western Florida in the East and to Louisiana in the West.

Importance.—Typically a weed tree. The fruit is occasionally used locally for preserves.

Buncombe Crab

Malus bracteata Rehd.

This small tree occurs sporadically from Missouri and Kentucky to Tennessee, western North Carolina, Georgia, Alabama, and Florida. Unlike most of our southern crabs (see also Louisiana and Missouri Crabs)

the leaves of this species are hairy below, a feature
that suffices to distinguish it from other related species
in most localities.

Louisiana and Missouri Crabs

These two forms are southern varieties of the prairie
crab (*Malus ioensis* Britt.) of the midwestern states.
Both are characterized by hairy leaves similar to those
of the Buncombe crab but differ from that species in
that their flower stalks and sepals are also hairy.
Louisiana crab (var. *creniserrata* Rehd.) is characterized by elliptical to ovate leaves with entire or finely
toothed margin, while in Missouri crab (var. *bushii*
Rehd.) the leaves are oblong to lance-shaped and
sharply toothed. The former is restricted to western
Louisiana, the latter to southern Missouri.

Biltmore Crab

Malus glabrata Rehd.

This is a shrub or small tree scarcely ever more than
20' tall, with a short trunk and compact, globular
crown. It is reported only from the mountains of
western North Carolina, where it occurs most frequently in rich, sheltered mountain valleys. Its
principal diagnostic features are triangular leaves with
coarsely serrate-lobed margins; pink, fragrant flowers;
obscurely angled fruits, $1\frac{1}{4}''$ to $1\frac{1}{2}''$ in diameter; and
twigs with stout spines, $1''$ or more in length.

Dunbar Crab

Malus glaucescens Rehd.

Usually a shrub, but occasionally becoming a small
tree, this plant occurs sporadically in the southern
Appalachian Mountains and extends northward into
Ohio, Pennsylvania, and New York. Triangular

leaves with glaucous lower surfaces serve to distinguish this form from other crabs with which it may be associated.

Wild Sweet Crab

Malus coronaria L.

The wild sweet crab is a small tree widely distributed through the northern United States but extending south along the Appalachian Mountains to North Carolina, where it is not infrequently found at altitudes above 3,200'. This tree is characterized by oval to ovate leaves with incised-serrate margins; fragrant, pinkish-white flowers; greenish, globular-depressed fruits, about 1¼" in diameter; and stout, reddish-brown, armed twigs. Wild sweet crab has a limited use as an ornamental, and the wood is employed locally for fuel and handle stock.

Bigfruit Crab

Malus × platycarpa Rehd.

This tree, which in some localities is scarcely more than a large shrub, produces the largest fruits of any of our southern crabs. It is found over widely separated areas from southeastern Ohio to Kentucky, West Virginia, Virginia, and western North Carolina. Its principal botanical features include ovate to elliptical leaves with finely serrate margins; pink, fragrant flowers; large, greenish fruits, 2" to 2½" in diameter; and stout, unarmed twigs.

Lanceleaf Crab

Malus lancifolia Rehd.

This small tree is easily recognized by its long, narrow, lance-shaped leaves (1½" to 3½" long) and small, green, globular fruits. Lanceleaf crab is wide-spread in moist valleys and gentle mountain slopes from western North Carolina to northeastern Pennsylvania, southern Ohio, and westward to Missouri.

THE MOUNTAIN-ASHES

Sorbus L.

These are a group of boreal trees and shrubs widely distributed through the cooler regions of Europe, Asia, and North America. At least three species are indigenous to the United States. One of these is a small tree that extends northward over the Appalachian highlands.

American Mountain-Ash

Sorbus americana Marsh.

Habit.—A tree or large spreading shrub, 20′ to 30′ in height and 8″ to 12″ in diameter; with many slender branches forming a narrow, round-topped crown.

Leaves.—Alternate, deciduous, odd–pinnately compound with 13 to 17 lance-shaped leaflets, borne on a grooved rachis, 6″ to 8″ long; leaflets, 2″ to 4″ long, ¼″ to 1″ wide, with long-tapered apices, unequally wedge-shaped bases, and sharply serrate margins; dark yellow-green above, paler and sometimes pubescent below; petioles, very short, the leaflets subsessile; stipules, triangular, toothed.

Flowers.—Perfect, in flat-topped, cymose clusters, 3″ to 4″ in diameter; calyx, with 5 triangular lobes; petals, 5, white; stamens, 20; pistil, with a 3-celled ovary surmounted by 3 styles.

Fruit.—A small, globular, orange-red pome with bitter flesh, about ¼″ in diameter; seeds, light brown, with rounded apices and pointed bases.

PLATE 90.—AMERICAN MOUNTAIN-ASH
1. Foliage and fruit $\times\frac{1}{2}$.   2. Flower cluster $\times\frac{1}{2}$.   3. Flower
$\times 3$.   4. Leaf scar $\times 1$.

Twigs.—Stout, at first hairy, ultimately reddish brown and smooth, dotted with prominent lenticels; terminal buds, conical, about ¾″ long, with several large, reddish-purple, resinous, overlapping scales; lateral buds, smaller (about ¼″ long), appressed; leaf scars, narrowly crescent-shaped, with 5 to 7 bundle scars; stipule scars, inconspicuous; pith, homogeneous.

Bark.—Thin, gray-brown or greenish-brown, irregularly scaly, aromatic when incised.

Habitat.—Near swamps and on rocky soils and mountain slopes.

Distribution.—Southern Appalachian Mountains, northward to Manitoba in the West; southern Labrador and Newfoundland in the East.

Importance.—Occasionally used as an ornamental. The fruit is a source of food for many small birds; its expressed juice is reported to be of some small medicinal value.

THE SERVICEBERRIES

Amelanchier Medic.

These are a genus of small trees and shrubs comprising about 25 species, which are inhabitants of widely separated regions in the Northern Hemisphere. Six species are indigenous to the ·South; 2 of them become arborescent.

KEY TO THE SOUTHERN ARBORESCENT SERVICEBERRIES

1. Flowers, appearing before the leaves; leaves, densely woolly-white while young; fruit, dry...............
Downy serviceberry (p. 334)
1. Flowers, appearing after the leaves; leaves, smooth or only slightly hairy; fruit, juicy.....................
Allegheny serviceberry (p. 336)

Downy Serviceberry

Amelanchier arborea (Michx. f.) Fern.

Habit.—A shrub, or tree 30′ to 50′ in height and 8″ to 18″ in diameter, with slender, spreading branches forming a narrow, rounded head..

Leaves.—Alternate, simple, deciduous, oval to oblong or rarely lance-shaped, 2″ to 4″ (rarely 6″) long, 1″ to 2″ wide; apex, short-pointed; base, rounded or remotely heart-shaped; margin, finely serrate; at first clothed with woolly hairs, silvery, becoming nearly glabrous, then yellow-green above, paler below; petiole, slender, 1″ to 2″ long.

Flowers.—Perfect, appearing before the leaves in silky, racemose clusters on short stalks; calyx, 5-lobed, bell-shaped, glabrous or hairy, persistent; petals, 5, obovate, white, small, somewhat clawlike at the base; stamens, usually 20; pistil, with a 5-celled ovary bearing 2 to 5 styles crowned with broad, flattened stigmas.

Fruit.—A nearly globular, reddish-purple, dry pome, up to ½″ in diameter, tasteless; seeds, numerous, small.

Twigs.—Slender, occasionally somewhat zigzag, at first slightly hairy, becoming glabrous, brown, with numerous pale lenticels; terminal buds, up to ¾″ long, conical, acuminate, the scales imbricate, greenish brown to reddish brown; lateral buds, similar but smaller; leaf scars, narrowly crescent-shaped, with 3 bundle scars; pith, homogeneous, often 5-angled in cross section.

Bark.—Thin, smooth, silvery gray to gray-brown to nearly black, becoming scaly with age.

Habitat.—On dry limestone soils on hillsides and ridges, on sandy loams, on riverbanks, and occasionally in swamps.

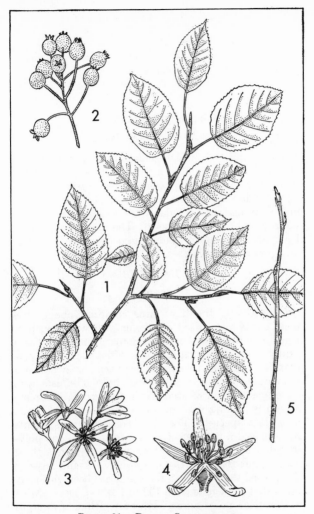

PLATE 91.—DOWNY SERVICEBERRY
1. Foliage ×½. 2. Fruit ×½. 3. Cluster of flowers ×1.
4. Flower ×1½. 5. Twig ×⅔.

Distribution.—New Hampshire west to Iowa, Kansas, and Missouri, south to Georgia and Louisiana.

Importance.—Occasionally planted as an ornamental. The wood is used in the manufacture of tool handles.

Allegheny Serviceberry

Amelanchier laevis Wieg.

This small tree, which seldom exceeds a height of 30' or diameter of 12", is essentially a plant of the Alleghany region. It extends northward over the Appalachian Mountains from Georgia to New England and southeastern Canada where it is found in moist ravines and protected slopes. The blue-black, succulent fruit is palatable and is used by mountain folks as a preserve and in pies.

THE HAWTHORNS

Crataegus L.

Collectively, the hawthorns comprise one of the most easily recognized groups of woody plants; but, because of the great botanical similarity many of them exhibit, specific identification often becomes perplexing. In fact, this genus has been somewhat of a taxonomic puzzle; even among those botanists who have spent years of study with the group, complete accord is lacking with respect to the botanical limits of certain species. The more conservative students have placed a number of similar forms into one polymorphic species, while others have adjudged these same forms to be worthy of species rank and have so designated them. Thus, the genus has been variously estimated to include from 100 to 1,200 species. Most authorities now agree, however, that *Crataegus* embraces at least 800 species of small trees and shrubs, the majority of which are indigenous to North America.

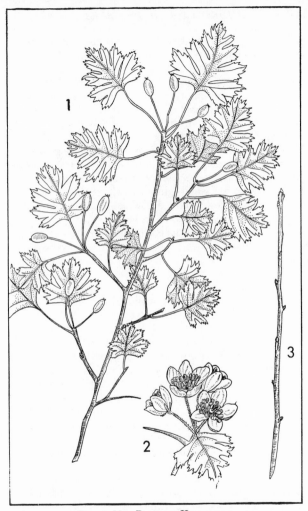

PLATE 92.—PARSLEY HAWTHORN
1. Foliage and fruit ×½. 2. Flowers ×1. 3. Twig ×⅔.

Of the 100 or more hawthorns encountered in the South, approximately 70 attain the stature of small trees. These are characterized by small, deciduous, alternate, simple, stipulate leaves, with toothed or lobed margins and short to long petioles, which are not infrequently winged and glandular. The perfect flowers, with showy, white petals, are borne in profusion in few- to many-flowered terminal and axillary clusters with the leaves or before they are fully grown. The fruit is a small, scarlet, orange, or rarely a blue pome, with 2 to 5 large, bony nutlets. The twigs are characterized by small globular winter buds, with reddish, often fleshy bud scales, and are profusely armed with thorns $\frac{1}{2}''$ to 6'' in length.

The southern hawthorns occur on a variety of sites. Some frequent pastures, meadows, and fallow fields, others margin forests of either pine or hardwoods or even occur under moderately dense forest canopies. Several attain their best development on dry, stony ridges and mountain slopes, while still others flourish in moist river bottoms and along the edges of swamps. It is also interesting to note that a number of the hawthorns are widespread throughout much of the eastern United States, while others, greatly restricted geographically, have been found in small, isolated regions. In fact, it is recorded that less than a dozen specimens of certain species have ever been observed.

Because of their lustrous foliage, showy blossoms, and clusters of brilliantly colored fruits, a number of the hawthorns enjoy widespread ornamental use. Notable is the widely cultivated English hawthorn (*C. oxyacantha* L.), with its many horticultural varities, several with rose-tinted petals. When planted in hedgerows, the hawthorns form an impenetrable barrier. The wood is hard and heavy, and it is said that the famous Irish shillelaghs were made from the black hawthorn.

Parsley hawthorn, *C. marshallii* Eggl., a tree of wide-spread distribution in the South, is the only member of the group here illustrated. Space does not permit the inclusion of descriptions of the many southern hawthorns, several of which are comparatively rare in occurrence and distribution. Most amateur naturalists are content merely to identify members of this genus as hawthorns, but those having a special interest in the group are referred to the excellent work of either Palmer (59) or Sargent (65).

THE CHERRIES AND PLUMS

Prunus L.

The genus *Prunus* comprises over 200 species of trees and shrubs widely distributed through the North Temperate Zone; a few extend into the tropics. Among the exotics that have long since become naturalized in many parts of the South, mention should be made of the peach [*P. persica* (L.) Stokes], originally a native of Asia, the European sour cherry (*P. cerasus* L.), the sweet cherry (*P. avium* L.), and the garden plum (*P. domestica* Stokes), also of European origin.

The apricot (*P. armeniaca* L.) and the almond (*P. amygdalus* Botsch.) are 2 other important members of this genus. Seeds of certain species are important sources of flavoring extracts, prussic acid, and a charcoal for gas masks; the fruits of several are used in the manufacture of brandies. The black cherry is the only American cherry of major importance to the lumber industry. The wood is highly prized for furniture and interior trim and is used extensively for backing blocks of engraver's plates as well as for many other purposes.

Of the more than 25 species native to the United States, 21 become arborescent, and 14 of these are found in our southern flora.

KEY TO THE SOUTHERN CHERRIES AND PLUMS

1. Flowers, borne in terminal racemes............... 2
1. Flowers, borne in axillary umbels................. 6

    2. Calyx, deciduous under the fruit..............
                Common chokecherry (p. 344)
    2. Calyx, persistent under the fruit.............. 3

3. Leaves, clothed below in reddish-brown, woolly hair.
            South Alabama chokecherry (p. 345)
3. Leaves, smooth or sparingly hairy below, occasionally hairy only on the midrib........................ 4

    4. Leaves, oblong to lance-shaped, with reddish, woolly hair along the midrib; flower stalks, smooth; fruit, purplish black..................
                Black cherry (p. 341)
    4. Leaves, oval, obovate, or elliptical, with scattered silky hairs on the lower surface; flower stalks, hairy; fruit, red or black...................... 5

5. Leaves, blunt or notched at the apex; fruit, red; twigs, woolly...............**Georgia chokecherry** (p. 345)
5. Leaves, acute at the apex; fruit, dark red to black; twigs, smooth or only slightly hairy...............
             Alabama chokecherry (p. 344)

    6. Fruit, without ventral grooves, about $\frac{1}{4}''$ in diameter, bright red; stone, globular or slightly elongated..................**Pin cherry** (p. 346)
    6. Fruit, ventrally grooved, usually $\frac{1}{2}''$ or more in diameter, purple, blue-black, yellow, or crimson; stone, more or less flattened (except in flatwoods plum)...................................... 7

7. Petioles, without glands; stone, globular or nearly so..
            Flatwoods plum (p. 348)
7. Petioles, glandular; stone, ovoid, usually noticeably flattened... 8

8. Fruit, deep reddish purple.................... 9
8. Fruit, yellow, orange, or bright red............10

9. Leaves, lance-shaped, hairy above, smooth below
   except for axillary tufts; flowers, appearing with the
   leaves, their stalks hairy....**Allegheny plum** (p. 348)
9. Leaves, oval to elliptical, smooth above, hairy below;
   flowers, appearing before the leaves, their stalks
   smooth....................**Mexican plum** (p. 348)

10. Leaves, narrow lance-shaped to elliptical........11
10. Leaves, broadly oval, ovate, to oblong..........12

11. Leaves, 2″ to 4″ long, ¾″ to 1¼″ wide; fruit, red,
    covered with a thick, waxy bloom.................
    ....**Wildgoose plum** (p. 349)
11. Leaves, 1″ to 3″ long, about ½″ wide; fruit, yellow
    or orange, blushed with red..**Chickasaw plum** (p. 349)

12. Flowers, strongly ill-scented...................
    ....**American plum** (p. 350)
12. Flowers, odorless or pleasantly scented.........13

13. Leaves, hairy above and blow...**Larissa plum** (p. 352)
13. Leaves, smooth above, hairy below...............14

14. Leaves, with soft, white hairs below; flower stalks,
    smooth; fruit, red with a waxy bloom..........
    ....**Inch plum** (p. 352)
14. Leaves, with yellowish or reddish hair along the
    midrib below; flower stalks, hairy; fruit, red
    or yellow, without a bloom....................
    ....**Hortulan plum** (p. 353)

Black Cherry

Prunus serotina Ehrh.

Habit.—A medium-sized tree, 50′ to 60′ in height
with a trunk 2′ to 3′ in diameter (occasionally much

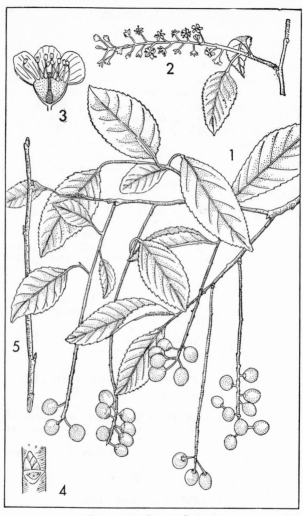

PLATE 93.—BLACK CHERRY
1. Foliage and fruit $\times\frac{1}{2}$. 2. Flower cluster $\times\frac{1}{2}$. 3. Single flower $\times 4$. 4. Leaf scar $\times 2$. 5. Twig $\times\frac{3}{4}$.

larger), with small, somewhat horizontal branches and a narrow, oblong head; the root system, wide-spreading.

Leaves.—Alternate, simple, deciduous, oval to oblong or lance-shaped, 2″ to 6″ long, 1″ to 1½″ wide; apex, abruptly sharp-pointed or long-tapered; base, acute to wedge-shaped; margin, finely serrate; lustrous dark green above, paler below, with a more or less rusty-red, pubescent midrib; petioles, slender, up to 1″ long, grooved and sometimes twisted.

Flowers.—Perfect, appearing with the leaves in many-flowered racemes, 4″ to 6″ long; calyx tube, 5-lobed, persistent; petals, 5, white; stamens, 15 to 20, in 3 ranks; pistil, with a 1-celled ovary, short style, and flattened stigma.

Fruit.—A nearly globular, black or purplish-black, edible drupe, with juicy, purplish flesh, about ½″ in diameter; stone, ⅓″ long, with a prominent ridge.

Twigs.—Slender, rigid, aromatic, with an acrid taste, at first coated with a bloom, becoming red-brown and glabrous; buds, up to ¼″ long, obtuse, dark brown, with several broad, overlapping scales; leaf scars, semicircular, with 3 bundle scars; pith, homogeneous.

Bark.—Thin, at first smooth, red-brown or black, with longitudinally elongated lenticels, becoming furrowed and forming persistent recurved scales, somewhat reticulated in appearance.

Habitat.—Most commonly found on deep, rich, moist soils in mixed stands with oaks, ashes, hickories, and yellowpoplar; less commonly on sandy soils; with conifers in the Adirondacks.

Distribution.—From Nova Scotia south to central Florida and west to Texas; also found through southern Canada to Lake Superior and on into North Dakota; becoming shrubby at the northern limits of its range; more or less scattered throughout the

eastern United States to a line connecting eastern
Texas with eastern North Dakota.

Importance.—An important hardwood, used in the
production of many types of wooden articles; among
the more important are furniture, boats, printing
blocks, and planing-mill products; hydrocyanic acid
is extracted from the bark; and the fruit is edible and
is sometimes used in flavoring brandy.

Common Chokecherry

Prunus virginiana L.

Common chokecherry is a small bushy tree of the
northeastern and midwestern states, extending south
into Kentucky and North Carolina. While usually
regarded as a weed tree, it has been found useful in
controlling soil erosion and has been successfully
propagated in the shelter-belt region of the plains
states. The tree may be recognized by its 2″ to 4″,
broadly obovate, doubly serrate, lustrous, dark-green
leaves with short petioles that are glandular at the
apex; small, 5-merous flowers, borne in 3″ to 6″
terminal racemes, which appear after leaf emergence;
bright-scarlet to wine-red fruit, and ⅓″ in diameter,
with dark, succulent, acidulous flesh and hard, singly
sutured stone; and dark, scaly, strongly ill-scented
bark.

Alabama Chokecherry

Prunus alabamensis (Mohr.) Small

This is a small tree of rare and sporadic occurrence
found only on the hills and low mountains of central
Alabama. The thick, dark, dull-green, oval to
broadly ovate leaves, 4″ to 5″ long, are somewhat
hairy below, particularly along the midribs, and are
characterized by finely glandular-toothed margins,

sharp-pointed apices, and obtuse or rounded bases; the petioles are short, stout, glandular, and hairy. The flowers, borne in 3″ to 4″ terminal racemes, appear when the leaves are about half grown. The nearly globular, dark-red to purplish-black fruits, about ⅓″ in diameter, are furnished with a thin, succulent, acidulous flesh and small, ovoid, compressed stone.

South Alabama Chokecherry

Prunus australis Beadle

This chokecherry, a moderately large tree, 60′ or more in height and 12″ to 15″ in diameter, is restricted to a localized area on the Alabama coastal plain in Conecuh County. It is readily distinguished from the Alabama chokecherry by its thinner leaves with rusty-red, hairy, lower surfaces, red, woolly petioles, and deep-purple fruit.

Georgia Chokecherry

Prunus cuthbertii Small

This is a small tree of the lower Piedmont plateau and coastal plain, ranging from eastern Georgia to north-central Florida. The leathery, obovate, dull-green leaves, 2″ to 4½″ long, are rounded or notched at the apex, wedge-shaped at the base, and covered below with a chalky-white bloom; the petioles are clothed with woolly hair. The flowers, borne in terminal racemes, are characterized by hairy stalks. The small, red, globular fruits are about ⅓″ in diameter. Of particular diagnostic importance are the slender twigs clothed in densely woolly, often matted hair.

Pin Cherry   Wild Red Cherry   Bird Cherry

Prunus pensylvanica L.

Habit.—Shrubby toward the northern limits of its range, but elsewhere usually appearing as a tree 25′ to 40′ in height with a trunk of 1′ to 2′ in diameter supporting a narrow, rounded or irregular crown.

Leaves.—Alternate, simple, deciduous, aromatic, but bitter to the taste; oblong-lanceolate, 3″ to 4½″ long, ½″ to 1¼″ wide; apex, long-pointed; base, wedge-shaped; margin, finely serrate (frequently with glandular teeth); lustrous bright green above, paler below; petioles, slender, glabrous, 1″ long; becoming bright yellow in the fall.

Flowers.—Perfect, regular, appearing with or after the leaves, borne in 4- to 5-flowered umbels or corymbs; individual flowers, about ½″ in diameter, borne on 1″ stalks; calyx, glabrous, with an orange-colored throat and red-tipped lobes; petals, 5, cream-colored, rounded above, narrowed into a claw below; stamens, 15 to 20; pistil, with a 1-celled ovary, slender style, and flattened stigma.

Fruit.—A bright-red, globose drupe, with acidulous flesh, about ¼″ in diameter; stone, globose or slightly elongated, pointed above, rounded below; often ridged on one side.

Twigs.—Slender, aromatic, bitter to the taste, light red, becoming darker with age, glabrous, with numerous pale lenticels; lateral spurs, appearing during the 2d year; inner bark, bright green; buds, small, ovoid, acute, reddish brown, clustered toward the tips of twigs; leaf scars, crescent-shaped, with 3 vascular scars; stipule scars, minute; pith, continuous.

Bark.—Thin, smooth, reddish brown, with horizontally elongated lenticels, at length separating into broad, persistent plates, covered with minute, persistent scales.

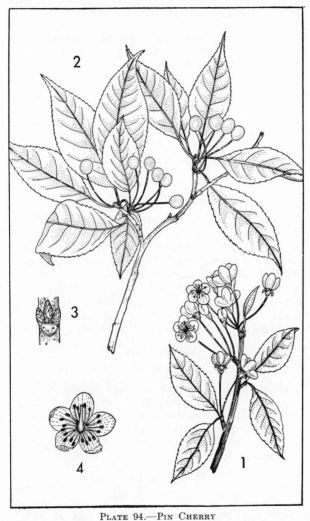

PLATE 94.—PIN CHERRY

1. Flowers and developing leaves ×1.   2. Mature foliage and
fruit ×½.   3. Leaf scar and buds ×1½.   4. Single flower ×2.

Habitat.—Usually on rich, moist soil in the open or in mixed stands, frequently forming more or less pure thickets on burned-over forest areas.

Distribution.—From Newfoundland to eastern British Colombia, south through New England into Pennsylvania and west to central Iowa; also in the mountains of Virginia, North Carolina, Tennessee, and Georgia.

Importance.—The fruit is occasionally used in the preparation of preserves and in the manufacture of commercial cough-sirups extracts.

Flatwoods Plum

Prunus umbellata Ell.

This large shrub or small tree frequents the southern coastal plains from North Carolina to eastern Texas and extends northward in the Mississippi Valley to southern Arkansas. Small, oblong-lance-shaped leaves with glandular teeth, large flowers, nearly 1″ in diameter, which appear before the leaves, variously colored fruits with globular stones, and spurlike twigs characterize this tree. The fruits are unusually rich in pectin and are used in jellies and preserves.

Allegheny Plum

Prunus alleghaniensis Porter

This is a small northern tree that extends south along the mountains through Virginia to North Carolina. The leaves are narrow, lance-shaped, 2″ to 3½″ in length; the flowers are in clusters of 2 to 4, and the fruit is globular, reddish purple, and about ½″ in diameter.

Mexican Plum

Prunus mexicana S. Wats.

Mexican plum is a tree of northern Mexico and extends north and eastward to western Louisiana,

Arkansas, Oklahoma, and southeastern Kansas. The large, purplish fruits of this tree are often gathered locally and used for preserves. Small, ovate to elliptical leaves 1″ to 3″ long, few-flowered umbels, which appear in advance of the leaves, and thornlike twigs are features of this species.

Wildgoose Plum

Prunus munsoniana Wight & Hedrick

Wildgoose plum is a small tree originally of the lower Ohio and lower Mississippi valleys and adjacent areas. It has commanded the interest of both horticulturist and pomologist and has, therefore, become naturalized over a much wider area. By careful selection, several hybrids of this and other plums have resulted in the production of palatable fruits of quality. In its natural habitats the tree is characterized by thin, light-green, elliptical to lance-shaped leaves, 2″ to 4″ long; flowers in clusters of 2 to 4; red fruits, ¾″ in length, often covered with a light, waxy bloom; and slender, not infrequently thorny twigs.

Chickasaw Plum

Prunus angustifolia Marsh.

The chickasaw plum, a small tree originally a native of Texas and Oklahoma, was introduced to the South Atlantic and Gulf states many years ago and now is thoroughly naturalized in these areas, where it often forms nearly impenetrable thickets in old fields and waste places. The tree is characterized by having somewhat lance-shaped leaves, spurlike lateral twigs, calyx lobes without glands, and small, red or yellow, juicy, palatable fruits. Numerous horticultural varieties have been developed for use in southern orchards, but the fruits are seldom placed on the market in any appreciable quantity.

American Plum

Prunus americana Marsh.

Habit.—A small tree, 20' to 35' in height, with a trunk becoming 1' in diameter; branching rather close to the ground into a broad, spreading head; often spreading by root shoots and forming dense thickets.

Leaves.—Alternate, simple, deciduous, oblong-ovate, 3" to 4" long, 1½" to 2" wide; apex, long-tapered; base, rounded or acute; margin, singly or doubly serrate, the teeth sharp-pointed; thick, rough, dark green above, paler below and usually glabrous; petioles, with or without glands.

Flowers.—Perfect, malodoriferous, in 2- to 5-flowered umbels, appearing before or with the leaves, about 1" in diameter; calyx tube, red, with 5 lance-shaped lobes; petals, 5, white, narrowing into a red, clawlike base; stamens, 20, in 3 rows; pistil, with a 1-celled ovary.

Fruit.—A bright-red, globular drupe, about 1" in diameter; with a tough skin and juicy, yellow flesh, acrid to the taste; stone, compressed.

Twigs.—Slender, glabrous, somewhat pointed, changing from orange to reddish brown with circular lenticels; lateral twigs, sometimes spurlike or ending in a thornlike structure; buds, small, acute, dark brown, the scales with irregular margins; leaf scars, shield-shaped, with 3 bundle scars; pith, homogeneous.

Bark.—Thin, brown, smooth, becoming separated into thin, appressed, persistent scales.

Habitat.—On rich, moist soils near swamps or streams; also in rich bottom lands and on gentle slopes.

Distribution.—Widely distributed from the east coast between New York and Florida, west to the Rocky Mountains.

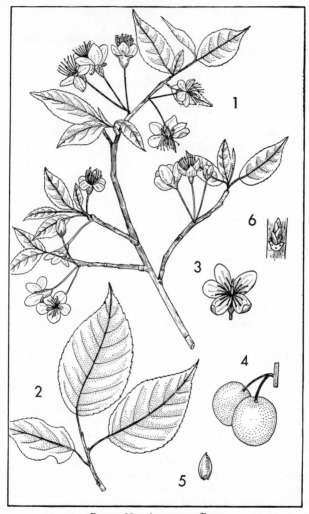

PLATE 95.—AMERICAN PLUM

1. Flowers and immature foliage ×½. 2. Mature foliage ×½
3. Single flower ×1. 4. Fruit ×½. 5. Pit ×½. 6. Leaf scar
and bud ×2.

Importance.—The fruit is sometimes used in the preparation of preserves.

Larissa Plum

Prunus tenuifolia Sarg.

Larissa plum is a small tree of southeastern Texas, found in mixed hardwood forests. Its principal distinguishing features are (1) dark-yellow-green, doubly serrate, oblong to elliptical leaves, 3″ to 4″ long; (2) 2- to 4-flowered, sessile umbels, the flower stalks hairy; (3) red, oblong to obovoid fruits, about ¾″ long, with a thin flesh and oblong, flattened, slightly grooved stone.

Inch Plum

Prunus lanata Mack. & Bush

Inch plum, so called because of the length of its fruit, is a small tree of the lower Ohio River Valley, Missouri, Arkansas, eastern Oklahoma, eastern Texas, Louisiana, and south-central Alabama. It is usually encountered along streams or in moist, rich river bottoms, although toward the northern limits of its range it is found on sheltered hills and ridges. The tree is characterized by broadly ovate to elliptical, light-yellow-green leaves, 2½″ to 4½″ long, with coarsely toothed or doubly toothed margins, hairy lower surfaces, and slender petioles that are commonly furnished with a single gland at the apex. The 5-merous flowers are borne in 2- to 5-flowered umbels, which appear in advance of the leaves. The bright-red, broadly ellipsoidal fruit, about 1″ long, is furnished with a waxy bloom, succulent flesh, and oblong, compressed stone.

Hortulan Plum

Prunus hortulana Bail.

This is a small tree of the central and southern midwestern states, extending eastward to northwestern Tennessee and central Kentucky.[1] The species, like the wildgoose plum, has been cross-bred with other plums to produce commercial fruits. Hortulan plum is characterized by lustrous-dark-green, oblong to lance-shaped, pointed leaves, 4″ to 6″ long, with slender, orange-tinted petioles; the flowers are borne in clusters of 2 to 4, appearing shortly after the leaves; the red or yellowish-red, ellipsoidal fruits are about 1″ long, with thin flesh and asymmetrical stone.

THE LAURELCHERRIES

Laurocerasus Reich.

The laurelcherries comprise a group of about 20 species of evergreen trees and shrubs that are inhabitants of tropical and warmer regions of both hemispheres. The English laurelcherry (*L. officinalis* Roem.) is probably the best-known member of this group and is used extensively for decorative purposes in many parts of the United States.

Four species, two of them restricted to southern California, the others small evergreen trees of the South, are the only American representatives of the group.

KEY TO THE SOUTHERN LAURELCHERRIES

1. Fruit, oblong to ovoid, black or blue-black; petals, shorter than calyx lobes. . **Carolina laurelcherry** (p. 354)
1. Fruit, globular or nearly so, orange-brown; petals, longer than calyx lobes. . . . .
   West Indies laurelcherry (p. 356)

[1] Reported from Georgia. See Small, J. K., (68) p. 649.

Carolina Laurelcherry　　Wild Orange

Prunus caroliniana (Ait.) Mill.

Habit.—A tree, 30′ to 40′ in height, with a trunk up to 10″ in diameter; branching more or less horizontally to form an oblong, narrow, open crown.

Leaves.—Alternate, simple, persistent until the 2d year; with a pleasant odor and taste; oblong-lanceolate, 2″ to 5″ long, ¾″ to 1½″ wide; apex, acuminate with a short, distinct point; base, wedge-shaped; margin, entire or remotely serrate, somewhat wavy; waxy, lustrous, dark green above, paler below; petioles, short, stout, orange; stipules, lanceolate.

Flowers.—Perfect, appearing in late winter and early spring in racemes on short axillary stalks; racemes, shorter than the leaves; calyx tube, narrow, with 5 small, rounded, undulate, early-deciduous lobes; petals, 5, small, creamy; stamens, 15 to 30, orange, longer than the petals; pistil, with a small ovary, the slender style enlarged into a subglobose stigma.

Fruit.—A lustrous, dry, black or blue-black, oblong drupe, ½″ in diameter, ripening in the late fall and persisting until the following spring; stone, ovoid, acute, with a rounded base and with a prominent dorsal groove.

Twigs.—Slender, glabrous, red to gray-brown, with few pale lenticels; buds, small, pointed, deep brown; leaf scars, crescent-shaped, with 3 bundle scars; pith, homogeneous.

Bark.—Thin, smooth, gray, becoming irregularly roughened.

Habitat.—Rich, moist soil.

Distribution.—From North Carolina to Florida and west to Louisiana and Texas.

Importance.—Cultivated as an ornamental. The leaves and branches contain considerable prussic acid and may be fatal to stock if browsed in quantity.

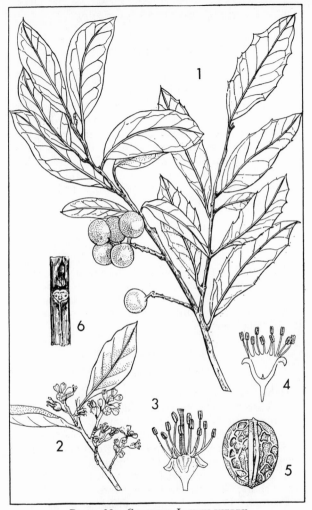

PLATE 96.—CAROLINA LAURELCHERRY
1. Foliage and fruit ×½.   2. Flower clusters ×½.   3. Flower
×4.   4. Section of flower showing mode of stamen attachment ×4.
5. Pit ×5.   6. Leaf scar ×1½.

West Indies Laurelcherry

Prunus myrtifolia (L.) Urban.

This is a small South American and West Indian tree that extends northward through the Florida Keys to lower peninsular Florida. It has a limited horticultural use, and the wood, although dense and highly colored, is of no industrial value. This species is readily distinguished from the Carolina laurelcherry by its elliptical leaves, small flowers with white petals, yellow at the base, and orange-brown fruits with cylindrical, bony pits.

THE COCO-PLUMS

Chrysobalanus L.

These are a small genus of evergreen trees and shrubs, mostly tropical. A single species (*C. icaco* L.) attains arborescent size in Florida (including the Keys). A shrubby form (*C. pellocarpus* Meyer) occurs in the same area.

Icaco Coco-Plum

Chrysobalanus icaco L.

Habit.—Usually a shrub, 10′ to 12′ high, growing into dense thickets; rarely treelike, with an erect or reclining stem 20′ to 30′ in length and 1′ in diameter.

Leaves.—Alternate, persistent, simple, obovate, 1″ to 3½″ wide; apex, rounded or slightly notched; base, wedge-shaped; margins, entire; dark lustrous green and glabrous above, yellow-green below; petioles, stout, short; stipules, short, acuminate.

Flowers.—Perfect, borne in terminal or axillary cymose panicles throughout the spring and summer months, with conspicuous deciduous bracts; calyx,

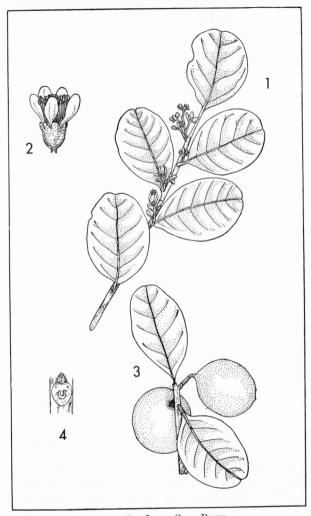

PLATE 97.—ICACO COCO-PLUM
1. Foliage and flowers ×½. 2. Flower ×2. 3. Fruit ×½.
4. Leaf scar ×2.

bell- to top-shaped; petals, 5, creamy white, spatulate, deciduous; stamens, numerous, with hairy filaments; pistil, with a 1-celled ovary, threadlike style, and minute, flattened stigma.

Fruit.—A fleshy, 1-seeded, pink, yellow, or white, globose drupe, about 2″ in diameter; juicy, sweet, the flesh adherent to the angled stone; seed, light brown.

Twigs.—Slender, dark brown, with numerous lenticels; buds, small, brown.

Bark.—Dark brown separating into long, thin scales.

Habitat.—On riverbanks, hammocks, and shores bordering on salt water.

Distribution.—On the southern Florida Keys, and in the West Indies, Brazil, and Africa.

Importance.—The fruits of this species are very juicy, although sometimes rather insipid, and in Cuba have been used for preserves. Various parts of the plant contain astringents used in compounding pharmaceutical preparations, particularly lotions.

THE PULSE OR PEA FAMILY

Leguminosae

This family, one of the largest of the flowering plants, consists of about 500 genera and over 15,000 species of trees, shrubs, lianas, and herbs with alternate, mostly compound leaves and podlike fruits. Among the herbaceous forms are included many valuable food and forage plants, of which alfalfa, vetches, beans, peas, dals, and various clovers should be mentioned. Gums, oils, tannins, resins, numerous drugs, and dyestuffs, such as haematoxylon and brazilin, are obtained from the various plant parts of arborescent members of this family. Because of their fragrant and often exquisitely tinted flowers, their delicate foliage, or their xerophilous habit, many legumes are prized ornamentals. The periodic use of many leguminous species, particularly clovers, lespedezas, soybeans, and vetches, to build up the available nitrogen content of the soil is a recognized and general practice that is pursued in agricultural regions throughout the world. Many valuable timbers such as the rosewoods, black locust, acacias, tulip-wood, black bean, koa, and others are traceable to this group.

Our southern flora embraces about 80 genera and nearly 400 species of the Leguminosae. Nine genera with arborescent forms are included.

Synopsis of Southern Genera

Genus	*Leaves*	*Flowers*	*Legume*	*Twigs*
Lysiloma	persistent, bipinnate, the rachis glandular	regular, usually perfect, in heads	borne in clusters, enlarged at the apex	unarmed, often warty
Gymnocladus	deciduous, bipinnate	regular, dioecious, in racemose clusters	tardily dehiscent, pulpy between the seeds	unarmed, stout, with large, pink pith
Gleditsia	deciduous, pinnate and bipinnate on the same tree	regular, polyg-amous, in racemes	tardily dehiscent, with or without pulp be-tween the seeds	armed with stout, branched thorns or unarmed
Robinia	deciduous, odd-pinnate	irregular, perfect, in racemes	dehiscent, dry and compressed, between the kidney-shaped seeds	armed with short, simple, stipular thorns

Genus	Leaves	Flowers	Legume	Twigs
Cercis	deciduous, simple	irregular, perfect, in sessile clusters	tardily dehiscent, compressed, and dry between the seeds	unarmed
Cladrastis	deciduous, odd-pinnate, the swollen rachis base enclosing the bud	irregular, perfect, in panicles	tardily dehiscent, thickened along the upper margin, not pulpy between seeds	moderately stout, unarmed
Erythrina	persistent, trifoliate	irregular, perfect, in racemes	readily dehiscent, greatly constricted between the kidney-shaped seeds	armed with short, broad, curved spines
Piscidia	deciduous, odd-pinnate	irregular, perfect, paniculate	dehiscent, constricted between the seeds, furnished with 4 broad, longitudinal wings	unarmed
Sophora	deciduous and persistent, odd-pinnate	irregular, perfect, in racemes	indehiscent, constricted between the seeds	unarmed

THE LYSILOMAS

Lysiloma Benth.

The lysilomas comprise a small group of about 10 species of trees and shrubs, largely confined to tropical America. *L. sabicu* Benth., the Cuban sabicu, produces a wood with many of the physical characteristics of mahogany and black walnut and in the past has been used extensively for furniture and interior trim.

Two species extend northward into the warmer regions of the United States. *L. watsonii* Rose is found in southern Arizona, while *L. bahamensis* Benth. appears quite commonly in the Florida Keys and elsewhere.

Bahama Lysiloma   Wild Tamarind

Lysiloma bahamensis Benth.

Habit.—A medium-sized tree, 40′ to 60′ in height, with a trunk 2′ to 3′ in diameter; with stout, horizontal branches forming a wide, more or less flattened head.

Leaves.—Alternate, persistent, bipinnately compound, 4″ to 5″ long, with 2 to 6 pairs of short-stalked pinnae, each with 20 to 60 sessile leaflets; leaflets, about ½″ long and ¼″ wide, somewhat obliquely oval, oblong, or ovate; obtuse or acute at the apex; the opposing pairs, more or less united at the base; margin, entire; pale green above, even paler below; the rachis, usually glandular; stipules, oval, acuminate, leaflike, about ½″ long.

Flowers.—Regular, perfect, vernal, appearing in compact, tomentose heads on axillary stalks, 1″ to 2″ long; calyx, bell-shaped, 5-toothed, half as long as the 5-lobed, funnel-shaped corolla; stamens, many, twice

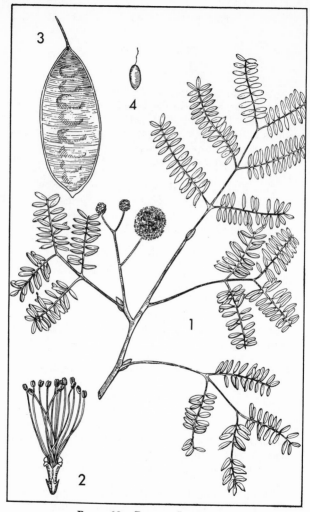

PLATE 98.—BAHAMA LYSILOMA
1. Foliage and flowers ×⅓. 2. Flower ×3. 3. Fruit ×⅓.
4. Seed ×⅓.

as long as the corolla, united below into a tube; pistil, sessile, with a slender style and minute stigma.

Fruit.—A legume, maturing in the fall but usually persisting until the following spring; in clusters of 2 or 3, 4″ to 5″ long, 1″ wide; with an acute tip and wedge-shaped base, borne on 1″ to 2″ stalks, brown; seeds, 8 to 15, oval, brown, lustrous.

Twigs.—Slender, glabrous, with conspicuous warts, reddish brown.

Bark.—At first thin, smooth, and gray, becoming brown with large flattened scales on older stems.

Habitat.—Sandy soil near salt water.

Distribution.—In southern Florida, on the Keys, and in the Bahama Islands and Cuba.

Importance.—Of some value for boat timbers.

THE COFFEETREES

Gymnocladus Lam.

This genus consists of two species, one a native of central China, the other the Kentucky coffeetree of the eastern United States.

Kentucky Coffeetree

Gymnocladus dioicus K. Koch

Habit.—A large tree, 100′ or more in height, with a trunk 2′ to 4′ in diameter; in the open, branching near the ground into a few ascending limbs forming a narrow, round-topped head; in the forest, often developing 50′ to 75′ of clear bole and a narrow, oval crown.

Leaves.—Alternate, deciduous, bipinnately compound, with 5 to 13 alternate pinnae, each with 6 to 14 leaflets; 1′ to 3′ long, 1′ to 2′ wide; leaflets, oval, 2″ to 2½″ long, about 1″ wide; with acuminate apices,

PLATE 99.—KENTUCKY COFFEETREE
1. Foliage $\times\frac{1}{3}$. 2. Female flower $\times 1$. 3. Male flower $\times 1$.
4. Fruit $\times\frac{1}{2}$. 5. Seed $\times\frac{1}{2}$. 6. Twig $\times\frac{3}{4}$.

rounded or unequal bases, and entire margins; dark green above, paler below and glabrous; rachis, long, slender, conspicuously swollen at the base; stipules, about ⅓″ long, glandular.

Flowers.—Regular, dioecious, appearing after the leaves in terminal, racemose clusters; staminate inflorescence, 3″ to 4″ long, many-flowered; pistillate inflorescence, 10″ to 12″ long, few-flowered, with long flower stalks; calyx, tubular, ½″ long, covered with whitish, woolly hairs, 10-angled, and 5-lobed; petals, oblong, white, longer than the calyx lobes; stamens, 10, not united into a tube, with hairy filaments and orange anthers; pistil, composed of a hairy ovary, short style, and an oblique stigma.

Fruit.—A large, flat, thick, woody legume, 4″ to 10″ long, 1″ to 2″ wide; borne on a stout stalk, 1″ to 2″ long, dark brown or red-brown, persistent until late winter; seeds, oval, compressed, stony, separated by a mass of brown, sweet pulp.

Twigs.—Stout, brown, with many orange-colored lenticels; terminal bud, lacking; lateral buds, superposed, 2 or 3 at each node, small, silky, indistinctly scaly; leaf scars, heart-shaped, with 3 or 5 often confluent, commonly divided bundle scars; pith, large, salmon-colored, continuous; stipule scars, minute, fringed.

Bark.—Up to 1″ thick, gray-brown, furrowed, forming scaly ridges.

Habitat.—On rich bottom lands, usually in mixed stands with honeylocust, hackberry, cottonwoods, and black ash; also on drier soil in the open or in parklike stands.

Distribution.—Central New York to Minnesota and Nebraska; also in Ohio, Kentucky, Tennessee, and Oklahoma; nowhere plentiful.

Importance.—Mostly used as an ornamental, but of some value for posts and crossties.

Remarks.—The seeds of this tree were once used by the early settlers of Kentucky and Tennessee as a coffee substitute, while the pulp of the green fruit was used in medicine.

THE HONEYLOCUSTS

Gleditsia L.

The honeylocusts comprise a group of 10 species of trees distributed through the forests of tropical Africa, eastern and central Asia, South America, and the eastern United States. The 3 North American species are all components of southern forests.

KEY TO THE SOUTHERN HONEYLOCUSTS

1. Legume, many-seeded, linear-oblong................ 2
1. Legume, 1- to 3-seeded, oval...**Waterlocust** (p. 369)

    2. Legume, 10″ to 20″ long, with a sweetish pulp between the seeds; twigs, armed with branched spines.....................**Honeylocust** (p. 366)
    2. Legume, 3″ to 5″ long, not pulpy between the seeds; twigs, unarmed..**Texas honeylocust** (p. 370)

Honeylocust

Gleditsia triacanthos L.

Habit.—A medium-sized tree, 60′ to 80′ in height and 2′ to 3′ in diameter, occasionally reaching 140′ by 6′; the thorny trunk, usually branching 5′ to 20′ above the ground into several stout, ascending limbs with spreading, pendulous branches forming a broad, rounded or flat-topped crown.

Leaves.—Alternate, deciduous, pinnate and bipinnately compound, 6″ to 8″ long; pinnate leaves, with 15 to 30 subopposite or alternate, nearly sessile leaf-

PLATE 100.—HONEYLOCUST
1. Foliage ×½. 2. Male flower ×3. 3. Female flower ×3.
4. Fruit ×2½. 5. Seed ×⅔.

lets; the leaflets, ovate to elliptical, 1″ to 2″ long, ½″ to 1″ wide; acute or rounded at the apex, broadly unequally wedge-shaped at the base; margin, remotely serrate or entire; lustrous dark green above, yellowish green below, glabrous; the rachis, grooved above, swollen below, pubescent; bipinnate leaves, with 4 to 7 pairs of pinnae, each pinna with 12 to 18 leaflets, smaller but otherwise similar to the unipinnate type.

Flowers.—Regular, perfect and imperfect, borne in axillary racemes, appearing when the pinnate leaves are fully developed or nearly so; staminate racemes, clustered, 2″ to 3″ long at maturity, pubescent, many-flowered; pistillate racemes, solitary, 2″ to 3″ long, slender, few-flowered; calyx, bell-shaped, with 5 hairy, acute lobes; petals, longer than calyx lobes, erect, oval, white; stamens, 10, inserted on calyx tube, the anthers green; pistil, composed of a white, hairy, linear ovary surmounted by a short, stout, style and headlike stigma.

Fruit.—A thin, flattened, thick-edged, twisted, dark-brown legume, 1′ to 1½′ long and about 1½″ wide; borne in 2's or 3's on short stalks, falling during the autumn and winter; seeds, many, oval, compressed, deep brown, ⅓″ long.

Twigs.—Moderately stout, zigzag, with thickened nodes, greenish or reddish brown, becoming somewhat gray-brown, armed with stout, rigid, simple or more commonly 3-branched thorns; terminal buds, wanting; lateral buds, minute, several at each node, more or less sunken, often covered by the leaf scar; leaf scars, irregularly shield-shaped, with 3 bundle scars; pith, continuous.

Bark.—Gray-brown to black, with deep, narrow, longitudinal fissures separating scaly ridges, usually with an abundance of stout, elongated, branched thorns traceable to adventitious buds along the bole.

Habitat.—On rich bottom lands and mountain slopes, along watercourses, and also on limestone soils; well adapted to prairie soils and suitable for planting in such areas.

Distribution.—From Pennsylvania west through Michigan and southern Minnesota to southeastern South Dakota; south along the mountains to Alabama in the East, and south through eastern Nebraska, Iowa, Kansas, and Oklahoma to eastern Texas in the West.

Importance.—Honeylocust is widely planted as an ornamental and for windbreaks and can be trimmed to form an impervious hedge. The wood is used in limited quantities for crossties, fence posts, and farm implements.

Remarks.—A spineless form (*G. triacanthos* var. *inermis*) is a common ornamental in certain localities in the South.

Waterlocust

Gleditsia aquatica Marsh.

The waterlocust, a small tree of modest proportions, is largely confined to moist situations and is not infrequently found on areas where inundation for long periods is fairly common. It occurs along the Atlantic and Gulf coastal plains from South Carolina to eastern Texas and extends northward through the Mississippi drainage basin to southern Illinois and southwestern Indiana. While exhibiting a habit very similar to that of honeylocust, it is readily distinguished from that species by its smaller leaves with fewer leaflets, more slender thorns, and its small, flattened, 1- to 3-seeded, nonpulpy pods. The trees are of little or no commercial value, although small quantities of the wood are used locally in cabinetry.

Texas Honeylocust

Gleditsia × *texana* Sarg.

Texas honeylocust is a large tree, often 100' or more in height and 2' to 3' in diameter. According to several authorities this form is a hybrid between the honeylocust and the waterlocust. The leaves are somewhat smaller than those of the honeylocust and have fewer, but similar leaflets. The flowers are perfect and imperfect and appear just before or with leaf emergence; the orange-red staminate flowers are borne in axillary racemes, pistillate flowers, on the other hand, being unknown. The fruit is several-seeded, although only about one-third as long as that of the honeylocust. The twigs, unlike those of either of the two previously described species, are unarmed. Texas honeylocust is found in Brazoria County (Texas), southern Louisiana, and southern Mississippi. It is of no economic significance.

THE LOCUSTS

Robinia L.

The locusts comprise a group of about 20 species of trees and shrubs, wholly restricted to the temperate regions of North America. Six species are found in southern woodlands, 2 of which become arborescent.

KEY TO THE SOUTHERN ARBORESCENT LOCUSTS

1. Flowers, white; leaf stalks and twigs, not sticky; fruit smooth and free of hair.........**Black locust** (p. 371)
1. Flowers, rose-tinted; leaf stalks and twigs, sticky; fruit, covered with stiff, glandular hairs.............
   Clammy locust (p. 373)

Black Locust

Robinia pseudoacacia L.

Habit.—A medium-sized tree, ordinarily 40' to 60' in height and 1' to 2½' in diameter; on the better sites, occasionally becoming 100' by 4'; the bole is usually short and divided 10' to 15' above the ground into several stout, ascending branches, which form an oblong or rather broad, irregular, open crown.

Leaves.—Alternate, deciduous, pinnately compound, 8" to 14" long, with 7 to 19 more or less alternate, nearly sessile leaflets; leaflets, ½" to 2" long, ½" to 1" wide; apex, with a small, abrupt tip or notched; base, rounded or broadly wedge-shaped; margin, entire; dull bluish green above, paler below, with a remotely pubescent midrib; rachis, smooth and glabrous.

Flowers.—Perfect, irregular, appearing just after leaf emergence in May or June, borne in drooping racemes, 4" to 5" in length; individual flowers, 1" long, fragrant, with slender stalks; calyx, persistent, bell-shaped, 5-lobed, with 1 lobe longer than the others; corolla, white, papilionaceous, with a standard, 2 wings, and a keel; stamens, 10, in 2 groups, the lower group forming a stamen tube; pistil, composed of an oblong ovary, a hairy style, and a small stigma.

Fruit.—A flattened, brown, oblong-linear, slightly curved legume, 2" to 4" long, about ½" wide, borne on a thick, short stalk, soon opening or persistent until winter; seeds, kidney-shaped, compressed, mottled, brown, 4 to 8 in each pod.

Twigs.—Rather stout, brittle, zigzag and somewhat angular, greenish brown, glabrous; terminal buds, absent; lateral buds, naked, sunken under the somewhat kidney-shaped leaf scars, accessory buds,

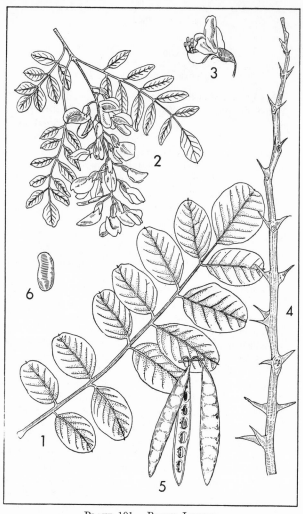

PLATE 101.—BLACK LOCUST

1. Leaf ×½. 2. Cluster of flowers ×½. 3. Flower ×¾.
4. Twig ×¾. 5. Fruit ×½. 6. Seed ×1.

present; stipules, modified to sharp-pointed spines; pith, homogeneous.

Bark.—Thick, gray, brown, or black, deeply furrowed with heavy, rounded, reticulate, scaly ridges.

Habitat.—Rich loam near streams and on bottom lands, on mountain slopes, or on limestone soils; adaptable to many soils and consequently widely distributed; spreading by means of seeds and root sprouts.

Distribution.—Originally found in the Appalachian region from Pennsylvania south to Georgia and in Arkansas, Indiana, and Illinois. It has been planted widely throughout the eastern United States and now occurs as an escape over an exceedingly wide area.

Importance.—The wood, because of its great durability, is used extensively for fence posts, wooden pegs, ship timbers, insulator pins, and piles. This locust is used widely for windbreaks and erosion-control projects and is of some value as an ornamental.

Remarks.—Black locust is associated with certain nitrogen fixing bacteria. The shipmast locust (var. *rectissima*) is a natural variety of this tree.

Clammy Locust

Robinia viscosa Vent.

The clammy locust is similar in many respects to black locust but has shorter leaves with more leaflets and fewer spines on the twigs; the flowers are rosy or flesh-colored. Glandular hairs on the narrow, winged pods, the twigs, and the leaf rachises render these parts clammy or sticky to the touch. This locust is restricted to the mountains of North Carolina and South Carolina and often occurs above altitudes of 3,000′. It has been introduced in many areas of the southern United States east of the Mississippi River and is hardy as far north as Massachusetts. It is most frequently encountered as an ornamental plant.

THE REDBUDS

Cercis L.

These are a small genus, with eight species of trees and shrubs distributed through the warmer regions of southern Europe, eastern Asia, and North America. Three species are indigenous to the United States, and one of them, eastern redbud, attains arborescent stature in the South.

Eastern Redbud   Judastree

Cercis canadensis L.

Habit.—Usually a shrub or small tree, occasionally becoming 40′ in height, with a trunk up to 1′ in diameter, branching 10′ to 15′ above the ground to form a narrow, erect or spreading, flattened or rounded head.

Leaves.—Alternate, deciduous, simple, kidney-shaped, 3″ to 5″ in diameter; apex, abruptly acute; base, heart-shaped or flattened; margin, entire; bright green above, paler below and glabrous except for axillary tufts of hairs; petioles, slender, 2″ to 5″ long, prominently swollen at the point of blade attachment.

Flowers.—Perfect, irregular, appearing before the leaves in clusters of 4 to 8; ½″ long, on ½″-long stalks; often found on the branches and trunks of young trees; calyx tube, dark red, bell-shaped with 5 short, rounded lobes; petals, 5, rose-pink, the upper enclosed by 2 lateral, winglike petals and 2 partly

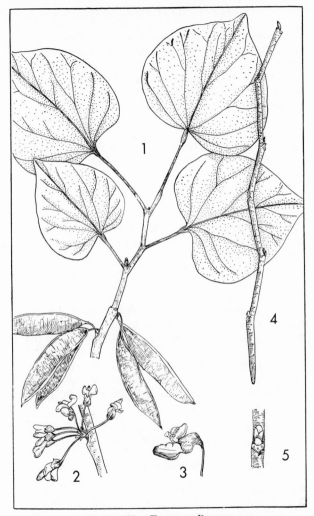

PLATE 102.—EASTERN REDBUD
1. Foliage and fruit ×½. 2. Cluster of flowers ×⅔.
3. Flower, lateral view ×1. 4. Twig ×½. 5. Leaf scar ×1.

fused, basal petals (keel); stamens, 10, shorter than the petals, in 2 rows; pistil, with a pubescent ovary, curved style, and obtuse stigma.

Fruit.—A small, linear-oblong legume, 2″ to 3½″ long, borne in lateral clusters along the twig, short-stalked, compressed; maturing from May to September but often persisting through the winter; seeds, ovate, compressed, brown, ¼″ long.

Twigs.—Slender, more or less angled or zigzag, at first light brown with many small lenticels, becoming gray-brown; terminal buds, absent; lateral buds, small, blunt, red; accessory buds, common; leaf scars, raised, with 2 large bundle scars; pith, continuous.

Bark.—Thin, brown, smooth, becoming darker and furrowed, then forming long, narrow plates, which are broken into thin scales.

Habitat.—Rich, moist soil near streams or in fertile bottoms on mountain slopes and in open woods; frequently forming thickets.

Distribution.—From New Jersey west through Pennsylvania and New York to Minnesota; south to Florida in the East and to eastern Texas in the West.

Importance.—A valuable ornamental species.

Remarks.—An Old World congener of this tree is, according to tradition, the one upon which Judas Iscariot hanged himself.

THE YELLOWWOODS

Cladrastis Raf.

This small genus includes only four species of trees. Two are natives of China, a third is found in Japan, and the fourth is indigenous to the forests of the southeastern United States.

American Yellowwood

Cladrastis lutea K. Koch

Habit.—A medium-sized tree, ordinarily 30' to 60' in height, with a trunk 1½' to 3' in diameter; commonly branching within 10' of the ground into a few ascending branches and forming a spreading, open, rounded head.

Leaves.—Alternate, deciduous, pinnately compound, with 5 to 11 subopposite leaflets, 8" to 12" long; leaflets, 3" to 4" long, 1" to 2" wide, obovate, with acute apices, wedge-shaped bases, and entire margins; dark yellow-green above, paler below; rachis, stout, with a much enlarged base, which covers the winter bud.

Flowers.—Perfect, irregular, appearing after the leaves in 12" to 14", stalked terminal panicles; individual flowers, on slender stalks; calyx, bell-shaped; the corolla, papilionaceous, with white petals; stamens, 10, free; ovary, bright red.

Fruit.—A glabrous, short-stalked, compressed, linear legume, 3" to 4" long; seeds, 4 to 6, compressed, dark brown.

Twigs.—Slender, somewhat pendulous and zigzag, brittle, becoming brown and glabrous, with numerous dark lenticels; terminal buds, lacking; lateral buds, naked, woolly, superposed; leaf scars, elevated, surrounding the small obtuse buds, with 3 to 5 raised bundle scars; pith, continuous.

Bark.—Thin, light gray or brown, smooth.

Habitat.—Rich soils, usually of limestone origin, along ridges, slopes, or cliffs near streams.

Distribution.—North Carolina, Tennessee, Kentucky, Alabama, and Missouri.

Importance.—Planted occasionally as an ornamental.

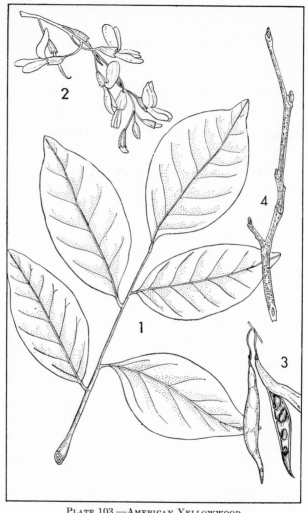

PLATE 103.—AMERICAN YELLOWWOOD
1. Leaf ×½.   2. Flowers ×¾.   3. Fruit ×½.   4. Twig ×¾.

Remarks.—Normally flowering only once every 2 years.

THE CORALBEANS

Erythrina L.

The coralbeans comprise a group of 106 species of trees, shrubs, or rarely herbs, widely distributed through the warmer regions of both hemispheres. The seeds of several species yield powerful alkaloids used in the preparation of pharmaceutical compounds. Two forms, one of which becomes arborescent, are indigenous to the lower Florida peninsula and neighboring Keys.

Eastern Coralbean

Erythrina herbacea L.

Habit.—A shrub or rarely a tree, up to 30′ in height, with a trunk 1′ in diameter; branches small, erect or spreading, and forming a rounded, open head.

Leaves.—Alternate, persistent, trifoliate, 6″ to 8″ long; leaflets, more or less triangular, 2″ to 3½″ long, 1½″ to 2½″ wide, borne on short stalks; apex, rounded; base rounded or broadly wedge-shaped; margin, entire; yellow-green above and below, glabrous; rachis, slender, much elongated, often spiny.

Flowers.—Perfect, irregular, borne in dense, long-stalked racemes, 8″ to 13″ long; flowers, papilionaceous, short-stalked; calyx, dark red; corolla, bright red; stamens, 10, in 2 groups; ovary, stalked.

Fruit.—A sharp-pointed, linear, stalked, brown legume, 4″ to 6″ long, constricted between the seeds; seeds, compressed, bright red, lustrous.

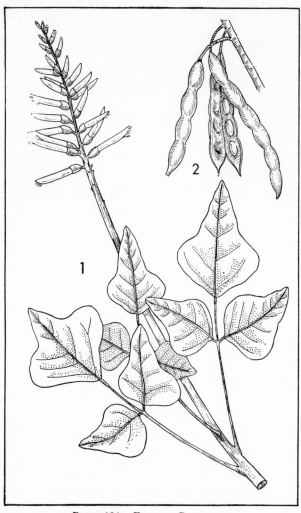

PLATE 104.—EASTERN CORALBEAN
1. Foliage and flowers ×½.   2. Fruit ×⅓.

Twigs.—Slender, greenish yellow and glabrous, armed with short, heavy, curved spines.

Bark.—Thin, red or red-brown, with conspicuous longitudinal rows of lenticels.

Habitat.—On sandy soil near salt water.

Distribution.—In Florida from Miami south and on the Keys.

Importance.—Used as an ornamental.

THE FISHPOISON-TREES

Piscidia L.

These are a small group of tropical American species comprising eight species of trees. The roots of several species yield piscida, a compound of limited medicinal use. A single species, *I. communis* Blake (*I. piscipula* A.S.H.), reaches its northern limits in the lower Florida peninsula.

Florida Fishpoison-Tree   Jamaica Dogwood

Piscidia piscipula L.

Habit.—A tree, 40′ to 50′ in height, with a trunk 1½′ to 3′ in diameter (rarely shrubby); branches, stout, erect, ascending or more or less contorted, forming an open, irregular, broad or narrow crown.

Leaves.—Alternate, tardily deciduous, pinnately compound, with 5 to 11 leaflets, 4″ to 9″ long; leaflets, 1½″ to 3″ long, opposite, obovate, with short, pubescent stalks, acute apices, rounded or wedge-shaped bases, and entire margins; at first rusty-hairy; becoming at maturity dark green and glabrous above, paler and more or less rusty-hairy below, particularly along the midrib; rachis, stout, expanded at the base.

Flowers.—Perfect, irregular, appearing in May before the leaves in several-flowered, axillary panicles;

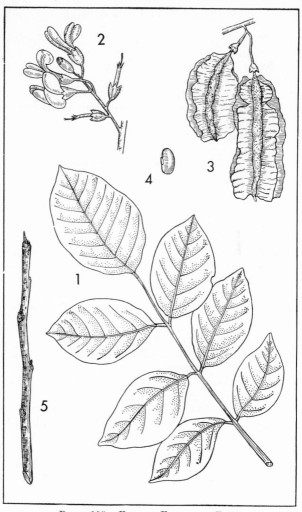

PLATE 105.—FLORIDA FISHPOISON-TREE
1. Leaf ×½. 2. Cluster of flowers ×⅔. 3. Fruit ×½.
4. Seed ×⅔. 5. Twig ×⅔.

calyx, gray, pubescent, 5-lobed; petals, white tinged with red, with a pubescent, green-blotched standard, 2 wing petals, and a keel; stamens, 10, united into a tube; pistil, with a slender, curved style and a capitate stigma.

Fruit.—A linear, compressed, long-stalked legume, constricted between the seeds and furnished with 2 pairs of wings, 1 pair arising from each suture; 3″ to 4″ long, 1″ to 1½″ broad (including wings); maturing in July and August; seeds, oval, compressed brown.

Twigs.—Slender, at first rusty-pubescent but becoming glabrous, brown with conspicuous, oblong lenticels; lateral buds, up to ¼″ long, ovoid-acute, brown and pubescent; leaf scars, large, rounded or somewhat heart-shaped, with numerous scattered bundle scars.

Bark.—Thin, gray with irregular, darker patches and many small, squarrose scales.

Habitat.—Sandy soil near salt water.

Distribution.—Common on the coast of Florida, the Keys, the Antilles, and southern Mexico.

Importance.—Of some value for fuel, charcoal, and boat timbers; somewhat resistant to rot. An extract of the bark has been used by the West Indies Indians to stupefy fish in order to catch them in nets more readily; hence the common name.

THE SOPHORAS

Sophora L.

These are a large genus of trees, shrubs, and herbs widely distributed through the milder regions of the world. Two arborescent species are natives of the southern United States.

KEY TO THE SOUTHERN SPECIES

1. Leaves, deciduous, with 13 to 19 leaflets; flowers, white, in axillary racemes...........**Texas sophora** (p. 384)
1. Leaves, persistent, with 7 to 9 leaflets; flowers, blue-violet, in terminal racemes........................
Mescalbean sophora (p. 386)

Texas Sophora

Sophora affinis J. & G.

Habit.—A large shrub or small tree, sometimes 20' to 25' in height and 6" to 10" in diameter; with a round-topped crown of graceful symmetry; the bole, sometimes dividing near the base.

Leaves.—Alternate, deciduous, odd–pinnately compound, with 13 to 19 leaflets borne on a slender, hairy rachis, 6" to 9" long; leaflets, elliptical, 1" to 1½" long, ½" wide, with acute or minutely spine-tipped apices, rounded bases, and entire or slightly undulate margins; pale yellow-green, smooth above, lighter and hairy below; petioles, short, stout.

Flowers.—Perfect, borne in axillary racemes, 3" to 5" in length; calyx, bell-shaped, the 5 toothlike lobes of nearly equal length; corolla, white, tinged with pink, with a large, nearly orbicular standard, oblong wings, and keel; stamens, 10, of which 9 are united into a tube and the remaining one is free; pistil, with a stalklike ovary surmounted by a long, contracted style and headlike stigma.

Fruit.—A rounded, black, often hairy, indehiscent legume, ½" to 3" long, greatly constricted between the seeds; seeds, 1 to 8 (mostly 4 to 8), globular or ovoid, chestnut-brown.

Twigs.—Slender, orange-brown, dark brown, or green, more or less zigzag, commonly swollen at the

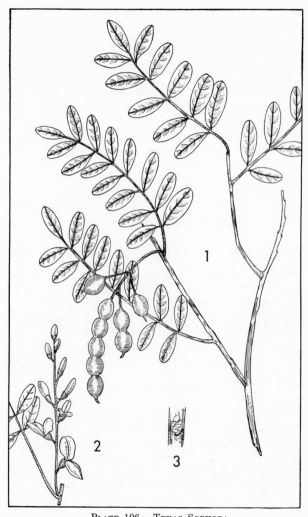

PLATE 106.—TEXAS SOPHORA
1. Foliage and fruit ×⅓. 2. Cluster of flowers ×⅓. 3. Leaf
scar ×1.

nodes; buds, depressed, covered by a netlike membrane; leaf scars, shield-shaped, with 3 bundle scars; pith, homogeneous, 3-angled, pale green; stipule scars, minute.

Bark.—Thin, dark brown and scaly, the scales oblong and shreddy at the surface.

Habitat.—Forming small groves or even thickets along streams and moist depressions; also on hillsides underlaid with limestone.

Distribution.—Northwestern Louisiana, southwestern Arkansas, southern Oklahoma, and Texas.

Importance.—None.

Mescalbean Sophora   Frijolito

Sophora secundiflora (Ortega) Lag.

This is a tree of the Southwest that occurs very sparsely in the western limits of our range. The botanical features listed in the key will serve to distinguish this tree from the Texas sophora. The seeds contain a powerful alkaloid, sophorin.

THE CALTROP FAMILY

Zygophyllaceae

The Caltrop Family comprises a group of about 21 genera and more than 150 species of tropical and subtropical trees, shrubs, and herbs with opposite, pinnate leaves. The group is represented in the United States by at least 5 genera. *Guajacum* L., however, is the only one with arborescent forms.

THE LIGNUMVITAES

Guaiacum L.

This genus includes seven or eight species distributed through the forests of Mexico, Central America, the West Indies, the Peruvian Andes, and southern Florida, where the holywood lignumvitae reaches its northern limits.

Holywood Lignumvitae

Guaiacum sanctum L.

Habit.—A small tree, sometimes 25′ to 30′ in height and 2′ to 3′ in diameter; with a short, gnarled trunk supporting a small, globelike crown of slender, pendulous branches.

Leaves.—Opposite, persistent, pinnately compound, 3″ to 4″ long, with 3 or 4 pairs of nearly sessile, leathery leaflets; leaflets, mostly obovate, about 1″ long, ½″ wide; with blunt or spine-tipped apices, unequally wedge-shaped bases, and entire margins; lustrous dark green both above and below; rachis, smooth; stipules, terminating in a pointed tip, deciduous or occasionally persisting through the summer.

Flowers.—Perfect, regular, borne in terminal clusters of 2 to 4 or rarely solitary; calyx, 5-lobed, the lobes hairy, obovate; petals, 5, blue, commonly twisted at their base; stamens, 10, opposite to and alternating with the petals; pistil, with an obovoid, 5-celled ovary, short style, and 5-lobed stigma.

Fruit.—A lustrous, orange-colored, obovoid, strongly 5-angled, fleshy capsule; at maturity splitting along 5 lines of suture, about ¾″ long; seeds, numerous, black, with a fleshy, scarlet outer coat.

Twigs.—Slender, greenish gray, hairy when they first appear, becoming grayish white in the 2d season;

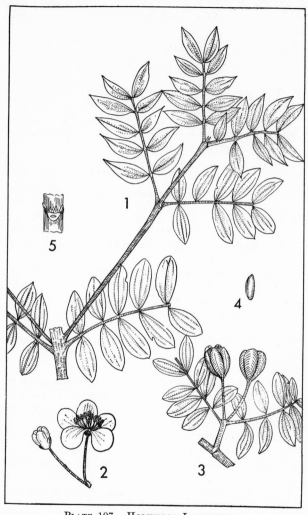

PLATE 107.—HOLYWOOD LIGNUMVITAE

1. Foliage ×½. 2. Cluster of flowers ×⅔. 3. Fruit ×½.
4. Seed ×⅔. 5. Leaf scar ×1½.

characterized by small excrescences, noticeably swollen at the nodes; buds, minute, naked; leaf scars, broadly crescent-shaped, with a single transverse bundle scar; stipules or stipule scars, evident; pith, white, terete, continuous.

Bark.—Thin, grayish white, superficially scaly.

Habitat.—A tidewater tree.

Distribution.—Southern Florida Keys, the Bahamas, Puerto Rico, Yucatan, Cuba, and Haiti.

Importance.—Lignumvitae produces a very hard, heavy, resinous wood adapted to many special uses. The resin content, which runs to about 30 per cent of the weight of the wood, renders the wood suitable for many purposes where the introduction of other lubricants is not practical. Because of this feature, it is ideal for ship propeller-shaft bearings and for food- and liquid-handling machinery where oil cannot be used without the possibility of contamination. The wood is also used for pulleys, neck bearings, mallets, bushings, bowling balls, and casters. The resin has a medicinal value as a diaphoretic in treating rheumatism and similar ailments.

THE RUE FAMILY
Rutaceae

The Rue Family comprises a group of 120 genera and about 1,000 species of trees, shrubs, and a few herbs, distributed through the temperate and warmer regions of the world. Several tropical species produce excellent structural and decorative woods, but the best-known members of the group belong to the genus *Citrus*, to which are traceable the orange, lemon, lime, kumquat, and grapefruit.

Four genera with arborescent forms are included in the silva of the United States, and 3 of them are represented by one or more forms in our southern woodlands.

Synopsis of Southern Genera

Genus	Leaves	Flowers	Fruit
Zanthoxylum	pinnate, alternate, usually with 5 or more leaflets	dioecious or polygamous	a capsule
Ptelea	alternate, trifoliate	polygamous	a disclike samara
Amyris	opposite, trifoliate	perfect or polygamous	a 1-seeded drupe

THE PRICKLY-ASHES

Zanthoxylum L.

The prickly-ashes number about 140 species of trees and shrubs with aromatic foliage, fruit, and bark, and usually with stipular spines. While the genus is widely distributed throughout the tropical and warmer regions of the world, it is most abundant in the forests of tropical America.

Five species, one a northern shrub (*Z. americanum* Mill.), are indigenous to the United States. The four arborescent species are all southern trees.

KEY TO THE SOUTHERN PRICKLY-ASHES

1. Leaf rachis, winged; flower clusters, axillary..........
   Lime prickly-ash (p. 391)
1. Leaf rachis, unwinged, sometimes armed with prickles; flower clusters, terminal............................ 2

2. Leaves, odd-pinnate, dull; flower parts, in 5's...... 3
2. Leaves, even-pinnate, shiny; flower parts, in 3's...
   Biscayne prickly-ash (p. 396)

3. Leaves, deciduous; twigs, armed with stout, stipular spines.......................**Hercules-club** (p. 393)
3. Leaves, persistent; twigs, unarmed..................
   Yellowheart (p. 394)

Lime Prickly-Ash   Wild Lime

Zanthoxylum fagara Sarg.

Habit.—Usually encountered as a shrub, but occasionally attaining arborescent proportions, then a tree 25′ to 30′ in height, with a slender, commonly inclined trunk 10″ to 20″ in diameter; crown, more or less cylindrical, with nearly erect, crowded branches.

Leaves.—Alternate, persistent, odd–pinnately compound, 3″ to 4″ long, with 7 to 9 nearly sessile or sub-sessile leaflets; leaflets, leathery, mostly obovate, about ½″ long; apex, rounded or notched; base, rounded and broadly wedge-shaped; margin, minutely scalloped above the middle; bright green and dotted with minute glands; rachis, winged; stipules, becoming hooked, woody spines, commonly deciduous.

Flowers.—Dioecious, borne in the leaf axils during late spring and early summer in cylindrical cymes, occasionally appearing from small, globular buds on twigs of the previous season; calyx, composed of 4 sepals; petals, 4, yellow-green, ovate, about twice as long as the sepals; stamens, 4, in the male flowers with slender, elongated filaments; pistils, 2 (rudimentary in the male flowers), with sessile, ovoid ovaries, short, stout styles, and single, fleshy, stigmatic lobes.

Fruit.—An obovoid, rusty-brown, wrinkled, and somewhat warty capsule, about ¼″ long; at maturity, splitting along 2 lines of suture and releasing the single. shining-black seed.

Twigs.—Slender, commonly zigzag, grayish yellow to reddish brown, sometimes with minute ridges between the nodes; buds, small, globelike, woolly and indistinctly scaly; leaf scars, half-round to broadly triangular, with 3 bundle scars; pith, continuous, white; stipular spines, hooked, often early deciduous.

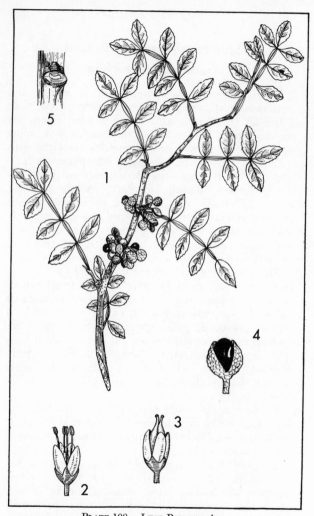

PLATE 108.—LIME PRICKLY-ASH

1. Foliage and fruit ×½. 2. Male flower ×2. 3. Female flower ×2. 4. Single fruit ×2. 5. Leaf scar ×2.

Bark.—Very thin, gray, on the larger stems broken into thin, closely appressed scales, sometimes featured by corky projections, 1″ or more in height.

Habitat.—Very abundant in southern Florida, arborescent on hammocks and well-drained, rich loams; commonly shrubby on sandy soils near the sea.

Distribution.—Southern Florida and the Keys and southeastern Texas to the Rio Grande; south through the West Indies, Mexico, and Central America to Peru and Brazil.

Importance.—None.

Hercules-Club   Toothache-Tree
Zanthoxylum clava-herculis L.

Habit.—A small tree, 30′ to 40′ in height and 12″ to 18″ in diameter, with a short bole and nearly globular crown of horizontally spreading branches.

Leaves.—Alternate, late deciduous, often persisting through the winter and sometimes until leaf emergence the following spring, odd–pinnately compound, 5″ to 9″ long, with 7 to 19 sessile or nearly sessile leaflets; leaflets, somewhat leathery, mostly ovate, sometimes scythe-shaped, 1″ to 2½″ long; apex, acute to long-tapered; base, unequally rounded or wedge-shaped; margin, with rounded teeth; lustrous bright green above, paler and more or less hairy below; rachis, unwinged, stout, hairy, and usually spiny; stipules, becoming woody spines.

Flowers.—Dioecious, borne in the early spring in terminal cymose clusters; calyx, composed of 5 minute sepals; petals, 5, oval, light green; stamens, 5, longer than the petals, sometimes present in rudimentary form in the pistillate flowers; pistils, 3-(rarely 2-) celled, each with an ovoid, sessile ovary, short, thick style, and 2-lobed stigma, rudimentary in the staminate flowers.

Fruit.—An ovoid to nearly globular, brown, wrinkled or roughed, 3- or 2-valved capsule, about ¼″ long, at maturity the single, shining-black seed commonly hanging by a slender thread from the husk.

Twigs.—Stout, at first clothed with brownish hairs, becoming gray-brown to yellow-brown and smooth in their 2d season, often glandular; buds, small, obtuse, smooth and indistinctly scaly, black or dark brown; leaf scars, broadly triangular to heart-shaped, with 3 bundle scars; armed with long, straight or curved, chestnut-brown spines commonly ½″ or more in length; pith, continuous, whitish.

Bark.—Very thin, even on the largest trunks, light gray and smooth except for conical, corky excrescences, 1″ or more in diameter across their base.

Habitat.—Sandy soils near the coast, riverbanks, and low, fertile valleys near streams in association with other hardwoods.

Distribution.—Atlantic coastal plain from southeastern Virginia to southern Florida; west through the Gulf states, Louisiana, Arkansas, Texas and to the Colorado River Valley.

Importance.—The wood of herculesclub is of no commercial value. The bark, however, contains analgesics, at one time used in quantity by the Negro slave when seeking relief from the pains of rheumatism and toothache.

Remarks.—A shrubby variety (*Z. clava-herculis* var. *fruticosum* Gray), commonly with trifoliate leaves, occurs in western Texas.

Yellowheart   Satinwood

Zanthoxylum flavum Vahl.

Habit.—A tree, 30′ to 40′ in height, with a modest, cylindrical bole 12″ to 20″ in diameter and a dense, round-topped, evergreen crown, which is often broader than tall.

Leaves.—Alternate, persistent, odd–pinnately compound, 6″ to 9″ long, with 5 to 11 (rarely 3) short-stalked leaflets; leaflets, leathery, oblong or ovate, sometimes scythe-shaped, 1½″ to 2″ long; apex, mostly obtuse; base, usually asymmetrical; margins, entire or minutely scalloped; yellowish green and characteristically dotted with a myriad of plainly visible, translucent glands; rachis, usually woolly.

Flowers.—Dioecious, borne in the early spring in terminal, spreading, cymose clusters; calyx, 5-lobed, the lobes triangular; petals, 5, greenish white; stamens, 5, longer than the petals (wanting in the pistillate flowers); pistils, 2 (rarely), with obovate ovaries, short styles, and spreading stigmas (rudimentary in the male flowers).

Fruit.—An ovoid, glandular-punctate, chestnut-brown capsule, about ⅓″ long; at maturity splitting along 2 lines of suture to release a single shining-black seed.

Twigs.—Stout, brittle, brown, covered with silky hairs in their 1st year, ultimately becoming gray, smooth or somewhat wrinkled; buds, narrow, elongated, covered with a coat of woolly hairs, indistinctly scaly, about ½″ long; leaf scars, broadly triangular, with 3 bundle scars; pith, continuous, whitish.

Bark.—About ¼″ thick, smooth and light gray on young stems, becoming fissured and separating into short, closely appressed scales on old trunks.

Habitat.—Seldom found far removed from salt water; ordinarily occurring as an occasional tree in association with other species.

Distribution.—The Florida Keys, the Bahamas, San Domingo, and Puerto Rico.

Importance.—This species produces a hard, rich, golden-yellow, highly figured wood that at present is not infrequently used in American cabinet shops for the fabrication of modern furniture.

Biscayne Prickly-Ash

Zanthoxylum coriaceum A. Rich.

This is a rare tropical shrub or small tree occurring in Florida only along Biscayne Bay and near Fort Lauderdale. It may be distinguished from other pricklyashes of the south by its even-pinnate leaves and flowers that have their parts in 3's.

THE HOPTREES

Ptelea L.

The hoptrees comprise a group of about 10 species of trees and shrubs restricted to North America and distributed from southern Canada to Mexico. Two species attain arborescent proportions in the United States, one of which is indigenous to the South.

Common Hoptree

Ptelea trifoliata L.

Habit.—A large shrub, or sometimes a small tree, 20′ to 25′ in height and 6″ to 12″ in diameter, with a straight, slender, trunk bearing a broad, rounded crown with numerous short, stout, erect, and ascending branches.

Leaves.—Alternate (rarely opposite), deciduous, glandular, trifoliate (rarely in part 5-foliate), 4″ to 6″ long; leaflets, 2½″ to 4″ long, nearly sessile, ovate to oblong; apex, acute; base, wedge-shaped; margins, entire or remotely scalloped; lustrous,

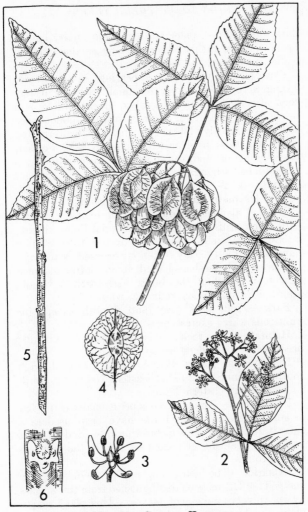

PLATE 109.—COMMON HOPTREE
1. Foliage and fruit ×½. 2. Cluster of flowers ⅓. 3. Single
flower ×2. 4. Single fruit ×1. 5. Twig ×⅔. 6. Leaf scar ×3.

dark green above, paler and commonly hairy on the lower surface; rachis, about as long as the terminal leaflet, swollen at the base.

Flowers.—Polygamous, appearing in the early spring in many-flowered, terminal, cymose clusters soon after leaf emergence; calyx, green, with 4 or 5 ovate lobes; petals, 4 or 5, greenish white, about twice as long as the calyx lobes; stamens, 4 or 5, alternating with the petals; pistil, raised, the ovary 2- or 3-celled, laterally compressed, the short style surmounted by a 2- or 3-lobed stigma.

Fruit.—A 2- or 3-celled, circular, compressed, yellowish samara with a broad, netted wing.

Twigs.—Slender, yellowish brown, exhaling a rank odor when bruised or broken; terminal buds, absent; lateral buds, small, globular, covered with whitish hairs, indistinctly scaly, often superposed; leaf scars, U-shaped to horseshoe-shaped, in the latter instance nearly surrounding the buds, each with 3 bundle scars; pith, continuous, rounded, whitish.

Bark.—Thin, dark gray and smooth except for numerous warty excrescences.

Habitat.—Dry, rocky soils margining woodlands; occasionally an understory species.

Distribution.—Long Island, N.Y., west through southern Minnesota to southeastern Nebraska, south to Florida and eastern Texas.

Importance.—The hoptree is occasionally employed as an ornamental. Its fruits have been used as a substitute for real hops in brewing beer, and its bark contains certain bitter principles used in the preparation of tonics.

Remarks.—The coast hoptree (*P. trifoliata* var. *mollis* T. & G.) may be distinguished from this species by its velvety, pubescent leaves. This plant ranges along the Atlantic coastal plain from North Carolina to Florida.

THE TORCHWOODS

Amyris L.

These are a group of about 15 species of trees and shrubs, with fragrant resinous juices, confined to tropical America and northern Mexico. A single arborescent form of the West Indies extends to the Florida Keys.

Sea Amyris   Torchwood

Amyris elemifera L.

Habit.—A small tree, 40′ to 50′ in height, with a slender bole 10″ to 15″ in diameter. (In many localities never more than a large, bushy shrub.)

Leaves.—Opposite, persistent, leathery, glandular, 3-foliate, 2″ to 4½″ long; leaflets, 1″ to 2½″ long, stalked, ovate to ovate-lanceolate; apex, long-tapered; base, rounded or broadly wedge-shaped; margins, entire or remotely scalloped; bright green, smooth, lustrous above, dull green, with dark, glandular dots below; rachis, about 1″ to 1½″ long, smooth.

Flowers.—Perfect (rarely polygamous), appearing in the late summer and throughout the autumn in terminal, panicled clusters; calyx, 4-lobed; petals, 4, white, about twice as long as the calyx lobes; stamens, 8, opposite and alternate with the petals; pistil, with a 1-celled ovoid ovary, short style, and headlike stigma.

Fruit.—A black, globular drupe, covered with a bluish, waxy bloom; 1-seeded by abortion; the flesh, thin, aromatic, and palatable.

Twigs.—Slender, unarmed, light brown, often warty; buds, acute, the shining scales usually keeled on the back; leaf scars, half-round, with 3 often crowded bundle scars; pith, continuous, white.

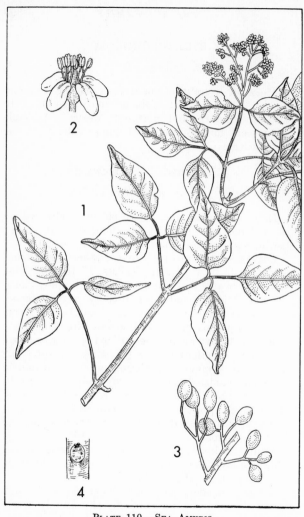

PLATE 110.—SEA AMYRIS
1. Foliage and flowers ×½. 2. Single flower ×3. 3. Fruit
×⅔. 4. Leaf scar ×1½.

Bark.—Thin, brownish gray and smooth; on the largest trunks, shallowly furrowed and broken into small, closely appressed scales.

Habitat.—On sandy and rocky shores immediately adjacent to the ocean and on high, rich hammocks farther inland.

Distribution.—Southern peninsular Florida, the Florida Keys, the Bahamas, and the West Indies.

Importance.—The very resinous wood of this species is occasionally used locally for fuel and the branches for torches. The wood oils have a limited pharmaceutical use.

THE QUASSIA FAMILY

Simaroubaceae

This is a group of tropical and subtropical plants with about 150 species included in 30 genera. The Chinese tree-of-heaven [*Ailanthus altissima* (Mill.) Swingle], introduced from Asia many years ago, belongs to this family. This tree has long since escaped cultivation and has become naturalized in many parts of the United States including large areas in the South.

Three genera are represented in our subtropical forests, each by a single species.

Synopsis of Southern Genera

Genus	Leaves	Flowers	Fruit
Alvaradoa	with 21 to 41 leaflets	in racemes	2-winged samara
Picramnia	with 5 to 9 leaflets	in racemes	a berry
Simarouba	with 10 to 14 leaflets	in panicles	a drupe

THE ALVARADOAS

Alvaradoa Liebm.

These are a genus of three or four species of trees and shrubs with bitter juices, confined to the tropics and subtropics of the Western Hemisphere. The cosmopolitan Mexican alvaradoa extends northward into Florida.

Mexican Alvaradoa

Alvaradoa amorphoides Liebm.

Habit.—A shrub or, toward the northern limits of its range, a small tree; in Florida, occasionally attaining a height of 20′ to 30′ and a diameter of 4″ to 8″.

Leaves.—Alternate, persistent, crowded at the ends of twigs, pinnately compound, with 21 to 41 leaflets borne on a slender, flexible rachis, 4″ to 12″ long; leaflets, oblong to obovate, ½″ to ¾″ long, about ¼″ wide, with obtuse or minutely spine-tipped apices, gradually narrowing, often somewhat asymmetrical bases, and entire, somewhat thickened, and slightly curled margins; dark green above, pale green and hairy below; petioles, extremely short, hairy.

Flowers.—Unisexual, each sex borne on separate trees, in many-flowered terminal or axillary racemes, 3″ to 8″ long; staminate flowers, with a 5-parted, bell-shaped calyx, 5 threadlike petals (petals sometimes wanting), and 10 stamens; pistillate flowers, without petals, the pistil with a 3-angled, 3-celled ovary, crowned with a pair of unequal, recurved styles, stigmatic above the middle.

Fruit.—A reddish, lanceolate, long-stalked, 2-winged samara, about ¾″ long, crowned at the summit by the persistent styles and furnished along the margin of the wings with long, spreading hairs; seeds, yellowish, pointed, about ¼″ long.

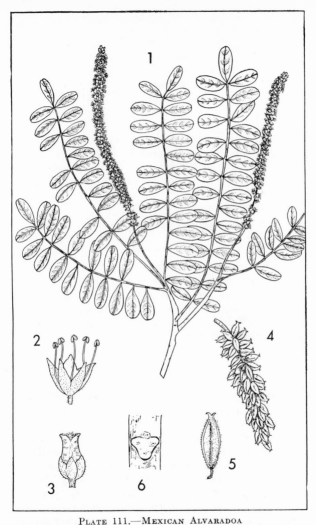

PLATE 111.—MEXICAN ALVARADOA
1. Leaves and male inflorescence ×⅓. 2. Male flower ×2.
3. Female flower ×2. 4. Fruit cluster ×⅓. 5. Single fruit ×1.
6. Leaf scar ×2.

Twigs.—Slender, densely clothed with white, woolly hairs during the 1st winter, later becoming smooth and dark reddish brown except for pale lenticels; buds, minute, globular, hairy; leaf scars, half-round to 3-lobed, with 3 bundle scars; pith, homogeneous.

Bark.—Thin, smooth, gray-brown, sometimes with a reddish tinge.

Habitat.—Hammocks and drier high ground.

Distribution.—Near Homestead and Miami, Fla., south over many of the Keys to Cuba; also reported from the Bahamas, Argentina, Central America, and southern Mexico.

Importance.—None.

THE BITTERBUSHES

Picramnia Sw.

The bitterbushes constitute a group of about 20 tropical and subtropical trees, many of which produce barks containing bitter principles of pharmaceutical value in the preparation of tonics. All are restricted to the New World, and one inhabits the Keys and forests of lower peninsular Florida.

Bitterbush

Picramnia pentandra Sw.

Habit.—A shrub or small, slender tree; in Florida seldom attaining a height of more than 20′ or a diameter of 6″.

Leaves.—Alternate, persistent, odd–pinnately compound, with 5 to 9 alternate or subopposite leaflets borne on a slender rachis, 8″ to 12″ long; leaflets, leathery, mostly oblong to ovate, 1″ to 3″ long, about 1″ wide, with long-tapered apices, wedge-shaped bases, and entire or slightly thickened, curled margins; dark green, smooth, lustrous above, paler below; petioles, very short, about $\frac{1}{10}$″ long.

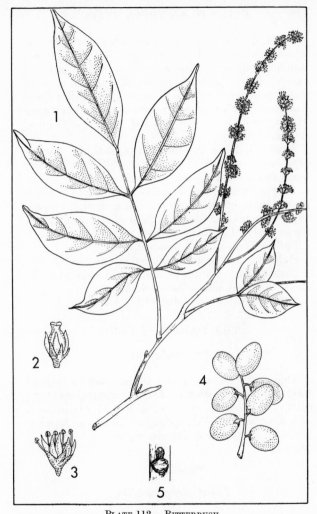

PLATE 112.—BITTERBUSH

1. Foliage and male flowers ×½. 2. Female flower ×2.
3. Male flower ×2. 4. Fruit cluster ×⅔. 5. Leaf scar ×1½.

Flowers.—Unisexual, greenish, each sex borne on separate trees in hairy racemes, 4″ to 8″ long; staminate flowers, with a 5-lobed, hairy calyx, 5 narrow, hairy, greenish petals, 5 stamens, and an abortive ovary; pistillate flowers, with similar calyx and corolla, 5 scalelike, abortive stamens, and pistil with a sessile ovary surmounted by a 2- or 3-lobed stigma.

Fruit.—A 1- or 2-seeded, lustrous-black, oblong-oval berry, about ½″ in length, ¼″ in diameter; seeds, lustrous, tawny.

Twigs.—Slender, hairy, yellowish brown to greenish brown; buds, ovoid, hairy; leaf scars, circular to oval, with 3 marginal bundle scars, the medial scar elongated transversely, the others circular; pith, homogeneous.

Bark.—Thin, smooth, yellow-brown.

Habitat.—Sandy shores bordering tidewaters.

Distribution.—Lower peninsular Florida and the Keys, the West Indies, and Colombia.

Importance.—Of no value within our range.

THE PARADISE-TREES

Simarouba Aubl.

This group of four species is restricted to tropical forests of the New World. Like other members of the family, the paradise-trees are also noted for resins, oils, and pharmaceutical compounds. Only one member of this genus occurs within our region.

Paradise-Tree

Simarouba glauca D.C.

Habit.—A tree, often 50′ or more in height and 1′ to 2′ in diameter, with a straight, columnar bole and

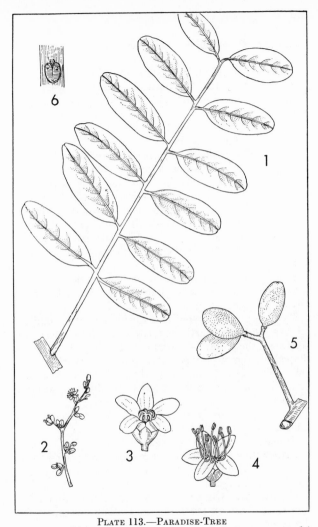

PLATE 113.—PARADISE-TREE

1. Leaf ×½. 2. Small portion of male inflorescence ×½.
3. Female flower ×2. 4. Male flower ×½. 5. Cluster of fruit ×½.
6. Leaf scar ×1½.

small, nearly globular crown with short, spreading branches.

Leaves.—Alternate, persistent, even–pinnately compound, with 10 to 14 opposite or alternate, leathery leaflets borne on a stout rachis, 6″ to 10″ long; leaflets, leathery, oblong, oval, or obovate, 2″ to 3″ long, about 1¼″ wide, with rounded or minutely spine-tipped apices, oblique, asymmetrical bases, and curled margins; dark green above, with a white bloom below; petioles, short, very stout, about ¼″ long.

Flowers.—Unisexual, the sexes borne on separate trees, in axillary or terminal panicles, 1′ to 1½′ long and 1′ to 2′ broad; staminate flowers, with a 5-lobed calyx, 5 yellow petals, and 10 stamens; pistillate flowers, with similar calyx and corolla parts and a 5-celled, nearly globular ovary with a minute, sessile stigma.

Fruit.—An ovoid, deep-purple or scarlet drupe, with thin flesh, about 1″ long; seed, orange-brown, about ¾″ long.

Twigs.—Stout, greenish brown, smooth; buds, minute, globular, partly embedded in the epidermal layers of the twig; leaf scars, heart-shaped, shield-shaped, or remotely triangular, sometimes with pale-yellowish, silky hairs along their margins, with 3 raised, bundle scars; pith, homogeneous, light brownish white.

Bark.—Moderately thick, reddish brown, scaly at the surface.

Habitat.—Coastal hammocks.

Distribution.—Southern peninsular Florida and the Keys, the West Indies, Mexico, central and tropical South America.

Importance.—Quassin, a bitter principle used for tonics, is obtained from this and other members of the genus.

THE TORCHWOOD FAMILY

Burseraceae

This is a tropical group of trees and shrubs with resinous, aromatic sap, comprising about 400 species distributed in 20 genera. The resinous exudations from the bark are used medicinally and for compounding incense. Frankincense is the product of several Arabian species of *Boswellia*, while myrrh is derived from *Commiphora myrrha* Eng., a small tree indigenous to the shores of the Red Sea. Several tropical American genera are productive of timber.

THE GUMBOS

Bursera Jacq.

The gumbos comprise a group of about 80 trees, mostly inhabitants of the American tropics. Two species occur in the United States, one in the Southwest, the other in the Southeast.

Gumbo-Limbo

Bursera simaruba (L.) Sarg.

Habit.—A moderately large tree, 50′ to 60′ in height and 2′ to 3′ in diameter, with a spreading, round-topped crown.

Leaves.—Alternate, persistent or tardily deciduous through the winter and early spring, crowded toward the tips of twigs, odd–pinnately compound, with 3 to 9 (mostly 5 or 7) leaflets borne on a smooth, slender rachis, 6″ to 8″ long; leaflets, leathery, oblong to ovate, except for the terminal leaflet, opposite in pairs, 2″ to 3″ long, 1″ to 2″ broad, with acute, long-tapered apices, unequally oblique bases, and entire or slightly

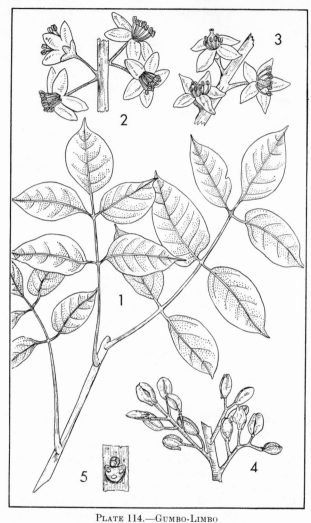

PLATE 114.—GUMBO-LIMBO
1. Foliage ×½. 2. Male flowers ×2. 3. Female flowers ×2.
4. Fruit cluster ×1. 5. Leaf scar ×1.

wavy margins; bright green above, paler below; petioles, about ½″ long.

Flowers.—Polygamous, borne in many-flowered racemes; sepals, 5; petals, 5; stamens, 8 to 12, longer than the petals, much reduced in the pistillate flowers; pistil, with 3- to 5-celled ovary, short style, and cushionlike stigma, abortive in the staminate flowers.

Fruit.—Drupaceous, ⅓″ long, dark red, 3-angled, leathery; at maturity, splitting along 3 lines of suture and releasing the single (occasionally 2) triangular, bony nutlet; seeds, minute, pinkish.

Twigs.—Stout, gray to light yellowish brown; buds, obtuse, reddish brown, scaly; leaf scars, heart-shaped, with 3 bundle scars; pith, homogeneous.

Bark.—Thin, light reddish brown, divided into thin, papery, birchlike scales.

Habitat.—Sandy soils and hammocks near tidewater.

Distribution.—Southern Florida including the Keys, and the West Indies.

Importance.—Of little commercial value. Small logs used in the round as fence posts have been known to take root and grow at an exceedingly rapid rate.

THE MAHOGANY FAMILY

Meliaceae

This family, widely distributed throughout the tropical and warmer regions of the world, includes about 40 genera and more than 600 species of trees, shrubs, and woody annuals Many of the world's finest cabinet woods are products of this family; a few are noted ornamentals. The West Indies mahogany (*Swietenia mahagoni* Jacq.), the baywood (*S. macrophylla* King), and the cigarbox cedar (*Cedrela odorata* L.) are the most noteworthy timbers of tropical America. The African mahoganies, which in recent years have been substituted quite generally for the American mahoganies, are products of several species of the genera *Khaya* and *Entandrophragma*. The chinaberry (*Melia azedarach* L.), widely used as a dooryard tree throughout the South, is also a member of this group.

THE MAHOGANIES

Swietenia Jacq.

These are a small genus of trees including five or six species distributed through the forests of southern Florida, Mexico, Central America, Venezuela, and Peru. The West Indies mahogany is our only representative of this family.

West Indies Mahogany

Swietenia mahagoni Jacq.

Habit.—A moderately tall tree; in Florida, seldom exceeding a height or diameter of 40′ to 60′ and 12″ 24″, respectively, but much larger in the tropics.

Leaves.—Alternate, persistent, even–pinnately compound, 4″ to 7″ long, with 3 or 4 pairs of leathery leaflets; leaflets, ovate to lance-shaped, often scythelike, 3″ to 4″ long, about 1″ broad; apex, long-tapered; base, asymmetrical, usually rounded on the upper side of the midrib, straight on the lower side; margin, entire; bright green above, pale yellow-green below, sometimes furnished with rusty-red hairs; rachis, slender except at the thickened base.

Flowers.—Perfect, minute, borne in panicles in the leaf axils; calyx, minute, cup-shaped, 5-lobed; petals, 5, white or greenish, about ⅛″ long, notched at the apex; stamens, forming a 10-lobed tube, the anthers, attached on the back below the sinuses of the tube; pistil, with a 5-celled, ovoid ovary surmounted by an

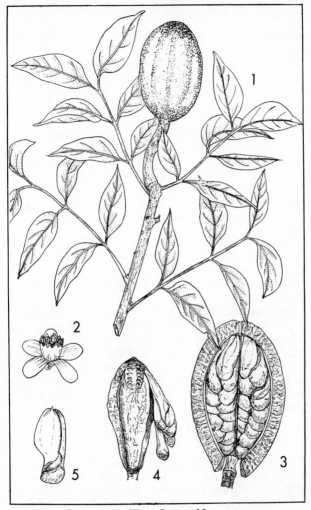

PLATE 115.—WEST INDIES MAHOGANY

1. Foliage and fruit ×⅓. 2. Flower ×2. 3. Longitudinal
section through fruit ×½. 4. Mode of seed attachment ×½.
5. Seed ×1.

erect, thick style crowned with a cushion or disclike stigma.

Fruit.—A dark-reddish-brown, ovoid, thick-walled capsule, about 3″ to 4″ long; 5-celled, 5-valved, at maturity splitting from base toward the rounded apex and separating from a 5-angled, club-shaped axis; seeds, squarish, winged, about ¾″ long, arranged in 2 rows on each side of the axis and suspended from near the summit by an attachment of the wing.

Twigs.—Stout or moderately slender, sometimes angled, light brown, warty; terminal buds, wanting; lateral buds, small, depressed, globular, with 2 or 3 outer scales; leaf scars, shield-shaped, with 3 bundle scars or 3 groups of bundle scars; pith, homogeneous, light brown.

Bark.—Moderately thick, dark brownish red to dark brown, divided at the surface into broad, short, thickened scales.

Habitat.—Hammocks and shore lines in Florida and the Keys.

Distribution.—Lower peninsular Florida and the Keys; abundant in the West Indies.

Importance.—One of the world's most valuable cabinet timbers. Excessive cutting in Florida has resulted in its almost complete extinction within our range except in a few very localized areas. The bark contains an astringent that has been used as a substitute for quinine.

THE SPURGE FAMILY

Euphorbiaceae

The Spurge Family embraces about 250 genera and nearly 5,000 species of trees, shrubs, herbs, and climbers with acrid and not infrequently poisonous sap. Many species are of great economic value. Among those plants used ornamentally or for decorative purposes are the Christmas poinsettia (*Euphorbia*

heterophylla L.), the crown-of-thorns (*E. splendens*
Bojer.), and many of the crotons (*Croton* spp.). The
principal source of rubber is from the latex of the
South American *Hevea brasiliensis* Arg., now widely
cultivated throughout the tropics; Pará rubber is
obtained from *H. guianensis* Aubl., also a native of
South America. The seeds of the castorbean (*Ricinus
communis* L.) are rich in an oil used in medicinal
preparations, for illuminative purposes, and as a
lubricant for airplane motors and other types of high-
speed machinery. The Chinese wood oil or tung oil
is expressed from the seeds of *Aleurites fordii* Hems.,
now widely planted in certain southern areas. Croton
oil is obtained from the seeds of *C. tiglium* L., and the
roots of *Manihot utilissima* Pohl. produce the tapioca
starch of commerce.

Thirty genera and about 135 species are components
of our southern flora. Three genera include arborescent forms.

Synopsis of Southern Genera

Genus	Leaves	Flowers	Fruit
Drypetes	persistent, with acute bases	dioecious, in axillary clusters	a 1-seeded drupe
Hippomane	tardily deciduous, with rounded or heart-shaped bases	monoecious, in terminal, bisexual spikes; the pistillate, basal	a many-seeded drupe
Gymnanthes	persistent, with acute bases	monoecious, both sexes appearing in the same leaf axils but on separate stalks	a 3-lobed capsule

THE DRYPETES

Drypetes Vahl.

These are a small, tropical American genus of trees distributed through the West Indies and South and Central America. Two extend northward into southern Florida.

KEY TO THE FLORIDIAN DRYPETES

1. Fruit, ovoid, ivory-white, with a thick, hard stone; staminate flowers, with a 5-lobed calyx, and 8 stamens; leaf scars, circular. . . . .**Milkbark** (p. 416)
1. Fruit, globular, scarlet, with a thin, brittle stone; staminate flowers, with a 4-lobed calyx, and 4 stamens; leaf scars, oval. . . . .**Guiana plum** (p. 418)

Milkbark

Drypetes diversifolia Krug. & Urg.

Habit.—A small tree or shrub, sometimes 30′ to 40′ in height and 8″ to 12″ in diameter, with an oblong crown of stout, ascending branches.

Leaves.—Alternate, simple, persistent, leathery, oblong to oval, 3″ to 5″ long, 1″ to 2″ wide; apex, acute, rounded, or minutely notched; base, rounded or wedge-shaped; margin, entire, sometimes with spiny teeth on young leaves or those of vigorous shoots; lustrous, dark green above, somewhat paler below; petioles, stout, about ½″ long, grooved above, often yellow; stipules, minute, triangular.

Flowers.—Unisexual, each sex appearing on separate plants in the axils of leaves from the previous season; staminate, in many-flowered clusters, with a 5-lobed calyx, no petals, and 8 stamens, variable in length; pistillate, solitary or occasionally in clusters of 2 or 3, with a 5-lobed calyx, no petals, and pistil

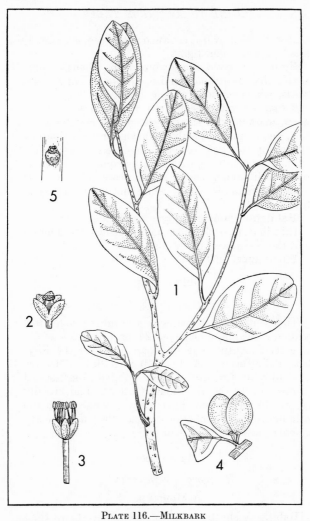

PLATE 116.—MILKBARK
1. Foliage ×⅓.   2. Female flower ×2.   3. Male flower ×2.
4. Fruit ×½.   5. Leaf scar ×1½.

with a 1-celled ovary, crowned with a sessile or nearly sessile, cushionlike stigma.

Fruit.—An ovoid, ivory-white drupe, about 1″ long; with a dry, mealy pulp and brown, hard, bony stone; seeds, 1 in each stone, oblong, about ½″ long.

Twigs.—Stout, greenish red, with widely separated hairs, marked with small, pale, raised, circular lenticels; buds, minute, partly embedded in the epidermal tissues of the twig, often resin-covered; leaf scars, circular, or nearly so, with 3 nearly equidistant bundle scars; pith, homogeneous; stipule scars, minute.

Bark.—Smooth, chalky white mottled with gray or brown.

Habitat.—Hammocks; rare in Florida.

Distribution.—Extreme lower peninsular Florida and the Keys; also in the Bahamas.

Importance.—None.

Guiana Plum

Drypetes lateriflora Urb.

The whitewood drypetes is a shrub or small tree seldom exceeding a height of 25′ or a diameter of 6″. It extends south along the coast and over the Keys from Palm Beach, Fla., to the West Indies. This tree is readily distinguished from milkbark on several count. Its leaves are about 1″ shorter and broadly elliptical; the flowers have only 4 sepals, and the staminate a like number of stamens; the fruit is nearly globular, scarlet, and about ¼″ long.

Manchineel

Hippomane mancinella L.

A Monotype

Habit.—A shrub or bushy tree, rarely more than 15′ in height or 6″ in diameter; characterized by

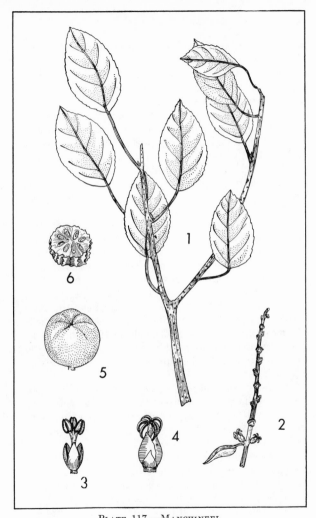

PLATE 117.—MANCHINEEL

1. Leaves ×⅓. 2. Flower cluster ×½. 3. Male flower ×3.
4. Female flower ×3. 5. Fruit ×½. 6. Transverse section of
stone ×½.

pendulous branches and a spreading, rounded crown
of pleasing symmetry.

Leaves.—Alternate, simple, tardily deciduous, usually falling with the appearance of the new spring
shoots, broadly ovate, 3″ to 4″ long, 1″ to 2″ wide;
apex, abruptly narrowed into a short, sharp, needle-
pointed tip; base, rounded or heart-shaped; margin,
with fine, rounded, glandular teeth, at least above the
middle; dark yellow-green above, paler below; petioles,
slender, slightly grooved above, with large, reddish
glands near the leaf blade, 2″ to 4″ long; stipules,
lance-shaped, broad at the base, often irregularly
toothed toward the apex.

Flowers.—Unisexual, both sexes appearing in terminal, bisexual spikes 4″ to 6″ in length; staminate
flowers, minute, in clusters of 8 to 15 along the upper
portion of the rachis in the axil of a bract, with a 3-
lobed, yellowish-green calyx, no petals, and 2 or 3
stamens united into a column; pistillate flowers,
solitary, inserted below the staminate near the base
of the rachis, each in the axil of a small bract, with a 3-
lobed calyx, no petals, and single pistil with a 6- to
8-celled ovary, surmounted by a short, columnar style
which is divided at the summit into 6 to 8 reflexed,
stigmatic lobes.

Fruit.—A pear-shaped, sometimes obscurely 6- to
8-lobed, yellow-green drupe, with a bright-yellow or
scarlet cheek, 1″ to 1½″ in diameter; with a thin skin,
milky flesh, and 6 to 8 large seeds in the globular stone;
seeds, oblong to ovoid, about ¼″ long.

Twigs.—Stout, reddish brown, dotted with numerous pale lenticels, exuding a milky sap when incised;
buds, ovoid, with several overlapping, chestnut-brown
scales; leaf scars, half round to somewhat oblong, with
a row of bundle scars; stipule scars, nearly encircling
the twig; pith, large, homogeneous.

Bark.—Thin, smooth, white, gray, or dark brown;

on the largest trunks, divided at the surface into small, appressed scales of irregular contour.

Habitat.—Sandy knolls, beaches, and hammocks immediately adjacent to tidewater.

Distribution.—Peninsular Florida and the Keys, the West Indies, Mexico, both coasts of Central America, and northeastern South America.

Importance.—Of no commercial value. A poison obtained from the caustic sap that caused serious skin lesions and complete destruction of mucous tissues was used by the aborigines as an arrow poison.

THE OYSTERWOODS

Gymnanthes Sw.

These are a tropical American genus comprising 10 species of evergreen trees, one of which extends into southern Florida.

Oysterwood

Gymnanthes lucida Sw.

Habit.—A small tree, never more than 35′ in height or 10″ in diameter.

Leaves.—Alternate, simple, persistent, leathery, elliptical to somewhat spatulalike, 2″ to 3″ long, ½″ to 1½″ wide; apex, acute or rounded; base, wedge-shaped; margin, entire or wavy, often obscurely toothed near the apex; dark green, lustrous above, lighter and paler below; petioles, grooved above, about ¼″ long; stipules, minute, hairy, ovate.

Flowers.—Unisexual, both sexes borne in the same leaf axils but on separate stalks; staminate flowers, abundant, appearing in clusters of 3 in the axil of a bract, the clusters spirally arranged on a 1½″ to 2″ rachis, with a rudimentary calyx and 2 or 3 stamens; pistillate flowers, solitary (rarely 2 or 3 at the node),

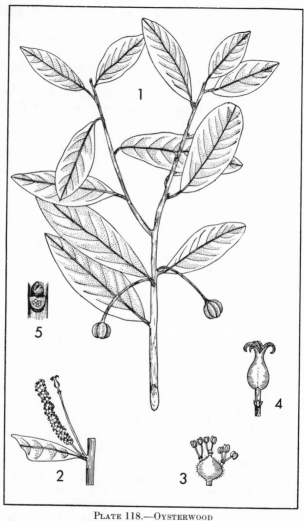

PLATE 118.—OYSTERWOOD

1. Foliage and fruit ×½. 2. Flower cluster ×½. 3. Male
flowers ×3. 4. Female flower ×3. 5. Leaf scar ×2.

terminating a long, slender, flexible stalk, with 3 bractlike sepals and a pistil with a 3-celled, 3-lobed ovary crowned with 3 recurved styles, which are stigmatic on their upper surface.

Fruit.—A reddish-brown to brownish-black, 3-lobed capsule, about ⅓″ in diameter; seeds, ovoid, about ⅛″ in length.

Twigs.—Slender, gray-red to gray-brown, dotted with pale, elongated lenticels, exuding a milky sap when cut or bruised; buds, ovoid, with several overlapping, lustrous, brown scales; leaf scars, half-round, with 4 bundle scars arranged in superposed pairs; pith, homogeneous.

Bark.—Very thin, separating at the surface into large, thin, reddish-brown scales; inner bark, light brown, darkening upon exposure.

Habitat.—Hammocks and wooded shores.

Distribution.—Lower peninsular Florida (near Miami); south over the Keys; in many of the West Indies.

Importance.—None.

THE SUMAC FAMILY

Anacardiaceae

The Sumac Family constitutes a group of approximately 65 genera and nearly 500 species of trees, shrubs, and woody climbers with resinous barks. A few species are endemic to temperate regions, but a large part of this family is characteristically tropical. Tannins, largely of the pyrogallol class, are obtained from the leaves, bark, wood, and even the fruits of almost all anacardiaceous species. Several plants are a source of valuable oils and oleoresins used in the manufacture of varnishes and lacquers. Mango fruits and cashew and pistachio nuts are other commercial products of the family. Certain species of this group are characterized by the presence of toxic substances in leaves and twigs that when handled cause epidermal irritations and in some instances serious skin lesions.

Four genera with 10 species attaining tree size occur in the forests of the United States. In the South this family is represented by 5 arborescent forms included in 3 genera.

Synopsis of Southern Genera

Genus	Leaves	Flowers	Fruit
Cotinus	simple, deciduous	pistillate flowers, with 3 separate styles	oblong-oblique, dry
Rhus	pinnately compound, deciduous	pistillate flowers, with 3 separate styles	globular, leathery or fleshy
Metopium	pinnately compound, persistent	pistillate flowers, with a single 3-lobed style	ovoid, resinous-fleshy

THE SMOKETREES

Cotinus L.

This genus includes but two species, both small trees. One occurs over a wide area through Europe and Asia; the other is found in the southern United States. Both are characterized by clusters of slender, hairy, sterile flower stalks that from a distance have the general appearance and color of a puff of smoke, hence the name *smoketrees*.

Smoketree   Chittamwood

Cotinus obovatus Raf.

Habit.—Commonly shrubby, but not infrequently a small tree, 25′ to 35′ in height and 12″ to 15″ in

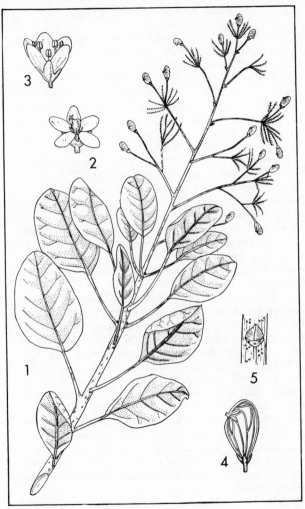

PLATE 119.—SMOKETREE

1. Foliage and fruit ×⅓. 2. Female flower ×3. 3. Male
flower ×3. 4. Fruit ×3. 5. Leaf scar ×2.

diameter. The bole is usually short and soon becomes lost in a crown with many wide-spreading, arching or slightly pendulous branches.

Leaves.—Alternate, simple, deciduous, 4″ to 6″ long, 2″ to 3″ wide, oval or obovate; apex, rounded or shallowly notched; base, obtuse or gradually tapering; margin, entire and commonly curled under; dark green above, pale green and hairy on the principal veins below; petioles, short, stout, about ¾″ to 2″ long.

Flowers.—Dioecious by abortion, appearing in the spring in few-flowered terminal clusters 5″ to 6″ in length; calyx, 5-lobed; petals, 5, greenish yellow; stamens, 5, shorter than and alternating with the petals; pistil, with an obovoid, compressed, sessile ovary and 3 short, stout, fleshy styles with large, obtuse stigmas; the many abortive flowers borne on elongated, hairy, filamentous stalks, which acquire a smoky hue about the time the fruits ripen, serve as an important diagnostic feature.

Fruit.—A rather dry, obliquely oblong, somewhat compressed drupe, with a light-brown, kidney-shaped, bony pit, about ¼″ long; borne on stalks 1″ to 2″ long and interspersed among the many purplish to brownish, hairy stems of the sterile flowers.

Twigs.—Slender, green or purplish or reddish brown, marked with prominent, whitish, corky lenticels, gummy and aromatic when bruised or crushed; terminal buds, about ¼″ long, ovoid, covered by several reddish-brown, overlapping scales; lateral buds, smaller, usually with 1 or 2 pairs of visible scales; leaf scars, crescent-shaped, triangular, or remotely 3-lobed, each with 3 bundle scars; pith, oval in cross section, whitish or golden brown, continuous; stipule scars, lacking.

Bark.—Very thin even on the largest stems, light gray or grayish brown, broken into thin, more or less oblong scales.

Habitat.—Rocky woodlands, knobs, and limestone glades, where it occurs as an occasional tree in admixture with hardwoods and eastern redcedar, or in nearly pure, spreading thickets.

Distribution.—Kentucky along the Ohio River, south to the Tennessee River Valley in Alabama, west through southern Missouri, Arkansas, and Oklahoma to western Texas.

Importance.—Smoketree has a limited ornamental use. Because of the durable nature of its wood, the tree was used at one time for fencing. The wood yields a water-soluble, orange-brown dye that was in great demand throughout the South during the period of the War between the States. As a result of excessive cutting, this species is much less abundant than formerly.

THE SUMACS

Rhus L.

The genus *Rhus*, which includes the sumacs, poison-ivy, and poisonoak, numbers about 100 species of trees, shrubs, and woody vines of wide distribution through temperate regions of both hemispheres. In the United States, 4 species attain the stature of small trees, and 3 of them occur in our southern timberlands.

KEY TO THE SOUTHERN ARBORESCENT SUMACS

1. Leaflet margins, entire; fruit, white, juicy............
   Poison sumac (p. 428)
1. Leaflet margins, toothed; fruit, red, rather dry....... 2

2. Leaf rachis, winged, with 9 to 21 leaflets; twigs, slender, with warty, red lenticels and watery juice; fruit, in open clusters......**Shining sumac** (p. 431)
2. Leaf rachis, unwinged, with 11 to 31 leaflets; twigs, stout, densely hairy, with a milky juice; fruit, densely clustered.........**Staghorn sumac** (p. 433)

Poison Sumac

Rhus vernix L.

Habit.—Usually a shrub, occasionally becoming arborescent and then 25′ to 30′ in height and 6″ to 8″ in diameter; in the forest, ordinarily an understory species with a narrow, rounded crown of pendulous branches.

Leaves.—Alternate, deciduous, odd–pinnately compound, 7″ to 15″ long, with 7 to 13 stalked leaflets; leaflets, oblong to obovate, thick and firm, 3″ to 4″ long, 1″ to 2″ wide; pointed or rounded at the apex, unequally wedge-shaped at the base, the margins entire; lustrous and dark green above, paler and smooth below; the rachis, smooth, slender, commonly bright red.

Flowers.—Polygamous, borne in axillary clusters in the early summer after the leaves are fully developed; calyx, 5-lobed, the lobes acute; petals, 5, yellowish green, about 3 times the length of the calyx lobes; stamens, 5, their anthers brilliant orange; pistil, with a nearly globular ovary surmounted by 3 short styles, each with an enlarged fleshy stigma.

Fruit.—A white or ivory-colored drupe, about ¼″ in diameter; with a thin, juicy flesh and bony pit having grooved walls; the fruit clusters, often persisting through the winter and serving as an excellent warning of the presence of this very poisonous tree.

Twigs.—Stout, glabrous, light brown to orange-brown, dotted with numerous, minute, raised lenticels; when bruised or crushed, exuding a watery, poisonous sap, which becomes black upon long exposure; terminal buds, about ¼″ long, conical, sessile, with a pair of smooth, purplish outer scales; lateral buds, similar to the terminal bud but smaller; leaf scars, broadly crescent- to shield-shaped, the bundle scars numerous,

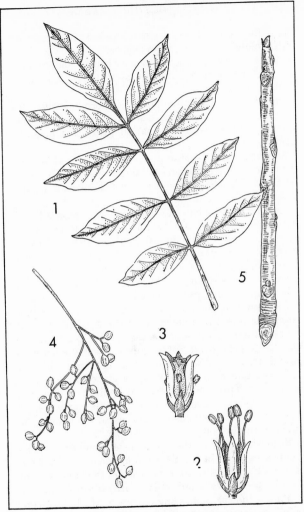

PLATE 120.—POISON SUMAC
1. Leaf ×⅓. 2. Male flower ×3. 3. Female flower ×3.
4. Fruit cluster ×½. 5. Twig ×1.

commonly more or less divided into 3 distinct groups; pith, yellowish brown, homogeneous.

Bark.—Very thin, gray to gray-brown and smooth except for elongated, horizontal lenticels and longitudinal striations.

Habitat.—Most abundant in permanently wet swamps and in peat bogs, where it occurs as an occasional bush or tree in association with other bottom-land species.

Distribution.—Northern New England westward through southern Canada to southeastern Minnesota; south to Florida in the East and Louisiana in the West.

Importance.—This tree contains a nonvolatile oil that is extremely poisonous and causes skin lesions to susceptible persons coming in contact with its leaves, twigs, or even other parts of the plant. If it is accidently handled, one should wash immediately with strong yellow soapsuds. After several hours or when skin eruption has once started, soap is no longer of value, but a 5 per cent water solution of potassium permanganate will relieve the itching (there are, of course, numerous lotions on the market that may be used). A preventive solution has recently been suggested that consists of 5 grams of ferric chloride dissolved in a mixture of 50 cc. of glycerin and 50 cc. of water. This solution may be rubbed on the skin as a protective agent prior to possible exposure, or even after exposure since it serves to neutralize the effect of the poison.

Remarks.—Two other poisonous members of this genus also occur in the South, and one should make a special effort to learn to recognize and then avoid them at all times. One, poison-ivy (*R. radicans* L.), is a trailing vine or sprawling shrub with light-green, trifoliate leaves, yellowish-white fruits, and naked winter buds. Poison-oak (*R. quercifolia* R. & F.), the other form, is a more erect, bushy shrub, very similar to poison-ivy except for its leaflets, which are more or less prominently 3- to 7-lobed. If contact is made with either of these plants, the treatment recommended for sumac poison may be applied with equally good results.

Shining Sumac   Winged Sumac
Rhus copallina L.

Habit.—Throughout much of its range, merely a shrub, but occasionally attaining heights of 20′ to 30′ and proportionate diameters; the crown, usually flat-topped and spreading; the root system shallow, with numerous root suckers.

Leaves.—Alternate, deciduous, odd–pinnately compound, 6″ to 12″ long, with 9 to 21 sessile or nearly sessile leaflets; leaflets, oblong to lance-shaped, thick, 1½″ to 4″ long, ¾″ to 1¼″ wide; long-tapered at the apex, wedge-shaped or inequilateral at the base; margins, entire or remotely toothed above the middle; dark green and shining above, paler and somewhat hairy below; with small, green, leaflike wings along the rachis.

Flowers.—Dioecious, borne in terminal or sub-terminal clusters when the leaves are fully developed; calyx, 5-lobed, the lobes ovate, hairy on their inner surface; petals, 5, greenish yellow, acute but reflexed above the middle; stamens, 5, exserted in the staminate flowers, abortive in the pistillate flowers; pistil composed of a pubescent, ovoid ovary with 3 short, stout styles, each terminating in a large, fleshy stigma, abortive in the staminate flowers.

Fruit.—A small, nearly ovoid, crimson drupe, about ¼″ long; with a large, kidney-shaped pit and rather dry flesh covered with dense, glandular hairs; the fruit clusters, often persistent through the fall and early winter.

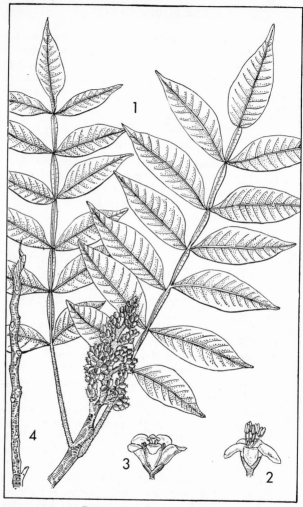

PLATE 121.—Shining Sumac
1. Foliage and fruit ✕½.   2. Male flower ✕3.   3. Female
flower ✕3.   4. Twig ✕⅔.

Twigs.—Stout, commonly zigzag, gray-brown to reddish brown, often hairy and dotted by many rusty-red, corky lenticels, exuding a watery, nonpoisonous sap when bruised or crushed; terminal buds, absent; lateral buds, occasionally superposed, nearly spherical, small, rusty-brown, hairy; leaf scars, U-shaped, with 5 to 11 scattered bundle scars; pith, yellowish brown, terete, homogeneous.

Bark.—Thin, reddish brown, and marked with prominent, horizontally elongated lenticels, at length sloughing off into large, papery scales.

Habitat.—In fallow fields and meadows, on dry, sandy slopes and ridges, in rare instances in wet bottoms; commonly in thickets produced by root suckers.

Distribution.—Northern New England west through southern Canada and southern Michigan to eastern Nebraska, south to Florida and Texas.

Importance.—Prized throughout many sections of the eastern United States as a decorative tree or shrub.

Staghorn Sumac

Rhus typhina L.

Habit.—Commonly shrubby, but sometimes encountered as a tree 25′ to 35′ in height and 6″ to 12″ in diameter. The bole is usually short, the leafy crown flat-topped and supported by numerous ascending branches. The roots are shallow and spreading and commonly give rise to new aerial stems (root suckers).

Leaves.—Alternate, deciduous, odd–pinnately compound, with 11 to 31 sessile or nearly sessile leaflets, 12″ to 24″ long; leaflets, oblong to lance-shaped, 2″ to 5″ long, about 1″ wide, long-tapered at the apex, rounded or slightly cordate at the base, the margins singly sharply serrate; dull green and smooth above, paler, and hairy along the midrib below; the rachis, stout, densely hairy.

Flowers.—Dioecious, borne in dense, terminal, panicled clusters after the leaves are fully developed; calyx, 5-lobed, the lobes long-tapered and woolly on their backs; petals, 5, greenish yellow, strap-shaped, reflexed above the middle in the staminate flowers, erect in the pistillate; stamens, 5, exserted in the staminate flowers and alternating with the petals, abortive in the female flowers; pistil composed of a hairy, conelike ovary surmounted by 3 short, thick styles, each with a fleshy stigma, abortive in the male flowers.

Fruit.—A small, hemispherical to nearly globular drupe, about ⅛″ in diameter; with a hard, kidney-shaped pit and thin layer of rather dry flesh, clothed in a dense coat of crimson, acidulous hairs; fruit clusters, often persistent throughout the winter.

Twigs.—Stout, brittle, clothed in a dense coat of greenish-brown to nearly black hairs (hence the name *staghorn*), dotted with conspicuous orange-brown lenticels, exuding a sticky, milky fluid when bruised or crushed; terminal buds, absent; lateral buds, small, conical, covered with matted, woolly hairs, nearly surrounded by the broad, C-shaped leaf scars; each leaf scar, with 3 clusters of bundle scars; pith, large, orange-brown, terete, homogeneous.

Bark.—Thin, dark brown, with horizontally elongated lenticels; superficially scaly on the largest trunks.

Habitat.—In old fields and abandoned pastures, also on rocky slopes, and occasionally in moist situations; forming thickets by means of numerous root suckers.

Distribution.—New Brunswick (Canada) west through southern Ontario to eastern North Dakota; south to Alabama and Georgia in the East and central Iowa in the West.

Importance.—Occasionally used as an ornamental. The highly colored wood has a limited use in the manufacture of novelties.

THE POISONTREES

Metopium P.Br.

This is a small genus with only three species, all confined to the forests of tropical America. One of these, the Florida poisontree, extends northward into southern Florida.

Florida Poisontree

Metopium toxiferum Kr. & Urb.

Habit.—A shrub, or sometimes a small tree rarely more than 25' to 35' in height or 10" to 15" in diameter; characterized by a short trunk with stout, arching limbs and pendulous branches, forming a spreading, round-topped crown. The sap exudations are extremely poisonous to the touch, and actual contact with this species should be avoided.

Leaves.—Alternate, persistent, pinnately compound, 6" to 10" long, with 5 to 7 (rarely 3) leaflets; leaflets, 3" to 4" long, 2" to 3" wide, mostly ovate, acute, or occasionally notched at the apex, rounded or wedge- or heart-shaped at the base, the margin somewhat thickened and slightly curled; dark green, smooth, and lustrous above, paler below; rachis, slender, smooth or finely hairy, swollen at the base.

Flowers.—Unisexual, each sex borne on separate trees in open, erect, panicled clusters in the axils of leaves crowded at the tips of twigs; calyx, 5-lobed, the lobes nearly circular; petals, 5, broadly oval or subrectangular, yellow-green, longitudinally striate above; stamens, 5, with filaments shorter than the anthers, rudimentary in pistillate flowers; pistil, with an ovoid ovary surmounted by a short style with 3 stigmatic lobes, abortive in the staminate flowers.

Fruit.—A small, ovoid, lustrous-orange drupe, about ¾" long; with a thick, resinous flesh and brittle pit.

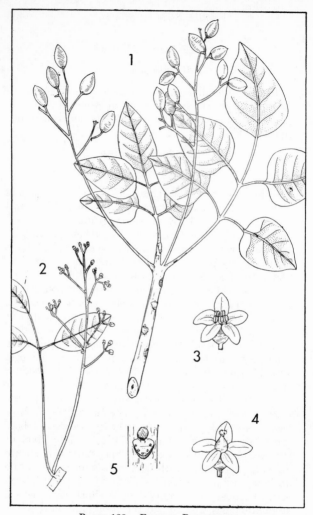

PLATE 122.—FLORIDA POISONTREE
1. Foliage and fruit ×⅓. 2. Cluster of flowers ×⅓. 3. Male
flower ×3. 4. Female flower ×3. 5. Leaf scar ×2.

Twigs.—Moderately stout, reddish brown, dotted with numerous large, orange-brown, warty lenticels, when crushed or bruised exuding a caustic, milky juice; buds, about ⅓″ long, covered by several slender, reddish-brown hairy scales; leaf scars, lunate to heart-shaped, with, 3 (sometimes divided) bundle scars; pith, pale brown, terete, homogeneous.

Bark.—Thin, reddish brown, and mottled with darker browns resulting from gummy exudations; on the largest trunks, divided into thin, scaly plates and exposing the bright-orange inner bark.

Habitat.—On shore lines adjacent to salt water; usually occurring as a solitary tree or in small groups in association with other hardwoods.

Distribution.—Southern tip of Florida, the Florida Keys, Honduras and the West Indies.

Importance.—The wood is of no commercial value. The resinous, gummy exudations of the bark have been used in the preparation of purgatives and medicinal emetics and diuretics.

THE CYRILLA FAMILY

Cyrillaceae

This is a small American family including only three genera (two are monotypic) and six species of small trees and shrubs of no economic value.

The two monotypic genera are widely distributed along the South Atlantic and Gulf coastal plains.

Synopsis of Southern Genera

Genus	Leaves	Flowers	Fruit
Cyrilla	tardily deciduous	in axillary racemes	capsulelike, ovoid, unwinged
Cliftonia	persistent	in terminal racemes	capsulelike, oblong, 2- to 4-winged

Swamp Cyrilla

Cyrilla racemiflora L.

A Monotype

Habit.—A small, graceful tree, sometimes 25′ to 35′ in height and 8″ to 16″ in diameter; the bole, usually dividing a short distance from the ground into several arching limbs, resulting in a spreading, round-topped crown of pleasing symmetry.

Leaves.—Alternate, simple, tardily deciduous, often clustered near the tips of twigs, oblong to oblong-obovate or elliptical, 2″ to 3″ long, ½″ to 1″ wide; apex, rounded or minutely notched, rarely acute; base, wedge-shaped; margin, entire; dark green above, paler below; petioles, moderately stout, ⅛″ to ¾″ long; stipules, wanting.

Flowers.—Perfect, fragrant, borne in erect racemes clustered near the ends of twigs of the previous season, 4″ to 6″ long; calyx, minute, 5-lobed; petals, 5, white or pinkish, furnished with nectar glands; stamens, 5, pistil, with an ovoid, 2-celled ovary, short, thick style, and spreading, 2-lobed stigma.

Fruit.—A minute, ovoid to conical, 2-celled, 2-seeded, dry, indehiscent, capsulelike structure, about ⅛″ long, crowned with the remnant of the style; seeds, minute, light brown.

Twigs.—Slender, smooth, lustrous brown, often 3-sided; terminal buds, present, ovoid, with several chestnut-brown, loosely overlapping scales, about ¼″ long; lateral buds, smaller, sometimes several superposed in an axillary groove; leaf scars, shield-shaped, with a large, curved, sometimes divided bundle scar, fringed across the top; pith, homogeneous, somewhat 3-angled in cross section.

Bark.—Thin, reddish brown, lustrous, divided at the surface into thin, shreddy scales; at the base of the bole, ridged.

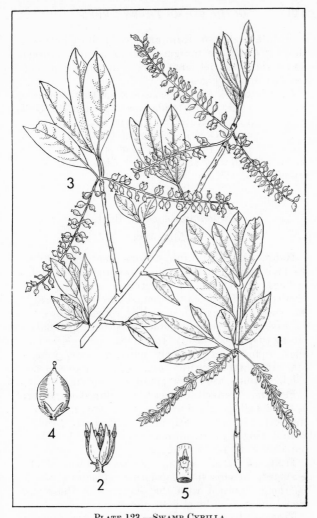

PLATE 123.—SWAMP CYRILLA

1. Foliage and flowers ×½.   2. Single flower ×3.   3. Foliage
and fruit clusters ×½.   4. Single fruit ×4.   5. Leaf scar ×1½.

Habitat.—Often forming nearly impenetrable thickets along the margins of swamps and pocosins and in rich river bottoms; in the Gulf states, found on exposed, sandy ridges.

Distribution.—Atlantic coastal plain from southern Virginia to northern Florida, west through the Gulf states to the Neches River Valley in Texas.

Importance.—Of no commercial value. It is said that the spongy bark at the base of larger boles is astringent and very absorbent and this is suitable as a styptic.

Buckwheat-Tree

Cliftonia monophylla Britt.

A Monotype

Habit.—A bushy shrub, or sometimes a tree 30′ to 40′ high and 6″ to 12″ in diameter; the bole, usually inclined, often somewhat contorted, and frequently divided a few feet from the ground into several spreading limbs, resulting in a spreading, rounded crown.

Leaves.—Alternate, simple, persistent, glandular, oblong to lance-shaped, 1″ to 2″ long, ½″ to ¾″ wide; apex, rounded or minutely notched; base, wedge-shaped; margin, entire; bright green above, paler below; petioles, very short; stipules, wanting.

Flowers.—Perfect, in erect terminal racemes; calyx, 5- to 8-lobed; petals, 5 to 8, white or pink, glandular; stamens, 10; pistil, with an oblong, 2- to 4-celled, 2- to 4-winged ovary surmounted by a nearly sessile, remotely 2- to 4-lobed stigma.

Fruit.—A small, oblong, 2- to 4-celled, 2- to 4-winged, indehiscent, capsulelike structure, about ¼″ long, crowned with the remnants of the style; seeds, about 1/16″ long, light brown.

Twigs.—Slender, reddish brown, occasionally obscurely 3-angled; buds, small, ovoid, appressed,

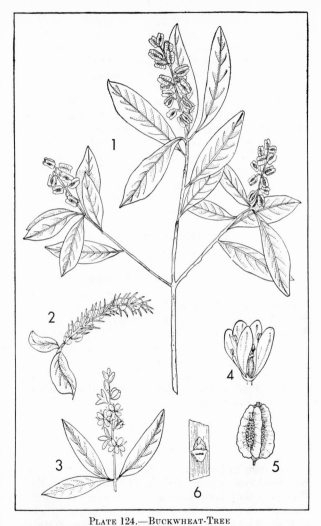

PLATE 124.—BUCKWHEAT-TREE

1. Foliage and fruit ×1.   2. Cluster of flower buds with attending bracts ×1.   3. Cluster of flowers ×1.   4. Single flower ×3.
5. Fruit ×3.   6. Leaf scar ×1½.

with 2 or rarely 3 outer scales; leaf scars, shield-shaped, with a single (sometimes divided) bundle scar; pith, homogeneous, occasionally somewhat 3-angled.

Bark.—Thin, dark reddish brown, divided at the surface into small, persistent, elongated scales.

Habitat.—Alluvial swamps, sandy or peaty soils, and river bottoms subject to short periods of inundation; an understory tree sometimes forming thickets.

Distribution.—Atlantic and Gulf coastal plains from near Savannah, Georgia, to eastern Louisiana.

Importance.—The wood has a high calorific value and is occasionally used for fuel.

THE HOLLY FAMILY

Aquifoliaceae

The Holly Family comprises 5 genera and over 300 species of woody plants indigenous to both temperate and tropical forests of all continents except Australia. Two genera represented by approximately 15 species are found in the United States. *Nemopanthus mucronata* Trel., a small shrub native to our eastern montane forests, is a monotype. The Aquifoliaceae are of little value in the production of commercial timber, although several species are important ornamentals.

THE HOLLIES

Ilex L.

This genus includes nearly 300 species of evergreen and deciduous shrubs and small trees widely distributed in both hemispheres. The evergreen American and English hollies, because of their thick, lustrous, dark-green foliage and contrasting, bright-red fruits, are prized for Christmas decorations; both

are widely cultivated ornamentals in many parts of
the United States and Canada.

Fourteen species of *Ilex* are native to the United
States, and 6 are southern trees. Only one, the
American holly, however, can be classed as a timber
tree of commercial importance.

KEY TO THE SOUTHERN HOLLIES

1. Leaves, evergreen; fruit stones, ribbed on all sides.... 2
1. Leaves, deciduous; fruit stones, ribbed only on the back 5

    2. Leaves, spiny-toothed...... **American holly** (p. 443)
    2. Leaves, not spiny-toothed........................ 3

3. Fruit, red or rarely yellowish; leaves, usually toothed,
    at least above the middle........................ 4
3. Fruit, purplish brown; leaves, entire...............
                  Tawnyberry holly (p. 446)

    4. Leaves, oblong-obovate; the margin, in part serrate
       above the middle...............**Dahoon** (p. 446)
    4. Leaves, elliptical to oblong-elliptical; the margin,
       coarsely serrate or more or less scalloped..........
                      Yaupon (p. 448)

5. Leaves, spatulalike to oblanceolate; the margin, finely
    toothed; fruit, orange-red, about ¼″ in diameter....
                   Possumhaw (p. 448)
5. Leaves, ovate to oblong-lanceolate; the margin,
    remotely glandular-serrate........................
                Mountain holly (p. 450)

American Holly

Ilex opaca Ait.

Habit.—A small or medium-sized tree, commonly
30′ to 50′ in height and 1′ to 2′ in diameter (occasionally 100′ by 4′), with tapering bole clothed in

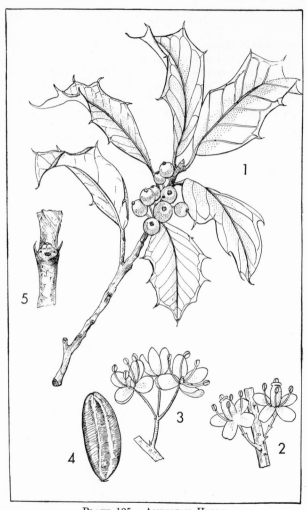

PLATE 125.—AMERICAN HOLLY

1. Foliage and fruit ×½. 2. Female flowers ×3. ·3. Male flowers ×3. 4. Pit ×7. 5. Leaf scar ×2.

short, slender, somewhat contorted branches, forming a more or less pyramidal crown.

Leaves.—Alternate, persistent, simple, leathery, oblong-ovate, 2″ to 4″ long, 1″ to 2″ wide; apex, acute, sharp-pointed; base, rounded or wedge-shaped; margin, wavy, with numerous stout, stiff, sharp-pointed spines (occasionally leaves with entire margins may be found); dull, yellowish green above, paler and decidely more yellowish below; petioles, short, stout, grooved, with noticeably swollen bases.

Flowers.—Regular, dioecious, axillary, appearing in the spring in cymose clusters on short stalks; staminate flowers, in clusters of 3 to 9; the pistillate, solitary or in clusters of 2 and 3; calyx, 4- to 6-lobed, the lobes acute and hairy on the margin; petals, 4 to 6, greenish white; stamens, as many as the petals and alternating with them, small and sterile in the pistillate flowers; pistil, with a 4- to 8-celled ovary, short style, and 4 to 8 stigmatic lobes, rudimentary and abortive in the staminate flowers.

Fruit.—A spherical, red, berrylike drupe, about ¼″ in diameter, containing several prominently ribbed, 1-seeded nutlets. [A form with yellow fruits (var. *xanthocarpa*) is occasionally encountered.]

Twigs.—Stout, glabrous, light brown, with numerous rather inconspicuous lenticels; terminal buds, acute, downy, with 2 to 4 overlapping scales; lateral buds, obtuse, smaller; leaf scars, crescent-shaped, with a single bundle scar; stipule scars, minute; pith, small, continuous.

Bark.—Gray, thin, often roughened by wartlike excrescences.

Habitat.—On rich, moist, bottom lands, borders of swamps, and dry but well-protected slopes; frequently found on sandy soils near the coast.

Distribution.—Along the coast from Massachusetts to Florida west to eastern Texas; northward through the Mississippi Valley drainage basin to southern Indiana and Illinois; rare in the region of the Appalachian Mountains.

Importance.—Holly wood is employed in cabinetry, particularly as an inlay, and in the manufacture of wooden novelties and souvenirs. The foliage and fruits are commonly used for holiday decorations.

Tawnyberry Holly

Ilex krugiana Loesen

This is a restricted species found only in Florida, the Keys, Haiti, the Bahamas, and San Domingo. It may be distinguished by its alternate, persistent, entire, lance-shaped leaves, lustrous-purplish-brown fruits with prominently ribbed nutlets, and whitish twigs. The tree is of no economic importance.

Dahoon

Ilex cassine L.

Habit.—A large shrub or small tree, 20′ to 30′ in height, with a trunk 12″ to 15″ in diameter; the slender, ascending branches forming a low, broad, rounded crown.

Leaves.—Alternate, persistent, simple, oblong-lanceolate, 1½″ to 3″ long, ½″ to 1″ wide; apex, blunt or acute, with a minute, terminal, spinose tip; base, wedge-shaped; margin, entire or toothed above the middle toward the apex: dark green above, paler below, at first pubescent but becoming glabrous; petioles, short, stout, swollen at the base.

Flowers.—Similar to those of American holly.

Fruit.—Similar to that of American holly.

Twigs.—Slender, pubescent through at least 3 seasons, then becoming brown and glabrous, with few inconspicuous lenticels; buds, minute, hairy; leaf

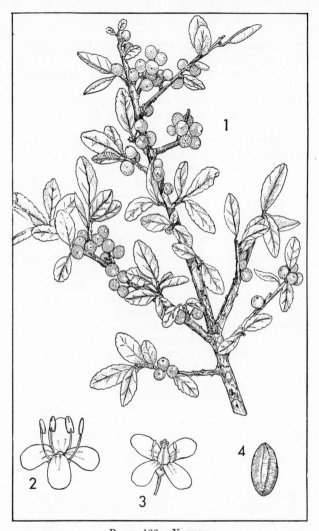

PLATE 126.—YAUPON
1. Foliage and fruit ×3. 2. Male flower ×3. 3. Female
flower ×3. 4. Pit ×½.

scars, crescent-shaped, with a single bundle scar; pith, small, continuous.

Bark.—Thin, gray, roughened by numerous lenticels.

Habitat.—In or near swamps, on moist, fertile soils with other hardwoods, and not infrequently on sandy ridges.

Distribution.—Southeastern Virginia south along the coast to Florida and the Keys and west to Louisiana; also in the Bahamas and in Cuba.

Importance.—Of limited ornamental value, particularly in the southeastern United States.

Yaupon

Ilex vomitoria Ait.

The yaupon is similar in many respects to the dahoon and is often found with it. However, the yaupon is more widely distributed, ranging as far west as Texas and Arkansas. The plant is treelike or shrubby, with persistent, elliptical, serrate leaves, smaller than those of the dahoon. The male inflorescence is a many-flowered cyme, while pistillate plants bear a profusion of flowers in 1's or 2's. The scarlet fruits are abundant and are borne in small clusters in the leaf axils. The twigs are nearly glabrous; the bark is red-brown and scaly.

The yaupon is used for Christmas decorations and is occasionally planted as a shrub for decorative purposes. Its leaves are emetic and purgative.

Possumhaw   Deciduous Holly   Winterberry

Ilex decidua Walt.

Habit.—A tall shrub with several erect stems, or a small tree, 20′ to 30′ in height and 4″ to 10″ in diameter; with stout, spreading branches, forming a ragged, open crown.

PLATE 127.—POSSUMHAW
1. Foliage and fruit ×½. 2. Male flowers ×2. 3. Female
flowers ×2. 4. Pit ×2. 5. Leaf scar ×3.

Leaves.—Alternate, deciduous, simple, on old growth clustered on spurlike, lateral twigs; ovate-lanceolate, 2″ to 3″ long, ½″ to 1″ wide; apex, obtuse or tapered; base, wedge-shaped; margin, finely serrate; light green above, paler below, somewhat hairy along the midrib; petiole, short, grooved, hairy; stipules, threadlike, deciduous.

Flowers.—As for the genus. See American Holly.

Fruit.—A spherical, red-orange, berrylike drupe, solitary or in clusters of 2 or 3, about ¼″ in diameter; nutlets, ribbed only on the back.

Twigs.—Slender, glabrous, light gray, lenticellate, with abundant spur growth after the 1st season; terminal buds, minute, obtuse, with 2 or 3 visible scales; lateral buds, similar but smaller; leaf scars, crescent-shaped, with a single bundle scar; pith, homogeneous; stipule scars, minute.

Bark.—Thin, rather smooth, gray, greenish gray, or light brown.

Habitat.—On lowlands, in swamps, near streams, or in moist, rich, upland soils; usually an understory tree in mixed hardwood forests.

Distribution.—Virginia south to western Florida, west through the Gulf states to Texas, north through Arkansas and Oklahoma to southern Missouri and southern Illinois.

Importance.—Sparingly used as an ornamental locally.

Mountain Holly

Ilex monticola A. Gray

The mountain holly is quite similar to possumhaw, which it superficially resembles. There are, however, several features that serve to identify this species. The leaves are larger than those of possumhaw and are characterized by marginal, glandular teeth and sunken veins on the upper surface. The bright-red fruits are about ½″ in diameter or nearly twice as large as those of possumhaw. This species occurs from southern New England south along the Appalachians to Georgia and Alabama and has also been reported from Florida. A shrubby form of mountain holly (var. *mollis*) exists near the coast in the Piedmont plateau and possibly elsewhere. It is of no commercial or economic value.

THE BITTERSWEET FAMILY
Celastraceae

The Bittersweet Family comprises about 45 genera and 450 species of trees, shrubs, and vines. Six arborescent forms, representing 6 separate genera, are indigenous to the United States; 5 of these inhabit the forests of the South. Perhaps the best-known member of this family is the bittersweet (*Celastrus scandens* L.). Its brilliant, orange-red fruits are easily preserved by drying and in some localities are commonly used as decorations in the home during the fall and winter.

Synopsis of Southern Arborescent Genera

Genus	Leaves	Flowers	Fruit
Euonymus	opposite, deciduous	perfect; in 7- to 15-flowered cymes	a 4-lobed capsule
Maytenus	alternate, persistent	polygamous; solitary or fascicled	a 4-angled capsule
Schaefferia	alternate, persistent	dioecious; solitary or fascicled	a scarlet drupe
Crossopetalum	opposite or whorled, persistent	perfect; solitary or in few-flowered cymes	a red or purple drupe
Gyminda	opposite, persistent	dioecious; in few-flowered cymes	a blue-black drupe

THE WAHOOS AND BURNINGBUSHES

Euonymus L.

These are a genus of about 65 species of trees, shrubs, and vines widely distributed through the North Temperate Zone, a few extending to Australia and the East Indies. Included are a number of well-known ornamental forms. The eastern wahoo is widespread in the South.

Eastern Wahoo   Spindletree   Burningbush

Euonymus atropurpureus Jacq.

Habit.—A shrub, or rarely a tree 25′ in height and 6″ in diameter, with a spreading, irregular, rounded crown.

Leaves.—Opposite, simple, deciduous, ovate to elliptical, 2″ to 5″ long, 1″ to 2″ wide; apex, long-tapered; base, acute; margin, finely serrate or doubly serrate; bright green above, paler below; petioles, stout, about ½″ long.

Flowers.—Perfect, about ½″ wide, in 7- to 15-flowered, axillary cymes; calyx, 4-lobed, the lobes rounded; petals, 4, dark purple, obovate, sometimes obscurely toothed on the margin; stamens, 4, spreading; pistil, with a 4-celled ovary, short style, and depressed stigma.

Fruit.—A deeply 4-lobed capsule, about ½″ in diameter, the valves purple; when opening, exposing the persistent seeds; seeds, surrounded by a thin, fleshy, scarlet aril; about ¼″ long.

Twigs.—Slender, purplish green, dotted with prominent, pale lenticels; terminal buds, ovoid, about ¼″ long, with 3 to 5 pairs of purplish, sharp-pointed scales; lateral buds, similar but smaller; leaf scars, half-round to half-oval, with a single bundle scar;

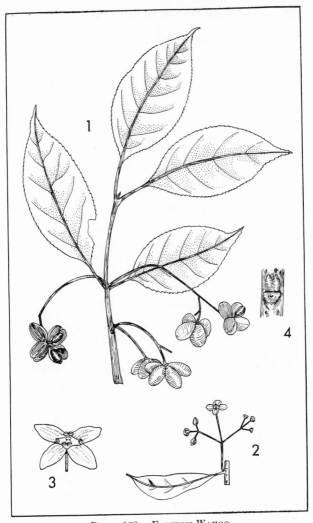

PLATE 128.—EASTERN WAHOO
1. Foliage and fruit ×½. 2. Flower cluster ×½. 3. Flower ×1.
4. Leaf scar ×1½.

pith, greenish, spongy; stipule scars, minute, often obscure.

Bark.—Very thin, ashy gray, scaly.

Habitat.—Woodlands and thickets, usually on moist, rich soils.

Distribution.—Widespread through the East; west of the Appalachian Mountains to the prairie states, but aborescent only in Texas and Arkansas.

Importance.—Occasionally used as an ornamental. The root bark contains principles used in medicine.

THE MAYTENS

Maytenus Molina

These are a tropical American genus of trees and shrubs embracing about 70 species. A single form extends into southern Florida.

Guttapercha Mayten

Maytenus phyllanthoides Benth.

Habit.—A low, sprawling shrub, or occasionally a small tree, rarely more than 18′ to 20′ in height or 12″ in diameter.

Leaves.—Alternate, simple, persistent, leathery, oblong to elliptical, 1″ to 1½″ long, ½″ to ¾″ wide; apex, acute, rounded, or minutely notched; base, wedge-shaped; margin, entire or wavy, often slightly thickened; lustrous, dark green tinged with red above, paler below; petioles, very short, about ⅕″ long; stipules, minute, early deciduous.

Flowers.—Polygamous, minute, solitary or in few-flowered, axillary clusters; calyx, 5-lobed; petals, 5, white; stamens, 5; pistil, with a 3- or 4-celled ovary, crowned with a 3- or 4-lobed stigma.

Fruit.—A broadly obovoid, 4-angled, bright-red capsule, about ⅓″ long; tipped at the apex with a

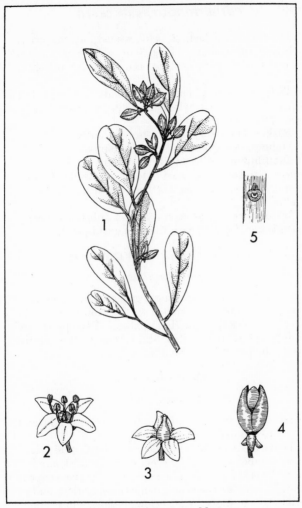

PLATE 129.—GUTTAPERCHA MAYTEN
1. Foliage and fruit ×1. 2. Male flower ×3. 3. Female
flower ×3. 4. Fruit ×3. 5. Leaf scar ×2.

short spine; 1-celled, 2- to 4-seeded; at maturity, splitting to the base along 3 or 4 lines of suture; seeds, minute, enclosed at the base in an open, scarlet aril.

Twigs.—Slender, pale gray; buds, minute; leaf scars, more or less half-round, with a single bundle scar; pith, homogeneous.

Bark.—Thin, gray to gray-brown, smooth.

Habitat.—Seacoast and near-by bluffs.

Distribution.—Coastal Texas, reappearing on both the east and the west coast of lower peninsular Florida and the Keys; also in northern Mexico and Lower California.

Importance.—The leaves yield a substance nearly chemically identical with the true gutta-percha.

THE WEST INDIES BOXWOODS

Schaefferia Jacq.

A small genus comprising a group of five evergreen trees or shrubs, all confined to the tropics and subtropics of the Western Hemisphere. Two species are indigenous to the United States, one to the Northwest, the other to the Southeast.

Florida-boxwood

Schaefferia frutescens Jacq.

Habit.—A tree, sometimes 30′ to 40′ in height and 6″ to 10″ in diameter.

Leaves.—Alternate, simple, persistent, oval, elliptical to obovate or oblanceolate, 2″ to 3″ long, ½″ to 1″ broad; apex, usually acute; base, wedge-shaped; margin, entire, thickened, sometimes curled under; bright green above, paler below; petiole, short, stout.

Flowers.—Unisexual, solitary or in few-flowered, axillary fascicles, each sex borne on separate trees;

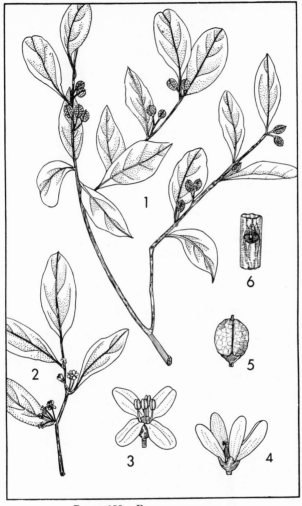

PLATE 130.—FLORIDA-BOXWOOD

1. Foliage and fruit $\times\frac{1}{2}$. 2. Flower clusters $\times\frac{1}{2}$. 3. Male flower $\times 3$. 4. Female flower $\times 3$. 5. Fruit $\times 2$. 6. Leaf scar $\times 1\frac{1}{2}$.

the staminate, mostly in clusters of 3 to 5, with 4 sepals, 4 greenish petals, 4 stamens, and an abortive pistil; the pistillate, with similar calyx and corolla, no stamens, and a pistil with a globular, 2-celled ovary with 2 reflexed, sessile stigmas.

Fruit.—A globular, acid, scarlet drupe, about ¼″ in diameter; stone, bony.

Twigs.—Slender, angled, greenish yellow to greenish gray, warty; buds, minute; leaf scars, variable, often oval or obscurely triangular, with a single raised bundle scar; pith, homogeneous.

Bark.—Thin, brown or reddish brown, dividing at the surface into tiny scales.

Habitat.—Hammocks and sandy soils near tidewater.

Distribution.—Lower Florida Keys, Cuba, Trinidad, Puerto Rico, and southern Mexico.

Importance.—None.

THE CROSSOPETALUMS

Crossopetalum P. Br.

These are a small group of evergreen trees and shrubs restricted to tropical America. Two species extend northward to southern Florida, one of these being a small tree.

Florida Crossopetalum

Crossopetalum rhacoma Crantz

Habit.—A shrub or small tree, sometimes 15′ to 20′ in height and 4″ to 6″ in diameter.

Leaves.—Opposite or in whorls of 3, simple, persistent, oval, obovate to elliptical, ½″ to 1½″ long, ¼″ to ½″ wide; apex, acute, rounded, or minutely notched; base, wedge-shaped; margin, with blunt or rounded teeth, at least above the middle; light

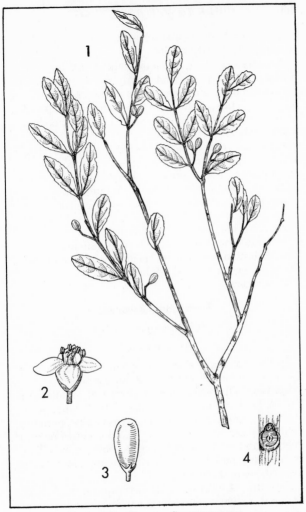

PLATE 131.—FLORIDA CROSSOPETALUM

1. Foliage and fruit ×½. 2. Flower ×3. 3. Fruit ×3.
4. Leaf scar ×1½.

green, smooth above, paler below; petiole, very short, or the leaves nearly sessile.

Flowers.—Perfect, in long-stalked, axillary, few-flowered cymes; calyx, 4-lobed; petals, 4, oval or nearly circular, purplish red; stamens, 4, alternating with the petals; pistil, with a broadly ovoid, 4-celled ovary and short, stout, columnar style crowned with 4 stigmatic lobes.

Fruit.—A red or reddish-purple, obovoid drupe, about ¼″ long; stone, bony; seeds, minute.

Twigs.—Slender, smooth, brown to ashy gray, more or less 4-angled; buds, minute; leaf scars, triangular to half-oval, with a single central bundle scar; pith, homogeneous.

Bark.—Thin, smooth, light brown.

Habitat.—Sand dunes, bluffs, and hammocks.

Distribution.—Southern peninsular Florida and Florida Keys and the West Indies.

Importance.—None.

West Indies Falsebox

Gyminda latifolia Urb.

A Monotype

Habit.—A large shrub or small tree, sometimes 20′ to 30′ in height and 6″ to 8″ in diameter.

Leaves.—Opposite, (rarely alternate) simple, persistent, leathery, mostly obovate, 1″ to 2″ long, ¾″ to 1″ wide; apex, rounded or occasionally minutely notched; base, wedge-shaped; margin, entire or with finely rounded teeth; light green above, pale yellow-green below; petiole, very short; stipules, minute, long-tapered, early deciduous.

Flowers.—Unisexual, each sex appearing in few-flowered, axillary cymes on separate trees; the staminate, with a minute, 4-lobed calyx, 4 white petals, 4 stamens inserted opposite the petals, and a rudimen-

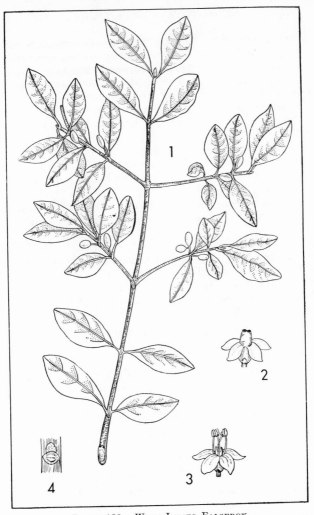

PLATE 132.—WEST INDIES FALSEBOX
1. Foliage and fruit ×½. 2. Female flower ×3. 3. Male
flower ×3. 4. Leaf scar ×1½.

tary pistil; the pistillate, with similar calyx and corolla, no stamens, and a pistil with a 2-celled ovary surmounted by a large, 2-lobed, sessile stigma.

Fruit.—An ovoid or obovoid, dark-blue or black, 2-celled, 1- or 2-seeded drupe, about ¼″ long; crowned with the remnants of the stigma, seated upon the persistent calyx; stone, thick but brittle; seeds, oblong, minute.

Twigs.—Slender, 4-angled, pale brown; buds, minute, sharp-pointed; leaf scars, somewhat diamond-shaped, with a single central, raised bundle scar; pith, homogeneous.

Bark.—Very thin, light brown, often mottled with red, divided at the surface into long, narrow, shreddy scales.

Habitat.—Hammocks.

Distribution.—Lower peninsular Florida and the Keys; the West Indies and Venezuela.

Importance.—The wood is occasionally used as a substitute for genuine boxwood in the fabrication of engraver's blocks.

THE MAPLE FAMILY

Aceraceae

The Maple Family includes only 2 genera, *Acer* L. and *Dipteronia* Oliv. The latter is an Asiatic monotype, while *Acer*, with its 114 or more species, is widespread throughout the Northern Hemisphere.

THE MAPLES

Acer. L.

This large genus of trees and shrubs includes many species that are noted particularly for the fine timbers they produce; many others are highly prized ornamentals. As a group they are characterized by simple, opposite leaves and doubly winged fruits.

Thirteen maples are found in the forests of the United States; 8 of these occur in the timbered areas of the South.

KEY TO THE SOUTHERN MAPLES

1. Leaves, simple, palmately 3- to 5-lobed.............. 2
1. Leaves, pinnately compound, with 3 to 9 entire, toothed, or lobed leaflets...........**Boxelder** (p. 464)

  2. Flowers, appearing in advance of the leaves from separate flower buds.......................... 3
  2. Flowers, appearing with the leaves or after they are fully developed................................ 4

3. Flowers, without petals, greenish yellow, nearly sessile; twigs, exhaling a fetid odor when bruised............
           Silver maple (p. 469)
3. Flowers, with red or orange petals, long-stalked; twigs, not exhaling a fetid odor when bruised..............
           Red maple (p. 466)

  4. Flowers, borne in lateral clusters, without petals; the sepals, forming a tube...................... 5
  4. Flowers, borne in terminal clusters, with petals; the sepals, not forming a tube...................... 7

5. Lobes of leaves, more or less toothed; bark, usually smooth and whitish............**Chalk maple** (p. 474)
5. Lobes of leaves, entire; bark, usually dark and furrowed... 6

  6. Leaves, glabrous below.......**Sugar maple** (p. 471)
  6. Leaves, hairy below........**Florida maple** (p. 474)

7. Flower clusters, erect; leaf margins, coarsely toothed; bark, gray...............**Mountain maple** (p. 477)
7. Flower clusters, drooping or pendulous; leaf margins, finely toothed; bark, green, streaked with white......
           Striped maple (p. 474)

Boxelder   Ashleaf Maple
Acer negundo L.

Habit.—A small to medium-sized tree, usually less than 50′ but occasionally becoming 75′ in height, with a trunk 2′ to 4′ in diameter; the bole is usually short and divides 6′ to 20′ above the ground into several stout, horizontal limbs and branches to form a wide, rounded, bushy crown.

Leaves.—Opposite, pinnately compound, 6″ to 15″ long; with 3 to 7 or sometimes 9 subopposite, short-stalked leaflets; leaflets, variable, occasionally lobed or rarely subdivided; ovate-obovate, oval, or ovate-lanceolate, 2″ to 4″ long, 1½″ to 2½″ wide, long-tapered at the apex, heart-shaped, rounded, or wedge-shaped at the base; margin, coarsely serrate; light green and remotely pubescent above, paler below, the veins pubescent; the rachis, noticeably swollen at the base.

Flowers.—Dioecious, appearing with or before the leaves on last year's twigs; the staminate, in drooping clusters, the pistillate, in drooping racemes; calyx, hairy, bell-shaped or tubular, 5-lobed; stamens, 4 to 6, exserted, with large anthers; pistil, short, pubescent, with 2 stout, elongated styles.

Fruit.—A reddish-brown, V-shaped, double samara with slightly convergent wings, 1″ to 1½″ long; maturing in the fall; fruit stalks, commonly persistent throughout the winter.

Twigs.—Stout, lustrous or with a conspicuous bloom, green to purplish green, with scattered, pale lenticels; terminal buds, ovoid, bluish white, tomentose, ⅛″ long; lateral buds, similar but smaller, very short-stalked, appressed; leaf scars, elevated, V-shaped, with 3 to 5 bundle scars; pith, white, homogeneous.

Bark.—Thin, gray-brown, with shallow fissures separating narrow, rounded, reticulate ridges.

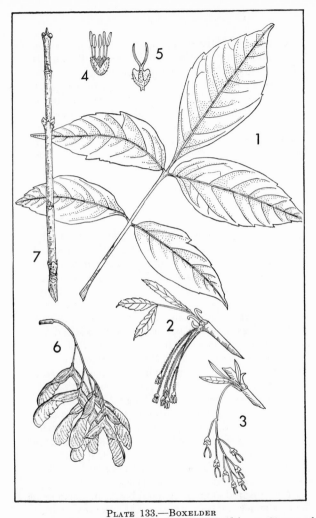

PLATE 133.—BOXELDER

1. Leaf $\times\frac{1}{3}$. 2. Cluster of male flowers $\times\frac{1}{2}$. 3. Cluster of
female flowers $\times\frac{1}{2}$. 4. Male flower $\times 2$. 5. Female flower $\times 2$.
6. Fruit cluster $\times\frac{1}{2}$. 7. Twig $\times\frac{1}{2}$.

Habitat.—Mostly on deep, moist soils near rivers, lakes, and swamps; also found occasionally on drier soils in association with many hardwoods.

Distribution.—From Vermont west through southern Ontario and Michigan to western Minnesota; south to Florida in the East and eastern Texas in the West.

Importance.—Of some value as a timber in the manufacture of cheap wooden products; widely planted as an ornamental and for windbreaks.

Red Maple

Acer rubrum L.

Habit.—A medium-sized tree, mostly 40′ to 50′ in height, with a trunk 1′ to 2′ in diameter, rarely 120′ by 4′; in the open, branching near the ground to form a dense, narrow, oblong head; in the forest, free of branches for 30′ or more and producing a narrow, short, rounded crown.

Leaves.—Opposite, simple, deciduous, circular, 2″ to 6″ in diameter, palmately 3- to 5-lobed with acute sinuses; apex of both terminal and lateral lobes, long-tapering; base, flat or somewhat heart-shaped; margin, coarsely and irregularly serrate; light green above, paler and glabrous below; petioles, red or reddish-green, 2″ to 4″ long.

Flowers.—Polygamous, appearing before the leaves in dense, stalked, axillary clusters, red, in one variety yellow (var. *pallidiflorum*); calyx, bell-shaped, deeply 5-lobed; petals, 5, as long as calyx lobes; stamens, 5 to 8, exserted in the male flowers, with red anthers; pistil, short, with 2 stout, divergent styles.

Fruit.—A red double samara borne in clusters on long, slender stalks; wings, short, broad, slightly divergent, ¾″ long; persistent until late spring, the seeds germinating soon after falling.

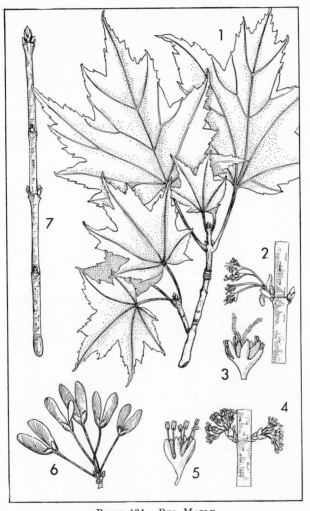

PLATE 134.—RED MAPLE

1. Foliage ×½. 2. Cluster of female flowers ×1. 3. Female
flower ×3. 4. Cluster of male flowers ×1. 5. Male flower ×3.
6. Cluster of fruit ×½. 7. Twig ×¾.

Twigs.—Slender, shining red, with minute, pale lenticels; terminal buds, obtuse, red, with 4 to 6 pairs of overlapping scales; lateral buds, similar but smaller, very short-stalked; flower buds, similar to and collateral with the leaf buds; leaf scars, V-shaped, with 3 conspicuous bundle scars; pith, white, homogeneous.

Bark.—At first thin, smooth, gray, becoming thicker and furrowed on older trunks, and ultimately divided into long, narrow ridges covered with scaly plates, which are free at their extremities.

Habitat.—Most common on moist bottom lands or in swamps; also found on drier soils on higher ground; frequently associated with cottonwoods, oaks, black ash, and black tupelo.

Distribution.—Southern Newfoundland west through Quebec and Ontario to northern Minnesota; south through eastern Iowa and Missouri to eastern Oklahoma and Texas in the West and to southern Florida in the East.

Importance.—Of some value as a source of timber for cheap furniture; most highly prized as an ornamental shade tree because of its rapid growth, highly colored flowers and fruit, and spectacular autumnal coloration.

Remarks.—A number of natural varieties of the red maple have been described. The trident red maple (*A. rubrum* var. *trilobum* K. Koch.) is widespread through the South. It may be separated from the species by its smaller, 3-lobed leaves, yellow flowers, and smaller fruits, the latter also occasionally yellow. Drummond red maple (*A. rubrum* var. *drummondi* Sarg.) is a variety frequently found in the deep swamps of the Mississippi Valley drainage basin. It is characterized by 5-lobed leaves, which are broader than long and woolly or hairy below; the petioles are likewise very hairy. The fruits, which are a brilliant red, are about twice as long as those of the species.

Silver Maple

Acer saccharinum L.

Habit.—A medium-sized tree, mostly 60′ to 80′ in height and 2′ to 3′ in diameter, rarely 120′ by 5′; the bole, commonly dividing near the ground into several stout, erect, divergent branches, forming a wide-spreading, rounded crown; roots, shallow and frequently very near the surface of the soil.

Leaves.—Opposite, simple, deciduous, circular, 6″ to 7″ in diameter, deeply palmately 5-lobed, with secondary lobes; sinuses, acute or rounded; apex, long-tapered; base, heart-shaped or flattened; margin, coarsely serrate; pale green above, silvery below; petioles, red, about 4″ long.

Flowers.—Polygamous; appearing before the leaves, in dense, sessile, axillary clusters on the previous year's twigs; calyx, 5-lobed, pubescent, urn- or tube-shaped; corolla, absent; stamens, 3 to 7, exserted, with red anthers; pistil, short, pubescent, with 2 conspicuous, divergent styles.

Fruit.—A wrinkled, reddish-brown, double samara with divergent wings, 1″ to 2″ long; maturing in the spring, the seed germinating soon after falling.

Twigs.—Brittle, slender, lustrous, reddish brown; with many conspicuous lenticels, with a rank odor when bruised; terminal buds, ovate, blunt, red, $\frac{1}{5}$″ long, with 2 to 4 pairs of overlapping scales; lateral leaf buds, similar, smaller; flower buds, large, globose, collaterally disposed; leaf scars, V-shaped, with 3 bundle scars; pith, homogeneous.

Bark.—At first, thin, smooth, silvery; at maturity, breaking into long, loose, scaly plates, which are more or less free at the ends.

Habitat.—Largely restricted to rich, moist bottom-land sites, but capable of development on dry soils, particularly when planted as an ornamental.

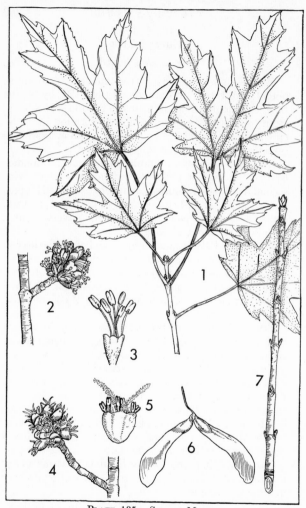

PLATE 135.—SILVER MAPLE
1. Foliage ×⅓. 2. Cluster of male flowers ×1. 3. Male
flower ×3. 4. Cluster of female flowers ×⅓. 5. Female flower
×3. 6. Fruit ×½. 7. Twig ×¾.

Distribution.—From northeastern Canada west through Ontario and Michigan to South Dakota; south to northern Florida in the East and Oklahoma and Arkansas in the West.

Importance.—Silver maple and certain of its varieties are widely used ornamental shade trees. Care should be employed, however, in the selection of this group for decorative use since their very brittle branches are easily and often severely damaged by sleet, heavy snows, and high winds.

Sugar Maple

Acer saccharum Marsh.

Habit.—A moderately large tree, often 70' to 80' in height and 2' to 3' in diameter or rarely up to 135' by 5'; in the open, branching a few feet from the ground to form a large, dense, pyramidal or rounded crown; in the forest, developing a clear bole for 50' or more of its length and crowned with a small, shallow, rounded head.

Leaves.—Opposite, simple, deciduous, circular, palmately 5- or rarely 3-lobed, 3" to 5" in diameter; apex, long-tapered; base, heart-shaped or flattened; margin of lobes, entire or irregularly toothed at wide intervals; rich green above, pale and glabrous below; petioles, slender, glabrous, 1½" to 3" long.

Flowers.—Polygamous, appearing with the leaves in dense, many-flowered corymbs, the staminate and pistillate flowers on the same or on different trees; individual flowers, on long, hairy, drooping, filamentous stalks; calyx, bell-shaped, 5-lobed, hairy; corolla, absent; stamens, 7 or 8; pistil, sessile, with 2 styles and long, exserted stigmas.

Fruit.—A reddish-brown, double samara, borne in clusters on slender stalks; with broad, parallel or slightly divergent, thin wings, about 1" long.

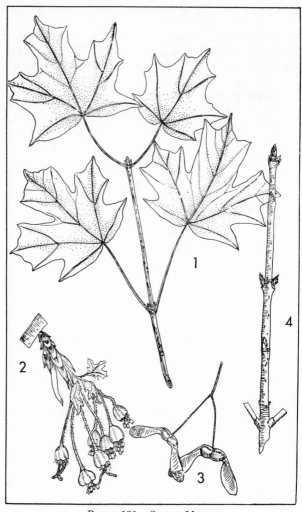

PLATE 136.—SUGAR MAPLE
1. Foliage ×⅓. 2. Flower cluster ×1. 3. Fruit ×½.
4. Twig ×¾.

Twigs.—Slender, shining, reddish brown, with many conspicuous lenticels; terminal buds, about $\frac{1}{5}''$ long, conical, reddish brown, with 6 to 8 pairs of overlapping scales; lateral buds, similar but smaller, partly surrounded by the V-shaped leaf scars in which are disposed 3 conspicuous, nearly equidistant bundle scars; pith, white, homogeneous.

Bark.—At first light gray and smooth, but becoming darker, thicker, and deeply furrowed into long, longitudinal scaly ridges on large trunks.

Habitat.—Most common on moist, rich soils of slopes and ridges; also on poorer soils and common on those of limestone origin; usually associated in the North with beech, yellow birch, red spruce, white pine, and hemlock; in the South, with oaks, hickories, yellowpoplar, and ashes.

Distribution.—From Newfoundland west through Manitoba to the Dakotas and Iowa; south to Texas and Louisiana in the West, and through Virginia to Alabama in the East.

Importance.—Extremely valuable as a timber tree. The wood is used principally for furniture, flooring, trim, and woodenware. With beech and birch it is used in the hardwood distillation industry as a source of wood alcohol, acetate of lime, and charcoal. It is the most important source of maple sirup and a highly prized ornamental.

Remarks.—Black maple, *Acer nigrum* F.A. Michx. (*A. saccharum* var. *nigrum* Britt.), has been reported as occurring very sparsely in the mountains of Virginia and North Carolina. It may be distinguished from the sugar maple by its pubescent, 3-lobed leaves, stout, purplish twigs with pubescent buds and prominent lenticels.

Florida Maple

Acer barbatum Michx.

The Florida maple is so much like *A. saccharum* as often to be mistaken for it. It is a smaller tree, however, with blue-green leaves that are more or less tomentose below. The leaf petioles are noticeably swollen at the base. This maple is found on moist soils or on limestone ridges on the coastal plain and Piedmont areas from southeastern Virginia to Florida and west to Texas and Arkansas.

The Florida maple is of little value as a timber species but is a source of maple sirup and makes an excellent shade tree.

Chalk Maple

Acer leucoderme Small

The chalk maple is another member of the southern sugar maple group. Ordinarily it is a large shrub or small tree, with 3- or occasionally 5-lobed leaves, yellow flowers, and small fruits with wide-spreading wings. It is easily recognized in the field by its smooth, chalky-white bark. This maple is restricted to small areas in North Carolina (Stanly County), Tennessee (Polk County), South Carolina, Georgia, Alabama, and Louisiana but is most abundant in Georgia and Alabama.

Striped Maple   Moose Maple

Acer pensylvanicum L.

Habit.—Frequently a shrub, or a small tree becoming 30' to 40' in height, with a short trunk up to 10'' in diameter; branches, small, upright, forming an oblong, rounded head.

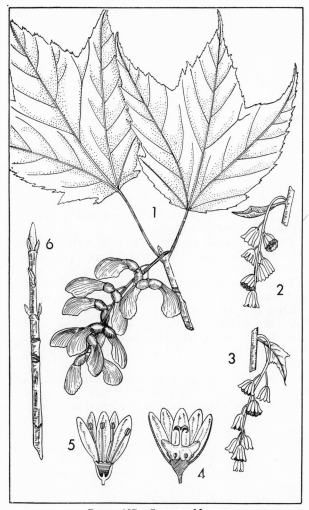

PLATE 137.—STRIPED MAPLE

1. Foliage and fruit ✕⅓.   2. Cluster of male flowers ✕1.
3. Cluster of female flowers ✕1.   4. Female flower, sectional
view ✕3.   5. Male flower, sectional view ✕3.   6. Twig ✕¾.

Leaves.—Opposite, simple, deciduous, ovate, 5″ to 6″ long, 4″ to 5″ wide; 3-lobed; apex, long-tapered; base, rounded or slightly heart-shaped; margin, doubly serrate; pale green above, paler and glabrous below, becoming light yellow in the fall; borne on stout, grooved, 1″ to 2″ petioles, which are swollen at their base.

Flowers.—Monoecious, appearing after the leaves in slender, drooping, long-stalked racemes, about 5″ long; staminate and pistillate flowers, in different racemes on the same tree; calyx, with 5 lanceolate sepals; petals, obovate, canary-yellow, longer than the sepals; stamens, 7 or 8, shorter than the petals; pistil, consisting of a purplish ovary with 2 united styles and divergent stigmas.

Fruit.—A double samara, with thin, widely divergent wings, ¾″ long; seeds, reddish brown and somewhat wrinkled.

Twigs.—Slender, smooth, becoming reddish brown and, after 2 years, striped with rather broad, light-colored lines; terminal buds, valvate, stalked, ½″ long, the scales conspicuously keeled; lateral buds, similar but much smaller; leaf scars, narrowly U-shaped, with 5 to 7 bundle scars; pith, white, homogeneous.

Bark.—Up to ¼″ thick; at first, smooth and bright green, with broad, longitudinal, whitish stripes; at maturity, becoming somewhat roughened and warty.

Habitat.—On sandy soil near fresh water from an altitude of a few feet above sea level to more than 5,000′ in the southern Appalachian Mountains; frequently on sandy loam in association with other species; usually shaded by larger trees of many other species.

Distribution.—From Quebec to northern Wisconsin, southward through the Atlantic states and the Appalachians to northern Georgia.

Importance.—Of slight value as an ornamental in the northern and northeastern United States and in Europe.

Mountain Maple

Acer spicatum Lam.

Habit.—A shrub, or sometimes a small tree up to 30' in height with a short bole 6" to 8" in diameter and then having several upright branches with many branchlets, forming a bushy head.

Leaves.—Opposite, simple, deciduous, rounded, 4" to 5" long, with 3 or rarely 5 tapering lobes; apex, abruptly long-tapered; base, flattened, rounded, or slightly heart-shaped; margin, coarsely glandular, serrate; at maturity, light green, glabrous above, paler and more or less pubescent below, becoming orange or red in the fall; petioles, slender, reddish, enlarged at base, 2" to 4" long.

Flowers.—Monoecious, appearing after the leaves in upright, pubescent racemes, with staminate flowers at the apex and pistillate at the base of each inflorescence; individual flowers, short-stalked, with a yellow, 5-lobed, pubescent calyx and 5 yellow petals; stamens, 7 or 8; pistil, consisting of a hairy ovary, long style, and 2 short-lobed stigmas.

Fruit.—A bright-red, yellow, or brown, glabrous, double samara with somewhat divergent wings, ½" long; seeds, reddish brown, smooth.

Twigs.—Slender, at first pubescent, becoming glabrous in their 1st season, red or brown; terminal buds, valvate, acute, ⅛" long, with bright-red, more or less pubescent scales; lateral buds, similar but smaller; leaf scars, narrowly U-shaped, with 5 to 7 bundle scars; pith, white, homogeneous.

Bark.—Thin, brown or reddish brown; smooth or at maturity becoming remotely furrowed.

Habitat.—Moist soil on slopes or rocky hillsides in the shade of other species; usually shrublike, but becoming arborescent on the mountains of Tennessee and North Carolina.

Distribution.—Newfoundland, Labrador, Manitoba, and Saskatchewan, south through New England, thence along the Appalachian Mountains to northern Georgia.

Importance.—Sometimes used as an ornamental.

THE BUCKEYE FAMILY

Hippocastanaceae

The Buckeye Family, a small one, consists of only 3 genera and about 25 species of trees and shrubs, widely distributed throughout the United States, Mexico, Central America, India, eastern Asia, and southern Europe. This family is not an important timber-contributing group although several of the species attain large size. A number are included among the better known ornamental shrubs and trees because of their showy, varicolored flowers and handsome foliage.

THE BUCKEYES

Aesculus L.

There are about 16 species of *Aesculus* widely distributed throughout North America, Europe, and Asia. The best-known species is probably the European horsechestnut (*A. hippocastanum* L.), now widely used in many parts of the United States as a street and shade tree.

Several other species, including the brilliant, red-flowering buckeye (*A. carnea* Hayne) and the shrubby buckeye (*A. parviflora* Walt.), are used for more formal decorative purposes.

Of the 10 American buckeyes and horsechestnuts, 5 attain tree size in the forests of the South.

KEY TO THE SOUTHERN BUCKEYES

1. Fruit, covered with distant, short, unbranched prickles; leaves and twigs, exhaling a fetid odor when bruised...
Ohio buckeye (p. 482)
1. Fruit, smooth, sometimes pitted, but never armed; leaves and twigs, not fetid......................... 2

  2. Calyx, bell-shaped, greenish yellow............... 3
  2. Calyx, tubular, reddish yellow or red............. 4

3. Stamens, exserted; leaves, 5-foliate; capsules, 1- to 3-(mostly 1-) seeded..........**Painted buckeye** (p. 482)
3. Stamens, not exserted; leaves, 5- to 7-foliate; capsules, 2- to 4-(mostly 2-) seeded....**Yellow buckeye** (p. 479)

  4. Flowers, dark red; leaves, smooth or only slightly hairy below; fruit, dark brown, lustrous...........
Red buckeye (p. 482)
  4. Flowers, rose-colored, often tinged with yellow; fruit, light brownish yellow......................
Southern buckeye (p. 483)

Yellow Buckeye

Aesculus octandra Marsh.

Habit.—A large tree, commonly 60′ to 90′ in height, with a trunk 2′ to 3′ in diameter; branches, somewhat pendulous, forming an oblong, rounded crown.

Leaves.—Opposite, deciduous, palmately compound, about 10″ in diameter, with 5 to 7 leaflets; leaflets, 4″ to 6″ long, 1½″ to 2½″ wide; nearly sessile, obovate; apex, acuminate; base, wedge-shaped; margin, serrate; at maturity, dark green and glabrous above, dull below, with a few tufts of hair in axils of the larger veins; rachis, stout, 4″ to 6″ long.

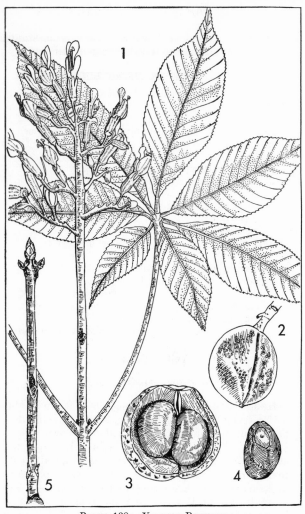

PLATE 138.—YELLOW BUCKEYE
1. Leaf and inflorescence ×½. 2. Fruit ×½. 3. Longitudinal section through fruit ×¾. 4. Seed ×¾. 5. Twig ×⅓.

Flowers.—Polygamous, irregular, yellow, appearing with the leaves in many-flowered panicles, 5″ to 7″ long; individual flowers, about 1″ long, borne on short, glandular, pubescent stalks; calyx, bell-shaped, glandular, pubescent; petals, 4, converging, of unequal lengths, remotely pubescent; stamens, 7, shorter than the petals; pistil, with a pubescent ovary, slender style, and terminal stigma.

Fruit.—A more or less globose, leathery capsule, about 2″ in diameter; husk, smooth; seeds, 2 to 4 (mostly 2), 1″ to 1½″ in diameter; lustrous, mahogany colored, with a large, gray hilum.

Twigs.—Stout, glabrous, light brown, with numerous lenticels; terminal buds, conical, stout, acute, about ⅔″ long, pale brown, with several pairs of imbricate scales; lateral buds, similar but much smaller and obtuse; leaf scars, large, with conspicuous bundle scars arranged in a V-shaped row; pith, large, white, continuous.

Bark.—Up to 1″ thick, gray-brown or dark brown; at maturity, becoming slightly furrowed and covered with small, thin, superficial scales.

Habitat.—On rich soil in river bottoms and on mountain slopes, usually occurring as an occasional tree in association with other hardwoods.

Distribution.—In the Appalachians from southeastern Pennsylvania, south through eastern Tennessee to northern Georgia and Alabama; also west through Pennsylvania, Ohio, and Indiana to southern Illinois.

Importance.—Of limited use in the manufacture of articles such as artificial limbs, woodenware, cigar boxes, luggage, and toys. The tree is also used as an ornamental.

Remarks.—The seeds of the buckeye were once carried in the pockets of persons who believed that they were effective in warding off attacks of rheumatism.

A form (var. *virginica* Sarg.) with pinkish flowers has been reported from West Virginia.

Ohio Buckeye   Fetid Buckeye

Aesculus glabra Willd.

The Ohio buckeye is similar in its general appearance to the yellow buckeye and is occasionally found associated with it in mixed hardwood stands. Its range is much more extensive, however, and it is found also in Iowa, Nebraska, Missouri, and Kansas. The fetid odor emanating from the bruised leaves and twigs of the Ohio buckeye, together with the spiny fruit husks, long stamens, and keeled bud scales, readily serve to distinguish this species in the field. The bark is also somewhat rougher than that of the yellow buckeye.

Painted Buckeye

Aesculus sylvatica Bartr.

The painted buckeye is a small southern tree rarely exceeding 30′ in height and 10″ in diameter. It is most common from North Carolina to Georgia and Alabama but is also found in Florida near Pensacola. Its more important botanical characters follow: leaflets, oblong-obovate; flowers, yellow or sometimes tinged with red, the calyx nearly glabrous; stamens, 7, short; ovary, very hairy; fruit husk, smooth, incasing a single or rarely 2 or 3 dark-brown seeds. Georgia buckeye is important only as an ornamental plant.

Red Buckeye

Aesculus pavia L.

This shrub or small tree occurs sparsely along the coastal plain from southeastern Virginia to western

Florida, thence, west through the Gulf states to western Louisiana. It has also been reported as indigenous to localized areas in Kentucky. The tree is characterized by beautiful, upright clusters of dark-red flowers and makes a handsome ornamental plant for use in parks and lawns.

Southern Buckeye

Aesculus discolor Pursh.

This is a small tree very similar to red buckeye in most of its characteristics, distinguished by red or yellowish-red flowers, with a red, tubular calyx and yellow or yellowish-red, glandular petals. The 5 leaflets are oblong-obovate and are borne on a slender, grooved, hairy rachis. The seeds are a light yellowish brown and usually occur in pairs in the 3-valved capsule. Southern buckeye is occasionally associated with red buckeye, but its distribution is somewhat wider since it occurs also in Texas, Arkansas, Missouri, and Tennessee.

THE SOAPBERRY FAMILY

Sapindaceae

The Soapberry Family, including approximately 125 genera and over 1,000 species of trees, shrubs, lianas, and herbs, is restricted largely to the warmer and tropical regions of the world. Many species have luxuriant foliage and large, showy clusters of delicately tinted flowers and hence are in demand for decorative purposes. In this connection, mention should be made of the balloonvine (*Cardiospermum halicacabum* L.), the southern soapberry (*Sapindus saponaria* L.), and the Chinese letchi (*Letchi chinensis* Sonn.). Fresh nuts of the latter are marketed in season throughout southeastern Asia and when dried or canned become an article of export trade.

Representatives of 6 genera of this family are found in the South, 4 of them with arborescent species.

Synopsis of Southern Arborescent Genera

Genus	Leaves	Flowers	Fruit
Sapindus	odd, rarely even-pinnate; margins, entire	petals, longer than sepals	an orange or yellow berry
Exothea	even-pinnate; margins, entire	petals, much shorter than sepals	a deep-purple berry
Hypelate	trifoliate; margins, entire	petals and sepals, of about equal length	a black drupe
Cupania	odd-pinnate; margins toothed	petals and sepals, of about equal length	a capsule

THE SOAPBERRIES

Sapindus (Tourn.) L.

These are a small genus comprising about 10 species of trees and shrubs indigenous to Asia and the New World. Three species are included within our range.

KEY TO THE SOUTHERN SOAPBERRIES

1. Leaf rachis, winged, with 5 to 9 leaflets. . . . .
	Wingleaf soapberry (p. 485)
1. Leaf rachis, unwinged. 2

  2. Leaves, persistent, with 7 to 13 leaflets. . . . .
	Florida soapberry (p. 487)
  2. Leaves, deciduous, with 8 to 18 leaflets. . . . . . .
	Western soapberry (p. 487)

Wingleaf Soapberry

Sapindus saponaria L.

Habit.—A small tree, occasionally 30′ in height and 12″ in diameter; with ascending branches and a narrow crown.

Leaves.—Alternate, persistent, pinnately compound with 4 to 9 leaflets borne on a stout, interrupted-winged rachis, 6″ to 8″ long; leaflets, leathery, oblong to elliptical, 2″ to 4″ long, about 1½″ wide, with rounded or minutely notched apices, acute bases, and entire or slightly wavy margins; yellow-green above, paler and with fine, woolly hairs below; petioles, extremely short, or leaflets subsessile.

Flowers.—Perfect and imperfect, minute, in many-flowered, terminal, and axillary panicles, 7″ to 12″ long; calyx, with 5 (rarely 4) sepals, hairy on the margin; petals, 5 (rarely 4), white, hairy, rounded at the apex, terminating below in a claw; stamens, 10 (rarely 8), their filaments hairy; pistil, with a 3-celled, slightly 3-lobed ovary, crowned with 3 short, stigmatic styles, exserted in the perfect flowers, abortive in the staminate flowers.

Fruit.—A globular, orange-brown berry, with a thin, juicy pulp, about ¾″ in diameter; seeds, black, obovoid, about ½″ long.

Twigs.—Slender, often angled or somewhat fluted, orange-green to brownish green, dotted with minute, pale lenticels; terminal buds, wanting; lateral buds, globular, with 2 outer scales, usually superposed; leaf scars, obscurely triangular to 3-lobed, with a streak-like bundle scar in the vortex of each angle or lobe, commonly indistinct; pith, large, homogeneous, pale brown or white.

Bark.—Thin, gray, furnished with many oblong excrescences, dividing at the surface into many thin, flakelike scales.

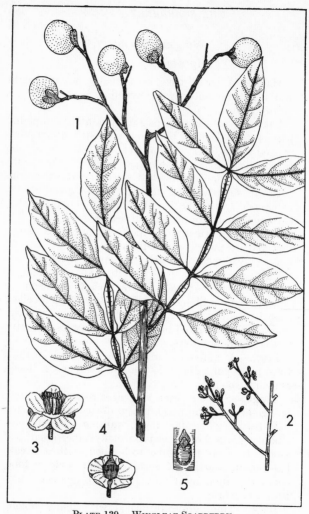

PLATE 139.—WINGLEAF SOAPBERRY

1. Foliage of fruit ×½. 2. Cluster of flowers ×½. 3. Male, flower ×5. 4. Perfect flower ×5. 5. Leaf scar ×2

Habitat.—Hammocks and shore lines.

Distribution.—Southern peninsular Florida, the Keys, the West Indies, Venezuela, and Ecuador.

Importance.—Soapberries derive their name from the fact that the pulp of their fruit, when crushed in water, develops a lather and makes a good substitute for soap. The bark of this tree contains astringents suitable for the preparation of tonics.

Florida Soapberry

Sapindus marginatus Willd.

The Florida soapberry is a small coastal tree extending from northern Georgia southward through Florida to Cuba. Nowhere is it abundant. It may be distinguished from the southern soapberry, with which it is sometimes associated, by its larger leaves with 7 to 13 falcate leaflets, supported on unwinged rachises, flowers with scaly petals, and yellow, keeled, ovoid fruits, about ¾″ long.

Western Soapberry Wild Chinatree

Sapindus drummondii Hook. & Arn.

This moderately large tree of the Southwest extends eastward into southern Texas and eastern Louisiana. Unlike the other soapberries within our region, the leaves of this species are deciduous and even-pinnate (with 8 to 18 leaflets). The flowers develop scaly petals similar to those of the Florida soapberry. The globular, orange-yellow fruits, only ½″ in diameter, are not keeled and turn black after ripening. The wood is used locally for basketry.

Butterbough

Exothea paniculata Radlk.

A Monotype

Habit.—A tree, occasionally 50' in height and 12" in diameter, with a narrow, rounded crown.

Leaves.—Alternate, persistent, even–pinnately compound, 4" to 8" long; with 2 to 6 (mostly 2 or 4) leaflets, supported on a slender, grooved rachis; leaflets, oblong to ovate or oval, 4" to 5" long, 1½" to 2" wide, with rounded, minutely notched, or acute apices, acute to wedge-shaped bases, and entire but slightly wavy margins; dark green, lustrous above, paler below; petioles, very short, some leaflets often subsessile.

Flowers.—Perfect and imperfect, borne in terminal or axillary, spreading panicles, clothed with rusty-orange hairs; sepals, 5, ovate; petals, 5, white, with a short, basal claw, much shorter than the sepals; stamens, 8 (rarely 7), much reduced in the pistillate flowers; pistil, with a broadly conical, 2-celled ovary, surmounted by a short, thick, gooseneck style with a thick, terminal stigma, abortive in the staminate flowers.

Fruit.—A 1-seeded, juicy, dark-purple (rarely orange), globular berry, about ½" long, crowned with the remnants of the style and seated upon the persistent calyx; seed, nearly spherical, about ¼" long.

Twigs.—Slender, orange-brown to reddish brown, profusely dotted with myriads of pale, circular lenticels; buds, minute, indistinct, partly embedded in the epidermal layers; leaf scars, shield-shaped, half-round or remotely 3-lobed, with 3 bundle scars; pith, homogeneous.

Bark.—Thin, brownish red, divided at the surface into large, thin, irregular scales.

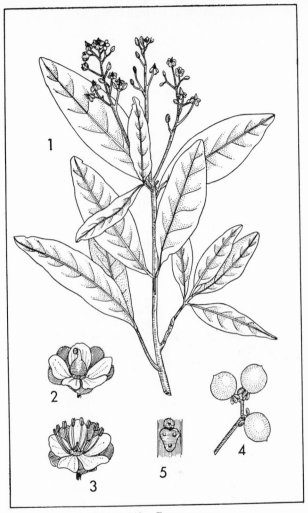

PLATE 140.—BUTTERBOUGH

1. Foliage and flowers $\times \frac{1}{3}$. 2. Female flower $\times 2$. 3. Male flower $\times 2$. 4. Fruit cluster $\times \frac{1}{2}$. 5. Leaf scar $\times 1\frac{1}{2}$.

Habitat.—Hammocks and marl soils.

Distribution.—Lower peninsular Florida, the Florida Keys, and many of the West Indies.

Importance.—The wood is used locally in the construction of small watercraft and novelties.

Inkwood

Hypelate trifoliata Sw.

A Monotype

Habit.—A shrub or small tree, occasionally 30′ to 40′ in height and 12″ to 18″ in diameter.

Leaves.—Alternate, persistent, trifoliate, leathery, 3″ to 5″ long; the rachis, 1½″ to 2″ long, with minute, lateral wings; leaflets, sessile, obovate, 1½″ to 2½″ long, ¾″ to 1½″ wide; apex, rounded, minutely notched, or acute; base, wedge-shaped; margin, entire, thickened, curled under; dark green, lustrous above, lighter green and lustrous below.

Flowers.—Perfect and imperfect, minute, borne in few-flowered, terminal and axillary panicles; calyx, 5-lobed; petals, 5, white, nearly circular; stamens, variable among the flowers, 7 to 10, reduced in the pistillate flowers; pistil, with a sessile, ovoid, 3-celled, slightly 3-lobed ovary surmounted by a short, stout, conical style and fleshy, 3-lobed stigma, abortive in the staminate flowers.

Fruit.—A black, sweet, fleshy, ovoid drupe, about ⅜″ in diameter, tipped with the remnant of a style and seated upon the persistent calyx; stone, thick but brittle, with an obovoid seed.

Twigs.—Pale gray-green, ultimately reddish brown and lustrous; buds, minute; leaf scars, half-round, remotely triangular, or shield-shaped, with 3 bundle scars; pith, homogeneous.

Bark.—Thin, pale brown, furnished with shallow, irregular depressions.

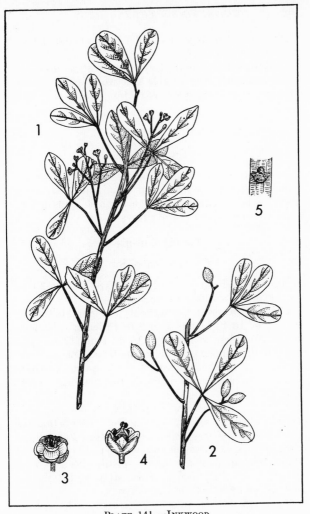

PLATE 141.—INKWOOD

1. Foliage and flowers ×⅓. 2. Fruit ×⅓. 3. Male flower
×2. 4. Female flower ×2. 5. Leaf scar ×1½.

Habitat.—Hammocks and flat pine woods; of very sporadic occurrence.

Distribution.—Florida Keys and West Indies.

Importance.—The durable heartwood is used locally for fence posts, marine construction, and tool handle stock.

THE CUPANIAS

Cupania L.

These are a tropical genus of trees and shrubs comprising about 35 species, all of them restricted to the Western Hemisphere. A single form extends northward to some of the Florida Keys.

Florida Cupania

Cupania glabra Sw.

Habit.—A shrub or small, bushy tree, 25' to 30' in height and 6" to 10" in diameter.

Leaves.—Alternate, persistent, odd–pinnately compound, 6" to 10" long, with 5 to 15 leaflets; leaflets, oblong to oblanceolate, $2\frac{1}{2}$" to 6" long, 1" to $1\frac{1}{2}$" wide, with rounded or minutely notched apices, acute bases, and toothed margins; dark green, lustrous above, dull green and hairy below; petioles, short, stout.

Flowers.—Perfect and imperfect, in few-flowered, axillary clusters; sepals, varying from 4 to 6 (mostly 4 or 5); petals, 4 or 5, green, tinged with red or yellow, about as long as the sepals; stamens, 5 to 12 (mostly 8), abortive in the pistillate flowers; pistil, with a 2- to 4- (mostly 3-) celled ovary, short, stout style, stigma, lobes as many as cells in the ovary.

Fruit.—A 2- to 4- (mostly 3-) lobed, leathery, top-like capsule, borne on a stout, stalklike base, about $\frac{1}{2}$" to $\frac{3}{4}$" long.

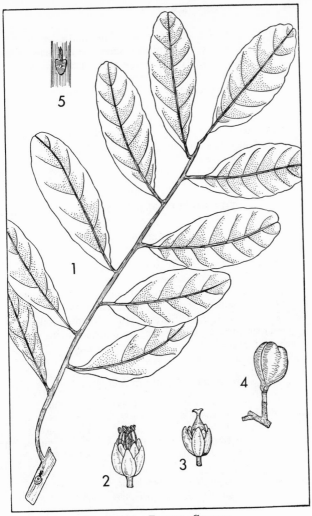

PLATE 142.—FLORIDA CUPANIA
1. Leaf ×½. 2. Male flower ×3. 3. Female flower ×3.
4. Fruit ×.1. 5. Leaf scar ×1½.

Twigs.—Slender, clothed with fine hairs, brown; buds, minute; leaf scars, 3-lobed, shield-shaped or half-round, with 1 or 3 bundle scars; pith, minute, homogeneous.

Bark.—Thin, smooth or scaly on the larger trunks, dark brown.

Habitat.—Hammocks.

Distribution.—In Florida, only on the lower Keys; abundant in Cuba and Jamaica; extending to Central and South America.

Importance.—None.

THE BUCKTHORN FAMILY

Rhamnaceae

The Buckthorn Family includes about 45 genera and over 500 species of trees, shrubs, and a few herbs, widely scattered through tropical and warmer regions of both hemispheres. Of the more than 100 species native to the United States, only 6 (included in 4 genera) attain arborescent proportions in our southern forests.

Synopsis of Southern Genera

Genus	*Leaves*	*Flowers*	*Fruit*
Krugiodendron	opposite or nearly so, persistent	petals, 0; sepals, crested	drupaceous, black, fleshy, with a single, bony pit
Reynosia	opposite or nearly so, persistent	petals, 0; sepals, not crested	drupaceous, purple, fleshy, with a single, bony pit

Genus	Leaves	Flowers	Fruit
Rhamnus	alternate or nearly sub-opposite, deciduous	petals, 5, ovate, notched at apex, partly enveloping the stamens	drupaceous, black, more or less leathery, with 2 or 3 small, bony pits
Colubrina	alternate, persistent	petals, 5, spreading	a capsule, orange-red to purple, dry and hard, splitting into 3 segments, each with a single, black, bony pit

Leadwood

Krugiodendron ferreum Urb.

A Monotype

Habit.—Ordinarily a large, bushy shrub, occasionally becoming arborescent, then attaining a height of 20′ to 30′ and a diameter of 6″ to 10″.

Leaves.—Opposite, or occasionally more or less alternate on the lower branches, simple, persistent for 2 or 3 years, 1″ to 1¾″ long, ½″ to 1½″ wide, broadly oval to ovate; apex, commonly notched; base, more or less rounded or tapered; margins, entire or slightly wavy; bright green, lustrous, and occasionally sparsely hairy above, pale green below; with a leathery texture; petioles, short, stout, about ¼″ long; stipules, thin, pointed, persistent.

Flowers.—Perfect, regular, greenish yellow, borne in 3 to 5 cymose, axillary clusters on branches of the current season; calyx, more or less conical, with 5 (occasionally 4 or 6) triangular sepals, united at the

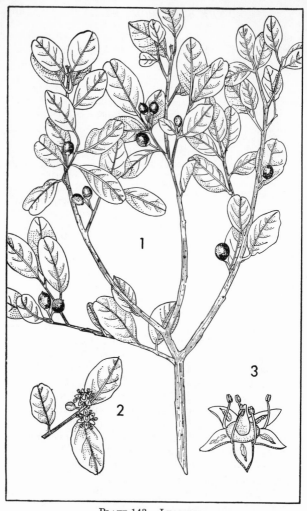

PLATE 143.—LEADWOOD

1. Foliage and fruit ×½. 2. Cluster of flowers· ×½.
3. Flower ×2.

base, each sepal crested on the inner surface; corolla, none; stamens, as many as the sepals and alternating with them; pistil, consisting of a short, stout style, terminating in a 2-lobed stigma and surmounting a 2-celled ovary.

Fruit.—An ovoid to nearly spherical, black drupe, often tipped with the base of the style; with a thin layer of flesh surrounding a rather large, thin-walled, bony pit, about ⅓″ long; seeds, small, ellipsoidal.

Twigs.—Slender, the new growth green and clothed with dense, velvety pubescence, at length becoming gray-brown and smooth except for numerous small and occasionally crowded lenticels; terminal buds, usually wanting; lateral buds, minute, ovoid, with grayish-brown, valvate scales; leaf scars, elevated, circular or nearly so, with 3 (occasionally 1 to 4) nearly equidistant, deeply sunken bundle scars; stipule scars, inconspicuous; pith, continuous.

Bark.—Gray, divided by narrow fissures into rounded, longitudinal ridges, which are scaly at the surface, about ¼″ thick.

Habitat.—Hammocks, commonly near tidewater.

Distribution.—Southern Florida from Cape Canaveral, south through the Keys and the West Indies from the Bahamas to St. Vincent and Jamaica.

Importance.—Leadwood is of no commercial value at the present time. It may be of interest to note, however, that it produces the heaviest wood grown in the United States (sp. gr. 1.3, or about 81 lb. to the cubic foot).

THE DARLING-PLUMS

Reynosia Griseb.

These are a small genus of trees and shrubs comprising nine species widely scattered through the forests of the West Indies. A single form (*R. septen-*

trionalis Urb.) extends to the North American mainland and has its northern limits in southern Florida.

Darling-Plum

Reynosia septentrionalis Urb.

Habit.—Scarcely ever more than a large shrub or a small tree, 20′ to 25′ in height and 6″ to 9″ in diameter.

Leaves.—Opposite or nearly so, simple, persistent for 1 or 2 years, 1″ to 1½″ long, ½″ to ¾″ broad, often quite variable in shape but mostly oblong, oval, or obovate; apex, notched or rounded, then commonly terminating in a minute bristle; base, tapering gradually; margin, entire, usually revolute; dark green above, paler and not infrequently with fine, reddish hairs below, thick and leatherlike; petioles, short, broad, about ¼″ long; stipules, small, falling away as the leaves unfold.

Flowers.—Perfect, regular, greenish yellow or green, borne in few-flowered, axillary umbels on the current season's branches; calyx, composed of 5 sharp-pointed, ovate sepals, united at the base; corolla, none; stamens, 5, alternating with the calyx lobes; pistil, the short, thick style terminating in a 2- or 3-lobed stigma and surmounting a 2- or 3-celled ovary, with a single ovule in each cell.

Fruit.—An ovoid, dark-purple drupe with a spinose apex, the thin, sweet, edible flesh, surrounding a single large, bony pit, ½″ long; sometimes ripening over winter; seed, small, nearly globular, somewhat albuminous.

Twigs.—Slender, occasionally somewhat angular, at first clothed in fine hair, but at length smooth and gray-brown; terminal buds, present, conical, with several overlapping scales; laterals buds, minute, ovoid; leaf scars, small, elevated, oval to crescent-shaped, with a single central bundle scar; stipule scars, barely discernible even with a lens; pith, continuous.

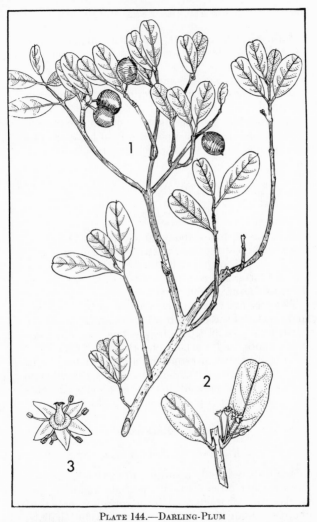

PLATE 144.—DARLING-PLUM

1. Foliage and fruit $\times\frac{1}{2}$.   2. Cluster of flowers $\times\frac{1}{2}$.   3. Flower $\times 2$.

Bark.—Reddish brown, splitting up into thin, scaly plates on the larger stems, rarely more than ⅛″ thick.

Habitat.—Hammocks and sand dunes.

Distribution.—Southern Florida and neighboring Keys and in the Bahamas.

Importance.—Darling-plum is of no commercial value at present. The wood is not so heavy as that of leadwood and when thoroughly dried will barely float in water (sp. gr. 1.07).

THE BUCKTHORNS

Rhamnus L.

Rhamnus includes about 60 species of small trees and shrubs; 5 of these are native to the United States. The barks and occasionally the fruits of most species are very bitter and contain powerful drugs suitable for the manufacture of purgatives.

Two species are components of our southern timberlands. One of these, shrubby buckthorn (*R. lanceolata* Pursh.), is a small shrub frequenting stream banks, moist slopes, and thickets underlaid with limestone. It is readily distinguished from the Carolina buckthorn (*R. caroliniana* Watt.), the remaining species, by its sweet-scented, unisexual flowers (dioecious) and nutlets that are deeply grooved on the back.

Carolina Buckthorn

Rhamnus caroliniana Walt.

Habit.—Commonly a shrub, but at times attaining tree size, then often 30′ to 40′ in height and 6″ to 10″ in diameter; characterized by a spreading crown of unarmed branches and a comparatively shallow, spreading root system.

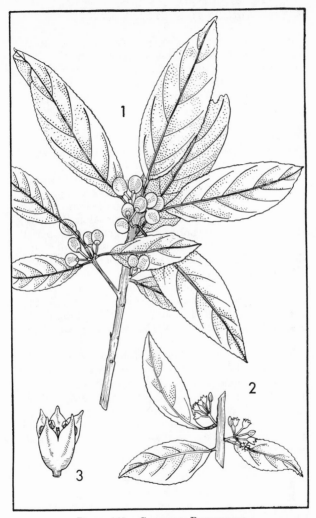

PLATE 145.—CAROLINA BUCKTHORN
1. Foliage and fruit $\times\frac{1}{2}$. 2. Flower cluster $\times\frac{1}{2}$. 3. Flower
$\times2$.

Leaves.—Alternate, simple, deciduous, 2½″ to 6″ long, 1″ to 2″ broad, oblong or broadly elliptical; apex, acute or gradually tapered; base, rounded or tapered; margin, obscurely toothed, the teeth sharp or rounded; dark yellow-green and shiny above, paler, smooth or occasionally hairy below; petioles, slender, flexible, ½″ to 1″ long; stipules, triangular. A variety (*R. caroliniana* var. *mollis*) occasionally associated with the species may be distinguished by its leaves, which are densely hairy on the lower surface.

Flowers.—Perfect, regular, borne in few-flowered, hairy umbels in the axils of leaves; calyx, composed of 5 nearly triangular, pointed sepals, united into a tube; petals, 5, whitish, ovate, deeply notched at the apex; stamens, 5, short, opposite the petals and partly enveloped by them; pistil, composed of a long, slender style terminating in a 3-lobed stigma and surmounting a 3-celled ovary.

Fruit.—A nearly spherical, black, leathery drupe, ⅓″ in diameter, often depressed at the apex; the thin, sweet, rather dry flesh, containing 3 bony pits, which are rounded on the back; seeds, reddish brown, about ⅕″ in length, albuminous.

Twigs.—Slender, at first reddish brown, with scattered, silky hairs or covered with a whitish bloom, ultimately smooth, gray, angled, and dotted with lenticels; terminal buds, present, elongated, naked, clothed with dense, woolly hair; lateral buds, ovoid; leaf scars, lunate to semioval, with 3 prominent bundle scars; stipule scars, slitlike; pith, terete, white, continuous.

Bark.—Ashy gray, smooth or shallowly furrowed, occasionally marked with dark blotches.

Habitat.—Most abundant on calcareous soils along streams and in rich bottom lands; also frequenting thickets, open, rocky woods, hillsides, and ridges.

Distribution.—Virginia south to western Florida;

west through the Ohio River Valley to eastern Kansas, Oklahoma, and Texas.

Importance.—Occasionally used for ornamental purposes.

THE COLUBRINAS

Colubrina L.C.R.

The colubrinas comprise a group of about 15 species of trees and shrubs, the majority[1] scattered through the tropical forests of the New World. Four species are to be found within the boundaries of the United States, 2 of which attain tree size. *C. texensis* Gray is a small, pubescent, profusely branched shrub endemic to the plains of Texas, New Mexico, and northern Mexico. *C. colubrina* Mill. (*C. arborescens* Sarg.), a tree in the West Indies, occurs in the Florida Keys as a large shrub. It may be distinguished from others of the group by its rusty-red, pubescent twigs and leathery leaves, which are also clothed with dense, rusty-red pubescence on their lower surfaces.

KEY TO THE ARBORESCENT COLUBRINAS

1. Leaves, thin, glandular at the base, smooth below....
   Soldierwood (p. 503)
1. Leaves, leathery, not glandular at the base, very hairy below.....................**Cuba colubrina** (p. 506)

Soldierwood

Colubrina reclinata Brong.

Habit.—A tree, 50′ to 60′ in height and 3′ to 4′ in diameter, with a trunk commonly characterized by deep, serpentine furrows. (This feature has given rise to the generic name, *coluber* meaning "serpent.")

[1] A single species (*C. asiatica* Brong.) is found in the Old World; 2 others are natives of India.

PLATE 146.—SOLDIERWOOD

1. Foliage and flowers ×½. 2. Single flower ×3. 3. Cluster
of fruits ×⅔.

Leaves.—Alternate, simple, persistent for 2 years, 2″ to 3½″ long, 1½″ to 2″ wide, ovate to lance-shaped or elliptical; apex, abruptly tapered to a blunt point; base, rounded or gradually tapered; margins, entire or remotely wavy, with 2 basal, marginal glands; yellow-green above and below, sometimes with fine, silky hairs below, thin and flexible; petioles, slender, about ½″ long; stipules, minute, dropping off as the leaves unfold.

Flowers.—Perfect, regular, borne in axillary, hairy cymes on branches of the current season; calyx, bell-shaped or tubular, with 5 triangular lobes; corolla, composed of 5 yellow petals; stamens, 5, opposite the petals and inserted with them; pistil, composed of a long, slender style crowned with 3 obtuse, stigmatic lobes and surmounting a 3-lobed, nearly globular ovary.

Fruit.—An orange-red capsule, splitting into 3 valves, each with a single black, oblong seed, about ¼″ in diameter.

Twigs.—Slender, occasionally somewhat angular, at first with a coat of fine, silky hairs, but soon becoming smooth and reddish brown; terminal buds, very small, ovoid, covered with several overlapping, hairy scales; lateral buds, similar to the terminal buds; leaf scars, almost circular, with 1 or 3 bundle scars; stipule scars, slitlike, barely discernible even with a lens; pith, white, continuous.

Bark.—Orange-brown, deeply and irregularly ridged and furrowed, sloughing off at the surface into large, paperlike scales.

Habitat.—Hammocks; ordinarily occurring as a scattered tree, but on Umbrella Key forming extensive woodlands.

Distribution.—North end of Key Largo, Umbrella Key, and small, neighboring islands near Elliott's Key in Florida; also Cuba, the Bahamas, Ste. Croix, the

Virgin Islands, and neighboring islands in the West
Indies.

Importance.—Like many other of the semitropical
trees of small stature and limited distribution, this
species has little utility at the present time.   According to Sargent, the leaves of this tree have been used in
Ste. Croix and the Virgin Islands in the preparation
of stomachic brews.

Cuba Colubrina

Colubrina cubensis Brong.

Habit.—A large shrub or small tree that under
optimum conditions for growth attains a height of 20'
to 30' and a diameter of 6" to 9".

Leaves.—Alternate, simple, persistent for 2 years,
3½" to 5½" long, 1" to 2" wide, oblong to broadly
elliptical; apex, acute or rounded and terminating in
a short bristle; base, rounded, tapered, or asymmetrical; margin, with broad, rounded teeth, not
infrequently remotely revolute; dark green and hairy
above, pale green and hairy below, with a leathery
texture; petioles, slender, yellowish, clothed with
dense, yellowish-brown hair, about ½" long; stipules,
inconspicuous, early deciduous.

Flowers.—Perfect, regular, very small, borne in
axillary clusters on branches of the current season,
calyx, extremely hairy, the 5 lobes triangular; petals,
5, yellow, about as long as the calyx lobes; stamens, 5, opposite the petals and inserted with them;
pistil, with a slender style, 3 stigmatic lobes, and a
3-celled ovary.

Fruit.—A reddish to purplish, globular capsule,
splitting along 3 lines of suture into 3 valves, each
with a black, oblong seed; about ⅓" in diameter.

Twigs.—Rather stouter than those of the preceding species, at first covered with yellowish-brown, silky hairs, at length smooth or nearly so, reddish brown to purplish brown, marked with prominent, slitlike lenticels; buds, naked; leaf scars, V-shaped or less frequently lunate, with 3 bundle scars; stipule scars, minute, slitlike; pith, white, homogeneous.

Bark.—Similar to that of the preceding species but not so deeply furrowed or scaly.

Habitat.—Hammocks and dry, sandy or gravelly soils.

Distribution.—The Everglade Keys of Florida, Cuba, the Bahamas, and Haiti.

Importance.—Of no commercial or ornamental value.

THE BASSWOOD FAMILY

Tiliaceae

The Basswood Family comprises a group of temperate and tropical trees, shrubs, and herbs, with about 300 species included in 35 genera. Jute, the bast fibers of which are used in cordage, fabrics, and paper, is obtained from several members of the genus *Corchorus* L. A few genera, notably those from the Southern Hemisphere, are productive of commercial timber.

Three genera are represented in the flora of North America, one of which includes a number of arborescent species.

THE BASSWOODS

Tilia L.

The basswoods comprise a group of about 50 species of trees widely distributed in Europe, central China, southern Japan, Mexico, and eastern North America.

Specific identification of the basswoods is fraught with difficulty. The American species, at least, have been found to be a puzzling group, and taxonomists are not in complete agreement regarding the limits of several species. Field identification is often complicated by the fact that, even within a species, there is manifested considerable variation between leaves which appear in the spring and those which develop during the summer. Thus, unless otherwise noted, all the ensuing leaf descriptions are of leaves produced in the spring on flower-bearing branches. The species of basswood here described follow closely the concepts of Small.[1]

At least 16 species, all trees, inhabit the forests of the South. A number of other doubtful species have been described but are not included here.

KEY TO THE SOUTHERN BASSWOODS[2]

1. Lower surface of mature leaves, free of hair or with only occasional axillary tufts...................... 2
1. Lower surface of mature leaves, clothed with silky or woolly hairs.................................... 9

   2. Lower surface of mature leaves, furnished with a whitish bloom............................... 3
   2. Lower surfaces of mature leaves, varying through shades of pale green to pale yellow-green........ 6

3. Bracts, hairy at period of floral opening............
                    Colonels Island basswood (p. 513)
3. Bracts, free of hair at period of floral opening....... 4

   4. Flower stalks, free of hair; bracts, about 1½″ wide
                 Appalachian basswood (p. 513)
   4. Flower stalks, hairy; bracts, ¾″ wide or less.... 5

[1] Small, J. K., Manual of the Southeastern Flora, pp. 840–846.

[2] It is recommended that only leaves from fruiting branches be examined in using this key.

5. Spring leaves, smooth or nearly so when unfolding, more or less copper-colored. .**Ashe basswood** (p. 513)
5. Spring leaves, woolly when unfolding. . . . .
Florida basswood (p. 514)

6. Spring leaves, smooth or nearly so when first unfolding. 7
6. Spring leaves, woolly when first unfolding. 8

7. Flowers, in clusters of 10 to 15, their stalks free from hair or nearly so. . . . . . .**American basswood** (p. 514)
7. Flowers, in clusters of 8 to 40, their stalks densely woolly. . . . .**Gulf basswood** (p. 515)

8. Mature leaves, more or less leathery, finely dentate, blue-green, flattened or rounded on one side at the base. . . . .**Louisiana basswood** (p. 515)
8. Mature leaves, more or less papery, finely serrate, yellow-green, unequally wedge-shaped or rounded at the base. . . .**Colonels Island basswood** (p. 513)

9. Leaves, with tawny, brown, or rusty-red, woolly hairs below. 10
9. Leaves, with white, gray, or silvery, silky or woolly hairs below. 16

10. Leaves, mostly obliquely cordate at the base. . . .11
10. Leaves, mostly obliquely truncate or broadly wedge-shaped at the base. .14

11. Hairs, on leaves, flowers, and twigs more or less erect, thus giving the parts a fuzzy appearance. . . . .
Hairy basswood.(p. 515)
11. Hairs, on leaves, flowers, and twigs more or less appressed. 12

12. Twigs of summer shoots, very hairy or woolly. . .
Carolina basswood (p. 515)
12. Twigs of summer shoots, free from hair or nearly so. 13

13. Bracts, 2″ to 5″ long; leaf margins, coarsely serrate
Quebec basswood (p. 516)
13. Bracts, 4″ to 6″ long; leaf margins, finely serrate...
White basswood (p. 510)

14. Leaves, elliptical, broadly wedge-shaped or rounded on one side at the base................
Okaloosa basswood (p. 516)
14. Leaves, ovate, truncate at the base............15

15. Bracts, nearly sessile, 2″ to 3½″ long..............
Georgia basswood (p. 516)
15. Bracts, stalked, 4″ to 6″ long.....................
White basswood (p. 510)

16. Leaves, with ivory-white hairs below..........
Ivory basswood (p. 517)
16. Leaves, with snowy-white or silvery-gray hairs below...................................17

17. Flowers, in glabrous cymes.......................
Highlands basswood (p. 517)
17. Flowers, in hairy cymes or corymbs...............18

18. Flowers, in corymbs of 10 to 20................
White basswood (p. 510)
18. Flowers, in cymes of 7 to 12....................
Michaux basswood (p. 517)

White Basswood

Tilia heterophylla Vent.

Habit.—A large tree, often 60′ to 80′ in height and 1′ to 2½′ in diameter, with a long, clear, cylindrical, sometimes buttressed bole and spreading root system.

Leaves.—Alternate, simple, deciduous, ovate, 3″ to 5½″ long, 2″ to 3″ broad; apex, long-tapered; base, obliquely heart-shaped or flattened; margin, finely glandular, dentately toothed; at maturity dark green

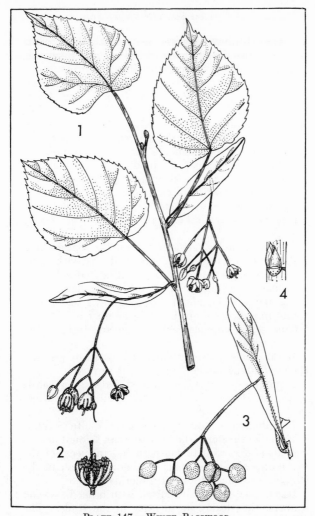

PLATE 147.—WHITE BASSWOOD
1. Foliage and flowers $\times\frac{1}{3}$. 2. Flower $\times 1$. 3. Cluster of fruit $\times\frac{1}{2}$. 4. Leaf scar $\times 1\frac{1}{2}$.

and smooth above, covered below with thick, white or pale-brown, woolly hairs; petioles, slender, smooth, about 1½" long; stipules, straplike.

Flowers.—Perfect, borne on drooping, hairy stalks, in corymbs of 10 to 20 flowers from a long, asymmetrical bract, 4" to 6" long and 1" to 1½" wide; sepals, 5, separate, long-tapered; petals, 5, pale yellow, alternating with the sepals; stamens, many, borne in clusters of 5, their filaments united at the base and attached to a petallike staminodium (sterile stamen), opposite the petals; pistil, with a 5-celled ovary and stout style crowned with a 5-lobed stigma.

Fruit.—Nutlike, leathery or woody, ellipsoidal, about ⅓" long, clothed with rusty-brown, woolly hairs.

Twigs.—Slender, sometimes slightly zigzag, reddish brown, red, or yellowish brown, dotted with small, pale lenticels; terminal buds, wanting; lateral buds, inequilateral, mucilaginous, with 2 outer scales; hairy along the margin, about ¼" long; leaf scars, half-round to crescent-shaped, with a number of scattered bundle scars; stipule scars, prominent; pith, white, homogeneous.

Bark.—Thick, deeply furrowed between grayish-brown, flattened ridges, scaly at the surface.

Habitat.—In mixed, hardwood forests; on gentle mountain slopes with moist but well-drained soils; rare on the coastal plains.

Distribution.—West Virginia near White Sulphur Springs south along the Appalachian Mountains to Alabama; westward to southern Indiana; east of the mountains along the upper Piedmont plateau in the Carolinas to Jackson County, Florida.

Importance.—Cut and mixed with other basswood timbers, thus losing its identity in the trade. The wood is of excellent quality and is used for many purposes, notably for drawing boards, excelsior, boxboards, cheap furniture, plywood, washing machines, and interior trim.

Colonels Island Basswood

Tilia littoralis Sarg.

This is a tree of greatly restricted distribution, inhabiting Colonel's and adjacent islands near the mouths of the Medway and North rivers of north-coastal Georgia. The tree is characterized by yellow-green, ovate leaves with asymmetrical, wedge-shaped, flattened or rounded bases, smooth or with a whitish bloom below; 9- to 15-flowered, hairy cymes supported on nearly sessile, long, narrow bracts, 3″ to 7″ in length and about ⅜″ in width; and nearly globular nutlets, about ¼″ in diameter, clothed with pale, woolly hairs.

Appalachian Basswood

Tilia australis Small

This is a small tree found on gentle slopes of the southern Appalachian Mountains from northern Alabama to southwestern Virginia. Its chief botanical features are oval to ovate leaves, 3″ to 6″ long, with heart-shaped or asymmetrically flattened bases, rounded, glandular, marginal teeth, and glaucous lower surfaces; bracts, 4″ to 6″ long and 1½″ wide, each supporting a many-flowered cyme; and fruit, about ¼″ long, nearly globular, woolly.

Ashe Basswood

Tilia ashei Bush

This is a small tree restricted to western Florida, where it has been observed along stream banks and on moist slopes. This form seems to be a very close botanical congener of the Florida basswood. It is characterized by ovate to oval leaves, which at maturity are practically free from hair except along the margin; the bracts are 2″ to 4″ in length and about ¾″ in width, rectangular, and nearly sessile and support a compact, few-flowered cyme; the fruits are about ¼″ in diameter, nearly globular, and coated with yellow-gray, woolly hairs.

Florida Basswood

Tilia floridana Small

According to some authorities this tree occurs only in or near Jackson County, Florida. Small[1] has greatly extended its range, however, and includes as part of the species two other forms, *T. crenoserrata* Sarg. and *T. alabamensis* Ashe. Thus, following Small's concept, Florida basswood extends from Florida westward to Texas and southeastern Oklahoma and northward to western North Carolina. Its principal botanical features are: broadly ovate leaves, 2″ to 4½″ long, with coarse, marginal teeth silvery-white lower surfaces; few-flowered cymes, borne on spatulalike or scythe-shaped bracts, 4″ to 6″ long; and yellowish to reddish-brown twigs.

American Basswood

Tilia glabra Vent.

This is a northern tree that extends southward to Maryland and west through Kentucky to Missouri. Useful features for its identification are: large, ovate leaves, 5″ to 6″ long, devoid of hair except for axillary tufts; few-flowered cymes, borne on bracts, 4″ to 5″ long; and nutlike fruits, sometimes ½″ long, with a gray woolly coat. Under optimum conditions

---

[1] Small, J. K., Manual of the Flora of the Southeastern States, p. 846.

for growth this tree will attain a height of 100′ to 125′ and a diameter of 2′ or 3′ and is an important source of commercial timber.

Gulf Basswood
Tilia leucocarpa Ashe

This is a small tree of the lower Mississippi Valley and adjacent Gulf states, extending from Alabama west to eastern Texas, thence north through southwestern Oklahoma and southeastern Arkansas. The large flower clusters (8 to 40), borne on long, narrow bracts, and the dark-green, glabrous leaves, 3″ to 6″ long, are reliable features for identification.

Louisiana Basswood
Tilia cocksii Sarg.

This is a small tree of very limited distribution found only in the vicinity of Lake Charles, Louisiana, where it frequents the banks of streams and moist flatwoods. It resembles closely the Florida basswood but is characterized by bluish-green, leathery leaves.

Hairy Basswood
Tilia lasioclada Sarg.

This is one of the most easily recognizable members of the group. Hairy basswood occurs along the coastal plain from southeastern South Carolina in the Savannah River Valley to Gadsden County, Florida. The spreading hairs on leaves, twigs, and parts of the inflorescence serve readily to distinguish this tree from other basswoods of the region.

Carolina Basswood
Tilia caroliniana Mill.

Carolina basswood is a large tree of the coastal plain extending from North Carolina near Wilmington to

Georgia, central and western Florida, western Louisiana, southern Arkansas, and eastern Texas to the Edwards Plateau. The broadly ovate leaves (3″ to 5″ long) with coarsely dentate margins, clothed with rusty-brown, woolly hairs on their lower surfaces, hairy, 8- to 15-flowered cymes, on nearly hairless bracts, and tiny globular fruits, about ⅛″ long, are its principal diagnostic features.

Quebec Basswood

Tilia neglecta Spach.

The Quebec basswood is a large tree often 90′ in height and 2′ to 3′ in diameter. While its name suggests that it is a northern species, it actually occurs in many sections of the South. It is found in the southern Appalachian Mountains and in northern Mississippi. This tree is very similar to the Carolina basswood but differs largely in the inflorescence bracts, which taper gradually from apex to base; those of the Carolina basswood are more nearly linear and taper abruptly at the base.

Okaloosa Basswood

Tilia porracea Ashe

This is a tree of very restricted range, reported only from Okaloosa County, Florida. It is characterized by elliptical leaves, asymmetrical at the base, and scythelike bracts supporting a hairy, 7- to 15-flowered corymb.

Georgia Basswood

Tilia georgiana Sarg.

This is a small coastal-plain tree extending from South Carolina to central Florida. The ovate leaves are mostly truncate at the base and the short bracts (2″ to 3½″ long) nearly sessile; the fruits are globular, often depressed at the summit, with 5 grooves or more rarely ridges, and are covered with a thick coat of rusty-brown, woolly hairs.

Ivory Basswood

Tilia eburnea Ashe

This is a tall tree confined to a small area from northwest coastal Florida to western North Carolina. The thick coat of ivory-white hairs on the lower sides of the leaves is its most reliable diagnostic feature.

Highlands Basswood

Tilia truncata Spach.

This is a large tree of the southern Appalachian Mountains found on moist slopes usually between 2,500′ and 3,000′ of elevation from Virginia to North Carolina and Tennessee. The leaves are 4″ to 7″ long, ovate to nearly oblong, and clothed below with matted, snowy-white hairs. The flowers are borne in glabrous cymes supported upon bracts, 4″ to 5″ long and 1″ wide. The ovoid to ellipsoid fruits are about ⅓″ long and covered with a dense, brown, woolly coat.

Michaux Basswood

Tilia michauxii Nutt.

This is a large tree of wide distribution through the eastern United States, in the South inhabiting parts of Georgia, Alabama, Mississippi, Arkansas, and Missouri. Michaux basswood is similar in character to white basswood, and some authorities consider it to be merely a variety of that species. The flowers of Michaux basswood are borne in cymes of 7 to 12, while those of white basswood are produced in 10- to 20-flowered corymbs.

THE TEA FAMILY

Theaceae

The Tea Family includes 16 genera and about 175 species of trees and shrubs, mostly evergreens. The majority of these are indigenous to eastern Asia. Commercial tea is the dried leaves of *Thea sinensis* L. and some of its improved varieties. Among the ornamentals, the camellias should be mentioned. These evergreen shrubs or small trees with large pink, purplish, or white blossoms and handsome foliage are prized decorative plants throughout the South.

Two genera, each with 2 arborescent species, inhabit southern forests.

Synopsis of Southern Genera

Genus	*Leaves*	*Flowers*	*Fruit*
Gordonia	deciduous or persistent	sepals, very unequal	a capsule, with many angular or winged seeds
Stewartia	deciduous	sepals, equal or nearly so	a capsule, with many lens-shaped seeds

THE GORDONIAS

Gordonia Ellis

The gordonias comprise a group of 17 trees of American and Asiatic distribution. The very rare Franklintree or Franklinia belongs to this group; however, some authorities have designated this form as a monotype and have given it the technical designation *Franklinia alatamaha* Marsh.

Loblolly-bay and the Franklinia are the southern representatives of this group.

KEY TO THE GORDONIAS

1. Leaves, persistent; flowers, long-stalked; capsule, ovoid, splitting from the apex to below the middle....
Loblolly-bay (p. 519)
1. Leaves, deciduous; flowers, nearly sessile; capsule, globular, splitting alternately from base and apex along 10 lines of suture..........**Franklinia** (p. 521)

Loblolly-Bay

Gordonia lasianthus (L.) Ellis

Habit.—A handsome, short-lived, evergreen tree, sometimes 60' to 70' in height and 12'' to 18'' in diameter; with ascending branches forming a narrow, ovoid crown; in exposed and sterile situations, often a low, sprawling shrub.

Leaves.—Alternate, simple, persistent, leathery, oblong to oblanceolate, 4'' to 6'' long, 1½'' to 2'' wide; apex, acute; base, wedge-shaped; margin, finely or obscurely toothed above the middle; dark green above, paler below, often with scattered, woolly hairs; petiole, stout, about ½'' long, grooved above and winged toward the apex.

Flowers.—Perfect, solitary in the leaf axils, about 2½'' wide, fragrant, long-stalked; sepals, 5, unequal, about ½'' long, hairy on the margin and clothed on the outer surface with dense, velvety hairs; petals, 5, white, about 1½'' long; stamens, many, united at the base of their filaments and forming a cup, which is inserted upon the base of the petals; pistil, with a 5-celled, ovoid ovary, crowned by a short, stout style and fleshy, minutely 5-lobed stigma.

Fruit.—A woody, ovoid, hairy capsule, about ¾'' long; seated upon a persistent calyx, and tipped with the remnants of the style; at maturity, splitting along 5 lines of suture to below the middle; seeds, minute, winged.

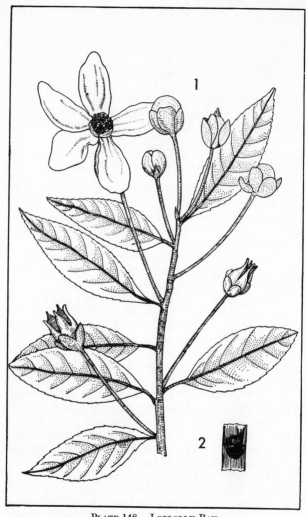

PLATE 148.—LOBLOLLY-BAY
1. Foliage, flowers, and fruit ×½.   2. Leaf scar ×1½.

Twigs.—Moderately stout, dark brown, the epidermal layers often wrinkled; buds, naked, ovoid or nearly globular; leaf scars, shield-shaped, with a line or broadly U-shaped row of bundle scars; pith, homogeneous; stipule scars, wanting.

Bark.—Thick, dark reddish brown, deeply furrowed, the intervening ridges superficially scaly.

Habitat.—Swamps, bays, and wet situations in the pine barrens of the coastal plains.

Distribution.—Southern coastal Virginia, south along the coastal plain to Florida and west to Louisiana; south in Florida to Lake Okeechobee.

Importance.—A tree of minor importance. The pinkish wood has been used locally for cabinetry, and the bark is known to contain suitable astringents for tanning. While having handsome foliage and showy flowers, this species is seldom used for decorative purposes.

Franklinia   Franklintree

Gordonia alatamaha Marsh.

Like the well-known ginkgo of China, this tree has not been found growing under natural conditions for many years. It is undoubtedly one of the world's rarest trees and is known today only as a cultivated plant.

Franklinia was first discovered in 1765 by John and William Bartram on the banks of the Altamaha River near Fort Barrington, Ga. Later (1773), one of the Bartrams returned and collected both plants and seeds, which were propagated at Philadelphia. In 1790 Dr. Moses Marshall rediscovered the same grove of trees. This appears to be the last time this species was observed growing naturally. This tree, however, may be propagated by both seed and cuttings so that its perpetuation seems reasonably assured.

Franklinia may be distinguished from the loblolly-bay by its deciduous leaves, nearly sessile flowers with barrellike ovaries, globular capsules, which split from both apex and base in alternating lines of suture, and large, coffee-colored pith. The tree is prized most highly by arboriculturists.

THE STEWARTIAS

Stewartia L.

The Stewartias comprise a group of American and Asiatic shrubs or small trees numbering five species. These are particularly noted for their large showy flowers, but because of the difficulty in propagating them in nurseries they are seldom offered for sale in any large numbers.

Two species, both small trees, occur in southern forests.

KEY TO THE SOUTHERN STEWARTIAS

1. Capsule, 5-angled, beaked at the summit; flowers, with yellow stamens and 5 distinct styles; winter buds, about ¼″ long..........**Mountain stewartia** (p. 522)
1. Capsule, globular, not beaked at the summit; flowers, with purple stamens and a single stout style; winter buds, minute.............**Virginia stewartia** (p. 524)

Mountain Stewartia

Stewartia ovata (Cav.) Weatherby

Habit.—A large shrub, or small tree with spreading branches; scarcely ever more than 25′ in height or 5″ in diameter.

Leaves.—Alternate, simple, deciduous, elliptical to ovate or oblong, 2″ to 5″ long, 1″ to 2½″ broad; apex, acute to long-tapered; base, wedge-shaped; margin, hairy, minutely toothed, at least above the middle; dark green above, paler and hairy below; petioles, hairy, about ½″ long.

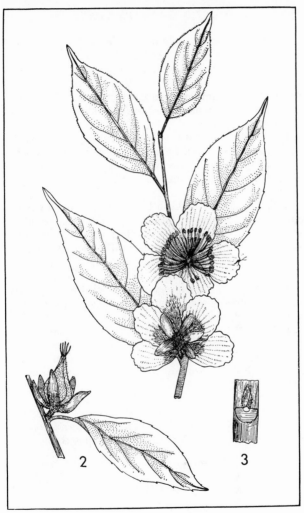

PLATE 149.—MOUNTAIN STEWARTIA
1. Foliage and flowers ×⅓.   2. Fruit ×1.   3. Leaf scar. ×2.

Flowers.—Perfect, solitary in the axils of leaves, about 4″ broad, nearly sessile; calyx, with 6 oblong-linear sepals; petals, 5, white, crimped and irregularly toothed along the margin; stamens, many, their filaments united at the base, their anthers yellow; pistil, with a broad, conical ovary surmounted by 5 distinct styles.

Fruit.—A 5-angled, ovoid, hairy capsule, about ¾″ long, seated upon the persistent calyx and tipped with the remnants of the styles; at maturity, splitting along 5 lines of suture and releasing the small, lenticular seeds.

Twigs.—Slender, reddish brown; buds, solitary and superposed, spindle-shaped, about ¼″ long, usually with 2 outer, often hairy scales; leaf scars, half-round, with a single raised bundle scar; pith, spongy; stipule scars, wanting.

Bark.—Dark brown, smooth.

Habitat.—An understory species of the southern montane forests, most abundant along watercourses and on moist, wooded slopes.

Distribution.—The Blue Ridge and Appalachian Mountains and adjacent areas from Virginia to Alabama; disjuncts have been reported from Wake County, North Carolina, and coastal Virginia near Williamsburg.

Importance.—Sparingly used as an ornamental.

Remarks.—A form (var. *grandiflora*) with purple stamens has been reported from northwestern Georgia and the Cumberland Mountains of Tennessee.

Virginia Stewartia

Stewartia malacodendron L.

This shrub or small tree is essentially a species of the coastal plains from Virginia to Florida and west to Louisiana. It appears to be even more exacting in its requirements than the mountain stewartia and is exceedingly difficult to propagate. Virginia stewartia may be distinguished from the preceding tree by its smaller leaves, 2″ to 3″ long, flowers with purple stamens, and nearly globular, beakless capsules.

THE WILD CINNAMON FAMILY

Canellaceae

This small tropical group of trees and shrubs comprising five genera ranges from Madagascar and southern Africa to tropical America. A single species inhabits the woodlands of southern Florida.

Canella

Canella winterana Gaertn.

A Monotype

Habit.—A moderately large tropical tree; in southern Florida, attaining a height of about 25′ and a diameter of about 10″; the crown, usually compact and more or less ovoid.

Leaves.—Alternate, simple, persistent, dotted with minute glands, leathery, obovate, 3″ to 5″ long, 1″ to 2″ wide; apex, rounded; sometimes with a shallow notch; base, narrowly wedge-shaped; margin, entire; bright green, lustrous above, paler below; petioles, stout, short, grooved; stipules, wanting.

Flowers.—Perfect, about ⅛″ in width, borne in terminal or subterminal cymes; calyx, composed of 3 nearly circular sepals; petals, 5, oblong, rounded at the apex, white or pinkish; stamens, 20, their filaments united into a tube, which encloses the pistil; ovary, conical to nearly cylindrical, crowned with a short style and a 2- or 3-lobed stigma.

Fruit.—A globular, bright-red, fleshy, 2- to 4-seeded berry, about ½″ in diameter, tipped with the

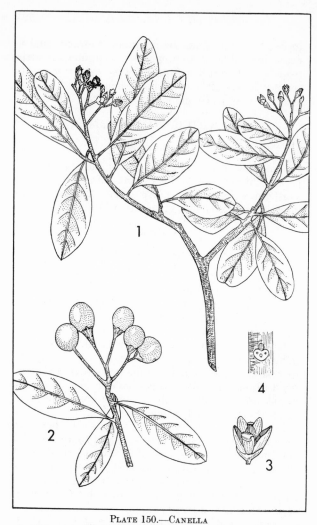

PLATE 150.—CANELLA
1. Foliage and flowers ×⅓. 2. Cluster of fruit ×⅓.
3. Flower ×½. 4. Leaf scar ×2.

remnant of a persistent style; seeds, kidney-shaped, with a black, shiny seed coat, about ⅛″ long.

Twigs.—Stout, ashy gray; buds, minute; leaf scars, heart-shaped to circular or nearly so, with 3 bundle scars; pith, homogeneous.

Bark.—Thin, light gray, scaly; when blazed, exhibiting a yellow inner bark; aromatic.

Habitat.—Hammocks and coastal forests; usually an understory species.

Distribution.—Monroe County, Florida, south over the Keys and in the West Indies.

Importance.—This tree furnishes the wild cinnamon bark of commerce.

THE PAPAYA FAMILY

Caricaceae

These are a small, tropical family of trees and shrubs with bitter, milky sap, consisting of 2 genera and about 30 species. A single representative, the papaya or custardapple, occurs within our limits.

THE PAPAYAS

Carica L.

These are a group of 20 short-lived evergreen trees restricted to the tropics and subtropics of the New World.

Papaya

Carica papaya L.

Habit.—In the tropics a tree, often 25′ to 35′ in height and about 12″ in diameter, but in Florida rarely more than 12′ to 15′ in height or 4″ to 6″ in diameter.

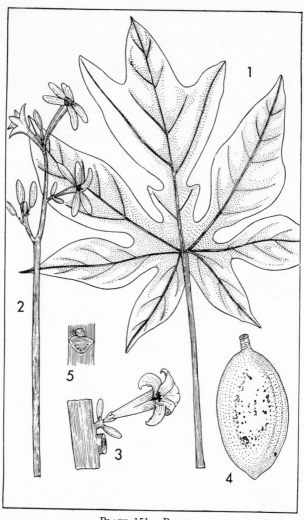

PLATE 151.—PAPAYA

1. Leaf ×⅕. 2. Cluster of male flowers ×¾. 3. Cluster of female flowers ×1. 4. Fruit ×⅓. 5. Leaf scar ×1.

Leaves.—Alternate, simple, persistent, ovate to nearly circular, palmately lobed, 12" to 24" in diameter; apex, acute, often ending in a short, sharp tip; base, deeply heart-shaped; margin of lobes, entire or deeply pinnately lobed; bright green above, paler below; petiole, very stout, hollow, often 3' to 4' long, greatly enlarged at the base.

Flowers.—Unisexual, both types appearing on the same tree; staminate, fragrant, in many-flowered, axillary, cymose panicles borne on long, hairy stalks; pistillate, in 1- to 3-flowered cymes borne on very short stalks, usually ½" or less in length; calyx, minute, 5-lobed; corolla of the staminate flowers, funnel-shaped, with 5 straplike lobes at the summit, yellow or with a reddish tinge, about 1" long; that of the pistillate flowers, composed of 5 erect, oblong-linear petals; stamens, 10, in 2 series, inserted upon the corolla of the staminate flowers; pistil, with a slightly 5-angled, 1-celled ovary, crowned with a short style and 5-parted stigma.

Fruit.—A yellow-green to orange, ovoid to ellipsoidal berry, about 4" long and 3" wide, solitary or in clusters of 2 or 3, with a thick skin and sweetish flesh; seed, about ¼" long, wrinkled.

Many of the horticultural forms propagated in Florida and elsewhere produce fruit of much greater size and abundance than that just described.

Twigs.—Stout, green, exuding a milky sap when bruised; buds, small, globular, essentially naked; leaf scars, broadly shield-shaped to 3-lobed, with many small bundle scars arranged in a U- to C-shaped line pith, large, 5-angled in cross section, hollow through the center; stipule scars, wanting.

Bark.—Smooth green, ultimately becoming gray.

Habitat.—Hammocks, pinelands, and cutover lands.

Distribution.—Lower peninsular Florida and the Keys, the West Indies, Mexico, Central and South America.

Importance.—Widely cultivated through the tropics for its fruit, which is highly regarded for its food value. The expressed juices make a very enjoyable, spicy, and thirst-quenching beverage. The milky sap contains papain, a substance capable of digesting albumin.

THE MANGROVE FAMILY

Rhizophoraceae

The Mangrove Family comprises a group of about 20 genera and 60 species of tropical, evergreen, maritime trees and shrubs. These plants develop large networks of stiltlike roots, which encourage the deposition of silt and mud carried in from the sea on incoming tides. In due course, a solid terrain is formed, and upon this soon begins to encroach the vegetation of the neighboring inland forests. An added feature of many members of this group is the seed, which germinates while still attached to the parent tree. The barks of most members of this family are rich in tannin.

A single genus, represented by one species, occurs within our region.

THE MANGROVES

Rhizophora L.

The mangroves comprise a group of three species, all small trees, distributed along tidal shores throughout the tropics. A single species is widespread over the Florida Keys and extends north along both coasts of the Florida mainland to Tampa Bay and Indian River.

Mangrove

Rhizophora mangle L.

Habit.—In the tropics, a tall tree, 70' to 80' in height, with a long, clear, columnar bole, 1' to 2' in

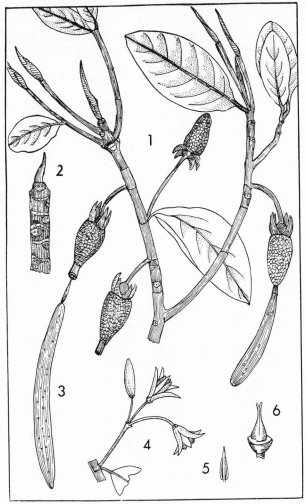

PLATE 152.—Mangrove

1. Foliage and fruit with embryo in various stages of development   ×½.   2. Twig   ×1.   3. Fully   grown   radicle ×½.
4. Flower cluster ×½.   5. Stamen detail ×1.   6. Pistil detail ×1.

diameter; in Florida, a short, bushy tree, about 20′ in height and 4″ to 8″ in diameter, characterized by a multitude of aerial, fleshy, adventitious roots, which arch out and downward into the mud, where they continue to grow.

Leaves.—Opposite, simple, persistent, leathery, ovate to elliptical, 3″ to 5″ long, 1″ to 2″ wide; apex, acute or rounded; base, broadly wedge-shaped; margin, entire, somewhat thickened; dark green, lustrous above, paler below; petioles, about 1″ long; stipules, lance-shaped, about 1½″ long, falling away as the leaves unfold.

Flowers.—Perfect, axillary about 1″ in diameter, in 2- or 3-flowered clusters, borne on stalks 1″ to 2″ in length, calyx, 4-lobed, persistent under the fruit; petals, 4, pale yellow, hairy on the inner surface; stamens, 8; pistil, with a 2-celled, conical ovary crowned with a pair of spreading, awl-shaped styles, stigmatic at their summit.

Fruit.—A leathery, rusty-brown, conical berry, about 1″ in length; surrounded at the base by the persistent calyx, roughened by minute bosses; developing at the summit a short, woody tube, ½″ or more in length, through which passes the developing embryo; seed, 1, germinating within the fruit before it becomes detached and sending through the terminal pore of the fruit a dark-brown radical, 6″ to 12″ in length and often ⅓″ in thickness at its summit; when released from the tree, the heavy end of the dartlike seedling lodges in the mud, and the aerial portion above high-water level immediately sends out leafy shoots. (This type of development exemplifies one of the most interesting cases of plant adaptation to environment.)

Twigs.—Stout, smooth, dark red-brown; buds, minute, more or less sunken; leaf scars, broadly elliptical to oval, with 3 bundle scars; stipule scars, conspicuous, encircling the twig, with evident bundle scars; pith, large, homogeneous, brown.

Bark.—Thick, gray to gray-brown, divided into irregular, scaly ridges by deep anastomosing furrows.

Habitat.—Brackish waters along creeks, bays, and lagoons.

Distribution.—Coasts of peninsular Florida and the Florida Keys, Mexico including Lower California, the West Indies, Central and South America.

Importance.—These trees are of great importance in the building up of new land surfaces. The wood has been used for fuel, piling, crossties, and charcoal. The bark contains 20 to 30 per cent of tannin by weight and is an important source of this commodity.

THE WHITE-MANGROVE FAMILY

Combretaceae

The White-mangrove Family constitutes a group of about 15 genera and 285 species of evergreen trees, shrubs, and vines. Many of them play an important role in building land surfaces along tidewaters. A few are productive of valuable fruits, astringents, and dye principles. The East Indian laurel (*Terminalia tomentosa* W. et A.) and the African limba (*T. superba* Eng. & Diels) supply appreciable quantities of valuable timber to the modern furniture industry. The East Indian almond (*T. catappa* L.) is used extensively as an ornamental in tropical countries of the New World and has become naturalized in parts of peninsular Florida.

Three monotypic genera are indigenous to our subtropics.

Synopsis of Arborescent Genera

Genus	Leaves	Flowers	Fruit
Bucida	alternate	in spikes; without petals	5-angled, urn-shaped

Genus	Leaves	Flowers	Fruit
Conocarpus	alternate	in heads; without petals	scalelike, in heads
Laguncularia	opposite	in spikes; with 5 petals	10-ribbed, obovoid

Oxhorn Bucida

Bucida buceras L.

A Monotype

Habit.—A tree of very unusual habit; occasionally with a single upright stem, but commonly producing a short, massive, prostrate bole, 2′ to 3′ in diameter, from which arise several large secondary trunks that are often 40′ to 50′ in height and 1′ to 2′ in diameter; the crown of these is composed of numerous horizontal branches.

Leaves.—Alternate, simple, persistent, leathery, crowded at the tips of the twigs, mostly obovate, 2″ to 3″ long, 1″ to 1½″ wide; apex, rounded, minutely notched, or with a short, pointed tip; base, wedge-shaped; margin, entire; blue-green above, yellow-green below, with rusty-red hairs on the midrib; petioles, stout, about ½″ long.

Flowers.—Perfect, in spikes, the supporting stalk flexible and hairy; calyx, surrounding the ovary and constricted above it, 5-lobed at the summit; greenish white; petals, none; stamens, 10, in 2 rows, the taller 5 inserted opposite the calyx lobes, the shorter 5 alternating with them; pistil, with a 1-celled ovary inserted in the calyx tube, surmounted by a slender style with minute stigma.

Fruit.—An ovoid or conical, 5-angled, light-brown, leathery drupe, about ¼″ long; crowned with a persistent calyx; seed, minute, chestnut-brown.

Twigs.—Slender, at first clothed with rusty-red hairs, later becoming reddish brown, and finally super-

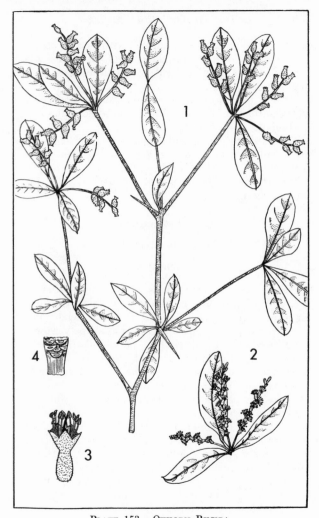

PLATE 153.—OXHORN BUCIDA
1. Foliage and fruit ×½. 2. Cluster of flowers ×½.
3. Flower ×3. 4. Leaf scars ×1½.

ficially shreddy, commonly armed with slender spines
1″ or more in length; buds, naked; leaf scars, crescent-
shaped, with a single central, oval bundle scar; pith,
homogeneous.

Bark.—Thick, gray-brown to reddish brown, divided
at the surface into small, closely appressed scales.

Habitat.—Brackish marshes.

Distribution.—In Florida reported only from Elliott's Key; common in the West Indies and along
tropical shores of the Caribbean Sea.

Importance.—Bark reported to be suitable for
tanning leather.

Button-Mangrove

Conocarpus erecta L.

A Monotype

Habit.—At the extremities of its range often a
low, sprawling shrub, but under favorable conditions
for growth becoming a tree, 40′ to 60′ in height and
1′ to 2′ in diameter, with a narrow, but shapely crown.

Leaves.—Alternate, simple, persistent, leathery,
ovate, oval, or obovate, 2″ to 4″ long, ½″ to 1½″
wide; apex, acute; base, wedge-shaped, with a pair of
marginal glands; margin, entire; dark green above,
paler below; petiole, short, stout, about ½″ long.

Flowers.—Perfect, minute, borne in dense, globular
heads, ⅓″ in diameter, the heads borne in terminal
panicles 3″ to 10″ long; calyx, bell-shaped, 5-lobed;
petals, none; stamens, 5 in 1 row (rarely 7 or 8 in 2
ranks); pistil, 1-celled, minute.

Fruit.—A minute, reddish, scalelike, leathery drupe
borne in heads to form a cone about 1″ in diameter;
seeds, minute, pale yellowish brown.

Twigs.—Slender, conspicuously angled, reddish
brown, smooth; buds, naked; leaf scars, half-round

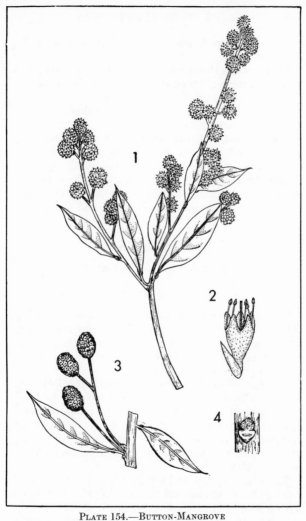

PLATE 154.—BUTTON-MANGROVE

1. Foliage and flowers ×¼. 2. Flower ×4. 3. Cluster of fruits ×¼. 4. Leaf scar ×2.

to crescent-shaped, with a single bundle scar; pith, homogeneous.

Bark.—Dark brown to nearly black, broken into broad, flattened, anastomosing ridges by irregular fissures; ridges, superficially scaly; scales, appressed.

Habitat.—The silty and muddy foreshores of tidewater bays and lagoons.

Distribution.—Tampa Bay and Cape Canaveral, Florida, south over the Keys to the West Indies and coasts of West Africa and Central and South America.

Importance.—The bark contains principles of medicinal value and is a suitable tannage. The wood is said to have a high calorific value and is used for fuel.

White-Mangrove

Laguncularia racemosa Gaertn.

A Monotype

Habit.—Like the previous species a low, sprawling shrub toward the northern limits of its range but, where growth is favorable, becoming a tree, 40′ to 60′ in height and 1′ to 2′ in diameter, with a narrow, rounded crown.

Leaves.—Opposite, simple, persistent, leathery, oblong to broadly elliptical, 1″ to 3″ long, 1″ to 1½″ wide; apex, obtuse or minutely notched; base, rounded or broadly wedge-shaped, with small tubercles or excrescences near the entire margin; petiole, red, about ½″ long, with a pair of conspicuous glands near the blade.

Flowers.—Perfect and unisexual, borne in terminal and axillary spikes; calyx, top-shaped, 10-ridged, with 5 lobes at the summit; petals, 5, whitish, nearly circular; stamens, 10, in 2 rows of 5; pistil, with a 1-celled ovary, short style, and 2-lobed stigma.

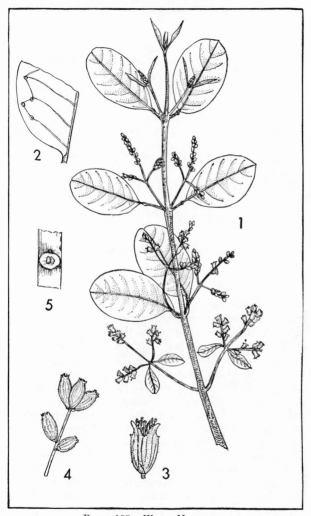

PLATE 155.—White-Mangrove
1. Foliage and flowers ×½. 2. Section of leaf surface ×1.
3. Flower ×3. 4. Fruit cluster ×¾. 5. Leaf scar ×2.

Fruit.—An obovoid, leathery, 10-ribbed, reddish-brown drupe, about ½″ long, crowned with the persistent calyx; seed, oblong to obovoid, dark red.

Twigs.—Slender, somewhat angular, dark reddish brown, often mottled, thickened at the nodes; buds, naked; leaf scars, nearly circular, with a central, sometimes divided bundle scar; pith, homogeneous.

Bark.—About 1″ thick, reddish brown, ridged and scaly.

Habitat.—Foreshores of tidal bays, swales, and lagoons.

Distribution.—Lower peninsular Florida south over the Keys to the West Indies, tropical Mexico, South and Central America, and the west coast of Africa.

THE MYRTLE FAMILY

Myrtaceae

The Myrtle Family embraces a group of about 70 genera and more than 2,800 species of aromatic trees and shrubs. Here are grouped the famous eucalypts of Australia; also traceable to this family are such well-known condiments as cloves, allspice, and guavas. Leaf oils from the eucalypts and other related trees are used extensively for industrial and medicinal purposes, as well as in the production of expensive perfumes. Several genera are productive of excellent timbers, which enjoy a wide diversity of uses.

Four genera, 3 with arborescent forms, are natives of the subtropical South. Guava (*Psidium guajava* Raddi), a native of Central America, has become naturalized in the lower Florida peninsular and adjacent Keys, as has the bottlebrush (*Melaleuca leucadendron* L.), originally from Australia.

Synopsis of Southern Arborescent Genera

Genus	*Leaves*	*Flowers*	*Fruit*
Eugenia	persistent	borne in racemes or fascicles; with petals	red or black, with a minute crown
Anamomis	persistent	born in cymes, the terminal flower sessile; with petals	red or brownish red, with a conspicuous crown
Calyptranthes	persistent	borne in cymes; without petals	reddish brown, with a conspicuous crown

THE EUGENIAS[1]

Eugenia L.

A group of about 600 species of aromatic evergreen trees and shrubs widely distributed through the warmer areas of the Americas, Asia, Africa, and Australia. Five[2] species attaining the size of small trees are listed for lower Florida and the Keys.

KEY TO THE EUGENIAS

1. Flowers, in racemes.............................. 2
1. Flowers, in fascicles or solitary.................... 4

   2. Fruit, ovoid to ellipsoidal, longer than broad, black; leaves, oblong to obovate................
                               Boxleaf eugenia (p. 544)
   2. Fruit, nearly globular, depressed at the summit, broader than long, red or black; leaves, oval to elliptical....................................... 3

[1] Formerly designated as the stoppers.
[2] The other shrubby species formerly included with this genus are now listed under *Mosiera* Small.

3. Petals, wider than long; fruit, black, about ½″ in diameter.............**White-stopper eugenia** (p. 542)

3. Petals, longer than wide; fruit, red or black, about ¼″ in diameter.................**Smalls eugenia** (p. 544)

    4. Petals, about as long as the sepals; fruit, orange, tinged with black or red, depressed at the summit, about ½″ in diameter..**Spiceberry eugenia** (p. 544)

    4. Petals, about twice as long as the sepals; fruit, scarlet, globular, about ¼″ in diameter..........
                   Redberry eugenia (p. 544)

White-Stopper Eugenia   White Stopper

Eugenia axillaris (Sw.) Willd.

Habit.—A small tree, sometimes 20′ to 30′ in height and 8″ to 12″ in diameter; often shrubby, particularly toward the northern limits of its range.

Leaves.—Opposite, simple, persistent, leathery, mostly oval, ovate, or elliptical, 1″ to 3″ long, ½″ to 1″ wide; apex, acute; base, rounded; margin, entire; dark green above, paler below and furnished with a multitude of minute black dots; petioles, stout, sometimes winged, about ¼″ long.

Flowers.—Perfect, minute, in short, axillary racemes; calyx, bell-shaped, 4-lobed, the lobes glandular; petals, 4, white, glandular; stamens, many, in several ranks; pistil, with a 2-celled ovary, slender style, and headlike stigma.

Fruit.—Berrylike, sweet and juicy, usually 1-seeded, black, glandular, about ½″ in diameter.

Twigs.—Slender or stout, iron-gray to reddish gray, often covered with small, warty excrescences; buds, minute, with 1 or 2 outer scales; leaf scars, nearly circular, with a single C-shaped to oval bundle scar; pith, homogeneous.

Bark.—Very thin, on the largest stems divided into light-brown, scaly ridges.

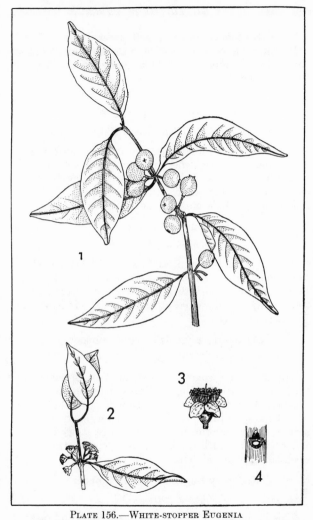

PLATE 156.—WHITE-STOPPER EUGENIA
1. Foliage and fruit ×½. 2. Cluster of flowers ×1. 3. Single
flower ×3. 4. Leaf scar ×1½.

Habitat.—Sandy soils near salt water.

Distribution.—Northward over the Keys to the St. Johns River, Florida; also on many of the West Indian islands.

Importance.—None.

Boxleaf Eugenia   Spanish Stopper

Eugenia buxifolia (Sw.) Willd.

This is a West Indian tree that extends northward to southern Florida, where it seldom becomes more than a large shrub.   It is characterized by very small, nearly sessile, obovate leaves and small, black, ellipsoidal fruits.   It is most abundant on cutover land.

Smalls Eugenia

Eugenia anthera Small

This is a small tree or large shrub found in hammocks along the coast of southern peninsular Florida. It may be distinguished by its very small leaves, $\frac{1}{2}''$ to $2''$ long, and dark-red or black fruits.   It is of no commercial value.

Spiceberry Eugenia   Red Stopper

Eugenia rhombea (Berg.) Urb.

The spiceberry eugenia is a small West Indian tree that occurs in the United States only in extreme southern Florida on Keys near Key West.   The flowers, often $\frac{1}{2}''$ in diameter, are borne in few-flowered, axillary fascicles; the fruits are orange, tinged with red or black, nearly globular, but depressed at the apex, and about $\frac{1}{2}''$ long.

Redberry Eugenia   Red Stopper

Eugenia confusa DC.

This is the largest of the native eugenias and often becomes a tree $60'$ in height and $1\frac{1}{2}'$ in diameter.

Like those of the former species, the flowers are borne in axillary clusters but are much smaller, about $\frac{1}{8}''$ in diameter; the fruits are scarlet and about $\frac{1}{8}''$ in diameter. This tree extends southward from Biscayne Bay over the Keys to many of the West Indies.

THE NAKEDWOODS

Anamomis Griseb.

These are a small group of West Indian and Floridian trees and shrubs including about eight species.

KEY TO THE FLORIDIAN SPECIES

1. Leaves, mostly oblong; cymes, several-flowered, the flowers with 60 to 70 stamens; fruit, red.............
   Simpson nakedwood (p. 545)
1. Leaves, mostly oval to obovate; cymes, 3-flowered, the flowers with 30 to 40 stamens; fruit, black...........
   Twinberry nakedwood (p. 547)

Simpson Nakedwood

Anamomis simpsonii Small

Habit.—A medium-sized tree, occasionally 50' or more in height and 1' in diameter, with a narrowly rounded crown of ascending branches.

Leaves.—Opposite, simple, persistent, leathery, oblong to elliptical, 1'' to 2'' long, $\frac{1}{2}''$ to 1'' wide; apex, rounded, with a shallow, apical notch or abruptly short-pointed; base, wedge-shaped; margin, entire, thickened, slightly curled backward; dark yellow-green and lustrous above, paler and duller below; petioles, slender, about $\frac{1}{4}''$ long.

Flowers.—Perfect, in 3- to 15-flowered, axillary cymes, fragrant, about $\frac{1}{2}''$ in diameter; calyx, urn-shaped, covered with white, silken hairs, 4-lobed, 1 pair more or less kidney-shaped, the other more nearly ovate; petals, 4, white, paired, nearly circular,

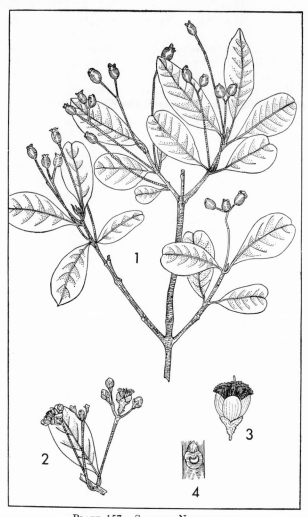

PLATE 157.—SIMPSON NAKEDWOOD
1. Foliage and fruit ×½. 2. Cluster of flowers ×½.
3. Flower ×1. 4. Leaf scar ×2.

with hairy, ragged margins; stamens, 60 to 70, in several ranks; pistil, ovoid, crowned with a spikelike style.

Fruit.—An ellipsoidal, usually 1-seeded, red berry, about ¼″ long, crowned with the remnant of a persistent calyx; seed, kidney-shaped.

Twigs.—Slender, at first clothed with milky-white, silken hairs, at length smooth and reddish brown; buds, naked, minute; leaf scars, circular or nearly so, with a single bundle scar; pith, homogeneous.

Bark.—Thin, smooth, reddish brown, often mottled.

Habitat.—Hammocks.

Distribution.—Lower east coast of Florida and the Everglade Keys.

Importance.—Of no commercial value. Distillations from the leaves contain an oil having the aroma of nutmegs.

Twinberry Nakedwood

Anamomis dicrana (Berg.) Britt.

The twinberry nakedwood is a much smaller tree than the preceding species, being seldom more than 25′ in height or 8″ in diameter. It is readily distinguished by its 3-flowered cymes and small, black, aromatic berries. It occurs from the lower middle Florida peninsula south over the Keys to Key West and the West Indies.

THE LIDFLOWERS

Calyptranthes Sw.

This is a small tropical American group of trees and shrubs comprising eight species characterized by an unusual floral structure, a deciduous, lidlike limb that caps the calyx before the flower opens. Two species, both small trees, inhabit lower Florida.

KEY TO THE FLORIDIAN SPECIES

1. Leaves, oblong to ovate, with petioles; flowers, sessile.
Pale lidflower (p. 548)
1. Leaves, elliptical, sessile or nearly so; flowers, stalked..
Myrtle-of-the-river lidflower (p. 550)

Pale Lidflower

Calyptranthes pallens Griseb.

Habit.—A shrub or small tree in Florida seldom more than 25′ in height and 4″ to 6″ in diameter, but attaining much larger proportions elsewhere.

Leaves.—Opposite, simple, persistent, leathery, ovate to oblong, 2″ to 3″ long, about ¾″ wide; apex, long-tapered; base, rounded or broadly wedge-shaped; margin, entire, curled backward; dark green, lustrous, with pale glands above, pale below but dotted with darker glands; petiole, stout, about ½″ long.

Flowers.—Perfect, borne in axillary cymes of about 3″ in length; calyx, closed in the bud by a nearly circular, lidlike, often deciduous limb; petals, wanting; stamens, many, in several ranks; pistil, with a 2- or 3-celled ovary, crowned with a spikelike style.

Fruit.—An oblong to nearly globular, reddish-brown berry, about ¼″ in diameter; with a hairy skin and thin layer of rather dry pulp; seeds, oblong.

Twigs.—Slender, woolly, angular between the nodes, later becoming rounded, reddish brown, and scaly; buds, naked; leaf scars, half-round, with a single bundle scar; pith, homogeneous.

Bark.—Very thin, grayish white, smooth or separating irregularly into large, platelike scales.

Habitat.—Hammocks and coastal soils of coral origin.

Distribution.—Southern peninsular Florida and the Keys, the West Indies, and southern Mexico.

Importance.—None.

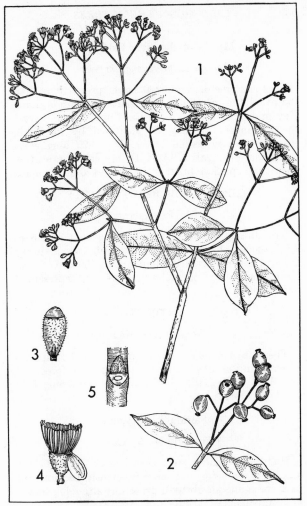

PLATE 158.—PALE LIDFLOWER

1. Foliage and flowers ×½. 2. Fruit cluster ×¾. 3. Closed
flower ×2. 4. Open flower (note lid) ×2. 5. Leaf scar ×2.

Myrtle-of-the-river Lidflower

Calyptranthes zuzygium Sw.

This is a tree of somewhat larger proportions than the pale lidflower occurring in southern Florida, Long Key and Paradise Key, Haiti, Cuba, Jamaica, and the Bahamas. It may be identified by its small, elliptical, nearly sessile leaves, 1″ to 2″ long, with wavy margins; calyx lids with nipplelike protuberances; and small globular fruits depressed at the apex.

THE MEADOW BEAUTY FAMILY

Melastomaceae

This family numbers about 165 genera and over 2,500 species of trees, shrubs, and herbs, the majority tropical and particularly abundant in South America. Two genera, 1 of them herbaceous, are represented in the South.

THE TETRAZYGIAS

Tetrazygia A. Rich.

These are a small genus comprising about 15 species of trees and shrubs, scattered through the forests of the West Indies, with a single form extending into southern Florida.

Florida Tetrazygia

Tetrazygia bicolor Cogn.

Habit.—A slender tree, occasionally 30′ in height and 6″ in diameter, but more frequently encountered as a spreading shrub with gracefully drooping leaves and branchlets.

Leaves.—Opposite, simple, persistent, with a characteristic ladderlike pattern between the midrib and

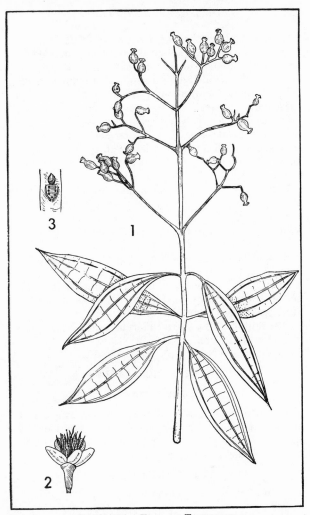

PLATE 159.—FLORIDA TETRAZYGIA

1. Foliage and fruit ×½. 2. Flower ×1½. 3. Leaf scar ×2.

2 large, submarginal veins, lanceolate, 3″ to 5″ long, 1″ to 2″ broad; apex, long-tapered; base, rounded or occasionally wedge-shaped; margin, entire, thickened, and rolled backward; dark green, smooth above, paler below; petiole, stout, about 1″ long.

Flowers.—Perfect, borne in large, many-flowered, terminal panicles; calyx, pitcher-shaped, attached to the ovary; petals, 4 or 5, white, attached to the ovary; stamens, 8 or 10; pistil, consisting of a 3-celled ovary and a 10-toothed sheath about the base of the slender style.

Fruit.—An ovoid, 3-celled, purplish-black berry, about ⅓″ long; crowned by the persistent calyx tube.

Twigs.—Slender, gray-brown, lenticellate; buds, minute, globular; leaf scars, shield-shaped, with 5 to 7 bundle scars; pith, homogeneous.

Bark.—Thin, gray-brown, smooth, or shallowly fissured on the largest stems.

Habitat.—Pinewoods and mixed broadleaved stands; in the former usually shrubby, attaining best development on the Everglade Keys.

Distribution.—Southern Florida, the Keys, the Bahamas, and Cuba.

Importance.—None.

THE GINSENG FAMILY

Araliaceae

This is a large family of trees, shrubs, vines, and herbs, comprising about 50 genera and more than 500 species. Three genera are represented in the South, 1 of which includes a small, spiny tree.

THE SPIKENARDS

Aralia L.

This is a small group of aromatic herbs, shrubs, and small trees numbering about 20 species. Four species inhabit our southern area, and one, the Devils-walking-stick, becomes arborescent in some localities.

Devils-walkingstick

Aralia spinosa L.

Habit.—A small, vigorous tree, commonly 25' to 35' in height and 6" to 10" in diameter, with a grotesque, flat-topped crown of spreading branches; in the juvenile stage, commonly reproducing from stolons.

Leaves.—Alternate, deciduous, odd–bipinnately compound, crowded at the tips of the stout twigs, 3' to 4' long, 2' to 3' wide; pinnae, with a long-stalked, terminal leaflet and 5 or 6 pairs of laterals; leaflets, mostly ovate, 2" to 4" long, about 1½" wide, with acute to long-tapered apices, rounded or wedge-shaped bases, and finely toothed margins; dark green, smooth above, paler below, smooth or with scattered hairs and occasionally a few stout prickles along the midrib; the leaf, supported by a stout, spiny rachis, 18" to 20" long, greatly enlarged at the base and clasping the twig.

Flowers.—Perfect or unisexual by abortion, borne on light-yellowish stalks in umbels, which are arranged so as to form large, terminal, compound panicles; calyx, attached to the ovary, 5-lobed at the summit; petals, 5, white, ovate; stamens, 5, about as long as and alternating with the petals; pistil, with a 5-celled ovary crowned by 5 styles, each with a small, headlike stigma, abortive in the staminate flowers.

Fruit.—A black, remotely 5-angled, 5-celled, berry-like drupe, about ⅜" in diameter, crowned with remnants of the blackened styles; seeds, oblong-flattened, embedded in the juicy, purplish pulp.

Twigs.—Very stout, often ½" to 1" in diameter, with pale-orange lenticels, armed with stout, irregu-

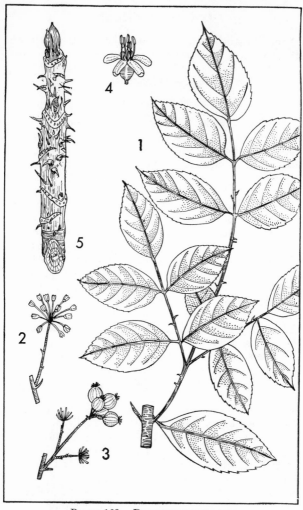

PLATE 160.—Devils-walkingstick

1. Portion of leaf ×¼. 2. Portion of flower cluster ×½.
3. Portion of fruit cluster ×½. 4. Flower ×2. 5. Twig ×⅔.

larly scattered prickles, which often form a crownlike row about the leaf scar; terminal buds, conical, with several outer, overlapping scales, $\frac{1}{2}''$ to $\frac{3}{4}''$ long; lateral buds, smaller, appressed, more or less triangular; leaf scars, U-shaped, nearly encircling the twig, with a single row of 7 to 15 bundle scars; pith, large, pale, homogeneous.

Bark.—Thin, brown, divided by shallow, irregular fissures into broad, flattened, anastomosing ridges; inner bark, bright yellow.

Habitat.—Moist soils of rich bottoms and gentle slopes; usually an understory species.

Distribution.—Southern New York west through southern Indiana to southeastern Iowa; south to Florida, thence west to eastern Texas.

Importance.—Used sparingly as an ornamental. Root, bark, and fruit contain compounds suitable for pharmaceutical preparations.

THE TUPELO FAMILY

Nyssaceae

The Tupelo Family includes only 3 genera and 10 species of trees and shrubs widely distributed in the southeastern United States, the Malayan Archipelago, Mongolia, and the Himalayas. According to some authorities the members of this group comprise a part of the Cornaceae and are so classified. Six species of the genus *Nyssa* are indigenous to the South.

THE TUPELOS AND BLACKGUMS

Nyssa L.

This group numbers eight species, six of which occur in our eastern and southern forests. The two remaining species are natives of the Indo-Malayan region and western China, respectively. All are characterized by small, inconspicuous flowers (poly-gamodioecious), drupelike fruits with ribbed seeds, and alternate, simple, dark-green leaves. All six American species occur in our southern forests, and four of them reach arborescent proportions.

KEY TO THE SOUTHERN TUPELOS

1. Pistillate flowers, in cluster of 2 to several; fruit, blue.. 2
1. Pistillate flowers, solitary; fruit, red or purple........ 3

    2. Flowers, appearing with the leaves; stone, with numerous poorly developed ribs.................
                              Black tupelo (p. 556)
    2. Flowers, appearing after the leaves; stone, conspicuously ribbed ....**Swamp tupelo** (p. 558)

3. Fruit, purple; stone, ridged ......**Water tupelo** (p. 559)
3. Fruit, red; stone, winged.....**Ogeechee tupelo** (p. 561)

Black Tupelo   Blackgum

Nyssa sylvatica Marsh.

Habit.—A moderately large tree, sometimes becoming 100′ or more in height and 3′ to 4′ in diameter; characterized by an unbuttressed, somewhat tapered bole, narrow, oblong crown, and spreading root system, which commonly produces vigorous sprouts.

Leaves.—Alternate, deciduous, simple, 2″ to 5″ long, 1″ to 3″ broad, mostly obovate and oval; apex, acute; base, rounded or wedge-shaped; margin, entire or sometimes with a few, coarse, scattered teeth; dark green and lustrous above, paler and with silky hairs on the lower surface; petiole, about 1″ long, terete or remotely winged, often red.

Flowers.—Regular, perfect and imperfect, axillary, appearing before the leaves have fully developed; staminate flowers, borne in many-flowered heads, supported on long, often pendulous, hairy stalks,

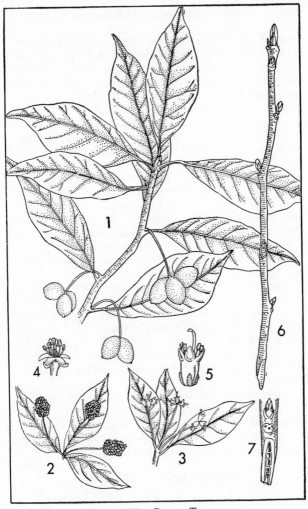

PLATE 161.—BLACK TUPELO

1. Foliage and fruit ×½.　2. Cluster of male flowers ×¾.
3. Cluster of female flowers ×¾.　4. Male flower ×3.　5. Female
flower ×3.　6. Twig ×¾.　7. Leaf scar ×1½.

and with a minute, disclike calyx, 5 thick, greenish-white, early-deciduous petals, and 5 to 12 exserted stamens; pistillate flowers, borne in clusters of 2 to several, with calyx and petals similar to those of the staminate flowers; stamens, 5 to 10, shorter than the petals, fertile or sterile; pistil, with a 1- to 2-celled ovary, tubular style, and exserted, reflexed stigma.

Fruit.—Drupelike, ovoid, dark blue, about ½″ long; flesh, thin and rather bitter; pit, indistinctly 10- to 12-ribbed.

Twigs.—Moderately stout, reddish brown, with numerous pale lenticels; terminal buds, present, ovoid, about ¼″ long, covered by several overlapping, reddish-brown scales; lateral buds, smaller, often conspicuously divergent; leaf scars, half-round, with 3 bundle scars; pith, white, diaphragmed.

Bark.—Gray to light brown, blocky and often having the appearance of alligator leather.

Habitat.—Variable, found on moist, rich soil near swamps, in mixed, upland hardwood forests and on lower mountain slopes; never in deep swamps or on lands subject to periodic inundation.

Distribution.—Southern Maine to southeastern Wisconsin near Lake Michigan; south to central and western Florida in the East and to eastern Texas in the West.

Importance.—For many years regarded as a weed tree; now in common use in the manufacture of plywood and commercial veneers, boxboards, crossties, paper pulp, cooperage, woodenware, handles, laundry appliances, and planing-mill products.

Swamp Tupelo　　　Blackgum

Nyssa sylvatica var. *biflora* (Walt.) Sarg.

This tree, common to wet situations and swamps of the southern coastal plains, so closely resembles the black tupelo that its presence in many localities has been overlooked. It is readily distinguished from that species, however, on several counts. The leaves are narrower and oblanceolate. The flowers appear after the leaves are about fully developed, and the pistillate are usually borne in pairs. The fruit pits are featured by prominent, longitudinal ridges or ribs, which alone suffice to distinguish this species from the black tupelo. The wood is used for the same purpose as that of the previous species, and the timbers of these two are commonly mixed indiscriminately in the trade.

Water Tupelo   Tupelogum

Nyssa aquatica L.

Habit.—A tree, often 100′ or more in height and 3′ to 4′ in diameter above a strongly buttressed base; with tapering bole and narrow, oblong head composed of small spreading branches.

Leaves.—Alternate, deciduous, simple, oblong-obovate, 5″ to 10″ long, 2″ to 4″ wide; apex, acute or tapering; base, wedge-shaped or occasionally rounded; margin, entire or sometimes scalloped-toothed; dark lustrous green above, paler and somewhat pubescent below; petiole, stout, grooved, hairy, swollen at the base, about 2″ long.

Flowers.—Regular, perfect and imperfect, axillary, appearing before or with the leaves; staminate flowers, in dense heads borne on long, slender, hair stalks; pistillate flowers, solitary, borne on short stalks; individual flowers, similar in structure and form to those of the black tupelo except for the calyx, which is cuplike.

Fruit.—Drupelike, oblong, purple, with a thick skin and thin, bitter flesh, about 1″ in length, borne on slender stalks 3″ to 4″ in length; maturing in

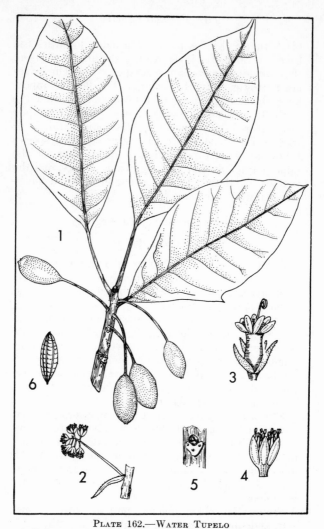

PLATE 162.—WATER TUPELO

1. Foliage and fruit ×½. 2. Cluster of male flowers ×¾.
3. Female flower ×3. 4. Male flower ×3. 5. Leaf scar ×2.
6. Pit ×1.

September and October; stone, light brown, with many conspicuous, acute, winglike ridges.

Twigs.—Stout, red or red-brown, with small, scattered lenticels; terminal buds, small, globose, yellowish; lateral buds, similar but much smaller; leaf scars, rounded to heart-shaped, with 3 conspicuous bundle scars; pith, diaphragmed.

Bark.—Thin, gray-brown or brown, with many longitudinal, scaly ridges.

Habitat.—In deep swamps and often in standing water, usually mixed with cypress; less commonly found on deep, moist soil with elms, sycamore, red maple, and green ash.

Distribution.—Along the Atlantic coast from southern Virginia to central Florida and west through the Gulf states to Texas, north through Arkansas, western Tennessee, and Kentucky to southern Illinois.

Importance.—The wood of water tupelo is used for the same purposes as that of the black tupelo. The rootwood is occasionally employed as a substitute for cork.

Ogeechee Tupelo   Sour Tupelo
Nyssa ogeche Marsh.

This is a small tree or merely a large shrub of rare occurrence along the margins of lakes and ponds and on inundated riverbanks from southeastern South Carolina through coastal Georgia to the lower valley of the Apalachicola River in western Florida. It may be distinguished by its hairy twigs, oblong-obovate leaves, short-stalked fruits, $\frac{1}{2}''$ or more in length, and fruit pits with numerous papery, winglike ridges. The wood is of little or no value, but the fruits have been used locally to make Ogeechee lime preserve.

Michaux's (51) statement, recorded in 1819, concerning the habit and sex of this tree is exceedingly interesting and is repeated here. "As a peculiarity witnessed in no other tree of North America, the male and female trees are easily distinguished by their general appearance when the leaves are fallen. The branches of the male are more compressed about the trunk, and rise in a direction more nearly perpendicular; those of the female diffuse themselves horizontally and form a larger and rounded summit."

THE DOGWOOD FAMILY

Cornaceae

The Dogwood Family comprises a group of about 100 species of trees, shrubs, and herbs included in about 10 genera. Geographically, the family is widespread, but the majority of the species are restricted to the Northern Hemisphere. Only representatives of *Cornus* and *Garrya* are found in the United States. Not one of the 22 American species included in these two groups is of any major importance as a timber producer, although several are used widely as ornamentals.

THE DOGWOODS

Cornus Tourn.

Most of the 50 odd members of this genus are shrubs or small trees, although a few are herbs. Eighteen species are native to this country, and several of them are important ornamentals. The common flowering dogwood (*C. florida*) is widely scattered throughout the eastern United States and is well known as one of our most attractive early-flowering trees. In the southern United States, 2 other small trees, the pagoda dogwood (*C. alternifolia*) and the roughleafed dogwood (*C. asperifolia*), are occasionally encountered.

KEY TO THE SOUTHERN ARBORESCENT DOGWOODS

1. Leaves, alternate; fruit, blue-black.................
                 Alternate-leaf dogwood (p. 563)
1. Leaves, opposite; fruit, red or white................ 2

  2. Flowers, in heads, surrounded by conspicuous bracts; fruit, red......**Flowering dogwood** (p. 565)
  2. Flowers, in cymes, without bracts; fruit, white....
                 Roughleaf dogwood (p. 568)

Alternate-Leaf Dogwood

Cornus alternifolia L.

Habit.—A small tree, up to 30′ in height with a short trunk 6″ to 8″ in diameter, or a dense shrub with numerous stout stems; when treelike, branching close to the ground into several, stout, spreading branches with slender twigs, forming a broad, flat-topped crown.

Leaves.—Alternate (rarely subopposite or opposite), deciduous, simple, 3″ to 5″ long, 2½″ to 3½″ wide, oval or ovate; apex, tapered; base, wedge-shaped or rounded; margin, entire; at maturity yellowish green, more or less glabrous above, pale and pubescent below, with a somewhat orange-colored midrib; primary veins, curved upward and more or less paralleling the margin; petioles, slender, grooved, pubescent, about 2″ long, with a swollen base.

Flowers.—Perfect, appearing after the leaves in flat-topped, many-flowered cymes on slender, jointed stalks; individual flowers, ¼″ long, consisting of an oblong, pubescent calyx, 4 white, oblong petals, 4 stamens, and a small ovary with a stout style.

Fruit.—A deep-blue or blue-black, subglobose drupe, about ⅓″ in diameter; borne in loose cymes on

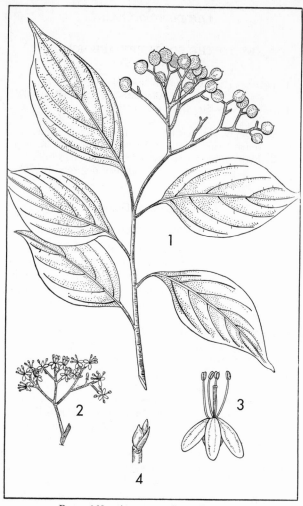

PLATE 163.—ALTERNATE-LEAF DOGWOOD
1. Foliage and fruit ×½. 2. Cluster of flowers ×½.
3. Flower ×3. 4. Leaf scar ×1.

red stalks, maturing in the fall; pit, obovoid, 1- to 2-seeded, with many longitudinal, compound grooves; seeds, lunate, about ¼″ long. A form with yellow fruits (var. *ochrocarpa* Rehd.) is used ornamentally.

Twigs.—Slender, glabrous, green or greenish brown, with numerous small, pale, scattered lenticels; acrid when broken; terminal buds, present, about ⅓″ long, with 2 or sometimes 3 visible, green, brown or purplish scales, about ¼″ long; lateral buds, smaller, oval, acute, often nearly covered by the persistent petiole bases; leaf scars, half-moon-shaped, with 3 bundle scars, during the 1st season raised on the petiole bases; pith, homogeneous.

Bark.—Thin, dark, reddish brown, at first smooth, then becoming longitudinally furrowed and forming narrow, somewhat scaly ridges on old stems.

Habitat.—Rich, moist soil along the margins of forests or near streams, mixed with other hardwoods and often in their shade, occasionally found in the open.

Distribution.—From Nova Scotia west to Minnesota, south through Iowa, Missouri, and the Appalachians to northern Alabama and Georgia.

Importance.—Occasionally propagated as an ornamental because of its showy flowers and brilliant autumnal foliage.

Flowering Dogwood

Cornus florida L.

Habit.—A small, bushy tree, 15′ to rarely 40′ in height, with a short trunk 6″ to 18″ in diameter, the several large, wide-spreading branches forming a low, dense, rounded head.

Leaves.—Opposite, simple, deciduous, 3″ to 6″ long, 1½″ to 2″ wide; usually oval, acute or slender; apex, pointed; base, wedge-shaped, often unequal;

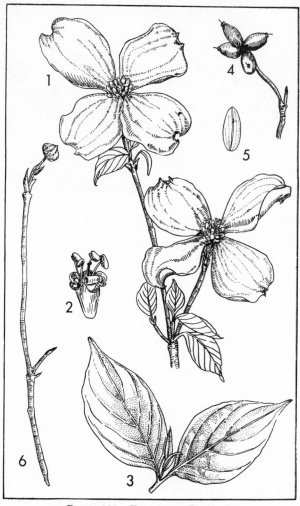

PLATE 164.—FLOWERING DOGWOOD

1. Flowers with attending bracts ×½. 2. Flower ×3.
3. Foliage ×½. 4. Fruit cluster ×¾. 5. Pit ×1½. 6. Twig ×¾.

margin, entire or remotely scalloped; primary veins, curved upward; light green and somewhat hairy above, whitish-pubescent below; upper surface, becoming scarlet in the fall; petioles, stout, grooved up to ¾″ long.

Flowers.—Perfect, appearing with the leaves in dense heads, which are surrounded by 4 large, white, or rarely reddish-white, notched, obovate, petallike bracts; mature inflorescence, 2″ to 4″ in diameter; individual flowers, ⅛″ in diameter; calyx, somewhat urn-shaped, remotely 4-angled, and 4-lobed, adhering to the ovary; petals, 4, strap-shaped, arising with the stamens from the top of the ovary; stamens, 4; pistil composed of a 2-celled ovary, slender style, and expanded stigma.

Fruit.—A bright-red, ovoid drupe, about ½″ long and ¼″ in diameter; borne in clusters of 2 to several, with the persistent calyx and style evident, ripening in the fall; pit, ovate, 2-celled, somewhat grooved; seeds, oblong.

Twigs.—Slender, at first red or yellowish green to purple and somewhat pubescent, becoming glabrous and brown or gray-brown; terminal leaf buds, acute, with 2 scales, about ¼″ long; terminal flower buds, nearly globular, each with 4 scales; lateral buds, very small, often enclosed by the persistent petiole bases; leaf scars, V-shaped, nearly encircling the twig, with 3 bundle scars; pith, homogeneous.

Bark.—Up to ⅜″ thick, dark brown or nearly black, soon breaking into many squarrose, polygonal, scaly blocks.

Habitat.—On moist, rich, deep soils near streams and on slopes, usually growing in the shade of other hardwoods; also found on open slopes and ridges.

Distribution.—From southern Maine west through Massachusetts and New York to southeastern

Kansas, south to central Florida and to eastern Texas, and occasionally found in northern Mexico.

Importance.—Of restricted value as a source of wood for small articles such as spindles, shuttles, hubs, and handles; of great importance as an ornamental, both the white- and the red-flowering varieties being widely planted. In colonial times a brew made from the bark was used in the treatment of fever.

Roughleaf Dogwood

Cornus drummondii C. A. Meyer

Roughleaf dogwood is much like *C. alternifolia* in habit, although, when arborescent, it may reach the height of 50′. The leaves of the two species are quite similar, but those of *C. drummondii* are always opposite. The flowers of this species are white and are borne in more open clusters than are those of *C. alternifolia*. Roughleaf dogwood occurs in a wider range than pagoda dogwood and is found from Ontario southward in a fanwise fashion, reaching Florida in the East and Texas in the Southwest. It also occurs in Nebraska, South Dakota, Oklahoma, and Arkansas. It is of no commercial importance but is used occasionally in decorative plantings.

THE HEATH FAMILY

Ericaceae

The Heath Family numbers about 70 genera and over 1,500 species of shrubs and trees widely distributed through the cooler regions of the world. Several members of this group, notably the azaleas, rhododendrons, and laurels, are prized decorative plants. Here are also included the blueberries, cranberries, and huckleberries. Tobacco pipes are made largely from the roots of briar (*Erica arborea* L.), a small European tree.

This family is represented in the South by 22 genera, 6 of which include arborescent forms.

Synopsis of Arborescent Genera

Genus	Leaves	Flowers	Fruit
Elliottia	deciduous	in panicles; corolla of 4 petals; stamens, 8	a 4-celled, globular capsule
Rhododendron	evergreen	in corymbs; corolla, 5-lobed; stamens, 8 to 12	a 5-celled, ovoid capsule
Oxydendrum	deciduous	in racemes; corolla, 5-lobed; stamens, 10	a 5-celled, pyramidal capsule
Kalmia	evergreen	in corymbs; corolla, 5-lobed; stamens, 10	a 5-celled, globular capsule
Lyonia	evergreen	in axillary fascicles; corolla, 5-lobed; stamens, 8 to 10	a 5-celled, oblong capsule
Vaccinium	deciduous or evergreen	in racemes; corolla, 5-lobed; stamens, 8 to 10	a berry

Elliottia

Elliottia racemosa Ell.

A Monotype[1]

Habit.—A large shrub or small tree, seldom more than 20′ in height or 6″ in diameter; usually self-propagating by root stocks.

[1] One of North America's rarest trees.

PLATE 165.—ELLIOTTIA

1. Foliage and flowers $\times\frac{1}{2}$.   2. Flower $\times\frac{3}{4}$.   3. Fruit cluster
$\times\frac{2}{3}$.   4. Leaf scar $\times1\frac{1}{2}$.

Leaves.—Alternate, simple, deciduous, oblong to ovate, 3″ to 4″ long, 1″ to 2″ wide; apex, acute; base, acute; margin, entire; dark green and smooth above, pale green and hairy below; petioles, slender, flattened, about ½″ long.

Flowers.—Perfect, borne in erect, terminal panicles; calyx, 4-lobed, reddish brown; petals, 4, straplike, white; stamens, 8; pistil, 4- (rarely 3- or 5-) celled.

Fruit.—A 4- (rarely 3- or 5-) celled, globular capsule, about ⅜″ in diameter.

Twigs.—Slender, brown or grayish brown, sometimes rather 3-sided; terminal buds, conical, about ⅛″ long, with 3 exposed, chestnut-brown scales; lateral buds, similar but smaller, usually divergent; leaf scars, shield-shaped, with a single bundle scar; pith, white, homogeneous.

Bark.—Thin, comparatively smooth, brown or grayish brown.

Habitat.—Occurring in a few isolated areas on oak ridges, sandy hills, and river valleys.

Distribution.—Southern South Carolina near the coast and eastern Georgia (Bullock, Burke, and Richmond Counties).

Importance.—Of particular interest to botanists because of its limited distribution, scarcity, and mode of propagation.

Remarks.—The fruits of this species are exceedingly rare and have been reported as unknown or not observed by many investigators. Cross-fertilization is necessary for the successful formation of the fruit of this species. However, the comparative scarcity of trees, together with the great distance between most of them, is such that this vital process is seldom accomplished.

THE RHODODENDRONS

Rhododendron L.

This is a large group of trees and shrubs numbering about 600 species, the majority Asiatic. Because of their very showy flowers and foliage, many of them are widely used ornamentals and their horticultural varieties are legion.

About 25 species are indigenous to the United States, one of which is a small southern tree.

Rosebay Rhododendron

Rhododendron maximum L.

Habit.—An evergreen, bushy tree, rarely more than 30′ in height or 10″ in diameter; characterized by a short bole, which is often contorted or prostrate, and a rounded crown with stout, twisted branches; in some localities, never more than a shrub.

Leaves.—Alternate, simple, persistent, firm and leathery, commonly clustered toward the tips of branches, mostly oval to ovate or obovate, 4″ to 12″ long, 2″ to 3″ wide; apex, acute or abruptly pointed; base, rounded or wedge-shaped; margin, entire, somewhat curled backward; dark green, lustrous above, paler, commonly with a whitish bloom below; petioles, stout, with a prominent ridge above, about 1½″ long.

Flowers.—Perfect, borne in 16- to 24-flowered, terminal, corymblike clusters, 4″ to 6″ in diameter; calyx, 5-lobed; corolla, white, pink, or rarely purplish, 5-lobed, the upper lobe marked with a cluster of greenish, yellowish, or orange-colored dots on the inner face, glandular at the base of the sinuses; stamens, 8 to 12, of two lengths; pistil, with a 5-celled ovary, long curving style, and headlike stigma.

PLATE 166.—ROSEBAY RHODODENDRON
1. Foliage and flowers ×⅓.   2. Fruit and flower bud ×½.
3. Leaf scar ×1½.

Fruit.—A dark-reddish-brown, 5-celled, ovoid capsule, about ½″ long and crowned with the remnants of the style; often persistent until the following season; seeds, flattened, oblong, winged at the ends.

Twigs.—Stout, dark green, smooth, turning reddish brown their 2d season; buds, of 2 sorts; (1) flower buds, terminal, conical, about 1½″ long; (2) leaf buds, of 2 sizes; the terminal buds, conical, about 1″ long, dark green, with many overlapping scales; lateral buds, much smaller; leaf scars, more or less heart-shaped, with 1 or 3 bundle scars; pith, homogeneous, brownish white.

Habitat.—In the North found in cool swamps; to the south commonly found on steep, rocky slopes and stream banks up to elevations of 4,500′; frequently forming extensive, nearly impenetrable thickets known locally as "rhododendron hells."

Distribution.—Nova Scotia to the northern shores of Lake Erie, south through Ohio, Pennsylvania, New York, and New England and along the Appalachian Mountains to northern Georgia.

Importance.—A tree of widespread ornamental use. The wood is used for tobacco pipes and tool handles and by the engraver as a substitute for boxwood.

THE LAURELS
Kalmia L.

These are a small group of shrubs and shrublike trees consisting of eight species and found in North America and the West Indies. A single arborescent form, the mountain-laurel, inhabits our southern mountains and adjacent areas.

Mountain-Laurel
Kalmia latifolia L.

Habit.—Commonly encountered as a shrub, but occasionally attaining arborescent proportions and

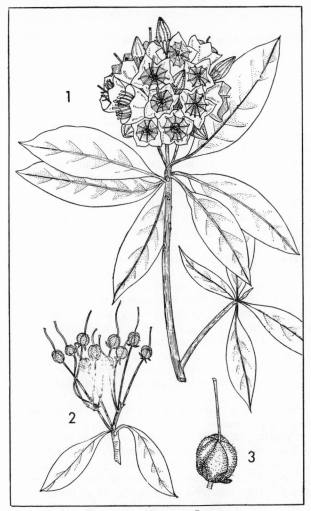

PLATE 167.—MOUNTAIN-LAUREL

1. Foliage and flowers ×½.   2. Cluster of fruits ×½.   3. Fruit
×2.

then a tree scarcely more than 30′ tall and 15″ in diameter; bole, usually short, the divergent branches forming a compact, rounded head.

Leaves.—Alternate (rarely opposite or in whorls of 3), leathery, simple, persistent, elliptical to lanceolate, 3″ to 4″ long, 1″ to 1½″ wide; apex, acute, sometimes ending in a sharp point; base, wedge-shaped; margin, entire; dull, dark green above, yellowish green below; petiole, stout, about ½″ long.

Flowers.—Perfect, borne in terminal and axillary corymbs; calyx, 5-lobed, the lobes thin, green; corolla, wheel-shaped or saucerlike, white, rose, or pink, 5-lobed at the summit, with 10 pouches in which the anthers are inserted prior to pollen release; stamens, 10; pistil, with a globular, 5-celled ovary and long, fiberlike style.

Fruit.—A 5-celled, globular capsule, crowned with the persistent style, about ¼″ in diameter; seeds, minute, oblong, terminally winged.

Twigs.—Slender, reddish green to reddish brown; buds, of 2 sorts; (1) flower buds, clustered at the tips of twigs, about 1″ long, covered by several glandular-hairy scales; (2) leaf buds, small, usually with 2 green outer scales; leaf scars, half-round to shield-shaped, with a single bundle scar; pith, homogeneous; the open capsules, often persistent on the twig through the winter.

Bark.—Thin, dark reddish brown, dividing into long, narrow scales.

Habitat.—In the North, found in swamps and bogs and on rich, wet bottom lands; farther south, ascending hillsides and mountain slopes, forming a dense understory in deciduous forests; in the southern Appalachians, occurring at elevations up to 4,000′.

Distribution.—New Brunswick to the northern shores of Lake Erie, south through New England, the Appalachian Mountains, the Piedmont plateau, and adjacent areas to western Florida and Louisiana; also reported from Indiana.

Importance.—Widely used as an ornamental. The leaves of this species contain appreciable amounts of andromedotoxin, a substance particularly poisonous to sheep, although cattle, horses, and goats are also susceptible. On the other hand, deer and other wild animals that have been known to browse on the foliage of this tree do not seem to be seriously affected.

Sourwood

Oxydendrum arboreum DC.

A Monotype

Habit.—A small to medium-sized tree, sometimes attaining a height of 60′ and a diameter of 20″, but usually much smaller; in dense forests usually producing a slender, columnar bole and short, oblong crown; in more open situations developing a short, often leaning trunk, which divides into several stout, ascending limbs, resulting in a broad crown of irregular contour.

Leaves.—Alternate, simple, deciduous, bitter to the taste, elliptical, 5″ to 7″ long, 1″ to 3″ wide; apex, acute to long-tapered; base, narrowly to broadly wedge-shaped; margin, finely toothed; bright yellow-green, lustrous above, paler, smooth below; petioles, slender, about 1″ long.

Flowers.—Perfect, borne in long, terminal or axillary, clustered racemes; calyx, divided nearly to the base into 5 lobes, persistent with the fruit; corolla, 5-lobed, cylindrical, white; stamens, 10; pistil, 5-celled, with a small, terminal stigma.

Fruit.—A 5-celled, pyramidal, many-seeded capsule, about ½″ long; seeds, minute, oblong.

Twigs.—Moderately stout, often zigzag, sometimes angled, green, orange-brown, or red, dotted with con-

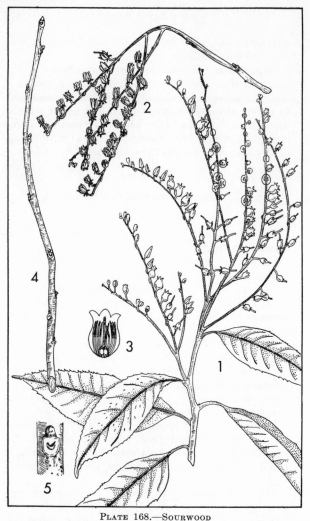

PLATE 168.—SOURWOOD

1. Foliage and flowers $\times\frac{1}{3}$.　2. Cluster of fruit $\times\frac{1}{3}$.　3. Longitudinal section through single flower $\times1\frac{1}{2}$.　4. Twig $\times\frac{2}{3}$.
5. Leaf scar $\times2$.

spicuous lenticels; terminal buds, wanting; lateral buds, nearly globular, scaly, about $\frac{1}{8}''$ in diameter; leaf scars, half-round to shield-shaped, with a single C-shaped bundle scar; pith, white, homogeneous.

Bark.—Silvery gray to gray-brown, furrowed, the ridges often interlacing and superficially scaly and those on the larger trunks usually divided transversely, resulting in a blocky aspect.

Habitat.—Usually occurring as an occasional tree in mixed hardwood stands on moist hillsides, ridges, and gentle mountain slopes; in the southern Appalachians ascending to elevations of 3,500'.

Distribution.—Western Pennsylvania west through Ohio to southern Indiana, thence south over the Piedmont plateau, the Appalachian Mountains, western Kentucky, and Tennessee to the Gulf of Mexico.

Importance.—Occasionally used as an ornamental. The flowers are sought by the honeybee, and sourwood honey is occasionally offered for sale locally. The wood produced is of poor quality and is seldom used except for fuel.

THE LYONIAS

Lyonia Nutt.

These are a small group of trees and shrubs restricted to tropical and warmer countries of the New World. Six species are indigenous to the United States and one of them attains tree size on the lower coastal plains.

Tree Lyonia

Lyonia ferruginea Hell.

Habit.—A large shrub, or small tree with a greatly contorted, often prostrate bole; under favorable conditions becoming 30' in height and about 10'' in diam-

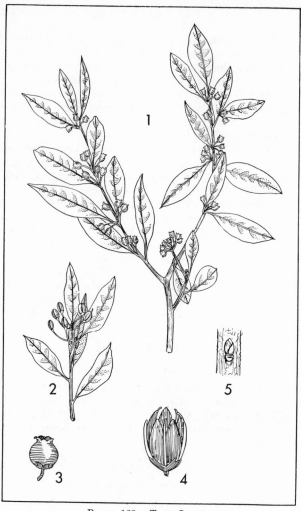

PLATE 169.—TREE LYONIA
1. Foliage and flowers ×½. 2. Foliage and cluster of fruits ×⅓.
3. Flower ×3. 4. Fruit ×1½. 5. Leaf scar ×2.

eter, then with a short trunk and stout, ascending limbs, forming an irregular, open, oblong crown.

Leaves.—Alternate, simple, persistent, leathery, obovate to somewhat diamond-shaped, 1″ to 3″ long, about 1″ wide; apex, rounded or pointed, usually tipped with a short, stiff point; base, wedge-shaped; margin, entire; pale green, shiny, and sometimes scaly above, covered with pale-rusty scales below; petioles, short, about ⅜″ long, swollen at the base.

Flowers.—Perfect, about ⅛″ long, borne in axillary fascicles; calyx, 5-lobed, persistent under the fruit; corolla, 5-lobed at the summit, white, hairy, globular; stamens, 10 (rarely 8); pistil, with a 5-celled ovary.

Fruit.—A 5-celled, oblong capsule, about ½″ long; seeds, light brown, about ⅛″ long.

Twigs.—Slender, often more or less 3-angled, reddish brown, often hairy, sometimes scaly; buds, minute, sharp-pointed, covered with 2 exposed scales, usually closely appressed against the twig; leaf scars, half-round, with a single oval bundle scar; pith, homogeneous.

Bark.—Reddish brown, divided into narrow, scaly ridges by shallow, longitudinal fissures.

Habitat.—Hammocks, acid humus, and sandy soils; commonly found at tidewater.

Distribution.—Coastal regions of South Carolina, Georgia, and Florida; also in the West Indies and Mexico.

Importance.—Of no commercial value.

THE SPARKLEBERRIES

Vaccinium L.

These are a group of shrubs and a few small trees comprising about 100 species. At least 35 forms are indigenous to the United States, and one of them becomes a small tree in the South. The cranberry

(*V. macrocarpum* L.) is probably the best-known member of this group.

Tree Sparkleberry

Vaccinium arboreum Marsh.

Habit.—A small, bushy tree, sometimes 30′ in height and 10″ in diameter, but usually much smaller; ordinarily characterized by a short, crooked bole, contorted branches, and dense, rounded head.

Leaves.—Alternate, simple, deciduous, or persistent for a single year (in the South), oblong, oval, or nearly circular, 1″ to 3″ long, about 1″ wide; apex, acute or rounded, sometimes with a short, pointed tip; base, wedge-shaped; margin, entire or furnished with minute, glandular teeth; dark green, lustrous above, paler below, sometimes with 5 scattered hairs along the midrib and principal veins; with a short petiole, or nearly sessile.

Flowers.—Perfect, borne in short, axillary racemes with small, leaflike bracts; calyx, 5-lobed; corolla, bell-shaped, white, slightly 5-lobed at the summit; stamens, 10; pistil, with a usually 5-celled ovary and hairlike style crowned with a minute stigma.

Fruit.—A globular, lustrous-black, many-seeded berry, about ¼″ in diameter; seeds, minute, more or less kidney-shaped.

Twigs.—Slender, brown to reddish brown, sometimes angled; buds, nearly globular, reddish brown to reddish purple, covered with several overlapping scales; leaf scars, half-round or nearly so, with a single oval bundle scar; pith, white, homogeneous.

Bark.—Dark brown, sometimes with a purplish tinge, divided into thin, elongated, shreddy, interlacing ridges.

Habitat.—An understory species frequenting moist soils near streams and lakes, along hillsides, and in

PLATE 170.—TREE SPARKLEBERRY
1. Foliage and fruit ×½. 2. Cluster of flowers ×⅔.
3. Flower ×2. 4. Seed ×1.

high mountain valleys. Unlike most other members of this family, tree farkleberry can maintain itself on soils of limestone origin.

Distribution.—Virginia coastal plain west to southern Illinois and Missouri, south to Florida and through the Gulf states to eastern Texas.

Importance.—An astringent extracted from root bark is sometimes used locally in the treatment of diarrhea; the bark from the bole is suitable for tanning leather. The wood has been used for tobacco pipes, woodenware, and novelties.

Remarks.—A form (*V. arboreum* var. *glaucescens* Sarg.) with glaucous leaves, large, leaflike bracts of the floral sprays, and nearly globular corollas is widespread through southern Missouri, eastern Oklahoma, Arkansas, eastern Texas, and western Louisiana.

THE THEOPHRASTA FAMILY

Theophrastaceae

This is a small tropical American family of little or no economic value, represented by 5 genera and about 70 species of trees and shrubs.

THE JOEWOODS

Jaquinia L.

This is the largest genus of the family and comprises about 35 species. Joewood, a small tree, extends northward from Cuba to southern Florida.

Joewood

Jaquinia keyensis Mez.

Habit.—A shrubby tree, 15' to 20' in height and 4" to 8" in diameter; with stout, often contorted, spreading branches, forming a dense, nearly globular crown.

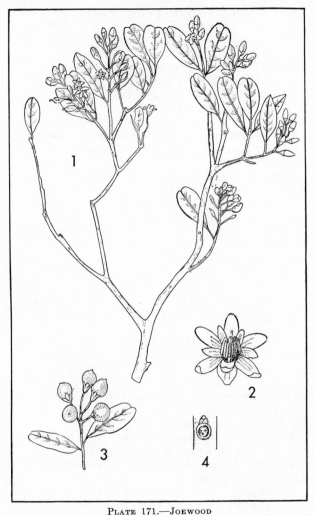

PLATE 171.—JOEWOOD
1. Foliage and flowers ×½. 2. Flower ×3. 3. Cluster of
fruit ×⅔. 4. Leaf scar ×2.

Leaves.—Alternate, or occasionally opposite, or nearly whorled, simple, persistent, leathery, the veins hardly in evidence, often crowded toward the tips of twigs; oblong, obovate, or spatula-shaped, 1″ to 3″ long, ½″ to 1″ broad; apex, ending in a short spine-like tip, shallowly notched, or merely rounded; base, wedge-shaped; margin, entire, often thickened; usually rolled backward; yellow-green above, paler and profusely glandular below; petiole, short, swollen at the base.

Flowers.—Perfect, fragrant, in terminal and axillary racemes; calyx, bell-shaped, 5-lobed, hairy along the margins; corolla, funnel-shaped, 5-lobed, the lobes longer than the tube, pale yellow; stamens, 5, inserted at the base of the corolla opposite the lobes; staminodia petallike, inserted on the corolla at the base of each sinus, thus alternating with the lobes; pistil, with a 1-celled ovary, slender style, and 5-lobed stigma.

Fruit.—A nearly globular, orange-red, many-seeded berry, about ⅓″ in diameter, tipped with the remnant of a persistent style and seated upon the persistent calyx.

Twigs.—Slender, many-angled, at first densely clothed with yellowish-brown to yellowish-green hairs, ultimately reddish brown and marked with conspicuous lenticels; terminal bud, absent; lateral buds, minute, globular, nearly completely embedded in the outer tissues of the twig; leaf scars, nearly circular, with 3 bundle scars; pith, homogeneous.

Bark.—Thin, comparatively smooth, blue-gray, often mottled with white or grayish white.

Habitat.—Dry, sandy and coral soils immediately adjacent to salt water.

Distribution.—Lower peninsular Florida, bordering the Everglades, on several of the Keys, Jamaica, the Bahamas, and Cuba.

Importance.—None.

THE MYRSINE FAMILY

Myrsinaceae

The Myrsine Family, with 30 genera and several hundred species of trees and shrubs, is distinctly a tropical group. There are at least 10 arborescent genera in tropical America, 2 of which are represented in Florida, each with a single species.

Synopsis of Southern Genera

Genus	Leaves	Flowers	Fruit
Ardisia	uniformly disposed along the twig	perfect, corolla marked with red	black
Rapanea	commonly crowded at the tips of twigs	unisexual, corolla marked with purple	blue-black

THE MARLBERRIES

Ardisia Sw.

The Marlberries comprise a group of nearly 200 species of trees and shrubs widely distributed through the tropical and subtropical forests of both hemispheres. A few species are employed ornamentally, and the wood of certain West Indian trees is used for furniture and cabinetry. A single species extends northward into southern Florida.

Marlberry

Ardisia escallonioides Cham. & Schlecht.

Habit.—A shrub or rarely a small tree, about 25′ in height and 4″ to 6″ in diameter, with slender, ascending branches, forming a narrow, columnar head.

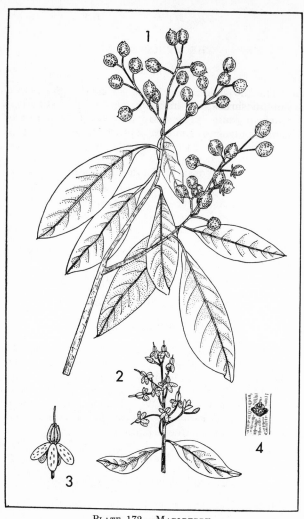

PLATE 172.—MARLBERRY

1. Foliage and fruit ×½. 2. Cluster of flowers ×1. 3. Flower
×4. 4. Leaf scar ×2.

Leaves.—Alternate, simple, more or less persistent, leathery, ovate, oblong, or obovate, rarely lanceolate, 3″ to 6″ long, 1″ to 2″ wide; apex, acute or rounded; base, wedge-shaped; margin, entire, thickened, and somewhat rolled backward; dark yellow-green above, conspicuously glandular-dotted below; petioles, stout, grooved, about ¼″ long; stipules, wanting.

Flowers.—Perfect, minute, fragrant, appearing through the summer and fall in many-flowered, terminal (rarely axillary), rusty-red, hairy panicles, 3″ to 5″ long; calyx, 5-lobed; corolla, 5-parted, the lobes furnished with red dots on their inner faces; stamens, 5, inserted on the throat of the corolla, each with a short, broad filament; pistil, with a nearly globular, glandular, 1-celled ovary, elongated style, and minute, terminal stigma.

Fruit.—A lustrous-black, globular drupe with a glandular-resinous skin, thin, dry flesh, and 1-seeded, hard, brittle stone, about ¼″ in diameter, usually tipped with a remnant of the slender style and seated upon the persistent calyx; seeds, with a basal lobe, red-brown, about ⅛″ long.

Twigs.—Stout, commonly contorted, orange-brown to rusty-red-brown, ultimately gray, dotted with numerous tiny, circular lenticels; terminal buds, long-tapered, nearly ¼″ long, rusty-brown; lateral buds, minute, globular, nearly completely embedded in the epidermal or cortical layers of the twig; leaf scars, shield-shaped to nearly circular, with a central group of 3 bundle scars; pith, homogeneous.

Bark.—Thin, light gray to pinkish white, dividing at the surface into thin, papery platelike scales.

Habitat.—Moist hammocks and sandy soils near the sea.

Distribution.—Near Lake Okeechobee, Florida, thence south along both east and west coasts, and on many of the Keys; also reported from the Bahamas, Cuba, and Mexico.

Importance.—None.

THE RAPANEAS

Rapanea Aubl.

The rapaneas are another tropical group consisting of approximately 150 species of evergreen trees and shrubs. These, too, are widely distributed through tropical forests of the world. Certain South American species are used extensively for pulpwood, furniture, and construction lumber, and their barks yield tannin extracts. A single species extends northward to southern Florida.

Guiana Rapanea

Rapanea guianensis Aubl.

Habit.—Scarcely ever more than a tall, slender shrub, but occasionally bordering on arborescent proportions; then 18′ to 25′ in height and 3″ to 5″ in diameter, with a short, contorted bole and narrow, irregularly open crown.

Leaves.—Alternate, simple, persistent, leathery, often more or less crowded toward the tips of twigs, obovate to oblong, 2″ to 4″ long, 1″ to 2″ wide; apex, obtuse or rounded, then with a shallow notch; base, wedge-shaped; margin, entire, thickened, rolled backward; bright green above, paler and usually somewhat scaly below; petioles, winged, about ¼″ long.

Flowers.—Minute, perfect or unisexual by abortion, borne in short-stalked, axillary clusters; calyx, 5-(rarely 4-) lobed; corolla, 5- (rarely 4-) lobed, white, striped with purple, hairy along the margin of the lobes; stamens, 5 (rarely 4), the anthers sessile and inserted on the corolla lobes, abortive and rudimentary

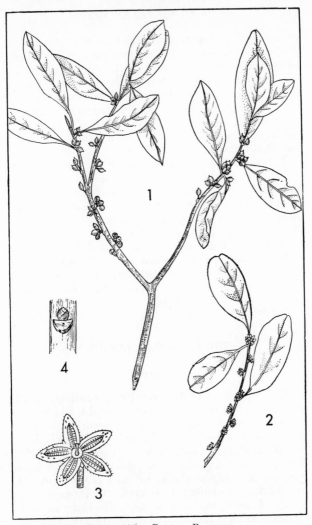

PLATE 173.—GUIANA RAPANEA
1. Foliage and fruit ×½. 2. Flower clusters ×½. 3. Flower
×5. 4. Leaf scar ×2.

in the pistillate flowers; pistil, abortive in the staminate flowers, in the perfect flowers consisting of a 1-celled ovary with narrow style and short, oblique stigma, in the pistillate flowers with a nearly globular, 1-celled ovary surmounted by a large, lobed, subsessile stigma.

Fruit.—A globular, dark, blue-black drupe, about ⅕″ in diameter, tipped with the remnants of a style and seated upon a persistent calyx; stone, white, 1-seeded, hard but brittle.

Twigs.—Slender, reddish brown to gray-brown; buds, minute, globular, deeply embedded in the epidermal layers of the twig; leaf scars, mostly half-round, with a single central bundle scar, which is occasionally divided; pith, homogeneous.

Bark.—Thin, gray, usually smooth.

Habitat.—Hammocks, flatwoods, and riverbanks.

Distribution.—Lake Okeechobee, Florida, thence south along the east and west coasts to the southern Keys; also reported from many of the West Indies, Mexico, Bolivia, and Brazil.

Importance.—None.

THE SAPODILLA FAMILY

Sapotaceae

The Sapodilla Family comprises approximately 50 genera and 500 species of trees and shrubs, widely distributed throughout the tropics of the world. Several fine cabinet timbers are produced by certain members of this family, but as a general rule they are used only locally. All these plants are laticiferous, and in a number of instances the milky juice is the source of products of importance to man. Gutta-percha is obtained from the sap of an Indo-Malayan tree (*Palaquium gutta* Burch.), and chicle, the basic material of much chewing gum, is procured from the tropical

American sapota (*Achras zapota* L.). The sapota is also cultivated for its fruit, which is palatable and acclaimed by many to be the finest in the New World. The seeds of several species are rich in oil, are a source of fat for soapmaking, and may be rendered suitable for food.

Eight arborescent species included in 5 genera are found in our semitropical forests.

Synopsis of Southern Genera

Genus	Leaves	Flowers	Fruit	Buds
Sideroxylon	evergreen	calyx, 5-lobed	ovoid to spherical, yellow	naked
Dipholis	evergreen	calyx, 5-lobed	nearly globular, black	naked
Bumelia	deciduous or evergreen, commonly borne on spurs	calyx, 5-lobed	variable in shape, black	scaly
Achras	evergreen, clustered at the ends of twigs	calyx, 6- to 8-lobed	globular, coated with minute, rusty-brown scales	naked
Chrysophyllum	evergreen, copper-colored below	calyx, 5-lobed	ovoid, purple	naked

THE FALSE-MASTICS

Sideroxylon L.

These are a genus of approximately 100 species of trees and shrubs widely distributed throughout the tropics. A single species extends northward to the southern tip of Florida.

False-Mastic　　　Jungleplum

Sideroxylon foetidissimum Jacq.

Habit.—A medium-sized tree, 60′ to 80′ in height and 2′ to 3′ in diameter; characterized by a long, clear trunk, ascending branches, and short, dense, irregular crown.

Leaves.—Alternate, simple, persistent, oval, 3″ to 5″ long, 1″ to 2″ broad; apex, notched, rounded or acute; base, broadly wedge-shaped; margin, rolled slightly inward; lustrous, bright green above, yellow-green below; petioles, slender, about 1¼″ long.

Flowers.—Perfect, minute, borne in many-flowered, axillary fascicles on twigs of the previous season; calyx, 5-lobed, yellow-green; corolla, 5-lobed, yellow; stamens, 5, opposite the corolla lobes; abortive stamens, 5, alternating with the corolla lobes; pistil, the ovary surmounted by a minutely 5-lobed stigma.

Fruit.—Berrylike, yellow, oval to nearly globular, the flesh thick and juicy, 1-seeded, about 1″ long; seed, obovoid, rounded at the apex, about ½″ long.

Twigs.—Stout, orange-brown, often tinged with red; buds, naked; leaf scars, nearly circular, with 3 bundle scars; pith, homogeneous.

Bark.—About ½″ thick, divided into thick, reddish-brown, platelike scales.

Habitat.—Hammocks and sandy soils adjacent to tidewater.

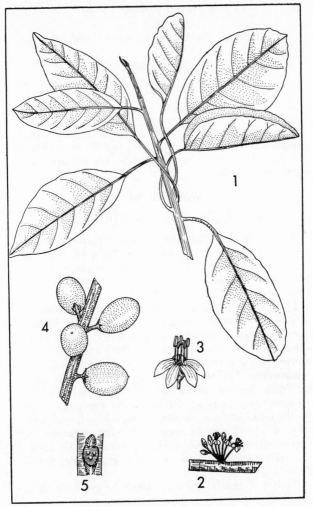

PLATE 174.—FALSE-MASTIC
1. Foliage ×⅓. 2. Flower cluster ×1. 3. Flower ×4.
4. Fruit ×½. 5. Leaf scar ×1½.

Distribution.—Southern peninsular Florida and the Keys.

Importance.—Of no commercial value.

THE BUSTICS

Dipholis A.DC.

These are a small group comprising only three species, all native to the tropics of the Western Hemisphere. A single form extends northward into southern Florida.

Willow Bustic

Dipholis salicifolia A.DC.

Habit.—A small tree, seldom more than 35′ in height or 15″ in diameter; the ascending branches forming a slender, symmetrical crown, which often makes possible the distinguishing of this tree at a considerable distance.

Leaves.—Alternate, simple, persistent, obovate to oblong or lanceolate, 3″ to 5″ long, 1″ to 2″ broad; apex, rounded, pointed, or long-tapered; base, wedge-shaped; margin, wavy, thickened; dark green, lustrous above, yellow-green below; petiole, about 1″ long.

Flowers.—Perfect, minute, borne in the leaf axils or from leafless nodes in few-flowered, fascicled clusters; calyx, deeply 5-lobed, with rusty-red hairs on the outer surface; corolla, white, 5-lobed, each lobe with a lateral pair of secondary lobes; stamens, 5, opposite the corolla lobes; abortive stamens, 5, petal-like, alternating with those which are fertile; pistil, flask-shaped.

Fruit.—A nearly globular, black berry, with thin, dry flesh; about ¼″ in diameter; seed, ovoid.

Twigs.—Slender, light gray to reddish brown, dotted with numerous circular lenticels; buds, naked;

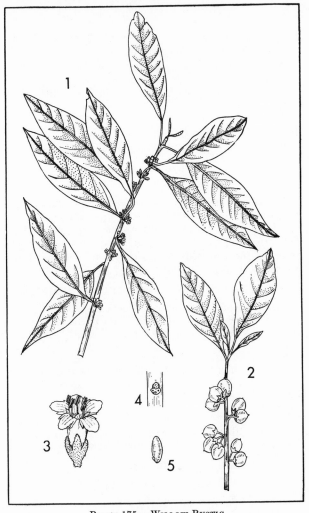

PLATE 175.—WILLOW BUSTIC

1. Foliage and flowers ×½. 2. Fruit ×½. 3. Flower ×4.
4. Leaf scar ×1½. 5. Seed ×½.

leaf scars, nearly circular to heart-shaped, with 3 bundle scars; pith, homogeneous.

Bark.—Thin, divided into reddish-brown, squarish, scablike scales.

Habitat.—Hammocks, sandy soils, and pinewood flats.

Distribution.—Southern peninsular Florida, the Keys, and the West Indies.

Importance.—Of no commercial value.

THE BUMELIAS
Bumelia Sw.

These are a genus comprising about 35 species of trees and shrubs, usually with thorny branches and restricted to the tropics and warmer regions of the Western Hemisphere. At least 10 species are indigenous to the United States, 4 of which become arborescent within our range.

KEY TO THE SOUTHERN ARBORESCENT BUMELIAS

1. Leaves, deciduous, about 5″ in length...............
   Buckthorn bumelia (p. 601)
1. Leaves, persistent, usually 3″ or less in length........ 2

  2. Leaves, smooth or with scattered hairs below, about 1½″ in length.......**Saffron-plum bumelia** (p. 601)
  2. Leaves, densely hairy or woolly below, about 2½″ in length...................................... 3

3. Leaves, woolly below..........**Gum bumelia** (p. 598)
3. Leaves, with yellow-red or copper-red hairs below....
   Tough bumelia (p. 601)

Gum Bumelia
Bumelia lanuginosa Pers.

Habit.—Usually a small tree, 40′ or more in height and 1′ to 2′ in diameter, with the greater part of the bole clothed in a long, narrow, oblong crown.

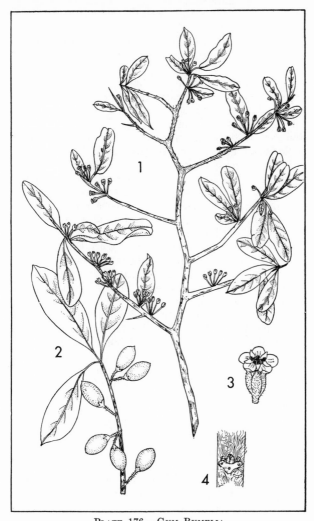

PLATE 176.—GUM BUMELIA

1. Foliage and flowers ×½. 2. Fruit ×⅔. 3. Flower ×5.
4. Leaf scar ×2.

Leaves.—Alternate, simple, persistent, often borne in false whorls on lateral spurs, ovate to oblong, 1″ to 3″ long, about 1″ wide; apex, rounded, sometimes ending abruptly in a short, sharp tip; base, wedge-shaped; margin, entire; dark green and lustrous above, with dull-silvery or rusty-brown, woolly hairs below; petioles, about ½″ long, coated with woolly hairs similar to those found on the lower side of the blade.

Flowers.—Perfect, minute, borne in many-flowered, axillary, fascicled clusters; calyx, 5-lobed, coated on the outer surface with rusty-red hairs; corolla, 5-lobed, each lobe furnished with a pair of smaller, straplike, secondary lobes; stamens, 5, opposite the corolla lobes; abortive stamens, 5, petallike, alternating with the fertile ones; pistil, conical.

Fruit.—A black, oblong berry, with thick flesh, about ½″ long; seed, oblong, about ¼″ long.

Twigs.—Stout, stiff, often zigzag, hairy or woolly, commonly armed with spines, which occasionally are themselves leafy, reddish brown to grayish brown; buds, about ⅛″ long, scaly, woolly, sometimes 3 at a node; leaf scars, variable, circular or more commonly broadly V-shaped, with 3 bundle scars; pith, homogeneous.

Bark.—About ½″ thick, divided into narrow, scaly ridges separated by narrow, shallow fissures, gray-brown to nearly black on the larger trunks.

Habitat.—On the coastal plain on rocky, gravelly, or dry, sandy soils and in river valleys.

Distribution.—Southeastern Georgia, Florida west to Texas; up the Mississippi Valley to southern Illinois.

Importance.—A thick, clear gum is produced upon scarification of the bole, but this substance has little or no utility at the present time.

Tough Bumelia

Bumelia tenax Willd.

This is a small tree found along the coast on dry, sandy soils from North Carolina to peninsular Florida and the Keys. It is readily distinguishable from other members of this group by its small, obovate to oblanceolate leaves, with shining, copper-colored, hairy lower surfaces, commonly armed twigs, and black, oblong fruits, about $\frac{1}{2}''$ in length.

Buckthorn Bumelia

Bumelia lycioides (L.) Pers.

This small tree is found over a wide area from southern Indiana and Illinois south through Kentucky and Tennessee to the Gulf states (eastern Texas to Florida), thence along the Atlantic seaboard to southern Virginia.

Buckthorn bumelia is characterized by deciduous, elliptical or oblanceolate leaves, $3''$ to $6''$ in length, twigs with stout, curved spines, and black, oval fruits, about $\frac{3}{4}''$ in length.

Saffron-Plum Bumelia

Bumelia angustifolia Nutt.

This is a shrub or small tree seldom exceeding a height of $20'$ and found only in lower peninsular Florida, the Keys, and neighboring islands of the West Indies. It is characterized by very short leaves, $1''$ to $1\frac{1}{2}''$ in length, and large, black, oblong or cylindrical fruits, about $1''$ in length.

THE SAPODILLAS

Achras L.

This genus comprises a group of nearly 150 species of trees widely distributed throughout the tropics of the world. To this group is traceable the well-known bulletwood. Balata, a valuable commercial gum, is derived from several species, but notably *A. globosa* Gaertn. of the Guianas and *A. darienensis* Pittier, a tree of Panama. A single species (*A. emarginata* Britt.) extends northward into southern Florida.

Wild-Dilly

Achras emarginata (L.) Britt.

Habit.—A tree, 30′ to 40′ in height and 12″ to 18″ in diameter; characterized by stout branches, a gnarled bole, and dense, nearly globular crown.

Leaves.—Alternate, simple, persistent, leathery, clustered at the ends of twigs, oblong to obovate, 3″ to 4″ long, 1″ to 2″ wide; apex, rounded or broadly but shallowly notched; base, rounded or broadly wedge-shaped; margin, slightly thickened and rolled under; bright green and covered with a light, waxy bloom above, with rusty-red hairs below; petiole, grooved, clothed with rusty-red hairs or smooth, about ¾″ long.

Flowers.—Perfect, borne in axillary clusters at the tips of twigs on long, rusty-red, hairy, drooping stalks; calyx, 6-lobed, the lobes in 2 series, woolly-red on the back; corolla, 6-lobed, light yellow, each lobed with 2 lateral, straplike appendages; stamens, 6, opposite the petals; abortive stamens, 6, triangular, scalelike, alternating with the fertile ones; pistil, conical.

Fruit.—A nearly globular, usually 1-seeded berry, about 1½″ in diameter; with a thick outer skin covered with minute, rusty-brown scabs and spongy flesh filled with a thick, milky-white juice; seed, about ½″ long.

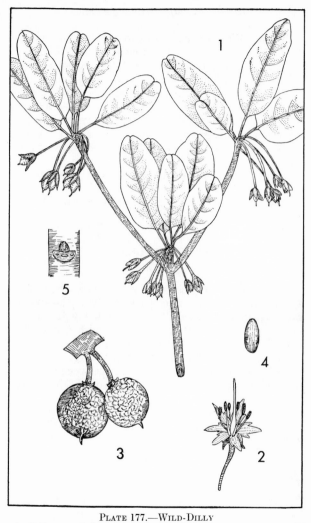

PLATE 177.—WILD-DILLY

1. Foliage and flowers ×⅓. 2. Flower ×2. 3. Fruit ×⅓.
4. Seed ×1. 5. Leaf scar ×2.

Twigs.—Stout, in characteristic crowded clusters at the end of twigs from the previous season, orange-brown, scaly in their 2d season; buds, naked, rusty-red, woolly; leaf scars, heart-shaped to semicircular, with 3 bundle scars, the medial usually the largest; pith homogeneous.

Bark.—Thin, reddish brown to grayish brown, separated by irregular furrows into narrow, rounded ridges, which are divided by transverse fissures into squarish, scaly blocks.

Habitat.—Hammocks and sandy soils near tide-water.

Distribution.—Florida Keys, and several West Indian islands.

Importance.—None.

THE SATINLEAFS

Chrysophyllum L.

These are a tropical genus including about 65 species of evergreen trees and shrubs. The West Indian satinleaf (*C. cainito* L.) is probably the most important species. Its bluish or purplish fruits, the size of our domestic apples, are said to possess an excellent flavor. This species is now widely cultivated in many parts of the tropics and has become naturalized in several tropical regions of the Western Hemisphere.

A single species from the American tropics extends north into lower peninsular Florida and adjacent keys.

Satinleaf

Chrysophyllum oliviforme L.

Habit.—A large shrub or small tree, often 25′ to 30′ in height and 8″ to 12″ in diameter; with ascending branches and a dense, oblong crown.

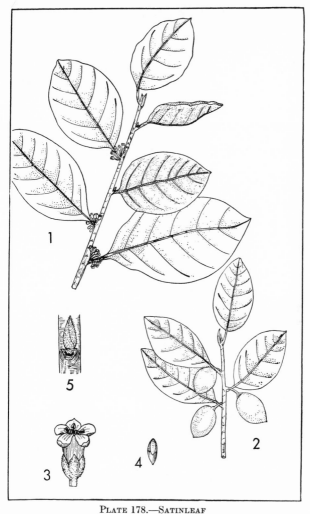

PLATE 178.—SATINLEAF

1. Foliage and flowers $\times\frac{1}{2}$.   2. Fruit $\times\frac{1}{2}$.   3. Flowers $\times 4$.
4. Seed $\times\frac{2}{3}$.   5. Leaf scar $\times 2$.

Leaves.—Alternate, simple, persistent, leathery, oval, 2″ to 3″ long, 1″ to 2″ wide; apex, rounded or abruptly acute; base, wedge-shaped; margin, entire or slightly wavy; blue-green, lustrous above, coated with lustrous, copper-colored hairs below; petioles, stout, about ½″ long.

Flowers.—Perfect, borne intermittently throughout the year in fascicled clusters in the leaf axils; calyx, 5-lobed; corolla, white, 5-lobed; stamens, 5; sterile or abortive stamens, none; pistil, ovoid, 5-celled, surmounted by 5 fleshy stigmas.

Fruit.—A dark-purple, oval berry, with a sweetish, light-purplish, juicy flesh, about ¾″ long; seeds, ellipsoidal, about ½″ long.

Twigs.—Slender, often zigzag, reddish brown, dotted with numerous circular lenticels; buds, naked; leaf scars, semicircular to shield-shaped, with a single, lunate bundle scar; pith, homogeneous.

Bark.—Thin, light reddish brown, separated by shallow fissures into thin, scaly plates.

Habitat.—Hammocks, flatwoods, and sandy plains.

Distribution.—Southern Florida, the Keys, and neighboring West Indian islands.

Importance.—None.

THE EBONY FAMILY

Ebenaceae

The Ebony Family embraces about 300 species included in 7 genera. This group is primarily tropical or subtropical in habit and is widely distributed in Africa and the Malay Peninsula. The true ebony (*Diospyros ebenum* Koenig) is highly prized for its black, hard, heavy wood, which has long been used in the manufacture of expensive bowls, candlesticks, piano keys, and furniture. Members of several other genera of the family produce a black or dark-brownish-black wood, which is also distributed under the name of ebony.

The genus *Diospyros* includes the only American representatives.

THE PERSIMMONS

Diospyros L.

The persimmons and ebonies are trees or shrubs numbering nearly 200 species found in Asia, Africa, the Malay Peninsula, and the United States. Several are important timber-producing species, many have ornamental value, and the fruits of several are edible.

Two persimmons are indigenous to the United States. One (*D. virginiana* L.) is a southern timber tree of secondary importance. The other (*D. texana* Scheele) occurs sparsely in southern and southwestern Texas.

KEY TO THE SOUTHERN PERSIMMONS

1. Flowers, on twigs of the current season; fruit, orange to reddish purple; seeds, oblong.........................
   Common persimmon (p. 607)
1. Flowers, on twigs from the previous season; fruit, black; seeds, triangular.... **Texas persimmon** (p. 610)

Common Persimmon

Diospyros virginiana L.

Habit.—A tree, usually 40′ to 60′ in height, with a trunk 1′ to 2′ in diameter (max. 130′ by 2½′). The bole commonly branches 10′ to 20′ above the ground with its slender, spreading, zigzag branches forming a broad, rounded, open head. Commonly a shrub toward the northern limits of its range.

Leaves.—Simple, alternate, deciduous, ovate-oblong, 4″ to 6″ long, 2″ to 3″ broad; apex, acuminate; base, wedge-shaped or rounded; margin, entire, often some-

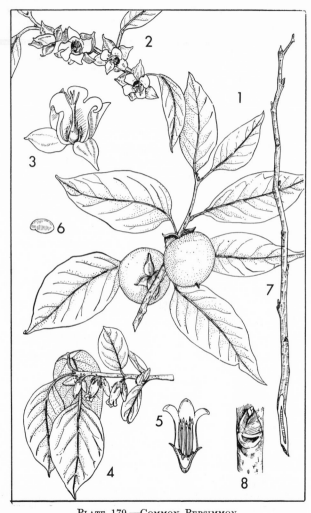

PLATE 179.—COMMON PERSIMMON
1. Foliage and fruit ×½. 2. Cluster of female flowers ×1.
3. Section through female flower ×2. 4. Cluster of male flowers
×1. 5. Section through male flower ×2. 6. Seed ×⅓. 7. Twig
×⅔. 8. Leaf scar ×2.

what wavy; dark green, leathery, and glabrous above, paler below; petioles, stout, 1″ long.

Flowers.—Dioecious; appearing with the leaves on twigs of the current season; calyx, 4-lobed; corolla, 4- (rarely 5-) lobed; staminate flowers, in 2- to several-flowered, hairy-stalked cymes, usually with 16 stamens; the pistillate, solitary, with a 4-celled ovary and 4 spreading, 2-lobed styles.

Fruit.—A subglobose, orange to reddish purple, several-seeded berry, with a persistent, woody calyx; flesh at first very astringent, but sweet and edible after ripening, about 1½″ in diameter; seeds, oblong, flattened, with rounded ends, the coat slightly wrinkled.

Twigs.—Slender, glabrous or pubescent, somewhat zigzag, with scattered, orange lenticels; terminal buds, absent; lateral buds, ovoid, acute, ⅛″ long, with 2 lustrous outer scales; leaf scars, half-moon-shaped, with 1 bundle scar; pith, continuous or diaphragmed.

Bark.—Gray-brown to nearly black, up to 1″ thick, and broken into squarrose, scaly blocks separated by narrow, deep fissures, thus having the appearance of alligator leather.

Habitat.—On deep, rich bottom lands or on higher, sandy, well-drained soil; usually found as an occasional tree in association with many other broadleaved trees.

Distribution.—Southern Connecticut and Long Island south to southern Florida; west through central Pennsylvania to southeastern Iowa, thence south to eastern Texas.

Importance.—The wood has been used for shuttles, shoe lasts, plane stocks, mallets, and wooden golf-club heads. The fruit is edible and is sometimes fermented into wine; the bark is the source of an astringent compound.

Texas Persimmon

Diospyros texana Scheele

The Texas persimmon is a restricted species found mainly in southern and western Texas on rich, moist soil or drier, rocky slopes. It is similar in size and appearance to the common persimmon, but the flowers are borne on last year's twigs, and the fruit is a black berry with triangular seeds. The leaves are blunt and are pubescent below. The bark is smooth and gray and exfoliates irregularly.

The Texas persimmon is of no economic importance. The fruit is edible and a source of a purple-black dye.

THE STORAX FAMILY

Styracaceae

The Storax Family embraces 6 genera and about 110 species of trees and shrubs with alternate, simple leaves and showy flowers. These are widely scattered through the Mediterranean basin, the Malay Archipelago, eastern Asia, and the Americas. Many, because of their beautiful floral displays and comparative ease of propagation, are widely used ornamentals. Two genera are represented in the South with one or more arborescent species.

Synopsis of Southern Genera

Genus	Flowers	Fruit
Styrax	corolla, 5- (rarely 6- or 7-) parted	drupaceous, ovoid, unwinged
Halesia	corolla, shallowly to deeply 4-lobed	nutlike, elongated, 2- to 4-winged

THE SNOWBELLS

Styrax L.

This genus comprises a group of trees and shrubs numbering about 100 species, the majority tropical. While not a timber-contributing group, certain species are important sources of benzoin, storax, and resins. Five species are native to the United States, and one of these is a small southern tree.

Bigleaf Snowbell

Styrax grandifolia Ait.

Habit.—A shrub or small tree, 6' to 40' tall; when treelike, with a trunk up to 8" in diameter and a narrow, rounded head.

Leaves.—Simple, alternate, deciduous, obovate, 2" to 5" long, 1" to 3" broad; apex, acute or acuminate; base, rounded or wedge-shaped; margin, remotely and then distantly serrate or entire; pale green and glabrous above, woolly along the veins; petiole, short, stout, hairy.

Flowers.—Perfect, appearing with the leaves, 1" long, white, in 6" axillary racemes with minute bracts; calyx, bell-shaped, woolly, 5-toothed; corolla, white, deeply 5-lobed; stamens, 10; ovary, 3-celled.

Fruit.—An obovoid, dry drupe with the remnant of a persistent style at the apex, enclosed below by the persistent calyx, about ⅓" long; seed, large, obovoid, brown.

Twigs.—Slender, at first pubescent, later becoming glabrous and brown; terminal buds, lacking; axillary buds, 1 to 3 at a node, naked, scurfy, superposed, ⅛" long; leaf scars, crescent-shaped, with a single central bundle scar, which is occasionally divided; pith, small, rounded, green, homogeneous.

Bark.—Thin, smooth, dark chestnut-brown to black.

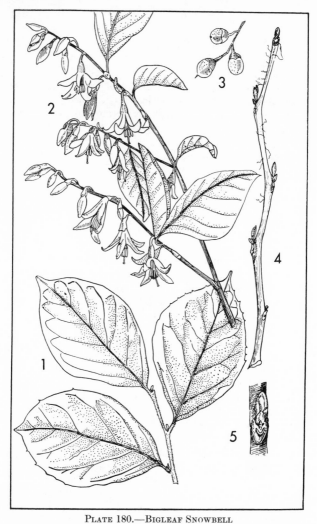

PLATE 180.—BIGLEAF SNOWBELL
1. Foliage $\times\frac{1}{2}$. 2. Flowers $\times\frac{1}{2}$. 3. Fruit $\times\frac{2}{3}$. 4. Twig
$\times 1$. 5. Leaf scar $\times 2$.

Habitat.—Rich, moist soil in woods near swamps or streams.

Distribution.—From Virginia south to Florida and west to Georgia, Louisiana, and Mississippi.

Importance.—Used sparingly as an ornamental.

THE SILVERBELLS

Halesia L.

This small group includes only five species of shrubs and trees. A single form occurs in eastern China, while the others are all indigenous to the southeastern United States. Because of their showy flowers and unusual fruits, all have been used for decorative purposes.

KEY TO THE SOUTHERN SILVERBELLS

1. Fruit, 2-winged.........**Two-wing silverbell** (p. 613)
1. Fruit, 4-winged.................................. 2

2. Flowers, 2″ or more in length....................
　　　　　　　　　Mountain silverbell (p. 617)
2. Flowers, 1″ or less in length..................... 3

3. Fruit, club-shaped; flowers, usually ¼″ or less in length
　　　　　　　　　Little silverbell (p. 618)
3. Fruit, oblong to obovate; flowers, ½″ to 1″ in length..
　　　　　　　　　Carolina silverbell (p. 615)

Two-Wing Silverbell

Halesia diptera Ellis

Habit.—A small tree, occasionally becoming 30′ in height, with a trunk 6″ to 12″ in diameter, supporting a small, rounded head; frequently occurring as a small, much-branched shrub.

Leaves.—Alternate, simple, deciduous, obovate, 3″ to 4″ long, about 2″ wide; apex, acute or acuminate;

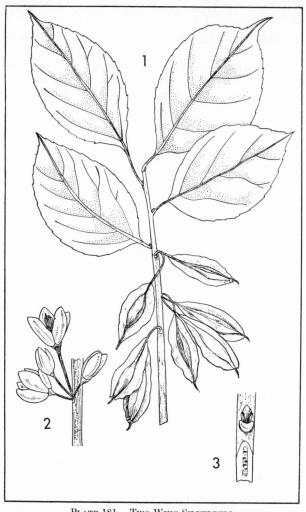

PLATE 181.—TWO-WING SILVERBELL

1. Foliage and fruit ×½. 2. Flowers ×⅔. 3. Leaf scar ×1½.

base, wedge-shaped; margin, remotely serrate; light green and more or less glabrous above, pale and hairy below; petioles, ¾″ long, hairy.

Flowers.—Perfect, appearing with the leaves in few-flowered clusters or racemes; calyx, woolly on the outer surface; corolla, white, divided nearly to the base into 4 lobes; stamens, 8 to 16 (mostly 8); pistil, 2- (rarely 4-) celled.

Fruit.—Nutlike, oblong to obovoid, 1″ to 2″ long, 1″ wide at the medial point; furnished with a pair of broad, longitudinal wings; stone, ellipsoidal, ridged; seeds, tapered at the ends.

Twigs.—Slender, at first hairy, with scattered lenticels; buds superposed, small, ovoid, obtuse, with hairy, reddish scales; leaf scars, large, elevated, heart-shaped, with a crescent-shaped bundle scar, which is often divided; pith, small, chambered, white.

Bark.—Thin, brown or reddish brown, with longitudinal fissures and scaly ridges.

Habitat.—Rich, moist soil in woods, on swamp borders, and on banks of streams.

Distribution.—From Florida west to Texas and southwestern Arkansas.

Importance.—Occasionally cultivated as an ornamental.

Carolina Silverbell

Halesia carolina L.

Habit.—A shrub or small tree, rarely more than 35′ in height; often featured by a short, stocky trunk, 12″ to 16″ in diameter, which divides near the ground into several, spreading limbs to form a broad, rounded crown.

Leaves.—Alternate, simple, deciduous, oblong to elliptical, 3″ to 5″ long, 1½″ to 3″ wide; apex, long-tapered; base, rounded or wedge-shaped; margin,

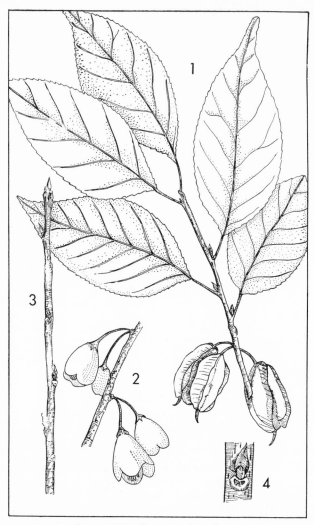

PLATE 182.—CAROLINA SILVERBELL
1. Foliage and fruit ×½. 2. Flowers ×½. 3. Twig ×1.
4. Leaf scar ×2.

dentate-serrate; dark yellow-green and glabrous above; paler and slightly hairy below; petioles, short, about ⅜″ long.

Flowers.—Perfect, appearing with the leaves, ½″ to 1″ long; calyx, 4-lobed, hairy on the margin; corolla, white (sometimes with a pinkish tinge), 4-lobed; stamens, 10 to 16; pistil, with a 4-celled ovary.

Fruit.—Nutlike, oblong, 1½″ to 2½″ long, ½″ to 1″ wide; furnished with 4 narrow, longitudinal wings; stone, ellipsoidal; seed, tapered at either end.

Twigs.—Slender, at first very hairy but becoming smooth during their 1st winter, with numerous pale lenticels; buds, superposed, ovoid, sometimes constricted at the base, with 4 outer, reddish scales; leaf scars, crescent-shaped, with a U-shaped bundle scar; pith, white, chambered.

Bark.—On young stems, reddish brown, with chalky-white streaks (a very distinctive feature); later, becoming about ½″ thick and divided into flattened, scaly ridges by shallow fissures.

Habitat.—Slopes and margins of streams.

Range.—Southern West Virginia through Kentucky to southern Illinois; south through the Piedmont plateau of the Carolinas to central Georgia, western Florida, and Alabama.

Importance.—Commonly used as an ornamental; hardy through central New York and southern New England.

Mountain Silverbell

Halesia monticola Sarg.

This tree is similar to the Carolina silverbell but may be distinguished by its larger leaves (8″ to 11″ long) and flowers (2″ long). Usually found at elevations above 2,500′, this tree often attains a height of 60′ to 90′, with proportionate diameters. It is of no value as a timber tree but, like other members of the group, is occasionally used ornamentally. This silverbell is a montane species ranging through the mountains of North Carolina, Tennessee, and Georgia. A variety with rose-colored flowers extends westward to Arkansas and eastern Oklahoma.

Little Silverbell
Halesia parviflora Michx.

This species, which is often not more than a large, bushy shrub, occurs sparsely in northern Florida, Alabama, Mississippi, and eastern Oklahoma on dry, sandy, upland sites. It may be distinguished from others of the group by its club-shaped fruits and small flowers, usually $\frac{1}{4}''$ in length. It has no commercial or ornamental value.

THE SWEETLEAF FAMILY
Symplocaceae

This is a monotypic family consisting of the single genus *Symplocos* L'Her., with about 300 species of shrubs or small trees having simple, alternate, deciduous leaves; perfect, or perfect and imperfect flowers in spikes or racemes; and dry, drupaceous fruits containing a 1-seeded stone. The leaves and bark of several forms produce yellow dyes, while the roots of others contain extractives used in the preparation of tonics.

A single species occurs in the southern states, another is native to the West Indies, while the remainder are scattered through the forests of Asia and Australia.

Common Sweetleaf   Horsesugar
Symplocos tinctoria L'Her.

Habit.—Usually a shrub, but occasionally a tree, up to 35′ in height, with a short trunk 6″ in diameter and a rounded, open head.

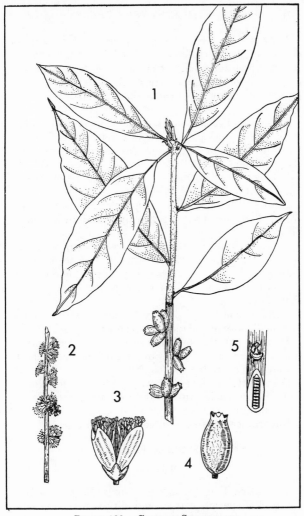

PLATE 183.—COMMON SWEETLEAF
1. Foliage and fruit ×½. 2. Cluster of flowers ×⅓.
3. Flower ×2. 4. Fruit ×1½. 5. Leaf scar ×1½.

Leaves.—Simple, alternate, more or less tardily deciduous, leathery, oblong, 5″ to 6″ long, 1″ to 2″ broad; apex, acuminate or acute; base, tapered; margin, wavy-toothed; dark green, glabrous above, pale, pubescent below; petioles, short, stout, remotely winged.

Flowers.—Perfect, clustered, at first surrounded by 3 oblong, overlapping bracts; individual flowers, fragrant, borne on short, stout, silky stalks; calyx, cup-shaped, remotely 5-lobed; corolla, white, 5-lobed, ½″ long; stamens, many, longer than petals, with orange anthers; ovary, 3-celled.

Fruit.—A small, brown, ovoid, dry drupe, ½″ long; crowned with remnants of the calyx; seed, ovoid, dark brown.

Twigs.—Stout, more or less pubescent, gray-brown, with a few small, elevated lenticels; leaf scars, half-round, with a single, large, horizontal bundle scar (sometimes divided); buds, ovoid, acute, brown; pith, chambered.

Bark.—Thin, gray, slightly furrowed, with numerous small, wartlike, corky excresences.

Habitat.—In the shade of larger trees on rich, moist soil in forests and along swamp margins; occurring at sea level to altitudes above 3,500′.

Distribution.—From Delaware, south through North and South Carolina to Florida, west to eastern Texas and southern Arkansas.

Importance.—Of no commercial importance.

THE OLIVE FAMILY

Oleaceae

The Olive Family embraces some 25 genera and nearly 500 species of trees and shrubs with opposite leaves, widely distributed in tropical and temperate forests of both North and South America, Europe, and Asia. The most important timber-producing species are included in the genus *Fraxinus* (the ashes), and the olive of commerce is obtained from the European *Olea europaea* L. Yellow jasmine, lilacs, privets, forsythias, and fringetree are numbered among the more common ornamentals of this group.

Four genera are represented in the southern forests by one or more arborescent species.

Synopsis of Southern Genera

Genus	Leaves	Flowers	Fruit
Fraxinus	compound, deciduous	dioecious, polygamous or perfect	a terminally winged samara
Forestiera	simple, deciduous	dioecious	a 1-celled (rarely 2), thin-skinned drupe
Chionanthus	simple, deciduous	dioecious or rarely perfect	a 1-celled (rarely 2, or 3), thick-skinned, rather dry drupe
Osmanthus	simple, persistent	perfect or polygamous	a 1-seeded, fleshy drupe

THE ASHES

Fraxinus L.

The ashes comprise a group of about 65 species scattered through the forests of both the Old and the New World. Several are important timber trees; others, because of their showy flowers, have a use as ornamentals. At least 2 species are productive of medicinal extracts.

About 20 ashes are native to the United States, 9 of which occur in our southern forests. These are featured by opposite, pinnately compound leaves and terminally winged samara fruits.

KEY TO THE SOUTHERN ASHES

1. Flowers, naked.................................. 2
1. Flowers, with a calyx........................... 3

    2. Flowers, perfect; leaflets, short-stalked; twigs, 4-angled, furnished with corky ridges; sap, turning blue upon exposure.............**Blue ash** (p. 623)
    2. Flowers, polygamous; leaflets, sessile; twigs, rounded, without corky ridges..**Black ash** (p. 624)

3. Fruit, flattened, the wing extending to the base of the seed cavity....................................... 4
3. Fruit, plump, more or less circular in cross section, the wing terminating the seed cavity or extending along it for varying lengths............................... 5

    4. Leaves, with 5 to 9 (mostly 7) thick, leathery leaflets, 7″ to 12″ long; fruits, long-stalked, commonly 3-winged.............**Carolina ash** (p. 625)
    4. Leaves, with 3 to 7 (mostly 5) thin leaflets, 4″ to 9″ long; fruits, short-stalked, with a single broad, terminal wing...............**Florida ash** (p. 627)

5. Leaves and twigs, smooth......................... 6
5. Leaves and twigs, densely hairy.................. 7

    6. Leaves, lustrous green above and below; lateral buds, inserted above the leaf scar.....**Green ash** (p. 632)
    6. Leaves, pale green above, sometimes silvery below; lateral buds, partly surrounded by the leaf scar...
                        White ash (p. 627)

7. Fruit, less than 2″ long, linear to oblong; the wing, terminal to the seed cavity.....**Biltmore ash** (p. 630)
7. Fruit, 2″ to 3″ long, spear-shaped to elliptical; the wing, extending along the seed cavity to below the middle... 8

8. Leaves, 10″ to 20″ long; fruit, about 3″ long and
   ½″ wide..................**Pumpkin ash** (p. 630)
8. Leaves, 10″ to 12″ long; fruit, about 2″ long and
   ¼″ wide......................**Red ash** (p. 630)

Blue Ash

Fraxinus quadrangulata Michx.

Habit.—A medium-sized tree, often 50′ to 70′ in
height and 2′ to 3′ in diameter (rarely 120′ by 4′);
the small branches, spreading and forming a slender,
open, more or less rounded head.

Leaves.—Opposite, deciduous odd–pinnately compound, 8″ to 12″ long, with 5 to 11 stalked leaflets;
leaflets, oblong-lanceolate, 3″ to 5″ long, 1″ to 2″
wide; apex, acuminate; base, wedge-shaped to
rounded; margin serrate; greenish yellow and glabrous
above, green below, with tufts of hairs along the
midrib and principal veins; rachis, slender, glabrous,
or sometime minutely hairy near the base.

Flowers.—Appearing before the leaves; perfect,
naked, in loose panicles; stamens, 2, purplish; pistil,
with an oblong ovary surmounted by a short, 2-lobed,
purplish style.

Fruit.—An oblong samara, 1″ to 2″ long; wing,
rounded, clasping the flattened seed to below the
middle.

Twigs.—Stout, rather conspicuously 4-angled; inter-
nodes, somewhat winged; at first reddish brown and
hairy, later becoming gray with scattered lenticels;
terminal buds, ovoid, acute, reddish brown, larger
than the lateral buds; leaf scars, U-shaped, with
a crescent-shaped row of bundle scars; pith, homogeneous; the expressed sap, turning blue upon
exposure.

Bark.—About ½″ thick, gray, with large, flattened
scales, which break up into smaller scales.

Habitat.—On rich, dry, limestone bottom lands and hills; less commonly on mountain slopes.

Distribution.—Most common in the Ohio and upper Mississippi River valleys but extending from Ontario through southern Michigan to Iowa and into Ohio, Indiana, Kentucky and Tennessee, Missouri, Kansas, Arkansas, and Oklahoma.

Importance.—Of some value in the manufacture of flooring, and once commonly used as a carriage wood. It is also the source of a blue dye; hence its common name. Blue ash is frequently planted as an ornamental.

Black Ash

Fraxinus nigra Marsh.

Habit.—A medium-sized tree, 40′ to 60′ in height and 1′ to 1½′ in diameter; with either a straight or a crooked bole and a small, narrow, shallow crown.

Leaves.—Opposite, deciduous, odd–pinnately compound, 12″ to 16″ long, with 7 to 11 sessile leaflets; leaflets, 4″ to 5″ long, 1½″ wide, oblong-lanceolate; apex, acute; base, wedge-shaped; margins, serrate; dark green and glabrous above, with axillary hairs and paler below; rachis, stout.

Flowers.—Appearing before the leaves; naked, polygamous, paniculate; staminate flowers, either on separate trees or appearing with perfect flowers in the same panicle; perianth, lacking; stamens, 2, with large, purple anthers; stigmas, purple, 2-lobed at the summit.

Fruit.—A more or less oblong, light-brown samara, 1″ to 2″ long; with a large seed and thin, oblong wing; wing, rounded or notched at the tip; seed, somewhat flattened.

Twigs.—Stout, glabrous, with flattened nodes and conspicuous lenticels; terminal buds, conical, brown to black, up to ½″ long; lateral buds, similar, but much smaller, the first pair inserted some distance below the terminal bud; leaf scars, nearly circular, with an oval ring of bundle scars; pith, white, homogeneous.

Bark.—Thin, gray to gray-black, with shallow fissures and interlacing, scaly ridges.

Habitat.—Most common on deep, rich, moist soils near streams and swamps, occasionally on mountain slopes; usually associated with other species such as arborvitae, maples, birches, boxelder, and tupelos.

Distribution.—Typically a northern species, but reaching its southern limits from Delaware to the mountains of West Virginia.

Importance.—An inferior timber species used mainly for baskets, chair bottoms, and chair splints and hoops and occasionally for interior trim in houses.

Carolina Ash

Fraxinus caroliniana Mill.

Habit.—A tree, occasionally becoming 40' in height, with a trunk 1' in diameter; with small branches, forming a somewhat rounded, narrow crown.

Leaves.—Opposite, deciduous, odd–pinnately compound, 7″ to 12″ long, with 5 to 7 stalked leaflets; leaflets, 3″ to 6″ long, 2″ to 3″ broad, oblong-ovate; apex, blunt or rounded; base, wedge-shaped; the margin, coarsely serrate-toothed; dark green above, paler below, glabrous; rachis, stout, circular in cross section.

Flowers.—Appearing before the leaves; dioecious, in panicles; the staminate, with a minute calyx and 2 to 4 stamens; the pistillate, with a small calyx and globular ovary surmounted by an elongated style, forked at its tip.

Fruit.—A broad, flattened, oblong-obovate samara, up to 3″ in length, ¾″ in width, often 3-winged;

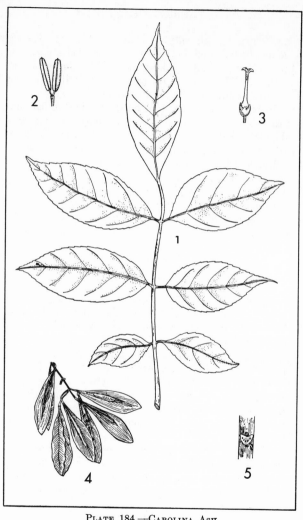

PLATE 184.—CAROLINA ASH

1. Leaf ×½. 2. Male flower ×3. 3. Female flower ×3.
4. Fruit cluster ×⅓. 5. Leaf scar ×1.

seed, elliptical, completely surrounded by the wing; wing, pointed or notched at the apex.

Twigs.—Slender, at first greenish pubescent, becoming brown or gray, with scattered lenticels; terminal buds, ⅛″ long, chestnut-brown; lateral buds, similar; leaf scars, semicircular, with a U-shaped row of bundle scars; pith, white, homogeneous.

Bark.—Thin, gray, with an irregularly scaly surface.

Habitat.—A swamp species; tolerant of excessive soil moisture and able to withstand periodic inundation; most commonly found in the shade of larger trees.

Distribution.—From Washington, D.C., south along the Atlantic coastal plain to Florida and west along the Gulf coastal plain to Texas; also in Cuba.

Importance.—Of no economic importance.

Florida Ash

Fraxinus pauciflora Sarg.

The Florida ash is a small tree confined to the swamps of southern Georgia and northern Florida. It is similar to the Carolina ash in that it develops flattened fruits with wide wings extending to the base of the seed cavity but may be distinguished from that species by its smaller leaves with 3 to 7 (mostly 5) leaflets and shorter fruit stalks. It is of no commercial value.

White Ash

Fraxinus americana L.

Habit.—An important tree, often 70′ to 80′ (rarely 125′) in height, with a 2′ to 3′ trunk; in the forest, developing a clear, straight bole, unbranched for many feet and supporting a narrow, pyramidal crown; open-grown trees, in contrast, produce branches within a few feet of the ground and form a broad, round-topped head of pleasing symmetry.

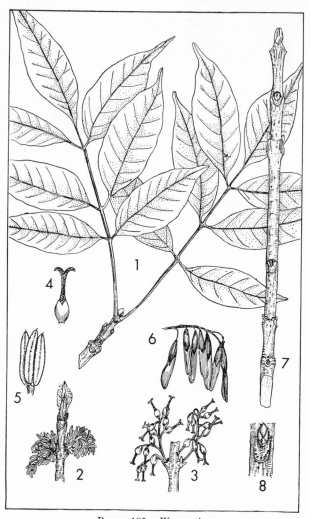

PLATE 185.—WHITE ASH

1. Foliage ×⅓. 2. Cluster of male flowers ×1. 3. Cluster of
female flowers ×1. 4. Female flower ×3. 5. Male flower ×3.
6. Fruit cluster ×⅓. 7. Twig ×¾. 8. Leaf scar ×1½.

Leaves.—Opposite, deciduous, odd–pinnately compound, 8″ to 13″ long, with 5 to 9 (mostly 7) stalked leaflets; leaflets, ovate-lanceolate, 3″ to 5″ long, 1½″ to 3″ wide; apex, acuminate; base, rounded or wedge-shaped; margin, toothed or entire; dark green and glabrous above, paler below and more or less pubescent; rachis, stout, grooved.

Flowers.—Appearing before the leaves, dioecious, apetalous, dark red, borne in dense panicles; the staminate, consisting of a minute, 4-lobed calyx and 2 stamens; pistillate flowers, with a deeply 4-lobed calyx and single pistil having a long, 2-parted style.

Fruit.—An oblong or somewhat spatulate, light-brown samara, up to 2″ long, borne in loose panicles; wing, slightly extended along the side of the spindle-shaped seed cavity.

Twigs.—Stout, dark green to greenish brown, with pale lenticels; terminal buds, dark brown, blunt, with 4 to 6 scales; lateral buds, smaller, with superposed buds sometimes present; leaf scars, broadly U-shaped, shallowly to deeply notched, with numerous bundle scars arranged in a U-shaped line; pith, white, continuous.

Bark.—Thick, gray-brown, becoming deeply and narrowly fissured by narrow, interlacing ridges, thus forming a somewhat diamond-shaped pattern.

Habitat.—Most commonly found on rich, moist, well-drained soils, in association with other species; in bottom lands near streams and often on low slopes.

Distribution.—Nova Scotia and New Brunswick west and south through northern Michigan to southern Minnesota; south to northern Florida and eastern Texas.

Importance.—A very important timber species prized as a source of wood for tool handles, implements, furniture, and refrigerators. White ash is planted as an ornamental as it is attractive, hardy, and relatively free of diseases.

Biltmore Ash

Fraxinus biltmoreana Bead.

Biltmore ash is very similar to white ash and is often mistaken for it. This species occurs principally in the southern Appalachian region and may be recognized by its hairy twigs and leaves, which otherwise resemble those of the white ash. Considerable variation in this species makes specific identification at times rather difficult.

Pumpkin Ash

Fraxinus profunda Bush.

This large tree with densely hairy leaves and twigs is most commonly observed in river bottoms subject to periodic and protracted inundations. It is found over large areas in both the northern and southern states but reaches its maximum development in the South, where trees 120′ in height and 3½′ in diameter have been reported. Some authorities recognize two forms. To the very hairy specimens they assign the technical name indicated above, but to those trees which develop smooth twigs and leaves, or leaves hairy only along the midrib of leaflets, they have given the name *F. profunda* var. *ashei* Palmer.

Pumpkin ash most nearly resembles red ash but may be separated from that species on the basis of leaf and fruit characteristics (see Key page 622).

Red Ash

Fraxinus pennsylvanica Marsh.

Habit.—A small to medium-sized tree, 30′ to 50′ in height and 12″ to 18″ in diameter; the base of the

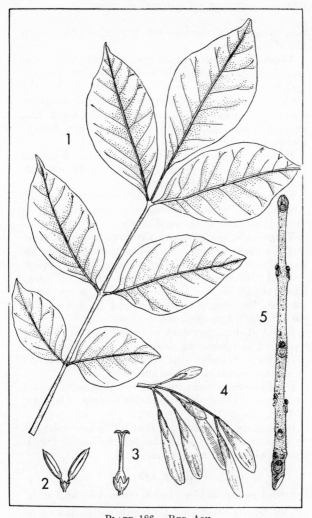

PLATE 186.—Red Ash
1. Leaf ×½. 2. Male flowers ×3. 3. Female flower ×3.
4. Fruit cluster ×½. 5. Twig ×¾.

bole occasionally more or less buttressed, the crown broad and irregular.

Leaves.—Opposite, deciduous, odd–pinnately compound, 8″ to 12″ long, with 7 to 9 stalked leaflets; leaflets, obovate, 4″ to 6″ long, about 1½″ wide; apex, acute; base, wedge-shaped; margin, entire or remotely (rarely sharply) serrate; yellow-green and smooth above, pale green and very hairy below; rachis, stout, hairy.

Flowers.—Appearing with the leaves; dioecious, apetalous, in woolly panicles; the staminate, purplish red; the pistillate, greenish red.

Fruit.—A light-brown, lanceolate samara, about 2″ long and ¼″ wide; the wing, tapering gradually to below the middle of the seed cavity.

Twigs.—Slender or stout, gray to gray-brown, those of the current season quite velvety, usually more or less flattened at the nodes; terminal buds, ovoid, covered with hairy, rusty-red scales, about ⅛″ long; lateral buds, similar but smaller; leaf scars, semi-circular, the bundle scars arranged in a U-shaped pattern; pith, homogeneous.

Bark.—Thin, gray-brown, with narrow fissures separated by interlacing ridges.

Habitat.—Widely distributed near streams and swamps, tolerant of inundation.

Distribution.—Nova Scotia to Manitoba, south to Kansas, Missouri, northern Mississippi, Alabama, and Georgia.

Importance.—Similar to that of white ash but developing a wood of somewhat inferior quality; occasionally cultivated as an ornamental.

Green Ash

Fraxinus pennsylvanica var. *lanceolata* (Borkh.) Sarg.

This tree is considered by many authorities to be merely a variety of the red ash, although there are those who accord it specific rank. It may be distinguished from red ash by its lustrous-green, sharply serrate, lanceolate leaflets and smooth twigs. There are numerous intergrading forms, and these make specific identification a matter of individual judgment. While green ash is commonly observed in moist situations, its ability to develop under the most adverse conditions has resulted in its widespread use for planting in the shelter-belt zone and similar areas. This form produces excellent timber; the tree is commonly used ornamentally.

THE FORESTIERAS

Forestiera Poir.

The genus *Forestiera* is represented by about 15 species of trees and shrubs found in the southern United States, Mexico, Central America, the West Indies, and South America. A single arborescent species (*F. acuminata* Poir.) occurs in the southeastern United States.

The forestieras have simple leaves, and some species are evergreen. The flowers, which are very small, are either dioecious or polygamous. The fruit is a more or less fleshy drupe, usually 1-seeded. While no great economic importance is attached to this genus, certain species are frequently cultivated as ornamentals.

Swamp-Privet

Forestiera acuminata Poir.

Habit.—A shrub or small to medium-sized tree, sometimes 50' in height, with a short trunk 8" to 12" in diameter; in the forest, producing a broad, open crown.

Leaves.—Opposite, deciduous, simple, elliptical, 2" to 4½" long, 1" to 2" broad; apex, acuminate;

base, wedge-shaped; margin, often remotely serrate above the middle, yellow-green and glabrous above, paler below; petiole, slender, ½″ long, occasionally obscurely winged.

Flowers.—Appearing before the leaves; dioecious, apetalous; staminate, in stalked clusters from the axils of yellow bracts, with 4 stamens, ovary abortive, inconspicuous; pistillate, in panicles 1″ long, ovary ovoid, narrowed into a slender style with a 2-lobed stigma, stamens absent or abortive.

Fruit.—An ovoid, purple, dry drupe, about 1″ long, narrowed at the base; stone, conspicuously ridged; seeds, compressed, striate, light brown.

Twigs.—Slender, light brown, warty, with numerous lenticels; terminal buds, ovoid, acute, ¹⁄₁₆″ long; lateral buds, smaller, similar, often superposed; leaf scars, small, circular and rounded, with a single U-shaped bundle scar; pith, homogeneous.

Bark.—Thin, dark brown, and remotely ridged.

Habitat.—On low-lying, moist soil near streams and swamps.

Distribution.—Scattered in suitable habitats in Indiana, Illinois, Tennessee, Missouri, Arkansas, Louisiana, and Texas; most common in Missouri, Arkansas, and Texas, but attaining largest size in Louisiana.

Importance.—Of some value as an ornamental.

THE FRINGETREES

Chionanthus L.

Chionanthus is a small genus represented by only two species. One of these is found in the United States; the other is a native of China.

The bark of the American species contains medicinal compounds. This form is also much planted as an ornamental.

Fringetree

Chionanthus virginicus L.

Habit.—A shrub, or sometimes attaining arborescent proportions and then becoming 20′ to 30′ in height with a short trunk 8″ to 12″ in diameter; with stout, ascending branches, forming a narrow, oblong head.

Leaves.—Opposite, deciduous, simple, ovate-oblong, 4″ to 8″ long, 1″ to 4″ broad; apex, acuminate; base, wedge-shaped; margin, entire, but often somewhat wavy; veins, forming a prominent, netlike pattern; dark green and glabrous above, paler below, with numerous hairs on the veins; petioles, stout, ¾″ long.

Flowers.—Appearing with the leaves; dioecious, fragrant; borne in loose, pendent, hairy, 3-flowered clusters, 4″ to 6″ long, subtended by bracts; perfect flowers, occasionally present; calyx, deeply 4-lobed; corolla, white, with 4 or sometimes with 5 or, 6, long, straplike lobes; stamens, 2 (rarely 4); ovary, 1-celled.

Fruit.—A dark-blue-black, oval drupe, occasionally covered with a whitish bloom, about 1″ long; seeds, ovoid, about ⅓″ long.

Twigs.—Stout, slightly angled, more or less pubescent, ashy gray, with subnodal thickenings; lenticels, large and scattered; terminal buds, broadly ovoid, acute, brown, ⅓″ long; lateral buds, smaller; leaf scars, elevated, semicircular, with numerous bundle scars arranged in a U-shaped pattern; pith, white, homogeneous.

Bark.—Thin, close, and with thin, appressed, brown, superficial scales.

Habitat.—On rich, moist soil near streams; occasionally found at altitudes up to 4,000′.

Distribution.—From Pennsylvania to Florida and west to Arkansas, Oklahoma, and Texas.

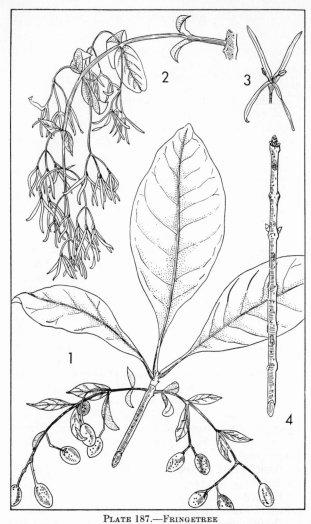

PLATE 187.—FRINGETREE

1. Foliage and fruit ×⅓. 2. Flower cluster ×½. 3. Flower ×1.
4. Twig ×¾.

Importance.—The bark is a source of a tonic and has been used as a diuretic and fever reductant; frequently cultivated for its ornamental value.

THE OSMANTHES

Osmanthus Lour.

The osmanthes comprise a group of about 10 species widely scattered in North America, Hawaii, and the Orient. The flowers of certain species are used in China to flavor tea, and several others are cultivated as ornamentals. Two species occur in the South.

KEY TO THE SOUTHERN SPECIES

1. Fruit, dark purple, about ½″ in diameter; flower stalks smooth........................**Devilwood** (p. 637)
1. Fruit, yellowish green, about ¾″ in diameter; flower stalks, hairy............**Bigfruit osmanthus** (p. 639)

Devilwood

Osmanthus americanus B. & H.

Habit.—A tree, becoming 50′ to 70′ in height, with a trunk 1′ in diameter; crown, long, narrow, and somewhat oblong (often shrubby).

Leaves.—Opposite, persistent, simple, oblong-lanceolate, 4″ to 5″ long, 1″ to 2½″ broad; apex, variable, acute, notched, or rounded; base, wedge-shaped; margin, entire and somewhat curled; bright green, leathery, and smooth above; paler below; petiole, stout, up to ¾″ long.

Flowers.—Appearing before the leaves; imperfect and perfect flowers on different plants; flowers, in 3-flowered cymes or racemes subtended by triangular bracts; calyx, 4-toothed; corolla, creamy white, tubular, 4-lobed at the summit; stamens, 2 (rarely 4); pistil, 1-celled (rudimentary on the male flowers).

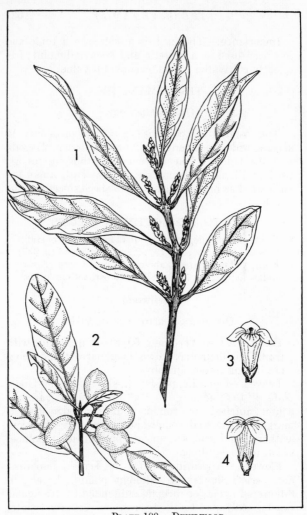

PLATE 188.—DEVILWOOD

1. Foliage and flowers ×½. 2. Fruit ×½. 3. Female flower
×2. 4. Male flower ×2.

Fruit.—A dark-blue, ovoid, thin-skinned drupe, about 1″ long, ½″ wide; seed, ovoid, brown, striate.

Twigs.—Slender, remotely angled, brown, with minute lenticels; terminal buds, lanceolate, reddish brown, ½″ long; lateral buds, smaller; leaf scars, elevated, circular, with a ring of small bundle scars; pith, white, homogeneous.

Bark.—Thin, close, gray-brown, with small, appressed scales, which exfoliate to reveal the reddish inner bark.

Habitat.—On moist, rich soil near swamps, ponds, and streams; less common on dry upland sites.

Distribution.—From North Carolina along the coast, south to Florida and west to Louisiana.

Importance.—Of value only as a cultivated ornamental.

Hammock Osmanthus

Osmanthus floridanus Chapm.

This small tree is restricted to hammocks of peninsular Florida and may be distinguished from devilwood osmanthus by its thicker, larger leaves, hairy flower stalks, and greenish-yellow fruits.

THE BORAGE FAMILY

Boraginaceae

The Borage Family, with 90 genera and about 1,500 species, is widely distributed through the warmer regions of both hemispheres. A few forms attain arborescent proportions, but the vast majority are herbaceous. Included in this group are the well-known forgetmenots, beggar's-lice, bluebells, and heliotropes.

Two genera, each represented by a single arborescent form, are included in our southern flora.

Synopsis of Southern Arborescent Genera

Genus	Leaves	Flowers	Fruit
Cordia	margins, often toothed above the middle	corolla, 1″ to 2″ across; style-branches forked	pear-shaped, partly or wholly covered by a persistent calyx
Bourreria	margins, entire from base to apex	corolla, ½″ to ¾″ across; style-branches not forked	globular, the calyx, small and basal

THE CORDIAS

Cordia L.

These are a group of about 250 species of trees and shrubs, the majority indigenous to tropical America. Some are productive of excellent timber, and others are propagated for their fruits. One of the 2 species native to the United States is a small tree of southern Florida and adjacent islands to the south and east.

Geiger-Tree

Cordia sebestena L.

Habit.—A large shrub or small tree, seldom more than 20′ to 30′ in height or 6″ to 8″ in diameter; in the forest, developing a small, ovoid crown composed of stout, ascending branches.

Leaves.—Alternate, simple, persistent, 5″ to 6″ long, 3″ to 4″ wide, mostly ovate; apex, acute or rounded; base, rounded or heart-shaped; margin, entire or occasionally toothed above the middle; dark green, with short, stiff hairs above, paler and usually smooth except along the principal veins below; petioles, stout, hairy, about 1½″ long.

Flowers.—Complete, borne in many-flowered, terminal clusters which appear irregularly throughout

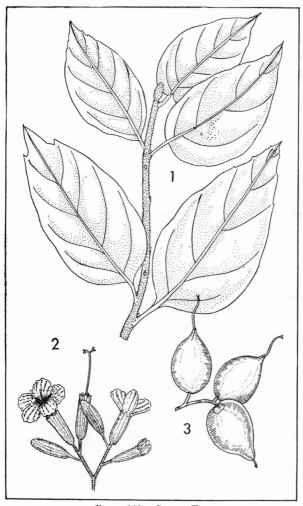

PLATE 189.—GEIGER-TREE
1. Foliage ×½.   2. Flowers ×½.   3. Fruit ×½.

the year; calyx, tubular, hairy, 5-lobed, the lobes tri-angular and toothlike, the tube characterized by many longitudinal ribs; corolla, 5-lobed, bright orange or deep yellowish orange, funnel-shaped, hairy on the outer surface, 1″ to 1½″ in diameter across the fully opened flower; stamens, 5, attached to the corolla tube; pistil, with a 4-celled ovary, the style-branches forked.

Fruit.—A pear-shaped, drupelike structure, com-pletely enclosed in a smooth, ivory-white, enlarged calyx, about 1¼″ long, the taillike remnant of the long exserted style commonly persistent.

Twigs.—Stout, changing from dark green to light gray during their 1st year; buds, naked; leaf scars, heart-shaped, with 2 central, circular clusters of bundle scars; pith, large, homogeneous.

Bark.—Dark brown to nearly black, with deep fissures separating narrow, superficially scaly ridges.

Habitat.—Hammocks and low ground near salt water.

Distribution.—Southern Florida, the Keys, and many of the West Indies.

Importance.—Used ornamentally throughout its range because of its showy, bright, flame-colored flowers.

THE STRONGBARKS
Bourreria P.Br.

These are a small group of 18 to 20 species of trees and shrubs restricted to the subtropics and tropics of the Americas. A single arborescent form occurs within our limits.

Bahama Strongbark
Bourreria ovata Meyers

Habit.—A moderately large tree, sometimes 40′ to 50′ in height and 10″ to 12″ in diameter, with a

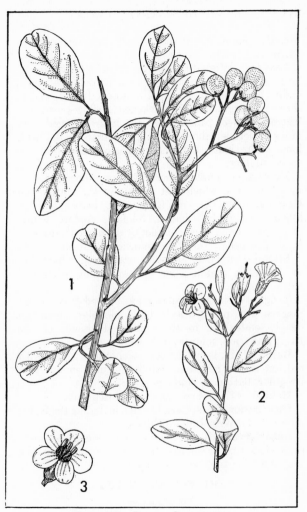

PLATE 190.—BAHAMA STRONGBARK
1. Foliage and fruit $\times \frac{1}{2}$. 2. Flower cluster $\times \frac{1}{2}$. 3. Flower $\times 1$.

broadly buttressed base, fluted bole, and narrow, irregular, rounded crown.

Leaves.—Alternate, simple, persistent, 2″ to 3″ long, 1″ to 2″ wide, mostly oval to obovate; apex, ending in a short tip, rounded, or notched; base, wedge-shaped; margin, entire, thickened; yellow-green and lustrous above, paler below, the midrib tinged with orange; petiole, about 1″ long, at first coated with long, white hairs, but becoming smooth during the early summer.

Flowers.—Complete, borne in many-flowered, terminal clusters, which first appear in the spring and then again in the late fall; calyx, bell-shaped, 5-lobed; corolla, bell-shaped, 5-lobed, creamy white, about ¾″ across when completely developed; stamens, 5; pistil, 4-celled, the style branches not forked.

Fruit.—Drupelike, globular, orange-red, about ½″ in diameter, seated upon the spreading persistent calyx.

Twigs.—Slender, orange-gray to red-gray, often marked with pale lenticels; buds, globular, seemingly deeply embedded in the epidermal tissues of the twig; leaf scars, minute; pith, continuous.

Bark.—Thin, brownish gray, sometimes tinged with red, on the larger stems exfoliating into small, thin, irregular, flattened, platelike scales.

Habitat.—Hammocks and moist, rich soils.

Distribution.—Southern Florida, including the Keys; many of the West Indian islands.

Importance.—Of no commercial value. A brew, somewhat similar to tea, has been made from the inner bark by the Bahama Island natives.

THE VERVAIN FAMILY
Verbenaceae

The Vervain Family includes about 80 genera and nearly 1,200 species of plants, the majority herbaceous.

East Indian teakwood is probably the best known and most valuable member of the group. Handsome foliage and showy flowers characterize many species. In the South, the monks pepperbush (*Vitex agnus-castus* L.) and certain of the lantanas are prized ornamentals.

Two genera, each represented by a single arborescent form, are found in our subtropical forests.

Synopsis of Southern Genera

Genus	Leaves	Flowers	Fruit
Avicennia	woolly below	in spikes; corolla 4-lobed	a capsule
Citharexylum	smooth below	in racemes; corolla, 5-lobed	a drupe

THE BLACK-MANGROVES

Avicennia L.

The black-mangroves comprise a small group of tidewater trees of widespread occurrence in the tropics of both the Old and the New World. These plants are unique both in their method of seeding and in their habit of growth. Each of the podlike fruit contains a large, heavy seed that continues to develop even after maturation. When released the developing seedling falls into the soft, mucky soils, which are often completely submerged at high tide, and immediately takes root. The young plant develops a system of submerged, lateral roots, from which arises a multitude of thick, leafless, unbranched knees. These are produced in such profusion that they actually form a network that retards the seaward flow of trash and debris brought in by incoming tidal waters and helps in the accumulation of silt and sand. In time, the foreshores of mangrove swamps are thus actually extended and new land surfaces formed.

Black-Mangrove

Avicennia nitida Jacq.

Habit.—A shrub, or small tree within the limits of our range, but through the West Indies often 60′ to 70′ in height and about 2′ in diameter; featuring a rounded widespread crown and spreading root system with numerous, aerating roots or knees.

Leaves.—Opposite, simple, persistent, mostly oblong to elliptical, 2″ to 4″ long, ¾″ to 1½″ wide; apex, acute or rounded; base, wedge-shaped; margin, entire, often slightly curled backward; dark green, lustrous above; gray and woolly below; petioles, about ½″ long, grooved above, swollen at the base.

Flowers.—Complete, borne regularly throughout the growing season in short, terminal, spikelike clusters; calyx, deeply 5-lobed; corolla, white, tubular, 4-lobed at the apex about ½″ wide; stamens, 4, attached to the corolla; ovary, 1-celled.

Fruit.—A small, somewhat compressed, egg-shaped, 2-valved, 1-seeded capsule, about 1½″ long and 1″ wide.

Twigs.—Slender, more or less 4-angled, at first finely hairy, ultimately orange-brown and smooth although often contorted; buds, minute, globular; leaf scars, U-shaped, with a central row of vascular scars; pith, homogeneous.

Bark.—Dark brown, with longitudinal and transverse fissures separating the flat, scaly, squarish blocks; when sloughing off, displaying an orange-red inner bark.

Habitat.—Low, tidal shores.

Distribution.—In the United States from St. Augustine, Florida, south through the Keys, the islands of Mississippi Sound, and Louisiana. Also abundant in the West Indies, on the Brazilian coast, across the Atlantic to the African west coast.

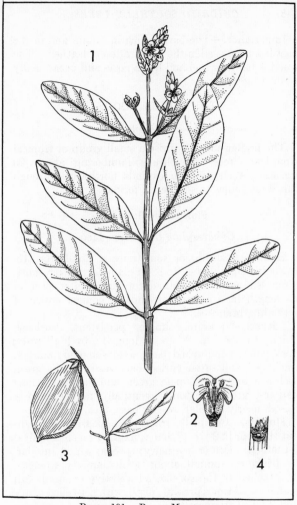

PLATE 191.—BLACK-MANGROVE

1. Foliage and flowers ×½. 2. Flower ×1. 3. Fruit ×¾.
4. Leaf scar ×1½.

Importance.—The bark is rich in tannin and in the past has been used in the preparation of leather. The wood is used for fuel and fence posts and occasionally as flooring.

THE FIDDLEWOODS

Citharexylum L.

The fiddlewoods comprise a small group of tropical American trees and shrubs numbering about 20 species. A single form extends northward through the West Indies to southern Florida.

Florida Fiddlewood

Citharexylum fruticosum Jacq.

Habit.—A shrub, or sometimes a small tree, 15′ to 30′ in height and 4″ to 8″ in diameter; with a short, often leaning bole, clothed for the greater part of its length in a narrow, irregularly conical crown of ascending branches.

Leaves.—Opposite, simple, persistent, leathery, oblong to obovate, 2″ to 4″ long, 1″ to 1½″ wide; apex, pointed or notched; base, wedge-shaped; margin, thickened and often curled backward; bright green and lustrous above, pale green and smooth below; petioles, grooved, stout, eventually falling from a raised, nearly circular, woody base, pith, continuous.

Flowers.—Complete, fragrant, appearing throughout the year in 2″ to 4″, hairy, axillary racemes; calyx; 5-toothed; more or less hairy; corolla, white, tubular, 5-lobed at the summit, about ⅛″ in diameter; stamens, 4, attached to the corolla, an abortive or sterile 5th stamen sometimes present; pistil, with a 4-celled ovary and 2-lobed stigma.

Fruit.—A nearly globular, reddish-brown to purplish-black, 2-stoned, 4-seeded drupe, about ⅓″ in

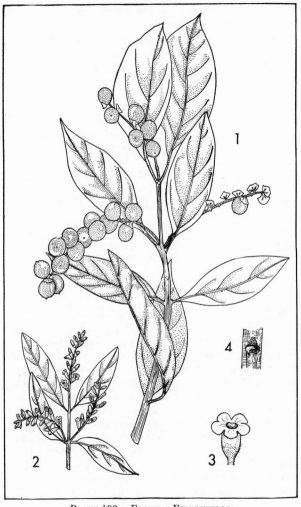

PLATE 192.—FLORIDA FIDDLEWOOD
1. Foliage and fruit ×⅔. 2. Cluster of flowers ×½.
3. Flower ×3. 4. Leaf scar ×2.

diameter; inserted upon the persistent, spreading, cuplike calyx.

Twigs.—Slender, ridged, angular in cross section, light grayish yellow, hairy; buds, globular, minute, hairy, more or less submerged in the twig; leaf scars, raised, woody, nearly circular, with a U-shaped band of bundle scars; pith, continuous.

Bark.—Very thin, light brown to reddish brown, separating at the surface into tiny, flat, closely appressed scales.

Habitat.—Shores and hammocks adjacent to tide-waters.

Distribution.—Southern peninsular Florida, the Keys, and the West Indies.

Importance.—Of no commercial value.

Remarks.—A form with hairy leaves (var. *villosum* Schulz) may not infrequently be encountered.

THE POTATO FAMILY

Solanaceae

This interesting family, with its numerous food and drug plants, comprises a group of about 85 genera and over 1,800 species, the majority herbaceous. Among the food plants mention should be made of the Irish potato, tomato, pepper, and eggplant. Belladonna, jimsonweed, and henbane are productive of powerful drugs used in pharmaceutical preparations. Tobacco, the principal cash crop of many of our southern farmers, is also included in the group. Among the plants of recognized ornamental value, are the petunias, matrimonyvine, and nightshade.

A single arborescent form of this family occurs in the South.

THE NIGHTSHADES

Solanum L.

This is a large genus, comprising about 1,200 species of herbs, vines, shrubs, and a few trees. A single arborescent form extends northward from the American tropics into southern Florida.

Mullein Nightshade

Solanum verbascifolium L.

Habit.—Ordinarily a shrub, but occasionally becoming about 20' in height with a single, erect stem, 4" to 6" in diameter; in the latter instance, with a broad, nearly flat-topped crown.

Leaves.—Alternate, simple, persistent, mostly ovate to elliptical, 4" to 7" long, 1" to 3" wide; apex, acute to long-tapered; base, rounded or wedgelike; margin, wavy, sometimes slightly thickened; yellow-green and hairy above, paler and more densely hairy below; petioles, about 1" long, densely hairy.

Flowers.—Complete, mostly in hairy, axillary clusters, 2" to 4" in length; calyx, hairy, 5-lobed, the teeth triangular; corolla, white, deeply 5-parted; stamens, 5, inserted on the corolla, their anthers much elongated; pistil, with a 2-celled ovary, slender style, and slightly thickened stigma.

Fruit.—Globular, yellow, berrylike, about ¾" in diameter, supported by the persistent, hairy calyx; seeds, numerous, minute, yellow, compressed.

Twigs.—Unarmed, stout, densely hairy, becoming smooth and orange-brown in their 2d winter; buds, hairy, small, and blunt; leaf scars, half-round, with 3 bundle scars; pith, spongy.

Bark.—Very thin, greenish yellow to yellowish gray, with numerous warty excrescences.

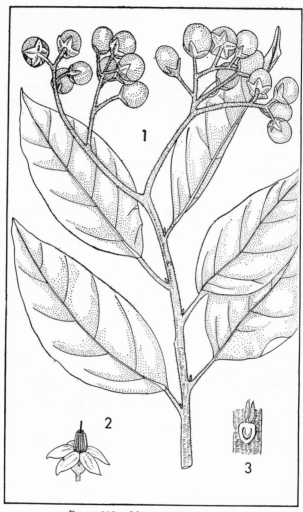

PLATE 193.—MULLEIN NIGHTSHADE
1. Foliage and fruit $\times \frac{1}{2}$.   2. Flower $\times 1$.   3. Leaf scar $\times 2$.

Habitat.—Shores and rich hummocks near the sea.

Distribution.—Widespread through the West Indies, Mexico, and Central America, and across the Pacific to southeastern China and tropics of the Old World; in the United States restricted to lower peninsular Florida and the Keys. Some authorities do not regard this as a truly indigenous Floridian species.

Importance.—None.

THE TRUMPETCREEPER FAMILY

Bignoniaceae

The Trumpetcreeper Family numbers about 100 genera and nearly 600 species of trees, shrubs, vines, and herbs, mostly tropical. Several of the arborescent species are productive of valuable cabinet woods, while others, because of their handsome foliage and showy flowers, are widely used for decorative purposes. Three of the 5 genera indigenous to the United States include tree species, and 2 of these, *Catalpa* and *Enallagma*, are represented in southern forests.

Synopsis of Southern Genera

Genus	*Leaves*	*Flowers*	*Fruit*	*Seeds*
Catalpa	opposite and whorled, deciduous, ovate	in panicles or corymbs; stamens, 2	a linear, woody capsule	winged
Enallagma	alternate, persistent, oblong	solitary or clustered; stamens, 4	**a berry**	**unwinged**

THE CATALPAS

Catalpa Scop.

These are a genus with seven species found in eastern China, the West Indies, and eastern United States. The two American species are both natives of the South.

KEY TO THE SOUTHERN CATALPAS

1. Fruit pods, slender, thin-walled; corolla, conspicuously blotched with yellow and purple on the inner surface..
 Southern catalpa (p. 654)
1. Fruit pods, stout, thick-walled; corolla, inconspicuously blotched with yellow on the inner surface, spotted externally with purple......**Northern catalpa** (p. 656)

Southern Catalpa   Indianbean

Catalpa bignonioides Walt.

Habit.—A medium-sized tree, rarely becoming 60′ in height, with a short bole 2′ to 4′ in diameter, separating into several oblique, heavy, brittle branches, forming a broad, rounded, open crown.

Leaves.—Opposite or whorled, deciduous, simple, broadly ovate, 5″ to 6″ long, 4″ to 5″ wide; apex, pointed or more or less rounded; base, heart-shaped; margin, entire or somewhat undulate (rarely lobed); light green, glabrous above, paler and pubescent below, with a conspicuous midrib; petioles, stout, 5″ to 6″ long.

Flowers.—Perfect, irregular, appearing after the leaves, in compact, many-flowered panicles, on slender stalks, 8″ to 10″ in length; individual flowers, about 2″ wide, with a small, glabrous, purplish calyx and a white, 5-lobed corolla with yellow and purple blotches on the inner surface; fertile stamens, 2; pistil, 2-celled, with a long style and 2 exserted stigmas.

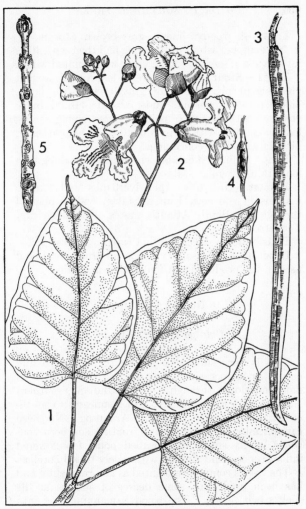

PLATE 194.—SOUTHERN CATALPA

1. Foliage ×½. 2. Flowers ×½. 3. Fruit ×½. 4. Seed
×¾. 5. Twig ×⅔.

Fruit.—A woody, linear, gray-brown capsule, 6″ to 20″ long, persistent until spring and then separating into 2 valves; seeds, 1″ long, gray, with pointed wings.

Twigs.—Stout, brittle, more or less forked, at first greenish purple, becoming gray-brown with large, pale lenticels; terminal buds, absent; lateral buds, globose, with about 6 pointed, overlapping scales; leaf scars, oval, with a circle of 10 to 12 bundle scars; pith, large, white, continuous.

Bark.—Thin, reddish brown or gray, breaking into long, thin, irregular scales.

Habitat.—Native to the riverbanks and swamp margins of southern United States; widely planted through the South Atlantic states, Kentucky, and Tennessee.

Distribution.—From Florida west to Mississippi.

Importance.—Of some value as an ornamental, and used in the production of fence posts and rails.

Northern Catalpa

Catalpa speciosa Engem.

This is very similar to the southern catalpa and occurs as an occasional tree in rich, moist soils on flats and slopes through southern Indiana, southern Illinois, western Kentucky, and Tennessee to southeastern Missouri and eastern Arkansas. Northern catalpa may be distinguished from its southern congener by its stout, thick-walled pods, few-flowered inflorescences, and flowers with palely tinted corollas.

The tree is commonly planted as an ornamental and has been used with some degree of success in the shelter-belt region. The wood is manufactured into cheap furniture, and quantities are used in the round for poles and posts.

THE CALABASHES

Enallagma Bail.

The calabashes comprise a small, tropical, American genus of trees indigenous to the West Indies, Central America, and Mexico. The blackcalabash reaches its northern limits in lower peninsular Florida.

Black-Calabash

Enallagma latifolia (Mill.) Small

Habit.—A small tree 20′ high, with a 4″ to 5″ trunk and slender, pendulous, warty branches forming a low, rounded head.

Leaves.—Alternate persistent, simple, oblong-ovate, 6″ to 8″ long, 1″ to 4″ wide; apex, short-pointed or rounded; base, narrowly wedge-shaped; margin, entire; at maturity leathery; lustrous, dark green above, yellow below, with a stout midrib, glabrous; petioles, short, stout, glandular.

Flowers.—Perfect, irregular, appearing with the leaves and again in the fall, solitary or in few-flowered clusters; calyx, green, with 2 large, prominent lobes; corolla, creamy white or purplish, about 2″ long, with purple bands on the lower side, obscurely 5-lobed; stamens, 4, in 2 ranks; pistil, with an ovoid, 2-celled ovary, narrow style, and 2-lobed stigma.

Fruit.—Berrylike, ovoid to oblong, 3″ to 4″ long, 1½″ to 2″ wide, remotely 4-ribbed; husk, dark green and somewhat roughened by minute spines; seeds, oblong, ½″ long.

Twigs.—Stout, somewhat angular, with enlarged nodes and persistent leaf bases; at first creamy white, becoming gray; buds, small, woody, persistent; pith, continuous.

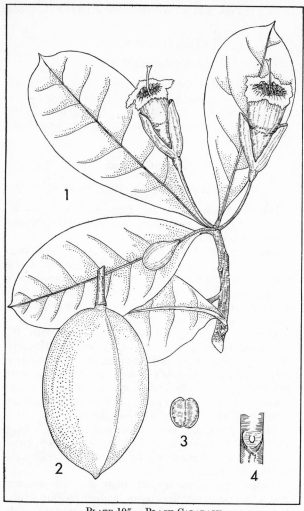

PLATE 195.—BLACK-CALABASH

1. Foliage and flowers ×½. 2. Fruit ×½. 3. Seed ×⅔.
4. Leaf scar ×1½.

Bark.—Thin, reddish brown, dividing into broad, thin scales.

Habitat.—Rich, moist soil near salt water.

Distribution.—In the region of the Bay of Biscayne in Florida; also on the Antilles, in Mexico, and south to Venezuela.

Importance.—None.

THE MADDER FAMILY

Rubiaceae

The Madder Family numbers about 350 genera and nearly 6,000 species of trees, shrubs, and herbs, some of them climbers. The best-known and most important member of the group is the coffee plant. Originally a native of Africa and Asia, this valuable plant and many of its horticultural varieties are now widely cultivated throughout the warmer regions of the world. Other commercial derivatives of this family include quinine, alizarin (a red dye principle), and lumber. The capejasmine and gardenias are members of this family and are prized for their beautiful and pleasantly scented flowers.

Four genera are represented in our subtropical forests by 1 or more arborescent species.

Synopsis of Southern Arborescent Genera

Genus	Leaves	Flowers	Fruit
Pinckneya	deciduous	in terminal and axillary clusters; calyx, unequally 5-lobed, the largest pinkish and petal-like	a capsule
Exostema	persistent	axillary, mostly solitary; calyx, equally 5-lobed	a capsule

Genus	*Leaves*	*Flowers*	*Fruit*
Cephalanthus	deciduous	in heads, solitary or clustered; calyx, 4- (rarely 5-) lobed	an achene
Guettarda	persistent	in axillary clusters; calyx, 4-lobed	drupaceous

Pinckneya   Fevertree

Pinckneya pubens Michx.

A Monotype

Habit.—A small tree, seldom more than 25′ to 30′ in height and 6″ to 10″ in diameter, with a narrow, rounded crown composed of numerous, slender, horizontal branches, an unbuttressed bole, and a shallow, fibrous root system.

Leaves.—Opposite, simple, deciduous, elliptical to ovate, 5″ to 8″ long, 3″ to 4″ broad; apex, acute; base, wedge-shaped; margin, entire; dark green, obscurely hairy above, pale green and hairy below; petioles, about 1″ long; stipules, extending between the petioles, awl-shaped, glandular.

Flowers.—Complete, borne in terminal and axillary, few-flowered clusters; calyx, 5-lobed, with 1 and sometimes 2 of the lobes becoming greatly enlarged and petallike, then rose-colored, up to 3″ long and 1½″ wide; corolla, trumpet-shaped, light yellow, 5-lobed at the summit, the lobes hairy, often recurved, marked on the inner surface with bright-red lines; stamens, 5, attached to the corolla, exserted; pistil, with a 2-celled ovary, long, narrow style, and remotely 2-lobed stigma, which extends above the stamens.

Fruit.—A 2-lobed, 2-valved, 2-celled, light-brown, papery, nearly globular capsule, about 1″ long; seeds, winged.

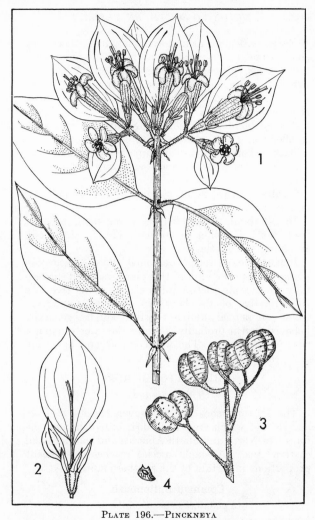

PLATE 196.—PINCKNEYA

1. Foliage and flowers $\times \frac{1}{3}$. 2. Detail of calyx showing much
enlarged petallike sepal $\times \frac{1}{2}$. 3. Fruit cluster $\times \frac{1}{2}$. 4. Seed
$\times \frac{1}{2}$.

Twigs.—Slender, at first extremely hairy, becoming smooth and reddish brown in their 2nd season; terminal buds, present, conical, with 1 or 2 pairs of exposed scales; lateral buds, much smaller, more nearly ovoid, and indistinctly scaly, leaf scars, crescent-shaped, with a crescent-shaped or occasionally C-shaped bundle scar, sometimes divided into many smaller scars; pith, chalky white, homogeneous.

Bark.—Thin, light brown, superficially scaly at the surface; scales, minute; inner bark, very bitter to the taste.

Habitat.—Margins of streams, wet bottomlands, and swamps.

Distribution.—Restricted; occurring along the coast from South Carolina to northern Florida (Leon and Washington Counties).

Importance.—In early colonial days a decoction prepared from the bark of this plant was used successfully in treating victims of malaria. This tree is a close relative of the Peruvian cinchona tree, from which commercial quinine is derived, and it is generally believed that it probably contains the same or similar curative products. The wood is soft and light and of no commercial value.

THE BUTTONBUSHES
Cephalanthus L.

The buttonbushes number seven species of trees and shrubs, which are widely distributed through the forests of North and South America and southern and eastern Asia. A single species reaches arborescent proportions in certain of the southern states.

Common Buttonbush
Cephalanthus occidentalis L.

Habit.—Throughout most of its range a profusely branched, often sprawling shrub, but in certain parts

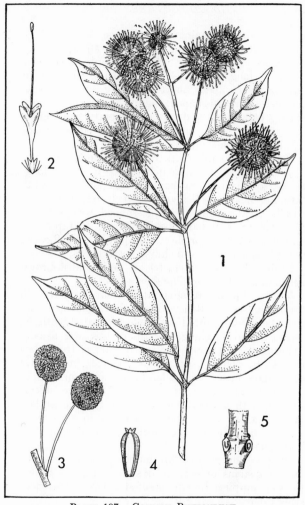

PLATE 197.—COMMON BUTTONBUSH
1. Foliage and flowers ×½. 2. Flower detail ×2. 3. Head
of fruit ×½. 4. Single fruit ×2. 5. Leaf scars ×½.

of the South becoming a small tree, 25′ to 35′ in height and 4″ to 8″ in diameter (max. 50′ by 1′).

Leaves.—Opposite or whorled, simple, deciduous, 4″ to 7″ long, 2″ to 3½″ wide, ovate, elliptical, or lance-shaped; apex, short- to long-tapered; base, rounded or wedge-shaped; margin, entire; dark green above, pale green and not infrequently hairy along the principal veins below; petioles, grooved, about ¾″ long; stipules, minute, triangular.

Flowers.—Complete, fragrant, borne in heads, 1″ to 1½″ in diameter, on slender stalks 1″ to 2″ long; heads, solitary or in racemose clusters of 2 to several, terminal or axillary; calyx tube, 4- (rarely 5-) lobed; corolla, creamy white, trumpet-shaped, with 4 (rarely 5) terminal, rounded lobes; stamens, 4 (rarely 5), seated upon the corolla tube; pistil, with 2-celled ovary, slender style, and club-shaped stigma.

Fruit.—A spheroid cluster of dark-reddish-brown achenes, about ¾″ in diameter.

Twigs.—Slender to moderately stout, dark reddish brown, glossy or often covered with a bloom during their 1st winter, dotted with pale, elongated lenticels; terminal buds, lacking, the tip of the twig usually dying back, or terminating in a cluster of fruits; lateral buds, solitary or paired, conical, indistinctly scaly, more or less embedded in the epidermal tissues of the twig; leaf scars, crescent-shaped to shield-shaped, with a C-shaped bundle scar, often broken into numerous small bundles arranged in a C- or U-shaped line; stipule scars, slitlike, often united; pith, homogeneous.

Bark.—Thin, gray-brown, and comparatively smooth on young stems, on older trunks becoming dark brown to deep purplish brown, fissured between flattened, scaly ridges.

Habitat.—Low ground; most abundant in swamps and along streams and margins of ponds; shrubby throughout much of its range, in some localities forming nearly impenetrable thickets.

Distribution.—Southeastern Canada; eastern United States from the coastal plains to the midwestern plains states; also through the Southwest to California and Mexico; south through peninsular Florida to Cuba.

Importance.—Occasionally used as an ornamental. The bark is said to contain products having pharmaceutical value.

THE PRINCEWOODS

Exostema Rich.

These are a group of about 20 species of trees and shrubs, all indigenous to the American tropics, but particularly abundant in the West Indies. A single species, Caribbean princewood, reaches its northern limit in southern Florida.

Caribbean Princewood

Exostema caribaeum R. & S.

Habit.—A shrub or small tree, 15′ to 25′ in height and 6″ to 10″ in diameter; with slender, ascending branches forming a narrow, rounded crown.

Leaves.—Opposite, simple, persistent through the 2d season, leathery, lance-shaped to oblong, 1″ to 3″ long, ½″ to 1½″ wide; apex, usually long-tapered, ending in a short, pointed tip; base, broadly wedge-shaped; margin, entire; dark green above, yellow-green below; petioles and midrib, orange, the former about ½″ long; stipules, triangular, sharp-pointed.

Flowers.—Complete, solitary in the leaf axils, fragrant, about 3″ long; calyx, in the form of a tube, 5-lobed at the summit, the lobes triangular; corolla, white, trumpet-shaped, with 5 spreading lobes; stamens, 5, attached to the corolla; pistil, with a 2-celled ovary, long, slender style, and headlike stigma.

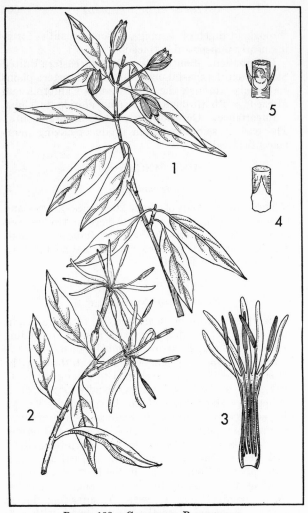

PLATE 198.—CARIBBEAN PRINCEWOOD

1. Foliage and fruit ×½.   2. Flower cluster ×½.   3. Longitudinal section through corolla showing attachment of stamens ×⅔.   4. Stipule ×2.   5. Leaf scar ×2.

Fruit.—A 2-celled, 2-valved, many-seeded capsule, about ¾″ long; seeds, oblong, winged, about ⅛″ long.

Twigs.—Slender, greenish brown to reddish brown, dotted with pale lenticels; buds, small, nearly globular, indistinctly scaly; leaf scars, essentially half-round to nearly circular, with a broad, C-shaped row of bundle scars; pith, homogeneous; stipule scars, encircling the twig between the nodes.

Bark.—Very thin, gray-white or nearly so, often mottled with orange; divided into squarish or rectangular plates.

Habitat.—Hammocks and sandy soils near tidewater.

Distribution.—Southern tip of Florida, the Keys, the West Indies, southern Mexico, and Central America.

Importance.—The bark was once used in the preparation of a tonic to reduce fever. Since the discovery of the cinchona bark (quinine), however, its use has been only local.

THE VELVETSEEDS

Guettarda Endl.

These are a group of about 50 shrubs and small trees found in wooded regions of tropical America, eastern tropical Africa, and Australia. Two arborescent forms occur in Florida.

KEY TO THE SOUTHERN VELVETSEEDS

1. Leaves, leathery, 2″ to 5″ long, their petioles and lower surfaces clothed with rusty-red, matted, woolly hairs; stone of fruit, 4- to 9-seeded.......................
      Roughleaf velvetseed (p. 668)
1. Leaves, thin, 1″ to 2½″ long, their petioles and lower surfaces clothed with silky, white hairs; stone of fruit, 2- to 4-seeded........**Everglades velvetseed** (p. 670)

Roughleaf Velvetseed

Guettarda scabra Lam.

Habit.—A small evergreen tree, seldom more than 20′ to 30′ in height or 12″ to 16″ in diameter, with an open, irregular crown, which often clothes the greater length of the bole.

Leaves.—Opposite, simple, persistent, leathery, oval to egg-shaped, 2″ to 5″ long, 1½″ to 3″ broad; apex, rounded, often ending abruptly in a short, pointed tip; base, rounded or somewhat heart-shaped; margin, entire, commonly curled under; dark green and somewhat roughened above, with rusty-red, matted hairs below; petioles, stout, about ½″ long, rusty-pubescent; stipules, awl-shaped, persistent.

Flowers.—Perfect, appearing intermittently during late winter and spring, borne in few-flowered, long-stalked, axillary cymes; calyx, oblong, 5- to 7-toothed, clothed with rusty-red hairs; corolla, white, tubular, about 1″ long, with 5 (rarely 7) expanding lobes at the summit; stamens, as many as the corolla lobes, not exserted; pistil, 4-celled, with a short style and head-like stigma.

Fruit.—A purplish drupe with a thin, rather dry flesh, and a 4- to 9-seeded stone, about ¼″ in diameter.

Twigs.—Moderately stout, clothed with rusty-red, woolly hairs; buds, globular, scarcely discernible; leaf scars, broadly U- to shield-shaped, with a U-shaped row of bundle scars; pith, homogeneous; stipules, awl-shaped, persistent.

Bark.—Dark brown, smooth or occasionally superficially scaly.

Habitat.—Dry, sandy soils near salt water.

Distribution.—Lower peninsular Florida, the Keys, and certain of the West Indian islands.

Importance.—None.

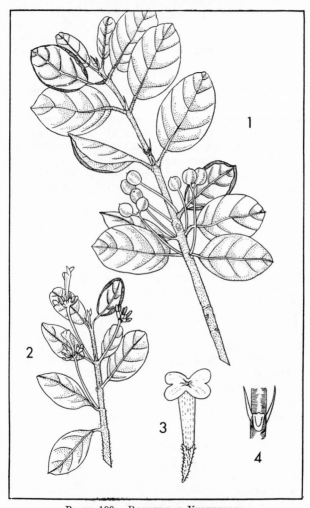

PLATE 199.—ROUGHLEAF VELVETSEED
1. Foliage and fruit ×½. 2. Cluster of flowers ×½.
3. Flower ×1. 4. Leaf scar ×1½.

Everglades Velvetseed

Guettarda elliptica Sw.

This is an even smaller tree than the preceding species, found in hammocks on the Everglade Keys and neighboring islands. Everglades velvetseed is characterized by small, silky leaves, 1″ to 2½″ long, and yellowish-white flowers, each with a 4-toothed calyx, 4-lobed, tubular corolla, and 4 stamens. The purplish drupe is fleshy and sweet and includes a single stone with 2 to 4 seeds. The tree is of no value.

THE HONEYSUCKLE FAMILY

Caprifoliaceae

The Honeysuckle Family includes 10 genera and about 275 species of trees, shrubs, lianas, and perennial herbs of wide distribution through the temperate regions of the world. The group is noted principally for the many fine shrubs with showy flowers and highly colored fruits, and many forms are prized ornamentals. While there are no timber trees of economic importance in this group, a few species are especially noted for the edible fruits they produce or for the medicinal compounds they contain.

Viburnum is the only genus with arborescent species indigenous to the South.

THE VIBURNUMS

Viburnum L.

This genus includes about 100 species of trees and shrubs, many with shapely leaves and showy flowers and fruit. Several species, 6 of which attain the stature of small trees, occur within our region.

KEY TO THE SOUTHERN ARBORESCENT VIBURNUMS

1. Flower clusters, long-stalked; fruit, globular; buds, brown-scurfy.........**Possumhaw viburnum** (p. 676)
1. Flower clusters, sessile or nearly so; fruit, oblong to ovoid; buds, red-scurfy to lead-colored............. 2

2. Leaves, sessile or nearly so...................... 3
2. Leaves, with petioles......................... 4

3. Stone of fruit, nearly globular; leaves, exhaling a strong scent when crushed.......**Walters viburnum** (p. 676)
3. Stone of fruit, flattened, more or less oblong; leaves, more or less scented........**Nashs viburnum** (p. 676)

4. Leaves, with long-tapered apices and sharply serrate margins.............**Nannyberry viburnum** (p. 676)
4. Leaves, with round, obtuse, or abruptly acute apices and entire, finely, or remotely toothed margins.... 5

5. Buds, rusty-red; leaves, dark green, glossy, with rusty-red hairs on petiole and principal veins.............
    Rusty blackhaw viburnum (p. 671)
5. Buds, lead-colored; leaves, dull, sometimes grayish green, without rusty-red hairs......................
    Blackhaw viburnum (p. 674)

Rusty Blackhaw Viburnum

Viburnum rufidulum Raf.

Habit.—A shrub, or occasionally a small tree, seldom more than 25′ in height and 6″ in diameter (max. 40′ by 1½′); in the forest, producing a short, clear bole, which supports an open, rounded or flat-topped head.

Leaves.—Opposite, simple, deciduous, mostly oval, 2″ to 3″ long, 1″ to 1½″ wide; apex, rounded or abruptly sharp-pointed; base, rounded or wedge-shaped; margin, finely, sometimes remotely, serrate;

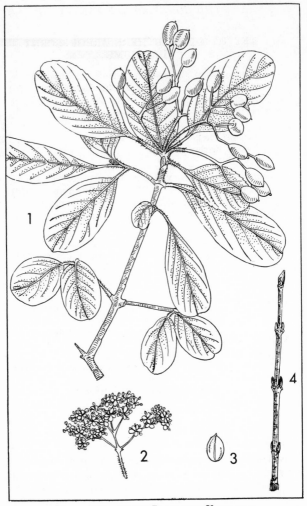

PLATE 200.—RUSTY BLACKHAW VIBURNUM
1. Foliage and fruit ×½. 2. Portion of flower cluster ×½.
3. Pit ×1. 4. Twig ×½.

dark green, glossy above, paler below, and with scattered, rusty-red hairs along the midrib and principal veins; petiole, stout, about $\frac{1}{2}''$ long, grooved, sometimes winged, often clothed with rusty-red hairs.

Flowers.—Perfect, appearing in flat-topped, sessile clusters, 4″ to 6″ in width; calyx, forming a cylindrical tube, crowned at the summit by 5 lobes, usually persistent under the fruit; corolla, white to cream-colored, with 5 spreading lobes; stamens, 5, attached to the corolla and alternating with the lobes; pistil, with a 1-celled ovary and 3 stigmatic lobes.

Fruit.—A more or less oblong, bright-blue drupe, sometimes covered with a whitish, waxy bloom, about $\frac{1}{4}''$ in diameter, borne on red stalks in drooping clusters; seed, globular or nearly so.

Twigs.—Stout, dotted with small, reddish-colored lenticels and clothed in woolly, rusty-red hairs, sometimes reduced to spurs; terminal buds, oblong, the scales valvate, covered with woolly, rusty-red hairs; lateral buds, similar but smaller; leaf scars, V-shaped to crescent-shaped, with 3 nearly equidistant bundle scars; pith, rounded or with an angular appearance when viewed in cross section, homogeneous.

Bark.—Dark brown to nearly black, divided transversely and longitudinally by narrow fissures, thus giving it the aspect of alligator leather; in this respect closely resembling that of the flowering dogwood.

Habitat.—An understory species found on a variety of sites but attaining its best development on moist, rich alluvium.

Distribution.—Southwestern Virginia west through southern Illinois to central Missouri and eastern Kansas; south to Florida and west through the Gulf region to eastern Texas.

Importance.—Used sparingly as an ornamental.

Blackhaw Viburnum

Viburnum prunifolium L.

Habit.—A shrub or small tree scarcely ever more than 25' in height or 6" in diameter; crown, usually irregular and composed of stiff, spreading branches.

Leaves.—Opposite, simple, deciduous, variable in shape but mostly oval to ovate, 1" to 3" long, about 1" to 2" wide; apex, rounded or abruptly short-pointed; base, rounded or wedge-shaped; margin, finely, sometimes remotely serrate; rather dull, often gray-green and smooth above, paler and smooth below; petiole, grooved, bright red, winged on vigorous growth, about ½" long.

Flowers.—Similar to those of the preceding species.

Fruit.—Similar to that of the preceding species except for the seed, which is oblong.

Twigs.—Slender, gray, sometimes tinged with red, rigid and often spinelike; terminal buds, commonly flask-shaped, lead-gray, the scales valvate, about ½" long; lateral buds, oblong and much smaller; leaf scars, V-shaped, with 3 bundle scars; pith, homogeneous.

Bark.—Similar to that of the preceding species.

Habitat.—Margins of forests, along fences and roads; often found in moist situations, but not so frequently encountered in such localities as the rusty blackhaw.

Distribution.—Southwestern Connecticut south through eastern Virginia and the Piedmont plateau of the Carolinas to southeastern Georgia; occurring intermittently through Kentucky, southern Ohio, southern Michigan, southern Illinois, Missouri, and eastern Kansas.

Importance.—Used sparingly as an ornamental.

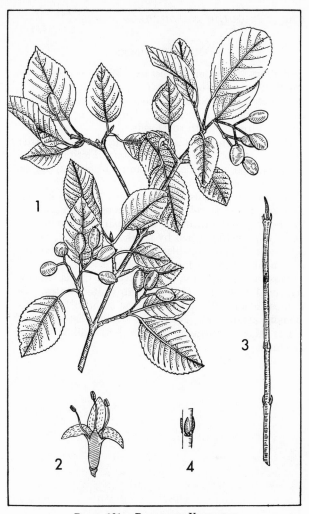

PLATE 201.—BLACKHAW VIBURNUM

1. Foliage and fruit ×½. 2. Flower ×3. 3. Twig ×½.
4. Whorled arrangement of buds ×⅔.

Other Viburnums

Walters viburnum (*V. obovatum* Walt.) is a shrub or small tree with sessile leaves and black fruit with nearly globular seeds. All parts of the plant exhale a strong scent when crushed. This tree occurs from coastal Virginia south to Florida.

Nashs viburnum (*V. nashii* Sm.) is a small tree endemic to the swamps of western Florida. It is characterized by sessile leaves and a black drupe with flattened, oblong seeds.

Nannyberry viburnum (*V. lentago* L.), also known as *wild raisin, sheepberry, nannyplum,* and *blackhaw,* reaches its southern limits within parts of the South. It may be distinguished by its sharply serrate, petiolate leaflets and blue-black fruits. It is a favorite ornamental plant in many localities.

Possumhaw viburnum (*V. nudum* L.) is widely scattered over much of the eastern United States. It is most commonly encountered as a shrub but occasionally attains tree size. It is readily distinguished from other viburnums by its long-stalked, floral clusters.

GLOSSARY

abortive—Barren or defective.

achene—A small, 1-celled, 1-seeded, unwinged fruit.

acidulous—Slightly acid; bitter.

acuminate—Long-tapering; attenuated.

acute—The shape of an acute angle.

aggregate—A cluster of ripened ovaries traceable to separate pistils of the same flower and all inserted on a common receptacle.

albumen—Nutritive substance surrounding the embryo of seeds.

ament—A catkin.

anastomosing—Interlacing.

anther—The pollen-bearing portion of the stamen.

apetalous—Without petals.

apophysis—Visible portion of a scale of a closed cone.

appressed—Lying flat; flattened.

arborescent—Treelike.

arcuate—Said of leaf venation where principal veins tend to parallel the margin.

arm—A thorn, spine, prickle, or bristle.

attenuate—Long-tapering.

aril—A fleshy appendage growing from the point of attachment of the seed.

axil—Upper edge between attached organ and its stem.

axile—Situated on the axis.

axillary—Situated in the axil.

axis—The center line of any organ.

baccate—Berrylike.

berry—A simple, fleshy fruit, with seeds embedded in the pulpy mass.

biglandular—With 2 glands.

bipinnate—Twice pinnate.

bisexual—Having both sex organs on the same individual.

blade—The expanded portion of a leaf.

boreal—Northern.

boss—A raised projection, usually pointed.

bract—Modified leaf of a flower cluster.

bud—An embryonic axis with its appendages.

calyx—The outer floral envelope.

capitate—In a head or headlike.

capsule—A simple, dry, dehiscent fruit, splitting along 2 or more lines of suture; the product of a compound pistil.

catkin—A flexible, usually pendent, scaly spike bearing apetalous, unisexual flowers.

ciliate—Descriptive of a margin fringed with hairs.

claw—Usually a hooklike structure, or in the shape of a hook.

collateral—Said of accessory buds arranged on either side of lateral buds.

compressed—Flattened.

cone—An inflorescence or fruit with overlapping scales.

cordate—Heart-shaped.

corolla—The inner floral envelope; composed of separate or united petals.

corymb—An indeterminate inflorescence; consisting of a central rachis bearing a number of branched, pedicelled (stalked) flowers; the lower pedicels much longer than the upper, thus resulting in a rounded or more or less flat-topped cluster.

crenate—Descriptive of a margin with blunt, rounded teeth.

crest—A crown, usually of hair.

cuneate—Wedge-shaped.

cyme—A determinate inflorescence consisting of a central rachis bearing a number of pedicelled flowers.

cymose—Cymelike.

deciduous—Not persistent; said of leaves falling in autumn or of certain floral parts after fertilization.

dehiscent—Descriptive of the opening of an anther, husk, or fruit by slits or valves.

deltoid—Triangular.

dentate—Descriptive of a margin with sharp teeth pointing outward.

depressed—Flattened from above.

determinate—Descriptive of an inflorescence in which the terminal flower opens slightly in advance of its nearest associates.

dimorphic—Occurring in 2 forms.

dioecious—Unisexual, with staminate and pistillate (or ovulate) flowers on separate plants.

disc—Flattened receptacle of a flower within calyx or corolla.

dorsal—Relating to the back.

drupaceous—Drupelike.

drupe—A simple, usually 1-seeded, fleshy fruit, the outer wall fleshy, the inner wall bony.

ellipsoid—The geometric figure obtained by rotating an ellipse on its longer axis.

elliptical—Resembling an ellipse.

emarginate—Having a shallow notch at the extremity.

entire—Wholly without teeth or other divisions such as lobes.

erose—Irregularly toothed or eroded.

excavated—Said of twigs in which the pith has disappeared as a result of the action of enzymes.

exserted—Extended; usually said of stamens extending beyond the corolla.

exstipulate—Without stipules.

falcate—Sickle- or scythe-shaped.

fascicled—In clusters or bundles.

fetid—Malodorous.

filament—That portion of the stamen which supports the anther.

fluted—Regularly marked by alternating ridges and groovelike depressions.

foliaceous—Leaflike in texture and appearance.

follicle—A dry fruit, the product of a simple pistil, dehiscing along 1 line of suture.

fruit—Seed-bearing part of a plant.

fusiform—Spindle-shaped.

glabrous—Smooth, free from hair of whatever form.

glandular—Furnished with glands, or of the nature of a gland.

glaucous—Covered with a white, waxy bloom.

globose—Globular, spherical.

head—A spherical or flat-topped inflorescence of sessile or nearly sessile flowers borne on a common receptacle.

hilum—Scar or point of attachment of the seed.

hirsute—With stiff, bristly hairs.

hoary—Densely grayish-white-pubescent.

hybrid—A natural or artificial cross, usually between 2 species.

imbricate—Overlapping.

imperfect—Said of flowers of 1 sex or in which the organs of 1 sex are abortive.

incised—More or less deeply and sharply cut.

incomplete—Descriptive of flowers in which 1 or more of the accessory or essential whorls are wanting.

indeterminate—Applied to inflorescences in which the flowers open progressively from the base upward.

indigenous—Native and original to an area.

inequilateral—Asymmetrical.

inflated—Bladderlike.

inflorescence—A characteristic floral arrangement.

inserted—Attached to or growing out of.

internode—That portion of a twig between the nodes.

involucre—A cluster of bracts subtending a flower, fruit, or inflorescence.

irregular—Said of flowers that are not bilaterally symmetrical.

keel—The united petals of a papilionaceous flower of the Leguminosae; a central, dorsal ridge.

laciniate—Cut into lobes separated by deep, narrow, irregular incisions.

lanceolate—Lance-shaped.

leaflet—A single unit of a compound leaf.

legume—A dry fruit, the product of a simple pistil, usually dehiscing along 2 lines of suture.

lenticular—Having the shape of a double convex lens.

linear—Long and narrow, with margins parallel or nearly so.

lobe—Any segment of an organ.

lobed—Divided into lobes, or having lobes.

lunate—Crescent-shaped.

midrib—The principal rib or central vein of a leaf.

monoecious—Having unisexual flowers, both sexes being borne on the same plant.

mucro—Short, narrow, and abrupt tip of a leaf or cone scale (bristle).

mucronate—Furnished with a mucro.

multiple—A cluster of ripened ovaries traceable to pistils of separate flowers.

naked bud—Bud without scales.

nectar—Sweet secretion of a flower.

nectareous—Nectar-producing.

nectar gland—Gland secreting nectar.

nectariferous—Nectar-producing.

nectiferous—Same as nectariferous.

node—That point upon a stem which bears a leaf or leaves, of whatever form.

nut—An idehiscent, usually 1-celled, 1-seeded fruit (usually the product of a compound ovary), with a bony, woody, leathery, or papery wall and generally partly or wholly incased in an involucre or husk.

nutlet—A diminutive nut.

ob——Prefix implying inversion.

obcordate—Inverted heart-shaped.

oblanceolate—Inverted lance-shaped.

oblong—Longer than broad, with the margins usually parallel.

obovate—Inverted ovate.

obovoid—Appearing as an inverted egg.

obtuse—Blunt.

ocrea—A basal sheath.

orbicular—Circular.

oval—Broadly elliptical.

ovate—Egg-shaped.

ovulate—Pertaining to the ovule; possessing ovules.

ovule—That which after fertilization becomes the seed.

palmate—Radially disposed.

panicle—A compound or branched raceme.

papilionaceous—Descriptive of the flowers of certain legumes having a standard, wings, and keel.

parted—Divided by sinuses that extend nearly to the midrib.

pedicel—The supporting stalk of a single flower.

peduncle—A primary flower stalk supporting either a cluster or a single flower.

peltate—Said of a cone scale that is shield-shaped and attached by its lower surface to the supporting stalk.

pendulous—Drooping, hanging, or declining.

perfect—Said of flowers having both sex organs present and functioning.

perianth—The floral envelope, of whatever form.

persistent—Said of leaves that are evergreen and of flower parts and fruits that remain attached to the plant for protracted lengths of time.

petal—The unit of the corolla.

petaloid—Resembling a petal.

petiole—The stalk of a leaf.

pinnate—Descriptive of compound leaves with the leaflets arranged on opposite sides along a common rachis.

pinnule—Blade or follaceous unit of a twice compounded leaf.

pistil—Seed-bearing organ of a flower.

pistillate—Furnished with pistils; generally descriptive of unisexual flowers.

pith—The central tissue of a twig.

pitted—Marked with small depressions.

plumose—Pubescent in a manner simulating a feather or plume.

polygamous—Bearing perfect and unisexual flowers on the same plant.

pome—A simple, fleshy fruit, the product of a compound pistil, with the seeds incased in a papery or cartilagenous wall.

preformed—Said of flowers and inflorescences that appear in the summer or early fall but that do not function until the following spring.

pubescent—Covered with short, fine, soft hairs.

punctate—Dotted with minute resin glands or cysts.

pyriform—Pear-shaped.

raceme—An indeterminate inflorescence consisting of a central rachis bearing a number of flowers with pedicels of nearly equal length, the basal flower opening slightly in advance of its nearest associates.

racemose—Resembling a raceme; in racemes.

rachis—The axis of a compound leaf or of an inflorescence.

receptacle—The expanded portion of the axis that bears the floral organs.

regular—Uniform in shape or distribution of parts.

reniform—Kidney-shaped.

repand—Wavy; undulate.

resin cyst—Cell or cavity containing resin.

reticulate—Forming a network.

revolute—Rolled backward.

rufous—Reddish brown.

rugose—Wrinkled; descriptive of leaf surfaces with sunken veins.

samara—A winged, achenelike fruit.

scabrous—With short, erect, stiff, bristly hairs.

seed—A ripened ovule.

sepal—A unit of the calyx.

serrate—Descriptive of sharp teeth pointing forward.

sessile—Without stalk of any kind.

sheath—A tubular envelope.

simple—In 1 piece or unit; not compound.

sinuate—Deeply or strongly wavy.

sinus—Recess, gap, or cleft between 2 lobes.

spatulate—Shaped like a spatula.

spike—An erect or rarely lax inflorescence consisting of an axis bearing a number of sessile flowers.

spine—A sharp, woody outgrowth from a stem.

spur—A short, compact twig with little or no internodal development.

stamen—The pollen-bearing organ of the flower.

staminodia—Plural of staminodium.

staminodium—An abortive or sterile stamen.

stellate—Having the shape of a star, or starlike.

stem—Main axis of the plant.

sterile—Unproductive.

stigma—That part of the pistil which receives the pollen.

stipule—A leafy appendage attached to the twig at the base of the petiole; usually borne in pairs.

stolon—A branch or shoot given off at the summit of a root.

striate—With fine grooves, ridges, or lines of color.

strobile—An inflorescence or cone featured by imbricated bracts or scales.

style—That part of the pistil which connects the ovary with the stigma.

succulent—Juicy or pulpy.

superposed—Inserted one above the other.

suture—Line of dehiscence.

terete—Circular in transverse section.

ternate—in 3's.

thorn—A sharp-pointed, modified branch.

tomentose—Furnished with dense, matted, usually woolly hairs.

trifoliate—Three-foliate; having 3 leaflets.

tubercle—A small, tuberlike body.

umbel—An indeterminate inflorescence consisting of several stalked flowers with a common point of attachment.

undulate—Wavy.

unisexual—Having functioning organs of only one sex.

valvate—Said of dehiscent fruits and buds whose valves or scales meet at the edges without overlapping.

ventral—Pertaining to the front or face of an organ.

whorl—Cyclic arrangement of like parts.

Selected References

1. ASHE, W. W. Loblolly or North Carolina Pine. *North Carolina Geological Economic Survey, Bull.* 24, 1915.

2. ————. Note on Magnolia and Other Woody Plants. *Torreya* **31**: 37–41, 1931.

3. ————. Black Walnut: Its Growth and Management. *U.S. Dept. Agr. Bull.* 933, 1921.

4. BATES, C. G. A Key to the Identification of Some Coniferous Seedlings. *Jour. Forestry* **23**: 278–281, 1925.

5. BERRY, E. W. Tree Ancestors. The Williams & Wilkins Company, Baltimore. 1923.

6. BLAKESLEE, A. F., and C. D. JARVIS. Trees in Winter. The Macmillan Company, New York. 1916.

7. BOISEN, A. T., and J. A. NEWLIN. The Commercial Hickories. *U.S. Dept. Agr. Bull.* 80, 1910.

8. BOWERS, C. G. Rhododendrons and Azaleas. The Macmillan Company, New York. 1925.

9. BRITTON, N. L. North American Trees. Henry Holt and Company, Inc., New York. 1908.

10. BROOKS, A. B. West Virginia Trees. *Agr. Exp. Sta. Bull.* 175, College of Agriculture of West Virginia University.

11. BROWN, H. P. Trees of the Northeastern States (a revised and enlarged Trees of New York State, Native and Naturalized). The Christopher Publishing House, Boston. 1937.

12. CHITTENDEN, A. K. The Red Gum. *U.S. Dept. Agr. Bull.* 58, 1906.

13. CLUTE, W. N. The Common Names of Plants and Their Meanings. W. N. Clute & Co., Indianapolis. 1931.

14. COKER, W. C., and H. R. TOTTEN. Trees of the Southeastern States. University of North Carolina Press, Chapel Hill. 1934.

15. DALLIMORE, W., and A. B. JACKSON. A Handbook of Coniferae. Edward Arnold & Co., London. 1923.

16. DAVIS, E. F. The Toxic Principle of *Juglans nigra* as Identified with Synthetic Juglone, and Its Toxic Effects on Tomato and Alfalfa Plants. *Amer. Jour. Botany* **15**: 620, 1928.

17. DYAL, S. C. A Key to the Species of Oaks of Eastern North America Based on Foliage and Twig Characters. *Rhodora* **38**: 53–63, 1936.

18. EDGERTON, D. P. The Forest—A Handbook for Teachers. *U.S. Dept. Agr. Misc. Circ.* 98, 1927.

19. FLETCHER, W. F. The Native Persimmon. *U.S. Dept. Agr. Farm Bull.* 685, new ed., 1935.

20. FOSTER, H. D., and W. W. ASHE. Chestnut Oak in the Southern Appalachians. *U.S. Dept. Agr. Circ.*, 135, 1908.

21. FROTHINGHAM, E. H. The Eastern Hemlock. *U.S. Dept. Agr. Bull.* 152, 1915.

22. GERRY, E., and others. A Naval Stores Handbook. *U.S. Dept. Agr. Misc. Pub.* 209, 1935.

23. GRANT, C. V., and H. A. HANSEN. Poison Ivy and Poison Sumach and Their Eradication. *U.S. Dept. Agr. Farm Bull.* 1166, 1929.

24. GRAY, ASA. Gray's Manual of Botany, 8th ed. American Book Company, New York. 1950.

25. GREELEY, W. B., and W. W. ASHE. White Oak in the Southern Appalachians. *U.S. Dept. Agr. Circ.* 105, 1907.

26. GREENWOOD, C. H. Trees of the South. University of North Carolina Press, Chapel Hill. 1939.

27. GROOM, P. Trees and Their Life Histories. Cassell & Co., Ltd., London. 1909.

28. HALL, W. L., and H. VAN SCHRENK. The Hardy Catalpa. *U.S. Dept. Agr. Bull.* 37, 1902.

29. HANSEN, A. A. Dangerous Poison Ivy. *Field & Stream* **34:** 19, 1930.

30. HARLOW, W. M. Identification of the Pines of the United States, Native and Introduced, by Needle Structure. *New York State Coll. Forestry Tech. Bull.* 32, 1931.

31. ———. Fruit Key and Twig Key. Dover Pub., 1946. 2 books: Fruit Key to Northeastern Trees and Twig Key to the Deciduous Woody Plants of Eastern N. America.

32. ——— and E. S. HARRAR. Textbook of Dendrology, 2d edition. McGraw-Hill Book Company, Inc., New York. 1941.

33. HARPER, R. M. Economic Botany of Alabama. *Univ. Ala. Mono.* 9, 1928.

34. HITCHCOCK, A. S. Descriptive Systematic Botany. John Wiley & Sons, Inc., New York. 1925.

35. HODSON, E. R., and J. H. FOSTER. Engelmann Spruce in the Rocky Mountains. *U.S. Dept. Agr. Forest Service Circ.* 170, 1910.

36. HOTTES, A. C. The Book of Shrubs. De La Mare Garden Books, New York. 1928.

37. ———. The Book of Trees. De La Mare Garden Books, New York. 1932.

38. HOUGH, R. B. Handbook of the Trees of the Northern States and Canada. Lowville, N.Y. 1907.

39. HUTCHINSON, J. The Families of Flowering Plants. Vol 1. Dicotyledons. Macmillan & Company, Ltd., London. 1926.

40. ILLICK, J. S.　Tree Habits: How to Know the Hardwoods. American Naturalist Association, Washington, D.C., 1924.
41. KORSTIAN, C. F., and W. D. BRUSH.　Southern White Cedar.　*U.S. Dept. Agr. Tech. Bull.* 251, 1931.
42. LAMB, G. N.　Willows: Their Growth, Use, and Importance.　*U.S. Dept. Agr. Bull.* 316, 1915.
43. LENHART, D. Y.　Initial Root Development of Longleaf Pine.　*Jour. Forestry* **32**: 459–461, 1934.
44. MATTOON, W. R.　Life History of Shortleaf Pine.　*U.S. Dept. Agr. Bull.* 244, 1915.
45. ———.　Longleaf Pine.　*U.S. Dept. Agr. Bull.* 1061, 1925.
46. ———.　Slash Pine—An Important Second-growth Tree. *Proc. Soc. Amer. Foresters* **11**: 405–416, 1916.
47. ———.　The Southern Cypress.　*U.S. Dept. Agr. Bull.* 272, 1915.
48. ———.　The Sprouting of Shortleaf pine in the Arkansas National Forest.　*Forestry Quart.* **6**: 158–159, 1908.
49. MCCARTHY, E. F.　Yellow Poplar: Characteristics, Growth and Management.　*U.S. Dept. Agr. Bull.* 356, 1933.
50. MEEHAN, T.　Historical Notes on the Arbor Vitae.　*Proc. Acad. Nat. Sci. Philadelphia* **34**: 110–111, 1882.
51. MICHAUX, F. A.　North American Sylva. Vols. 1, 2, and 3, D. Rice and A. N. Hart, Philadelphia, 1857.
52. MOHR, C., and F. ROTH.　The Timber Pine of the Southern United States.　*U.S. Dept. Agr. Bull.* 13, 1897.
53. MUENSCHER, W. C.　Keys to Woody Plants. Ithaca, N.Y. 1922.
54. NUTTALL, T.　North American Sylva. Vols. 1 and 2. D. Rice and A. N. Hart, Philadelphia. 1859.
55. OMAN, A. E.　Hardy Catalpa.　*Proc. Soc. Amer. Foresters* **6**: 45–52, 1911.
56. OTIS, C. H.　Michigan Trees. University of Michigan, Ann Arbor. 1926.
57. PALMER, E. J.　On Nuttall's Trail through Arkansas. *Jour. Arnold Arboretum* **8**: 24–55, 1927.
58. ———.　The Spontaneous Flora of the Arnold Arboretum. *Jour. Arnold Arboretum* **6**: 5–128, 1925.
59. ———.　Synopsis of North American Crataegi.　*Jour. Arnold Arboretum* **6**: 5–128, 1925.
60. PEATTIE, D. C.　The Romance of Andre Michaux.　*Nature Magazine* **10**: 259–260, 1927.
61. POOL, R. J.　Flowers and Flowering Plants. McGraw-Hill Book Company, Inc., New York. 1929.

62. PUTNAM, J. A., and H. BULL. The Trees of the Bottomlands of the Mississippi River Delta Region. U.S. Department of Agriculture unnumbered (mimeographed) publication, 1932.

63. REHDER, A. Manual of Cultivated Trees and Shrubs. The Macmillan Company, New York. 1927.

64. ROGERS, W. E. Tree Flowers of Forest, Park, and Street. Published by the author, Appleton, Wis. 1935.

65. SARGENT, C. S. Manual of the Trees of North America. Dover Publications, New York. 1961.

66. ———. Notes on North American Trees. II. *Carya. Botan. Gaz.* **66**: 229–258, 1918.

67. ———. The Silva of North America. 14 vols. Houghton Mifflin Company, Boston. 1890–1902.

68. SMALL, J. K. Manual of the Southeastern Flora. Published by the author, New York. 1933.

69. STEPHENS, E. L. How Old Are the Live Oaks? *Amer. Forestry* **37**: 739–742, 1931.

70. STERRETT, W. D. The Ashes: Their Characteristics and Management. *U.S. Dept. Agr. Bull.* 299, 1915.

71. STEVENSON, N. I. A Pocket Guide to Sixty Distinctive Tropical Trees. Published by the author, Fayette, Iowa. 1933.

72. SUDWORTH, G. B. Forest Atlas. Part I. Pines, 1913.

73. ———. Check List of Forest Trees of the United States. *U.S. Dept. Agr. Misc. Circ.* 92, 1927.

74. TRELEASE, W. Winter Botany. Urbana, Ill. 1918.

75. WEIGLE, W. G., and E. H. FROTHINGHAM. The Aspens. *U.S. Dept. Agr. Bull.* 93, 1911.

76. WETHNER, W. B. Some American Trees. The Macmillan Company, New York. 1935.

77. WILLIAMSON, A. W. Cottonwood in the Mississippi Valley. *U.S. Dept. Agr. Bull.* 24, 1913.

78. WISE, L. E. Drug from the Forest. *Amer. Forestry* **41**: 322–324, 1935.

79. ZIMMERMAN, P. W., and A. E. HITCHCOCK. Selection, Propagation, and Growth of Holly. *Floral Exchange,*.**81**: 19–20, 1933.

80. ZON, R. Loblolly Pine in Eastern Texas. *U.S. Dept. Agr. Bull.* 64, 1905.

81. KELSEY, H. P., and W. A. DAYTON. Standardized Plant Names. J. Horace McFarland Co., Harrisburg, 1942.

INDEX

Page numbers in **boldface** are for illustration pages.

A

Abies, 46, 78
Abies balsamea, 81
  fraseri, 79, **80**
Acer, 462
Acer barbatum, 474
  leucoderme, 474
  negundo, 464, **465**
  nigrum, 473
  pensylvanicum, 474
  rubrum, 466, **467**
  rubrum var. *drummondii*, 468
  rubrum var. *pallidiflorum*, 466
  rubrum var. *trilobum*, 468
  saccharinum, 469, **470**
  saccharum, 471, **472**
  saccharum var. *nigrum*, 473
  spicatum, 477
Aceraceae, 462
Achras, 593
Achras darienensis, 602
  emarginata, 602, **603**
  globosa, 602
  zapota, 593
Aerial roots, 260, 642
Aesculus, 478
Aesculus carnea, 478
  discolor, 483

Aesculus glabra, 482
  hippocastanum, 478
  octandra, 479, **480**
  pavia, 482
  sylvatica, 482
African limba, 533
African mahogany, 411
Ailanthus altissima, 401
Alabama chinkapin, 173
Alabama chokeberry, 344
Aleurites fordii, 415
Allegheny chinkapin, 170, **171**
Allegheny plum, 348
Allegheny serviceberry, 336
Alligator pear, 298
Almond, 339
  East Indian, 533
Alnus rubra, 148
Alternate-leaf dogwood, 563, **564**
Alvaradoa, 401, 402
Alvaradoa amorphoides, 402
Amelanchier, 324, 333
Amelanchier arborea, 334
  laevis, 336
American basswood, 514
American beech, 164, **165**
American chestnut, 168, **169**
American elm, 231, **232**
American holly, 443, **444**

689

American hornbeam, 158, **159**
American mountain-ash, 331, **332**
American plum, 350, **351**
American sapota, 593
Amyris, 390, 399
Amyris elemifera, 399
Amyris, sea, 399, **400**
Anacardiaceae, 423
Anamomis, 541, 545
Anamomis dicrana, 547
    simpsonii, 545
Aniba panurensis, 298
Annona, 292, 295
Annona glabra, 295
Annonaceae, 291
Appalachian basswood, 513
Apricot, 339
Aquifoliaceae, 442
Aralia, 552
Aralia spinosa, 553
Araliaceae, 552
Ardisia escallonioides, 587
Arkansas oak, 226
Ash, Biltmore, 630
    black, 624
    blue, 623
    Carolina, 625, **626**
    Florida, 627
    green, 632
    pumpkin, 630
    red, 630, **631**
    white, 627, **628**
Ashe basswood, 513
Ashe chinkapin, 172
Ashe hickory, 134
Ashe magnolia, 288
Ashes, 621
Ashleaf maple, 464
Asiminia triloba, 292

Aspen, bigtooth, 112
Aspens, 106
Atlantic white-cedar, 90, **91**
Austrian pine, 47
Avicennia nitida, 646
Avocado, 298
Azaleas, 568

B

Bahama lysiloma, 503, **504**
Bahama strongbark, 642, **643**
Baldcypress, 83, **84**
Baldcypress family, 82
Baloonvine, 483
Balsam firs, 78, 81
Bark, features of, 25
Basket oak, 194
Basswood, American, 514
    Appalachian, 513
    Ashe, 513
    Carolina, 515
    Colonel's Island, 513
    Florida, 514
    Georgia, 516
    gulf, 515
    hairy, 515
    highland, 517
    ivory, 517
    Louisiana, 515
    Michaux, 517
    Okaloosa, 516
    Quebec, 516
    white, 510, **511**
Basswood family, 507
Basswoods, 507
Baywood, 411
Bear oak, 203
Beaverwood, 251
Beech, American, 164, **165**
    bronze, 163

Beech, European, 163
Beech family, 162
Betula, 148, 149
Betula alleghaniensis, 154
   lenta, 152
   nigra, 149
   papyrifera var. *cordifolia*, 157
Bigfruit crab, 330
Bigfruit osmanthus, 639
Bigleaf magnolia, 288
Bigleaf shagbark hickory, 126
Bigleaf snowbell, 611, **612**
Bignoniaceae, 653
Bigtooth aspen, 112
Biltmore ash, 630
Biltmore crab, 329
Birch, black, 152, **153**
   mountain paper, 157
   river, 149, **150**
   yellow, 154, **155**
Birch family, 148
Bird cherry, 346
Biscayne prickly-ash, 396
Bitter pecan, 147
Bitterbush, 404, **405**
Bitternut hickory, 141, **142**
Bittersweet, 451
Bittersweet family, 451
Black ash, 624
Black birch, 152, **153**
Black-calabash, 657, **658**
Black cherry, 341, **342**
Black cottonwood, 110
Black hickory, 135
Black locust, 371, **372**
Black-mangrove, 646, **647**
Black maple, 473
Black oak, 208, **209**
Black spruce, 74
Black tupelo, 556, **557**

Black walnut, 118, **119**
Black willow, 103, **104**
Blackgum, 556, 558
Blackhaw viburnum, 674, **675**
Blackjack oak, 224, **225**
Blolly, longleaf, 273, **274**
Blue ash, 623
Bluebeech, 158
Blueberries, 568
Bluejack oak, 219
Bluff oak, 190
Boise de Rose, 298
Borage family, 639
Boraginaceae, 639
Boswellia, 409
Bottlebrush, 540
Bougainvilleas, 273
Bourreria, 640, 642
Bourreria ovata, 642
Boxelder, 464, **465**
Boxleaf eugenia, 544
Boxwoods, West Indies, 456
Briar, 568
Broadleaf evergreens, 2
Bronze beech, 163
Bucida, 533
Bucida buceras, 534
Bucida, oxhorn, 534, **535**
Buckeye, fetid, 482
   Ohio, 482
   painted, 482
   red, 482
   redflowering, 478
   southern, 483
   yellow, 479, **480**
Buckeye family, 478
Buckthorn, Carolina, 500, **501**
   shrubby, 500
Buckthorn bumelia, 601
Buckthorn family, 494
Buckwheat-tree, 440, **441**

Bumelia angustifolia, 601
 lanuginosa, 598
 lycioides, 601
 tenax, 601
Bumelia, buckthorn, 601
 gum, 598, **599**
 saffron-plum, 601
 tough, 601
Bumelias, 598
Buncombe crab, 328
Bur oak, 185, **186**
Burningbushes, 452
Burseraceae, 409
Bustic, willow, 596, **597**
Butterbough, 488, **489**
Butternut, 121, **122**
Buttonbush, 662, **663**
Button-mangrove, 536, 537
Buttonwood, 321

C

Caltrop family, 386
Calyptranthes, 541, 547
Calyptranthes pallens, 548
 zuzygium, 550
Camphor, 298
Canella, 525, **526**
Canella winterana, 525
Canellaceae, 525
Caper, dog, 313
 Jamaica, **312**, 313
Caper family, 311
Capparidaceae, 311
Capparis, 311
Capparis cynophyllophora, 313
 flexulosa, 313
 spinosa, 313
Caprifoliaceae, 670
Cardiospermum halicacabum,
 483

Caribbean princewood, 665,
 666
Carica papaya, 527
Carolina ash, 625, **626**
Carolina basswood, 515
Carolina buckthorn, 500, **501**
Carolina hemlock, 78
Carolina laurelcherry, 354, 355
Carolina red hickory, 141
Carolina silverbell, 615, **616**
Carpinus, 148, 157
Carpinus caroliniana, 158
Carya, 117, 123
Carya aquatica, 147
 ashei, 134
 carolinae-septentrionalis, 131
 cordiformis, 141
 floridana, 141
 glabra, 135
 glabra var. *angulata*, 138
 glabra var. *megacarpa*, 138
 glabra var. *reniformis*, 138
 illinoensis, 144
 lasiniosa, 126
 × *lecontei*, 147
 leiodermis, 134
 myristicaeformis, 144
 ovalis, 138
 ovalis var. *hirsuta*, 141
 ovalis var. *obcordata*, 141
 ovalis var. *obovalis*, 140
 ovata, 128
 pallida, 133
 texana, 135
 tomentosa, 131
 villosa, 138
Cashew, 423
Cassia bark, 298
Castanea, 153, 166
Castanea alabamensis, 173
 alnifolia, 173

Castanea alnifolia var.
  floridana, 173
  dentata, 168
  floridana, 173
  ozarkensis, 173
  pumila, 170
  pumila var. *ashei*, 172
Castorbean, 415
Catalpa bignonioides, 654
  speciosa, 656
Catalpa, northern, 656
  southern, 654, **655**
Cedar, cigarbox, 411
  pencil, 95
Cedar, elm, 242
Cedar family, 86
Cedrela odorata, 411
Celastraceae, 451
Celastrus scandens, 451
Celtis, 229, 248
Celtis laevigata, 252
  occidentalis, 249
  tenuifolia, 253
Cephalanthus, 660, 662
Cephalanthus occidentalis, 662
Cercis, 360, 374
Cercis canadensis, 374
Chalk maple, 474
Chamaecyparis, 86, 90
Chamaecyparis thyoides, 90
Chapman oak, 199
Cherries, 339
Cherry, bird, 346
  black, 341, **342**
  European sour, 339
  pin, 346, **347**
  sweet, 339
  wild red, 346
Cherrybark oak, 206
Chestnut, American, 168, **169**
Chestnut oak, 196, **197**

Chestnuts, 166
Chickasaw plum, 349
Chinaberry, 412
Chinatree, wild, 487
Chinese letchi, 483
Chinese tree-of-heaven, 401
Chinese tuliptree, 288
Chinkapin, Allegheny, 170, **171**
  Alabama, 173
  Ashe, 172
  Florida, 172
  Ozark, 173
Chinkapin oak, 192, **193**
Chinkapins, 166
Chionanthus, 631, 634
Chionanthus virginicus, 635
Chittamwood, 424
Chokeberry, Alabama, 344
  common, 344
  Georgia, 345
  South Alabama, 345
Christmas poinsettia, 414
Chrysobalanus, 325, 356
Chrysobalanus icaco, 356
  pellocarpus, 356
Chrysophyllum, 393, 604
Chrysophyllum cainito, 604
  oliviforme, 604
Cigarbox cedar, 411
Cinnamomum camphora, 298
  cassia, 298
  zeylandicum, 298
Citharexylum, 645, 648
Citharexylum fruticosum, 648
  fruticosum var. *villosum*, 650
Citrus, 389
Citrus fruits, 389
Cladrastis, 360, 376
Cladrastis lutea, 377
Clammy locust, 373
Classification of trees, 3

Cliftonia, 437
Cliftonia monophylla, 440
Coast hoptree, 398
Coastalplain willow, 106
Coccoloba, 268
Coccoloba laurifolia, 271
    uvifera, 269
Coco-plum, icaco, 356, **357**
Coco-plums, 356
Coffeetree, Kentucky, 363, **364**
Colonel's Island basswood, 513
Colorado blue spruce, 71
Colubrina arborescens, 503
    cubensis, 506
    reclinata, 503
    texensis, 503
Commiphora myrrha, 409
Common buttonbush, 662, **663**
Common chokecherry, 344
Common hoptree, 396, **397**
Common persimmon, 607, **608**
Common sweetleaf, 618, **619**
Common witchhazel, 318, **319**
Conifers, 2, 45
Conocarpus erecta, 536
Coralbean, eastern, 379, **380**
Corchorus, 507
Cordia sebestena, 640
Corkwood, Florida, 115, **116**
Corkwood family, 115
Cornaceae, 563
Cornus alternifolia, 563
    drummondii, 568
    florida, 565
Corylus, 148
Cotinus obovatus, 424
Cottonwood, black, 110
    eastern, 107
Cow oak, 194
Crab, bigfruit, 330

Crab, Biltmore, 329
    Buncombe, 328
    Dunbar, 329
    lanceleaf, 330
    Louisiana, 329
    Missouri, 329
    prairie, 329
    southern, 326, **327**
    wild sweet, 330
Crabapples, 326
Cranberries, 568
Crataegus marshallii, 339
    oxycantha, 338
Crossopetalum, Florida, 458, **459**
Crossopetalum rhacoma, 458
Croton tiglium, 415
Crown-of-thorns, 415
Cuba colubrina, 506
Cuban sabicu, 361
Cucumber-tree, 282, **283**
    yellow, 284
Cupania glabra, 492
Cupressaceae, 86
Custard-apple family, 291
Cyrilla family, 437
Cyrilla, swamp, 438, **439**
Cyrilla racemiflora, 437
Cyrillaceae, 437

D

Dahoon, 446
Darling-plum, 498, **499**
Deciduous holly, 448, **449**
Demerara greenheart, 299
Devilwood, 637, **638**
Devils-walkingstick, 553, **554**
Diamondleaf oak, 224
Diospyros, 607
Diospyros ebenum, 606

Diospyros texana, 610
  virginiana, 607
Dipholis, 593, 596
Dipholis salicifolia, 596
Dipteronia, 462
Dog caper, 313
Dogwood, alternate-leaf, 563, **564**
  flowering, 565, **566**
  roughleaf, 568
Dogwood family, 562
Doveplum, 271
Downy serviceberry, 334, **335**
Drummond red maple, 468
Drypetes, 415, 416
Drypetes diversifolia, 416
  lateriflora, 418
Dunbar crab, 329
Durand oak, 199

E

East Indian almond, 533
East Indian laurel, 533
Eastern coralbean, 379, **380**
Eastern cottonwood, 107
Eastern hemlock, 75, **76**
Eastern hophornbeam, 160, **161**
Eastern poplar, 107, **108**
Eastern redbud, 374, **375**
Eastern wahoo, 452, **453**
Eastern white pine, 49, **50**
Ebenaceae, 606
Ebony, 606
Ebony family, 606
Elaphrium simaruba, 409
Elliottia racemosa, 569
Elm, American, 231, **232**
  cedar, 242
  moose, 239
  September, 234, **235**

Elm, slippery, 237, **238**
  winged, 239, **240**
Elm family, 229
Enallagma, 653, 657
Enallagma cucurbitina, 657
Endiandra palmerstoni, 298
English hawthorn, 338
English laurel cherry, 353
Entandrophragma, 412
Erica arborea, 568
Ericaceae, 568
Erythrina, 360, 379
Erythrina herbacea, 379
Eugenia, 541
Eugenia anthera, 544
  axillaris, 542
  buxifolia, 544
  confusa, 544
  rhombea, 544
Eugenia, boxleaf, 544
  redberry, 544
  Smalls, 544
  spiceberry, 544
  white-stopper, 542, **543**
Euonymus, 451, 452
Euonymus atropurpureus, 452
Euphorbia heterophylla, 414
  splendens, 415
Euphorbiaceae, 414
European horsechestnut, 478
European sour cherry, 339
Everglades velvetseed, 670
Evergreens, 2
Exostema, 659, 665
Exostema caribaeum, 665
Exothea, 484
Exothea paniculata, 488

F

Fagaceae, 162
Fagus, 163

Fagus grandifolia, 164
  sylvatica var. *atropunicea*, 163
Falsebox, West Indies, 460,
  461
False-mastic, 594, **595**
Family, botanical concept of, 4
Fetid buckeye, 482
Fevertree, 660
Ficus, 254, 259
Ficus aurea, 260
  carica, 259
  laevigata, 262
Fiddlewood, Florida, 648, **649**
Fig, Florida strangler, 260, **261**
  shortleaf, 262
Fir, balsam, 78
Fishpoison-tree, 381, **382**
Flatwoods plum, 348
Florida ash, 627
Florida basswood, 514
Florida boxwood, 456, **457**
Florida chinkapin, 172
Florida corkwood, 115, **116**
Florida crossopetalum, 458, **459**
Florida cupania, 492, **493**
Florida fiddlewood, 648, **649**
Florida poisontree, 435, **436**
Florida soapberry, 487
Florida strangler fig, 260, **261**
Florida tetrazygia, 550, **551**
Florida torreya, 97, **98**
Fir, balsam, 81
  Fraser, 79, **80**
Florida trema, 246, **247**
Florida yew, 99, **100**
Flowering dogwood, 565, **566**
Flowers, organization of, 14–16,
  17
Forestiera, 621, 633
Forestiera acuminata, 633
Four-o'clock family, 272

Frankincense, 93
Franklinia, 521
Franklintree, 521
Fraser fir, 79, **80**
Fraser magnolia, 285, **286**
Fraxinus, 621
Fraxinus americana, 627
  biltmoreana, 630
  caroliniana, 625
  nigra, 624
  pauciflora, 627
  pennsylvanica, 630
  pennsylvanica var. *lanceolata*,
    632
  profunda, 630
  profunda var. *ashei*, 632
  quadrangulata, 623
Fringetree, 635, **636**
Fruits, of broadleaf trees, 18–
  19, **20**, 21
  of coniferous trees, 16

G

Garden plum, 339
Garrya, 562
Geiger-tree, 640, **641**
Genus, concept of, 4
Georgia basswood, 516
Georgia chokecherry, 345
Georgia hackberry, 253
Georgia oak, 213
Ginseng family, 552
Gleditsia, 359, 366
Gleditsia aquatica, 369
  × *texana*, 370
  triacanthos, 366
  triacanthos var. *inermis*, 369
Golden willow, 102
Gordonia, 518
Gordonia alatamaha, 521
  lasianthus, 519

Grass stage of longleaf pine, 53
Graytwig, gulf, 266, **267**
Green ash, 632
Greenheart, demerara, 299
Guaiacum, 387
Guaiacum sanctum, 387
Guava, 540
Guettarda, 660, 667
Guettarda elliptica, 670
 scabra, 668
Guiana rapanea, 590, **591**
Guianaplum, 418
Gulf basswood, 515
Gulf graytwig, 266, **267**
Gulf licaria, 309, **310**
Gum bumelia, 598, **599**
Gumbo-limbo, 409, **410**
Guttapercha, 592
Guttapercha mayten, 454, **455**
Gyminda, 451
Gyminda latifolia, 460
Gymnanthes, 415, 421
Gymnanthes lucida, 421
Gymnocladus, 359, 363
Gymnocladus dioicus, 363, **364**

H

Hackberry, 249, **250**
Hackberry, Georgia, 253
Hairy basswood, 515
Halesia, 610, 613
Halesia carolina, 615
 diptera, 613
 monticola, 617
 parviflora, 618
Hamamelidaceae, 314
Hamamelis, 314, 317
Hamamelis macrophylla, 320
Hamamelis virginiana, 318
Harbison willow, 106
Hardwoods, 2

Hawthorn, English, 338
 parsley, **337**, 339
Hawthorns, 336
Heath family, 568
Hemlock, Carolina, 78
 eastern, 75, **76**
Hercules-club, 393
Hevea brasiliensis, 415
 guianensis, 415
Hickory, Ashe, 134
 bigleaf shagbark, 126
 bitternut, 141, **142**
 black, 135
 northern red, 141
 nutmeg, 144
 pearnut red, 140
 pignut, 135, **136**
 red, 138, **139**
 scrub, 141
 shagbark, 128, **129**
 shellbark, 126, **127**
 southern shagbark, 131
 swamp, 134
 valley, 138
 water, 147
Highlands basswood, 517
Hippocastanaceae, 478
Hippomane, 415
Hippomane mancinella, 418
Hog-plum, 263
Holly, American, 443, **444**
 deciduous, 448
 mountain, 450
 tawnyberry, 446
Holly family, 442
Holywood lignumvitae, 387, **388**
Honeylocust, 366, **367**
 Texas, 370
Honeysuckle family, 670

Hophornbeam, eastern, 160, **161**
Horsechestnut, European, 478
Horsesugar, 618
Hortulan plum, 353
Huckleberries, 568
Hyperlate, 484
Hyperlate trifoliata, 490

I

Icaco coco-plum, 356, **357**
Ilex, 442
Ilex cassine, 446
  decidua, 448
  Krugiana, **446**
  monticola, **450**
  monticola var. *mollis*, 451
  opaca, 443
  opaca var. *xanthocarpa*, 445
  vomitoria, 448
Inch plum, 352
Indian bean, 654
Inkwood, 490, 491
Ivory basswood, 517

J

Jaquinia, 584
Jaquinia keyensis, 584
Jamaica caper, **312**, 313
Jamaica dogwood, 381
Jamaica nectandra, 303, **304**
Joewood, 584, **585**
Judastree, 230
Juglandaceae, 117
Juglans, 117, 118
Juglans cinerea, 121
  nigra, **118**
Jungleplum, 594
Junipers, 92
Juniperus, 86, 92

Juniperus communis, 92
  communis var. *montana*, 92
  phoenica, 93
  silicola, 95
  virginiana, 93

K

Kalmia, 574
Kalmia latifolia, 574
Kentucky coffeetree, 363, **364**
Keys to generic groups, 26–44
Khaya, 412
Kinds of trees, 2
Knotweed family, 268
Krugiodendron, 494
Krugiodendron ferrum, 495

L

Laguncularia, 534
Laguncularia racemosa, 538
Lanceleaf crab, 330
Larissa plum, 352
Lauraceae, 298
Laurel, East Indian, 533
Laurel family, 298
Laurel oak, 200, **201**
Laurel cherries, 353
Laurelcherry, Carolina, 354, **355**
  English, 353
  West Indies, 356
Leadwood, 495, **496**
Leaves, features of, 8–14
Leguminosae, 358
Leitneria floridana, 115
Leitneriaceae, 115
Letchi chinensis, 483
Letchi, Chinese, 483
Licaria, gulf, 309, **310**

Lidflower, myrtle-of-the-river, 550
  pale, 548, **549**
Lignumvitae, holywood, 387, **388**
Limba, African, 533
Lime prickly-ash, 391, **392**
Lime, wild, 391
Liquidambar, 314
Liquidambar styraciflua, 315
Liriodendron, 276, 288
Liriodendron tulipifera, 289
Little silverbell, 618
Live oak, 179, **180**
Loblolly-bay, 519, **520**
Loblolly pine, 55, **56**
Locust, black, 371, **372**
  clammy, 373
  shipmast, 373
Longleaf blolly, 273, **274**
Longleaf pine, 51, **52**
Louisiana basswood, 515
Louisiana crab, 329
Lyonia, 579
Lyonia ferruginea, 579
Lyonia, tree, 579, **580**
Lysiloma, 359, 361
Lysiloma bahamensis, 361
  sabicu, 363
  watsonii, 363
Lysiloma, Bahama, 361, **362**

M

Maclura, 254, 256
Maclura pomifera, 257
Madder family, 659
Magnolia, Ashe, 288
  bigleaf, 288
  Fraser, 285, **286**
  mountain, 285

Magnolia, pyramid, 287
  southern, 277, **278**
  umbrella, 285
Magnolia, 276
Magnolia acuminata, 382
  ashei, 288
  cordata, 284
  fraseri, 285
  grandiflora, 277
  macrophylla, 288
  pyramidata, 287
  tripetala, 285
  virginiana, 280
  virginiana var. *australis*, 282
Magnolia family, 275
Magnoliaceae, 275
Mahogany, African, 411
  West Indies, 412, **413**
Mahogany family, 411
Malus, 324, 325
Malus angustifolia, 326
  bracteata, 328
  coronaria, 330
  glabrata, 329
  glaucescens, 329
  ioensis, 329
  ioensis var. *bushii*, 329
  ioensis var. *creniserrata*, 329
  lancifolia, **330**
  × *platycarpa*, 330
  pumila, 325
Manchineel, 418, **419**
Mango, 423
Mangrove, 530, **531**
Mangrove family, 530
Manihot utilissima, 415
Maple, ashleaf, 464
  black, 473
  chalk, 474
  Drummond red, 468
  Florida, 474

Maple, moose, 474
  mountain, 477
  red, 466, **467**
  silver, 469, **470**
  striped, 474, 475
  sugar, 471, **472**
  trident red, 468
Maple family, 462
Maritime pine, 47
Marlberry, 587, **588**
Mayten, guttapercha, 454, **455**
Maytenus, 451, 454
Maytenus phyllanthoides, 454
Meadow beauty family, 550
Melaleuca leucadendron, 540
Melastomaceae, 550
Melia azedarach, 412
Meliaceae, 411
Metopium, 424, 435
Metopium toxiferum, 435
Mexican alvaradoa, 402, **403**
Mexican plum, 348
Michaux basswood, 517
Milkbark, 416, **417**
Missouri crab, 329
Mistletoe, 174
Mockernut hickory, 131, **132**
Monks pepperbush, 645
Moose elm, 239
Moraceae, 253
Morus, 253, 254
Morus alba, 254
  rubra, 254
Mossycup oak, 185
Mountain-ash, American, 331,
  332
Mountain holly, 450
Mountain-laurel, 574
Mountain magnolia, 285
Mountain maple, 477
Mountain paper birch, 157

Mountain silverbell, 617
Mountain stewartia, 522, **523**
Mulberry, red, 253, **254**
  white, 254
Mullein nightshade, 651, **652**
Myrica, 112
Myrica caroliniensis, 112
  cerifera, 113
Myricaceae, 112
Myrrh, 409
Myrsinaceae, 587
Myrsine family, 587
Myrtle oak, 202
Myrtle-of-the-river, lidflower,
  550

N

Nakedwood, Simpson, 545, **546**
  twinberry, 547
Nannyberry viburnum, 676
Nannyplum, 676
Nashs viburnum, 676
Nemopanthus mucronata, 442
Nightshade, Mullein, 651, **652**
Northern catalpa, 656
Northern red hickory, 141
Northern red oak, 206, **207**
Northern white-cedar, 87, **88**
Nutmeg hickory, 144
Nuttall oak, 219
Nyctaginaceae, 273
Nyssa, 555
Nyssa aquatica, 559
  aquatica var. *biflora*, 558
  ogeche, 561
  sylvatica, 556
Nyssaceae, 555

O

Oak, Arkansas, 226

Oak, basket, 194
  bear, 203
  black, 208, **209**
  blackjack, 224, **225**
  bluejack, 219
  bluff, 190
  bur, 185, **186**
  Chapman, 199
  cherrybark, 206
  chestnut, 196, **197**
  chinkapin, 192, **193**
  cow, 194
  diamond leaf, 224
  Durand, 199
  Georgia, 213
  laurel, 200, **201**
  live, 179, **180**
  mossycup, 185
  myrtle, 202
  northern red, 206, **207**
  Nuttall, 219
  Oglethorpe, 199
  overcup, 183, **184**
  pin, 214, **215**
  post, 181, **182**
  rock, 196
  scarlet, 216, **217**
  scrub, 203
  shingle, 220, **221**
  Shumard red, 213
  southern red, 203, **204**
  swamp chestnut, 194, **195**
  swamp white, 190, **191**
  swamp red, 205
  Texas, 213
  turkey, 211, **212**
  water, 227, **228**
  white, 187, **188**
  willow, 222, **223**
  yellow, 192
Ogeechee tupelo, 561

Oglethorpe oak, 199
Ohio buckeye, 482
Okaloosa basswood, 516
Olacaceae, 263
Olea europaea, 621
Oleaceae, 620
Olive family, 620
Orange, wild, 354
Oriental spruce, 71
Oriental walnut, 298
Osage-orange, 257, **258**
Osmanthus, bigfruit, 639
Osmanthus americanus, 637
  floridanus, 639
Ostrya, 148, 160
Ostrya knowltonii, 160
  virginiana, 160
Overcup oak, 183, **184**
Oxhorn bucida, 534, **535**
Oxydendrum arboreum, 577
Oysterwood, 421, **422**
Ozark chinkapin, 173

P

Painted buckeye, 482
Palaquium gutta, 592
Pale lidflower, 548, 549
Papaya, 527, **528**
Papaya family, 527
Paper-mulberry, 253
Paradise-tree, 406, **407**
Parsley hawthorn, **337**, 339
Pawpaw, 292, **293**
Pea family, 358
Peach, 339
Pear, 324
  alligator, 298
Pearnut red hickory, 140
Pecan, 144, **145**
  bitter, 147

Pecan hickories, 123
Pencil cedar, 95
Pepperbush, monks, 645
Persea, 299, 300
Persea borbonia, 300
    gratissima, 298
    palustris, 303
Persimmon, common, 607, **608**
    Texas, 610
Picea mariana, 74
    orientalis, 71
    pungens, 71
    rubens, 72
    sitchensis, 71
Picramnia, 401, 404
Picramnia pentandra, 404
Pignut hickory, 135, **136**
Pin cherry, 214, **215**
Pinckneya, 660, **661**
Pinckneya, 659
Pinckneya pubens, 660
Pinaceae, 45
Pine, Austrian, 47
    eastern white, 49, **50**
    loblolly, 55, **56**
    longleaf, 51, **52**
    pitch, 60, **61**
    sand, 70
    shortleaf, 67, **68**
    slash, 58, **59**
    Sonderegger, 55
    spruce, 70
    sugar, 46
    table-mountain, 63, **64**
    Virginia, 65, **66**
Pine family, 45
Pinus, 45
Pinus clausa, 70
    echinata, 67
    elliottii, 58
    glabra, 70

Pinus nigra, 47
    palustris, 51
    pungens, 63
    rigida, 60
    rigida var. *serotina*, 62
    serotina, 62
    strobus, 49
    sylvatica, 47
    taeda, 55
    thunbergii, 47
    virginiana, 65
Piscidia, 360, 381
Piscidia piscipula, 381
Pistachio, 229
Pitch pine, 60, 61
Planera, 229
Planera aquatica, 244
Planertree, 244, **245**
Planetree, 321
Platanaceae, 321
Platanus occidentalis, 321
    racemosa, 321
    wrightii, 321
Plum, Allegheny, 348
    American, 350, **351**
    Chickasaw, 349
    flatwoods, 348
    garden, 339
    hortulan, 353
    inch, 352
    larissa, 352
    Mexican, 348
    wildgoose, 349
Poinsettia, Christmas, 414
Poison-ivy, 430
Poison-oak, 430
Poison sumac, 428, **429**
    treatment for, 430
Poisontree, Florida, 435, **436**
Polygonaceae, 268
Pond pine, 62

Pond-apple, 295, **296**
Pondcypress, 85
Ponderosa pine, 46
Poplar eastern, 107, **108**
  Lombardy, 107
  swamp, 110, **111**
Populus, 106
Populus deltoides, 107
  grandidentata, 112
  heterophylla, 110
Possumhaw, 448, **449**
Possumhaw viburnum, 676
Post oak, 181, **182**
Potato family, 650
Prairie crab, 329
Prairie willow, 106
Prickly-ash, Biscayne, 396
  lime, 391, **392**
Princewood, Caribbean, 665, **666**
Prunus, 325, 339
Prunus alabamensis, 334
  alleghaniensis, 348
  americana, 350
  amygdalus, 339
  angustifolia, 349
  armeniaca, 339
  australis, 345
  avium, 339
  caroliniana, 354
  cerasus, 339
  domestica, 339
  hortulana, 353
  lantana, 352
  mexicana, 348
  munsoniana, 349
  myrtifolia, 356
  pensylvanica, 346
  persica, 339
  serotina, 341
  tenuifolia, 352

Prunus umbellata, 348
  virginiana, 344
Psidium guajava, 540
Ptelea trifoliata, 396
  trifoliata var. *mollis*, 398
Pulse family, 358
Pumpkin ash, 630
Pussy willow, 106
Pyramid magnolia, 287

Q

Quassia family, 401
Quebec basswood, 516
Quercus, 163, 173
Quercus alba, 187
  alba var. *latiloba*, 188
  arkansana, 226
  austrina, 190
  bicolor, 190
  chapmanii, 199
  cinerea, 219
  coccinea, 216
  durandii, 199
  falcata, 203
  falcata var. *leucophylla*, 206
  falcata var. *pagodaefolia*, 205
  georgiana, 213
  ilicifolia, 203
  imbricaria, 220
  laevis, 211
  laurifolia, 200
  laurifolia var. *tridentata*, 200
  lyrata, 183
  macrocarpa, 158
  marilandica, 224
  montana, 196
  -muehlenbergii, 192
  myrtifolia, 202
  nigra, 227
  nuttallii, 219

Quercus obtusa, 224
  oglethorpensis, 199
  palustris, 214
  phellos, 222
  prinus, 194
  rubra, 206
  shumardii, 213
  stellata, 181
  stellata var. *margaretta*, 183
  texana, 213
  velutina, 208
  virginiana, 179

R

Rapanea, Guiana, 590, **591**
Rapanea, 590
Rapanea guianensis, 590
Red ash, 630, **631**
Red buckeye, 482
Red hickory, 138, **139**
Red maple, 466, **467**
Red mulberry, 254, **255**
Red oaks, 174
Red spruce, 72, **73**
Red stopper, 544
Red bay, 300, **301**
Redberry eugenia, 544
Redbud eastern, 374, 375
Redcedar, eastern, 93, **94**
  southern, 95
  western, 87
Redflowering buckeye, 478
Redgum, 315
Redwood, 82
Reynosia, 494, 497
Reynosia septentrionalis, 498
Rhamnaceae, 494
Rhamnus, 494, 500
Rhamnus caroliniana, 500
  caroliniana var. *mollis*, 502
  lanceolata, 500

Rhizophora, 530
Rhizophora mangle, 530
Rhizophoraceae, 530
Rhododendron, 572
Rhododendron maximum, 572
Rhododendron, rosebay, 572
Rhus, 424, 427
Rhus copallina, 431
  quercifolia, 430
  radicans, 430
  typhina, 433
  vernix, 428
Ricinus communis, 415
River birch, 149, **150**
Robinia, 359, 370
Robinia pseudoacacia, 371
  pseudoacacia var. *rectissima*, 373
  viscosa, 373
Rock oak, 196
Rosaceae, 323
Rose family, 323
Rosebay rhododendron, 572, **573**
Roughleaf dogwood, 568
Roughleaf velvetseed, 668, **669**
Rubiaceae, 659
Rue family, 389
Rusty blackhaw viburnum, 671, **672**
Rutaceae, 389

S

Sabicu, Cuban, 361
Saffron-plum bumelia, 601
Salicaceae, 101
Salix, 101
Salix alba, 102
  alba var. *vitellina*, 102
  babylonica, 102
  discolor, 106

Salix harbisonii, 105
  humilis, 106
  longipes, 106
  longipes var. *wardii*, 106
  nigra, 103
Sand hickory, 133
Sand pine, 70
Sand post oak, 183
Sapindaceae, 483
Sapindus, 484
Sapindus drummondii, 487
  marginatus, 487
  saponaria, 485
Sapodilla family, 592
Sapota, American, 593
Sapotaceae, 592
Sassafras, 299, 306
Sassafras albidum, 306
Sassafras, 306, **307**
Satinleaf, 604, **605**
  West Indian, 602
Satinwalnut, 317
Satinwood, 394
Scarlet oak, 216, **217**
Schaefferia, 451, 456
Schaefferia frutescens, 456
Schoepfia, 263, 266
Schoepfia chrysophylloides, 266
Scotch pine, 71
Scrub hickory, 141
Scrub oak, 203
Sea amyris, 399, **400**
Seagrape, 269, 270
September elm, 234, **235**
Sequoia, 82
Serviceberry, Allegheny, 336
  downy, 334, **335**
Shagbark hickory, 128, **129**
Sheepberry, 676
Shellbark hickory, 126, **127**
Shingle oak, 220, **221**

Shining sumac, 431, **432**
Shipmast locust, 373
Shortleaf fig, 262
Shortleaf pine, 67, **68**
Shrubby buckthorn, 500
Shumard red oak, 213
Sideroxylon, 593, 594
Sideroxylon foetidissimum, 594
Silver maple, 469, **470**
Silverbell, Carolina, 615, **616**
  little, 618
  mountain, 617
  two-wing, 613, **614**
Simarouba, 401, 406
Simarouba glauca, 406
Simaroubaceae, 401
Simpson nakedwood, 545, **546**
Sitka spruce, 71
Slash pine, 58, **59**
Slippery elm, 237, **238**
Smalls eugenia, 544
Smoketrees, 424
Snowbell, bigleaf, 611, **612**
Soapberry, Florida, 487
  western, 487
  wingleaf, 485, **486**
Soapberry family, 483
Softwoods, 2
Solanaceae, 650
Solanum, 651
Solanum verbasifolium, 651
Soldierwood, 503, **504**
Sonderegger pine, 55
Sophora, mescal-bean, 386
  Texas, 384, **385**
Sophora, 380, 383
Sophora affinis, 384
  secundiflora, 386
Sorbus, 324, 331
Sorbus americana, 331
Sour tupelo, 561

Sourwood, 577, **578**
South Alabama chokecherry, 345
Southern bayberry, 113, **114**
Southern buckeye, 483
Southern catalpa, 654, **655**
Southern crab, 326, **327**
Southern forests, 1
Southern magnolia, 277, **278**
Southern red oak, 203, **204**
Southern redcedar, 95
Southern shagbark hickory, 131
Southern witchhazel, 320
Spanish stopper, 544
Sparkleberry, 582, **583**
Species, concept of, 4
Spiceberry eugenia, 544
Spikenards, 552
Spruce, black, 74
    red, 72, **73**
    Sitka, 71
Spurge family, 414
Staghorn sumac, 433
Stewartia, 518, 522
Stewartia malacodendron, 524
    ovata, 522
Stewartia, mountain, 522, **523**
    Virginia, 524
Stinking cedar, 97
Stinkwood, 299
Stopper, red, 544
    Spanish, 544
    white, 542
Storax family, 610
Striped maple, 474, **475**
Strongbark, Bahama, 642, **643**
Styracaceae, 610
Styrax, 610, 611
Styrax grandiflora, 611
Sugar maple, 471, **472**

Sugar pine, 46
Sugarberry, 252
Sumac, poison, 428, **429**
    shining, 431, **432**
    staghorn, 433
    winged, 431
Sumac family, 423
Swamp chestnut oak, 194, **195**
Swamp cyrilla, 438, **439**
Swamp hickory, 134
Swamp poplar, 110, **111**
Swamp-privet, 633
Swamp red oak, 205
Swamp tupelo, 558
Swamp white oak, 190, **191**
Swamp bay, 303
Sweet-cherry, 339
Sweet gale family, 112
Sweet bay, 280, **281**
Sweetgum, 315, **316**
Sweetleaf, common, 618, **619**
Sweetleaf family, 618
Swietenia, 412
Swietenia macrophylla, 411
    mahagoni, 412
Sycamore, 321, **322**
Sycamore family, 321
Symplocaceae, 618
Symplocos tinctora, 618

T

Table-mountain pine, 63, **64**
Tallowwood, 263, **264**
Tallowwood family, 263
Tamarind, wild, 361
Tawnyberry holly, 446
Taxaceae, 96
Taxodiaceae, 82
Taxodium distichum, 83
    distichum var. *nutans*, 85
    mucronatum, 82

Taxus, 96
Taxus floridana, 99
Tea family, 518
Teakwood, 645
Terminalia catappa, 533
   superba, 533
   tomentosa, 533
Tetrazygia, 500
Tetrazygia bicolor, 550
Tetrazygia, Florida, 550, **551**
Texas honeylocust, 370
Texas oak, 313
Texas persimmon, 610
Texas sophora, 384, **385**
Thea sinensis, 518
Theaceae, 518
Theophrasta family, 584
Theophrastaceae, 584
Thuja, 86, 87
Thuja occidentalis, 87
   plicata, 87
Tilia, 507
Tilia ashei, 513
   australis, 513
   caroliniana, 515
   cocksii, 515
   eburnea, 517
   floridana, 514
   georgiana, 516
   glabra, 514
   heterophylla, 510
   lasioclada, 515
   leucocarpa, 515
   littoralis, 513
   michauxii, 517
   neglecta, 516
   porracea, 516
   truncata, 517
Tiliaceae, 650
Toothache tree, 393
Torchwood family, 409

Torreya, Florida, 97, **98**
Torreya, 96
Torreya californica, 96
   taxifolia, 97
Torrubia, 272
Torrubia longifolia, 273
   obtusata, 275
Tough bumelia, 601
Tree fruits, 16
Tree habits, 7
Tree lyonia, 579, **580**
Tree names, 4
Tree-of-heaven, Chinese, 401
Trema, Florida, 246, **247**
Trema, 229, 246
Trema micrantha, 246
Trident red maple, 468
True hickories, 123
Trumpetcreeper family, 653
Tsuga, 46, 75
Tsuga canadensis, 75
   caroliniana, 78
Tuliptree, 289
   Chinese, 288
Tupelo, black, 556, **557**
   Ogeechee, 561
   sour, 561
   swamp, 558
   water, 559, **560**
Tupelo family, 555
Tupelo gum, 559
Turkey oak, 211, **212**
Twigs, features of, 21–25
Twinberry nakedwood, 547
Two-wing silverbell, 613, **614**

U

Ulmaceae, 229
Ulmus, 229, 230
Ulmus alata, 239

Ulmus americana, 231
  crassifolia, 242
  rubra, 237
  serotina, 234
Umbrella magnolia, 285

V

Vaccinium, 581
Vaccinium arboreum, 582
  arboreum var. *glaucesens*, 584
  macrocarpum, 582
Valley hickory, 138
Velvetseed, everglades, 670
  roughleaf, 668, **669**
Verbenaceae, 644
Vervain family, 644
Viburnum, blackhaw, 674, 675
  nannyberry, 676
  Nashs, 676
  possumhaw, 676
  rusty blackhaw, 671, **672**
  Walters, 676
Viburnum, 670
Viburnum lentago, 676
  nashii, 676
  nudum, 676
  obovatum, 676
  prunifolium, 674
  rufidulum, 671
Virginia pine, 65, **66**
Virginia stewartia, 524
Vitex agnus-castus, 645

W

Wahoo, eastern, 452, **453**
Walnut, black, 118, **119**
  white, 121
Walnut family, 117
Walters viburnum, 676

Ward willow, 106
Water hickory, 147
Water oak, 227, **228**
Water tupelo, 559, **560**
Waterelm, 244
Waterlocust, 369
Weeping willow, 102
West Indian satinleaf, 604
West Indies boxwoods, 456
West Indies falsebox, 460, **461**
West Indies laurelcherry, 356
West Indies mahogany, 412, **413**
Western redcedar, 87
Western soapberry, 487
Western white pine, 46
White ash, 627, **628**
White basswood, 510, **511**
White-cedar, Atlantic, 90, **91**
  northern, 87, **88**
White-mangrove, 538, **539**
White-mangrove family, 533
White mulberry, 254
White oak, 187, 188
White stopper, 542
White-stopper eugenia, 542
White walnut, 121
White willow, 102
Whitewood, 266
Wild chinatree, 487
Wild cinnamon family, 525
Wild-dilly, 602, **603**
Wild lime, 391
Wild orange, 354
Wild raisin, 676
Wild red cherry, 346
Wild sweet crab, 330
Wild tamarind, 361
Wildgoose plum, 349
Willow, black, 103, **104**
  coastalplain, 106

Willow, golden, 102
  Harbison, 105
  prairie, 106
  pussy, 106
  Ward, 106
  weeping, 102
  white, 102
Willow bustic, 596, **597**
Willow family, 102
Willow oak, 222, **223**
Winged elm, 239, **240**
Winged sumac, 431
Wingleaf soapberry, 485
Winterberry, 448
Witchhazel, common, 318, **319**
  southern, 320
Witchhazel family, 314

X

Ximenia, 263
Ximenia americana, 263

Y

Yaupon, **447**, 448
Yellow birch, 154, **155**
Yellow buckeye, 479, **480**
Yellow cucumber-tree, 284
Yellow oak, 192
Yellow-poplar, 289, **290**
Yellowheart, 394
Yellowwood, 377, **378**
Yew, Florida, 99, 100
Yew family, 96

Z

Zanthoxylum, 390
Zanthoxylum americanum, 390
  clava-herculis, 393
  clava-herculis var. *fruticosum*,
    394
  coriaceum, 396
  fagara, 391
  flavum, 394
Zygophyllaceae, 386

THE STORY OF GARDENING:

From the Hanging Gardens of Babylon to the Hanging Gardens of New York

by Richardson Wright

The author of this book was the editor of "House and Garden Magazine" for 35 years and a member of the board of directors of New York's Horticultural Society. He was also one of the most widely-read writers on gardening, for his love of the subject shows through every page of his books. This warm and informative text, one of Wright's best, covers 6,000 years of gardening history, from the earliest efforts of primitive men to the gardens high atop New York's skyscrapers.

There are discussions of Chinese and Japanese gardens; the formal Mohammedan gardens with their water pools; early Greek and Roman gardens and their statuary; Italy's monastic and villa gardens; Spanish patios, the source of present-day gardens in California, Florida, and the Southwest; formal gardens of France; Dutch tulip gardens; three centuries of English gardening and their influences on American styles; the beginnings of Naturalism; American gardening from early Colonial times to the city gardens of today. These discussions involve the gardening literature and philosophy of the various eras, the plants and flowers that enjoyed special favor, and the fascinating personalities that played important roles.

And they are all illustrated with more than 100 photographs and drawings, including a Byzantine tree fountain, a medieval may tree, examples of topiary art and hedge sculpture, an early Japanese garden, Tudor garden layouts, a modern German version of the traditional rock garden, summer houses in an Indian garden, a New York terraced garden, winter and summer treatment of orange trees in 17th-century Holland, Renaissance Florentine formal gardens, and many other uncommon gardens, furnishings, and decorative embellishments used through the centuries.

Full of exciting garden ideas as well as a wealth of gardening lore, this history of the long and surprisingly complex evolution of garden types and techniques is certain to please all amateur and professional horticulturists. It is surely a must for the shelves of everyone who has a home garden of his own—or would like to have one.

"No contemporary American could have told the story so well . . . delightful reading," Saturday Review of Lit. "A rare pleasure," Boston Transcript. "An amazing, a superb book . . . a masterpiece of writing," Books.

Unaltered, unabridged republication of original edition. List of full-page illustrations. Total of 104 illustrations. Extensive bibliography. Index. x + 475pp. 5⅜ x 8½.

21105-3 Paperbound **$2.50**

LIFE HISTORIES OF NORTH AMERICAN BIRDS

by Arthur Cleveland Bent

The all-inclusiveness of Bent's volumes on North American birds has made them classics of our time. Arthur Cleveland Bent was one of America's outstanding ornithologists, and his twenty-volume series on American birds, published under the auspices of the Smithsonian Institute, forms the most comprehensive, most complete, and most-used single source of information in existence. No ornithologist, conservationist, amateur naturalist or birdwatcher should be without a copy; yet copies are increasingly hard to come by. Now, however, Dover Publications is republishing at inexpensive prices the entire series.

It is unlikely that Bent's monumental work will ever be superseded, or even equalled. It was compiled through the lifetime work of a remarkable scientist, and it had behind it the resources of a government agency. It will be used perpetually, not only as a reference work, but as an unequalled introduction.

Despite its scholarly stature, however, this set of volumes is delightful to read. It is easy in its presentation, personable and chatty in style, often narrative, and will offer hours of delightful reading to anyone interested in birds. No previous knowledge of biology or ornithology is needed to follow it in all its detail.

Volumes will appear in approximately this order:

Birds of Prey   (2 volumes)
Shore Birds   (2 volumes)
Diving Birds
Gulls and Terns
Petrels, Pelicans, etc.
Wild Fowl   (2 volumes)
Marsh Birds
Gallinaceous Birds
Woodpeckers

Cuckoos, Goatsuckers, Hummingbirds, etc.
Flycatchers, Larks, Swallows, etc.
Jays, Crows, Titmice
Thrushes, Kinglets, etc.
Nuthatches Wrens, Thrashers, etc.
Wagtails, Shrikes, Vireos, etc.
Wood Warblers
Blackbirds, Orioles, Tanagers, etc.

All volumes are complete and unabridged, printed upon quality paper, sewnbound so that pages will never fall out, with all illustrations of the originals. Approximately **$2.75** per volume.

WOODCRAFT AND CAMPING
by George W. Sears ("Nessmuk")

Written at a time when woodlore and woodcraft were vital skills, and when America's wilderness regions offered a true opportunity for "roughing it," this book has remained a classic through three or four generations of readers. The author, George W. Sears, is best known as "Nessmuk," and if ever there was a Daniel Boone, this must have been the man! His knowledge of how to get along on camping, hiking, and hunting trips—and of how to get the most out of such experiences—is unsurpassed.

No book has ever inspired so many readers to get out and try out-door living for themselves. Nessmuk is so sincerely appreciative of the pleasures and peace of mind that come from direct contact with nature that the appeal of the woods becomes almost irresistible as you read through his pages. A treasure-chest of useful, specific information, instructions, and suggestions on every aspect of woodcraft, his book is also an inspiration that cannot fail to arouse genuine enthusiasm among Scouts, day-school students, young campers, and other youth groups. And adult readers find its appeal just as exciting.

The author's straightforward devotion to out-door life and recreation provides refreshing reading whether you are a nature enthusiast or not. But it is to the confirmed outdoorsman, to the reader in charge of group nature activity, and to the novice camper or hiker that the book is primarily directed. With its fund of practical advice and its contagious spirit, it should be a constant companion on trips and woodland outings, just as it has been for countless other readers for over fifty years.

Slightly abridged and altered republication of 1920 edition. Index. 12 illustrations. ix + 105pp. 5⅜ x 8½.   21145-2 Paperbound **$1.25**

THE PUMA: MYSTERIOUS AMERICAN CAT

By Stanley P. Young and Edward A. Goldman

The puma (alias "cougar," "mountain lion," "panther," "catamount," etc.) is perhaps the most successful and dangerous of American predators. A deadly hunter of wild animal prey, he is best known to us through the fearsome tales of his attacks on man and livestock; as such he has been the legitimate object of predator control activities from the Yukon to the Straits of Magellan. Yet this magnificent animal's destructiveness and his threat to man's well-being has been somewhat overestimated. This book offers a better understanding of the puma and his mysterious ways. Prepared by two of America's outstanding mammalogists, it is the definitive study of the life-form.

Part I (by S. P. Young) is a comprehensive survey of the puma's history, life habits, and its relationship to man. Making full use of the reports of hundreds of naturalists and woodsmen of the present and past (including Daniel Boone, Lewis and Clark, Darwin, etc.) and the results of numerous government-sponsored field studies spanning more than a quarter-century, the author furnishes exhaustive information on the animal's physical features (coloration, size, weight, strength, etc.), abilities, geographical distribution, breeding habits, enemies, tracks, diseases, food, economic and ecological value, and extensive details on the hunting, trapping, and control of the puma by man. No other book gives you such a complete portrait of this fascinating beast.

The second half of the book (Classification of the Races of the Puma, by the late E. A. Goldman) lists 30 subspecies of Felis concolor, with full descriptions of the distinguishing characteristics of each variety. Also covered are the evolutionary history of the species and its general physical attributes, including photographs and tabulated data on cranial differences, etc. Throughout the book there is a wealth of illustrative material: distribution maps, photos of pumas in their natural habitats, characteristic poses, treed by dogs and hunters, their food, tracks, traps, and the like.

Trappers and hunters, stock raisers, outdoorsmen, natural historians, students, and others will find this an extremely useful and authoritative study of methods of control, identification, and classification, as well as an engrossing account of the puma's life history. Here is also a strong argument—despite the animal's reputation as the leading predator of the New World—for a reasonable conservation approach to this distinctive American species.

Unaltered, unabridged reproduction of original (1946) edition. Foreword. 50-page bibliography of 746 entries. Index. 93 plates, including 165 black-and-white photographic illustrations. 6 figures. 13 tables. xiv + 358pp. 5⅜ x 8⅜. 21184-3 Paperbound **$3.00**

THE BEHAVIOUR AND SOCIAL LIFE OF HONEYBEES
By C. Ronald Ribbands

This outstanding book offers a definitive survey of all the facets of honeybee life and behavior. The industrious lives of these insects and their highly-efficient, interdependent patterns of social organization have made them fascinating objects of study for centuries, and, because they are easily kept and observed, we know more about their ways and habits than we do about any other insect. In this work, Professor Ribbands has brought together the results of experimentation and research from scientific journals and widely-scattered sources from all over the world, and he has presented this accumulated knowledge in interesting, everyday terms that both scientist and layman will appreciate.

Beginning with a basic coverage of physiology, anatomy and sensory equipment—including a full description of the structural differences between worker, queen, and drone, the author also gives a thorough account of the behavior of honeybees in the field. He deals with such questions as how temperature, rain, wind, etc., affect foraging activity and how bees find their way home and back to food areas, covering the details of pollen and nectar gathering, foraging range, mating habits, etc. An important section explains how individuals communicate in various field and hive situations: recruitment to feeding areas (with a discussion of the intricate dances which indicate where these areas are), selection of a home, recognition of companions, the defense of the community, and the like.

There is also an extensive treatment of life within the community, considering the activities of food sharing, wax production, comb building, and brood rearing, the causes of swarming, the queen, her life and relationship with the workers, the evolution of the community and adaptation to a restricted food supply, and many other matters. This is an invaluable book for the beekeeper, natural historian, biologist, entomologist, social scientist, et al. The general reader will find the nontechnical exposition extremely informative and engrossing.

"A 'MUST' for every scientist, experimenter and educator, and a happy and valuable selection for all interested in the honeybee," AMERICAN BEE JOURNAL. "Recommended in the strongest of terms," AMERICAN SCIENTIST. "Erudite, as well as interesting . . . well-documented," NATURAL HISTORY MAGAZINE. "An indispensable reference," J. Hambleton, BEES.

Unabridged, unaltered republication of original edition. 9 photographic plates. 66 figures. Indices. 693-item bibliography. 352pp. 5⅜ x 8½. 21137-1 Paperbound $3.00

LIFE HISTORIES OF NORTH AMERICAN DIVING BIRDS

by Arthur Cleveland Bent

The all-inclusiveness of Bent's volumes on North American birds has made them classics of our time. Arthur Cleveland Bent was one of America's outstanding ornithologists, and his twenty-volume series on American birds, published under the auspices of the Smithsonian Institution, forms the most comprehensive, most complete, and most-used single source of information in existence. No ornithologist, conservationist, amateur naturalist or birdwatcher should be without a copy.

In this volume, the reader will find an encyclopedic collection of information about thirty-six different diving birds (grebe, loon, auk, murre, puffin, etc.). Not a group of general descriptions but a collection of detailed, specific observations of individual flocks throughout the country, it describes in readable language and copious detail the nesting habits, plumage, egg form, distribution, food, behavior, swimming and diving habits, voice, enemies, winter habits, range, courtship procedures, molting information, and migratory habits of every known North American diving bird.

Completely modern in its approach, the study was made with the full recognition of the difficulties inherent in the observation and interpretation of wild life behavior. For that reason, not only the reports of hundreds of contemporary observers throughout the country were utilized, but also the writings of America's great naturalists of the past — Audubon, Burroughs, William Brewster. The complete textual coverage is supplemented by 12 full-page black-and-white plates showing types of eggs, and 43 plates containing 80 photographs of young at various stages of growth, nesting sites, etc.

Unabridged republication of 1st edition. Index. Bibliography. 55 full-page plates. xiv + 239pp. of text. 5⅜ x 8½. 21091-X Paperbound **$3.00**

LIFE HISTORIES OF NORTH AMERICAN GULLS AND TERNS
by Arthur Cleveland Bent

The all-inclusiveness of Bent's volumes on North American birds has made them classics of our time. Arthur Cleveland Bent was one of America's outstanding ornithologists, and his twenty-volume series on American birds, published under the auspices of the Smithsonian Institution, forms the most comprehensive, most complete, and most-used single source of information in existence. No ornithologist, conservationist, amateur naturalist or birdwatcher should be without a copy.

In this volume the reader will find an encyclopedic collection of information about 50 different gulls and terns. Not a group of general descriptions, but a collection of detailed, specific observations of individual flocks throughout the country, it describes in readable language and copious detail the nesting habits, plumage, egg form and distribution, food, behavior, field marks, voice, enemies, winter habits, range, courtship procedures, molting information, and migratory habits of every known North American gull and tern.

Completely modern in its approach, the study was made with the full recognition of the difficulties inherent in the observation and interpretation of wild life behavior. For that reason, not only the reports of hundreds of contemporary observers throughout the country were utilized, but also the writings of America's great naturalists of the past—Audubon, Burroughs, William Brewster. The complete textual coverage is supplemented by 16 full-page black-and-white plates showing 99 types of eggs, and 77 plates containing 149 photographs of young at various stages of growth, nesting sites, etc.

Unabridged republication of 1st edition. Index. Bibliography. 93 plates. xii + 337pp. of text. 5⅜ x 8½.   21029-4 Paperbound **$3.00**

LIFE HISTORIES OF NORTH AMERICAN MARSH BIRDS
by Arthur Cleveland Bent

The all-inclusiveness of Bent's volumes on North American birds has made them classics of our time. Arthur Cleveland Bent was one of America's outstanding ornithologists, and his twenty-volume series on American birds, published under the auspices of the Smithsonian Institution, forms the most comprehensive, most complete, and most-used single source of information in existence. No ornithologist, conservationist, amateur naturalist or birdwatcher should be without a copy.

In this volume, the reader will find an encyclopedic collection of information about fifty-four different kinds of marsh bird (flamingo, ibis, bittern, heron, egret, crane, crake, rail, coot, etc.). Not a group of general descriptions but a collection of detailed, specific observations of individual flocks throughout the country, it describes in readable language and copious detail the nesting habits, plumage, egg form and distribution, food, behavior, field marks, voice, enemies, winter habits, range, courtship procedures, molting information, and migratory habits of every known North American marsh bird.

Completely modern in its approach, the study was made with the full recognition of the difficulties inherent in the observation and interpretation of wild life behavior. For that reason, not only the reports of hundreds of contemporary observers throughout the country were utilized, but also the writings of America's great naturalists of the past — Audubon, Burroughs, William Brewster. The complete textual coverage is supplemented by 98 full-page plates containing 179 black-and-white photographs of nesting sites, eggs, and the young of important species at various stages in their growth, etc.

Unabridged republication of 1st edition. Index. Bibliography. 98 full-page plates. xiv + 392pp. of text. 5⅜ x 8½.   21082-0 Paperbound **$4.00**

WESTERN FOREST TREES
By James B. Berry

For years this work has been a standard guide to the trees of the Western United States. Anyone who enjoys nature walks or hikes will want to own a copy of this woodlore classic, as will campers, vacationers, and all lovers of the outdoors.

This handy manual covers over 70 different subspecies of trees, ranging from the Pacific shores to the Rocky Mountain forests—as far east as Western South Dakota. All pertinent information is supplied for each type of tree: range, occurrence, growth habits, appearance and particularities of leaves, bark, fruit, twigs, etc., its wood, distinguishing features, and uses.

The book is divided into sections based on leaf characteristics: trees with needle-like leaves (pine, fir, spruce, redwood, hemlock, larch); trees with scale-like leaves (cedar, cypress, juniper); compound broadleaf trees (walnut, ash, locust, mesquite, California buckeye); lobed or divided broadleaf trees (maple, oak, sycamore); and simple broadleaf trees—including leaves with toothed margins (poplar, birch, alder, cherry, black willow) and with entire margins (desert willow, mahogany, gum, dogwood, laurel, madroña). This arrangement, together with the nearly 100 accompanying illustrations (mostly full-size) of buds, branches, twigs, leaves, and the like, provides an easily-used identification key covering virtually every tree of the area.

A long introductory section explains proper procedures in tree and wood identification and describes the general properties and structure of the various woods. An analytical key to porous and non-porous woods is also furnished, as are several subsidiary fruit, bark, leaf, and twig keys within the text for helpful reference purposes. All persons interested in the trees of the American West will find this little handbook just the thing to help them increase their knowledge and appreciation of their favorite woodlands.

Revised edition. Preface. 12 photographs. 85 fine line illustrations by Mary E. Eaton. Index. xii + 212pp. 5⅜ x 8 .   21138-X Paperbound **$2.00**

LIFE HISTORIES OF NORTH AMERICAN GALLINACEOUS BIRDS

by Arthur Cleveland Bent

The all-inclusiveness of Bent's volumes on North American birds has made them classics of our time. Arthur Cleveland Bent was one of America's outstanding ornithologists, and his twenty-volume series on American birds, published under the auspices of the Smithsonian Institution, forms the most comprehensive, most complete, and most-used single source of information in existence. No ornithologist, conservationist, amateur naturalist or birdwatcher should be without a copy.

In this volume, the reader will find an encyclopedic collection of information about eighty-eight different gallinaceous birds (partridge, quail, grouse, ptarmigan, pheasant, pigeon, dove, etc.). Not a group of general descriptions but a collection of detailed, specific observations of individual flocks throughout the country, it describes in readable language and copious detail the nesting habits, plumage, egg form and distribution, food, behavior, field marks, voice, enemies, winter habits, range, courtship procedures, molting information, and migratory habits of every known North American gallinaceous bird.

Completely modern in its approach, the study was made with the full recognition of the difficulties inherent in the observation and interpretation of wild life behavior. For that reason, not only the reports of hundreds of contemporary observers throughout the country were utilized, but also the writings of America's great naturalists of the past—Audubon, Burroughs, William Brewster. The complete textual coverage is supplemented by 93 full-page plates containing 170 black-and-white photographs of nesting sites, eggs, and the young of important species at various stages in their growth.

Unabridged republication of 1st edition. Index. Bibliography. 93 full-page plates. xiii + 490pp. of text. 5⅜ x 8½.   21028-6 Paperbound **$5.00**

HOW TO BECOME EXTINCT

by Will Cuppy

"The last two Great Auks in the world were killed June 4, 1844, on the island of Eldey, off the coast of Iceland. The last Passenger Pigeon, an old female named Martha, died September 1, 1914, peacefully, at the Cincinnati Zoo. I became extinct on August 23, 1934. I forget where I was at the time, but I shall always remember the date."

So wrote Will Cuppy, chronicler of "The Decline and Fall of Just About Everybody" and author of nearly a dozen other classics of American humor, including "How to Attract the Wombat" (Dover, $1.00). In this collection, Cuppy discusses the extinction of the dinosaur, the plesiosaur, the pterodactyl, the wooly mammoth, the dodo, and the giant ground sloth, and does a pretty good job on quite a few other, less extinct fish and reptiles.

The result is a deliriously funny anthology of 40 short pieces, each stamped with the unmistakable and indelible style of a master humorist. "Do Fish Think, Really?," "Note on Baron Cuvier," "Fish Out of Water," "Own Your Own Snake," "Aristotle, Indeed!," and an appendix containing "Are the Insects Winning?" and "Thoughts on the Ermine" are some of the longer essays interspersed among Cuppy's wry observations, sassy descriptions, and downright disrespectful comments on the cod (who has no vices but whose virtues are awful), the perch ("You have the mind of a perch" is the worst thing you can say to a fish), the tortoise (who is slow, plodding, herbivorous, and against all modern improvements), the boa constrictor, the cobra, and others.

The stamp of the author's style, which kept America amused for two decades, is not the only thing that is indelible about this book. The humor, too, defies the years and comes down to us, in this first reprint in 25 years, still fresh and still very much funnier than practically anyone else has ever been in writing. Complementing Cuppy's text are 51 line drawings by the incomparable William Steig, who is still among our most popular cartoonists.

Complete, unabridged republication of original (1941) edition. 51 illustrations by William Steig. x + 106pp. 5⅜ x 8½.   21273-4 Paperbound **$1.00**

HOW TO KNOW THE WILDFLOWERS
by Mrs. William Starr Dana

This well-known classic of nature lore has introduced hundreds of thousands of readers to the wonder and beauty of the wild flowers of most of the United States and Canada. Written with grace and charm, it is not only the handiest field guide to wild flowers, it is also a most pleasant and delightful book, packed full of interesting lore about plants and flowers.

To enable the reader to identify any given flower as easily as possible, Mrs. Dana has first classified plants by the color of their typical flowers: white, red, green, blue, yellow, pink, etc. She has then arranged the flowers within each color group according to their time of blossoming. As a result, if you should come upon a blue flower in June, you can turn instantly to the blue flowers, early section, and see a clear illustration of the plant you want to find—even if you have never had any botanical training at all. This combination of color and time classification makes this the easiest wild flower guide to use.

Mrs. Dana's coverage of the wild flowers of the Eastern and Central United States and Canada is very thorough, all in all more than 1,000 important flowering, berry-bearing and foliage plants. More than 170 full-page plates illustrate the most important and most typical plants (showing foliage, flower, growth habit, roots, fruit, and whatever else is needed), so that you can identify your find at a glance. These illustrations by Marion Satterlee are famous as being both the most realistic and most interesting of modern floral drawings. Many readers have colored them as they have found individual flowers, thus keeping a permanent record of their field trips.

A full text provides you with complete botanical information about each important plant, information about the history, uses, folklore, habitat and other material for each plant, while introductory chapters explain principles of botanical classification and description for those interested.

Unabridged reproduction of enlarged (1900) edition, with additional illustrations. Nomenclature modernized by Clarence J. Highlander. 174 full-page illustrations, more than 150 figures. xlii + 438pp. 5⅜ x 8½.   20332-8 Paperbound $2.75

GUIDE TO SOUTHERN TREES

by Ellwood S. Harrar

Dean of the School of Forestry, Duke University

and Dr. J. G. Harrar

President, Rockefeller Foundation

On nature walks, on hikes, while camping out, or even while you're driving through a wooded area, this 700-page manual will be your unfailing guide. With it, you'll be able to recognize any one of more than 350 different kinds of trees, from the common pine, cypress, walnut, beech, and elm to such seldom-seen species as Franklinia (one of the world's rarest trees, last seen growing naturally in 1790).

"Guide to Southern Trees" covers the entire area south of the Mason-Dixon line from the Atlantic Ocean to the Florida Keys and western Texas. An astonishing amount of information is packed into the description of each tree: habit, leaves, flowers, twigs, bark, fruit, habitat, distribution, and importance, as well as information of historical or commercial significance. Conifers and broadleaved trees are both fully covered, in readable and non-technical language—an especially helpful feature for the beginner and the amateur.

There are 200 full-page delineations (primarily of leaf structure) all carefully drawn to provide the maximum amount of precise, detailed information necessary for identification purposes. In addition, there is a 20-page synoptic key to the generic groups, which will help you find what family a particular tree belongs to, and finding keys for each family as well. Thus, you can use just two keys to find any unfamiliar tree in a matter of minutes. Finally there is a full explanatory introduction covering nomenclature, classification procedures, and important botanical functions for the layman.

The features listed above make this perhaps the most comprehensive guide available at such an inexpensive price. Amateur naturalists, teachers of natural science, Scout Masters, camp counselors, foresters, botanists, conservationists, gardeners, hikers, hunters, and everyone concerned with and interested in trees, from beginner to expert, will find this book an indispensable companion.

Unabridged republication of 1st (1946) edition. Index. 81-item bibliography. Glossary. 200 full-page illustrations. x + 712pp. 4½ x 6½.   T945 Paperbound **$3.00**

MANUAL OF THE TREES OF NORTH AMERICA

by Charles Sprague Sargent

The greatest dendrologist America has ever produced was without doubt Charles Sprague Sargent, Professor of Arboriculture at Harvard and Director of the Arnold Arboretum in Boston until his death in 1927. His monumental "Manual of the Trees of North America," incorporating the results of 44 years of original research, is still unsurpassed as the most comprehensive and reliable volume on the subject. Almost every other book on American trees is selective, but this one assures you of identifying any native tree; it includes 185 genera and 717 species of trees (and many shrubs) found in the United States, Canada, and Alaska. 783 sharp, clear line drawings illustrate leaves, flowers, and fruit.

First, a 6-page synoptic key breaks trees down into 66 different families; then, an unusually useful 11-page analytical key to genera helps the beginner locate any tree readily by its leaf characteristics. Within the text over 100 further keys aid in identification. The body of the work is a species by species description of leaves, flowers, fruit, winterbuds, bark, wood, growth habits, etc., extraordinary in its fullness and wealth of exact, specific detail. Distinguishing features of this book are its extremely precise locations and distributions; flower and leaf descriptions that indicate immaturity variations; and a strong discussion of varieties and local variants.

Additional useful features are a glossary of technical terms; a system of letter keys classifying trees by regions; and a detailed index of both technical and common names (index, glossary, and introductory keys are printed in both volumes.) Students and teachers of botany and forestry, naturalists, conservationists, and all nature lovers will find this set an unmatched lifetime reference source. "Still the best work," Carl Rogers in "The Tree Book."

Unabridged and unaltered reprint of the 2nd enlarged 1926 edition. Synopsis of Families. Analytical Key of Genera. Glossary. Index. 783 illustrations, 1 map. Total of 982pp. 5⅜ x 8.   T277 Vol I Paperbound **$2.50**
                                                            T278 Vol II Paperbound **$2.50**
                                                            The set **$5.00**

FRUIT KEY AND TWIG KEY TO TREES AND SHRUBS

FRUIT KEY TO NORTHEASTERN TREES
TWIG KEY TO THE DECIDUOUS WOODY PLANTS OF
EASTERN NORTH AMERICA

by W. M. Harlow

(Professor of Wood Technology, College of Forestry,
State University of New York, Syracuse)

Bound together for the first time in one volume, these handy, accurate, and easily used keys to fruit and twig identification are the only guides of their sort with photographs—over 350 of them, of nearly every twig and fruit described—making them especially valuable to the novice.

The fruit key (dealing with both deciduous trees and evergreens) begins with a concise introduction, explaining simply and lucidly the process of seeding, and identifying the various organs involved: the cones and flowers, and their component parts and variations. Next, the various types of fruits are described—drupe, berry, pome, legume, follicle, capsule, achene, samara, nut—and fruiting habits, followed by a synoptic summary of fruit types.

The introduction to the twig key tells in plain language the process of growth, and its relation to twig morphology through leaf scars, branch scars, buds, etc. For the benefit of the unwary, poison-ivy, poison-oak, and poison-sumac are immediately and fully described.

Identification in both books is easy. There is a pair of alternative descriptions of each aspect of the specimens. Your choice of the fitting one leads you automatically to the next proper pair. At the end of the chain is the name of your specimen and, as a double check, a photograph. More than 120 different fruits and 160 different twigs are distinguished.

This exceptional work, widely used in university courses in botany, biology, forestry, etc., is a valuable tool and instructor to the naturalist, woodsman, or farmer, and to anyone who has wondered about the name of a leafless tree in winter, or been intrigued by an interestingly shaped fruit or seed.

Over 350 photographs, up to 3 times natural size. Bibliography, glossary, index of common and scientific names, in each key. Total of xvii + 126pp. 5⅜ x 8½. Two volumes bound as one.   20511-8 Paperbound **1.35**